ESSENTIALS OF ORAL
COMMUNICATION

Pearson
Custom
Publishing

ESSENTIALS OF ORAL COMMUNICATION

ESSENTIALS OF HUMAN COMMUNICATION
THIRD EDITION

Joseph A. DeVito

COMMUNICATING TODAY
SECOND EDITION

Raymond Zeuschner

Compiled by ITT Educational Services, Inc.

Pearson
Custom
Publishing

Excerpts taken from:

Chapter 1–11, Glossary
Essentials of Human Communication, Third Edition
by Joseph A. DeVito
Copyright © 1999 by Addison Wesley Longman, Inc.
Reading, MA 01867

Chapters 11–14
Communicating Today, Second Edition
by Raymond Zeuschner
Copyright © 1997, 1993 by Allyn & Bacon
Needham Heights, MA 02494

Appendix A
Communication: Making Connections, Fourth Edition
by William J. Seiler and Melissa L. Beall
Copyright © 1999 by Allyn & Bacon

Charts (5)
*Thinking Through Communication: An Introduction to the
Study of Human Communication,* Second Edition
by Sarah Trenholm
Copyright © 1999, 1995 by Allyn & Bacon

Appendix C
Public Speaking: An Audience-Centered Approach, Third Edition
by Steven A. Beebe and Susan J. Beebe
Copyright © 1997, 1994, 1991 by Allyn & Bacon

Chapter 14 (partial)
Public Speaking in the Age of Diversity, Second Edition
by Teri Kwal Gamble and Michael W. Gamble
Copyright © 1998, 1994 by Allyn & Bacon

Pages 300–303
Mastering Public Speaking, Third Edition
by George L. Grice and John F. Skinner
Copyright © 1998, 1995, 1993 by Allyn & Bacon

This special edition published in cooperation with
Pearson Custom Publishing

Printed in the United States of America

10 9 8 7 6 5 4 3 2

Please visit our website at www.pearsoncustom.com

ISBN 0–536–02314–X

BA 990091

 PEARSON CUSTOM PUBLISHING
75 Arlington Street, Boston, MA 02116
A Pearson Education Company

Credits

PHOTOS

Chapter One
2 © Jeff Hunter/The Image Bank. 10 © Tony Freeman/Photo Edit. 15 © Pedrick/The Image Works. 17 Atlanta Committee.

Chapter Two
30 © Chris Close/The Image Bank. 35 © John Coletti/The Picture Cube. 42 © Mike Ansell—Touchstone/Reuters/Archive Photos.

Chapter Three
50 © I. Digiacomo/The Image Bank. 58 Steve Niedorf/The Image Bank. 61 Jeff Greenberg/Photo Researchers.

Chapter Four
70 © W. McNamee/Sygma. 81 © Michael Newman/Photo Edit. 84 © Dagmar Fabricius/Uniphoto.

Chapter Five
90 © Tom McCarthy/Unicorn Stock Photos 95 (left) © Ullmann/ Monkmeyer; (right) © Michael Newman/Photo Edit. 109 © Jeffrey Meyers/Uniphoto.

Chapter Six
118 © Bob Daemmrich/Stock Boston. 126 © Jason Mahshie/The Picture Cube. 134 © AP/Wide World Photos.

Chapter Seven
150 © Bob Daemmrich/Stock Boston. 161 © Bruce Ayers/Tony Stone Worldwide. 170 © Bob Daemmrich/The Image Works.

Chapter Eight
188 © Yellow Dog Productions/The Image Bank. 192 © Bob Daemmrich/Stock Boston. 215 © Richard Lord/The Image Works.

Chapter Nine
220 © R. Lord/The Image Works. 225 © Robert Brenner/Photo Edit. 240 (top) © Bill Horsman/Stock Boston; (bottom) © Jim Pickrell/The Image Works. 241 © Jeff Greenberg/Photo Edit.

Chapter Ten
244 © Ira Block/The Image Bank. 247 © H. Dratch/The Image Works. 261 © Sisse Brimberg/Woodfin Camp & Associates.

Chapter Eleven
268 © Michelle Bridwell/Photo Edit. 274 Michael Newman/Photo Edit. 280 © C. J. Allen/Stock Boston.

Chapter Twelve
288 Courtesy of Sygma/Larry Downing.

Chapter Fifteen
362 Courtesy of AP/Wide World Photos

Replacement photo for Appendix A
403 Courtesy of Prentice-Hall

Appendix B
312 Courtesy of Tony Stone Images

UPI/Corbis-Bettmann; p. 224, Don Farber/Woodfin Camp & Associates; p. 235, Elizabeth Crews/Stock, Boston; p. 236, F. Pedrick/The Image Works; p. 242, Robert Harbison; p. 244, Lawrence Migdale/Stock, Boston; p. 268, Jeff Greenberg/The Picture Cube; p. 278, John Coletti; p. 287, The Image Works Archives; p. 292, UPI/Corbis-Bettmann; p. 303, Bob Daemmrich/The Image Works.

Contents

Preface

It's an honor and a pleasure to introduce the first edition of *Essentials of Oral Communication* to those who have used previous editions and to newcomers alike. The purpose of this book is to foster the development and improvement of practical real-world skills in interpersonal communication (including interviewing), small group communication, and public speaking, without neglecting the theoretical foundations on which these skills are based. This goal is accomplished through the text's integrated features and pedagogical apparatus.

MAJOR FEATURES

Essentials helps students master the concepts and skills of human communication by integrating coverage throughout the book of six important elements: skill development, cultural awareness, listening, critical thinking, the importance of power, and ethics.

Emphasis on Skill Development

Communication skills are consistently rated among those most crucial for success in college, for establishing and maintaining productive relationships, for functioning effectively in business, and for exerting leadership in the small group and public arenas. *Essentials of Oral Communication* teaches students those skills.

In Part One, "Foundations of Human Communication" (Chapters 1–6), *Essentials* helps students with self-awareness and self-esteem, interpersonal perception, listening, and sending and receiving verbal and nonverbal messages. Part Two, "The Contexts of Human Communication" (Chapters 7–11), covers communication skills in context. **Interpersonal** communication skills are discussed in the context of conversations, conflict, and in developing, maintaining, repairing, and even dissolving close relationships. Guidance for improving **interviewing** skills is presented in the coverage of informative and employment interviews. Students learn to apply **small group** communication skills as both member and leader, and when generating ideas, sharing information, and solving problems in a variety of formats, such as quality circles and focus groups. In Part Three **Public speaking** skills are discussed in the context of preparing and presenting speeches designed to serve a variety of informative and persuasive goals.

These skills are discussed within the appropriate chapters as well as covered in the Skill Development Experiences, which appear at the end of each chapter. These activities provide opportunities for students to apply these principles to specific situations. Discussion questions are provided at the end of each experience. Skills are introduced in the chapter opening grids and reinforced by the chapter summaries.

Emphasis on Cultural Awareness

We live in a world defined by its cultural diversity—differences in gender, age, affectional orientation, societal position, race, religion, and nationality. Cultural issues, in fact, always influence communication. For this reason, culture is fully integrated throughout this edition as an integral part of human communication. "Cultural Viewpoint" material is marked by a globe icon in the margin. Each chapter contains discussions of culture relevant to the chapter topics. These major discussions include culture and competence, culture in self-concept formation, personality theory and culture, gender and cultural differences, culture and nonverbal communication, culture and conflict, culture and interpersonal relationships, cultural norms in small group communication, and cultural considerations in the language of public speaking, among others. In addition, a number of Skill Development Experiences, Listen to This boxes, and many of the critical thinking questions and quotations focus on culture.

Integrative Coverage of Listening

With only a few notable exceptions, communication textbooks have given almost exclusive emphasis to speaking, relegating listening to one chapter and, in many cases, even less. Yet, listening is an essential part of communication and much more attention needs to be paid to it in our coverage of interpersonal, small group, and public communication. *Essentials* takes listening out of the closet and gives it prominence in two ways.

First, a complete chapter is devoted to listening (Chapter 4) and covers the process of listening (from receiving to responding), listening effectiveness, the functions and techniques of active listening, and a new section on the influence of culture and gender on listening. Second **Listen to This** boxes are presented throughout the text. These boxes focus on specific listening skills as they relate to the text. For example, "Listening to Other Perspectives" appears in the chapter on perception (3) and "Sexist, Heterosexist, and Racist Listening" in the chapter on verbal language.

Comprehensive Coverage of Critical Thinking

If communication is to be accurate, responsible, intelligent, and well-reasoned, then it must rest on the principles and skills of critical thinking. *Essentials,* therefore, offers students many opportunities to learn critical thinking skills. For example, the last major heading in each chapter focuses on critical thinking in reference to topics in the chapter. Self-tests and Skill Development Experiences also feature elements of critical thinking containing questions for analysis, evaluation, and application of principles and skills of human communication. Quotations and probes in the margins, as well as photo captions that encourage students to stop and think critically about the chapter topics, also reinforce critical thinking (5).

Unique Coverage of Power in Communication

All communication transactions, all interpersonal relationships, all small groups, and all public communication situations are influenced by differences in power. The importance of power in communication is emphasized in *Essentials* with Power Perspective boxes. Power Perspectives in the early chapters explain the nature of power, its role in human communication, and the different types of power. Perspectives in subsequent chapters focus more on the skills of recognizing and using power and are more closely related to the concepts discussed in the text. For example, "Power Through Listening" is presented in the listening chapter (Chapter 4), "Recognizing" and "Avoiding Sexual Harassment" in the chapter on verbal messages (5), and "Résumé Power" in the chapter on interviewing (9).

Coverage of Ethical Issues

Ethical considerations have been a part of communication training for more than 2000 years. Aristotle, Cicero, and Quintilian—three great classical theorists—viewed ethics as an integral part of communication instruction. *Essentials of Oral Communication* follows in that tradition, incorporating Ethical Issue boxes throughout the text which discuss the ethical implications of communication concepts and skills presented throughout the book.

The boxes in the early chapters discuss the relationship of ethics to human communication, some popular approaches to ethics, and ethical standards. Boxes in subsequent chapters attempt to relate ethics more closely to the chapter contents. For example, "Lying" is discussed in the chapter on verbal messages (5), and "Secrets" in the chapter on interpersonal relationships (8).

PEDAGOGICAL APPARATUS

Essentials' pedagogical apparatus makes learning the essential principles and skills of human communication enjoyable and efficient for students. As in previous editions, the pedagogy is highly interactive.

- **Chapter Contents, Goals, and Skills.** Chapter opening grids link the major concepts of each chapter with their corresponding goals and skills, introducing students to the cognitive and behavioral learning objectives covered in the text.
- **Listen to This Boxes.** These boxes discuss specific listening skills as they apply to the topics of the chapter in which they appear. Each box identifies the page on which the next Listen to This box appears, allowing students to read them in sequence. Many boxes contain exercises or critical thinking probes designed to promote active learning.
- **Ethical Issue Boxes.** Ethical Issue boxes explain ethical concepts and emphasize ethical responsibility in all communication. Each box ends with a note identifying the location of the next Ethical Issue box so that students can read them in sequence.

Power Perspective Boxes. Power Perspective boxes explain the nature and principles of power as well as its different types and also identify power skills, uses, and management techniques. The Power Perspectives underscore the relationship between power distribution and effective interpersonal, small group, and public communication. Again, each box identifies the location of the next Power Perspective box allowing students to read them in sequence.

Self-Tests. *Essentials* contains Self-Tests including the standard research instruments for measuring apprehension, love, self-monitoring, time orientation, and argumentativeness, among others. Other tests are more pedagogical in purpose and designed primarily to help students understand the concepts discussed in the text, such as cultural beliefs, confirmation, gender differences in language, effective criticism, and credibility.

Quotations and Probes. Quotations and probes appear in the text margin near the content they expand upon. The quotations emphasize literary, philosophical, and often controversial observations on communication promoting critical thinking and discussion. The questions are designed to encourage students to analyze, evaluate, or apply the concepts covered in the text. There are now more questions dealing with specific research findings and theories than in previous editions in order to present these findings in a more provocative and practical context.

Key Word Quizzes. New to this edition are 10-item key word quizzes presented at the end of most chapters to help students review the significant vocabulary terms introduced in the chapter. The quizzes present true and false statements and ask students not only to identify false statements but to correct them. Suggested answers are provided upside down immediately after each exercise.

Chapter Summaries. Chapter summaries include both a Conceptual Summary and a Skills Summary. The conceptual summary provides a brief paragraph recalling the chapter's major topics and an itemized list of statements that summarize the essential content of the chapter. The skills summary identifies the major skills covered in the chapter and is presented as a checklist to allow the student to determine his or her current level of mastery and also to identify skills requiring further practice.

Skill Development Experiences. A wide variety of Skill Development Experiences allow students the opportunity to practice specific communication skills in an enjoyable and supportive atmosphere. Sixteen Experiences are new to this edition; others have been streamlined and updated.

CHAPTER 1

Introduction to Human Communication

CHAPTER CONCEPTS	CHAPTER GOALS	CHAPTER SKILLS
	After completing this chapter, you should be able to	After completing this chapter, you should be able to
Communication Models and Concepts	1. define communication and its essential components	communicate as speaker/listener with an awareness of the varied components involved in the communication act
Communication Principles	2. explain and give examples of the principles of human communication	communicate as speaker/listener with a recognition of the principles of human communication
Culture and Human Communication	3. explain the relationship of culture to human communication	communicate with an understanding of cultural influences and differences
Thinking Critically About Human Communication	4. explain the suggestions for approaching the study of human communication and for transferring skills	follow the suggestions for approaching human communication and for transferring skills of critical thinking

Of all the knowledge and skills you have, those concerning communication are among your most important and useful. Whether in your personal, social, or work life, your communication ability is your most vital asset. Through **intrapersonal communication,** you talk with, learn about, and judge yourself. You persuade yourself of this or that, reason about possible decisions to make, and rehearse messages that you plan to send to others. Through **interpersonal communication,** you interact with others, learn about them and yourself, and reveal yourself to others. Whether with new acquaintances, old friends, lovers, or family members, it's through interpersonal communication that you establish, maintain, sometimes destroy, and sometimes repair personal relationships. You also communicate interpersonally during interviews—when applying for a job, gathering information, and counseling.

Through **small group communication,** you interact with others in groups. You solve problems, develop new ideas, and share knowledge and experiences. You live your work and social lives largely in groups, from the employment interview to the executive board meeting, from the informal social group having coffee to the formal meeting discussing issues of international concern. Through **public communication,** others inform and persuade you. In turn, you inform and persuade others—to act, to buy, or to think in a particular way, or to change an attitude, opinion, or value. See Table 1.1.

This book focuses on these forms of communication and on you as both message sender and receiver. It has three major purposes. First, it explains the concepts and principles, the theory, and research in human communication.

Second, it explains the skills of interpersonal, small group, and public communication that help to increase your own communication competence and effectiveness in a world that is becoming increasingly multicultural. Third, it enhances your ability to think critically, in general, and about communication, in particular.

The differences between effective and ineffective communication are all around you. They're the differences between:

- the self-confident and the self-conscious speaker
- the person who gets hired and the one who gets passed over because of a poor showing in a job interview
- the couple who argue constructively and the couple who argue by hurting each other and eventually destroying their relationship
- the group member who is too self-focused to listen openly and contribute to the group and the member who serves both the task and the interpersonal needs of the group
- the public speaker who lacks credibility and persuasive appeal and the speaker audiences believe and follow
- the culturally isolated and the person who enjoys, profits from, and grows from effective and satisfying intercultural experiences

A good way to begin your study of human communication is to examine your own beliefs about communication. The accompanying self-test provides a stimulus for such an examination.

Communication is power. Those who have mastered its effective use can change their own experience of the world and the world's experience of them.

—Anthony Robbins

Table 1.1 Areas of Human Communication

This table identifies and arranges the forms of communication in terms of the number of persons involved, from one (in intrapersonal communication) to hundreds, thousands, and even millions (public speaking on television, for example). It also echoes (in general) the development of topics in this book.

Areas of Human Communication	Some Common Purposes	Some Theory-Related Concerns	Some Skills-Related Concerns
Intrapersonal: communication with oneself	To think, reason, analyze, reflect	How does self-concept develop? How does it influence communication? How can problem-solving and analyzing abilities be improved and taught? What's the relationship between personality and communication?	Increasing self-awareness, improving problem-solving and analyzing abilities, increasing self-control, reducing stress, managing interpersonal conflict
Interpersonal: communication between two persons	To discover, relate, influence, play, help	What's interpersonal effectiveness? What holds friends, lovers, and families together? What tears them apart? How can relationships be repaired? How do online relationships compare to those established face-to-face?	Increasing effectiveness in one-to-one communication, developing and maintaining effective relationships, improving conflict resolution abilities, interviewing for information or employment
Small group: communication within a small group of people	To share information, generate ideas, solve problems, help	What makes a leader? What type of leadership works best? What roles do members play in groups? How can groups be made more effective? How can virtual groups be most effectively used in the organization?	Increasing effectiveness as a group member, improving leadership abilities, using groups to achieve specific purposes (for example, solving problems, generating ideas)
Public: communication of speaker to audience	To inform, persuade, entertain	How can audiences be most effectively analyzed and adapted to? How can ideas be best developed for communication to an audience? How can public postings be made more effective?	Informing and persuading more effectively; developing, organizing, styling, and delivering messages with greater effectiveness; communicating on the Internet

Test Yourself | What Do You Believe About Human Communication?

Instructions: Respond to each of the following statements with T (true) if you think the statement is always or usually true and F (false) if you think the statement is always or usually false.

_____ 1. Good communicators are born, not made.

_____ 2. The more you communicate, the better your communication will be.

_____ 3. Unlike effective speaking, effective listening really cannot be taught.

_____ 4. Opening lines such as "Hello, how are you?" or "Fine weather today" serve no useful communication purpose.

_____ 5. The best way to communicate with someone from a different culture is exactly as you would with someone from your own culture.

_____ 6. When verbal and nonverbal messages contradict each other, people believe the verbal message.

_____ 7. Complete openness should be the goal of any meaningful interpersonal relationship.

_____ 8. Interpersonal conflict is a reliable sign that your relationship is in trouble.

_____ 9. Like good communicators, leaders are born, not made.

_____ 10. Fear of speaking is detrimental and the effective speaker must learn to eliminate it.

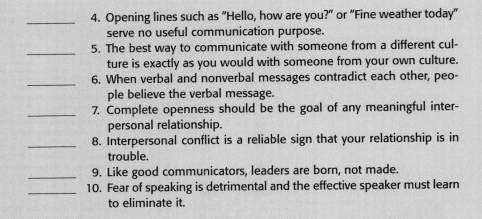

Thinking Critically About Communication Beliefs   If you're like most people, you were probably told lots of things about communication—like the statements above—that are simply not true. In fact, none of the above statements are true, so hopefully you answered "false" to all or most. As you read this book, you'll discover not only why these statements are false but some of the problems that can arise when you act on the basis of such misconceptions. This is perhaps, then, a good place to start practicing the critical thinking skill of questioning commonly held assumptions—about communication and about yourself as a communicator. What other beliefs do you hold about communication and about yourself as a communicator? How do these influence your communication behavior?

COMMUNICATION MODELS AND CONCEPTS

In early models or theories, communication was seen as traveling in a straight line from speaker to listener. In this **linear** view of communication the speaker spoke and the listener listened. Speaking and listening were seen as taking place at different times; when you spoke, you didn't listen and when you listened, you didn't speak (Figure 1.1).

This linear model fails to capture the give and take between the individuals that characterizes, for example, conversation or small group interaction. But it does provide a useful way of looking at certain forms of mass media communication such as television, newspapers and magazines, and billboards, as well as much computer communication such as certain types of bulletin boards and websites that send messages to you but don't allow you to add your own thoughts. In some instances, of course, you do eventually have an impact on these mediated messages when, for example, you buy the advertised product or watch the television show, or visit the website.

The linear view was soon replaced with an **interactional** view in which the speaker and listener were seen as exchanging turns at speaking and listening. For example, A spoke while B listened and then B spoke in response to what A said and A listened (Figure 1.2). Speaking and listening were still viewed as separate acts that did not overlap and that were not performed at the same time by the same person.

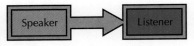

Figure 1.1 The Linear View of Human Communication

Communication researchers Judy Pearson and Paul Nelson (1994) suggest that you think of the speaker as passing a ball to the listener who either catches it or fumbles it. Can you think of another analogy or metaphor for this view of communication?

Power Perspective 1.1

Power and Human Communication

Power is the ability to influence the attitudes or behaviors of another person. It permeates all interactions, whether you're speaking with one person or in a group or giving a public speech. Because of its central importance to human communication and to your ultimate success as a communicator, each chapter contains at least one sidebar devoted to power. These discussions explain how power operates and spell out the skills of power.

Understanding how power operates in these settings will enable you to be more critical in dealing with the power of others and also more effective (persuasive, discriminating, reasonable, ethical) in your own exercise of power.

[The next Power Perspective appears on page 17.]

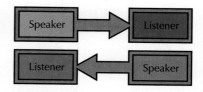

Figure 1.2 The Interactional View

In this view, continuing with the ball-throwing analogy, the speaker would pass the ball to the listener who would then pass the ball back or fumble (Pearson & Nelson, 1994). What other analogy would work here?

A more satisfying view, and one held currently, sees communication as a **transactional** process in which each person serves simultaneously as speaker and listener. At the same time that you send messages, you're also receiving messages from your own communications and from the reactions of the other person (Figure 1.3).

The transactional viewpoint sees each person as both speaker and listener, as simultaneously communicating and receiving messages (Barnlund, 1970; Watzlawick, Beavin, & Jackson, 1967; Watzlawick, 1977, 1978; Wilmot, 1987). In face-to-face conversation, small group communication, and public speaking, the speaking and listening take place simultaneously. You receive the messages as they're being sent. In computer-mediated communication, this real-time interaction occurs only sometimes. In E-mail (and snail mail) and newsgroup communication, for example, the sending and receiving may be separated by several days or much longer. In IRC groups, on the other hand, communication takes place in real time; the sending and receiving take place (almost) simultaneously.

The transactional view also sees the elements of communication as interdependent (never independent). Each exists in relation to the others. A change in any one element of the process produces changes in the other elements. For example, you're talking with a group of your coworkers and your boss enters the room. This change in "audience" will lead to other changes. Perhaps you'll change what you're saying or how you're saying it. Regardless of what change is introduced, other changes will be produced as a result.

Through communication, people act and react on the basis of the present situation as well as on the basis of their histories, past experiences, attitudes, cultural beliefs, and a host of related factors. One implication of this is that actions and reactions in communication are determined not only by what is said, but also by the way the person interprets what is said. Your responses to a movie, for example, don't depend solely on the words and pictures in the movies; they also depend on your previous experiences, present emotions, knowledge, physical well-being, and a lot more. Because of this two people listening to the same message will often derive two very different meanings. Although the words and symbols are the same,

In what ways does the public speaker receive messages from the audience? In what ways do audience members send and receive messages to each other?

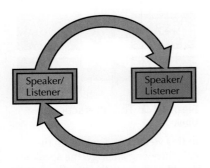

Figure 1.3 The Transactional View

In this view there would be a complex ball game under way in which each player could send and receive any number of balls at any time. Players would be able to throw and catch balls at the very same time (Pearson & Nelson, 1994). Any analogies for this view?

If your lips would keep from slips
Five things observe with care;
To who you speak, of whom you speak,
And how, and when, and where.
                                   —*W. E. Norris*

each person interprets them differently simply because each person is different and has had different experiences.

With this transactional model in mind, we can define communication as occurring when you send or receive messages and when you assign meaning to another person's signals. Human communication always is distorted by noise, occurs within a context, has some effect, and involves some opportunity for feedback. We can expand the basic transactional model by adding these essential elements as shown in Figure 1.4.

Throughout the explanation of these elements or components—and in fact, throughout this text—we make reference to both face-to-face and electronic communication. No matter how sophisticated, electronic communication is still very similar to ordinary face-to-face interactions. For example, electronic communication allows for the same types of communication as does face-to-face interaction, whether interpersonal, small group, or public speaking. You can put your thoughts into words through your keyboard and send them via modem in a way that is very similar to what you do when you send your thoughts into words through the air. When you write and send a letter (through the post office or E-mail connections) you're also engaging in interpersonal communication though the immediacy of response is absent. Similarly, you have interpersonal communication when in Internet Relay Chat (IRC) groups, you "whisper" or single out just one person to receive your message instead of the entire group.

As in face-to-face communication, in IRC groups you can also expand your two-person group to a small group with anywhere from 2 to 40 or 50 people, and technically far beyond that. There are literally thousands of IRCs that you can join, many more groups that you'd ever be able to join face-to-face. Of course, you can always open your own IRC group and invite those who are interested in, for example, old movies, carpentry, new software, or communication, to join your group.

The closest equivalent to public speaking in cyberspace is the newsgroup where you can post a message for anyone to read and then read their reactions to your message, and so on. Here you would post messages that are appropriate to the specific newsgroup just as you would, in face-to-face public speaking, select a topic appropriate to your audience. These

Figure 1.4 The Essentials of Human Communication

This is a general model of communication between two persons and most accurately depicts interpersonal communication. It puts into visual form the various elements of the communication process. How would you revise this model to depict small group interaction? To depict public speaking?

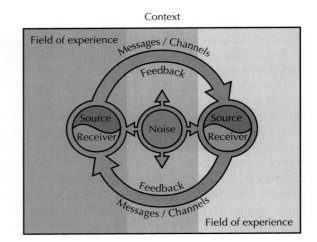

computer-mediated forms are discussed in depth in Chapters 7 (E-mail), 10 (IRC groups), and 12 (newsgroups).

Communication Context

Communication exists in a context and that context, to a large extent, determines the meaning of any verbal or nonverbal message. The same words or behaviors may have totally different meanings when they occur in different contexts. For example, the greeting, "How are you?" means "Hello" to someone you pass regularly on the street, but means "How's your health?" when said to a friend in the hospital. A wink to an attractive person on a bus means something completely different from a wink that signifies a put-on or a lie. Similarly, the meaning of a given signal depends on the other behavior it accompanies or is close to in time. Pounding a fist on the table during a speech in support of a politician means something quite different from that same gesture in response to news of a friend's death. Divorced from the context, it's impossible to tell what meaning was intended from just examining the signals. Of course, even if you know the context in detail, you still might not be able to decipher the intended meaning.

The context, which influences what you say and how you say it, has at least four aspects: physical, cultural, social–psychological, and temporal (or time):

- The **physical context** is the tangible or concrete environment, the room, park, or auditorium; you don't talk the same way at a noisy football game as at a quiet funeral.
- The **cultural context** includes the lifestyles, beliefs, values, behavior, and communication of a group; the rules of a group of people for considering something right or wrong.
- The **social–psychological context** refers to the status relationships among speakers, the formality of the situation, the emotional dimension of the interaction; you don't talk the same way in the cafeteria as you would at a formal dinner at your boss's house.
- The **temporal context** refers to the position in which a message fits into a sequence of events; you don't talk the same way after someone tells of the death of a close relative as you do after someone tells of winning the lottery.

These four contexts interact—each influences and is influenced by the others. For example, arriving late for a date (temporal context) may lead to changes in the degree of friendliness (social–psychological context), which would depend on the cultures of you and your date (cultural context), and which may lead to changes in where you go on the date (physical context).

Sources and Receivers

Each person involved in communication is both a source (speaker) and a receiver (listener). You send messages when you speak, write, gesture, or smile. You receive messages in listening, reading, seeing, smelling, and so on. At the same time that you send messages, you're also receiving messages. You're receiving your own messages (you hear yourself, you feel your own movements, you see many of your own gestures) and, at least in face-to-face communication, you're receiving the messages of the other person—visually,

Do you agree that E-mail and whispering in IRCs are similar to interpersonal conversation, that IRCs are similar to small groups, and that newsgroups are similar to public speaking? What other similarities can you identify? What differences can you identify?

How would you describe the communication context (physical, cultural, social–psychological, and temporal) in which you find yourself right now?

How might the failure to recognize the influence of any one of these four contexts (physical, cultural, social–psychological, and temporal) prevent or hinder meaningful communication?

auditorily, or even through touch or smell. As you speak, you look at the person for responses—for approval, understanding, puzzlement, sympathy, agreement, and so on. As you decipher these nonverbal signals, you're performing receiver functions.

Encoding and Decoding   When you put your ideas into speech, you're putting them into a code, hence *en*coding. When you translate the sound waves (the speech signals) that impinge on your ears into ideas, you take them out of the code they're in, hence *de*coding. Thus, speakers or writers are referred to as *encoders*, and listeners or readers as *decoders*.

Usually you encode an idea into a code that the other person understands, for example, English, Spanish, Indonesian depending on the shared knowledge that you and your listener possess. At times, however, you may want to exclude others and so, for example, you might speak in a language that only one of your listeners knows or use jargon to prevent others from understanding. Adults, when speaking of things they don't want children to understand, might spell out key words—a code that young children don't yet understand. Computer communication enables you to do a similar thing. For example, when sending your credit card number to a vendor you might send it in encrypted form, coded into a symbol system that only authorized receivers will be able to understand (decode). Similarly, in IRC groups you might do the same thing and write in a language that only certain of your readers will understand.

Communication Competence   *Communication competence* refers to your knowledge of how communication works and your ability to use communication effectively (Spitzberg & Cupach, 1989). It includes such knowledge as the role the context plays in influencing the content and

Competence, like truth, beauty and a contact lens, is in the eye of the beholder.
        —*Laurence J. Peter*

form of communication messages—for example, the knowledge that in certain contexts and with certain listeners one topic is appropriate and another is not. Knowledge about the rules of nonverbal behavior—for example, the appropriateness of touching, vocal volume, and physical closeness—is also part of communication competence. One of the major goals of this text and this course is to spell out the nature of and to thereby increase your own communication competence.

By increasing your competence, you'll have available a greater number of performance options. In other words, the more you know about communication or the greater your competence, the more choices you will have available for your day-to-day communications. The process is comparable to learning vocabulary: The more vocabulary you know, the more ways you have for expressing yourself. Thus, the aim of this book is to increase your communicative competence so you'll have a broader range of options in performing your various communication activities. The process is displayed in Figure 1.5.

 What noted personality would you nominate for the "Communication Competence Hall of Fame"?

Culture and Competence Communication competence is specific to a given culture. The principles of effective communication vary from one culture to another; what proves effective in one culture may prove ineffective in another. Thus, in American culture you would call a person you wish to date 3 or 4 days in advance. In certain Asian cultures, you might call the person's parents weeks or even months in advance. In American culture, as a kind of general friendly gesture, you might say, "Come over and pay us a visit." To members of some cultures, this comment is sufficient to prompt them to actually visit at their own convenience.

United States business executives will discuss business during the first several minutes of a meeting. However, Japanese business executives interact socially for an extended period of time and in the process learn about each other. Thus, the small group communication principle influenced by American culture would advise participants to attend to the meeting's agenda during the first 5 or 10 minutes. The principle in Japanese culture would advise participants to avoid dealing with business until all have socialized sufficiently and feel they know each other well enough to begin business negotiations. Note that neither principle is right or wrong. Each is effective within and ineffective outside its own culture. Incorporating an awareness of and sensitivity to and appropriately adjusting to such cultural differences is a first step to achieving competence in intercultural communication.

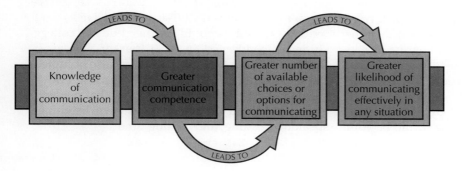

Figure 1.5 From knowledge to effectiveness.

Some researchers (for example, Beier, 1974) argue that the impulse to communicate two different feelings (for example, "I love you" and "I don't love you") creates messages in which the nonverbal contradicts the verbal message. Do you think this idea has validity? What other explanations might you offer to account for contradictory messages?

Field of Experience   The field of experience represents all your knowledge, beliefs, and values, what you have seen, heard, and done—your past experiences and your memory of them that together influence what you say, how you say it, what you allow yourself to receive, and how you respond to what you receive. When the fields of experience of two people overlap greatly, it's relatively easy for them to communicate. They will have more common experiences and hence attach more similar meanings to each other's words and gestures. When people have totally different fields of experience or when their fields overlap only slightly (as would people from widely differing cultures), they stand a greater chance of missing each other with their meanings, of failing to understand what the other person means, or of not being able to understand the values and attitudes expressed.

Messages

Communication messages take many forms and are transmitted or received through one or a combination of sensory organs. You communicate verbally (with words) and nonverbally (without words). Your meanings or intentions are conveyed with words (Chapter 5) and with the clothes you wear, the way you walk, and the way you smile (Chapter 6). Everything about you communicates. Three special types of messages should be noted here: metamessages, feedback, and feedforward.

Metamessages   A **metamessage** is a message that refers to another message; it's communication about communication. Verbally, you can say, for example, "This statement is false" or "Do you understand what I am trying to tell you?" These refer to communication and are, therefore, "metacommunicational."

Nonverbal behavior may also be metacommunicational. Obvious examples include crossing your fingers behind your back or winking when telling a lie. On a less obvious level, consider the frequent blind date. As you say "I had a really nice time," your nonverbal messages—the lack of a smile, the failure to maintain eye contact, the extra-long pauses—metacommunicate

Listen to This

Listening: The Flip Side of Speaking

In the popular mind, communication is often taken as synonymous with speaking. Listening is either neglected or regarded as something apart from "real communication." But, as emphasized in the model of communication presented earlier and as stressed throughout this book, listening is integral to all communication; it is a process that is coordinate with speaking.

If you measured importance by the time you spend on an activity, then listening would be your most important communication activity. In one

study, conducted in 1929 (Rankin), listening occupied 45% of a person's communication time; speaking was second with 30%; reading (16%) and writing (9%) followed. In another study of college students, conducted in 1980 (Barker, Edwards, Gaines, Gladney, & Holley), listening also occupied the most time: 53% compared to reading (17%), speaking (16%), and writing (14%). What percentages would you assign for your own listening, speaking, reading, and writing time?

[The next Listen to This box appears on page 40.]

and contradict the verbal "really nice time" and tell your date that you did not enjoy the evening. Nonverbal messages may also metacommunicate about other nonverbal messages. The individual who, upon meeting a stranger, both smiles and extends a totally lifeless hand shows how one nonverbal behavior may contradict another.

Feedback Messages   When you send a message—for example, in speaking to another person—you also hear yourself. That is, you get **feedback** from your own messages; you hear what you say, you feel the way you move, you see what you write. In addition to this self-feedback, you also get feedback from others. A frown or a smile, a yea or a nay, a pat on the back, or a punch in the mouth are all types of feedback.

Feedback tells the speaker what effect he or she is having on listeners. On the basis of this feedback—for example, boos or wild applause in public speaking—the speaker may continue on course or adjust, modify, strengthen, or change the content or form of the message. Smiles, head nods, and comments such as "I understand" and "right on" are examples of **positive feedback**—feedback that tells you to continue as you've been communicating. Similarly, the message you get back from a robot-administered mailing list (Chapter 10) telling you that it doesn't understand your "plain English" is feedback. When the robot answers your "Please enter my subscription to the communication and gender mailing list" with "Command 'please' not recognized" it is **negative feedback**—telling you something is wrong. Sometimes negative feedback comes with advice on how to correct the problem. A good example of this is the robot's "Commands must be in message BODY, not in HEADER" or your friend telling you, "You'd look better in a blue suit."

Feedforward Messages   **Feedforward** is information you provide before sending your primary messages (Richards, 1951). Feedforward reveals something about the messages to come and includes, for example, the preface or table of contents to a book, the opening paragraph of a chapter, movie previews, magazine covers, and introductions in public speeches.

Feedforward may be verbal ("Wait until you hear this one") or nonverbal (a prolonged pause or hands motioning for silence to signal that an important message is about to be spoken). Or, as is most often the case, it's some combination of verbal and nonverbal signals. Feedforward may refer to the content of the message to follow ("I'll tell you exactly what they said to each other") or to the form ("I won't spare you the gory details"). In E-mail, feedforward is given in the header where the name of the sender, the date, and the subject of the message are identified. Caller-ID, as illustrated in the cartoon on page 14, is another good example of feedforward. The cartoon is also an effective reminder that the assumptions you make about a speaker will greatly influence the ways you receive his or her messages.

Channel

The communication channel is the medium through which messages pass. Communication rarely takes place over only one channel. Rather, two, three, or four different channels are used simultaneously. In face-to-face conversations, for example, you speak and listen (vocal channel), but you

Usually when nonverbal behavior metacommunicates, it reinforces other verbal or nonverbal behavior. You may literally roll up your sleeves when talking about cleaning up the room. Can you think of examples where the nonverbal messages contradicted the verbal?

What kinds of feedforward can you find in this textbook? What specific functions do these feedforwards serve? Can you find examples of feedback in this text? What functions do these serve?

also gesture and receive these signals visually (visual channel). You also emit and smell odors (olfactory channel) and often touch one another, and this, too, is communication (tactile channel).

The different means of communication can also be viewed as channels. Thus, face-to-face contact, telephones, E-mail, movies, television, smoke signals, and telegraph would be types of channels.

Noise

Noise interferes with your receiving a message someone is sending or with their receiving your message. Noise may be physical (others talking loudly, cars honking), psychological (preconceived ideas, wandering thoughts), or semantic (misunderstood meanings). Technically, noise is anything that distorts the message, that is, anything that prevents the receiver from receiving the message.

A useful concept in understanding noise and its importance in communication is "signal-to-noise ratio." *Signal* refers to information that you would find useful and *noise* refers to information that is useless (to you). For example, a mailing list or newsgroup that contains lots of useful information would be high on signal and low on noise; those that contained lots of useless information would be high on noise and low on signal.

Since messages may be visual as well as spoken, noise too may be visual. Thus, the sunglasses that prevent someone from seeing the nonverbal messages from your eyes would be considered noise as would blurred type on a printed page or garbage on your computer screen. Table 1.2 identifies the four major types of noise in more detail.

All communications contain noise. Although noise cannot be totally eliminated, its effects can be reduced. Making your language more precise, sharpening your skills for sending and receiving nonverbal messages, and improving your listening and feedback skills are some ways to combat the influence of noise.

In Internet language, "channel" refers to a discussion group or an IRC group devoted to a specific topic. These groups are gathering places for discussion via the Internet. A "channel operator" establishes the channel and acts, in some ways, as a leader or moderator (see Chapter 10). How is a channel operator similar to or different from a face-to-face small group leader?

Effects

Communication always has some effect on those involved in the communication act. For every communication act, there is some consequence. For example, you may gain knowledge or learn how to analyze, synthesize, or evaluate something or how to communicate positively or emphatically. These are intellectual or **cognitive effects.** Or, you may acquire new attitudes

Table 1.2 Four Types of Noise

One of the most important skills in communication is to recognize the types of noise and to develop ways to combat them. Consider, for example, what kinds of noise occur in the classroom? In your family communications? At work? What can you do to combat these kinds of noise?

Types of Noise	Definition	Example
Physical	Interference that is external to both speaker and listener; interferes with the physical transmission of the signal or message	Screeching of passing cars, hum of computer, sunglasses
Physiological	Physical barriers within the speaker or listener	Visual impairments, hearing loss, articulation disorders, memory loss
Psychological	Cognitive or mental interference	Biases and prejudices in senders and receivers, closed-mindedness, inaccurate expectations, extreme emotionalism (anger, hate, love, grief)
Semantic	Speaker and listener assigning different meanings	People speaking different languages, use of jargon or overly complex terms not understood by listener

How would you describe noise in Internet communication? What types of noise can you identify in Internet communication?

or beliefs or change existing ones (**affective effects**). Or, you may learn new bodily movements such as how to throw a curve ball, paint a picture, or type (**psychomotor effects**).

PRINCIPLES OF COMMUNICATION

Several communication principles are essential to understanding interpersonal, small group, and public communication. These principles, although significant in terms of explaining theory, also have very practical applications. These principles will provide insight into issues such as:

Important principles may and must be flexible.
—Abraham Lincoln

- why some people communicate quickly and effectively while others have difficulty, even after a long acquaintance
- why some messages are easily believed and others disbelieved
- why disagreements seem to center on trivial issues and yet prove so difficult to resolve
- why people can experience the "same" event and yet disagree on what happened
- why people can so easily interpret each other's intentions
- why things said in anger or haste have such lasting effects

Communication is a Process of Adjustment

Communication takes place only to the extent that communicators use the same system of signals (Pittenger, Hockett, & Danehy, 1960). You will not be able to communicate with another person to the extent that your communication systems differ. In reality, however, no two persons use identical signal systems, so this principle is relevant to all forms of communication. Parents and children, for example, not only have largely different vocabularies but also have different meanings for the terms they share. Different cultures, even when they use a common language, often have different nonverbal communication systems. To the extent that these systems differ, meaningful and effective communication will not prove difficult.

Part of communication competence is being able to identify the other person's signals, and understanding how they're used and what they mean. Those in close relationships soon come to realize that learning the other person's signals takes a great deal of time and often a great deal of patience. If you want to understand what another person means (by a smile, by saying "I love you," by arguing about trivia, by self-deprecating comments), you have to learn that person's system of signals.

This principle is especially important in intercultural communication, largely because people from different cultures use different signals and sometimes similar signals to mean quite different things. Focused eye contact means honesty and openness in much of the United States. That same behavior may signify arrogance or disrespect in Japan, Indonesia, and many Hispanic cultures if engaged in by a youngster with someone significantly older. An illustration of the same signals meaning quite different things in other cultures is provided in the accompanying graphic.

The new source of power is not money in the hands of a few but information in the hands of many.
—John Naisbitt

Power Perspective 1.2

Power Can Be Increased or Decreased

Although people differ greatly in the amount of power they wield at any time and in any specific situation, everyone can increase their power in some ways. You can lift weights and increase your physical power. You can learn the techniques of negotiation and increase your power in group situations. You can learn the principles of communication and increase your persuasive power.

Power can also be decreased. Probably the most common way to lose power is by unsuccessfully trying to control another's behavior. For example, if you threaten someone with punishment and then fail to carry out your threat, you will lose power. Another way to lose power is to allow others to control you, for example, to take unfair advantage of you. When you don't confront these power tactics of others, you lose power yourself.

[The next Power Perspective appears on page 45.]

Have you done anything in the last few days to increase your power? If not, why not?

Communication Accommodation An interesting theory largely revolving around adjustment is communication accommodation theory. This theory holds that speakers adjust to or accommodate to the speaking style of their listeners to gain, for example, social approval and greater communication efficiency (Giles, Mulac, Bradac, & Johnson, 1987). For

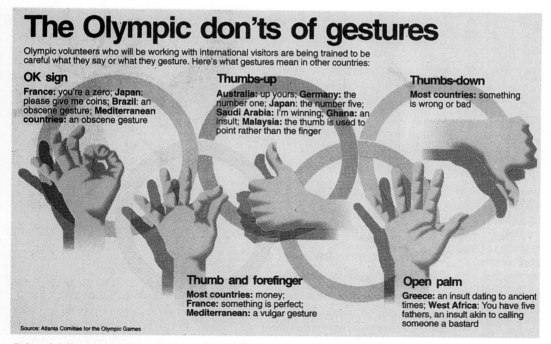

The Olympic don'ts of gestures

Olympic volunteers who will be working with international visitors are being trained to be careful what they say or what they gesture. Here's what gestures mean in other countries:

OK sign
France: you're a zero; **Japan:** please give me coins; **Brazil:** an obscene gesture; **Mediterranean countries:** an obscene gesture

Thumbs-up
Australia: up yours; **Germany:** the number one; **Japan:** the number five; **Saudi Arabia:** I'm winning; **Ghana:** an insult; **Malaysia:** the thumb is used to point rather than the finger

Thumbs-down
Most countries: something is wrong or bad

Thumb and forefinger
Most countries: money; **France:** something is perfect; **Mediterranean:** a vulgar gesture

Open palm
Greece: an insult dating to ancient times; **West Africa:** You have five fathers, an insult akin to calling someone a bastard

Source: Atlanta Comittee for the Olympic Games

Cultural differences in the meanings of nonverbal gestures are often great. The over-the-head clasped hands that signifies victory to an American may signify friendship to a Russian. To an American, holding up two fingers to make a V signifies victory or peace. To certain South Americans, however, it is an obscene gesture that corresponds to the American's extended middle finger. This figure highlights some additional nonverbal differences. Can you identify others?

Do you accommodate to the communication styles of those with whom you interact? Do doctors, nurses, and patients accommodate to each other's communication style? Who is most likely to make the accommodation?

example, when two people have a similar speech rate, they seem to be more attracted to each other than to those with dissimilar rates (Buller, LePoire, Aune, & Eloy, 1992). Speech rate similarity has also been associated with greater sociability and intimacy between communicators (Buller & Aune, 1992).

Similarly, the speaker who uses language intensity similar to that of the listeners, is judged to have greater credibility than the speaker who uses a level of intensity different from that of the listeners (Aune & Kikuchi, 1993). Still another study found that roommates who had similar communication attitudes (both roommates were high in communication competence and willingness to communicate and low in verbal aggressiveness) were highest in roommate liking and satisfaction (Martin & Anderson, 1995). Although this theory has not been tested on computer communication, it would predict that styles of written communication in E-mail or in IRC groups would also evidence accommodation and that you would find it more satisfying interacting with those who had a similar communication style.

As you'll see throughout this text, communication characteristics are influenced greatly by culture (Albert & Nelson, 1993). Thus, the communication similarities that lead to attraction and more positive perceptions are more likely to be present in *intra*cultural communication than in *inter*cultural encounters. This may present an important (but not insurmountable) obstacle to intercultural communication.

Communication Is a Package of Messages

Communication normally occurs in "packages" of verbal and nonverbal messages (Pittenger, Hockett, & Danehy, 1960). Usually, verbal and nonverbal signals reinforce or support each other. You don't usually express fear with words while the rest of your body relaxes. You don't normally express anger with your bodily posture while your face smiles. Your entire being works as a whole—verbally and nonverbally—to express your thoughts and feelings.

It's been argued that both the therapist and the client with disabilities send contradictory messages that create "double-binds" for each other (Esten & Wilmot, 1993). The client communicates both the desire to focus on the disability but also the desire to disregard it. If the therapist focuses on the disability, it is in violation of the client's desire to ignore it and if the therapist ignores it, it is in violation of the client's desire to concentrate on it. What guidelines would you offer the therapist or the client, based on your understanding of contradictory messages?

Usually, little attention is paid to the packaged nature of communication. It goes unnoticed. However, when the messages contradict each other—when eye avoidance belies the "I'm telling the truth," and when the nervous posture contradicts the focused stare—you take notice. Invariably you begin to question the person's sincerity and honesty.

Communication Involves Content and Relationship Dimensions

Communication can refer to something external to both speaker and listener (for example, the weather) as well as to the relationships between speaker and listener (for example, who is in charge). These two aspects are referred to as content and relationship dimensions of communication (Watzlawick, Beavin, & Jackson, 1967).

For example, let's say that a supervisor asks a worker to stop by the office after the meeting. The content aspect refers to what the supervisor wants the worker to do, namely, see him or her after the meeting. The relationship aspect, however, is different and refers to the relationship between the supervisor and the worker; it states how the communication is to be interpreted. For example, the use of the command indicates a status difference between the two parties: the supervisor can command the worker. If the worker commanded the supervisor, it would appear awkward and out of place because it would violate the normal relationship between employer and worker.

Some research shows that women engage in more relationship talk than men; they talk more about relationships, in general, and about the present relationship, in particular. Men engage in more content talk; they talk more about things external to the relationship (Wood, 1994; Pearson, West, & Turner, 1993). The accompanying cartoon cleverly captures this gender difference.

Problems often result from the failure to distinguish between the content and the relationship levels of communication. Consider a couple: Pat and Chris. Pat made plans to study with friends during the weekend without first asking Chris and an argument ensued. Probably both would have agreed that to study was the right choice to make. Thus, the argument is not centered on the content level. The argument, instead, centers on the relationship level. Chris expected to be consulted about plans for the weekend. Pat, in not doing this, rejected this definition of the relationship.

Examine the following interchange and note how relationship considerations are ignored.

People don't care how much we know until they know how much we care.
—*Dutch Boling*

"*If you want to talk, get a paper, and we'll talk about what's in the paper.*"

Based on your own experience, do you find this cartoon a generally accurate depiction of the male's preference for talking about matters external to the relationship? Would the cartoon be humorous if the woman were the speaker?

> Pat: I'm going to the rally tomorrow. The people at the health center are all going to voice their protest and I'm going with them. [Pat focuses on the content and ignores any relational implications of the message.]
>
> Chris: Why can't we ever do anything together? [Chris responds primarily on a relational level and ignores the content implications of the message, expressing displeasure at being ignored in this decision.]
>
> Pat: We can do something together anytime; tomorrow's the day of the rally. [Again, Pat focuses almost exclusively on the content.]

Here is essentially the same situation, but with something added: sensitivity to relationship messages.

> Pat: The people at the center are going to the rally tomorrow and I'd like to go with them. Would it be all right if I went to the rally? [Although Pat focuses on content, there is always an awareness of the relational dimensions by asking if this would be a problem. Pat also shows this in expressing a desire rather than a decision to attend this rally.]
>
> Chris: That sounds great but I'd really like to do something together tomorrow. [Chris focuses on the relational dimension but also acknowledges Pat's content orientation. Note too, that Chris does not respond defensively, as if there was a necessity to defend oneself or the emphasis on relational aspects.]
>
> Pat: How about your meeting me at La Cantina for dinner after the rally? [Pat responds to the relational aspect—without abandoning the desire to attend the rally. Pat tries to negotiate a solution that will meet the needs of both of them.]
>
> Chris: That sounds great. I'm dying for tacos. [Chris responds to both messages, approving of both Pat's attending the rally but also of their dinner date.]

Can you think of a specific example from your own experience where the differences between content and relationship messages caused a misunderstanding? Was this misunderstanding eventually clarified? If so, how?

Communication Sequences Are Punctuated

Communication events are continuous transactions with no clear-cut beginning or ending. As a participant in or an observer of communication, you divide this continuous, circular process into causes and effects, or stimuli and responses. That is, you segment or **punctuate** this continuous stream of communication into smaller pieces (Watzlawick, Beavin, & Jackson, 1967). Some of these you label causes (or stimuli), and others effects (or responses).

Consider this example: This manager lacks interest in the employees, seldom offering any suggestions for improvement or any praise for jobs well done. The employees are apathetic and morale is low. Each action (the manager's lack of involvement and the employees' low morale) stimulates the other. Each serves as the stimulus for the other but there may be no identifiable initial stimulus. Each event may be seen as a stimulus or as a response.

To understand what another person means from his or her point of view, you have to see the sequence of events as punctuated by the other person. Recognize too that your punctuation does not reflect what exists in reality. Rather, it reflects your own unique, subjective, and fallible perception.

Communication Is Purposeful

You communicate for a purpose; some motivation leads you to communicate. When you speak or write, you're trying to send your ideas to another; you're trying to accomplish some goal. Although different cultures will emphasize different purposes and motives (Rubin & Fernandez-Collado, 1992), five general purposes seem relatively common to most if not all forms of communication: to learn, to relate, to help, to influence, and to play:

to learn	to acquire knowledge of others, the world, and yourself
to relate	to form relationships with others, to interact with others as individuals
to help	to assist others by listening, offering solutions
to influence	to strengthen or change the attitudes or behaviors of others
to play	to enjoy the experience of the moment

Communication Is Inevitable, Irreversible, and Unrepeatable

Communication is **inevitable** and often takes place even though a person may not want to communicate. For example, take a student sitting in the back of the room with an "expressionless" face, perhaps staring out the window. Although the student might claim not to be communicating with the instructor, the instructor may derive any number of messages from this behavior—perhaps that the student lacks interest, is bored, or is worried about something. In any event, the teacher is receiving messages even though the student might not intentionally be sending any (Watzlawick, Beavin, & Jackson, 1967; Motley, 1990a, 1990b; Bavelas, 1990). This does not mean that all behavior is communication. For instance, if the student looked out the window and the teacher did not notice, no communication would have taken place. The two people must be in an interactional situation and the behavior must be perceived by some other person for the principle of inevitability to operate.

Notice too, that when you're in an interactional situation, you cannot *not* respond to the messages of others. For example, if you notice someone winking at you, you must respond in some way. Even if you don't respond actively or openly, that lack of response is itself a response, and it communicates.

Communication is also **irreversible.** Once you say something or press that send key on your E-mail, you cannot uncommunicate it. You can, of course, try to reduce the effects of your message. You can say, for example, "I really didn't mean what I said" or "Let me explain." But, regardless of how hard you try to negate or reduce the effects of your message, the message itself, once it has been received, cannot be taken back. In a public speaking situation in which the speech is recorded or broadcast,

Can you describe an argument that revolved around the difference in the way two people punctuated a sequence of events? Are men and women equally sensitive to the differences in the way people punctuate an interaction?

Will the new communication technologies (for example, E-mail, working at computer terminals, and telecommuting) change the basic purposes of communication identified here?

inappropriate messages may have national or even international effects. Here, attempts to put a positive spin on what one has said (for example, trying to offer clarification) often have the effect of further publicizing the original statement.

In face-to-face communication, the actual signals (the movements in the air) are evanescent; they fade almost as they are uttered. Some written messages, especially computer mediated messages such as those sent through E-mail, are unerasable. E-mails that are sent among employees in a large corporation, are often stored on disk or tape. Currently much litigation is proceeding using the evidence of racist or sexist E-mails that senders thought were erased, but weren't.

Because of irreversibility (and unerasability), be careful not to say things you may be sorry for later. Especially in conflict situations, when tempers run high, avoid saying things you may later wish to withdraw. Commitment messages—the "I love you" messages and their variants—need also to be monitored. Messages that can be interpreted as sexist, racist, or homophobic, which you thought private, might later be retrieved by others and create all sorts of problems for you and your organization. In group and public communication situations, when the messages are received by many people, it's especially crucial to recognize irreversibility.

Communication is also **unrepeatable.** A communication act can never be duplicated. The reason is simple: everyone and everything is constantly changing. As a result, you can never recapture the exact same situation, frame of mind, or relationship dynamics that defined a previous communication act. You can never repeat meeting someone for the first time, comforting a grieving friend, leading a small group for the first time, or giving a public speech.

CULTURE AND HUMAN COMMUNICATION

A walk through any large city, many small towns, and through just about any college campus will convince you that the United States is largely a collection of a lot of different cultures (see Figure 1.6). These cultures coexist somewhat separately but also with each influencing the other. This coexistence has led some researchers to refer to these cultures as cocultures (Samovar & Porter, 1991; Jandt, 1995). Many Internet groups (IRC groups or mailing list groups, for example) are even more multicultural, often drawing members from countries spanning the entire globe. Many of these groups have their own language, rituals, rules, and sanctions for violating them and are therefore much like cultures themselves. Try to see communication, whether face-to-face or via the Internet, with this cultural dimension in mind.

The Relevance of Culture

There are many reasons for the cultural emphasis you will find in this book. Most obviously, perhaps, are the vast demographic changes taking place throughout the United States. Whereas, at one time, the United States was largely a country populated by Europeans, it is now a country greatly influenced by the enormous number of new citizens from Latin and South America, Africa, and Asia. The same, as already noted, is even more true

With very good intentions, you tell your partner "I guess you'll just never learn how to dress." To your surprise your partner becomes extremely offended. Although you know you can't take the statement back (communication really is irreversible), you want to lessen its negative tone and its effect on your partner. What do you say?

Never say anything on the phone that you wouldn't want your mother to hear at your trial.
—Sydney Biddle Barrows

E Pluribus Unum—it was a good idea when our country was founded, and it's a good idea today. From many, one. That still identifies us.
—Barbara Jordan

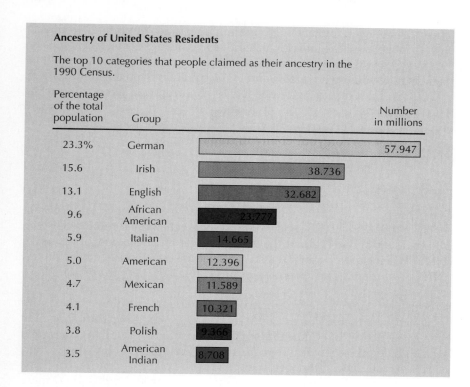

Ancestry of United States Residents

The top 10 categories that people claimed as their ancestry in the 1990 Census.

Percentage of the total population	Group	Number in millions
23.3%	German	57.947
15.6	Irish	38.736
13.1	English	32.682
9.6	African American	23.777
5.9	Italian	14.665
5.0	American	12.396
4.7	Mexican	11.589
4.1	French	10.321
3.8	Polish	9.366
3.5	American Indian	8.708

Figure 1.6 Ancestry of United States Residents

With immigration patterns changing so rapidly, the portrait illustrated here is likely to look very different in the coming years. What do you think the top 10 categories that people claim as their ancestry will be in the census for the year 2000? For the year 2020?

in colleges and universities throughout the United States and in much Internet communication. With these changes have come different ways of communicating and the need to understand and adapt to new ways of looking at communication.

We're also living in a time when people have become increasingly sensitive to cultural differences. American society has moved from an originally assimilationist perspective (people should leave their native culture behind and adopt their new culture) to one that values cultural diversity and recognizes the contributions of people with different cultural backgrounds and the value of a multicultural society and believes that people should retain their native cultural ways. With some notable exceptions—hate speech, racism, sexism, homophobia, and classism come quickly to mind—we're more concerned with saying the right thing and with ultimately developing a society where all cultures can co-exist and enrich each other. At the same time, the ability to interact effectively with members of other cultures often translates into financial gain and increased employment opportunities and advancement prospects. The increased economic interdependence of the United States and widely different cultures makes it essential to gain the needed intercultural communication understanding and skills.

Do your other college courses and textbooks integrate a multicultural perspective? How is this reflected?

The Aim of a Cultural Perspective

Because culture permeates all forms of communication, it's necessary to understand its influences if you're to understand and master effective communication. Culture influences what you say to yourself and how you talk with coworkers, friends, lovers, and family in everyday conversation. It

No culture can live, if it attempts to be exclusive.

—Mahatma Gandhi

In what ways would communication (interpersonal, small group, or public speaking) between or among people from the same culture and people from widely different cultures be the same? In what ways would they differ?

Are your local media more or less "culturally integrated" than the national media?

influences how you interact in groups and how much importance you place on the group versus the individual. It influences the topics you talk about and the strategies you use in communicating information or in persuading. It influences how you use the media and in the credibility you attribute to them.

Cultural understanding is needed to communicate effectively in the wide variety of intercultural situations. Success in interpersonal, small group, or public speaking—on your job and in your social life—will depend in great part on your ability to communicate with persons who are culturally different from yourself.

Ethnocentrism

One of the problems that hinders cultural awareness and sensitivity is **ethnocentrism,** the tendency to see others and their behaviors through your own cultural filters and to evaluate the values, beliefs, and behaviors of your own culture as being more positive, logical, and natural than those of other cultures.

Ethnocentrism exists on a continuum (Table 1.3). People are not ethnocentric or non-ethnocentric; rather, we are all somewhere between these polar opposites. Your degree of ethnocentrism varies depending on the group on which you focus. For example, if you're Greek American, you may have a low degree of ethnocentrism when dealing with Italian Americans but a high degree when dealing with Turkish Americans or Japanese Americans. Your degree of ethnocentrism (and we're all ethnocentric to at least some degree) will influence your interpersonal, group, public, and mass communication behaviors.

Table 1.3 The Ethnocentrism Continuum

This table, which draws from a number of researchers (Lukens, 1978; Gudykunst & Kim, 1984; Gudykunst, 1991), summarizes some of the interconnections. In this table five degrees of ethnocentrism are identified; in reality, of course, there are as many degrees as there are people. The "communication distances" are general terms that highlight the attitude that dominates that level of ethnocentrism. Under "communications" are some of the major ways people might interact given their particular degree of ethnocentrism.

Degree of Ethnocentrism	Communication Distance	Communications
Low	Equality	Treats others as equals; views different customs and ways of behaving as equal to your own
	Sensitivity	Wants to decrease distance between self and others
	Indifference	Lacks concern for others; prefers to interact in a world of similar other
	Avoidance	Avoids and limits communications, especially intimate ones with interculturally different others
High	Disparagement	Engages in hostile behavior; belittles others; views different cultures and ways of behaving as inferior to your own

Ethical Issue

Ethics and Human Communication

Because communication has effects, it also involves questions of ethics. There is a right-versus-wrong aspect to any communication act (Jaksa & Pritchard, 1994; Bok, 1978; Johannesen, 1990). For example, while it may be effective to lie in selling a product, most would agree that it would not be ethical.

Because of the central importance of ethics to all forms and functions of communication, ethical issues are integrated throughout this text. Here are just a few issues we consider throughout the text. As you read down the list consider what you *would* do if confronted with this issue and what you feel you *should* do (if this is different from what you *would* do). What general principle of ethics are you using in making these *would* and *should* judgments?

- Would it be ethical to not tell your romantic partner that you had an affair last week to avoid an argument and ill-feelings?
- Would it be ethical to reveal to a mutual acquaintance that Pat had served time in prison?
- Would it be ethical to exaggerate your virtues and minimize your vices to get a job? To get a promotion that you deserve? To get a date?
- Would it be ethical to assume leadership of a group to get the group to do as you wish?
- Would it be ethical to persuade an audience by scaring or threatening them if your goal was to get them to do something that would be beneficial to them, for example, getting them to stop smoking? To get them to follow a particular religious belief? To get them to do something that would benefit, say, the poor and homeless?

[The next Ethical Issue box appears on page 34.]

THINKING CRITICALLY ABOUT HUMAN COMMUNICATION

Suggestions for beginning your study of communication and for making your skills useful in a wide variety of contexts are provided in this chapter's critical thinking section.

What ethical principles do you follow in communicating with others? What ethical principles do you wish others would follow more often when communicating with you? What would be the most unethical communication you can think of?

Approaching the Study of Communication

In approaching the study of human communication, keep the following in mind. Realize, first, that the study of human communication involves both theory and research *and* practical skills for increasing communication effectiveness. Seek to understand the theories and research *and* to improve your communication skills. Each will assist in understanding the other: A knowledge of theory will help you better understand the skills and a knowledge of skills will help you better understand theory.

The concepts and principles discussed throughout this book and this course directly relate to your everyday communications. Try, for example, to recall examples from your own communications that illustrate the ideas considered here. This will help to make the material more personal and easier to assimilate.

Analyze yourself as a critical thinker and a communicator. Self-understanding is essential if you're to use this material in any meaningful sense, for example, to change some of your own behaviors. Be open to new ideas, even those that may contradict your existing beliefs.

Become willing to change your ways of communicating and even your ways of thinking. Carefully assess what you should and should not change, what you should strengthen or revise, and what you should leave as is.

Transferring Skills

Throughout this text, a wide variety of skills for improving interpersonal, small group, and public speaking are presented. Try not to limit these skills to the situations described here, but instead apply these to a wide variety of situations. You will find that skills learned here will transfer to other areas of your life if you do three things (Sternberg, 1987):

First, think about the principles flexibly and recognize exceptions to the rule. Consider where the principles seem useful and where they need to be adjusted. Recognize especially that the principles discussed here are largely the result of research conducted on college students in the United States. Ask yourself if they apply to other groups and other cultures.

Second, seek analogies between current situations and those you experienced earlier. What are the similarities? What are the differences? For example, most people repeat relationship problems because they fail to see the similarities (and sometimes the differences) between the old and destructive relationship and the new and soon-to-be equally destructive relationship.

Third, look for situations at home, work, and school where you could apply the skills discussed here. For instance, how can active listening skills improve your family communication? How can brainstorming and problem-solving skills help you deal with challenges at work?

> I am convinced that it is of primordial importance to learn more every year than the year before. After all, what is education but a process by which a person begins to learn how to learn?
> —*Peter Ustinov*

SUMMARY OF CONCEPTS AND SKILLS

In this chapter the nature of communication, the major models and concepts, some major communication principles, and the relevance of culture to human communication were considered.

1. Communication is best viewed as transactional (rather than linear or interactional). Communication is a process of interrelated parts.
2. Communication is the act, by one or more persons, of sending and receiving messages that are distorted by noise, occur within a context, have some effect (and some ethical dimension), and provide some opportunity for feedback.
3. The essentials of communication—the elements present in every communication act—are: context (physical, cultural, social–psychological, and temporal), source–receiver, competence, field of experience, messages, channel, noise (physical, physiological, psychological, and semantic), sending or encoding processes, receiving or decoding processes, effects, and ethics.
4. Communication messages may be of varied forms and may be sent and received through any combination of sensory organs. Communication messages may also metacommunicate—communicate about other messages. The communication channel is the medium through which the messages are sent.
5. Feedback refers to messages or information that is sent back to the source. It may come from the source itself or from the receiver. Feedforward refers to messages that preface other messages.
6. Noise is anything that distorts the message; it is present to some degree in every communication.
7. Communication ethics refers to the moral rightness or wrongness of a message and is an integral part of every effort to communicate.
8. Communication is a process of adjustment where each person must adjust his or her signals to the understanding of the other if meaning is to be transmitted from one person to another. In fact, communication accommodation theory holds that people imitate the speaking style of the other person as a way of gaining social approval.
9. Normally, communication is a package of signals, each reinforcing the other. When these signals oppose each other, we have contradictory messages.
10. Communication involves both content dimensions and relationship dimensions.
11. Communication sequences are punctuated for processing. Individuals divide the communication sequence into stimuli and responses in different ways.
12. Communication is purposeful. Through communication, you learn, relate, help, influence, and play.

13. In any interactional situation, communication is inevitable (you cannot not communicate nor can you not respond to communication), irreversible (you cannot take back any message), and unrepeatable (you cannot exactly repeat any message).

14. Culture permeates all forms of communication and intercultural communication is becoming more and more frequent as the United States becomes home and business partner to numerous different cultures.

15. Ethnocentrism, existing on a continuum, is the tendency to evaluate the beliefs, attitudes, and values of one's own culture positively and those of other cultures negatively.

Several important communication skills, emphasized in this chapter, are presented here in summary form (as they are in every chapter). These skill checklists don't include all the skills covered in the chapter but rather are representative of the most important skills. You'll gain most from this brief experience if you think carefully about each skill and try to identify instances from your recent communications in which you did or did not act on the basis of the specific skill. Use a rating scale such as the following: (1) = always, (2) = often, (3) = sometimes, (4) = rarely, (5) = hardly ever.

_____ 1. I'm sensitive to contexts of communication. I recognize that changes in the physical, cultural, social–psychological, and temporal contexts will alter meaning.

_____ 2. I look for meaning not only in words but in nonverbal behaviors as well.

_____ 3. I am sensitive to the feedback that I give to others and that others give to me.

_____ 4. I combat the effects of physical, physiological, psychological, and semantic noise that distort messages.

_____ 5. Because communication is transactional, I recognize the mutual influence of all elements and that messages are sent and received simultaneously by each speaker/listener.

_____ 6. Because communication is a process of adjustment, I make an effort to learn the other person's system of signals and meanings.

_____ 7. Because communication is a package of signals, I use my verbal and nonverbal messages to reinforce rather than contradict each other and I respond to contradictory messages by identifying and openly discussing the dual meanings communicated.

_____ 8. I listen to the relational messages that I and others send, and respond to the relational messages of others to increase meaningful interaction.

_____ 9. I actively look for the punctuation pattern that I and others use in order to better understand the meanings communicated.

_____ 10. Because communication is purposeful, I look carefully at both the speaker's and the listener's purposes.

_____ 11. Because communication is inevitable, irreversible, and unrepeatable, I look carefully for hidden meanings, am cautious in communicating messages that I may later wish to withdraw, and am aware that any communication act occurs only once.

_____ 12. I am sensitive to cultural variation and differences and see my own cultural teachings and those of other cultures without undue bias.

KEY WORD QUIZ

Write T for those statements that are true and F for those that are false. For those that are false, replace the boldface term with the correct term.

_____ 1. **Intrapersonal communication** refers to communication with oneself.

_____ 2. The tendency to see others and their behaviors through your own cultural filters and to evaluate your cultural values and beliefs as more positive than those of other cultures is known as **ethnocentrism.**

_____ 3. The process of putting ideas into a code, for example, thinking of an idea and then describing it in words is known as **decoding.**

_____ 4. The knowledge of how communication works and the ability to use communication effectively is called **communication competence.**

_____ 5. Messages that refer to other messages are called **metamessages.**

_____ 6. The messages you get back from your own messages and from the responses of others to what you communicate are known as **feedforward.**

_____ 7. Communication that refers to matters external to both speaker and listener is known as **relationship communication.**

_____ 8. The ways in which the sequence of communication is divided up into, for example, causes and effects or stimuli and responses is known as **punctuation.**

_____ 9. The view of communication that sees each person serving both speaker and listener roles simultaneously is an **interactional one.**

_____ 10. Interpersonal communication is **inevitable, reversible,** and **unrepeatable.**

Answers: TRUE: Numbers 1, 2, 4, 5, and 8. FALSE: 3 (encoding), 6 (feedback), 7 (content communication), 9 (transactional one), 10 (irreversible).

SKILL DEVELOPMENT EXPERIENCES

1.1 Models of Human Communication

The model presented in this chapter is only one possible representation of how communication takes place. Because it was introduced to explain certain foundation concepts, it was simplified to focus on two people in conversation. Either alone or in groups, construct your own diagrammatic model of the essential elements and processes involved in any one of the following situations. Your model's primary function should be to describe the elements involved and what processes operate in the specific situation chosen. You may find it useful to define the situation in more specific terms before you begin constructing your model.

1. Sitting silently on the bus trying to decide what you should say in your job interview.
2. Asking for a date on the phone to someone you've only communicated with on the Net.
3. Participating in a small work group to decide how to reduce operating costs.
4. Talking with someone who speaks a different language (which you don't know and who does not know your language) and comes from a culture very different from your own.
5. Delivering a lecture to a class of college students.
6. Performing in a movie.
7. Calling someone to try to get him or her to sign up with your telephone service.
8. Persuading an angry crowd to disband.
9. Writing a speech for a political candidate.
10. Watching television.

How adequately does your model explain the process of human communication? Would it help someone new to the field to get a clear picture of what communication is and how it operates? On the basis of this model, how might you revise the model presented earlier in this chapter in Figure 1.4?

1.2 Comparing Communication Channels

Here are several examples of face-to-face and computer communication situations. For each pair, draw a simple communication model for each communication situation and identify the ways in which each form of communication differs from its counterpart.

1. Sending (and receiving) E-mail and snail mail.
2. Talking (and listening) on the phone and sending (and receiving) E-mail.
3. Communicating in a small face-to-face group and in an IRC group.
4. Reading a commercial website and a print catalog or brochure.

5. Using a search engine such as Yahoo! or Excite and a print reference work such as *Reader's Guide to Periodical Literature* or *Psychological Abstracts* to search for information on a specific topic.
6. Posting (reading) a newsgroup message and giving (listening to) a public speech.

What general principle can you formulate that distinguishes "traditional" channels of communication from the newer electronic channels? In what ways do the different channels influence the messages you communicate? For example, do you communicate the same way when you compose a letter and when you send E-mail? Do you talk in a face-to-face group in the same way you communicate in an electronic chat room?

1.3 What's Happening?

How would you use the principles of human communication to *describe* what is happening in each of the following situations? Do note that these scenarios are extremely brief and are written only as aids to stimulate you to think more concretely about the axioms. The objective is not to select the one correct principle (each scenario can probably be described by reference to several), but to provide an opportunity to think about how the principles can be applied to specific situations.

1. A couple, together for 20 years, argues constantly about the seemingly most insignificant things—who takes the dog out, who does the shopping, who decides where to go to dinner, and so on. It has gotten to the point where they rarely have a day without argument and both are seriously considering separating.
2. Tanya and her grandmother can't seem to agree on what Tanya should do or not do. Tanya, for example, wants to go away for the weekend with her friends from college. Her grandmother fears she will get in with a bad crowd and end up in trouble and refuses to allow her to go.
3. In the heat of a big argument, Harry says he didn't want to ever see Peggy's family again. "They don't like me and I don't like them." Peggy reciprocated and said she felt the same way about his family. Now, weeks later, there remains a great deal of tension between them especially when they find themselves with one or both families.
4. Grace and Mark are engaged to be married and are currently senior executives at a large advertising agency. Recently, Grace made a presentation that was not received positively by the other members of the team. Grace feels that Tom—in not defending her proposal—created a negative attitude and actually encouraged others to reject her ideas. Tom says

that he felt he could not defend her proposal because others in the room would have felt his defense was motivated by their relationship and not by his positive evaluation of her proposal. So, he felt it was best to say nothing.

5. Pat and Chris have been online friends for the last 2 years, communicating with each other at least once a day. Recently, Pat wrote a number of things that Chris interpreted as insulting and as ridiculing Chris's feelings and dreams. Chris wrote back that these last messages were greatly resented and then stopped writing. Pat has written every day for the last 2 weeks to try to patch things up; Chris won't respond.

6. Margo has just taken over as vice president in charge of sales for a manufacturing company. Margo is extremely organized and refuses to waste time on nonessentials. In her staff meetings, she is business only. Several top sales representatives have requested to be assigned to other VPs. Their reason: They feel she works them too hard and doesn't care about them as people.

Although the purpose of this exercise was to describe what is happening, many people have a tendency to evaluate why things are going wrong and to suggest what they should do about it. Did you? If so, do you also do this when listening to someone talk about personal problems? What happens?

CHAPTER 2

The Self in Communication

CHAPTER CONCEPTS	CHAPTER GOALS	CHAPTER SKILLS
	After completing this chapter, you should be able to	After completing this chapter, you should be able to
Self-Concept	1. define *self-concept* and explain how it develops	communicate with an understanding of your self-concept, your strengths and weaknesses
Self-Awareness	2. define *self-awareness* and explain how you can increase it	increase your own self-awareness
Self-Disclosure	3. define *self-disclosure,* the factors influencing it, and its potential rewards and dangers	evaluate the costs and rewards of self-disclosure
Thinking Critically About the Self in Communication	4. explain the role of the self in communication	regulate your self-disclosures on the basis of the potential rewards and dangers

In all communications, the most important part is yourself. Who you are and how you see yourself influence the way you communicate and how you respond to others. In this chapter, we explore the self: the self-concept and how it develops; self-awareness and ways to increase it; and self-disclosure, communication that reveals who you are and how to regulate it effectively.

SELF-CONCEPT

Your self-concept is your image of who you are. It's how you perceive yourself: your feelings and thoughts about your strengths and weaknesses, your abilities and limitations. Self-concept develops from the image that others have of you; the comparisons between yourself and others; your cultural teachings; and your evaluation of your own thoughts and behaviors (Figure 2.1).

Other's Images of You

If you wished to see the way your hair looked, you'd probably look in a mirror. What would you do if you wanted to see how friendly or how assertive you are? According to the concept of the *looking-glass self* (Cooley, 1922), you would look at the image of yourself that others reveal to you through their behaviors and especially through the way they treat you and react to you.

Of course, you would not look to just anyone. Rather, you would look to those who are most significant in your life—to your *significant others*. As a child you would look to your parents and then to your elementary school teachers, for example. As an adult you might look to your friends, romantic partners, or children, as illustrated in the accompanying cartoon. If these significant others think highly of you, you will see a positive self-image reflected in their behaviors; if they think little of you, you will see a more negative image.

Even when we are quite alone, how often do we think with pleasure or pain of what others think of us—of their imagined approbation or disapprobation.

—*Charles Darwin*

Figure 2.1 The Sources of Self-Concept

This diagram depicts the four sources of self-concept, the four contributors to how you see yourself. As you read about self-concept, consider the influence of each factor throughout your life. Which factor influenced you most as a pre-teen? Which influences you the most now? Which will influence you the most 25 or 30 years from now?

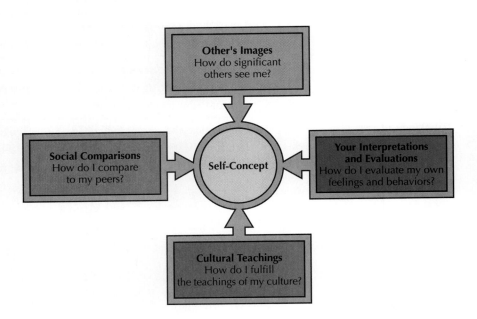

"Is everything all right, Jeffrey? You never call me 'dude' anymore."

Comparisons with Others

Another way you develop your self-concept is to compare yourself with others, to engage in what is called social comparisons (Festinger, 1954). Again, you don't choose just anyone. Rather, when you want to gain insight into who you are and how effective or competent you are, you compare yourself to your peers. For example, after an examination you probably want to know how you performed relative to the other students in your class. This gives you a clearer idea as to how effectively you performed. If you play on a baseball team, it's important to know your batting average in comparison with the batting average of others on the team. Absolute scores on the exam or of your batting average may be helpful in telling you something about your performance, but you gain a different perspective when you see your scores in comparison with those of your peers.

Cultural Teachings

Through your parents, teachers, and the media, your culture instills in you a variety beliefs, values, and attitudes—about success (how it should be defined and how you should achieve it), the relevance of a person's religion, race, or nationality, the ethical principles you should follow in business and in your personal life. These teachings provide benchmarks against which you can measure yourself. For example, your success in achieving what your culture defines as success will contribute to a positive self-concept. Your failure to achieve what your culture teaches (for example, not being married by the time you're 30) can contribute to a negative self-concept.

Especially important in self-concept are the teachings about gender roles, about how a man or woman should act. In fact, a popular classification of cultures is in terms of their masculinity and femininity (Hofstede, 1996). In

Some research (for example, Swann, 1984, 1987) shows that people adopt strategies and enter relationships that will confirm their self-concepts, even when these self-concepts are negative (Jones, 1990). People, Swann (1987) notes, "gravitate toward social relationships in which they are apt to receive self-confirmatory feedback." Do you do this? Do those you know do this?

Research (Brody, 1991) shows that girls and boys as young as 2 years old respond differently to success and failure. Boys show more pride in their successes than do girls. Girls, on the other hand, react to failure with greater shame. Girls also allow a single failure to affect the way they feel about themselves more than do boys. What implications would you draw from these findings?

a highly "masculine" culture, men are viewed as assertive, oriented to material success, and strong; women, on the other hand, are viewed as modest, focused on the quality of life, and tender. In a highly "feminine" culture, both men and women are encouraged to be modest, oriented to maintaining the quality of life, and tender. On the basis of Hofstede's research, the 10 countries with the highest masculinity score (beginning with the highest) are: Japan, Austria, Venezuela, Italy, Switzerland, Mexico, Ireland, Jamaica, Great Britain, and Germany. The 10 countries with the highest femininity score (beginning with the highest) are: Sweden, Norway, Netherlands, Denmark, Costa Rica, Yugoslavia, Finland, Chile, Portugal, and Thailand. Out of 53 countries ranked, the United States ranks 15th most masculine.

Masculine cultures emphasize individual success and so socialize their people to be assertive, ambitious, and competitive. For example, members of masculine cultures are more likely to confront conflicts directly and to competitively fight out any differences; they're more likely to emphasize conflict strategies in which they win and the others lose. Feminine cultures emphasize the quality of life and so socialize their people to be modest and to emphasize close interpersonal relationships. Feminine cultures are more likely to emphasize compromise and negotiation in resolving conflicts; they're more likely to emphasize conflict strategies in which both parties win.

Similarly, organizations can be viewed as masculine or feminine. Masculine organizations emphasize competitiveness and aggressiveness. They emphasize the bottom line and reward their workers on the basis of their contribution to the organization. Feminine organizations are less competitive and less aggressive. They're more likely to emphasize worker

Ethical Issue

Approaches to Ethics

In analyzing the ethics of a particular message or act, some people take the position that the question of ethics is objective and some that it's subjective. An **objective view** of ethics argues that the morality of an act—say a communication message—is absolute and exists apart from the values or beliefs of any individual or culture. An objective view holds that there is a set of standards that apply to all people in all situations at all times. Lying, false advertising, using false evidence, or revealing secrets you've promised to keep—to cite just a few examples—are unethical according to the objective view, regardless of the circumstances, and the values and beliefs of the culture in which they occur.

A **subjective view** of ethics argues that absolute statements of morality are ethnocentric and that the ethics of a message depends on the culture's values and beliefs as well as the particular communication circumstances. Thus, a subjective position would claim that lying is wrong to win votes or sell cigarettes, but that it may be ethical if the end result is positive, such as trying to make someone feel better by telling them they look great or that they will get well soon.

As you progress through your study of human communication and analyze your own communications, think about whether you hold objective or subjective views on ethics. Did your culture teach you that one of these views was correct and the other incorrect? Which view do you feel is supported in your typical college class? Consider, too, how the approach you take will yield different answers about the ethics of a particular message or act.

[The next Ethical Issue box appears on page 63.]

satisfaction and reward their workers on the basis of need; those who have large families, for example, may get better raises than single people, even if the singles have contributed more to the organization.

When you demonstrate the qualities that your culture (or your organization) teaches, you will see yourself as a cultural success and will be rewarded by other members of the culture (or organization). Seeing yourself as culturally successful and getting rewarded by others will contribute positively to your self-concept. When you fail to demonstrate such qualities, you are more likely to see yourself as a cultural failure and to be punished by other members of the culture, contributing to a more negative self-concept.

Your Own Interpretations and Evaluations

You also react to your own behavior—you interpret it and evaluate it. These interpretations and evaluations contribute to your self-concept. For example, let's say you believe that lying is wrong. If you lie, you'll probably evaluate this behavior in terms of these internalized beliefs and will react negatively to your behavior. You might, for example, experience guilt as a result of your behavior contradicting your beliefs. On the other hand, let's say that you pulled someone out of a burning building at great personal risk. You would probably evaluate this behavior

Generally, you are advised by your culture to not betray the trust of the person making the disclosures by telling others or using the information against that person. However, this injunction might, depending on the disclosure, create an ethical dilemma for you. For example, what should you do if your friend reveals in the strictest confidence that he or she intends to commit suicide? Would you keep this a secret or would you, perhaps, reveal this to a professional who might help your friend?

Is your place of employment basically masculine or feminine? What beliefs, attitudes, and values does it teach? What kinds of rewards or punishments do they administer for following and not following these teachings?

Research has shown that when people are made self-aware (for example, sitting them in a room facing a large mirror and having them listen to their own voices), they're more likely to resist the temptation to engage in unethical behavior (for example, cheat on a test) (Diener & Walbom, 1976). While 7% of the self-aware group cheated, 71% of the not-self-aware group cheated. Are you less likely to engage in unethical behavior when you are especially aware of yourself? Do you make more accurate judgments when self-aware?

I believe that when all the dreams are dead, you're left only with yourself. You'd better like yourself a lot.

—Rita Mae Brown

positively; you would feel good about this behavior and, as a result, about yourself.

The more you understand why you view yourself as you do, the better you'll understand who you are. You can gain additional insight into yourself by looking more closely at self-awareness and especially at the Johari model of the self.

SELF-AWARENESS

Self-awareness, basic to all communication, can be explained with the Johari window, a metaphoric division of the self into four areas (Figure 2.2).

Your Four Selves

Each has his past shut in him like the leaves of a book known to him by heart and his friends can only read the title.

—Virginia Woolf

Divided into four areas or "panes," the window shows different aspects or versions of the self. The four versions are the open self, blind self, hidden self, and unknown self. These areas are not separate from one another, but rather, *inter*dependent. As one dominates, the others recede; or, to stay with our metaphor, as one window pane becomes larger, one or another becomes smaller.

The Open Self   This self represents all the information, behaviors, attitudes, and feelings about yourself that you know. This could include your name, skin color, sex, age, religion, and political beliefs, among other matters. The "size" of the open self varies according to your personality and the people to whom you're relating. You are probably selectively open—open about some things, but not about others; open with some people, but not with others. You might want to take a brief detour and look at your own communication openness, especially at how it operates in intercultural settings by taking the accompanying self-test, "How Open Are You Interculturally?"

Figure 2.2 The Johari Window

This diagram is a commonly used tool for examining what we know and don't know about ourselves. It will also prove effective in explaining the nature of self-disclosure (covered later in this chapter). The window gets its name from its inventors, *Joseph* Luft and *Harry* Ingham. From *Group Process: An Introduction to Group Dynamics,* by Joseph Luft. Reprinted by permission.

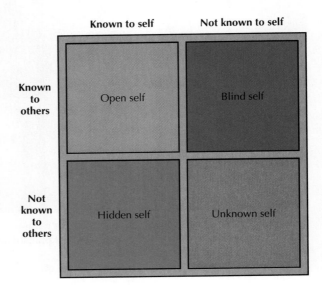

Instructions: Select a specific culture (national, racial, or religious) different from your own, and substitute this culture for the phrase *culturally different person* in each of the questions below. Indicate how open you would be to communicate in each of these situations, using the following scale:

> 5 = very open and willing
> 4 = open and willing
> 3 = neutral
> 2 = closed and unwilling
> 1 = very closed and unwilling

_____ 1. Talk with a culturally different person in the presence of those who are culturally similar to you.

_____ 2. Have a "best friendship" with a culturally different person.

_____ 3. Have a long-term romantic relationship with a culturally different person.

_____ 4. Adopt a child from a different culture.

_____ 5. Participate in a problem-solving or consciousness-raising group that is composed predominantly of people who are culturally different from you.

_____ 6. Listen openly and fairly to a speech by a culturally different person.

_____ 7. Listen fairly to a public speaker describing a different cultural group.

_____ 8. Ascribe a level of credibility to a culturally different person identical to that ascribed to a culturally similar person—all other things being equal.

Thinking Critically About Your Openness to Intercultural Communication This test was designed to raise questions rather than to provide answers. The questions refer to various aspects of interpersonal, small group, and public communication. High scores for any question or group of questions indicate considerable openness and a large open self; low scores indicate a lack of openness and a small open self. Use these numbers for purposes of thinking critically about the following questions rather than to indicate any absolute level of openness or closedness.

• Did you select the group on the basis of how positive or negative your attitudes were? What group would you be most open to interacting with? Least open?
• In which form of communication are you most open? Least open?
• How open are you to learning about the importance of greater intercultural understanding and communication?
• How open are you to learning what members of other groups think of your cultural groups?

I am an invisible man. . . . I am a man of substance, of flesh and bone, fiber and liquids—and I might even be said to possess a mind. I am invisible, understand, simply because people refuse to see me.

—Ralph Ellison

The Blind Self The blind self represents knowledge about you that others have but you don't. This might include your habit of finishing other people's sentences or rubbing your nose when you become anxious. It may include your tendency to overreact to imagined insults or to compete for attention. A large blind self indicates low self-awareness and interferes with accurate communication. Thus, it's important to reduce your blind self and learn what others know about you.

The Unknown Self The unknown self represents those parts of yourself that neither you nor others know. This is information that is buried in your subconscious and that has somehow escaped awareness. You gain insight into the unknown self in several ways. Sometimes this area is revealed through hypnosis, dreams, psychological tests, or psychotherapy. Another way to reveal this self is to explore yourself in an open, honest, and understanding way with those whom you trust—parents, lovers, and friends.

The Hidden Self The hidden self represents all the knowledge you have of yourself but keep from others. This window pane includes all your successfully kept secrets, for example, your dreams and fantasies, embarrassing experiences, unethical business practices, and any attitudes, beliefs, and values of which you may be ashamed. You probably keep secrets from some people and not from others. For example, you might not tell your parents you are dating someone of another race or religion, but you might tell a close friend. So too, you might not let your friends know you have difficulty asking for a date, but you might discuss this problem with a brother or sister.

Men can starve from a lack of self-realization as much as they can from a lack of bread.

—Richard Wright

We Wear the Mask
We wear the mask that grins and lies,
It hides our cheeks and shades
    our eyes—
This debt we pay to human guile:
With torn and bleeding hearts we smile,
And mouth with myriad subtleties.
Why should the world be otherwise,
In counting all our tears and sighs?
Nay, let them only see us, while
    We wear the mask.
We smile, but, O great Christ, our cries
To thee from tortured souls arise.
We sing, but oh the clay is vile
Beneath our feet, and long the mile;
But let the world dream otherwise,
    We wear the mask!

—Paul Laurence Dunbar

Growing in Self-Awareness

Because self-awareness is so important in communication, try to increase awareness of your own needs, desires, habits, beliefs, and attitudes. Here are a few suggestions:

Conveniently, others are constantly giving you the very feedback you need to increase self-awareness. In every interpersonal interaction, people comment on you in some way—on what you do, what you say, how you look. Sometimes these comments are explicit: "loosen up," "don't take things so hard," "you seem angry." Often they are "hidden" in the way in which others look at you or in what they talk about. Pay close attention to this kind of information (both verbal and nonverbal) and use it to increase your own self-awareness.

Revealing yourself to others will help increase your self-awareness. At the very least, you will bring into focus what you may have buried within. As you discuss yourself, you may see connections that you had previously missed. With feedback from others, you may gain still more insight. Also, by increasing your open self, you increase the chances that others will reveal what they know about you.

Seek out information to reduce your blind self. Encourage people to reveal what they know about you. You need not be so blatant as to say, "Tell me about myself," or "What do you think of me?" You can, however, use some situations that arise every day to gain self-information. "Do you think I came down too hard on the kids today?" "Do you think I was assertive enough when asking for the raise?" Seek this self-awareness in moderation. If you do it too often, your friends will soon look for someone else to talk with.

Still another way to seek information about yourself is to dialogue with yourself. No one knows you better than you know yourself. Ask yourself self-awareness questions: What motivates you to act as you do? What are your short- and long-term goals? How do you plan to achieve them? What are your strengths and weaknesses?

SELF-DISCLOSURE

Self-disclosure is a type of communication in which you reveal information about yourself, in which you move information from the hidden self into the open self (Jourard, 1968, 1971a, 1971b). Overt statements about the self as well as slips of the tongue, unconscious nonverbal movements, and public confessions would all be considered forms of self-disclosure. Usually, however, the term "self-disclosure" is used to refer to the conscious and overt revealing of information that you would normally keep hidden.

Self-disclosure is information previously unknown by the receiver. This may vary from the relatively commonplace ("I'm really afraid of that French exam") to the extremely significant ("I'm so depressed, I feel like committing suicide"). For self-disclosure to occur, the communication must involve at least two persons. You cannot self-disclose to yourself; the information must be received and understood by another individual.

In addition to disclosing information about yourself, you might also disclose information about those close to you, if it has a significant bearing on your life, social status, or professional capabilities. Thus, self-disclosure could refer to your own actions or the actions of, say, your parents or children, since these have a direct relationship to who you are.

Never let well enough alone.
—*Joyce Brothers*

I never intended to become a run-of-the-mill person.
—*Barbara Jordan*

Self-expression must pass into communication for its fulfillment.
—*Pearl S. Buck*

Factors Influencing Self-Disclosure

A number of factors influence whether or not you disclose, what you disclose, and to whom you disclose. Among the most important factors are who you are, your culture, your gender, your listeners, and your topic.

Who You Are Highly sociable and extroverted people self-disclose more than those who are less sociable and more introverted. People who are apprehensive about talking in general also self-disclose less than do those who are more comfortable in communicating.

Competent people engage in self-disclosure more than less competent people. Perhaps competent people have greater self-confidence and more positive things to reveal. Similarly, their self-confidence may make them more willing to risk possible negative reactions (McCroskey & Wheeless, 1976).

Your Culture Different cultures view self-disclosure differently. People in the United States, for example, disclose more than do people in Great Britain, Germany, Japan, or Puerto Rico (Gudykunst, 1983). American students also

In order to have a conversation with someone you must reveal yourself.
—*James Baldwin*

Listening to Yourself

Self-talk is important because it influences the way you feel about yourself, the degree to which you like yourself, and the extent to which you consider yourself a valuable person. By listening carefully to what you tell yourself, you'll gain in both self-awareness and self-esteem. Listen especially to two types of statements: self-destructive statements and self-affirming statements.

Self-destructive statements damage your self-esteem and prevent you from building meaningful and productive relationships. They may be about yourself ("I'm not creative"; "I'm boring"), your world ("The world is an unhappy place"; "People are out to get me"), or your relationships ("All the good people are already in relationships"; "If I ever fall in love, I know I'll be hurt").

Recognizing that you may have internalized such beliefs is a first step to eliminating them. A second step involves recognizing that these beliefs are in fact unrealistic and self-defeating. Cognitive therapists (for example, Ellis, 1988; Ellis & Harper, 1975; Beck, 1988) argue that you can accomplish this by understanding why these beliefs are unrealistic and substituting more realistic ones. For example, you might try substituting the unrealistic belief that you have to please others (always and in

everything you do) with a more realistic belief that it would be nice if others were pleased with you, but it certainly is not essential (Ellis, 1988).

Self-affirming statements, on the other hand, are positive and supportive. Remind yourself of your successes. Focus on your good deeds, positive qualities, strengths, and virtues. Also, look carefully at the good relationships you have with friends, coworkers, and relatives. Concentrate on your potential, not your limitations (Brody, 1991). Here is just a small sampling of self-affirmations that you may wish to try to say to yourself and, most important, listen to:

1. I'm a competent person.
2. I'm worth loving and having as a friend.
3. I'm growing and improving.
4. I'm empathic and supportive.
5. I facilitate open communication.
6. I can accept my past but can also let it go.
7. I can forgive myself and those who have hurt me.
8. I'm open-minded and listen fairly to others.
9. I can apologize.
10. I'm flexible and can adjust to different situations.

[The next Listen to This box appears on page 55.]

disclose more than do students from nine different Middle East countries (Jourard, 1971a). Similarly, American students self-disclose more on a variety of controversial issues and also self-disclose more to different types of people than do Chinese students (Chen, 1992). Singaporean–Chinese students consider more topics to be taboo and inappropriate for self-disclosure than their British colleagues (Goodwin & Lee, 1994). Among the Kabre of Togo, secrecy is a major part of everyday interaction, so they seldom engage in significant self-disclosure (Piot, 1993).

Some cultures (especially those high in masculinity) view the disclosing of one's inner feelings as a weakness. Among some groups, for example, it would be considered "out of place" for a man to cry at a happy occasion like a wedding while that same display of emotion would go unnoticed in some Latin cultures. Similarly, in Japan it's considered undesirable for colleagues to reveal personal information whereas in much of the United States it's expected (Barnlund, 1989; Hall & Hall, 1987).

In some cultures—for example, Mexican—there is a strong emphasis on discussing all matters in a positive mode, and this undoubtedly influences the way Mexicans approach self-disclosure as well. Negative self-disclosures, in contrast, are usually made to close intimates and then only after considerable time has elapsed in a relationship. This pattern is consistent with evidence showing that self-disclosure and trust are positively related (Wheeless & Grotz, 1977). Additional research, for example, finds that the Hispanic reluctance to disclose negative issues (for example, one's HIV+ status) is creating serious problems in preventing and in treating HIV infection (Szapocznik, 1995).

There are also important similarities across cultures. For example, people from Great Britain, Germany, the United States, and Puerto Rico are all more apt to disclose personal information about hobbies, interests, attitudes, and opinions on politics and religion than information on finances, sex, personality, and interpersonal relationships (Jourard, 1970). Similarly, one study showed self-disclosure patterns between American males to be virtually identical to those between Korean males (Won-Doornink, 1991).

Your Gender   The popular stereotype of gender differences in self-disclosure emphasizes the male reluctance to speak about himself. For the most part, research supports this generally accepted view and shows that women disclose more than men. Men and women, however, make negative disclosures approximately equally (Naifeh & Smith, 1984). Specifically, women disclose more than men about their previous romantic relationships, their feelings about their closest same-sex friends, their greatest fears, and what they don't like about their partners (Sprecher, 1987). Women also seem to increase the depth of their self-disclosures as the relationship becomes more intimate, while men seem not to change their disclosure levels. Men also have more taboo topics that they will not disclose to their friends than do women (Goodwin & Lee, 1994). Women also self-disclose more to members of the extended family than do men (Argyle & Henderson, 1985; Komarovsky, 1964; Moghaddam, Taylor, & Wright, 1993). One notable exception occurs in initial encounters. Here men will disclose more intimately than women, perhaps "in order to control the relationship's development" (Derlega, Winstead, Wong, & Hunter, 1985).

Both men and women avoid self-disclosure out of fear that they will project an unfavorable image. In a society in which image is so important—in

With him for a sire and her for a dam,
What should I be but just what I am?
—*Edna St. Vincent Millay,* A Few Figs from Thistles, *1920*

An interesting twist on the general finding that women self-disclose more than men is the finding that among married couples, both husbands and wives self-disclosed equally, but wives reported that they made more emotional disclosures than did their husbands (Shimanoff, 1985). Why do you think this is so?

Judy Pearson (1980) has argued that it's sex role, not biological gender, that accounts for the differences in self-disclosure. "Masculine women," for example, self-disclosed to a lesser extent than did women who scored low on masculinity scales. Further, "feminine men" self-disclosed to a greater extent than those who scored low on femininity scales. Do your own observations and experiences support this idea?

which one's image is often the basis for success or failure—this reason is not surprising. Other reasons for avoiding self-disclosure, however, are unique to men or women. Lawrence Rosenfeld (1979) summarizes males' reasons for self-disclosure avoidance: "If I disclose to you, I might project an image I do not want to project, which could make me look bad and cause me to lose control over you. This might go so far as to affect relationships I have with people other than you." Men's principal objective in avoiding self-disclosure is to maintain control. The general reason women avoid self-disclosure, says Rosenfeld, is that "if I disclose to you, I might project an image I do not want to project, such as my being emotionally ill, which you might use against me and which might hurt our relationship." Women's principal objective for avoiding self-disclosure is "to avoid personal hurt and problems with the relationship."

Your Listeners   Self-disclosure occurs more readily in small groups than in large groups. Dyads or groups of two people are the most hospitable setting for self-disclosure. With one listener, you can attend to the responses carefully. You can monitor your disclosures, continuing if there is support from your listener and stopping if there isn't. With more than one listener, such monitoring becomes difficult since the listeners' responses are sure to vary.

Sometimes self-disclosure takes place in group and public speaking situations. In consciousness-raising groups and in meetings, like those of

Increasingly television talk shows feature self-disclosure: men and women disclosing for the first time previous affairs, secret pregnancies, and intentions to seek divorce in front of a studio audience and a remote audience of millions. Recently, the sitcom character Ellen Morgan on *Ellen* disclosed being a lesbian. Comedian and actor Ellen DeGeneres also disclosed being a lesbian herself through a variety of media. How do you feel about public self-disclosure? What topics would you be willing to disclose on a television talk show? Which topics would you definitely not disclose in a public forum?

Alcoholics Anonymous, members may disclose their most intimate problems to ten or perhaps hundreds of people at one time. In these situations, group members are pledged to be totally supportive. These and similar groups are devoted specifically to encouraging self-disclosure and to giving each other support for the disclosures.

Because you disclose, generally at least, on the basis of support you receive, you probably disclose to people you like (Derlega, Winstead, Wong, & Greenspan, 1987) and to people you trust (Wheeless & Grotz, 1977). You probably also come to like those to whom you disclose (Berg & Archer, 1983). At times, self-disclosure occurs more in temporary than permanent relationships—for example, between strangers on a train or plane, a kind of "in-flight intimacy" (McGill, 1985). In this situation, two people set up an intimate self-disclosing relationship during a brief travel period, but don't pursue it beyond that point. In a similar way, you might set up a relationship with one or several people on the Internet and engage in significant disclosure. Perhaps knowing you'll never see these other people and that they will never know where you live or work or what you look like makes it easier.

You're more likely to disclose when the person you're with discloses. This **dyadic effect** (what one person does, the other person does likewise) probably leads you to feel more secure and reinforces your own self-disclosing behavior. Not surprisingly, disclosures are also more intimate when they're made in response to the disclosures of others (Berg & Archer, 1983).

The dyadic effect may not be universal. For example, some research (Won-Doornick, 1985) finds that while Americans are likely to follow the dyadic effect, Koreans do not. Does this dyadic effect operate in cultures with which you are familiar? What problems might be created by the failure to recognize that the dyadic effect does not hold for members of all cultures?

Your Topic   You're also more likely to disclose about some topics than others. For example, you're probably more likely to self-disclose information about your job or hobbies than about your sex life or financial situation (Jourard, 1968, 1971a). You're also more likely to disclose favorable information than unfavorable information. Generally, the more personal and negative the topic, the less likely you would be to self-disclose.

The accompanying self-test, "How Willing to Self-Disclose Are You?" focuses on the influences of the five factors just discussed: you, your culture, your gender, your listeners, and your topic.

Test Yourself   How Willing to Self-Disclose Are You?

Instructions: Respond to each of the following statements by indicating the likelihood that you would disclose such items of information to, say, other members of this class in an **interpersonal** situation, one-on-one; in a **small group** situation with five or six others; and in a **public communication** setting where you speak to all members of the class. Use the following scale to fill in all three columns:

1 = would definitely self-disclose
2 = would probably self-disclose
3 = don't know
4 = would probably not self-disclose
5 = would definitely not self-disclose

Information	Interpersonal Communication	Small Group Communication	Public Communication
1. My attitudes toward other religions, nationalities, and races			
2. My financial status, how much money I earn, how much I owe, how much I have saved			
3. My feelings about my parents			
4. My sexual fantasies			
5. My physical and mental health			
6. My ideal romantic partner			
7. My drinking and/or drug behavior			
8. My most embarrassing moment			
9. My unfulfilled desires			
10. My self-concept			

Thinking Critically About Self-Disclosure This test, and ideally its discussion with others who also complete it, should get you started thinking about your own self-disclosing behavior and especially the factors that influence it. How does your own personality influence your self-disclosure behavior? How has your culture and gender influenced your responses? Are you more likely to disclose interpersonally than in small group or public situations? Are you more likely to disclose in small groups than in public situations? Are there certain people to whom you feel relatively free to disclose and others to whom you feel much less free? What distinguishes these two groups of people? Are there certain topics you are less willing to disclose than others? Are you more likely to disclose positive secrets than negative ones? Are there topics about which you wish you had the opportunity to self-disclose but somehow can't find the right situation for such self-disclosing? As a listener, are there topics you would rather not hear about from certain people?

The Rewards and Dangers of Self-Disclosure

Self-disclose often brings rewards, but it can also create problems. Whether or not you self-disclose will depend on your assessment of the possible rewards and dangers. Here are some of the most important.

Rewards of Self-Disclosure   Self-disclosure contributes to self-knowledge; it helps you gain a new perspective on yourself and a deeper understanding of your own behavior. In therapy, for example, insight often comes while you're disclosing. Through self-disclosure, then, you may come to understand yourself more thoroughly.

Self-disclosure improves your coping abilities; it helps you to deal with problems, especially guilt. You may, for example, fear that you will not be accepted because of something you've done or because of some feeling or attitude you have. Because you feel these things are a basis for rejection, you may develop guilt. By self-disclosing such a feeling and receiving support rather than rejection, you may be better able to deal with guilt, perhaps reducing or even eliminating it.

Self-disclosure often improves communication. You understand the messages of others largely to the extent that you understand the individuals. You can tell what certain nuances mean, when the person is serious or joking, and when the person is being sarcastic out of fear or out of resentment. You might study a person's behavior or even live together for years, but if that person rarely self-discloses, you're far from understanding that individual as a complete person.

Self-disclosure helps you establish meaningful relationships. Without self-disclosure, relationships of any meaningful depth seem impossible. By self-disclosing, you tell others that you trust, respect, and care enough about them and your relationship to reveal yourself. This, in turn, leads the other individual to self-disclose and forms at least the start of a meaningful relationship, one that is honest and open and allows for more complete communication.

Dangers of Self-Disclosure   The many advantages of self-disclosure should not blind you to its very real risks (Bochner, 1984). When you self-disclose you risk personal and social rejection. You usually self-disclose to a person you expect will be supportive. But this may not always be true; the person you think will be supportive may turn out to reject you. Parents, normally

> Add a third to your two ears even if it be an imaginary one, for the news is so enchanting that two ears is not enough.
> —*Hausa Proverb*

Power Perspective 2.1

Referent Power

You have *referent power* over another person when that person wishes to be like you or identified with you. For example, an older brother may have referent power over a younger brother because the younger wants to be like his older brother. The assumption made by the younger brother is that he will be more like his older brother if he behaves and believes as his brother does. Your referent power increases when you're well liked and well respected, when you're seen as attractive and prestigious, when you're of the same sex, and when you have similar attitudes and experiences as this other person. This is why role models are so important; role models, by definition, possess referent power and exert great influence on those looking up to them. Referent power will more likely be ascribed to people who have positive self-concepts, who possess a high degree of self-awareness, and who disclose moderately and positively.

[The next Power Perspective appears on page 60.]

> The new source of power is not money in the hands of a few but information in the hands of many.
> —*John Naisbitt*

the most supportive of all interpersonal relations, frequently reject children who self-disclose their homosexuality, their plans to marry someone of a different race, or their belief in another faith. Your best friends, your closest intimates, may reject you for similar self-disclosures.

Self-disclosure may result in material losses. Politicians who disclose that they have been in therapy may lose the support of their own political party and find that voters are unwilling to vote for them. Teachers who disclose disagreement with the school administrators may find themselves denied tenure, teaching undesirable schedules, and victims of "budget cuts." In the business world, self-disclosures of alcoholism or drug addiction are often met with dismissal, demotion, or social exclusion.

Remember that self-disclosure, like any communication, is irreversible (Chapter 1). You cannot self-disclose and then take it back, nor can you erase the conclusions and inferences listeners have made on the basis of your disclosures. Remember, too, to examine the rewards and dangers of self-disclosure in terms of the particular cultural rules. As with all cultural rules, following them brings approval and violating them brings disapproval.

THINKING CRITICALLY ABOUT THE SELF IN COMMUNICATION

Because the self is so crucial in every communication act, it's essential that you carefully weigh the role of the self in your communication decisions. Your self-concept, self-awareness, and self-esteem will influence how positively or negatively you communicate and how defensive or supportive you will be. They will also influence how others communicate with you. Thus, when you want to determine ways of improving your own communications, consider the self-image that you're projecting. Attacking your self-destructive beliefs and engaging in self-affirmation, for example, will not only help you to increase self-esteem but will also make you a more effective communicator.

Similarly, think critically about the consequences of self-disclosing. As we noted earlier, attitudes toward self-disclosure vary from culture to culture and these must be considered in deciding whether to, and how to, self-disclose. Moreover, decisions to self-disclose will also be based on several other factors. Among these is your concern for your relationship with the person or persons to whom you are self-disclosing: Will this add tension to the relationship? Might it place an unfair burden on the friendship? Also consider the appropriateness of the context in which you are self-disclosing: Is this the right time, place, and circumstance? Should you disclose interpersonally, in a small group, or more publicly? Consider, too, the way in which the person to whom you're self-disclosing is responding (sympathetically? supportively? indifferently?). In addition, weigh the consequences of your self-disclosure. Can you afford to lose your job? Might it cause your friend some pain?

There are times when you may find yourself receiving the self-disclosures of others. Here, too, you need to consider the cultural rules and customs. In addition, remember that when someone is disclosing to you, he or she is simultaneously seeking your support and placing enormous trust in you. Listen attentively, not only to what is said, but also to the feelings that underlie the words. Paraphrase the speaker (restate in your own words what you think the speaker means) so that you can check your understanding and at the same time show that you're really listening. Openly express your support

> Never reveal all of yourself to other people; hold back something in reserve so that people are never quite sure if they really know you.
> —Michael Korda

As a parent would you share with your children your financial and personal worries? The answer, it seems, would depend at least in part on your socioeconomic status and on whether you are a single parent or one of two parents (McLoyd & Wilson, 1992). Research finds that members of middle-class two-parent families are reluctant to share financial problems with their children, preferring to shelter them from some of life's harsher realities. Low-income single mothers, however, feel that sharing this information with their children will help teach them how difficult life is and what to expect. The researchers argue that this practice of disclosing such difficulties actually creates problems for the child; such children often exhibit aggressiveness, difficulties in concentrating on learning in school, and anxiety disorders. What would your general advice be to parents about disclosing such matters?

Table 2.1 A Summary of Self-Disclosure Guidelines

Have you ever been involved in a self-disclosure experience where these general principles were violated? What happened?

In Self-Disclosing:	*In Responding to the Self-Disclosing of Others:*
1. Is the motivation to improve the relationship?	1. Are you trying to feel what the other person is feeling?
2. Does the self-disclosure impose burdens on your listener?	2. Are you using effective and active listening skills?
3. Is the self-disclosure appropriate to the context and the relationship between yourself and your listener?	3. Are you communicating supportiveness (verbally and nonverbally) to the discloser?
4. Is the other person disclosing also? If not, might this be a sign of disinterest?	4. Are you refraining from criticism and evaluation?
5. Might the self-disclosure place too heavy a burden on you?	5. Will you maintain confidentiality?

What do you think of "outing"—the process of making public that a noted personality is gay or lesbian? Under what conditions do you think outing is acceptable? Unacceptable?

during and after the disclosures with both words and gestures. Refrain from criticizing or passing judgments on the speaker.

It's interesting to note that one of the netiquette rules of E-mail is that you shouldn't forward mail to third parties without the writer's permission. This rule is a useful one for self-disclosure generally: Maintain confidentiality; don't pass on disclosures made to you to others without the discloser's permission. Table 2.1 summarizes some questions you might think about in self-disclosing and in responding to the disclosures of others.

SUMMARY OF CONCEPTS AND SKILLS

In this chapter we looked at the most important part of the communication process: the self. We discussed (1) self-concept and how it develops, (2) self-awareness and how to increase it, and (3) self-disclosure and how you might engage in it more effectively.

1. Self-concept refers to the image that you have of yourself and is composed of feelings and thoughts about both your abilities and your limitations. Self-concept develops from the image that others have of you, the comparisons you make between yourself and others, your cultural teachings, and your own interpretations and evaluations of your thoughts and behaviors.

2. The Johari Window model of the self is one way to view self-awareness. In this model there are four major areas: the open self, the blind self, the hidden self, and the unknown self. To increase self-awareness analyze yourself, listen to others to see yourself as they do, actively seek information from others about yourself, see yourself from different perspectives, and increase your open self.

3. Self-disclosure refers to a form of communication in which information about the self that is normally kept hidden is communicated to one or more other people.

4. Self-disclosure is more likely to occur when the potential discloser (a) feels competent, is sociable and extroverted, and is not apprehensive about communication; (b) comes from a culture that encourages self-disclosure; (c) is a woman; (d) is talking to supportive listeners who also disclose; and (e) talks about impersonal rather than personal topics and reveals positive rather than negative information.

5. The rewards of self-disclosure include increased self-knowledge, the ability to cope with difficult situations and guilt, communication efficiency, and the chances for more meaningful relationships. The dangers of self-disclosure include personal and social rejection, material loss, and intrapersonal difficulties.

6. Before self-disclosing, consider the cultural rules operating, the motivation for the self-disclosure, the possible burdens you might impose on your listener or yourself, the appropriateness of the self-disclosure, and the disclosures of the other person.

7. When listening to disclosures, take into consideration the cultural rules governing the communication situation, try to understand what the discloser is feeling, support the discloser, refrain from criticism and evaluation, and keep the disclosures confidential.

The skills for increasing self-awareness and for effective self-disclosure are critical to effective communication in all its forms. Check your ability to apply these skills. If you wish, use the following rating scale: (1) = almost always, (2) = often, (3) = sometimes, (4) = rarely, (5) = hardly ever.

_____ 1. I seek to understand my self-concept and be realistic about my strengths and my weaknesses.

_____ 2. I actively seek to increase self-awareness by talking with myself, listening to others, reducing my blind self, seeing myself from different perspectives, and increasing my open self.

_____ 3. I regulate my disclosures on the basis of the unique communication situation.

_____ 4. In deciding whether or not to self-disclose take into consideration (a) the cultural rules, (b) my motivation, (c) the possible burdens on my listener, (d) the appropriateness to the other person and the context, (e) the other person's disclosures, and (f) the possible burdens the disclosures may impose on me.

_____ 5. I respond to the disclosures of others by trying to feel what the other person is feeling, using effective and active listening skills, expressing supportiveness, refraining from criticism and evaluation, and keeping the disclosures confidential.

KEY WORD QUIZ

Write T for those statements that are true and F for those that are false. For those that are false replace the boldface term with the correct term.

1. The process by which you compare yourself with others, most often your peers, is known as **social comparison.**
2. A way of looking at yourself largely through the image that others reveal to you through their behaviors and especially through the way they treat you and react to you is known as **the looking-glass self.**
3. Your **self-concept** is your image of who you are.
4. Your self-evaluation is your **self-esteem.**
5. All the information that you know about yourself but that others don't know is in your **blind self.**
6. All the information that others know about you but that you don't know is in your **hidden self.**

7. Raising your self-esteem by saying and concentrating on the good things about yourself is known as **self-affirmation.**
8. **Lying** is a process of deliberately misleading another person.
9. The process of talking to others about yourself, of revealing things that you normally keep hidden, is known as **interpersonal communication.**
10. The **dyadic effect** describes the tendency for one person in a dyad to do essentially what the other person does.

Answers: TRUE: Numbers 1, 2, 3, 7, 8, 10. FALSE: 4 (self-awareness), 5 (hidden self), 6 (blind self), 9 (self-disclosure).

2.1 I'd Prefer to Be

This exercise should enable members of the class to get to know one another better and at the same time get to know themselves better. The questions should encourage each individual to increase awareness of some facet(s) of his or her thoughts or behaviors. The "I'd Prefer to Be" game is played in a group of four to six people.

1. Each person individually rank-orders each of the 10 clusters of preferences presented below using 1 for the most-preferred and 3 for the least-preferred choice.
2. The players then consider each of the 10 categories in turn, with each member giving his or her rank order.
3. Members may refuse to reveal their rankings for any category by saying, "I pass." The group is not permitted to question the reasons for any member's passing.
4. When a member has revealed his or her rankings for a category, group members may ask questions relevant to that category. These questions may be asked after any individual member's account or may be reserved until all members have given their rankings for a particular category.

1. _____ intelligent
   _____ wealthy
   _____ physically attractive
2. _____ movie star
   _____ senator
   _____ successful businessperson
3. _____ blind
   _____ deaf
   _____ mute
4. _____ on a date
   _____ surfing the net
   _____ watching television

5. _____ loved
   _____ feared
   _____ respected
6. _____ alone
   _____ with a group of people
   _____ with one person
7. _____ the loved
   _____ the lover
   _____ the good friend
8. _____ introvert
   _____ extrovert
   _____ ambivert
9. _____ a tree
   _____ a rock
   _____ a flower
10. _____ a leader
    _____ a follower
    _____ a loner

- What do the choices reveal about the individual? Why would it be dangerous to categorize people or draw conclusions about people on the basis of these choices?
- What is the degree of similarity of the group as a whole? Were cultural differences evident? Do the members show relatively similar choices or wide differences? What does this mean in terms of the members' ability to communicate with one another?
- Do the members accept/reject the choices of other members? Are some members disturbed by the choices other members make? If so, why? Are some apathetic? Why? Did hearing the choices of one or more members make you want to get to know them better?

2.2 Deciding About Self-Disclosure
Should you self-disclose or not? Here are several instances of impending self-disclosure. For each, indicate whether or not you think the self-disclosure would be appropriate. Specify your reasons for each of your judgments. In making your decision, consider each of the guidelines identified in this chapter.

1. Cathy has fallen in love with another man and wants to end her relationship with Tom, a coworker. She wants to call Tom on the phone, break the engagement, and disclose her new relationship.
2. Gregory plagiarized a term paper in anthropology. He is sorry, especially since the plagiarized paper only earned a grade of C+. He wants to disclose to his instructor and redo the paper.
3. Shandra is 27 years old and has been living in a romantic relationship with another woman for the past several years. Shandra wants to tell her par-

ents, with whom she has been very close throughout her life, but can't seem to get up the courage. She decides to tell them in a long letter.
4. Roberto, a college sophomore, has just discovered he is HIV+. He wants to tell his parents and his best friends but fears their rejection. In his Mexican-American culture, information like this is rarely disclosed, especially by men. His major advisor at school seems sensitive and empathic and he wonders if he should tell this instructor. He wants the support of his friends and family and yet doesn't want them to reject him or treat him differently.
5. Mary and Jim have been married for 12 years. Mary has disclosed a great deal to Jim—about her past romantic encounters, fears, insecurities, ambitions, and so on. Yet, Jim doesn't reciprocate. He almost never shares his feelings and has told Mary almost nothing about his life before they met. Mary wonders if she should begin to limit her disclosures.

2.3 Self-Defeating Drivers
Another approach to unrealistic beliefs is to focus on what Pamela Butler (1981) calls "drivers," beliefs that may motivate you to act in ways that are self-defeating. Consider each of these:

- the drive to **be perfect** impels you to try to perform at unrealistically high levels. Whether it's work, school, athletics, or appearance, this belief tells you that anything short of perfection is unacceptable and that you are to blame for any imperfections
- the drive to **be strong** tells you that weakness and any of the more vulnerable emotions like sadness, compassion, or loneliness are wrong
- the drive to **please others** leads you to seek approval from others. Pleasing yourself is secondary and, in fact, self-pleasure comes from pleasing others. The logic is that if you gain the approval of others then you are a worthy and deserving person; if others disapprove of you, then surely you must be worthless and undeserving
- the drive to **hurry up** compels you to do things quickly, to do more than can be reasonably expected in any given amount of time; it leads you to be impatient and to always rush
- the drive to **try hard** makes you take on more responsibilities than any one person can be expected to handle

Either alone or in small groups of five or six, create a scenario for each of these drivers to illustrate its use in a self-defeating, unproductive way and a scenario to illustrate how, in more moderate form, these drivers can be used in a self-enhancing, productive way.

Perception

CHAPTER CONCEPTS	CHAPTER GOALS After completing this chapter, you should be able to	CHAPTER SKILLS After completing this chapter, you should be able to
Perception	1. define perception and describe its stages: sensation, organization, and evaluation	perceive others with the knowledge that perceptions are influenced by who you are and by external stimuli
Processes Influencing Perception	2. explain the processes that influence interpersonal perception	avoid common perceptual barriers while perceiving others
Thinking Critically About Perception: Increasing Accuracy	3. explain the suggestions for increasing accuracy in perception	perceive others more accurately, using a variety of strategies

erception is the process by which you become aware of the many messages impinging on your senses. It influences what messages you take in and the meaning you give them. Perception is, therefore, central to the study of communication in all its forms. Here we look at how perception works, the processes that influence it, and how you can make your perceptions more accurate.

PERCEPTION

Perception is complex. There is no one-to-one relationship between the messages that occur—in the sounds of the voice, the marks on paper—and the messages that eventually reach your brain. Further, although two people may be exposed to the same stimulus, each will interpret it differently—not unlike our heroes in the accompanying cartoon. The three steps involved in the process explain how perception works: sensation, organization, and interpretation–evaluation (see Figure 3.1). These stages are not separate—they are continuous and blend into and overlap one another.

The first stage is **sensation.** At this stage, one or more of your five senses responds to a stimulus: you hear, see, smell, taste, feel, or use all of these senses at the same time. For example, when you meet another person you might feel the person's handshake, see the person's smile and body appearance, hear the person's voice, and perhaps even smell the person's breath or body odor.

At the **organization** stage, you organize the sensory stimulations according to various principles. One principle is that of proximity: The *proximity principle* means that you perceive people or messages that are physically close to one another as a unit. For example, you perceive people you often see together as a unit (such as a couple). You also assume that the verbal and nonverbal signals sent at about the same time (*temporal principle*) are related and constitute a unified whole. Another principle is *closure:* You perceive as a complete whole, a message that is actually incomplete. For example, you

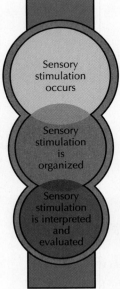

Figure 3.1 The Perception Process

This diagram identifies the three stages in the process of perception. It also shows how each stage overlaps with the next one and how the perception process moves from the general to the more specific.

see someone gesturing angrily, but can't quite make out the words. Thus, you assume that the verbal message is an expression of anger. You may even fill in specific words on the basis of the words you do hear. You use the principle of *contrast* when you note that some items (people or messages, for example) don't belong together; they are too different from each other to be part of the same perceptual organization. So, for example, in a conversation or a public speech listeners will focus their attention on changes in intensity or rate since these contrast with the rest of the message.

At the **interpretation–evaluation** stage you give the stimulus meaning and evaluate or judge it. This step is highly subjective; your interpretations and evaluations are not based solely on the outside stimulus, but also are greatly influenced by your own experiences, needs, wants, value systems, and beliefs about the way things are or should be, current physical or emotional states, expectations, and so on. Similarly, they are influenced by cultural factors—your cultural training and values. Two men walking arm-in-arm, young children competing in school and on the sports field, and someone in a leopard-skin coat will all be evaluated differently depending on your cultural values.

> Everyone complains of the badness of his memory, but nobody of his judgment.
>
> —LaRochefoucauld

Do you find that children are more accurate judges of people than adults? How would you go about testing the accuracy of this commonly held assumption?

| Test Yourself | How Accurate Are You at People Perception? |

Instructions: Respond to each of the following statements with T (true) if the statement is usually accurate in describing your behavior, or F (false) if the statement is usually inaccurate. Resist the temptation to give the "preferred" or "desirable" answers; respond, instead, as you behave.

_____ 1. I base most of my impressions of people on the first few minutes of our meeting.

_____ 2. When I know some things about another person, I fill in what I don't know.

_____ 3. I make predictions about people's behaviors that generally prove to be true.

_____ 4. I have clear ideas of what people of different national, racial, and religious groups are really like.

_____ 5. I reserve making judgments about people until I learn a great deal about them and see them in a variety of situations.

_____ 6. On the basis of my observations of people, I formulate guesses (that I am willing to revise), rather than firmly held conclusions.

_____ 7. I pay special attention to people's behaviors that might contradict my initial impressions.

_____ 8. I delay formulating conclusions about people until I have lots of evidence.

_____ 9. I avoid making assumptions about what is going on in someone else's head on the basis of their behaviors.

_____ 10. I recognize that people are different and don't assume that everyone is like me.

PROCESSES INFLUENCING PERCEPTION

Between the occurrence of the stimulation (the uttering of the message, presence of the person, smile, or wink) and its interpretation–evaluation, perception is influenced by five major psychological processes: implicit personality theory, the self-fulfilling prophecy, primacy–recency, stereotyping, and attribution (Cook, 1971; Rubin, 1973; Rubin & McNeil, 1985). These five processes (Figure 3.2) influence what you see and fail to see, and what you assume to be true or false about another person.

Personality Theory

Note the characteristic in parentheses that best seems to complete the following sentences:

> John is energetic, eager, and (intelligent, unintelligent).
> Mary is bold, defiant, and (extroverted, introverted).
> Joe is bright, lively, and (thin, fat).

Figure 3.2 Processes Influencing Perception

This diagram previews the five perception processes we consider in this chapter. Each of these perceptions, as we will see, also contain potential barriers that may prevent or obscure accurate perception. Can you recall perceptions you have of others that were influenced by one or more of these processes?

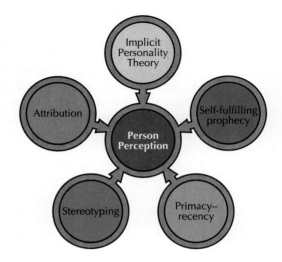

Listening to Other Perspectives

"Galileo and the Ghosts" is a technique for seeing a problem or person or situation through the eyes of a particular group of people (DeVito, 1996). It involves setting up a mental "ghost-thinking team," much like executives and politicians hire ghostwriters to write their speeches or corporations and research institutes maintain think-tanks. In this ghost-thinking technique, you select a team of four to eight "people" you admire, for example, historical figures like Aristotle or Picasso, fictional figures like Wonder Woman or Captain Picard, or persons from other cultures or of a different sex or affectional orientation.

You pose a question or problem and then ask yourself how this team of ghosts would answer your question or solve your problem, allowing yourself to listen to what they have to say. Of course, you're really listening to yourself, but you're acting in the role of another person. The technique forces you to step outside your normal role and to consider the perspective of someone totally different from you. If you wish, visualize yourself and your ghost-thinking team seated around a conference table, in a restaurant having lunch, or even jogging in the park. Choose the team members and the settings in any way you would like. Use whatever works for you and change it any time you want.

Your ghost-team analyzes your problem with perspectives different from your own. In the ghost-thinking technique each team member views your problem from his or her unique perspective. As a result, your perception of the problem will change. Your team members then view this new perception and perhaps analyze it again. As a result, your perception of the problem changes again. The process continues until you achieve a solution or decide that this technique has yielded all the insight it's going to yield.

In interpersonal communication and relationships, this technique might be used to see an issue or problem from the point of view of your romantic partner, parent, or child. In a small group setting, it might help you to see an issue from management or the employees' points of view. In public speaking, it could help you visualize your task from the perspective of different audiences.

Try creating your own think-tank or your own ghost-thinking team. Share your selections with others and then, if you wish, trade team members with others from your class to revise your team. Limiting your team to four to eight people will keep it more manageable. Once you have your ghost-team in place, try asking their advice on such questions as these: How can I become a more responsive relationship partner? How can I become less apprehensive in formal communication situations, such as interviewing or public speaking? How can I increase my assertive communication?

[The next Listen to This box appears on page 107.]

Jane is attractive, intelligent, and (likable, unlikable).
Susan is cheerful, positive, and (attractive, unattractive).
Jim is handsome, tall, and (interesting, boring).

What implicit personality theory do others have of you? Do the theories held by your close friends differ from those held by your casual acquaintances? Who has the more accurate theory?

Certain choices seem right and others seem wrong. What makes some seem "right" is your implicit personality theory, a system of rules identifying which characteristics go with which other characteristics. Most people's rules tell them that a person who is energetic and eager is also intelligent. Of course, there is no logical reason an unintelligent person could not be energetic and eager.

As you might expect, the implicit personality theories that people hold differ from culture to culture, group to group, and even person to person. For example, the Chinese have a concept called *shi gu* that refers to "someone who is worldly, devoted to his or her family, socially skillful, and somewhat reserved" (Aronson, 1994, p. 190). This concept is not easily encoded in English

Can you describe a specific instance of your using the halo effect in making a judgment about another person? A reverse halo effect?

as you can tell by trying to find a general concept that covers this type of person. In English, on the other hand, we have a concept of the "artistic type," a generalization that seems absent in Chinese. Thus, although it is easy for speakers of English or Chinese to refer to specific concepts—such as socially skilled or creative—each language creates its own general categories. Thus, in Chinese the qualities that make up *shi gu* are more easily seen as going together than they might be for an English speaker; they are part of the implicit personality theory of more Chinese speakers than English speakers.

Similarly, consider the different personality theories that "graduate students" and "blue-collar high-school dropouts" might have for "college students." Likewise, an individual may have had great experiences with doctors and so may have a very positive personality theory of doctors, whereas another person may have had negative experiences and might thus have developed a very negative personality theory.

The widely documented **halo effect** is a function of the implicit personality theory. If you believe an individual has several positive qualities, you're likely to conclude that she or he has other positive qualities. The "reverse halo effect" operates similarly. If you know a person has several negative qualities, you're likely to conclude that the person also has other negative qualities.

Beware: Potential Barriers   The tendency to develop a personality theory and then to perceive an individual as conforming to the theory can create barriers to perceptual accuracy and can lead you to:

- perceive qualities in an individual that your "theory" tells you should be present when they actually are not. For example, you see "goodwill" in the "charitable" acts of a friend when tax reduction may be the real motive.
- ignore or distort qualities or characteristics that do not conform to your theory. For example, you may ignore negative qualities in your friends that you would easily notice in your enemies.

Self-Fulfilling Prophecy

A **self-fulfilling prophecy** occurs when you make a prediction or formulate a belief that comes true because you made the prediction and acted as if it were true (Merton, 1957; Insel & Jacobson, 1975). There are four basic steps in the self-fulfilling prophecy:

It has been argued that the self-fulfilling prophecy may be used in organizations to stimulate higher performance (Eden, 1992; Field, 1989). For example, managers could be given the belief that workers can perform at extremely high levels; managers would then act as if this were true and thus promote this high-level behavior in the workers. How might it be used in the college classroom? How might it be used in parenting? Would you consider this behavior ethical?

1. You make a prediction or formulate a belief about someone (often, ourselves) or a situation. For example, you predict that Pat is awkward in interpersonal situations.
2. You act toward that person or situation as if the prediction or belief is true. For example, you act toward Pat as if she were, in fact, awkward.
3. Because you act as if the belief were true, it becomes true. Because of the way you act toward Pat, she becomes tense and manifests awkwardness.
4. Your effect on the person or the resulting situation strengthens your beliefs. Seeing Pat's awkwardness reinforces your belief that Pat is, in fact, awkward.

If you expect people to act in a certain way, the self-fulfilling prophecy will frequently make your predictions come true. Consider, for instance, people who enter a group situation convinced that other members will dislike them. Almost invariably they're proved right, perhaps because they act in a way that encourages people to respond negatively. Such people fulfill their own prophecies.

Beware: Potential Barriers   The tendency to fulfill your own prophecies can lead you to:

- influence another's behavior to conform to your prophecy
- see what you predicted rather than what really is. For example, it can lead you to perceive yourself as a failure because you made this prediction rather than because of any actual failures

Primacy–Recency

If what comes first exerts the most influence over how you perceive subsequent events or behavior, you have a primacy effect. If what comes last (or is the most recent) exerts the most influence on your perceptions, you have a recency effect. A classic study on primacy–recency effects in interpersonal perception showed that order was a significant factor in forming impressions of another person. In this study students were read a list of adjectives describing a person and were asked to evaluate the person. The students more positively evaluated a person described as "intelligent, industrious, impulsive, critical, stubborn, and envious" than a person described as "envious, stubborn, critical, impulsive, industrious, and intelligent" (Asch, 1946). The assumption is that you use early information to provide a general idea of what a person is like, then use later information to make the general idea more specific. The obvious practical implication of primacy–recency is that the first impression you make is likely to be the most important. Through this first impression, you filter additional information to formulate a "complete" picture of the person.

Beware: Potential Barriers   Your tendency to give greater weight to early information and to interpret later information in light of these early impressions can lead you to:

- formulate a "total" picture of an individual on the basis of initial impressions that may not be typical or accurate. For example, you might form an image of someone as socially ill at ease. If you based this impression on watching the person at a stressful job interview or during the first few minutes of a long political campaign, it's likely to be wrong.
- discount or distort later perceptions to avoid disrupting your initial impression. For instance, you may fail to see signs of deceit in someone who made a good first impression.

Stereotyping

A frequently used shortcut in perception is stereotyping. The term **stereotype** originated in printing and referred to the plate that printed the same image over and over. A sociological or psychological stereotype is therefore a fixed impression of a group of people. We all have attitudinal stereotypes—of national, religious, and racial groups, of men and women, of criminals, prostitutes, teachers, or plumbers, of heterosexuals, gay men, and lesbians.

A widely known example of the self-fulfilling prophecy is the *Pygmalion effect.* In one study, for example, teachers were told that certain pupils—whose names were actually selected at random—were expected to do exceptionally well, that they were late bloomers. At the end of the term, these students actually performed at a higher level than the others (Insel & Jacobson, 1975; Rosenthal & Jacobson, 1968). The teacher's expectations probably generated extra attention to the students, thereby positively affecting their performance. Has someone's predictions about you ever influenced you?

Assume that you are taking a course in which half the classes are extremely dull and half are extremely exciting. At the end of the semester, you evaluate the course and the instructor. Would your evaluation be more favorable if the dull classes came during the first half of the semester and the exciting classes during the second half? Or would it be more favorable if the order were reversed?

In a study of stereotypes on British television it was found that gender stereotypes hadn't changed much over the past 10 years and that these were comparable to those found on North American television (Furnham & Bitar, 1993). Other research suggests that these stereotypes have changed and that television depictions of men and women are erasing the stereotypes (Vernon, Williams, Phillips, & Wilson, 1990). Do you find gender stereotypes on television? How many can you identify?

Manage every second of a first meeting. Do not delude yourself that a bad impression can be easily corrected. Putting things right is a lot harder than getting them right first time.
—*David Lewis*

The primacy–recency principle is useful to a wide variety of communicators. For example, because public speaking audiences first form a general impression of the speaker and filter the rest of the speech through this initial impression, it's often wise for speakers to first focus on their most compelling argument to more strongly convince their listeners. If you were about to enter the group pictured above, what insights would primacy–recency offer you?

If you have these fixed impressions, you might, upon meeting a member of a particular group, see that person primarily as a member of that group. When you see that person as possessing all the characteristics you assign to the group as a whole, you run the risk of missing a great deal that is unique to the individual. If you meet someone who is homeless, for example, you might have a host of characteristics for "homeless" that you are ready to apply. You may also see various characteristics in this person's behavior that you would not see if you did not know this person was homeless. Stereotypes prevent you from seeing an individual as an individual.

Beware: Potential Barriers   Grouping people into categories and then responding to them primarily as members of that group can lead you to:

- perceive someone as having those qualities (usually negative) that you believe characterize the particular group (for example, all feminists are . . . or all gay men are . . . or all South Africans are . . .) and, therefore, fail to appreciate the multifaceted nature of all people and all groups.
- ignore the unique characteristics of an individual and, therefore, fail to benefit from the special contributions each can bring to an encounter.

Attribution

Attribution is a process by which you try to explain the motivation for a person's behavior. One way to do this is to ask yourself whether the person was in control of the behavior. For example, you invited your friend Desmond to dinner for seven o'clock and he arrives at nine. Consider how you would respond to each of these reasons:

What stereotypes do others have of you? (You may wish to ask several of your friends and acquaintances for help with this question.) How did these people develop these stereotypes? How accurate are they?

It is with our judgments as with our watches; no two go just alike, yet each believes his own.

—Alexander Pope

Modern Maturity

"It's all according to your point of view. To me, you're a monster."

Reason 1: I just couldn't tear myself away from the beach. I really wanted to get a great tan.

Reason 2: I was driving here when I saw some young kids mugging an old couple. I broke it up and took the couple home. They were so frightened that I had to stay with them until their children arrived. Their phone was out of order, so I had no way of calling to tell you I'd be late.

Reason 3: I got in a car accident and was taken to the hospital.

Assuming you believe all three explanations, you would attribute very different motives to Desmond's behavior. With reasons 1 and 2, you would conclude that Desmond was in control of his behavior; with reason 3, that he was not. Further, you would probably respond negatively to reason 1 (Desmond was selfish and inconsiderate) and positively to reason 2 (Desmond was a Good Samaritan). Because Desmond was not in control of his behavior in reason 3, you would probably not attribute either positive or negative motivation to his behavior. Instead you would probably feel sorry that he got into an accident.

You probably make similar judgments based on controllability in numerous situations. Consider, for example, how you would respond to the following situations:

- Doris fails her history midterm exam.
- Sidney's car is repossessed because he failed to keep up the payments.
- Margie is 150 pounds overweight and is complaining that she feels awful.
- Thomas's wife has just filed for divorce and he's feeling depressed.

Can you recall a recent inter-action where one or more of these strategies were used? What happened?

Power Perspective 3.1

Strategic Self-Presentation

How do you get others to like you and to perceive you as a competent and capable person? Here are four strategies and the pitfalls of each (Jones & Pittman, 1982; Jones, 1990):

Use **ingratiation.** Express lots of agreement with the opinions of the other person, compliment the other, or do favors for this person. Or you might emphasize your positive qualities. In using these strategies, however, you run the risk of being seen as a sycophant, someone who will stop at nothing to be liked.

Use **self-promotion.** Try to present yourself as exceptionally competent so that the other person will respect you. The obvious problem with this tactic is that you may be perceived as incompetent given the theory that competent people *demonstrate* competence rather than talk about it.

Use **exemplification.** Present yourself as worthy, moral, and virtuous. The downside to this is that you may appear as sanctimonious, or "holier than thou," a quality that most people dislike.

Use **supplication.** Present yourself as helpless and in need of assistance: "Can you type my paper? I'm such a bad typist." The supplicant runs the risk, however, of being seen as demanding, incompetent, or perhaps lazy.

[The next Power Perspective appears on page 73.]

You would most likely be sympathetic to each of these people if you feel that they were not in control of what happened. For example, if the examination was unfair, if Sidney lost his job because of employee discrimination, if Margie has a glandular problem, and if Thomas's wife wants to leave him for a wealthy drug dealer. On the other hand, you probably would not be sympathetic toward these people if you felt they were in control of what happened. For example, if Doris partied instead of studied, if Sidney gambled his payments away, if Margie ate nothing but junk food and refused to exercise, and if Thomas has been repeatedly unfaithful and his wife finally gave up trying to reform him.

Generally, research shows that if you feel a person was in control of negative behaviors, you will come to dislike him or her. If you believe the person was not in control of negative behaviors, you will come to feel sorry and not blame the person.

Beware: Potential Barriers Three major attribution problems can interfere with accuracy in perception. The **self-serving bias** operates when you evaluate your own behaviors and take credit for the positive and deny responsibility for the negative. Thus, you're more likely to attribute your own negative behaviors to uncontrollable factors. For example, after getting a D on an exam, you're more likely to attribute it to the difficulty or unfairness of the text. However, you're likely to attribute your positive behaviors to controllable factors, to your own strength or intelligence or personality. For example, after getting an A on an exam, you're more likely to attribute it to your ability or hard work (Bernstein, Stephan, & Avis, 1979). So, this self-serving bias may distort your attributions.

Other men's sins are before our eyes; our own are behind our backs.
—*Seneca*

Vanity is the quicksand of reason.
—*George Sand*

Can you explain, with the concept of controllability, the attitudes that many people have about the homeless? What attitudes do people have about drug addicts or alcoholics? What do they feel about successful politicians, scientists, or millionaires?

The second problem is **overattribution.** This is the tendency to single out one or two obvious characteristics of a person and attribute everything that person does to this one or two characteristics. For example, if the person had alcoholic parents or is blind or was born into great wealth, there is often a tendency to attribute everything that person does to such factors. So we say, Sally has difficulty forming meaningful relationships because she grew up in a home of alcoholics, Alex overeats because he's blind, and Lillian is irresponsible because she never had to work for her money. Most behaviors and personality characteristics result from a lot of factors, and you almost always make a mistake when you select one factor and attribute everything to it.

A third problem is called the **fundamental attribution error,** the tendency to conclude that people do what they do because that's the kind of people they are, not because of the situation they're in. When Pat is late for an appointment, you're more likely to conclude that Pat is inconsiderate or irresponsible or "scatterbrained" rather than attribute the lateness to the bus breaking down or to a traffic accident. When you commit the fundamental attribution error you overvalue the contribution of internal factors and undervalue the influence of external factors.

When you explain your own behavior you're likely to use more external explanations than you do when explaining the behaviors of others (Martin & Klimoski, 1990). One reason for giving greater weight to external factors in explaining your own behavior than you do in explaining the behavior of others is that you know the situation surrounding your own behavior. You know, for example, what's going on in your love life, and you know your financial condition, so you naturally see the influence of these factors. But you

To understand one's self is the classic form of consolation; to delude one's self is the romantic.
—*George Santayana*

rarely know as much about others, so you're likely to give less weight to the external factors in their cases.

This fundamental attribution error is at least in part culturally influenced. For example, in the United States people are more likely to explain behavior by saying that people did what they did because of who they are. But when Hindus in India were asked to explain why their friends behaved as they did, they gave greater weight to external factors than did Americans in the United States (Miller, 1984; Aronson, 1994). Further, Americans have little hesitation in offering causal explanations of a person's behavior ("Pat did this because . . ."). Hindus, on the other hand, are generally reluctant to explain a person's behavior in causal terms (Matsumoto, 1994).

THINKING CRITICALLY ABOUT PERCEPTION: INCREASING ACCURACY

Successful communication depends largely on the accuracy of your perception. As a preface it's important to realize that in addition to your perception of another's behaviors (verbal or nonverbal), you can also perceive what you think another person is feeling or thinking (Laing, Phillipson, & Lee, 1966; Littlejohn, 1996). You can, for example, perceive Pat kissing Chris. This is a simple, relatively direct perception of some behavior. But you can also sense (or perceive)—on the basis of the kiss—that Pat loves Chris. Notice the difference: You have observed the kiss, but have not observed the love. (Of course, you could continue in this vein and, from your conclusion that Pat loves Chris, conclude that Pat no longer loves Terry. That is, you can always formulate a conclusion on the basis of a previous conclusion. The process is unending.)

The important point to see here is that when your perceptions are based on something observable (here, the kiss), you have a greater chance of being accurate when you describe this kiss or even when you interpret and evaluate it. As you move further away from your actual observation, however, your chances of being accurate decrease—for example, when you try to describe or evaluate the love. Generally, when you draw conclusions on the basis of what you think someone is thinking as a result of the behavior, you have a greater chance of making errors than when you stick to conclusions about what you observe yourself.

We have already identified the potential barriers that can arise with each of the perceptual processes, for example, the self-serving bias,

Ethical Issue

Choice as An Ethical Standard

One approach to the ethics of communication can be found in the notion of choice. The underlying assumption is that people have a right to make their own choices. Communications are ethical when they facilitate a person's freedom of choice by presenting that person with accurate information. Communications are unethical when they interfere with the individual's freedom of choice by preventing the person from securing information that will help him or her make choices. Unethical communications, therefore, are those that force a person (1) to make choices he or she would not normally make or (2) to decline to make choices he or she would normally make or both. The ethical communicator provides others with the kind of information that is helpful in making their own choices.

You have the right to information about yourself that others possess and that influences the choices you will make. Thus, for example, you have the right to face your accusers, to know the witnesses who will be called to testify against you, to see your credit ratings, and to know what Social Security benefits you will receive. On the other hand, people do not have the right to information that is none of their business such as information about whether you and your partner are happy or argue a lot or receive food stamps.

You also have the right to remain silent; you have a right to privacy, to withhold information that has no bearing on the matter at hand. Thus, for example, your previous relationship history, affectional orientation, or religion is usually irrelevant to your ability to function as a doctor or police officer, for example, and may thus be kept private in most job-related situations. If these issues become relevant—you are about to enter a new relationship—then there *may be* an obligation to reveal your relationship history, affectional orientation, or religion.

In this ethic based on choice, however, there are a few qualifications that may restrict your freedom. The ethic assumes that persons are of an age and mental condition that allows free choice to be reasonably executed and that the choices they make do not prevent others from doing likewise. A 5- or 6-year-old child is not ready to make certain choices, so someone else must make them. Similarly, some people with mental disabilities need others to make certain decisions for them.

Furthermore, the choices you make must not prevent others from making their legitimate choices. You cannot permit a thief to steal, because in granting that freedom you would be imposing on the rights of potential victims. Similarly, certain information may be restricted because it could be potentially dangerous to society. Thus, for example, information on how to construct bombs, most would agree, is information that the average citizen does not have a right to know.

Think about this approach to ethics as you consider the questions raised in future ethics boxes as well as ethical dilemmas you face every day. Is the notion of choice helpful? Is it consistent with your own feelings about what is right and what is wrong? Would you add additional qualifications?

[The next Ethical Issue box appears on page 103.]

overattribution, and the fundamental attribution error in attribution and the numerous potential problems in each of the other four perceptual processes. There are, however, additional suggestions we want to offer.

Become Aware of Your Perceptions

Subject your perceptions to logical analysis—to critical thinking. Here are a few suggestions:

- Recognize your own role in perception. Your emotional and physiological state will influence the meaning you give to your perceptions. The sight of raw clams may be physically upsetting when you have a stomachache, but mouthwatering when you're hungry.

- Avoid early conclusions. On the basis of your observations of behaviors, formulate hypotheses to test against additional information and evidence rather than drawing conclusions you then look to confirm. Delay formulating conclusions until you've had a chance to process a wide variety of cues.
- Avoid the one-cue conclusion. Look for a variety of cues pointing in the same direction. The more cues pointing to the same conclusion, the more likely your conclusion will be correct. Be especially alert to contradictory cues, ones that refute your initial hypotheses. It's relatively easy to perceive cues that confirm your hypotheses but more difficult to acknowledge contradictory evidence. At the same time, seek validation from others. Do others see things in the same way you do? If not, ask yourself if your perceptions may be in some way distorted.
- Avoid mind reading. Regardless of how many behaviors you observe and how carefully you examine them, you can only *guess* what is going on in someone's mind. A person's motives are not open to outside inspection; you can make assumptions based on only overt behaviors.
- Beware of your own biases. Know when your perceptual evaluations are unduly influenced by your own biases: for example, perceiving only the positive in people you like and only the negative in people you do not like.

Check Your Perceptions

Perception checking is another way to reduce uncertainty and to make your perceptions more accurate. In its most basic form, perception checking consists of two steps:

1. Describe what you see or hear, recognizing that even descriptions are not really objective but are heavily influenced by who you are, your emotional state, and so on. At the same time, you may wish to describe what you think is happening. Again, try to do this as descriptively (not evaluatively) as you can. Sometimes you may wish to offer several possibilities.

   - You've called me from work a lot this week. You seem concerned that everything is all right at home.
   - You've not wanted to talk with me all week. You say that my work is fine but you don't seem to want to give me the same responsibilities that other editorial assistants have.

2. Ask the other person for confirmation. Do be careful that your request for confirmation doesn't sound as though you already know the answer. Avoid phrasing your questions defensively. Avoid saying, for example, "You really don't want to go out, do you; I knew you didn't when you turned on that lousy television." Instead, ask for confirmation in as supportive a way as possible: "Would you rather watch TV?" "Are you worried about me or the kids?" "Are you pleased with my work? Is there anything I can do to improve my job performance?"

As these examples illustrate, the goal of perception checking is not to prove that your initial perception is correct but to further explore the

What cues do you rely on most heavily in making initial judgments of people? Generally, how accurate are these initial judgments?

In the eyes of a lover, pockmarks are dimples.

—*Japanese proverb*

How would you use perception checking in such situations as these: (a) your friend says he wants to drop out of college, (b) your cousin hasn't called you in several months though you have called her at least six times, (c) another student seems totally detached from everything that happens in class?

thoughts and feelings of the other person. With this simple technique, you lessen your chances of misinterpreting another's feelings. At the same time, you give the other person an opportunity to elaborate on his or her thoughts and feelings.

Reduce Uncertainty

Reducing uncertainty enables you to achieve greater accuracy in perception. In large part you learned about uncertainty and how to deal with it from your culture.

Culture and Uncertainty   People from different cultures differ greatly in their attitudes toward uncertainty and how to deal with it. These attitudes and ways of dealing with uncertainty have consequences for perceptual accuracy.

People in some cultures do little to avoid uncertainty and have little anxiety about not knowing what will happen next. Uncertainty to them is a normal part of life. Members of these cultures don't feel threatened by unknown situations. Other cultures do much to avoid uncertainty and have a great deal of anxiety about not knowing what will happen next; uncertainty is seen as threatening and something that must be counteracted. Table 3.1 presents the countries that have the greatest anxiety over or feel most threatened by uncertainty, and those that have the lowest.

The potential for communication problems when people come from cultures with different attitudes toward uncertainty can be great. For example, managers from cultures with weak uncertainty avoidance will accept workers who work only when they have to and will not get too upset when workers are late. Managers from cultures with strong uncertainty avoidance will expect workers to be busy at all times and will have little tolerance for lateness.

The choice of a point of view is the initial act of a culture.
—*José Ortega y Gasset*

Because weak uncertainty-avoidance cultures have great tolerance for ambiguity and uncertainty, they minimize the rules governing communication and relationships (Hofstede, 1997; Lustig & Koester, 1996). People who do not follow the same rules as the cultural majority are readily tolerated. Different approaches and perspectives may even be encouraged in cultures with weak uncertainty avoidance. Strong uncertainty-avoidance cultures create very clear-cut rules for communication. It is considered unacceptable for people to break these rules.

Students from weak uncertainty-avoidance cultures appreciate freedom in education and prefer vague assignments without specific timetables. These students will want to be rewarded for creativity and will easily accept the teacher's (sometime) lack of knowledge. Students from strong uncertainty-avoidance cultures prefer highly structured experiences where there is very little ambiguity—specific objectives, detailed instructions, and definite timetables. These students expect to be judged on the basis of the right answers and expect the teacher to have all the answers all the time (Hofstede, 1997).

Geert Hofstede (1997, p. 119), who conducted much of the cultural research reported here, claims that those cultures that have strong uncertainty avoidance believe "What is different, is dangerous." Weak uncertainty-avoidance cultures believe "What is different, is curious." Does your experience support this distinction?

Strategies for Reducing Uncertainty   Communication involves a gradual process of reducing uncertainty about each other (Berger & Bradac, 1982; Gudykunst, Ting-Toomey, Sudweeks, & Stewart, 1995). A variety of

Table 3.1 Uncertainty Avoidance and Culture

There are wide differences within each culture as well as between cultures. These rankings are based on average scores obtained by members of these cultures. The countries are listed in order: Greece had the strongest uncertainty score (they worry about uncertainty), Portugal was second, Guatemala third, and so on. Singapore had the weakest uncertainty score (they worry little about uncertainty), Jamaica was second, Denmark third, and so on. Countries listed together had the same score.

Strong Uncertainty Avoidance	*Weak Uncertainty Avoidance*
Greece	Singapore
Portugal	Jamaica
Guatemala	Denmark
Uruguay	Sweden
Belgium, El Salvador	Hong Kong
Japan	Ireland
Yugoslavia	Great Britain
Peru	Malaysia
France, Chile, Spain, Costa Rica, Panama, and Argentina	India
Turkey and South Korea	Philippines
	United States

Here are three theorems, paraphrased from the theory of uncertainty reduction, a theory concerned with how communication reduces the uncertainty you have about another person (Berger & Calabrese, 1975): (1) the more people communicate, the more they like each other; (2) the more people communicate, the more intimate their communications will be; and (3) the more nonverbally expressive people are, the more they like each other. Do your own experiences support these assumptions? Can you give a specific example for one of the propositions?

strategies can help reduce uncertainty. Observing another person while he or she is engaged in an active task, preferably interacting with others in more informal social situations, will often reveal a great deal about the person, since people are less apt to monitor their behaviors and more likely to reveal their true selves in informal situations.

You can also manipulate the situation in such a way that you observe the person in more specific and more revealing contexts. Employment interviews, theatrical auditions, and student teaching are some of the ways situations are created to observe how the person might act and react and, hence, to reduce uncertainty about the person. New members of Internet chat groups usually lurk before joining the group discussion. Lurking, reading the exchanges between the other group members without saying anything yourself, will help you learn about the people in the group and about the group itself.

Another way to reduce uncertainty is to collect information about the person through asking others. You might, for example, inquire of a colleague if a third person finds you interesting and might like to have dinner with you.

Of course, you can interact with the individual. For example, you can ask questions: "Do you enjoy sports?" "What did you think of that computer science course?" "What would you do if you got fired?" You also gain knowledge of another by disclosing information about yourself. Your self-disclosure can help to create an environment that encourages disclosures from the person about whom you wish to learn more.

You probably use these strategies all the time to learn about people. Unfortunately, many people feel that they know someone well enough after observing the person only from a distance or from rumors. A combination of information—including and especially your own interactions—is most successful at reducing uncertainty.

Be Culturally Sensitive

You can increase your accuracy in perception by recognizing and being sensitive to cultural differences, especially those concerning values, attitudes, and beliefs. You can easily see and accept different hairstyles, clothing, and foods. In basic values and beliefs, however, you may assume that deep down we are really all alike. We aren't. When you assume similarities and ignore differences, you may fail to perceive a situation accurately. Take a simple example. An American invites a Filipino coworker to dinner. The Filipino politely refuses. The American is hurt and feels that the Filipino does not want to be friendly. The Filipino is hurt and concludes that the invitation was not extended sincerely. Here, it seems, both the American and the Filipino assume that their customs for inviting people to dinner are the same when, in fact, they aren't. A Filipino expects to be invited several times before accepting a dinner invitation. When an invitation is given only once it's viewed as insincere.

Within every cultural group there are wide and important differences. As all Americans are not alike, neither are all Indonesians, Greeks, Mexicans, and so on. When you make assumptions that all people of a certain culture are alike, you're thinking in stereotypes. Recognizing differences between another culture and your own *and* recognizing differences among members of a particular culture, will help you perceive the situation more accurately.

Can you identify a specific behavior that is permissible in one culture and frowned on in another? To what do you attribute these differences?

SUMMARY OF CONCEPTS AND SKILLS

In this chapter we discussed the way we receive messages through perception and explained how perception works, the processes that influence it, and how to make your perceptions more accurate.

1. Perception refers to the process by which you become aware of the many stimuli impinging on your senses. It occurs in three stages: sensory stimulation occurs, sensory stimulation is organized, and sensory stimulation is interpreted–evaluated.
2. The following processes influence perception: (1) implicit personality theory, (2) self-fulfilling prophecy, (3) primacy–recency, (4) stereotyping, and (5) attribution.
3. Implicit personality theory refers to the private personality theory that you hold and that influences how you perceive other people.
4. The self-fulfilling prophecy occurs when you make a prediction or formulate a belief that comes true because you have made the prediction and acted as if it were true.
5. Primacy–recency refers to the relative influence of stimuli as a result of their order. If what occurs first exerts greater influence, you have a primacy effect. If what occurs last exerts greater influence, you have a recency effect.
6. Stereotyping refers to the tendency to develop and maintain fixed, unchanging perceptions of groups of people and to use these perceptions to evaluate individual members, ignoring their individual, unique characteristics.
7. Attribution refers to the process by which you try to explain the motivation for a person's behavior. Whether or not the person was in control of the behavior will influence how you evaluate the behavior or explain the motivation for a person's behavior.
8. Increase the accuracy of your interpersonal perceptions by becoming aware of your perceptions, checking your perceptions, reducing uncertainty, and becoming aware of cultural differences and influences on perception.

Throughout this discussion of perception, a variety of skills were identified and are presented here in summary. Check your ability to apply these skills: (1) = almost always, (2) = often, (3) = sometimes, (4) = rarely, (5) = hardly ever.

_____ 1. Recognizing how primacy–recency works, I actively guard against first impressions that might prevent accurate perceptions of future events; I formulate hypotheses rather than conclusions.

_____ 2. To guard against the self-fulfilling prophecy, I take a second look at my perceptions when they conform too closely to my expectations.

_____ 3. I bring to consciousness my implicit personality theories.

4. I recognize stereotyping in the messages of others and avoid it in my own communications.

5. I am aware of and am careful to avoid the self-serving bias, overattribution, and the fundamental attribution error in trying to account for another person's behavior.

6. I am aware of my perceptions and subject them to logical and critical analysis, check perceptions, reduce uncertainty, and am culturally sensitive in drawing conclusions about others.

KEY WORD QUIZ

Write T for those statements that are true and F for those that are false. For those that are false replace the boldface term with the correct term.

1. The process by which you become aware of the many stimuli impinging on your senses is called **uncertainty reduction.**

2. Concluding that a person has positive qualities because you know that he or she has other positive qualities is known as **mind reading.**

3. The process by which we try to explain the motivation for a person's behavior is known as **attribution.**

4. A fixed impression of a group of people is known as a **stereotype.**

5. Expressing lots of agreement, complimenting, and doing favors for someone in order to get him or her like you is known as **ingratiation.**

6. The tendency to conclude that people do what they do because of the kind of people they are (rather than the situation they're in) is referred to as **exemplification.**

7. Taking credit for the positive things you do and attributing your negative actions to external uncontrollable factors is often the result of the **self-serving bias.**

8. When what comes first exerts the most influence, we have a **recency effect.**

9. When you make a prediction and it comes true because you made the prediction and acted as if it were true, the process is called the **self-fulfilling prophecy.**

10. Attributing just about everything a person does to one or two obvious characteristics is known as **personality theory.**

Answers: TRUE: Numbers 3, 4, 5, 7, 9. FALSE: 1 (perception), 2 (the halo effect), 6 (the fundamental attribution error), 8 (primacy effect), 10 (overattribution).

SKILL DEVELOPMENT EXPERIENCES

3.1 Understanding the Processes of Perception

For the next several days, record all personal examples of people perception, instances in which you drew a conclusion about another person. Try to classify these in terms of the processes identified in this chapter, for example, implicit personality theory, stereotyping, attribution. Record, also, the specific context in which they occurred. After you have identified the various processes, share your findings in groups of five or six or with the entire class. As always, disclose only what you wish to disclose. You may find it worthwhile to discuss some or all of these questions:

1. What process seems to be used most frequently?
2. Did the perception process entail any possible barriers?

3.2 Who? An Exercise in Interpersonal Perception

The purpose of this exercise is to explore some of the cues that people give and that others perceive and use in formulating inferences about the knowledge, abilities, and personality of these others. The exercise should serve as a useful summary of the concepts and principles of perception.

The entire class should form a circle so that each member may see each other member without straining. If members do not know all the names of their classmates, name tags should be used.

Each student should examine the following list of phrases and should write the name of one student to whom he or she feels each statement applies in the column marked "Who." Be certain to respond to all statements. Although one name may be used more than once, the experience will prove more effective if a wide variety of names are chosen. Unless the class is very small, no name should be used more than two times. Write in the names before reading any further.

Who?

1. Goes to the professional theater or opera a few times a year
2. Has traveled to at least three different countries
3. Watches soap operas on a regular basis
4. Has recently seen a pornographic (XXX-rated) movie
5. Is a member of an organized sports team
6. Surfs the Net (almost) daily.
7. Owns a state-of-the-art personal computer.

8. Fluently speaks a foreign language
9. Has many close friends
10. Knows how potatoes should be planted
11. Knows the difference between a hacksaw and a jigsaw
12. Knows the ingredients of a Bloody Mary
13. Know the meaning of ROM, RAM, and CACHE.
14. Can name all 12 signs of the zodiac
15. Has a car in the immediate family costing more than $35,000
16. Would aid a friend even at great personal sacrifice
17. Would like, perhaps secretly, to be a movie star
18. Writes poetry
19. Knows where Rwanda is
20. Knows the political status of Puerto Rico
21. Watches television talk shows whenever possible
22. Knows what prime rate means
23. Will prove an exceptional public speaker
24. Is very religious
25. Wants to go to graduate, law, or medical school
26. Would vote in favor of legalizing same-sex marriage
27. Is going to make a significant contribution to society
28. Is going to be a millionaire
29. Is a real romantic
30. Would emerge as a leader in a small group situation

After the names have been written for each statement by each student, the following procedure might prove useful. The instructor selects a statement (there is no need to tackle the statements in the order they are given here), and asks someone specifically, or the class generally, what names were put down. Before the person whose name was put down is asked whether the phrase is correctly or incorrectly attributed to him or her, some or all of the following questions may be considered.

- What was there about this person that led you to think that this phrase applied to him or her? What specific verbal or nonverbal cues led you to your conclusion?
- What additional cues would you need to raise your degree of certainty?
- Is your response at all a function of a stereotype you might have of this individual's ethnic, religious, racial, or sexual identification?
- Did anyone give contradictory cues? Explain the nature of these contradictory cues.
- How do you communicate your "self" to others? How do you communicate what you know, think, feel, and do to your peers?

3.3 Cultural Perceptions

Anonymously on an index card write one of your cultural identities (for example, race, religion, nationality) and three strengths that you feel a significant number of members of this cultural group possess. The cards should be collected, randomized, and read aloud.

This brief experience—along with any discussion it generates—should have made the following clear:

1. People have diverse cultural identities; each person has several.
2. Each identity has its own perceived strengths, though the "strengths" themselves may not be perceived as "strengths" by members of other cultures, for example, a man's willingness to cry and reveal emotional weakness may be considered a strength in some cultures but a weakness in others.
3. The most effective individual is likely to be the one who recognizes and welcomes the strengths of different cultures.

CHAPTER 4

Listening

CHAPTER CONCEPTS	CHAPTER GOALS	CHAPTER SKILLS
	After completing this chapter, you should be able to	After completing this chapter, you should be able to
The Listening Process	1. define listening and explain the five steps in the listening process	listen more effectively during each of the five listening stages
Effective Listening	2. explain the three dimensions of listening and the guidelines for regulating them	adjust your listening on the basis of: empathic and objective, nonjudgmental and critical, and surface and depth listening
Active Listening	3. define active listening and explain its functions and techniques	use active listening when appropriate
Listening, Culture, and Gender	4. explain how culture and gender influence listening	communicate with an awareness of cultural and gender differences in listening
Thinking Critically About Listening	5. explain the guidelines for listening for truth and accuracy	listen critically for truth and accuracy

How would you explain the similarities and the differences between perception and listening?

They [higher management] believe more and more that listening skills are crucial to job performance and are demanding that managers do something about it. Listening can no longer be sloughed off as just one more item in the vocabulary of communication.

—Warren Reed

Perception and listening are the two major ways in which you receive and make sense of messages. Taken together, the skills of perception and listening enable you to more accurately perceive, to better understand, and to more accurately interpret and evaluate these messages. Perception, as explained in the previous chapter, is the process by which you sense, organize, and interpret a wide variety of stimuli. It's the basic process that underlies your receiving any and all stimuli. Listening is a more specialized process, a type of perception, by which you receive and deal with auditory signals and is the subject of this chapter.

There can be little doubt that you listen a great deal. Upon awakening you listen to the radio. On the way to school you listen to friends, people around you, screeching cars, singing birds, or falling rain. In school you listen to the instructor, to other students, and, of course, to yourself. You listen to friends at lunch and return to class to listen to more instructors; you go to work and listen to coworkers, supervisors, or customers; you arrive home and again listen to family and friends. You listen to CDs, radio, or television. All in all, you probably listen for a good part of your waking day.

Another way to appreciate the importance of listening is to look at the benefits you derive from effective listening. Five of these benefits, organized around the five purposes of communication considered in Chapter 1, are to learn, to relate, to influence, to play, and to help.

Effective listening helps you to **learn:** to acquire knowledge of others, the world, and yourself; to avoid problems and difficulties; and to make more reasoned and reasonable decisions. It enables you to profit from the insights of others, to hear and be able to respond to warnings of impending problems, and to acquire more information relevant to decisions you'll be called upon to make. Listening to Peter talk about his travels to Cuba will help you learn more about Peter and about life in Cuba; listening to student reactions will help the teacher plan more relevant classes; listening to the difficulties your sales staff encounters may help you offer more pertinent sales training.

Effective listening helps you to **relate** to others. Because people come to like those who are attentive and supportive, you're likely to gain social acceptance and popularity through listening. Once people see your genuine concern for them, communicated through attentive and supportive listening, their liking for you will increase.

Through listening you can **influence** the attitudes and behaviors of others. People are more likely to respect and follow those they feel have listened to and understood them. For example, people are more likely to follow your advice as a leader, in both personal and professional contexts, if they feel you listen carefully to their contributions and concerns.

Your ability to listen effectively enables you to engage in communication as enjoyment, as **play.** Knowing when to suspend critical and evaluative thinking and when to simply engage in appreciative and accepting listening is crucial to effective communication. For example, listening to the anecdotes of coworkers will allow you to gain a more comfortable balance between the world of work and the world of play.

Effective listening enables you to **help** others—you'll hear more, empathize more, and come to understand others more deeply. Listening to your child's complaints about her teacher (instead of saying "Now what did you do wrong?") will increase your ability to help your child cope with school and her teacher.

THE LISTENING PROCESS

The listening process is a complex one that occurs in five stages: receiving, understanding, remembering, evaluating, and responding (Figure 4.1). The process is circular: The responses of person A serve as the stimuli for person B whose responses, in turn, serve as the stimuli for person A, and so on.

Receiving

Hearing, which is *not* the same as listening, begins and ends with this first stage of receiving. Hearing happens when you open your ears or get within range of auditory stimuli. Listening, on the other hand, is different. Listening begins (but does not end) with receiving (or hearing) messages the speaker sends.

In what ways are listening in public speaking and listening interpersonally the same? In what ways are they different?

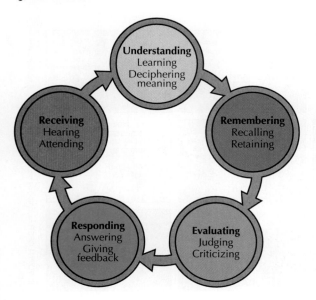

Figure 4.1 A Five-Stage Model of the Listening Process

This model depicts the various tags involved in listening. Note that receiving or hearing is not the same thing as listening but is, in fact, only the first in a five-step process. This model draws on a variety of previous models that listening researchers have developed (for example, Barker, 1990; Steil, Barker, & Watson, 1983; Brownell, 1987; Alessandra, 1986). In what other ways might you visualize the listening process?

At this receiving stage you note not only what is said (verbally and nonverbally) but also what is omitted. You not only receive the politician's summary of accomplishments in education, but also the omission of failures in improved health care programs or services to the homeless, for example.

This receiving stage of listening can be made more effective by:

- focusing your attention on the speaker's verbal and nonverbal messages, on what is said and what is not said
- avoiding distractions in the environment
- focusing your attention on the speaker's messages, not on what you will say next
- maintaining your role as listener; avoiding interrupting the speaker until he or she is finished
- confronting mixed messages—messages that communicate different and contradictory meanings—something the "Born Loser" cartoon characters might profit from

Understanding

Understanding occurs when you decode the speaker's signals—when you learn what the speaker means. Understanding includes both the thoughts that are expressed, as well as the emotional tone that accompanies them, for example, the urgency or the joy or sorrow expressed in the message.

The understanding phase of listening can be made more effective by:

- relating the speaker's new information to what you already know (In what way will this new proposal change our present health care?)
- seeing the speaker's messages from the speaker's point of view; avoid judging the message until it's fully understood *as the speaker intended it*

There is no such thing as a worthless conversation, provided you know what to listen for.

—*James Nathan Miller*

THE BORN LOSER reprinted by permission of Newspaper Enterprise Association, Inc.

- asking questions for clarification, if necessary; asking for additional details or examples if needed
- rephrasing (paraphrasing) the speaker's ideas

Is it not also arrogant to assume that we can fully understand what the other person intends without giving full attention to that person?
—Carley H. Dodd

Remembering

Messages that you receive and understand need to be retained at least for some period of time. In some small group and public speaking situations you can augment your memory by taking notes or by taping the messages. In most interpersonal communication situations, however, such note taking would be considered inappropriate, although you often do write down a phone number or an appointment or directions.

What you remember is not what was actually said, but what you think (or remember) was said. You don't simply *reproduce* in your memory what the speaker said; rather, you *reconstruct* the messages you hear into a system that makes sense to you—a concept noted in the discussion of perception in Chapter 3. To illustrate this important concept, try to memorize the list of 12 words presented below (Glucksberg & Danks, 1975). Don't worry about the order; only the number remembered counts. Take about 20 seconds to memorize as many words as possible. Don't read any further until you've tried to memorize the list.

Word List

bed	awake
dream	night
comfort	slumber
rest	tired
wake	eat
sound	snore

Now close the book and write down as many words from the list as you can remember. Don't read any further until you've tested your own memory.

If you're like my students, you not only remembered most of the words, but also added at least one word: "sleep." Most people recall "sleep" being on the list, but, as you can see, it wasn't. What happened was that you didn't just reproduce the list; you reconstructed it. In this case you gave the list meaning by including the word "sleep." This happens with all types of messages; they're reconstructed into a meaningful whole and, in the process, a distorted version is often remembered.

You can make this remembering phase of listening more effective by:

- identifying the central ideas and the major support advanced
- summarizing the message in an easier to retain form, but without ignoring crucial details or qualifications
- repeating names and key concepts to yourself or, if appropriate, aloud
- identifying the pattern and using it to organize what the speaker is saying (if this is a formal talk with a recognizable organizational structure)

Have you ever "remembered" something that was *not* said in an interpersonal, group, or public communication situation?

A good memory and a tongue tied in the middle is a combination which gives immortality to conversation.
—Mark Twain

Evaluating

Evaluating consists of judging the messages. At times you may try to evaluate the speaker's underlying intent, often without much conscious awareness. For example, Elaine tells you she is up for a promotion and is really excited about it. You may then try to judge her intention. Does she want you to use your influence with the company president? Is she preoccupied with the possible promotion and, thus, telling everyone? Is she looking for a pat on the back? Generally, if you know the person well, you'll be able to identify the intention and respond appropriately.

In other situations, the evaluation is more in the nature of a critical analysis. For example, in a business meeting you would evaluate proposals while listening to them. Are they practical? Will they increase productivity? What is the evidence? Are there more practical alternative proposals?

This evaluation stage of listening can be made more effective by:

- resisting evaluation until you fully understand the speaker's point of view
- assuming that the speaker is a person of goodwill and giving the speaker the benefit of any doubt by asking for clarification on issues you object to. (Are there any other reasons for accepting this new proposal?)
- distinguishing what is factual from what is opinion or personal interpretation by the speaker
- identifying any biases, self-interests, or prejudices that may lead the speaker to unfairly slant information presented

Responding

Responding occurs in two phases: (1) responses you make while the speaker is talking and (2) responses you make after the speaker has stopped talking. Responses made while the speaker is talking should, in most cases, be supportive and should acknowledge that you're listening. These responses (called "backchanneling cues") are messages (words and gestures) that let the speaker know you're paying attention, for example, nodding in agreement or saying "I see" or "uh-huh."

Responses after the speaker has stopped talking are generally more elaborate and might include empathy ("I know how you must feel"); asking for clarification ("Do you mean this new health plan will replace the old one?"); challenging ("I think your evidence is weak"); and agreeing ("You're absolutely right; I'll support your proposal when it comes up for a vote").

You can improve this responding phase of listening by:

- being supportive of the speaker throughout the talk by using varied backchanneling cues; using only one cue—for example, saying "uh-huh" throughout—will make it appear that you're not listening but are merely on automatic pilot
- expressing support for the speaker in your final responses
- taking ownership of your responses—stating your thoughts and feelings as your own; using "I" messages, saying "I think the new proposal will entail greater expense than you outlined" rather than "Everyone will object to the plan's cost."

EFFECTIVE LISTENING

Before reading about the principles of effective listening, examine your own listening behavior by taking the accompanying self-test. The "desirable" answers are obvious, of course, but try to give responses that are true for you in most of your listening experiences.

From listening comes wisdom, and from speaking repentance.

—*Italian Proverb*

Test Yourself — How Good a Listener Are You?

Instructions: Respond to each question using the following scale:

1 = always
2 = frequently
3 = sometimes
4 = seldom
5 = never

_____ 1. I listen to what the speaker is saying and feeling; I try to feel what the speaker feels.

_____ 2. I listen objectively; I focus on the logic of the ideas rather than on the emotional meaning of the message.

_____ 3. I listen without judging the speaker.

_____ 4. I listen critically; I rarely suspend my critical, evaluative faculties.

_____ 5. I listen to the literal meaning, to what the speaker says rather than play psychiatrist and focus on the hidden or deeper meanings.

_____ 6. I listen for the speaker's hidden meanings, to what the speaker means but isn't verbalizing.

Thinking Critically About Listening These statements focus on the ways of listening discussed in this chapter. All of these ways are appropriate at some times but not at other times. It depends. The only responses that are really inappropriate are "always" and "never." Effective listening is listening that is tailored to the specific communication situation. Review these statements and try to identify situations in which each statement would be appropriate and situations in which each statement would be inappropriate.

As should be apparent from the self-test, effective listening involved your making adjustments on the basis of the specific situation along the dimensions of empathic–objective, nonjudgmental–critical, and surface–depth.

Empathic and Objective Listening

If you want to understand what a person means and what a person feels, listen with empathy. When you empathize with others you see the world as they see it, you feel what they feel. Only when you achieve some degree of empathy can you begin to understand another's meaning.

How would you rate yourself on a 1 to 10 scale of empathy, with 1 being "usually very unempathic" to 10 being "usually very empathic"? How would your close friends rate you on the same scale?

Achieving empathy is not easy, but it's something worth working toward. It's important, for example, that a student see the teacher's point of view. It's equally important for the teacher to see the student's point of view. Popular students might intellectually understand why an unpopular student feels depressed, but that will not enable them to understand emotionally the feelings of depression. To accomplish that, they must put themselves in the position of the unpopular student, role play, and begin to feel that student's feelings and think his or her thoughts. It's only then that the popular students will be in a position to understand what that student feels and to genuinely empathize. (Chapter 7 offers more specific suggestions for developing and communicating empathy.)

Although empathic listening is the preferred type of listening in most communication situations, there are times when you need to go beyond empathy and listen objectively. While it's important to listen to a colleague tell you how the entire company fails to value his or her contributions and to understand how this employee feels and why, there are situations when you need to look a bit more objectively at both your colleague and the company and perhaps see the unrealistic expectations or the negative view your colleague has of the company. Sometimes you have to put your empathic responses aside and listen with objectivity and detachment.

In adjusting your empathic and objective listening focus, seek to understand both thoughts and feelings. Your listening task isn't finished until you have understood what the speaker is feeling as well as thinking.

Beware of the "friend-or-foe" factor that may lead you to distort messages because of your attitudes toward another person. For example, if you think Freddy is stupid, then it will take added effort to listen objectively to Freddy's messages and to hear anything that is clear or insightful.

Do you find yourself falling into the friend-or-foe fallacy, where you listen with positive expectations to a friend and negative expectations to an enemy? How might this tendency get you into trouble?

Nonjudgmental and Critical Listening

Effective listening is both nonjudgmental and critical. It involves listening with an open mind with the goal of reaching a greater level of understanding. However, it also involves listening critically to be able to make an evaluation or judgment. Clearly, listening for understanding, rather than to make a judgment, is the first step. Only after you have fully understood the message should you evaluate or judge. Listening with an open mind is often difficult. It's not easy, for example, to listen to arguments against your cherished belief or to criticisms of something you value highly. Listening often stops when a hostile or critical remark is made. Admittedly, to continue listening with an open mind is difficult, yet it's in precisely these situations that this type of listening is especially important.

Supplement open-minded listening with critical listening. This is especially helpful in the college environment. It's easy to simply listen to an instructor and take down what is said. Yet, it's important that you also evaluate and critically analyze what is said. Instructors have biases too; at times consciously and at times unconsciously, these biases creep into scholarly discussions. Listening critically can help you identify these biases and bring them to the surface. The vast majority of teachers appreciate critical responses. These responses demonstrate that you're listening and help to stimulate closer examination of the ideas being discussed.

Listening, not imitation, may be the sincerest form of flattery.

—*Joyce Brothers*

In adjusting your nonjudgmental and critical listening, keep an open mind. Avoid prejudging; delay evaluation until you have fully understood the intent and the content of the message.

Listen to the message in its entirety without blocking or filtering out difficult portions. Avoid distorting messages through oversimplification or **leveling,** the tendency to eliminate details and to simplify complex messages so that they are easier to remember. Avoid filtering out unpleasant or undesirable messages—you may miss the very information you need to change your assumptions or your behaviors.

Recognize your own biases that may interfere with accurate listening. Biases can often cause you to distort message reception through the process of **assimilation**, the tendency to interpret what you hear or think you hear according to your own prejudices and expectations. For example, are your cultural or gender biases preventing you from appreciating the speaker's point of view? Biases may also lead to **sharpening**, the tendency for a particular item of information to be given increased importance because it confirms your stereotypes or prejudices.

Finally, know when to listen critically and when to listen nonjudgmentally: Use critical listening when evaluations and judgments are called for and use nonjudgmental listening to express support and to encourage the speaker to continue talking.

Have you ever observed *sharpening?* What happened?

Surface and Depth Listening

In most messages there is an obvious meaning that a literal reading of the words and sentences reveals. This is the surface meaning. However, there is often another level of meaning. Sometimes it's the opposite of the expressed literal meaning; sometimes it's totally unrelated. In reality, few messages have only one level of meaning. Most function on two or three levels at the same time. Consider the parent who seems, on the surface, to be complaining about working too hard. On a deeper level, he or she may be asking for some expression of appreciation. The child who talks about the unfairness of the other children in the playground may be asking for affection and love, for some expression of caring, for some indication that you understand. To appreciate these other (deeper) meanings you need to engage in depth listening.

There is only one cardinal rule: one must always listen to the patient.
—*Oliver Sacks*

If you respond only to the surface-level communication (the literal meaning), you'll miss the opportunity to make meaningful contact with the other person's feelings and real needs. If you say to your parent, "You're always complaining. I bet you really love working so hard," you may be failing to answer this very real call for understanding and appreciation.

In regulating your surface and depth listening, focus on both verbal and nonverbal messages. Recognize both consistent and inconsistent "packages" of messages and take these cues as guides for inferring the meaning the speaker is trying to communicate. When in doubt, ask questions.

Listen for both content and relational messages (Chapter 1). The employee who constantly challenges the supervisor is on one level communicating disagreement over content; the employee is debating the issues. However, on another level—the relationship level—the employee may well be voicing objections to the supervisor's authority or authoritarianism.

If the supervisor is to deal effectively with the employee, he or she must listen and respond to both types of messages.

Don't disregard the literal (surface) meaning of interpersonal messages in your attempt to uncover the more hidden (deep) meanings. If you do, you'll quickly find that your listening problems disappear—because no one will talk to you anymore. Balance your attention between the surface and the underlying meanings. Respond to the various levels of meaning in the messages of others as you would like others to respond to yours—sensitively, but not obsessively, readily, but not overambitiously.

ACTIVE LISTENING

Consider the following exchange:

Speaker: I can't believe I have to redo this entire budget report. I really worked hard on this project and now I have to do it all over again.

Listener 1: That's not so bad; most people find they have to redo their first reports. That's the norm here.

Listener 2: So what? You don't intend to stay at this job. Anyway, you're getting paid by the hour, so what do you care?

Listener 3: You should be pleased that all you have to do is a simple rewrite. Both Peggy and Michael had to completely redo their entire projects.

Listener 4: You have to rewrite that report you've worked on for the last 3 weeks? You sound really angry and frustrated.

All four listeners are probably trying to make the speaker feel better, but they go about it in very different ways and, we can be sure, with very different results. Listeners 1 and 2 try to lessen the significance of the rewrite. These well-intended responses are extremely common but do little to promote meaningful communication and understanding. Listener 3 tries to give the situation a positive spin. With these responses, however, all three listeners are also suggesting that the speaker should not be feeling as he or she does. They're also saying the speaker's feelings are not legitimate and should be replaced with more logical feelings.

Listener 4's response, however, is different. Listener 4 uses active listening. Active listening, which owes its development to Thomas Gordon (1975) who made it a cornerstone of his P-E-T (Parent-Effectiveness-Training) technique, is a process of sending back to the speaker what you as a listener think the speaker meant—both in content and in feelings. Active listening, then, is not merely repeating the speaker's exact words, but rather putting your understanding of the speaker's total message into some meaningful whole.

Functions of Active Listening

Active listening serves several important functions. First, it helps you, as a listener, check your understanding of what the speaker said and, more important, what he or she meant. Reflecting back your understanding of

80   PART I: Foundations of Human Communication

what you think the speaker means gives the speaker an opportunity to offer clarification. In this way, future messages will have a better chance of being relevant.

Second, through active listening you let the speaker know that you acknowledge and accept his or her feelings. In the sample responses given, the first three listeners challenged the speaker's feelings. The active listener (Listener 4), who reflected back to the speaker what he or she thought was said, accepted what the speaker was feeling. In addition to accepting the speaker's feelings, Listener 4 also explicitly identifies them ("You sound angry and frustrated") allowing the speaker an opportunity to correct the listener.

Third, active listening stimulates the speaker to explore feelings and thoughts. Listener 4's response encourages the speaker to elaborate on his or her feelings. This exploration also helps the speaker to deal with these feelings through the opportunity to talk them through.

Techniques for Active Listening

Three simple techniques may prove useful in learning the process of active listening: paraphrase the speaker's meaning, express understanding, and ask questions.

Paraphrase the Speaker's Meaning   Stating in your own words what you think the speaker means and feels helps ensure understanding and also shows interest in the speaker. Further, it demonstrates that you're listening to both thoughts and feelings. Paraphrasing gives the speaker a chance to extend what was originally said. Thus, when Listener 4 echoes the speaker's thought, the speaker may elaborate on why rewriting the budget report meant so much. Perhaps the speaker fears that his or her other

Active listening is not always preferable. You may not want to listen actively, for example, when you know the person is lying or being abusive. In these cases you may decide to listen critically or even end the interaction. In what cases would you decide against listening actively?

reports will be challenged or that this now means a much-anticipated promotion will not be forthcoming. In your paraphrase, be especially careful not to lead the speaker in the direction you think he or she should go. Paraphrases should be objective descriptions.

Finally, do be careful that you don't overdo a paraphrase; only a very small percentage of statements need paraphrasing. Paraphrase when you feel there is a chance for misunderstanding or when you want to express support for the other person and keep the conversation going.

Express Understanding of the Speaker's Feelings In addition to paraphrasing the content, echo the feelings the speaker expressed or implied ("You must have felt horrible"). This expression of feelings will help you further check your perception of the speaker's feelings. This will also allow the speaker to see his or her feelings more objectively. This is especially helpful when the speaker feels angry, hurt, or depressed.

When you echo the speaker's feelings, you also offer the speaker a chance to elaborate. Most of us hold back our feelings until we're certain they (and, by extension, we) will be accepted. When we feel acceptance, we then feel free to go into more detail. Active listening gives the speaker this important opportunity. In echoing feelings, be careful not to over-or-understate the speaker's feelings; try to be as accurate as you can.

Ask Questions Asking questions ensures your own understanding of the speaker's thoughts and feelings and secures additional information ("How did you feel when you read your job appraisal report?"). Your questions should provide just enough stimulation and support for the speaker to feel he or she can elaborate on these thoughts and feelings. These questions further confirm your interest and concern for the speaker. Be careful, however, not to pry into unrelated areas or challenge the speaker in any way.

LISTENING, CULTURE, AND GENDER

Listening is difficult, in part, because of the inevitable differences in the communication systems between speaker and listener. Because each person has had a unique set of experiences, each person's communication and meaning system is going to be different from each other person's. When speaker and listener come from different cultures or are of different genders, the differences and their effects are naturally much greater. Let's look first at culture.

Listening and Culture

The culture in which you were raised will influence your listening in a variety of ways. Here we look at some of these: language and speech, nonverbal differences, direct and indirect styles, feedback, balance of story versus evidence, and credibility.

Language and Speech Even when speaker and listener speak the same language, they speak it with different meanings, different styles, and different pronunciation and articulation. No two speakers speak exactly the same language. Every speaker speaks an *idiolect*—a unique variation of the language (King & DiMichael, 1992).

Speakers and listeners who have different native languages and who may have learned English as a second language will have even greater differences in meaning. Translations are never precise and never fully capture the meaning in the other language. If your meaning for "house" was learned in a culture in which everyone lived in their own house with lots of land around it, then communicating with someone for whom the meaning of "house" was learned in a neighborhood of high-rise tenements is going to be imprecise. Although you'll each hear the same word, the meanings you'll each develop will be drastically different. In adjusting your listening—especially in an intercultural setting—understand that the speaker's meanings may be very different from yours although you're speaking the "same" language.

Still another part of speech is that of accents. In many classrooms throughout the country, there will be a wide range of accents. Those whose native language is a tonal one such as Chinese (where differences in pitch signal important meaning differences) may speak English with variations in pitch that may seem puzzling to others. Those whose native language is Japanese may have trouble distinguishing "l" from "r" since Japanese does not include this distinction. The native language acts as a filter and influences the accent given to the second language.

Nonverbal Behavioral Differences   Speakers from different cultures have different display rules, cultural rules that govern what nonverbal behaviors are appropriate and inappropriate in a public setting. As you listen to another person, you also "listen" to their nonverbals. If these are drastically different from what you expect on the basis of the verbal message, they may be seen as a kind of noise or interference or they may be seen as contradictory messages. In addition, different cultures may give very different meanings to the same nonverbal gesture; the thumb and forefinger forming a circle means "OK" in most of the United States, but it means "money" in Japan, "zero," in some Mediterranean countries, and "I'll kill you" in Tunisia.

Direct and Indirect Styles   Some cultures—Western Europe and the United States, for example—favor a direct style in communication; they advise us to "say what you mean and mean what you say." Many Asian cultures, on the other hand, favor an indirect style; they emphasize politeness and maintaining a positive public image rather than absolute truth. Listen carefully to persons with different styles of directness, a topic covered in Chapter 5. The possibility that the meanings the speaker wishes to communicate with, for example, directness, may be very different from the meanings you would communicate with indirectness.

Feedback   Members of some cultures give very direct and very honest feedback. Speakers from these cultures—the United States is a good example—expect the feedback to be an honest reflection of what their listeners are feeling. In other cultures—Japan and Korea are good examples—it's more important to be positive than to be truthful and so

Have you ever witnessed listening problems caused by a failure to recognize cultural differences? What could have been done to prevent such listening failures?

In what ways have you experienced men and women listening differently? Do you find that members of different cultures listen differently?

people may respond with positive feedback (for example, in commenting on a business colleague's proposal) even though they don't agree with it. Listen to feedback, as you would all messages, with a full recognition that various cultures view feedback very differently.

Balance of Story Versus Evidence   In the United States, most people want evidence before making decisions. In fact, you're taught this cultural value for evidence throughout the critical thinking emphasis in many of your courses. You're taught to seek good reasons, hard evidence, and reliable testimony before making a decision. Members of other cultures, however, may be more influenced by a story told with complete conviction or simply by the word of a high credibility source.

Credibility   What makes a speaker credible or believable will vary from one culture to another. In some cultures, people would claim that competence is the most important factor in, for example, choosing a teacher for their preschool children. In other cultures, the most important factor might be the goodness or morality of the teacher. Similarly, members of different cultures may perceive the credibility of the various media very differently. Members of a repressive society in which the government controls television news, for example, may come to attribute little credibility to such broadcasts. After all, this person might reason that television news is simply what the government wants you to know. This may be hard to understand or even recognize by someone raised in the United States, where the media are free of such political control. Credibility, also an effective mode of persuasion, is discussed in further detail in Chapter 15, "The Persuasive Speech."

Listen to information on subjects you are unacquainted with, instead of always striving to lead the conversation to some favorite one of your own. By the last method you will shine, but will not improve.

—*William Hazlitt*

Listening and Gender

Deborah Tannen opens her chapter on listening in her best selling *You Just Don't Understand: Women and Men in Conversation* with several anecdotes illustrating that when men and women talk, men lecture and women listen. The lecturer assumes the role of the superior, the teacher, the expert. The listener is then made to assume the role of the inferior, the student, the nonexpert.

Women, according to Tannen, seek to build rapport and establish a closer relationship and so use listening to achieve these ends. For example, women use more listening cues, that let the other person know they are paying attention and are interested, a difference humorously illustrated in the accompanying cartoon. Men not only use fewer listening cues but interrupt more and will often change the topic to one they know more about or one that is less relational or people-oriented to one that is more factual, for example, sports statistics, economic developments, or political problems. Men, research shows, play up their expertise, emphasize it, and use it to dominate the conversation. Women play down their expertise.

You might be tempted to conclude from this that women play fair in conversation and that men don't. However, that may be too simple an explanation. For example, research shows that men communicate with women in the same way they do with other men. Men are not showing disrespect for their female conversational partners but are simply communicating as they normally do. Women, too, communicate as they do, not only with men, but also with other women.

Does Deborah Tannen, in her description of the listening behavior of men and women, accurately describe your own listening tendencies?

"I'm sorry, I didn't hear what you said. I was listening to my body."

Tannen argues that the goal of a man in conversation is to be accorded respect and so he seeks to display his knowledge and expertise even if he has to change the topic from one he knows little about to one he knows a great deal about. A woman, on the other hand, seeks to be liked and so she expresses agreement and less frequently interrupts to take her turn as speaker.

Men and women also show that they're listening in different ways. A woman is more apt to give lots of listening cues, such as interjecting *yeah, uh-uh*, nodding in agreement, and smiling. A man is more likely to listen quietly, without giving lots of listening cues as feedback. Tannen also argues, however, that men do listen less to women than women listen to men. The reason, says Tannen, is that listening places the person in an inferior position whereas speaking places the person in a superior position.

There is no evidence to show that these differences represent any negative motives on the part of men to prove themselves superior or of women to ingratiate themselves. Rather, these differences in listening are largely the result of the way in which men and women have been socialized. It's another question whether men and women can (or should) change these habitual ways of listening (and speaking).

Which listening guidelines do you have the most difficulty following in interpersonal communication? In small groups? In public speaking?

We can, if we are able to listen as well as to speak, become better informed and wiser as we grow older, instead of being stuck like some people with the same little bundle of prejudices at 65 that we had at 25.

—*S. I. Hayakawa*

THINKING CRITICALLY ABOUT LISTENING

Earlier we noted the importance of regulating your listening between nonjudgmental and critical listening. In addition, however, listening critically depends also on assessing the truth and accuracy of the information and the honesty and motivation of the speaker. Thus, in addition to keeping an open mind and delaying judgments, it's necessary to focus on other issues as well:

- Is what the speaker says the truth as far as you understand it? For example, is this car really that great? Are there any disadvantages to this particular car?
- Has the speaker presented the information in enough detail? Have crucial parts been left out? For example, has the speaker identified all the costs?
- Is the speaker being honest? Is the speaker's motivation merely self-gain? For example, might this speaker be distorting the facts merely to make a sale and earn a commission?
- Does the speaker use fallacious reasoning such as stating that X causes Y when the evidence merely confirms that X and Y occur together? Are conclusions about "all" or "most people" based on a sample that is both large and representative of the population?
- Does the speaker rely too heavily on emotional appeals? Are these appeals legitimate?
- Has the speaker the credibility you want and expect? For example, is the speaker competent and knowledgeable about the topic?

Asking and answering these questions will help promote critical listening and more responsible communication.

SUMMARY OF CONCEPTS AND SKILLS

In this chapter we discussed the way we listen, how listening may be made more effective, the functions and techniques of active listening, and the influence of culture and gender on listening.

1. Listening serves a variety of purposes: we listen to learn, to relate to others, to influence the attitudes, beliefs, and behaviors of others, to play, and to help.
2. Listening is a five-step process consisting of receiving, understanding, remembering, evaluating, and responding. Receiving is essentially the hearing process; the messages from another person are received at this stage. Understanding is the stage of comprehension; you make sense out of the messages. The remembering stage refers to the fact that messages and your understanding of them are retained in your memory for at least some time. In evaluating you judge the messages and apply your critical thinking skills to them. The final stage, responding, includes both the responses you make while the speaker is speaking and the responses you may make after the speaker has stopped talking.
3. Effective listening involves a process of making adjustments—depending on the situation—along such dimensions as empathic and objective listening, nonjudgmental and critical listening, and surface and depth listening.
4. Active listening is a special type of listening that enables you to check your understanding of what the speaker means, express your acceptance of the speaker's feelings, and stimulate the speaker to further explore his or her thoughts and feelings.
5. Active listening techniques include paraphrasing, expressing understanding of the speaker's feelings, and asking questions.
6. Culture influences listening in a variety of ways. Contributing to listening difficulties are cultural differences in language and speech, nonverbal behaviors, direct and indirect styles, differences in giving feedback, preference for story versus evidence, and credibility differences.
7. Men and women listen differently and perhaps for different reasons. For example, women give more listening cues that say "I'm listening" than do men. According to some theorists women use listening to show empathy and to build rapport; men minimize listening because it puts one in a subordinate position.

Throughout this discussion of listening, a variety of skills were identified and are presented here in summary. Check your ability to apply these skills: (1) = almost always, (2) = often, (3) = sometimes, (4) = rarely, (5) = hardly ever.

_____ 1. I recognize that listening serves a variety of purposes and I adjust my listening on the basis of my purposes, for example, to learn, relate, influence, play, and help.

_____ 2. I realize that listening is a multistage process and I regulate my listening behavior as appropriate in receiving, understanding, remembering, evaluating, and responding.

_____ 3. In receiving messages, I seek to increase my chances of effective listening by, for example, focusing attention on the speaker's verbal and nonverbal messages, avoiding distractions, and focusing attention on what the speaker is saying and not on what I'm going to say next.

_____ 4. I facilitate understanding in listening by relating new information to what I already know and trying to see the messages from the speaker's point of view.

_____ 5. In remembering the speaker's messages I try to identify the central ideas and the major supporting materials, summarize the main ideas, and repeat important concepts to etch them more firmly in my mind.

_____ 6. In evaluating messages I first make sure I understand the speaker's point of view and seek to identify any sources of bias or self-interest.

_____ 7. In responding, I am supportive of the speaker and own my own thoughts and feelings.

_____ 8. I am especially careful to adjust my listening on the basis of the immediate situation between empathic and objective, nonjudgmental and critical, and surface and depth listening.

_____ 9. I practice active listening when appropriate by paraphrasing the speaker's meaning, expressing my understanding of the speaker's feelings, and asking questions.

_____ 10. I recognize the influence of culture on listening and the cultural differences in listening and take these into consideration when listening in intercultural situations.

_____ 11. I recognize gender differences in listening and take these into consideration when communicating with members of the opposite sex.

KEY WORD QUIZ

Write T for those statements that are true and F for those that are false. For those that are false replace the boldface term with the correct term.

_____ 1. The communication activity on which most people spend the most time is **talking**.

_____ 2. Listening, unlike speaking, is a **passive process**.

3. The first step in the listening process is **understanding.**

4. Memory for speech is a **reproductive process.**

5. Listening to understand and to feel what the other person is feeling is called **empathic listening.**

6. Research generally supports the finding that compared to men women give more **listening cues.**

7. Generally, compared to men, women engage in less conversational **interruption.**

8. The tendency for a particular item of information to take on increased importance because it seems to confirm what the listener believes is known as **sharpening.**

9. The tendency to interpret what you hear or think you hear according to your own biases and expectations is known as **assimilation.**

10. The process of restating in your own words your understanding of the speaker's thoughts and feelings is known as **paraphrasing.**

Answers: TRUE: Numbers 5, 6, 7, 8, 9, 10. FALSE: Numbers 1 (listening), 2 (active process), 3 (receiving, hearing, or attending), 4 (reconstructive process).

SKILL DEVELOPMENT EXPERIENCES

4.1 Paraphrasing to Ensure Understanding

For each of the messages presented below, write a paraphrase that you think would be appropriate. After you complete the paraphrases, ask another person if he or she would accept them as objective restatements of thoughts and feelings. Rework the paraphrases until the other person agrees that they're accurate. A sample paraphrase is provided for Number 1.

1. I can't deal with my parents' constant fighting. I've seen it for the last 10 years and I really can't stand it anymore.
   Paraphrase: You have trouble dealing with their fighting. You seem really upset by this last fight.

2. Did you hear I got engaged to Jerry? Our racial and religious differences are really going to cause difficulties for both of us. But we love each other. We'll work it through.

3. I got a C on that paper. That's the worst grade I've ever received. I just can't believe that I got a C. This is my major. What am I going to do?

4. I can't understand why I didn't get that promotion. I was here longer and did better work than Thompson. Even my two supervisors said I was the next in line for the promotion. Now it looks like another one won't come along for at least a year.

5. That rotten, inconsiderate pig just up and left. He never even said goodbye. We were together for 6 months and after one small argument he leaves without a word. And he even took my bathrobe—that expensive one he bought for my last birthday.

6. I'm just not sure what to do. I really love Fiona. She's the sweetest kid I've ever known. I mean she'd do anything for me. But, she really wants to get married. I do, too, and yet I don't want to make such a commitment. I mean—that's a long-term thing. Much as I hate to admit it, I don't want the responsibility of a wife, a family, a house. I really don't need that kind of pressure.

4.2 Reducing Barriers to Listening

Visualize yourself ready to talk with the following people on the topics noted. What barriers to listening (from any stage: receiving, understanding, remembering, evaluating, and responding) might arise in each encounter? What might you do to prevent these barriers from interfering with effective listening?

1. Doctors on the legitimacy of the AMA endorsing products for a fee.
2. Gloria Steinem on the contemporary women's movement.
3. President Bill Clinton on the role of the U.S. military in defending the world.
4. Spike Lee on ways to improve race relations.
5. A catholic priest on the need to remain a virgin until marriage.
6. A person with AIDS on the need for lower drug prices.
7. A lesbian mother on the unfairness of current adoption laws.
8. Oprah Winfrey on the mistakes of modern psychology.
9. A homeless person on the need to use public spaces.
10. A religious fundamentalist on the need to return to fundamentalist values.

In thinking about these situations, consider, for example: How would your initial expectations influence your listening? How would your assessment of the person's credibility (even before you begin to talk)? How will this influence your listening? Will you begin listening with a positive, a negative, or a neutral attitude? How might these attitudes influence your listening?

4.3 Regulating Your Listening Perspective

What type(s) of listening (emphatic, objective, nonjudgmental, critical, surface, depth, or active) would you use in each of the following situations? What types of listening would be obviously inappropriate in each situation?

1. Your steady dating partner for the last 5 years tells you that spells of depression are becoming more frequent and more long lasting.
2. Your history instructor's lecture on the contribution of the Ancient Greeks to modern civilization.
3. Your 12-year-old son says he wants to become a nurse.
4. Your sister tells you she's been accepted into Harvard's MBA program.
5. A salesperson tells you of the benefits of the new computer.
6. A blind person asks your assistance in getting off a bus.
7. Your supervisor explains the new Intranet mail system.
8. A newscaster reports on a recent Arab–Israeli meeting.
9. A gossip columnist details the secret lives of the stars.
10. The television advertiser explaining the benefits of the new Volvo.

4.4 Experiencing Active Listening

For each of the situations described below, supply at least one appropriate active listening response.

1. Your friend Phil has just broken up a love affair and is telling you about it. "I can't seem to get Chris out of my mind," he says. "All I do is daydream about what we used to do and all the fun we used to have."
2. You and your friend are discussing the recent chemistry examination. Your friend says: "I didn't get an A. I got a B+. What am I going to do now? I feel like a failure."
3. A young nephew tells you that he cannot talk with his parents. No matter how hard he tries, they just don't listen. "I tried to tell them that I can't play baseball and I don't want to play baseball," he confides. "But they ignore me and tell me that all I need is practice."
4. A friend just won $20,000 on a quiz show but is depressed because she lost the championship and the chance to compete for the grand prize of $150,000. She says: "I knew the answer, but I just couldn't think fast enough. That money could have solved all my problems."
5. Your mother has been having a difficult time at work. She was recently passed up for a promotion and received one of the lowest merit raises given in the company. "I'm not sure what I did wrong," she tells you. "I do my work, mind my own business, don't take my sick days like everyone else. How could they give that promotion to Helen who's only been with the company for 2 years? Maybe I should just quit."
6. Your friend, looking real depressed, meets you on the street and says: "I can't believe it, I just got a phone call from the clinic. I'm HIV+ and I don't know what to do."

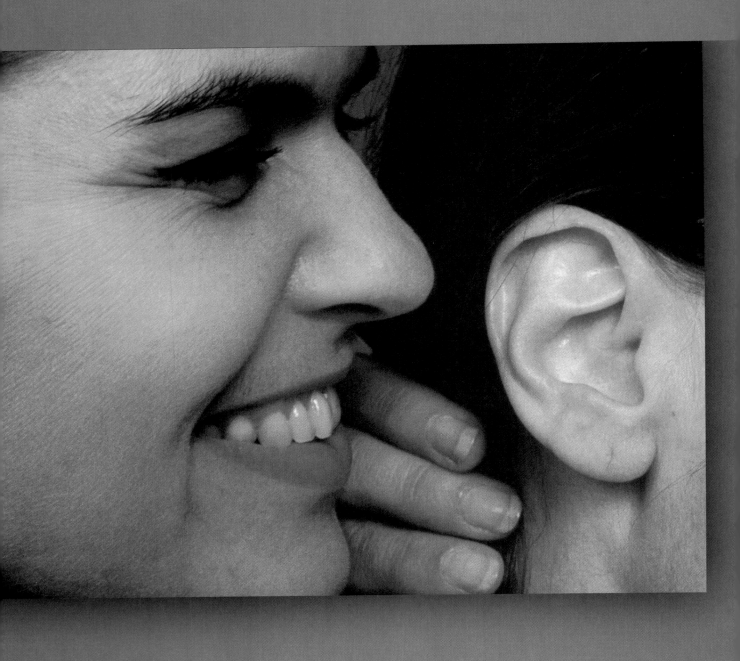

CHAPTER 5

Verbal Messages

CHAPTER CONCEPTS	CHAPTER OBJECTIVES After completing this chapter, you should be able to	CHAPTER SKILLS After completing this chapter, you should be able to
The Nature of Language	1. identify the characteristics of language and their implications for human communication	communicate with a recognition of denotation and connotation, variations in abstraction, differences in directness, the rules of language, and the principle that language meanings are in people
Disconfirmation	2. define *disconfirmation* and explain the nature of sexism, heterosexism, and racism	regulate your confirmations while avoiding language that puts down other groups, such as sexist, racist, and heterosexist language
Thinking Critically About Verbal Messages	3. explain the four principles for thinking critically about verbal messages	avoid the major barriers to effective language usage

In communication you use two major signal systems—the verbal and the nonverbal. The verbal system consists largely of signals (words) you send through the air that are received through hearing. The nonverbal system consists of just about every other way you can communicate meaning, for example, by gestures, facial expressions, and touch. In this chapter we focus on the verbal system, and in Chapter 6 we focus on the nonverbal. Do realize that in actual communication, the two systems function together.

THE NATURE OF LANGUAGE

The nature of language—what it is and how it works—can be appreciated by looking at five general principles: language is both denotative and connotative, varies in abstraction, varies in directness, is rule based, and its meanings are best viewed as being in people rather than just in the words.

Language is Both Denotative and Connotative

What differences in meaning might exist for such words as *woman* to an American and an Iranian, *religion* to a born-again Christian and an atheist, and *lunch* to a Chinese rice farmer and a Wall Street executive? What communication principles might help you communicate your meaning effectively in these situations?

You speak both denotatively and connotatively. **Denotation** refers to the objective meaning of a term, the meaning you'd find in a dictionary. It's the meaning that members who share a common language assign to a word. **Connotation** refers to the subjective or emotional meaning that specific speakers/listeners give to a word. Take as an example the word *death*. To a doctor this word might mean (or denote) the time when the heart stops. This is an objective description of a particular event. On the other hand, to the dead person's mother (upon being informed of her son's death), the word means (or connotes) much more. It recalls her son's youth, ambition, family, illness, and so on. To her, it's a highly emotional, subjective, and personal word. These emotional, subjective, or personal reactions are the word's connotative meaning.

Semanticist S. I. Hayakawa (Hayakawa & Hayakawa, 1990) coined the terms **snarl words** and **purr words** to further clarify the distinction between denotation and connotation. Snarl words are highly negative: "She's an idiot." "He's a pig." "They're a bunch of losers." Purr words are highly positive: "She's a real sweetheart." "He's a dream." "They're the greatest." Snarl and purr words, although they may sometimes seem to have denotative meaning and to refer to the "real world," are actually connotative in meaning. These terms do not describe people or events in the real world but rather the speaker's feelings about these people or events.

Using the concepts of connotation and denotation and of snarl and purr words, how would you define and explain such terms as "pejorative language," "hate speech," "slander," "libel," "whitewash," and "spin"?

Language Varies in Abstraction

Consider the following list of terms:

- entertainment
- film
- American film
- recent American film
- *Titanic*

At the top is the general or abstract entertainment. Note that entertainment includes all the other items on the list plus various other items—

television, novels, drama, comics, and so on. Film is more specific and concrete. It includes all of the items below it as well as various other items such as Indian film or Russian film. It excludes, however, all entertainment that is not film. American film is again more specific than film and excludes all films that are not American. Recent American film further limits American film to a time period. *Titanic* specifies concretely the one item to which reference is made.

Effective verbal messages include words from a wide range of abstractions. At times a general term may suit your needs best; at other times a more specific term may serve better. Generally, however, the specific term will prove the better choice. As you get more specific—less abstract—you more effectively guide the images that come to your listeners' minds.

Language Varies in Directness

Think about how you would respond to someone saying the following sentences.

1A. I'm so bored; I have nothing to do tonight.
2A. I'd like to go to the movies. Would you like to come?
1B. Do you feel like hamburgers tonight?
2B. I'd like hamburgers tonight. How about you?

Statements 1A and 1B are relatively indirect; they're attempts to get the listener to say or do something without committing the speaker. Statements 2A and 2B are more direct—they clearly state the speaker's preferences and then ask listeners if they agree. A more obvious example of an indirect (nonverbal) message occurs when you glance at your watch to communicate that it's late and that you had better be going. Indirect messages have both advantages and disadvantages.

Indirect messages allow you to express a desire without insulting or offending anyone; they allow you to observe the rules of polite interaction. Instead of saying, "I'm bored with this conversation," you say, "It's getting late and I have to get up early tomorrow," or you look at your watch and pretend to be surprised by the time. Instead of saying, "This food tastes like cardboard," you say, "I just started my diet," or "I just ate." In each instance you are stating a preference but are saying it indirectly so as to avoid offending someone. Not all direct requests, however, should be considered impolite. In one study of Spanish and English speakers, for example, no evidence was found to support the assumption that politeness and directness were incompatible (Mir, 1993).

Sometimes indirect messages allow you to ask for compliments in a socially acceptable manner, such as saying, "I was thinking of getting a nose job." You hope to get the desired compliment: "A nose job? You? Your nose is perfect."

Indirect messages, however, can also create problems. Consider the following dialog in which an indirect request is made:

Pat: You wouldn't like to have my parents over for dinner this weekend, would you?

Chris: I really wanted to go to the shore and just relax.

How would you describe youself in terms of direct versus indirect? Can you identify situations where you are almost always direct? Almost always indirect?

Pat: Well, if you feel you have to go to the shore, I'll make the dinner myself. You go to the shore. I really hate having them over and doing all the work myself. It's such a drag shopping, cooking, and cleaning all by myself.

Given this situation, Chris has two basic alternatives. One is to stick with the plans to go to the shore and relax. In this case Pat is going to be upset and Chris is going to be made to feel guilty for not helping with the dinner. A second alternative is to give in to Pat, help with the dinner, and not go to the shore. In this case Chris is going to have to give up a much-desired plan and is likely to resent Pat's "manipulative" tactics. Regardless of which decision is made, one person wins and one person loses. This win–lose situation creates resentment, competition, and often an "I'll get even" attitude. With direct requests, this type of situation is much less likely to develop. Consider:

Pat: I'd like to have my parents over for dinner this weekend. What do you think?

Chris: Well, I really wanted to go to the shore and just relax.

Regardless of what develops next, both individuals are starting out on relatively equal footing. Each has clearly and directly stated a preference. Although, at first, these preferences seem mutually exclusive, it might be possible to meet both persons' needs. For example, Chris might say, "How about going to the shore this weekend and having your parents over next weekend? I'm really exhausted; I could use the rest." Here is a direct response to a direct request. Unless there is some pressing need to have Pat's parents over for dinner this weekend, this response may enable each to meet the other's needs.

Gender and Cultural Differences in Directness   The popular stereotype in much of the United States holds that women are indirect in making requests and in giving orders. This indirectness communicates a powerlessness and discomfort with their own authority. Men, the stereotype continues, are direct, sometimes to the point of being blunt or rude. This directness communicates power and comfort with one's own authority.

Deborah Tannen (1994) provides an interesting perspective on these stereotypes. Women are, it seems, more indirect in giving orders and are more likely to say, for example, "It would be great if these letters could go out today" than "Have these letters out by 3." However, Tannen (1994, p. 84) argues that "issuing orders indirectly can be the prerogative of those in power" and does in no way show powerlessness. Power, to Tannen, is the ability to choose your own style of communication.

Men, however, are also indirect but in different situations. For example, men are more likely to use indirectness when they express weakness, reveal a problem, or admit an error (Rundquist, 1992; Tannen, 1994). Men are more likely to speak indirectly in expressing emotions other than anger. Men are also more indirect when they refuse expressions of increased romantic intimacy. Men are thus indirect, the theory states, when they are saying something that goes against the masculine stereotype.

Many Asian and Latin American cultures stress the values of indirectness largely because it prevents overt criticism and losing face. A somewhat

Many people who communicate directly see those who communicate indirectly as being manipulative. According to Tannen (1994, p. 92), however, "'manipulative' is often just a way of blaming others for our discomfort with their styles." Do you agree with Tannen? Or do you think that indirectness is very often intended to be manipulative?

different kind of indirectness is seen in the greater use of third parties or mediators to resolve conflict among the Chinese than among North Americans (Ma, 1992). In most of the United States, however, directness is the preferred style. "Be up front" and "tell it like it is" are commonly heard communication guidelines. Contrast these with the following two principles of indirectness found in the Japanese language (Tannen, 1994):

omoiyari, close to empathy, says that listeners need to understand the speaker without the speaker being specific or direct. This style places a much greater demand on the listener than would a direct speaking style.

sassuru advises listeners to anticipate a speaker's meanings and use subtle cues from the speaker to infer his or her total meaning.

In thinking about direct and indirect messages, it's important to realize how easy it is for misunderstandings to occur. For example, a person from a culture that values an indirect style of speech may be doing so to be polite. If, however, you're from a culture that values a more direct style of speech, you might assume that the person is using indirectness to be manipulative, because your culture regards it so.

Language Is Rule-Based

Language is a system of interconnected parts that is based on a wide variety of rules. Two especially important sets of rules are grammatical and cultural. You learned the grammatical rules—the rules for combining words into sentences (the rules of syntax), the rules for using words meaningfully (semantics), and the rules for combining sounds (phonology)—as you were growing up, by exposure to a particular language. If you grew up in a Chinese-speaking environment, you would have learned the rules for Chinese; if you grew up in an English-speaking environment, you would have learned the rules of English.

Cultural rules, on the other hand, focus on the principles that your culture considers important. When the principles are followed, you're seen as

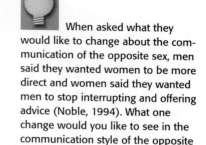

When asked what they would like to change about the communication of the opposite sex, men said they wanted women to be more direct and women said they wanted men to stop interrupting and offering advice (Noble, 1994). What one change would you like to see in the communication style of the opposite sex? Of your own sex?

Because the emphasis in E-mail is on speed, people prefer directness and brevity in these messages. This cultural preference is evident in the elimination of introductory and concluding comments and the use of abbreviations to express common phrases (BTW for "by the way"). In what other ways does E-mail encourage directness and brevity? What roles do directness and brevity play in other forms of computer communication, for example, IRC groups or newsgroups?

a properly functioning member of the culture. When you violate these principles, you risk being seen as deviant or perhaps as insulting.

Each culture has its own style of communication, its own principles or maxims governing communication. For example, in much of the United States we operate with the maxim of quality (communication must be truthful); that is, we expect that what the other person says will be the truth and we no doubt follow that maxim by telling the truth ourselves. Similarly, we operate with the maxim of relevance—what we talk about should be relevant to the conversation. Thus, if you're talking about A, B, and C and someone brings up D, you would assume that there is a connection between A, B, and C, on the one hand, and D, on the other. Of course, not all of the maxims followed in the United States are given equal importance throughout the rest of the world, or vice versa. Here are four that are not common in much of the United States.

The Maxim of Peaceful Relations   In Japanese conversations and group discussions, a maxim of keeping peaceful relationships with others operates (Midooka, 1990). This maxim is much more important to observe in public than it is in private conversations where it is at times violated.

The Maxim of Politeness   The maxim of politeness is probably universal across cultures (Brown & Levinson, 1988). Cultures differ, however, in how they define politeness and in how important politeness is compared with, for example, openness or honesty (Mao, 1994; Strecker, 1993).

In Asian cultures, especially Chinese and Japanese, politeness is especially important and violators of this maxim meet with harsher social punishments than would be the case in most of the United States or Western Europe (Fraser, 1990). In Asian cultures, this maxim may overshadow others. For example, it may require that you not tell the truth, a situation that would violate the maxim of quality.

There are also gender differences (and some similarities) in the expression of politeness (Holmes, 1995). Generally, studies from a number of different cultures show that women use more polite forms than men (Brown, 1980; Holmes, 1995; Wetzel, 1988). For example, in informal conversation and in conflict situations women tend to seek areas of agreement more than men. Young girls are more apt to try to modify disagreements while young boys are more apt to express more "bald disagreements" (Holmes, 1995). There are also similarities. For example, men and women in the United States and New Zealand pay compliments in similar ways (Holmes, 1986, 1995; Manes & Wolfson, 1981) and use politeness strategies when communicating bad news in an organization (Lee, 1993).

Politeness also varies with the type of relationship. One researcher has proposed that politeness is greatest with friends and considerably less with strangers and intimates and depicts this relationship as in Figure 5.1 (Wolfson, 1988; Holmes, 1995).

In Internet communication, politeness is covered in its rules of netiquette, rules that are clearly stated in most computer books (see discussion in Chapter 7). For example, find out what a group is talking about before breaking in with your own comment, don't send duplicate messages, don't attack other people.

The Maxim of Saving Face   This maxim tells you not to embarass or cause others to lose face. It is extremely important in **collectivist cultures**, where

Every action done in company ought to be with some sign of respect to those that are present.
—*George Washington*

In New York City, to take one example, politeness between cab drivers and riders has never been especially high and has prompted a great deal of criticism. In an attempt to combat this negative attitude, cab drivers have been given 50 polite phrases and are instructed to use these frequently: "May I open (close) the window for you?" "Madam (Sir), is the temperature okay for you?" "I'm sorry, I made a wrong turn. I'll take care of it, and we can deduct it from the fare" (*The New York Times*, May 6, 1996, p. B1). What do you think of this policy?

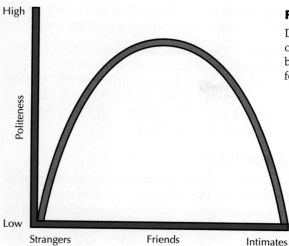

Figure 5.1 Wolfson's Bulge Model of Politeness

Do you find this model a generally accurate representation of your own level of politeness in different types of relationships? Can you build a case for an inverted **U** theory (where politeness would be high for both strangers and intimates and low for friends)?

great importance is placed on the group, the family, and the organization and less on the individual. Collectivist cultures (for example, Guatemala, Ecuador, Panama, Venezuela, Columbia, and Indonesia) teach cooperation rather than competition, and responsibility for the entire group rather than merely for oneself (Hofstede, 1997). The maxim is less important (but not absent) in **individualist cultures** (for example, the United States, Australia, Great Britain, Canada, New Zealand, and Italy) where greater im-

> Never give advice in a crowd.
> —*Arab proverb*

Power Perspective 5.1

Recognizing Sexual Harassment

Sexual harassment occurs when someone uses sexually inappropriate verbal or nonverbal messages. So, in these two chapters on messages, this power perspective along with two others deal with sexual harassment: avoiding (5.3) and responding to sexual harassment (6.2).

Recognizing what is sexual harassing behavior is a first step to avoiding it and responding appropriately to it. Attorneys Petrocelli and Repa (1992) note that under the law "sexual harassment is any unwelcome sexual advance or conduct on the job that creates an intimidating, hostile, or offensive working environment." Behavior constitutes sexual harassment, according to these attorneys, when it is:

1. Sexual in nature—for example, sexual advances, showing pornographic pictures, telling jokes that revolve around sex, comments on anatomy.
2. Unreasonable—for example, behavior that a reasonable person would object to.
3. Severe or pervasive—for example, physical molestation or creating an intimidating environment.
4. Unwelcome and offensive—for example, behavior that you let others know offends you and that you want stopped.

[The next Power Perspective appears on page 101.]

> All human beings are born free and equal in dignity and rights.
> —*United Nations Declaration of Human Rights, Article 1*

portance is placed on the individual and individuality, and members are taught to be competitive and responsible primarily for themselves.

The Maxim of Self-Denigration This maxim, observed in the conversations of Chinese speakers, although not unknown in other cultures as well, requires that a speaker avoid taking credit for accomplishments or make less of an ability or talent (Gu, 1990). To put oneself down here is a form of politeness in which you downplay your own abilities and strengths in order to elevate the person to whom you're speaking.

Language Meanings Are in People

To discover the meanings people try to communicate, examine the people as well as the words. An example of the confusion that can result when this relatively simple fact is not taken into consideration is provided by Ronald D. Laing, H. Phillipson, and A. Russell Lee (1966) and analyzed with insight by Paul Watzlawick (1977). A couple on the second night of their honeymoon are sitting at a hotel bar. The woman strikes up a conversation with the couple next to her. The husband refuses to communicate with the couple and becomes antagonistic toward his wife and the couple. The wife then grows angry because he has created such an awkward and unpleasant situation. Each becomes increasingly disturbed, and the evening ends in a bitter conflict with each convinced of the other's lack of consideration. Eight years later, they analyze this argument. Apparently *honeymoon* had meant different things to each. To the husband it was a "golden opportunity to ignore the rest of the world and simply explore each other." He felt his wife's interaction with the other couple implied there was something lacking in him. To the wife honeymoon meant an opportunity to try out her new role as wife. "I had never had a conversation with another couple as a wife before," she said. "Previous to this I had always been a 'girlfriend' or 'fiancée' or 'daughter' or 'sister.'"

Recognize also, that as you change, you also change the meanings you created out of past messages. Thus, although the message sent may not have changed, the meanings you created from it yesterday and the meanings you create today may be quite different. Yesterday, when a special someone said, "I love you," you created certain meanings. Today, when you learn that the same "I love you" was said to three other people or when you fall in love with someone else, you drastically change the meanings you perceive from those three words.

DISCONFIRMATION

Before reading about disconfirmation, take the self-test (right) to examine your own behavior.

A useful way to introduce disconfirmation and its alternatives, confirmation and rejection, is to consider a specific situation: Pat arrives home late one night. Chris is angry and complains about Pat's coming home so late. Consider some responses Pat might make:

1. Stop screaming. I'm not interested in what you're babbling about. I'll do what I want, when I want. I'm going to bed.
2. What are you so angry about? Didn't you delete my entire budget report last week? So, knock it off.

"When *I* use a word," Humpty Dumpty said in rather a scornful tone, "it means just what I choose it to mean; neither more nor less.

—*Lewis Carroll*

How Confirming Are You?

Instructions: In your typical communications, how likely are you to display the following behaviors? Use the following scale in responding to each statement:

5 = always
4 = often
3 = sometimes
2 = rarely
1 = never

_____ 1. I acknowledge the presence of another person both verbally and nonverbally.

_____ 2. I acknowledge the contributions of the other person by, for example, supporting or taking issue with what the person says.

_____ 3. During the conversation, I make nonverbal contact by maintaining direct eye contact, touching, hugging, kissing, and otherwise demonstrating acknowledgment of the other person.

_____ 4. I communicate as both speaker and listener, with involvement, and with a concern and respect for the other person.

_____ 5. I signal my understanding of the other person both verbally and nonverbally.

_____ 6. I reflect back the other person's feelings as a way of showing that I understand these feelings.

_____ 7. I ask questions as appropriate concerning the other person's thoughts and feelings.

_____ 8. I respond to the other person's requests, by, for example, returning phone calls and answering letters within a reasonable time.

_____ 9. I encourage the other person to express his or her thoughts and feelings.

_____ 10. I respond directly and exclusively to what the other person says.

Thinking Critically About Confirmation and Disconfirmation

All 10 statements are phrased so that they express confirming behaviors. Therefore, high scores (above 35) reflect a strong tendency to engage in confirmation. Low scores (below 25) reflect a strong tendency to engage in disconfirmation. Don't assume, however, that all situations call for confirmation and that only insensitive people are disconfirming. You may wish to consider the situations in which disconfirmation could be an appropriate response.

3. You have a right to be angry. I should have called when I was going to be late, but I got involved in an argument at work and I couldn't leave until it was resolved.

In response 1 Pat dismisses Chris's anger and even indicates a dismissal of Chris as a person. In response 2 Pat rejects the validity of Chris's reasons for being angry but does not dismiss Chris's feelings of anger or Chris as a person. In response 3 Pat acknowledges Chris's anger and the reasons for being

angry. In addition, Pat provides some kind of explanation and in doing so shows that Chris's feelings and Chris as a person are important and deserve to know what happened. The first response is an example of disconfirmation, the second of rejection, and the third of confirmation.

Psychologist William James once observed that "No more fiendish punishment could be devised, even were such a thing physically possible, than that one should be turned loose in society and remain absolutely unnoticed by all the members thereof." In this often-quoted observation, James identifies the essence of disconfirmation (Veenendall & Feinstein, 1996; Watzlawick, Beavin, & Jackson, 1967).

Disconfirmation is a communication pattern in which you ignore someone's presence as well as that person's communications. You say, in effect, that this person and what this person has to say are not worth serious attention or effort—that this person and this person's contributions are so unimportant or insignificant that there is no reason to concern yourselves with them.

Note that disconfirmation is not the same as *rejection*. In rejection you disagree with the person; you indicate your unwillingness to accept something the other person says or does. In disconfirming someone, however, you deny that person's significance; you claim that what this person says or does simply does not count.

Confirmation is the opposite communication pattern. In confirmation you not only acknowledge the presence of the other person but you also indicate your acceptance of this person, of this person's definition of self, and of your relationship as defined or viewed by this other person. Disconfirmation and confirmation may be communicated in a wide variety of ways. Table 5.1 (see page 102) shows just a few and parallels the self-test presented earlier so that you can see clearly not only the confirming but also the opposite disconfirming behaviors.

Power Perspective 5.2

Powerful Speech

One of the ways you communicate power is by using powerful language. Here are some suggestions for communicating power, based largely on research in the United States (Molloy, 1981; Kleinke, 1986; Johnson, 1987; Ng & Bradac, 1993).

1. Avoid hesitations; they make you sound unprepared and uncertain.
2. Avoid uncertainty expressions; these communicate a lack of commitment, direction, and conviction.
3. Avoid overpoliteness; such forms signal your subordinate status.
4. Avoid disqualifiers (*I didn't read the entire article, but . . .*); they may call into question the validity of your statements.
5. Avoid tag questions (questions that ask for agreement: *That was great, wasn't it?*); these may signal your own uncertainty.
6. Avoid slang and vulgar expressions; these usually signal low social class and little power.

[The next Power Perspective appears on page 104.]

Can you identify any additional powerless and powerful expressions?

You can gain insight into a wide variety of offensive language practices by viewing them as types of disconfirmation, as language that alienates and separates and prevents effective communication. The three common practices are sexism, heterosexism, and racism.

Sexism

Sexism is language that puts down someone because of her or his gender. Usually, the term refers to language that denigrates women, but it can also legitimately refer to language that denigrates men. Usually, sexist language is used by one sex against the other, but it need not be limited to these cases; women can be sexist against women and men can be sexist against men. The National Council of Teachers of English has proposed guidelines for nonsexist (gender-free, gender-neutral, or sex-fair) language. These concern the use of generic "man," the use of generic "he" and "his," and sex role stereotyping (Penfield, 1987).

Generic Man　The word *man* refers most clearly to an adult male. To use the term to refer to both men and women emphasizes "maleness" at the expense of "femaleness." Similarly, the terms *mankind* or *the common man* or even *cavemen* imply a primary focus on adult males. Gender-neutral terms can easily be substituted. Instead of *mankind,* you can say *humanity, people,* or *human beings.* Instead of *the common man,* you can say the *average person* or *ordinary people.* Instead of *cavemen,* you can say *prehistoric people* or *cave dwellers.*

　　Similarly, the use of such terms as *policeman* or *fireman* and other terms that presume maleness as the norm and femaleness as a deviation from this norm are clear and common examples of sexist language. Using nonsexist alternatives for these and similar terms and making these alternatives (for

We hold these truths to be self-evident, that all men and women are created equal.
—Elizabeth Cady Stanton

Table 5.1 Confirmation and Disconfirmation

As you review this table, try to imagine a specific illustration for each of the ways of communicating disconfirmation and confirmation (Pearson, 1993; Galvin & Brommel, 1996).

Confirmation	Disconfirmation
1. Acknowledge the presence and the contributions of the other by either supporting or taking issue with what the other says (self-test items 1 and 2)	1. Ignore the presence and the messages of the other person; ignore or express (nonverbally and verbally) indifference to anything the other says
2. Make nonverbal contact by maintaining direct eye contact, touching, hugging, kissing, and otherwise demonstrating acknowledgment of the other; engage in dialogue—communication in which both persons are speakers and listeners, both are involved, and both are concerned with each other (items 3 and 4)	2. Make no verbal contact; avoid direct eye contact; avoid touching other person; engage in monologue—communication in which one person speaks and one person listens; there is no real interaction, and there is no real concern or respect for each other
3. Demonstrate understanding of what the other says and means and reflect these feelings to demonstrate your understanding (items 5 and 6)	3. Jump to interpretation or evaluation rather than working at understanding what the other means; express your own feelings, ignore feelings of the other, or give abstract intellectualized responses
4. Ask questions of the other concerning both thoughts and feelings and acknowledge the questions of the other, return phone calls, answer E-mails and letters (items 7 and 8)	4. Make statements about yourself, ignore any lack of clarity in the other's remarks; ignore the other's requests; fail to answer questions, return phone calls, answer E-mails and letters
5. Encourage the other to express thoughts and feelings and respond directly and exclusively to what the other says (items 9 and 10)	5. Interrupt or otherwise make it difficult for the other to express himself or herself; respond only tangentially or by shifting the focus in another direction

What alternatives can you offer for such terms as these: man, mankind, countryman, man-made, the common man, manpower, repairman, doorman, fireman, stewardess, waitress, salesman, mailman, and actress?

Some quotations in this text use "man" and "he" generically. How would you reword them in today's language? Look through one of your textbooks. Can you find examples of sexist language? Sexist photos? Can you find examples of sexist language in your own speech? In the speech of your classmates? Your co-workers?

example, *police officer* and *firefighter* instead of *policeman* and *fireman*) a part of your active vocabulary will include the female sex as "normal" in such professions. Similarly, using "female forms" such as *actress* or *stewardess* is considered sexist since these are derivations of *actor* and *steward*, that, again emphasize that the male form is the norm and the female is the deviation from the norm.

Generic He and His The use of the masculine pronoun to refer to any individual regardless of sex is certainly declining. It was only as far back as 1975 that all college textbooks, for example, used the masculine pronoun as generic. There is no legitimate reason why the feminine pronoun could not alternate with the masculine pronoun in referring to hypothetical individuals, or why such terms as *he and she* or *her and him* could not be used instead of just *he* or *him*. Perhaps the best solution is to restructure your sentences to eliminate any reference to gender. Here are a few examples from the NCTE Guidelines (Penfield, 1987):

Sexist	*Gender-Free*
The average student is worried about his grades.	The average student is worried about grades.
Ask the student to hand in his work as soon as he is finished.	Ask students to hand in their work as soon as they are finished.

Deception researcher Paul Ekman (1985, p. 28) says lying occurs when "one person intends to mislead another, doing so deliberately, without prior notification of this purpose, and without having been explicitly asked to do so by the target [the person the liar intends to mislead]." As this definition implies, lying may involve overt statements but may also be committed by omission. When you omit something relevant, leading others to draw incorrect inferences, you are lying just as surely as if you had stated an untruth.

Similarly, although most lies are verbal, some are nonverbal; in fact, most lies involve at least some nonverbal elements. The innocent facial expression—despite the commission of some wrong—and the knowing nod instead of the honest expression of ignorance are common examples of nonverbal lying (O'Hair, Cody, & McLaughlin, 1981). Lies may range from the "white lie" and truth stretching to lies that form the basis of infidelity in a relationship, libel, and perjury.

Using the notion of choice explained in the Ethical Issue box in Chapter 3, lying or otherwise hiding the truth would be considered unethical because it prevents another person from learning about possible alternative choices. Consider the situation in which a patient has 6 months to live. Is it ethical for the doctor or family members to tell the patient that he or she is doing fine? Applying the notion of choice, you would have to conclude that it is not. In not telling the patient the truth, these people are making choices for him or her. They are in effect preventing the patient from living these last 6 months as he or she might want to, given the knowledge of imminent death. People may, of course, give up their right to hear all the information that concerns them. A patient may make it known that he or she does not want to know when death will occur. Relationship partners may make an agreement not to disclose their affairs. When this is the case, there is no lying, no deceit, and hence no unethical behavior in withholding such information.

Consider the following situation: Your friend arrives wearing a new outfit, looking pretty awful and asks you what you think of the new look. If you see the question asking you to evaluate the new outfit, then your obligation is to focus on this and give your honest opinion in as kind and responsive (but truthful) a manner as possible. Thus, instead of saying, "It makes you look old and sickly," you can more appropriately say, "I think you'd look much better in something more colorful." If, however, the question is simply a way to get positive stroking, you may wish to address that need and provide the kind of positive response the person is seeking. Thus you say, "You look great! You've been working out." Put in terms of the content–relationship axioms discussed in Chapter 1, the question is a relationship one, not a content one; the question really focuses on the person, not on the outfit. You are therefore not lying when you say, for example, "You look great" because the question really asked you to say something positive, and you have done so with your compliment.

Consider your own feelings about lying. Would you consider lying in each of the following situations to be ethical or unethical?

1. Lying to enable the other person to save face, for example, to agree with an idea you find foolish or to compliment someone when it is undeserved.
2. Lying to get someone to do something in his or her own best interest, for example, to diet, to stop smoking, or to study harder.
3. Lying to get what you deserve but can't get any other way, for example, a well-earned promotion or raise or another chance with your relationship partner.
4. Lying to keep hidden information about yourself that you simply don't want to reveal to anyone, for example, your financial situation, your affectional orientation, or your religious beliefs.
5. Lying to get yourself out of unpleasant situations, for example, to get out of an extra office chore, a boring conversation, or a conflict with your partner.

[The next Ethical Issue Box appears on page 162.]

Julia Stanley researched terms indicating sexual promiscuity and found 220 terms referring to a sexually promiscuous woman but only 22 terms for a sexually promiscuous man (Thorne, Kramarae, & Henley, 1983). Assuming the widely held assumption that the importance of a concept to a culture is reflected in the number of terms for the concept that the language has, how would you explain this difference in terms for promiscuity for men and for women?

I don't see the big deal about sexual behavior. Why do we need this excuse to hate? It should be a nonissue.
—*Cybill Shepherd*

Sex Role Stereotyping   The words we use often reflect a sex role bias, the assumption that certain roles or professions belong to men and others belong to women. In eliminating sex role stereotyping, avoid, for example, making the hypothetical elementary school teacher female and the college professor male. Avoid referring to doctors as male and nurses as female. Avoid noting the sex of a professional with terms such as "female doctor" or "male nurse." When you are referring to a specific doctor or nurse, the person's sex will become clear when you use the appropriate pronoun: *Dr. Smith wrote the prescription for her new patient* or *The nurse recorded the patient's temperature himself.*

Heterosexism

A close relative of sexism is heterosexism. The term is a relatively new addition to our list of linguistic prejudices. As the term implies, heterosexism refers to language used to disparage gay men and lesbians. As with racist language, we see heterosexism in the derogatory terms used for lesbians and gay men as well as in more subtle forms of language usage. For example, when you qualify a profession—as in "gay athlete" or "lesbian doctor"—you are, in effect, stating that athletes and doctors are not normally gay or lesbian. Further, you are highlighting the affectional orientation of the athlete and the doctor in a context in which it may have no relevance, in the same way that gender or racial distinctions often have no relevance to the issue at hand.

Still another instance of heterosexism—and perhaps the most difficult to deal with—is the presumption of heterosexuality. Usually, people assume the person they are talking to or about is heterosexual. Usually, they are correct since the majority of the population is heterosexual. At the same time, however, note that it denies the lesbian and gay identity a certain legitimacy. The practice is similar to the presumption of whiteness

We cannot live by power, and a culture that seeks to live by it becomes brutal and sterile.
—*Max Lerner*

Power Perspective 5.3

Avoiding Sexual Harassment

Here are three suggestions for avoiding behaviors that might be considered sexual harassment (Bravo & Cassedy, 1992):

1. Begin with the assumption that others at work are not interested in your sexual advances, sexual stories and jokes, or sexual gestures.
2. Listen and watch for negative reactions to any sex-related discussion. Use the suggestions and techniques discussed throughout this book (for example, perception checking, critical listening) to become aware of such reactions. When in doubt, find out; ask questions, for example.
3. Avoid saying or doing what you think your parent, partner, or child would find offensive in the behavior of someone with whom she or he worked.

[The next Power Perspective appears on page 125.]

and maleness that we have made significant inroads in eliminating. Here are a few suggestions for avoiding heterosexist or what some call "homophobic language."

- Avoid offensive nonverbal mannerisms that parody stereotypes when talking about gays and lesbians.
- Avoid "complimenting" gay men and lesbians because "they don't look it." To gays and lesbians, it's not a compliment. Similarly, expressing disappointment that a person is gay—often thought to be a compliment when said in such comments as "What a waste!"—is not really a compliment.
- Avoid the assumption that every gay or lesbian knows what every other gay or lesbian is thinking. It's very similar to asking a Japanese why Sony is investing heavily in the United States or, as one comic put it, asking an African American "What do you think Jesse Jackson meant by that last speech?"
- Avoid denying individual differences. Saying things like *lesbians are so loyal* or *gay men are so open with their feelings,* which ignore the reality of wide differences within any group, are potentially insulting to all groups.
- Avoid "overattribution"—the tendency to attribute just about everything a person does, says, and believes to being gay or lesbian. This tendency helps to recall and perpetuate stereotypes (see Chapter 3).
- Remember that relationship milestones are important to all people. Ignoring anniversaries or birthdays of a relative's partner is resented by everyone.

It's interesting to note that the terms denoting some of the major movements in art, for example, *impressionism* and *cubism,* were originally applied negatively. The terms were taken on by the artists and eventually became positive. A parallel can be seen in the use of the word *queer* by some lesbian and gay organizations. Their purpose in using the term is to make it lose its negative connotation. Can you think of other examples where certain groups have done this? Do you think this is a generally effective technique? Would it work with racist, sexist, and heterosexist terms equally?

Racism

According to Andrea Rich (1974), "any language that, through a conscious or unconscious attempt by the user, places a particular racial or ethnic group in an inferior position is racist." Racist language expresses racist attitudes. It also, however, contributes to the development of racist attitudes in those who use or hear the language. This, of course, is similar to sexist and heterosexist language perpetuating sexist and heterosexist attitudes.

Racist terms are used by members of one culture to disparage members of other cultures—their customs or their accomplishments—and to establish and maintain power over other groups. Racist language emphasizes differences rather than similarities and separates rather than unites members of different cultures. The social consequences of racist language in terms of employment, education, housing opportunities, and general community acceptance are well known.

It has often been pointed out (Davis, 1973; Bosmajian, 1969) that there are aspects of language that may be inherently racist. For example, in one examination of English, 134 synonyms for *white* were found. Of these, 44 had positive connotations (for example, "clean," "chaste," and "unblemished") and only 10 had negative connotations (for example, "whitewash" and "pale"). The remaining were relatively neutral. Of the 120 synonyms

Racism is the dogma that one ethnic group is condemned by nature to congenital inferiority and another group is destined to congenital superiority.
—*Ruth Benedict*

For a black writer in this country to be born into the English language is to realize that the assumptions on which the language operates are his enemy. . . . I was forced to reconsider similes: as black as sin, as black as night, blackhearted.
—*James Baldwin*

for *black,* 60 had unfavorable connotations ("unclean," "foreboding," and "deadly") and none had positive connotations.

Consider the following phrases:

- the Korean doctor
- the Chicano prodigy
- the African American mathematician
- the white nurse

In some cases, of course, the racial identifier may be relevant as in, say, "The Korean doctor argued for hours with the French [doctors] while the Mexicans tried to secure a compromise." Here the aim might be to identify the nationality of the doctor or the specific doctor (as you would if you forgot her or his name).

One of the interesting things about cultural identifiers is that some people want to know them and others don't seem to care what a person's race or religion or affectional orientation is. In most cases, the degree to which a person wants a cultural identifier will vary with the topic. Consider, for example, how you feel about each of the following sentences. Would you want to know the cultural identifiers? Would such identifiers influence the way you thought about or evaluated what a speaker says? Indicate which cultural identifiers concerning the speaker you would consider relevant and which you'd consider irrelevant in each of these situations.

1. The affectional orientation of someone who argues that gays and lesbians should (not) be allowed the same adoption rights as heterosexuals.
2. The religion of someone arguing that religious schools should (not) be publicly supported.
3. The sex of a person arguing that men need to learn to communicate with women/The sex of a person arguing that women need to learn to communicate with men.
4. The race of someone arguing that the school should (not) be named in honor of Malcolm X.
5. The religion or affectional orientation of someone arguing that the city must (not) recognize domestic partnerships as equal under the law to marriage.
6. The religion, sex, or age of someone arguing that condoms must (not) be made available to junior high school students without any restrictions based on parental objections.
7. The race or nationality of someone arguing that affirmative action programs must be retained (abolished).
8. The sex, age, or affectional orientation of someone arguing that sexual harassment is (not) a real problem in the workplace.
9. The religion or affectional orientation of someone arguing that AIDS education must stress abstinence, not safe sex/The religion or affectional orientation of someone arguing that AIDS education must stress safe sex, not abstinence.
10. The race or sex of someone arguing that interracial marriages and interracial adoptions should be encouraged (discouraged).

Andrea Rich (1974) observes: "The language of racism is not merely reflective of racist thought and attitude in the culture; its use also produces racist thought in those exposed to it and helps to shape certain forms of racist behavior." Do you agree with this? Do you think this also holds when members of a particular culture refer to themselves with terms that are considered by many to be racist?

Is it wrong for me to love my own? Is it wicked for me because my skin is red? Because I am a Sioux; because I was born where my father lived; because I would die for my people and my country?

—*Sitting Bull*

Sexist, Heterosexist, and Racist Listening

Just as racist, sexist, and heterosexist attitudes will influence your language, they also influence your listening. In this type of listening you hear what the speaker is saying through the stereotypes you hold. You assume that what the speaker is saying is influenced by the speaker's gender, affectional, or racial orientation.

Sexist, racist, and heterosexist listening occur in a wide variety of situations. For example, when you dismiss a valid argument or attribute validity to an invalid argument, when you refuse to give someone a fair hearing, or when you give less (or more) credibility to a speaker because the speaker is of a particular sex, race, or affectional orientation, you are practicing sexist, racist, or heterosexist listening. Stated differently, sexist, racist, or heterosexist listening occurs when you listen differently to a person because of his or her sex, race, or affectional orientation when these characteristics are irrelevant to the communication.

However, there are many instances where these characteristics are relevant and pertinent to your evaluation of the message. For example, the sex of the speaker talking on pregnancy, fathering a child, birth control, or surrogate fatherhood is, most would agree, probably relevant to the message. In these cases it is not sexist listening to hear the topic through the sex of the speaker. It is, however, sexist listening to assume that only one sex can be an authority on a particular topic or that one sex's opinions are without value. The same is true when listening through a person's race or affectional orientation.

How would you define sexist, heterosexist, and racist listening? Do you find these concepts useful in understanding effective communication? Do you find these types of listening operating in your classes? In your family? On your job? How would you reduce these types of listening?

[The next Listen to This box appears on page 139.]

Cultural Identifiers

Perhaps the best way to develop sexist-, heterosexist-, and racist-free language is to examine the preferred cultural identifiers to use in talking to and about members of different cultures. Remember, however, that preferred terms frequently change over time, so keep in touch with the most currently preferred language. The preferences and many of the specific examples identified here are drawn largely from the findings of the Task Force on Bias-Free Language of the Association of American University Presses (Schwartz, 1995).

Generally: The term *girl* should be used only to refer to very young females and is equivalent to *boy*. Neither term should be used for people older than 13 or 14. *Girl* is never used to refer to a grown woman, nor is *boy* used to refer to persons in blue-collar positions, as it once was. *Lady* is negatively evaluated by many because it connotes the stereotype of the prim and proper woman; *woman* or *young woman* is preferred. *Older person* is preferred to *elder, elderly, senior,* or *senior citizen* (which technically refers to someone older than 65).

Generally: *Gay* is the preferred term to refer to a man who has an affectional preference for other men and *lesbian* is the preferred term for a woman who has an affectional preference for other women (Lever, 1995). (*Lesbian* means "homosexual woman," so the phrase *lesbian woman* is redundant.) *Homosexual* refers to both gays and lesbians but more often to a sexual orientation to members of one's own sex. *Gay* and *lesbian*, on the other hand, refer to a broad cultural identification and not just to sexual orientation. *Gay* as a noun, although widely used, may prove offensive in some contexts, for

Throughout this text, gender differences are discussed in a wide variety of contexts. Holmes (1995) distinguishes three perspectives on gender differences in communication: (1) Gender differences are due to innate biological differences; (2) gender differences are due to different patterns of socialization that lead to different forms of communication; and (3) gender differences are due to the inequalities in social power; for example, because of women's lesser social power, they are more apt to communicate with greater deference and politeness than are men. What do you think of these three positions? Can you find arguments to support or contradict any of these positions?

example, "We have two gays on the team." Because most scientific thinking holds that sexuality is not a matter of choice, the term *sexual orientation* rather than *sexual preference* or *sexual status* (which is also vague) is preferred. An even more preferred expression is *affectional orientation*, which includes a range of emotional attachments rather than just sexual.

Generally: Most African Americans prefer *African American* to *black* (Hecht, Ribeau, & Collier, 1993) although *black* is often used with *white* and is used in a variety of other contexts (for example, Department of Black and Puerto Rican Studies, the *Journal of Black History,* and Black History Month). The American Psychological Association recommends that both terms be capitalized but the *Chicago Manual of Style* (the manual used by most newspapers and publishing houses) recommends using lower case. The terms *negro* and *colored,* although used in the names of some organizations (for example, the United Negro College Fund and the National Association for the Advancement of Colored People) are not used outside of these contexts.

White is generally used to refer to those whose roots are in European cultures and usually doesn't include Hispanics. Based on the analogy of *African American,* comes the phrase *European American.* Few *European Americans,* however, would want to be called that; most would prefer their national origins emphasized, for example, *German American* or *Greek American.* This preference may well change as Europe moves into a more cohesive and united entity. *People of color*—a more literary-sounding term appropriate perhaps to public speaking but sounding awkward in most conversations—is preferred to *nonwhite* which implies that whiteness is the norm and non-whiteness is a deviation from that norm. The same is true of the term *non-Christian.*

Generally: *Hispanic* is used to refer to anyone who identifies himself or herself as belonging to a Spanish-speaking culture. *Latina* (female) and *Latino* (male) refer to those whose roots are in one of the Latin American countries, for example, Haiti, Dominican Republic, Nicaragua, or Guatemala. *Hispanic American* refers to those United States residents whose ancestry is a Spanish culture and includes Mexican, Caribbean, and Central and South Americans. In emphasizing a Spanish heritage the term is really inadequate in referring to those large numbers in the Caribbean and in South America whose origins are French or Portuguese. *Chicana* (female) and *Chicano* (male) refer to those with roots in Mexico, although it often connotes a nationalist attitude (Jandt, 1995) and is considered offensive by many Mexican Americans; *Mexican American* is preferred.

Inuk (pl. *Inuit*), was officially adopted at the Inuit Circumpolar Conference to refer to the group of indigenous people of Alaska, Northern Canada, Greenland, and Eastern Siberia. This term is preferred to *Eskimo* (a term the U.S. Census Bureau uses) which was applied to the indigenous peoples of Alaska by Europeans and derives from a term that means "raw meat eaters" (Maggio, 1997).

Indian refers only to someone from India and is incorrectly used when applied to members of other Asian countries or to the indigenous peoples of North America. *American Indian* or *Native American* are preferred, even though many Native Americans refer to themselves as *Indians* and *Indian people.* In Canada, indigenous people are called "first people." The term *native American* (with a lower case *n*) is most often used to refer to persons born in the United States. Although the term technically could refer to anyone born in North or South America, people outside the United States

The first need of a free people is to be able to define their own terms and have those terms recognized by their oppressors.

—*Stokley Carmichael*

Words can destroy. What we call each other ultimately becomes what we think of each other, and it matters.

—*Jeanne J. Kirkpatrick*

generally prefer more specific designations such as *Argentinean, Cuban,* or *Canadian.* The term *native* means an indigenous inhabitant; it is not used to mean "someone having a less-developed culture."

Muslim is the preferred form (rather than the older *Moslem*) to refer to a person who adheres to the religious teachings of Islam. *Quran* (rather than *Koran*) is the preferred term for the scriptures of Islam. The terms "Muhammadan" or "Muhammadanism" are not considered appropriate since they imply worship of Muhammad, the prophet, "considered by Muslims to be a blasphemy against the absolute oneness of God" (Maggio, 1997, p. 277).

Although there is no universal agreement, generally *a Jewish person* is preferred to *a Jew* and *Jewish people* to *Jews; Jewess* (a Jewish female) is considered derogatory. If *Jew* is used, it should be used only as a noun; it is never correctly used as a verb or an adjective (Maggio, 1997).

When history was being written with a European perspective, it was taken as the focal point and the rest of the world was defined in terms of its location from Europe. Thus, Asia became the east or the orient and Asians became *Orientals*—a term that is today considered inappropriate or "Eurocentric." Thus, people from Asia are *Asians* just as people from Africa are *Africans* and people from Europe are *Europeans.*

What cultural identifiers do you prefer? Have these preferences changed over time? How can you let other people know the designations that you want and those that you don't want to be used to refer to you? An interesting exercise—especially in a large and multicultural class—is for each member to write anonymously his or her preferred cultural identification on an index card and have them all read aloud.

THINKING CRITICALLY ABOUT VERBAL MESSAGES

Four general principles will help you think more critically about verbal messages: (1) language *symbolizes* reality, but it is not the reality itself; (2) language can express both facts and inferences, yet often obscures the important distinction between them; (3) language is relatively

The greatest obstacle to discovery is not ignorance—it is the illusion of knowledge.
—Daniel Boorstein

What cultural identifiers do you use when thinking about yourself? When talking about yourself?

static and unchanging, but the world and the people it describes are changing all the time; and (4) language can obscure important distinctions among people. These four principles all concern what critical thinking theorists call "conceptual distortions" or thinking errors.

Language Symbolizes Reality (Partially)

Language describes the objects, people, and events in the world with varying degrees of accuracy. However, words and sentences are not objects, people, or events, even though we sometimes act as if they are. Two ways in which we sometimes act as if words and things were the same is when we think and speak intensionally or with an allness attitude.

Thinking Intensionally   Have you ever reacted to the way something was labeled or described rather than to the actual item? Have you ever bought something because of its name rather than because of the actual object? If so, you were probably responding intensionally.

Intensional orientation (the *s* in *intensional* is intentional) refers to the tendency to view people, objects, and events in the way they are talked about—the way they are labeled. For example, if Sally is labeled "uninteresting," and you responded intensionally, you would evaluate her as uninteresting before listening to what she had to say. You would see Sally through a filter imposed by the label "uninteresting." The opposite tendency, extensional orientation, is the tendency to look first at the actual people, objects, and events and only afterward at their labels. In this case, it would mean looking at Sally without any preconceived labels, guided by what she says and does, and not by the words used to label her.

The way to avoid intensional orientation is to extensionalize. You can do this by focusing your attention on the people, things, and events in the world as you see them and not as they are presented in the words of others. For example, when you meet Jack and Jill, observe and interact with them. Then form your impressions. Don't respond to them as "greedy, money-grubbing landlords" because Harry labeled them this way. Don't respond to Carmen as "lazy and inconsiderate" because Elaine told you she was.

Thinking in Allness Terms   No one can know all or say all about anything. The parable of the six blind men and the elephant is an excellent example of an "allness" orientation and its problems. You may recall the John Saxe poem that tells of six blind men of Indostan who examine an elephant, an animal they had only heard about. The first blind man touched the elephant's side and concluded the elephant was like a wall. The second felt the tusk and said the elephant must be like a spear. The third held the trunk and concluded the elephant was like a snake. The fourth touched the knee and knew the elephant was like a tree. The fifth felt the ear and said the elephant was like a fan. The sixth grabbed the tail and said that the elephant was like a rope.

Each reached his own conclusion; each argued that he was correct and that the others were wrong. Each was correct, and, at the same time, wrong.

Whatever we call a thing, whatever we say it is, it is not. For whatever we say is words, and words are words and not things. The words are maps, and the map is not the territory.
—Harry Weinberg

My doctor is wonderful. Once, in 1955, when I couldn't afford an operation, he touched up the x-rays.
—Joey Bishop

Visualize yourself seated with a packet of photographs before you. You are asked to scratch out the eyes in each photograph. You are further told that this is simply an experiment and that the individuals (all strangers) whose pictures you have will not be aware of anything that has happened here. As you progress through the pictures, scratching out the eyes, you come upon a photograph of your mother. Are you able to scratch out the eyes as you have done with the pictures of the strangers? Are you responding intensionally or extensionally?

We are all in the position of the six blind men. We never see all of anything. We never experience anything fully. We see a part, then conclude what the whole is like. We have to draw conclusions on the basis of insufficient evidence (and we always have insufficient evidence). We must recognize that when we make judgments based only on a part, we are making inferences that can later prove wrong once we have more complete information.

A useful device to help remember the non-allness orientation is to end each statement, verbally or mentally, with *etc.*—a reminder that there is more to learn, more to know, and more to say—that every statement is inevitably incomplete. Do be careful, however, that you do not use the *etc.* as a substitute for being specific.

Language Expresses Both Facts and Inferences

Often, when you listen or speak, you don't distinguish between statements of fact and those of inference. Yet, there are great differences between the two. Barriers to clear thinking can be created when inferences are treated as facts.

For example, you can say, "She's wearing a blue jacket," as well as "He's harboring an illogical hatred." Although the sentences have similar structures, they are different. You can observe the jacket and the blue color, but how do you observe "illogical hatred"? Obviously, this is not a descriptive but an inferential statement. It is one you make on the basis not only of what you observe, but on what you infer. For a statement to be considered factual it must be made by the observer after observation and must be limited to what is observed (Weinberg, 1958).

There is nothing wrong with making inferential statements. You must make them to talk about much that is meaningful to you. The problem arises when you act as if those inferential statements are factual. Consider the following anecdote (Maynard, 1963). A woman went for a walk one day and met a friend whom she had not seen, heard from, or heard about in 10 years. After an exchange of greetings, the woman said: "Is this your little boy?" and her friend replied, "Yes, I got married about 6 years ago." The woman then asked the child, "What is your name?" and the little boy replied, "Same as my father's." "Oh," said the woman, "then it must be Peter."

How did the woman know the boy's father's name when she had no contact with her friend in the last 10 years? The answer is obvious, but only after we recognize that in reading this short passage we have made an unconscious inference. Specifically, we have inferred that the woman's friend is a woman. Actually, the friend is a man named Peter.

You may test your ability to distinguish facts from inferences by taking the fact-inference test below (based on the tests constructed by Haney, 1973).

Test Yourself | Can You Distinguish Facts from Inferences?

Instructions: Carefully read the following report and the observations based on it. Indicate whether you think the observations are true, false, or doubtful on the basis of the information presented in the report. Write T if the observation is definitely true, F if the observation is definitely false, and ? if the observation may be either true or false. Judge each observation in order. Do not reread the observations after you have indicated your judgment, and do not change any of your answers.

A well-liked college teacher had just completed making up the final examinations and had turned off the lights in the office. Just then a tall, broad figure with dark glasses appeared and demanded the examination. The professor opened the drawer. Everything in the drawer was picked up and the individual ran down the corridor. The dean was notified immediately.

_____ 1. The thief was tall, broad, and wore dark glasses.
_____ 2. The professor turned off the lights.
_____ 3. A tall figure demanded the examination.
_____ 4. The examination was picked up by someone.
_____ 5. The examination was picked up by the professor.
_____ 6. A tall, broad figure appeared after the professor turned off the lights in the office.
_____ 7. The man who opened the drawer was the professor.
_____ 8. The professor ran down the corridor.
_____ 9. The drawer was never actually opened.
_____ 10. Three persons are referred to in this report.

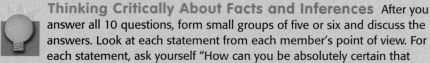

Thinking Critically About Facts and Inferences After you answer all 10 questions, form small groups of five or six and discuss the answers. Look at each statement from each member's point of view. For each statement, ask yourself "How can you be absolutely certain that the statement is true or false?" You should find that only one statement can be clearly identified as "true" and only one as "false"; eight should be marked "?"

Make your inferential statements tentatively. When you make inferential statements, leave open the possibility of your being wrong. If, for example, you treat the statement "Our biology teacher was fired for poor teaching" as factual, you eliminate alternative explanations. When making inferential statements, be psychologically prepared to be proved wrong. In this way, you'll be less hurt if you're shown to be wrong.

Be especially sensitive to this distinction when you're listening. Most talk is inferential. Beware of the speaker (whether in interpersonal, group, or public speaking) who presents everything as fact. Analyze closely and you'll uncover a world of inferences.

Language is Relatively Static

"Static evaluation" is a conceptual distortion in which we retain evaluations without change while the reality to which they refer is constantly changing. Often a verbal statement we make about an event or person remains static, while the event or person may change enormously. Consider this example (Korzybski, 1933).

> In a tank we have a large fish and many small fish, the natural food for the large fish. Given freedom in the tank, the large fish will eat the small fish. If we partition the tank, separating the large fish from the small fish by a clear piece of glass, the large fish will continue to attempt to eat the small fish but will fail, knocking instead into the glass partition.
>
> Eventually, the large fish will "learn" the futility of attempting to eat the small fish. If we now remove the partition, the small fish will swim all around the big fish, but the big fish will not eat them. In fact, the large fish will die of starvation while its natural food swims all around. The large fish has learned a pattern of behavior, and even though the actual territory has changed, the map remains static.

While we would probably all agree that everything is in a constant state of flux, do we act as if we know this? Do we act in accordance with the notion of change or just accept it intellectually? Do we realize, for example, that because we have failed at something once, we need not fail again? Our evaluations of ourselves and of others must keep pace with the rapidly changing real world, otherwise our attitudes and beliefs will be about a world that no longer exists.

To guard against static evaluation, date your statements and especially your evaluations. Remember that Pat Smith$_{1984}$ is not Pat Smith$_{1999}$; academic abilities$_{1992}$ are not academic abilities$_{1999}$. In listening, pay close attention to messages that claim that what was true still is. It may or may not be. Look for change.

Language Can Obscure Distinctions

Language can obscure distinctions among people or events that are covered by the same label but are really quite different (indiscrimination) and by making it easy to focus on extremes rather than on the vast middle ground between opposites (polarization).

Indiscrimination Indiscrimination refers to the failure to distinguish between similar but different people, objects, or events. It occurs when we focus on classes of things and fail to see that each is unique and needs to be looked at individually.

> The only man who behaves sensibly is my tailor; he takes my measure anew each time he sees me, whilst all the rest go on with their old measurements and expect them to fit me.
> —George Bernard Shaw

> People change and forget to tell each other.
> —Lillian Hellman

> What we know of other people is only our memory of the moments during which we knew them. And they have changed since then. . . . at every meeting we are meeting a stranger.
> —T. S. Eliot

Our language, however, provides us with common nouns, such as teacher, student, friend, enemy, war, politician, and liberal. These lead us to focus on similarities—to group together all teachers, all students, and all politicians. At the same time, the terms divert attention away from the uniqueness of each person, each object, and each event.

This misevaluation is at the heart of stereotyping on the basis of nationality, race, religion, sex, and affectional orientation. A stereotype, you'll remember from Chapter 3, is a fixed mental picture of a group that is applied to each individual in the group without regard to his or her unique qualities.

Most stereotypes are negative and denigrate the group to which they refer. Some, however, are positive. A particularly glaring example is the popular stereotype of Asian American students. The stereotype is that of a person who is successful, intelligent, and hardworking.

Whether the stereotypes are positive or negative, they create the same problem. They provide us with shortcuts that are often inappropriate. For instance, when you meet a particular person, your first reaction may be to pigeonhole him or her into some category—perhaps religious, national, or academic. Then you assign to this person all the qualities that are part of your stereotype. Regardless of the category you use or the specific qualities you are ready to assign, you fail to give sufficient attention to the individual's unique characteristics. Two people may both be Christian, Asian, and lesbian, for example, but each will be different from the other. Indiscrimination is a denial of another's uniqueness.

A useful antidote to indiscrimination is the index. This verbal or mental subscript identifies each individual as an individual although both may be covered by the same label. Thus, politician$_1$ is not politician$_2$, and teacher$_1$ is not teacher$_2$. The index helps us to discriminate among without discriminating against.

Polarization   Polarization is the tendency to look at the world in terms of opposites and to describe it in extremes—good or bad, positive or negative, healthy or sick, intelligent or stupid. It is often referred to as the fallacy of "either–or" or "black and white." Most people exist somewhere between the extremes. Yet we have a strong tendency to view only the extremes and to categorize people, objects, and events in terms of these polar opposites.

We create problems when we use the absolute form in inappropriate situations. For example, "The politician is either for us or against us." These options do not include all possibilities. The politician may be for us in some things and against us in other things, or may be neutral.

In correcting this tendency to polarize, beware of implying (and believing) that all individuals and events must fit into one extreme or the other, with no alternatives in between. Most people, most events, and most qualities exist between polar extremes. When others imply that there are only two sides or alternatives, look for the middle ground.

SUMMARY OF CONCEPTS AND SKILLS

In this chapter we considered verbal messages. We looked at the nature of language and identified several major ways in which language works and we looked at the concept of disconfirmation and especially how it relates to sexism, heterosexism, and racist language.

1. Language is both denotative (objective and generally easily agreed upon) and connotative (subjective and generally highly individual in meaning).
2. Language varies in abstraction; language can vary from extremely general to extremely specific.
3. Language varies in directness; language can state exactly what you mean or it can hedge and state your meaning very indirectly.
4. Language is rule-based; grammatical and cultural rules guide performance.
5. Language meanings are in people, not simply in words.
6. Disconfirmation refers to the process of ignoring the presence and the communications of others. Confirmation refers to accepting, supporting, and acknowledging the importance of the other person.
7. Racist, sexist, and heterosexist language disconfirms and puts down and negatively evaluates various cultural groups.
8. Thinking critically about verbal messages involves realizing that language symbolizes reality, it is not the reality itself; language can express both facts and inferences but doesn't indicate this grammatically; language is relatively static but people and events are forever changing; and language can obscure distinctions as when it provides lots of extreme terms but few terms to describe the middle ground.

The study of verbal messages and how meaning is communicated from one person to another have important implications for developing the skills of effective communication. Check your ability to apply these skills. Use a rating scale such as: (1) = almost always, (2) = often, (3) = sometimes, (4) = rarely, (5) = hardly ever.

_____ 1. I try to understand not only the objective, denotative meanings but also the subjective, connotative meanings.

_____ 2. I recognize that snarl and purr words describe the speaker's feelings and not objective reality.

_____ 3. I take special care to make spoken messages clear and unambiguous, especially when using terms for which people will have very different connotative meanings.

_____ 4. I recognize the gender and cultural differences in directness and can adjust my style of speaking and listening as appropriate to such variations.

_____ 5. I communicate with a clear recognition of the grammatical and the cultural rules (and maxims, especially that of politeness) of the language.

_____ 6. I focus attention not only on words but on the person communicating, recognizing that meanings are largely in the person.

_____ 7. I avoid disconfirmation and instead use responses that confirm the other person.

_____ 8. I avoid sexist, heterosexist, and racist language and, in general, language that puts down other groups.

_____ 9. I use the cultural identifiers that facilitate communication and avoid those that set up barriers to effective interaction.

_____ 10. I avoid responding intensionally, to labels as if they are objects; instead, I respond extensionally and look first at the reality and secondarily at the words.

_____ 11. I end my statements with an implicit *etc.*, in recognition that there is always more to be known or said.

_____ 12. I distinguish facts from inferences and respond to inferences with tentativeness.

_____ 13. I mentally date my statements and thus avoid static evaluation.

_____ 14. I avoid indiscrimination by viewing the uniqueness in each person and situation.

_____ 15. I avoid polarization by using "middle ground" terms and qualifiers in describing the world, especially people.

KEY WORD QUIZ

Write T for those statements that are true and F for those that are false. In addition, for those that are false, replace the boldface term with the correct term.

_____ 1. The meaning of a word that you would find in a dictionary is the word's **connotative meaning.**

_____ 2. "Mona Lisa," "art," "painting," and "contribution to civilization" differ in **abstraction.**

_____ 3. Questions that ask for agreement such as "That meal was great, don't you think?" are known as **tag questions.**

_____ 4. A pattern of communication in which you ignore someone's presence as well as that person's communication is known as **confirmation.**

_____ 5. When expressing weakness, revealing a problem, or admitting an error, men, as compared to women—according to Deborah Tannen— are more likely to use **direct speech.**

_____ 6. Language that puts down either sex is known as **sexist language.**

_____ 7. The tendency to look at the world in terms of opposites and to describe it in extremes—good or bad, positive or negative, young or old—is known as **static evaluation.**

_____ 8. The tendency to look first at the actual person, object, or event and only afterward at their labels or the way they are talked about is known as **intensional orientation.**

_____ 9. The rules for politeness on the Internet are referred to as **netiquette.**

_____ 10. The failure to distinguish between similar but different people, objects, or events is known as **discrimination.**

5. Happiness is a dry nose.
6. Love is a useless abstraction.
7. Is this book meaningful?
8. Was the movie any good?
9. Dick and Jane are no longer children.
10. This class is boring.

SKILL DEVELOPMENT EXPERIENCES

5.1 Thinking with E-Prime

The expression *E-prime* (*E'*) refers here to the mathematical equation E - e = E' where E = the English language and e = the verb *to be*. E', therefore, stands for normal English without the verb *to be*. D. David Bourland, Jr. (1965–1966; Bourland & Johnston, 1998; Wilson, 1989) argued that if you wrote and spoke without the verb *to be,* we would describe events more accurately. (A symposium of 18 articles on E-prime appears in the Summer 1992 issue of *ETC.: A Review of General Semantics.*) The verb *to be* often suggests that qualities are in the person or thing rather than in the observer making the statement. It is easy to forget that these statements are evaluative rather than purely descriptive. For example, when you say, "Johnny is a failure," you imply that failure is somehow within Johnny instead of a part of someone's evaluation of Johnny. This type of thinking is especially important in making statements about yourself. When you say, for example, "I'm not good at mathematics" or "I'm unpopular" or "I'm lazy," you imply that these qualities are *in* you. However, these are simply evaluations that may be incorrect or, if at least partly accurate, may change. The verb *to be* implies a permanence that is simply not true of the world in which we live.

To appreciate further the difference between statements that use the verb *to be* and those that do not, try to rewrite the following sentences without using the verb *to be* in any of its forms—*is, are, am, was,* etc.

1. I'm a poor student.
2. They are inconsiderate.
3. What is meaningful communication?
4. Is this valuable?

5.2 Confirming, Rejecting, and Disconfirming

Classify the following responses as confirmation, rejection, or disconfirmation and develop original responses to illustrate all three types of responses. Enrique receives this semester's grades in the mail; they are a lot better than previous semesters' grades, but are still not great. After opening the letter, Enrique says: "I really tried hard to get my grades up this semester." Enrique's parents respond:

_____ Going out every night hardly seems like trying very hard.

_____ What should we have for dinner?

_____ Keep up the good work.

_____ I can't believe you've really tried your best; how can you study with the stereo blasting in your ears.

_____ I'm sure you've tried real hard.

_____ That's great.

_____ What a rotten day I had at the office.

_____ I can remember when I was in school; got all B's without ever opening a book.

Pat, who has been out of work for the past several weeks, says: "I feel like such a failure; I just can't seem to find a job. I've been pounding the pavement for the last 5 weeks and still nothing." Pat's friend responds:

_____ I know you've been trying real hard.

_____ You really should get more training so you'd be able to sell yourself more effectively.

_____ I told you a hundred times, you need that college degree.

_____ I've got to go to the dentist on Friday. Boy, do I hate that.

_____ The employment picture is real bleak this time of the year, but your qualifications are really impressive. Something will come up soon.

_____ You are not a failure. You just can't find a job.

_____ What do you need a job for? Stay home and keep house. After all, Chris makes more than enough money to live in style.

_____ What's 5 weeks?

_____ Well, you'll just have to try harder.

5.3 Recognizing Gender Differences

The best way to start thinking about gender differences in language is to think about your own beliefs. The following self-test will help.

Instructions: Here are 10 statements about the "differences" between the speech of women and men. For each of the following statements, indicate whether you think the statement describes women's speech (W), men's speech (M), or women's and men's speech equally (=).

_____ 1. This speech is logical rather than emotional.

_____ 2. This speech is vague.

_____ 3. This speech is endless, less concise, and jumps from one idea to another.

_____ 4. This speech is highly businesslike.

_____ 5. This speech is more polite.

_____ 6. This speech uses weaker forms (for example, the weak intensifiers like *so* and *such*) and fewer exclamations.

_____ 7. This speech contains more tag questions (for example, questions appended to statements that ask for agreement, such as "Let's meet at ten o'clock, *okay*?").

_____ 8. This speech is more euphemistic (contains more polite words as substitutes for some taboo or potentially offensive terms) and uses fewer swear terms.

_____ 9. This speech is generally more effective.

_____ 10. This speech is less forceful and less in control.

After responding to all 10 statements, consider the following:

1. On what evidence did you base your answers?
2. How strongly do you believe that your answers are correct?
3. What do you think might account for sex differences in verbal behavior? Namely, how did the language differences that might distinguish the sexes, come into existence?
4. What effect might these language differences (individually or as a group) have on communication (and relationships generally) between the sexes?

Do not read any further until you have responded to the above statements and questions.

The 10 statements were drawn from the research of Cheris Kramarae (1974a, 1974b, 1977, 1981; also see Coates & Cameron, 1989), who argues that these "differences"—with the exception of statements 5 and 8 (research shows that women's speech is often more "polite")—are actually stereotypes of women's and men's speech that are not confirmed in analyses of actual speech. According to Kramarae, then, you should have answered "Women's and Men's Speech Equally" (=) for statements 1, 2, 3, 4, 6, 7, 9, and 10, and "Women's Speech" (W) for statements 5 and 8. Perhaps we see these "differences" in the media and believe that it accurately reflects real speech.

Reexamine your answers to the above 10 statements. Were your answers based on your actual experience with the speech of women and men or might they have been based on popular beliefs (or myths) about women's and men's speech?

CHAPTER 6

nonverbal Messages

CHAPTER CONCEPTS	CHAPTER GOALS After completing this chapter, you should be able to	CHAPTER SKILLS After completing this chapter, you should be able to
Body Messages	1. explain the five kinds of body movements	regulate your own body movements to communicate meaning
Facial and Eye Movements	2. describe the types of information communicated by the face and the eyes	use facial and eye expressions appropriately
Spatial and Territorial Communication	3. explain the four spatial distances 4. define *territoriality* and *marker*	communicate with space and territory
Artifactual Communication	5. explain artifactual communication	use artifacts to communicate and interpret meanings
Touch Communication	6. explain the major meanings communicated by touch	use appropriate touch to communicate varied meanings
Paralanguage and Silence	7. explain paralanguage	vary stress, rate, volume, rhythm, and pausing to communicate
Time Communication	8. explain how time communicates	use and interpret time cues appropriately
Thinking Critically About Nonverbal Messages	9. explain the suggestions for thinking critically about nonverbal communication	combine the nonverbal (and verbal) cues in interpreting meaning

nonverbal communication is communication without words; it is the communication that takes place through bodily gestures, facial expressions, eye movements, spatial relationships, clothing and color, touch, vocal rate and volume, and even the way in which you treat time.

What would your life be like if you were able to read a person's nonverbal behavior and tell what the person was thinking and feeling? What would it be like with your friends? Your coworkers? Your family? What if others could do the same with you? What would your interpersonal and professional lives be like if everyone could read your thoughts and feelings from simply observing your nonverbal messages? This kind of mind reading is obviously impossible. Yet, we do know a great deal about nonverbal messages and how they are used in communication—the focus of this chapter.

BODY MESSAGES

The body communicates with movements and gestures and with just its general appearance.

Body Movements

Nonverbal researchers identify five major types of body movements: emblems, illustrators, affect displays, regulators, and adaptors (Ekman & Friesen, 1969; Knapp & Hall, 1996).

Emblems are body gestures that directly translate into words or phrases, for example, the okay sign, the thumbs-up for "good job," and the "V" for victory. You use these consciously and purposely to communicate the same meaning as the words. Emblems are culture-specific—so, be careful when using your culture's emblems in other cultures. For example, when President Nixon visited Latin America and gestured with the okay sign he thought communicated something positive, he was quickly informed that this gesture was not universal. In Latin America the gesture has a far more negative meaning. Here are a few differences in meaning across cultures of the emblems you may commonly use (Axtell, 1991):

- In the United States, to say "hello" you wave with your whole hand moving from side to side, but in a large part of Europe that same signal means "No." In Greece, however, this would be considered insulting to the person to whom you are waving.
- The "V" for victory is common throughout much of the world, if used in England with the palm facing your face, it is as insulting as the raised middle finger is in the United States.
- In Texas the raised fist with little finger and index finger raised is a positive expression of support because it represents the Texas longhorn steer. However, in Italy it is an insult that means "cuckold." In parts of South America it is a gesture to ward off evil, and in parts of Africa it is a curse: "May you experience bad times."
- In the United States and in much of Asia hugging is rarely exchanged among acquaintances, but among Latins and Southern Europeans hugging is a common greeting gesture that, if withheld, may communicate unfriendliness.

Illustrators enhance (literally "illustrate") the verbal messages they accompany. For example, when referring to something to the left, you might gesture toward the left. Most often you illustrate with your hands, but you can also illustrate with head and general body movements. You might, for example, turn your head or your entire body toward the left. You might also use illustrators to communicate the shape or size of objects you're talking about.

Affect displays are movements of the face (smiling, frowning, for example) but also of the hands and general body (body tenseness, relaxing posture, for example) that communicate emotional meaning. You use affect displays to accompany and reinforce your verbal messages and also as substitutes for words, for example, you might just smile while saying how happy you are to see your friend or you might just smile. Because affect displays are primarily centered in the facial area, we consider these in more detail in the next section.

Regulators are behaviors that monitor, control, coordinate, or maintain the speaking of another individual. When you nod your head, for example, you tell the speaker to keep on speaking; when you lean forward and open your mouth, you tell the speaker that you would like to say something.

Adaptors are gestures that satisfy some personal need, for example, scratching to relieve an itch or moving your hair out of your eyes. *Self-adaptors* are self-touching movements (for example, rubbing your nose). *Alter adaptors* are movements directed at the person with whom you're speaking, for example, removing lint from a person's jacket or straightening their tie or folding your arms in front of you to keep others a comfortable distance from you. *Object adaptors* are those gestures focused on objects, for example, doodling on or shredding a Styrofoam coffee cup. Table 6.1 summarizes these five movements.

Body Appearance

Your general body appearance also communicates. Height, for example, has been shown to be significant in a wide variety of situations. Tall presidential candidates have a much better record of winning the election than do their shorter opponents. Tall people seem to be paid more and are favored by interviewers over shorter applicants (Keyes, 1980; DeVito & Hecht, 1990; Knapp & Hall, 1992).

Your body also reveals your race through skin color and tone and may also give clues as to your more specific nationality. Your weight in proportion to your height will also communicate messages to others as will the length, color, and style of your hair.

Your general attractiveness is also a part of body communication. Attractive people have the advantage in just about every activity you can name. They get better grades in school, are more valued as friends and lovers, and are preferred as co-workers (Burgoon, Buller, & Woodall, 1995). Although we normally think that attractiveness is culturally determined—and to some degree it is—recent research seems to be showing that definitions of attractiveness are becoming universal (Brody, 1994). A person rated as attractive in one culture is likely to be rated as attractive in other cultures—even cultures that are widely different in appearance.

Table 6.1 Five Body Movements

What other examples can you think of for these five movements?

	Name and Function	Examples
	EMBLEMS directly translate words or phrases; especially culture specific	"Okay" sign, "come here" wave, hitchhiker's sign
	ILLUSTRATORS accompany and literally "illustrate" verbal messages	Circular hand movements when talking of a circle; hands far apart when talking of something large
	AFFECT DISPLAYS communicate emotional meaning	Expressions of happiness, surprise, fear, anger, sadness, disgust/contempt
	REGULATORS monitor, maintain, or control the speaking of another	Facial expressions and hand gestures indicating "keep going," "slow down," or "what else happened?"
	ADAPTORS satisfy some need	Scratching one's head

FACIAL AND EYE MOVEMENTS

The facial area, including the eyes, is probably the single most important source of nonverbal messages.

Facial Communication

The power of one fair face makes my love sublime, for it has weaned my heart from low desires.
—*Michelangelo*

Throughout your interpersonal interactions, your face communicates, especially your emotions. In fact, facial movements alone seem to communicate the degree of pleasantness, agreement, and sympathy felt; the rest of the body doesn't provide any additional information. However, for other aspects, for example, the intensity with which an emotion is felt, both facial and bodily cues are used (Graham, Bitti, & Argyle, 1975; Graham & Argyle, 1975). So important are these cues in communicating your full meaning that graphic representations are now commonly used in Internet communication. In some Internet Relay Chat groups (those that are GUI, Graphic User Interface), buttons are available to help you encode your emotions graphically. Table 6.2 identifies some of the more common "emoticons," icons that communicate emotions.

Some nonverbal researchers claim that facial movements may communicate at least the following eight emotions: happiness, surprise, fear, anger, sadness, disgust, contempt, and interest (Ekman, Friesen, & Ellsworth, 1972). Others propose that, in addition, facial movements may also communicate bewilderment and determination (Leathers, 1976).

Try to communicate surprise using only facial movements. Do this in front of a mirror and try to describe, in as much detail as possible, the specific movements of the face that make up surprise. If you signal surprise like most people, you probably use raised and curved eyebrows, long horizontal forehead wrinkles, wide-open eyes, a dropped-open mouth, and lips parted with no tension. Even if there were differences—and clearly

Table 6.2 Some Popular Emoticons

These are some of the popular emoticons used in computer communication. The first six are popular in the United States; the last three are popular in Japan and illustrate how culture influences such symbols. Since Japanese culture considers it impolite for women to show their teeth when smiling, the emoticon for a woman's smile shows a dot signifying a closed mouth.

Emoticon	Meaning
:-)	Smile; I'm kidding
:-(	Frown; I'm feeling down
;-)	Winking
*	Kiss
{}	Hug
{*****}	Hugs and kisses
^.^	Woman's smile
^_^	Man's smile
^o^	Happy

there would be from one person to another—you could probably recognize the movements listed here as indicative of surprise.

Of course, some emotions are easier to communicate and to decode than others. For example, in one study, happiness was judged with an accuracy ranging from 55 to 100%, surprise from 38 to 86%, and sadness from 19 to 88% (Ekman, Friesen, & Ellsworth, 1972). Research finds that women and girls are more accurate judges of facial emotional expression than men and boys (Hall, 1984; Argyle, 1988).

Facial Management Techniques   As you learned the nonverbal system of communication you also learned certain facial management techniques; for example, to hide certain emotions and to emphasize others. Here are four types of facial management techniques that are frequently and widely used:

- Intensifying to exaggerate a feeling, for example, exaggerating surprise when friends throw you a party
- Deintensifying to underplay a feeling, for example, covering up your own joy in the presence of a friend's bad news
- Neutralizing to hide a feeling, for example, covering up your sadness so as not to depress others
- Masking to replace or substitute the expression of one emotion for another, for example, expressing happiness to cover up disappointment or, as in the cartoon on page 124, substituting an expression of confidence for worry

You probably learned these facial management techniques along with the display rules that dictate what emotions to express when; these are the rules of appropriate behavior. For example, when someone gets bad news in which you may secretly take pleasure, the display rule dictates that you frown and otherwise nonverbally signal your displeasure. If you violate these display rules, you will be judged insensitive.

Research shows that women smile more than men when making negative comments or expressing negative feelings (Shannon, 1987). What implications does this have for male–female communication? What implications might this have for child rearing? For teaching?

The Facial Feedback Hypothesis According to the facial feedback hypothesis your facial expression influences your level of physiological arousal. People who exaggerate their facial expressions show higher physiological arousal than those who suppress these expressions. Those who neither exaggerated nor suppressed their expressions had arousal levels between these two extremes (Lanzetta, Cartwright-Smith, & Kleck, 1976; Zuckerman, Klorman, Larrance, & Spiegel, 1981). In one interesting study, subjects held pens in their teeth in such a way as to simulate a sad expression. They were then asked to rate photographs. Results showed that mimicking sad expressions actually increased the degree of sadness the subjects reporting feeling when viewing the photographs (Larsen, Kasimatis, & Frey, 1992). Further support for this hypothesis comes from a study that compared subjects who (1) feel emotions such as happiness and anger and (2) feel and express these emotions. In support of the facial feedback hypothesis, subjects who felt and expressed the emotions became emotionally aroused faster than did those who only felt the emotion (Hess, Kappas, McHugo, & Lanzetta, 1992). So, not only does your facial expression influence the judgments and impressions that others have of you, they also influence your own level of emotional arousal (Cappella, 1993).

The Influence of Context and Culture The same facial expressions are seen differently if people are given different contexts. For example, in one experiment when a smiling face was presented looking at a glum face, the smiling face was judged to be vicious and taunting. However, when the same smiling face is presented looking at a frowning face, it's judged peaceful and friendly (Cline, 1956).

The wide variations in facial communication that we observe in different cultures seem to reflect which reactions are publicly permissible, rather than a difference in the way emotions are facially expressed. For example, Japanese

"Look at me. Do I look worried?"

and American students watched a film of an operation (Ekman, 1985). The students were videotaped in both an interview situation about the film and alone while watching the film. When alone, the students showed very similar reactions, but in the interview, the American students displayed facial expressions indicating displeasure, whereas the Japanese students did not show any great emotion. Similarly, it is considered "forward" or inappropriate for Japanese women to reveal broad smiles and so will hide their smiles, sometimes with their hands (cf. Ma, 1996). Women in the United States, on the other hand, have no such restrictions and so are more likely to smile openly. Thus, the difference may not be in the way different cultures express emotions but rather in the cultural rules for displaying emotions in public (cf. Matsumoto, 1991).

Similarly, cultural differences exist in decoding the meaning of a facial expression. For example, American and Japanese students judged the meaning of a smiling and a neutral facial expression. The Americans rated the smiling face as more attractive, more intelligent, and more sociable than the neutral face. The Japanese, however, rated the smiling face as more sociable but not as more attractive. They did, however, rate the neutral face as the more intelligent one (Matsumoto & Kudoh, 1993).

Eye Communication

From Ben Jonson's poetic observation "Drink to me only with thine eyes, and I will pledge with mine" to the scientific observations of contemporary researchers (Hess, 1975; Marshall, 1983), the eyes are regarded as the most important nonverbal message system.

> An eye can threaten like a loaded and leveled gun, or it can insult like hissing or kicking; or, in its altered mood, by beams of kindness, it can make the heart dance for joy.
> —*Ralph Waldo Emerson*

Power Perspective 6.1

Persuasive Power Signals

Much research has addressed the issue of the nonverbal factors related to your ability to persuade and influence others (Burgoon, Buller, & Woodall, 1995; Lewis, 1989). Here are a few ways to communicate power nonverbally.

- Other things being equal, dress relatively conservatively if you want to influence others; conservative clothing is associated with power and status.
- Engage in affirmative nodding; it shows others you're paying attention.
- Use facial expressions and gestures as appropriate; these help you express your concern for the other person and for the interaction and help you establish your charisma, a quality that makes you appear believable.
- Self-manipulations (playing with your hair or touching your face, for example) and backward leaning will damage your persuasiveness; they communicate a lack of comfort and feeling ill-at-ease.
- As a public speaker, consider standing relatively close to your listeners; it will create greater immediacy and is likely to be more persuasive.

[The next Power Perspective appears on page 130.]

In what other ways can you express power nonverbally?

The messages communicated by the eyes vary depending on the duration, direction, and quality of the eye behavior. For example, in every culture there are rather strict, although unstated, rules for the proper duration for eye contact. In one study conducted in England, the average length of gaze is 2.95 seconds. The average length of mutual gaze (two persons gazing at each other) is 1.18 seconds (Argyle & Ingham, 1972; Argyle, 1988). When eye contact falls short of this length of time, members (of some cultures) may think the person is uninterested, shy, or preoccupied. When the appropriate amount of time is exceeded, members might perceive the person as showing unusually high interest or even hostility.

The direction of the eye also communicates. In the United States it is considered appropriate to glance alternatively at the other person's face, then away, then again at the face, and so on. The rule for the public speaker is to scan the entire audience—not focusing on one area for too long or ignoring any one area of the audience. When you break these directional rules, you communicate different meanings—abnormally high or low interest, self-consciousness, nervousness over the interaction, and so on. The quality—how wide or how narrow your eyes get during interaction—also communicates meaning, especially interest level and such emotions as surprise, fear, and disgust.

In the 15th and 16th centuries in Italy, women put belladonna (which literally means "beautiful woman"), a botanical extract, in their eyes to dilate their pupils so they'd look more attractive. Contemporary research supports the logic of these women; dilated pupils are seen as more attractive, a finding that advertisers are quick to make use of. Notice how large the fashion model's pupils are in photos such as the one pictured here. Your pupils enlarge when you're interested in something or you're emotionally aroused. Conversely, your pupils constrict when you're viewing something you care little about, feel negatively about, or when you're not emotionally aroused (Hess, 1975, 1985). When you're in a conversation with others, do you notice their pupils dilating or constricting? If so, do you give meaning to these pupillary responses?

The Functions of Eye Movements With eye movements you communicate a variety of messages. For example, with eye movements you can seek feedback. In talking with someone, you look at her or him intently, as if to say, "Well, what do you think?"

You can also inform the other person that the channel of communication is open and that he or she should now speak. You see this in the college classroom, when the instructor asks a question and then locks eyes with a student. Without saying anything, the instructor expects that student to answer the question and the student knows it.

Eye movements may also signal the nature of a relationship, whether positive (an attentive glance) or negative (eye avoidance). You can also signal your power through "visual dominance behavior" (Exline, Ellyson, & Long, 1975). The average speaker, for example, maintains a high level of eye contact while listening and a lower level while speaking. When people want to signal dominance, they may reverse this pattern—maintaining a high level of eye contact while talking but a lower level while listening.

Eye contact can also change the psychological distance between yourself and another person. When you catch someone's eye at a party, for example, you become psychologically close even though far apart. By avoiding eye contact—even when physically close as in a crowded elevator—you increase the psychological distance between you.

Because messages vary from one culture to another, you risk breaking important rules when you communicate with eye movements. Americans, for example, consider direct eye contact an expression of honesty and forthrightness, but the Japanese often view this as a lack of respect. The Japanese will glance at the other person's face rarely and then only for very short periods of time (Axtell, 1990).

Women make eye contact more and maintain it longer (both in speaking and in listening) than do men. This holds true whether the woman is interacting with other women or with men. This difference in eye behavior may result from women's tendency to display their emotions more than men (Wood, 1994).

When you avoid eye contact or avert your glance, you help others maintain their privacy. You might engage in this "civil inattention" when you see a couple arguing in public (Goffman, 1967). You turn our eyes away (although your eyes may be wide open) as if to say, "I don't mean to intrude; I respect your privacy."

Eye avoidance can also signal lack of interest—in a person, a conversation, or some visual stimulus. At times, you might hide your eyes to block off unpleasant stimuli or close your eyes to block out visual stimuli and thus heighten other senses. For example, you might listen to music with your eyes closed. Lovers often close their eyes while kissing, and many prefer to make love in a dark or dimly lit room.

SPATIAL AND TERRITORIAL COMMUNICATION

Your use of space speaks as surely and loudly as words and sentences. Speakers who stand close to their listener, with their hands on the listener's shoulders and their eyes focused directly on those of the listener, communicate something very different from speakers who stand in a corner with arms folded and eyes downcast. Similarly, the executive office suite on the top floor with huge windows, private bar, and plush carpeting communicates something totally different from the 6 × 6 foot cubicle occupied by the rest of the workers.

Spatial Distances

The way in which you treat space, an area called *proxemics,* communicates a wide variety of messages. Edward Hall (1959, 1966) distinguishes four distances that define the type of relationship between people and identifies the various messages that each distance communicates.

In **intimate distance,** ranging from actual touching to 18 inches, the presence of the other individual is unmistakable. Each person experiences the sound, smell, and feel of the other's breath. You use intimate distance for lovemaking, wrestling, for comforting, and protecting. This distance is so short that most people do not consider it proper in public.

Personal distance refers to the protective "bubble" that defines your personal distance, ranging from 18 inches to 4 feet. This imaginary bubble keeps you protected and untouched by others. You can still hold or grasp another person at this distance, but only by extending your arms, allowing you to take certain individuals such as loved ones into your protective bubble. At the outer limit of personal distance, you can touch another person only if both of you extend your arms.

Social distance, ranging from 4 to 12 feet, you lose the visual detail you have at personal distance. You conduct impersonal business and interact at a social gathering at this social distance. The more distance you maintain in your interactions, the more formal they appear. In offices of high officials, the desks are positioned so the official is assured of at least this distance from clients.

Public distance, from 12 to more than 25 feet, protects you. At this distance you could take defensive action if threatened. On a public bus or train, for example, you might keep at least this distance from a drunkard. Although at this distance you lose fine details of the face and eyes, you are still close enough to see what is happening. These four distances are summarized in Table 6.3.

Influences on Space Communication

Several factors influence the way we relate to and use space in communicating. Below are a few examples of how status, culture, context, subject matter, sex, and age influence space communication (Burgoon, Buller, & Woodall, 1989).

People of equal **status** maintain shorter distances between themselves than do people of unequal status. When status is unequal, the higher-status person may approach the lower-status person more closely than the lower-status person would approach the higher-status person.

Members of different **cultures** treat space differently. For example, those from northern European cultures and many Americans stand fairly far apart when conversing, compared with those from southern European and Middle Eastern cultures who stand much closer. It's easy to see how those who

Some nonverbal researchers (Burgoon & Hale, 1988) argue that when people violate the expected distance in conversation, attention shifts from the topic to the person. Do you notice this? What else happens when expected distances are violated?

Research on space shows that the larger the physical **context** you are in, the smaller the interpersonal space you will maintain between yourself and those you are talking with (Burgoon, Buller, & Woodall, 1994). Do you find this to be true? Why do you assume this relationship exists?

Table 6.3 Relationships and Proxemic Distances

Note that these four distances can be further divided into close and far phases and that the far phase of one level (say, personal) blends into the close phase of the next level (social). Do your relationships also blend into one another or are your personal relationships totally separate from your social relationships?

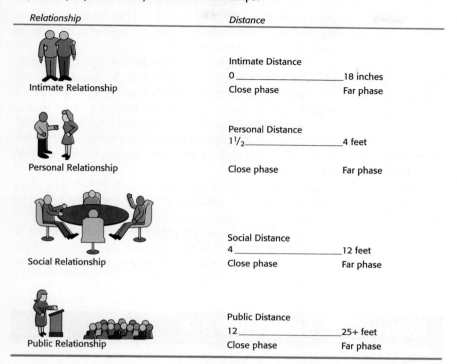

Relationship	Distance	
Intimate Relationship	**Intimate Distance** 0 _____ 18 inches	
	Close phase	Far phase
Personal Relationship	**Personal Distance** 1½ _____ 4 feet	
	Close phase	Far phase
Social Relationship	**Social Distance** 4 _____ 12 feet	
	Close phase	Far phase
Public Relationship	**Public Distance** 12 _____ 25+ feet	
	Close phase	Far phase

Protection theory holds that you establish a body buffer zone around yourself as protection against unwanted touching or attack (Dosey & Meisels, 1969; Albas & Albas, 1989). When you feel that you may be attacked, your body buffer zone increases; you want more space around you. For example, if you found yourself in a dangerous neighborhood at night, your body buffer zone would probably expand well beyond what it would be if you were in familiar and safe surroundings. If someone entered this buffer zone, you would probably feel threatened and seek to expand that distance by walking faster or crossing the street. In contrast, when you are feeling secure and protected, your buffer zone becomes much smaller. For example, if you are with a group of close friends and feel secure, your buffer zone shrinks, and you may welcome the close proximity and mutual touching. How would you go about testing this theory?

normally stand far apart may interpret the close distances of others as pushy and overly intimate. It's equally easy to appreciate how those who normally stand close may interpret the far distances of others as cold and unfriendly.

In the United States, if you live next door to someone, you are almost automatically expected to be friendly and to interact with that person. It seems so natural that we probably don't even consider that this is a cultural expectation not shared by all cultures. In Japan, however, the fact that your house is next to another's does not imply that you should become close or visit each other. Consider, therefore, the situation in which a Japanese buys a house next to an American. The Japanese may well see the American as overly familiar and as taking friendship for granted. The American may see the Japanese as distant, unfriendly, and unneighborly. Yet, each person is merely acting according to the expectations of his or her own culture (Hall & Hall, 1987).

When discussing personal **subjects** you maintain shorter distances than with impersonal subjects. In addition, you stand closer to someone praising you, than to someone criticizing you.

Your **sex** also influences your spatial relationships. Women generally stand closer than men. As people **age** there is a tendency for the spaces to become larger. Children stand much closer than do adults. This is some evidence that these distances are learned behaviors.

Why do you suppose people who are angry or tense need greater space around them? Do you find this true from your personal experience?

Territoriality

Another aspect of communication having to do with space is territoriality, a term that comes to us from ethology (the study of animals in their natural habitat). Territoriality refers to the ownership-like reaction toward a particular space or object. The size and location of human territory also say something about status (Sommer, 1969; Mehrabian, 1976). An apartment or office in midtown Manhattan or downtown Tokyo is extremely high-status territory since the cost restricts it to the wealthy.

Status is also indicated by the unwritten law granting the right of invasion. In some cultures and in some organizations, for example, higher-status individuals have more of a right to invade the territory of others than vice versa. The president of a large company can invade the territory of a junior executive by barging into her or his office, but the reverse would be unthinkable.

Like the dog in the cartoon, many animals mark their territory. Humans do as well. We make use of three types of markers: central, boundary, and ear (Hickson & Stacks, 1988).

Central markers signify that the territory is reserved. When you place a drink on a bar, books on your desk, and a sweater over the chair, you let others know that this territory belongs to you.

Boundary markers distinguish your territory from that belonging to others. Examples include: the dividers in the supermarket checkout line, the armrests separating your chair from those on either side, and the fence around your house or the door to your apartment.

Elbonics. The actions of two people maneuvering for one armrest in a movie theatre.

—*Rich Hall*

Power Perspective 6.2

Responding to Sexual Harassment

If you think you're being sexually harassed and feel a need to do something about it, consider these suggestions recommended by workers in the field (Petrocelli & Repa, 1992; Bravo & Cassedy, 1992; Rubenstein, 1993):

1. Talk to the harasser. Tell this person, assertively, that you do not welcome the behavior and that you find it offensive. This will often solve the problem. If it doesn't, then consider the next suggestion.
2. Collect evidence—corroboration from others who have experienced similar harassment at the hands of the same individual, perhaps a log of the offensive behaviors.
3. Use the channels within the organization that are probably already established to deal with such grievances. This step will, in most cases, eliminate any further harassment. In the event that it doesn't, you may consider going further.
4. File a complaint with an organization or governmental agency or perhaps take legal action.
5. Don't blame yourself. Like many who are abused, you may tend to blame yourself, feeling that you are responsible for being harassed. You aren't; however, you may need to secure emotional support from friends or perhaps from trained professionals.

[The next Power Perspective appears on page 140.]

Every power is subject to another power

—*Shona proverb*

"It's quite natural, you know,
he's just marking territory."

© Andre Noel

Ear markers identify your possessions. Trademarks, initials, nameplates, and initials on a shirt or attaché case specify that this particular object belongs to you.

ARTIFACTUAL COMMUNICATION

Artifactual messages are those made or arranged by human hands. Thus, color; your decoration of space; your clothing, jewelry, and bodily scents; and even the gifts you give would be considered artifacts. Let's look at each of these briefly.

Color Communication

When you're in debt, you speak of being "in the red"; when you make a profit, you're "in the black." When you're sad, you're "blue"; when you're healthy, you're "in the pink"; and when you're jealous, you're "green with envy." To be a coward is to be "yellow" and to be inexperienced is to be "green." When you talk a great deal, you talk "a blue streak"; and when

"Yes," I answered you last night;
"No," this morning, sir, I say:
Colors seen by candlelight
Will not look the same by day.
—*Elizabeth Barrett Browning*

Table 6.4 Some Cultural Meanings of Color

This table, constructed form the research reported by Henry Dreyfuss (1971), Nancy Hoft (1995), and Norine Dresser (1996), illustrates only some of the different meanings that colors may communicate and especially how they are viewed in different cultures. As you read this table, consider the meanings you give to these colors and where your meanings came from.

Color	Cultural Meanings and Comments
Red	In China red signifies prosperity and rebirth and is used for festive and joyous occasions; in France and the United Kingdom, masculinity; in many African countries, blasphemy or death; and in Japan it signifies anger and danger. Red ink, especially among Korean Buddhists, is used only to write a person's name at the time of death or on the anniversary of the person's death and creates lots of problems when American teachers used red ink to mark homework.
Green	In the United States green signifies capitalism, go ahead, and envy; in Ireland, patriotism; among some Native Americans, femininity; to the Egyptians, fertility and strength; and to the Japanese, youth and energy.
Black	In Thailand black signifies old age; in parts of Malaysia, courage; and in much of Europe and North America, death.
White	In Thailand white signifies purity; in many Muslim and Hindu cultures, purity and peace; and in Japan and other Asian countries, death and mourning.
Blue	In Iran blue signifies something negative; in Egypt, virtue and truth; in Ghana, joy; among the Cherokee, it signifies defeat.
Yellow	In China yellow signifies wealth and authority; in the United States, caution and cowardice; in Egypt, happiness and prosperity; and in many countries throughout the world, femininity.
Purple	In Latin America purple signifies death; in Europe, royalty; in Egypt, virtue and faith; in Japan, grace and nobility; and in China, barbarism.

you are angry, you "see red." As revealed through these time-worn clichés, language abounds in color symbolism.

Colors vary greatly in their meanings from one culture to another. Some of these cultural differences are illustrated in Table 6.4, but before looking at the table, think about the meanings your own culture(s) gives to such colors as red, green, black, white, blue, yellow, and purple.

There is some evidence that colors affect us physiologically. For example, respiratory movements increase in the presence of red light and decrease in the presence of blue light. Similarly, eye blinks increase in frequency when eyes are exposed to red light and decrease when exposed to blue. This seems consistent with our intuitive feelings that blue is more soothing and red more provocative. After changing a school's walls from orange and white to blue, the students' blood pressure decreased and their academic performance improved.

Colors surely influence our perceptions and behaviors (Kanner, 1989). People's acceptance of a product, for example, is largely determined by its package. For example, among consumers in the United States the very same coffee taken from a yellow can was described as weak, from a dark brown can it was described as too strong, from a red can it was described as rich, and from a blue can it was described as mild. Even our acceptance of a person may depend on the colors worn. Consider, for example, the comments of one color expert (Kanner, 1989): "If you have to pick the wardrobe for your defense lawyer heading into court and choose anything but blue, you deserve to lose the case . . . ." Black is so powerful that it can work against the lawyer with the jury. Brown lacks sufficient authority. Green will probably elicit a negative response.

Clothing, Body Adornment, and Odor

People make inferences about who you are—in part—by the way you dress. Whether these inferences are accurate or not, they will influence what people think of you and how they react to you. Your social class, your seriousness, your attitudes (for example, whether you are conservative or liberal), your concern for convention, your sense of style and, perhaps, even your creativity will all be judged—in part at least—by the way you dress.

College students will perceive an instructor dressed informally as friendly, fair, enthusiastic, and flexible, the same instructor dressed formally is perceived as prepared, knowledgeable, and organized (Malandro, Barker, & Barker, 1989).

Your jewelry also communicates messages about you. Wedding and engagement rings are obvious examples that communicate specific messages. College rings and political buttons likewise communicate specific messages. If you wear a Rolex watch or large precious stones, for example, others are likely to infer that you're rich. Men who wear earrings will be judged differently from men who don't. Body piercing and tattoos likewise communicate something about the individual.

The way you wear your hair communicates about who you are— from caring about being up-to-date to a desire to shock, to perhaps a lack of concern for appearances. Men with long hair, to take just one example, will generally be judged as less conservative than those with shorter hair.

Space Decoration

The way you decorate your private spaces also tells a lot about you. The office with the mahogany desk and bookcase set and oriental rugs communicates your importance and status within the organization, just as the metal desk and bare floors indicate an entry-level employee worker much further down in the company hierarchy.

Similarly, people will make inferences about you based on the way you decorate your home. The expensiveness of the furnishings may communicate your status and wealth, their coordination, and your sense of style. The magazines may reflect your interests while the arrangement of chairs around a television set may reveal how important watching television is to you. Bookcases lining the walls reveal the importance of reading. In fact, there is probably little in your home that would not send messages that others could use in making inferences about you. Computers, wide-screen televisions, well-equipped kitchens, and oil paintings of great grandparents, for example, all say something about the people who live in the home.

Costly thy habit as thy purse can buy, But not express'd in fancy; rich, not gaudy; for the apparel often proclaims the man.

—*Polonius to Laertes,* Hamlet, *Act 1, Scene III*

I think that I shall never see A billboard lovely as a tree. Indeed, unless the billboards fall I'll never see a tree at all.

—*Ogden Nash*

This is the 27,000 square-foot home of the Los Angeles Lakers' Shaquille O'Neal. What specific items in this photo tell you that this home belongs to someone extremely wealthy?

Similarly, the lack of certain items will communicate something about you. Consider what messages you would get from a home where there is no television, telephone, or books.

Smell Communication

Smell communication, or olfactics, is extremely important in a wide variety of situations and is now "big business" (Kleinfeld, 1992). There is some evidence (although clearly not very conclusive evidence), for example, that the smell of lemon contributes to a perception of health, the smell of lavender and eucalyptus seems to increase alertness, and the smell of rose oil seems to reduce blood pressure. Findings such as these have contributed to the growth of aromatherapy and to a new profession of aromatherapists (Furlow, 1996). Because humans possess "denser skin concentrations of scent glands than almost any other mammal" it has been argued that it only remains for us to discover how we use scent to communicate a wide variety of messages (Furlow, 1996, p. 41). Two particularly important messages scent communicates are those of attraction and identification.

Attraction Messages   In many animal species the female gives off a scent that draws males, often from far distances, and thus ensures the continuation of the species. Humans use perfumes, colognes, after-shave lotions, powders, and the like to (perhaps similarly) enhance attractiveness. Sophia Loren, Elizabeth Taylor, Cher, and, more recently, Billy Dee Williams, all sell perfumes by associating their own attractiveness with the fragrance. The implication is that others can smell likewise and can therefore appear equally attractive.

You also use odors to make yourself feel better; after all, you also smell yourself. When the smells are pleasant, you feel better about yourself.

When the smells are unpleasant, you feel less good about yourself and probably shower and perhaps put on some cologne.

Identification Messages Smell is often used to create an image or an identity for a product. Advertisers and manufacturers spend millions of dollars each year creating scents for cleaning products and tooth pastes, for example, which have nothing to do with their cleaning power. Instead, they function solely to create an image for the product. There is also evidence that we can identify specific significant others by smell. For example, young children were able to identify the T-shirts of their brothers and sisters solely on the basis of smell (Porter & Moore, 1981). One researcher goes so far as to advise: "If your man's odor reminds you of Dad or your brother, you may want genetic tests before trying to conceive a child" (Furlow, 1996, p. 41).

Gifts

Gift giving is a little discussed aspect of nonverbal communication but actually communicates a great deal. A gift can signify the level of intimacy you attribute to the relationship. If you perceive your relationship to be a very close one then you might give personal items like pajamas and underwear, which would be highly inappropriate if given between, say, two persons who just started dating. A gift can also signify the level of commitment; an expensive gift of jewelry would signify a level of commitment much greater than would a scarf or an umbrella.

Consider, for example, the "Pygmalion gift." This type of gift is designed to change the person into what you want that person to become. The parent who gives a child books or science equipment may be asking the child to be a scholar. The romantic partner who gives a gift of stylish clothing may be asking the person to dress differently.

Not surprisingly, gift giving is a practice in which rules and customs vary according to each culture. Even with good intentions, gift giving without sensitivity to cultural norms can backfire. Here are a few situations where gift giving created barriers rather than bonds. What might have gone wrong in each of these situations? These few examples should serve to illustrate the wide variations that exist among cultures in the meaning given to artifacts and in the seemingly simple process of giving gifts (Axtell, 1990; Dresser, 1996).

1. You bring chrysanthemums to a Belgian colleague and a clock to a Chinese colleague. Both react negatively.
2. Upon meeting an Arab businessman for the first time—someone with whom you wish to develop business relationships—you present him with a gift. He seems to become disturbed. To smooth things over, when you go to visit him and his family in Oman, you bring a bottle of your favorite brandy for after dinner. Your host seems even more disturbed now.
3. Arriving for dinner at the home of a Kenyan colleague, you present flowers as a dinner gift. Your host accepts them politely but looks puzzled. The next evening you visit your Swiss colleague and bring 14 red roses. Your host accepts them politely but looks strangely at

> Culture is communication, and communication is culture.
> —*Edward T. Hall*

Do you give Pygmalion gifts? Have you received such gifts? Were they effective?

you. Figuring that the red got you in trouble, on your third evening out you bring yellow roses to your Iranian friend. Again, there was a similar reaction.

4. You give your Chinese friend a set of dinner knives as a gift but she does not open it in front of you; you get offended. After she opens it, she gets offended.
5. You bring your Mexican friend a statue of an elephant drinking water from a lake. Your friend says he cannot accept it; his expressions tell you he really doesn't want it.

Possible reasons:

1. Chrysanthemums in Belgium and clocks in China are both reminders of death and that time is running out.
2. Gifts given at the first meeting with Arabs (or in the Middle East generally) may be interpreted as bribes. Further, since alcohol is prohibited by Islamic law, it should be avoided when selecting gifts for most Arabs or religious Muslims.
3. In Kenya, flowers are only brought to express condolence. In Switzerland red roses are a sign of romantic interest. In addition, an even number of flowers (or 13) is generally considered bad luck, so should be avoided. Yellow flowers to Iranians signify the enemy and send a message that you dislike them.
4. The Chinese custom is simply not to open gifts in front of the giver. Knives (and scissors) symbolize the severing of a relationship.
5. Among many Latin Americans the elephant's upward trunk symbolizes a holding of good luck; an elephant's downward trunk symbolizes luck slipping away.

TOUCH COMMUNICATION

Touch communication (also called haptics) is perhaps the most primitive form of nonverbal communication (Montagu, 1971). Touch develops before the other senses; even in the womb the child is stimulated by touch. Soon after birth the child is fondled, caressed, patted, and stroked. In turn, the child explores its world and quickly learns to communicate a variety of meanings through touch.

Touching varies greatly from one culture to another. For example, African Americans touch each other more than European Americans. Similarly, touching declines from kindergarten to the sixth grade for European Americans but not for African American children (Burgoon, Buller, & Woodall, 1994). Japanese touch each other much less than do Anglo-Saxons who in turn touch much less than do southern Europeans (Morris, 1977; Burgoon, Buller, & Woodall, 1994).

The Meanings of Touch

Nonverbal researchers have identified the major meanings of touch (Jones & Yarbrough, 1985). Here are five of the most important.

Who would touch whom—say, by putting an arm on the other person's shoulder or by putting a hand on the other person's back—in the following pairs: teacher and student, doctor and patient, manager and worker, minister and parishioner, police officer and accused, business executive and secretary? What reasons might you offer to explain these differences?

"There is a very simple rule about touching," the manager continued. "When you touch, don't take. Touch the people you manage only when you are giving them something—reassurance, support, encouragement, whatever."
—Kenneth Blanchard and Spencer Johnson

- Touch may communicate such **positive emotions** as support, appreciation, inclusion, sexual interest or intent, and affection.
- Touch often communicates **playfulness,** affectionately or aggressively.
- Touch may also **control** or direct the behaviors, attitudes, or feelings of the other person. In attention-getting, for example, you touch the person to gain his or her attention, as if to say "look at me" or "look over here."
- **Ritual** touching centers on greetings and departures, for example, shaking hands to say "hello" or "goodbye" or hugging, kissing, or putting your arm around another's shoulder when greeting or saying farewell.
- **Task-related** touching occurs while you are performing some function, for example, removing a speck of dust from another person's face or helping someone out of a car.

Nancy Henley (1977) argues that touching demonstrates the assertion of male power over women. Men may, says Henley, touch women during their daily routine. In the restaurant, office, and school, for example, men touch women and thus indicate "superior status." When women touch men, on the other hand, the interpretation that it designates a female-dominant relationship is not acceptable (to men). Men may explain and interpret this touching as a sexual invitation. What do you think of Henley's observations?

Cultural Differences and Touch

The several functions and examples of touching discussed here have been based on studies in North America; in other cultures these functions are not served in the same way. In some cultures, for example, some task-related touching is viewed negatively and is to be avoided. Among Koreans, it is considered disrespectful for a store owner to touch a customer in handing back change; it is considered too intimate a gesture. Members of other cultures, used to such touching, may consider the Korean's behavior cold and aloof. Muslim children are are socialized not to touch members of the opposite sex that can easily be interpreted as unfriendly by American children who are used to touching each other (Dresser, 1996).

For example, in one study on touch, college students in Japan and in the United States were surveyed (Barnlund, 1975). Students from the United States reported being touched twice as much as did the Japanese students. In Japan, there is a strong taboo against strangers touching, and the Japanese are, therefore, especially careful to maintain sufficient distance.

Some cultures, such as Southern European and Middle Eastern, are contact cultures, while others, such as Northern European and Japanese, are noncontact cultures. Members of contact cultures maintain close distances, touch each other in conversation, face each other more directly, and maintain longer and more focused eye contact. Members of noncontact cultures maintain greater distance in their interactions, touch each other rarely if at all, avoid facing each other directly, and maintain much less direct eye contact. As a result, northern Europeans and Japanese may be perceived as cold, distant, and uninvolved by southern Europeans, who may, in turn, be perceived as pushy, aggressive, and inappropriately intimate.

When one person has access to another person's body, but the first person is not allowed the same privilege in return, touch becomes an indicator of status rather than of solidarity.
—*Judy Cornelia Pearson*

Touch Avoidance

Much as we have a tendency to touch and be touched, we also have a tendency to avoid touch from certain people or in certain circumstances. Researchers in nonverbal communication have found some interesting relationships between touch avoidance and other significant communication variables (Andersen &

In one of O'Henry's stories, the narrator says: "She plucked from my lapel the invisible strand of lint (the universal act of woman to proclaim ownership)." What do you think of this observation? Is this an act proclaiming ownership? You'll notice this ploy used regularly in popular films and television dramas and sitcoms. Is it limited to women? Do men use similar gestures to proclaim ownership?

Leibowitz, 1978). For example, touch avoidance is positively related to communication apprehension; those who fear oral communication also score high on touch avoidance. Touch avoidance is also high with those who self-disclose little. Both touch and self-disclosure are intimate forms of communication; thus people who are reluctant to get close to another person by self-disclosing also seem reluctant to get close by touching.

Older people have higher touch-avoidance scores for opposite-sex persons than do younger people. As we get older we are touched less by members of the opposite sex. This decreased frequency may lead us to further avoid touching.

Males score higher on same-sex touch avoidance than do females, which matches our stereotypes. Men avoid touching other men, but women may and do touch other women. On the other hand, women have higher touch-avoidance scores for opposite-sex touching than do men.

PARALANGUAGE AND SILENCE

Paralanguage refers to the vocal (but nonverbal) dimension of speech. It refers to *how* you say something rather than what you say. While silence is the absence of sound, it is not the absence of communication.

Paralanguage

An old exercise to increase a student's ability to express different emotions, feelings, and attitudes was to have the student repeat a sentence while accenting or stressing different words each time. Placing the stress on different words easily communicates significant differences in meaning. Consider the following variations of the sentence: "Is this the face that launched a thousand ships?"

1. **Is** this the face that launched a thousand ships?
2. Is **this** the face that launched a thousand ships?
3. Is this **the face** that launched a thousand ships?
4. Is this the face that **launched** a thousand ships?
5. Is this the face that launched **a thousand ships?**

Each sentence communicates something different. In fact, each asks a different question even though the words are the same. All that differentiates the sentences are the words stressed, which is one aspect of paralanguage.

In addition to stress, paralanguage includes such vocal characteristics as rate, volume, and rhythm. It also includes vocalizations you make in crying, whispering, moaning, belching, yawning, and yelling (Trager, 1958, 1961; Argyle, 1988). A variation in any of these vocal features communicates. When you speak quickly, for example, you communicate something different from when you speak slowly. Even though the words might be the same, if the speed (or volume, rhythm, or pitch) differs, the meanings people receive will also differ.

Judgments About People Do you make judgments about another's personality on the basis of the person's paralinguistic cues? For example, do you conclude that those who speak softly feel inferior and believe that no

Some Difficult Listeners

Poet Walt Whitman once said, "To have great poets, there must be great audiences too." The same is true of conversation: To have great conversation, there must be great listeners as well as great talkers. So much of ineffective listening is communicated nonverbally that it seems appropriate to identify some general types of listeners that make conver-sation difficult. As you read this table, ask yourself what you can do as a speaker to help your listeners become less difficult. As a listener, what can you do to prevent yourself from becoming ones of these difficult listeners?

[The next Listen to This box appears on page 167.]

Listen Type	Listening Behavior	(Mis)interpreting Thoughts
The static listener	Gives no feedback, remains relatively motionless and expressionless	Why isn't she reacting? Can't she hear me?
The monotonous feedback giver	Seems responsive but the responses never vary; regardless of what you say, the response is the same	Am I making sense? Why is he still smiling? I'm being dead serious.
The overly expressive listener	Reacts to just about everything with extreme responses	Why is she so expressive? I didn't say anything that provocative. She'll have a heart attack when I get to the punch line.
The reader/writer	Reads or writes, while "listening" and only occasionally glances up	Am I that boring? Is last week's newspaper more interesting than what I'm saying?
The eye avoider	Looks all around the room and at others but never at you	Why isn't he looking at me? Do I have spinach in my teeth?
The preoccupied listener	Listens to other things at the same time, often with headphones with the sound so loud that it interferes with your own thinking	When is she going to shut that music off and really listen? Am I so boring that my talk needs background music?
The waiting listener	Listens for a cue to take over the speaking turn	Is he listening to me or re-hearsing his next interruption?
The thought completing listener	Listens a little and then finishes your thought	Am I that predictable? Why do I bother saying anything? He already knows what I'm going to say.

Power Perspective 6.3

Power Signals in Business

Communicating power in business is essential if you want to exert influence and if you want to advance within the organization. Here are some common suggestions, most of which are based on Lewis's (1989) work. Can you provide specific examples of these suggestions and how they might work (or not work) in business, at home, or at school?

- Be sure to respond in kind to another's eyebrow flash (raising the eyebrow as a way of acknowledging another person).
- When you break eye contact, direct your gaze downward; otherwise you will communicate a lack of interest in the other person.
- Use consistent packaging; be especially careful that your verbal and nonverbal messages don't contradict each other.
- When sitting, select chairs you can get in and out of easily; avoid deep plush chairs which you sink into and have trouble getting out of.
- To communicate dominance with your handshake, exert more pressure than usual and hold the grip a bit longer than normal. But be careful. Too much pressure may make you appear aggressive in parts of Europe and the Middle East (Starkey, 1997).
- Walk slowly and deliberately. To appear hurried is to appear as without power, as if you were rushing to meet the expectations of another person who had power over you.

[The next Power Perspective appears on page 159.]

one wants to listen to them? Do you assume that people who speak loudly have over-inflated egos? Do those who speak with no variation, in a complete monotone, seem uninterested in what they are saying? Might you generalize to their having a lack of interest in life in general? All these conclusions are based on little evidence; yet they seem to persist in much popular talk.

Research has found that people can accurately judge the status (whether high, middle, or low) of speakers from 60-second voice samples (Davitz, 1964). Many listeners made their judgments in fewer than 15 seconds. Speakers judged to be of high status were also given higher credibility than speakers rated middle and low.

Listeners can also accurately judge the emotional states of speakers from vocal expression alone. In these studies, speakers recite the alphabet or numbers while expressing emotions. Some emotions are easier to identify than others; it is easy to distinguish between hate and sympathy, but more difficult to distinguish between fear and anxiety. Of course, listeners vary in their ability to decode, and speakers in their ability to encode emotions (Scherer, 1986).

Judgments About Communication Effectiveness   In one-way communication (when one person is doing all or most of the speaking and the other person is doing all or most of the listening), those who talk fast (about 50% faster than normal) are more persuasive. People agree more with a fast speaker than with a slow speaker and find the fast speaker more intelligent and objective (MacLachlan, 1979).

When we look at comprehension, rapid speech shows an interesting effect. When the speaking rate is increased by 50%, the comprehension level drops by only 5%. When the rate is doubled, the comprehension level drops only 10%. These 5 and 10% losses are more than offset by the increased speed; thus, faster speech rates are much more efficient in communicating information. If the speeds are more than twice that of normal speech, however, the comprehension level begins to fall dramatically.

Do exercise caution in applying this research to all forms of communication (MacLachlan, 1979). While the speaker is speaking, the listener is generating or framing a reply. If the speaker talks too rapidly, there may not be enough time to compose this reply and the listener may become resentful. Furthermore, the increased rate may seem so unnatural that the listener may focus on the speed rather than the message being communicated.

Silence

"Speech," wrote Thomas Mann, "is civilization itself. The word, even the most contradictory word, preserves contact; it is silence which isolates." Philosopher Karl Jaspers, on the other hand, observed that "the ultimate in thinking as in communication is silence," and philosopher Max Picard noted that "silence is nothing merely negative; it is not the mere absence of speech. It is a positive, a complete world in itself." The one thing on which these contradictory observations agree is that silence communicates. Your silence communicates just as intensely as anything you verbalize (see Jaworski, 1993).

Functions of Silence   Silence allows the speaker *time to think*, time to formulate and organize his or her verbal communications. Before messages of intense conflict, as well as those confessing undying love, there is often silence. Again, silence seems to prepare the receiver for the importance of these future messages.

Some people use silence as a weapon to *hurt* others. We often speak of giving someone "the silent treatment." After a conflict, for example, one or both individuals might remain silent as a kind of punishment. Silence used to hurt others may also take the form of refusing to acknowledge the presence of another person, as in disconfirmation (see Chapter 5); in this case silence is a dramatic demonstration of the total indifference one person feels toward the other.

Sometimes silence is used as a *response to personal anxiety*, shyness, or threats. You may feel anxious or shy among new people and prefer to remain silent. By remaining silent you preclude the chance of rejection. Only when the silence is broken and an attempt to communicate with another person is made do you risk rejection.

Silence may be used to *prevent communication* of certain messages. In conflict situations, silence is sometimes used to prevent certain topics from surfacing and to prevent one or both parties from saying things they may later regret. In such situations, silence often allows us time to cool off

How would you read each of these sentences, first to praise and second to criticize: (1) Now that looks good on you; (2) You're an expert; (3) You're so sensitive, I'm amazed. How would you characterize the paralanguage differences between praising and criticizing?

Women like silent men. They think they're listening.

—Marcel Archanil

before expressing hatred, severe criticism, or personal attacks, which, we know, are irreversible.

Like the eyes, face, or hands, silence can also be used to *communicate emotional responses* (Ehrenhaus, 1988). Sometimes silence communicates a determination to be uncooperative or defiant; by refusing to engage in verbal communication, you defy the authority or the legitimacy of the other person's position. Silence is often used to communicate annoyance, usually accompanied by a pouting expression, arms crossed in front of the chest, and nostrils flared. Silence may express affection or love, especially when coupled with long and longing stares into each other's eyes.

Of course, you may also use silence when you simply have *nothing to say,* when nothing occurs to you, or when you do not want to say anything. James Russell Lowell expressed this well: "Blessed are they who have nothing to say, and who cannot be persuaded to say it."

Do you use silence to serve these varied functions? Are there other functions of silence that you've observed and that are not mentioned here?

Cultural Differences and Silence   All cultures, however, do not view silence as functioning in the same way. In the United States, for example, silence is often interpreted negatively. At a business meeting or even in informal social groups, the silent member may be seen as not listening, having nothing interesting to add, not understanding the issues, being insensitive, or being too self-absorbed to focus on the messages of others. Other cultures, however, view silence more positively. In many situations in Japan, for example, silence is a response that is considered more appropriate than speech (Haga, 1988).

The traditional Apache, for example, regard silence very differently than European Americans (Basso, 1972). Among the Apache, mutual friends do not feel the need to introduce strangers who may be working in the same area or on the same project. The strangers may remain silent for several days. This period enables them to observe each other and come to a judgment about the other person. Once this assessment is made, the individuals talk. When courting, especially during the initial stages, the Apache remain silent for hours; if they do talk, they generally talk very little. Only after a couple has been dating for several months will they have lengthy conversations. These periods of silence are generally attributed to shyness or self-consciousness. The use of silence is explicitly taught to Apache women, who are especially discouraged from engaging in long discussions with their dates. Silence during courtship is a sign of modesty to many Apache.

What nonverbal cues do you find generally reliable in showing that someone likes you? In showing that someone dislikes you?

TIME COMMUNICATION

Temporal communication (or chronemics) concerns the use of time—how you organize it, react to it, and the messages it communicates (Bruneau, 1985, 1990). Cultural and psychological time are two aspects of particular interest in human communication.

Cultural Time

Two types of cultural time are especially important: formal and informal time. In the United States and in most of the world, **formal time** is divided into seconds, minutes, hours, days, weeks, months, and years. Some cultures, however, may use phases of the moon or the seasons to delineate time periods. In the United States, if your college is on the semester system, your courses are divided into 50- or 75-minute periods that meet two or three times a week for 14-week periods. Eight semesters of 15 or 16 50-minute periods per week equal a college education. As these examples illustrate, formal time units are arbitrary. The culture establishes them for convenience.

Informal time refers to the use of general time terms—for example, "forever," "immediately," "soon," "right away," "as soon as possible." This type of time creates the most communication problems because the terms have different meanings for different people.

Attitudes toward time vary from one culture to another. In one study, for example, the accuracy of clocks was measured in six cultures—Japan, Indonesia, Italy, England, Taiwan, and the United States. Japan had the most accurate and Indonesia had the least accurate clocks. The speed at which people in these six cultures walked was also measured and results showed that the Japanese walked the fastest; the Indonesians walked the slowest (Levine & Bartlett, 1984).

Monochronism and Polychronism Another important distinction is that between monochronic and polychronic time orientations (Hall, 1959, 1976, 1987). Monochronic people or cultures such as the United States, Germany, Scandinavia, and Switzerland schedule one thing at a time. In these cultures, time is compartmentalized and there is a time for everything. Polychronic people or cultures such as Latin Americans, Mediterranean people, and Arabs, on the other hand, schedule a number of things at the same time. Eating, conducting business with several different people, and taking care of family matters may all be conducted at the same time. No culture is entirely monochronic or polychronic; rather, these are general tendencies that are found across a large part of the culture. Some cultures combine both time orientations; Japanese and parts of American culture are examples where both orientations are found. Table 6.5, based on Hall (1987), identifies some of the distinctions between these two time orientations.

Are you basically monochronic or polychronic? Can you identify the sources from which you developed this orientation? How comfortable are you with it?

The Social Clock An especially interesting aspect of cultural time is your "social clock" (Neugarten, 1979). Your culture and your more specific society within that culture maintains a time schedule that dictates the right time to do a variety of important things, for example, the right time to start dating, to finish college, to buy your own home, to have a child. Most people are taught about this clock as they grow up and internalize these lessons. On the basis of this social clock, you then evaluate your own social and professional development. If you are on time with the rest of your peers—for example, you all started dating at around the same age or you're all finishing college at around the same age—then you will feel well adjusted, competent, and a part of the group. If you are late, you will probably experience feelings of dissatisfaction and inadequacy.

Gather ye rose-buds while ye may.
Old Time is still aflying,
And this same flower that smiles today,
Tomorrow will be dying.
—*Robert Herrick*

Table 6.5 Monochronic and Polychronic Time

As you read down this table, note the potential for miscommunication that these differences might create when M-time and P-time people interact. Have any of these differences ever created communication misunderstandings for you?

The Monochronic-Time Person	The Polychronic-Time Person
Does one thing at a time	Does several things at once
Treats time schedules and plans very seriously; feels they may only be broken for the most serious reasons	Treats time schedules and plans as useful (not sacred); feels they may be broken for a variety of causes
Considers the job the most important part of one's life, ahead of even family	Considers the family and interpersonal relationships more important than the job
Considers privacy extremely important, seldom borrows or lends to others, works independently	Is actively involved with others, works in the presence of and with lots of people at the same time

Psychological Time

Psychological time refers to the importance placed on the past, present, and future. With a past orientation, you have a particular reverence for the past. You relive old times and regard the old methods as the best. You see events as circular and recurring and find that the wisdom of yesterday is applicable also to today and tomorrow. With a present orientation, you live in the present—without planning for tomorrow. With a future orientation, you look toward and live for the future. You save today, work hard in college, and deny yourselves luxuries because you are preparing for the future. Before reading about some of the consequences of the way you view time, take the following test to assess your own psychological time orientation.

Know the true value of time; snatch, seize, and enjoy every moment of it. No idleness, no laziness, no procrastination; never put off till tomorrow what you can do today.
—*Lord Chesterfield*

Test Yourself | What Time Do You Have?

Instructions: Indicate whether each statement is true (T) or untrue (F) of your general attitude and behavior. A few statements are repeated to facilitate interpreting your score.

_____ 1. Meeting tomorrow's deadlines and doing other necessary work comes before tonight's partying.

_____ 2. I meet my obligations to friends and authorities on time.

_____ 3. I complete projects on time by making steady progress.

_____ 4. I am able to resist temptations when I know there is work to be done.

_____ 5. I keep working at a difficult, uninteresting task if it will help me get ahead.

_____ 6. If things don't get done on time, I don't worry about it.

_____ 7. I think that it's useless to plan too far ahead because things hardly ever come out the way you planned anyway.

_____ 8. I try to live one day at a time.

_____ 9. I live to make better what is rather than to be concerned about what will be.

_____ 10. It seems to me that it doesn't make sense to worry about the future, since fate determines that whatever will be, will be.

_____ 11. I believe that getting together with friends to party is one of life's important pleasures.

_____ 12. I do things impulsively, making decisions on the spur of the moment.

_____ 13. I take risks to put excitement in my life.

_____ 14. I get drunk at parties.

_____ 15. It's fun to gamble.

_____ 16. Thinking about the future is pleasant to me.

_____ 17. When I want to achieve something, I set subgoals and consider specific means for reaching those goals.

_____ 18. It seems to me that my career path is pretty well laid out.

_____ 19. It upsets me to be late for appointments.

_____ 20. I meet my obligations to friends and authorities on time.

_____ 21. I get irritated at people who keep me waiting when we've agreed to meet at a given time.

_____ 22. It makes sense to invest a substantial part of my income in insurance premiums.

_____ 23. I believe that "A stitch in time saves nine."

_____ 24. I believe that "A bird in the hand is worth two in the bush."

_____ 25. I believe it is important to save for a rainy day.

_____ 26. I believe a person's day should be planned each morning.

_____ 27. I make lists of things I must do.

_____ 28. When I want to achieve something, I set subgoals and consider specific means for reaching those goals.

_____ 29. I believe that "A stitch in time saves nine."

Thinking Critically About Your Time Orientation This test measures seven factors. If you selected true (T) for all or most of the questions within any factor, you're probably high on that factor. If you selected untrue (F) for all or most of the questions within any factor, you're probably low on that factor.

The first factor, measured by questions 1–5, is a future, work motivation, perseverance orientation. These people have a strong work ethic and are committed to completing a task despite difficulties. The second factor (questions 6–10) is a present, fatalistic, worry-free orientation. High scorers live one day at a time, not necessarily to enjoy the day but to avoid planning for the future. The third factor (11–15) is a present, pleasure-seeking orientation. These people enjoy the present, take risks, and engage in impulsive actions. The fourth factor (16–18) is a future, goal-seeking, and planning orientation. The fifth factor (19–21) is a time-sensitivity orientation. People who score high are especially sensitive to time and its role in social obligations. The sixth factor (22–25) is a future, practical action orientation. These people do what they have to do to achieve the future they want. The seventh factor (26–29) is a future, somewhat obsessive daily planning orientation. High scorers make daily "to do" lists and devote great attention to specific details.

Source: From Alexander Gonzalez and Philip G. Zimbardo, "Time in Perspective," _Psychology Today 19_ (March 1985). Copyright © 1985 by Sussex Publishers, Inc. Reprinted by permission.

Consider some of the findings on psychological time (Gonzalez & Zimbardo, 1985). Future income is positively related to future orientation; the more future oriented you are, the greater your income is likely to be. Present orientation is strongest among lowest income males.

The time orientation you develop depends on your socioeconomic class and your personal experiences. The researchers who developed this scale and upon whose research these findings are based, observe: "A child with parents in unskilled and semiskilled occupations is usually socialized in a way that promotes a present-oriented fatalism and hedonism. A child of parents who are managers, teachers, or other professionals learns future-oriented values and strategies designed to promote achievement" (Gonzalez & Zimbardo, 1985). Similarly, the future-oriented person who works for tomorrow's goals will frequently look down on the present-oriented person as lazy and poorly motivated for enjoying today and not planning for tomorrow. In turn, the present-oriented person may see those with strong future orientations as obsessed with amassing wealth or rising in status.

Different time perspectives also account for much intercultural misunderstanding since different cultures often teach their members drastically different time orientations. For example, members from some Latin cultures would rather be late for an appointment than end a conversation abruptly. While the Latin sees this behavior as politeness toward the person with whom he or she is conversing, others may see this as impolite to the person with whom he or she had the appointment (Hall & Hall, 1987).

What is your own psychological time orientation? Will this help you achieve your goals? Are you generally satisfied with this orientation? Dissatisfied? If dissatisfied, what do you intend to do about it?

When I look at the future, it's so bright it burns my eyes.

—*Oprah Winfrey*

THINKING CRITICALLY ABOUT NONVERBAL MESSAGES

In thinking critically about nonverbal communication try following these suggestions.

Analyze your own nonverbal communication patterns. If you are to use this material in any meaningful way, for example, to change some of your behaviors, then self-analysis is essential.

Observe. Observe. Observe. Observe the behaviors of those around you as well as your own. See in everyday behavior what you read about here and discuss in class.

Resist the temptation to draw conclusions from nonverbal behaviors. Instead, develop hypotheses or educated guesses about what is going on and test their correctness on the basis of other evidence.

Connect and relate. Although the areas of nonverbal communication are presented separately in textbooks and in many class lectures, in actual communication situations, all of these areas work together.

SUMMARY OF CONCEPTS AND SKILLS

In this chapter we explored nonverbal communication—communication without words—and looked at the ways in which messages are communicated by body movements, facial and eye movements, space and territoriality, artifacts, touch, paralanguage and silence, and time.

1. Five types of body movements are especially important: emblems (nonverbal behaviors that rather directly translate words or phrases), illustrators (nonverbal behaviors that accompany and literally "illustrate" the verbal messages), affect displays (nonverbal movements that communicate emotional meaning), regulators (nonverbal movements

that coordinate, monitor, maintain, or control the speaking of another individual), and adaptors (nonverbal behaviors that are emitted without conscious awareness and that usually serve some kind of need, as in scratching an itch).

2. Facial movements may communicate a wide variety of emotions. The most frequently studied are happiness, surprise, fear, anger, sadness, and disgust/contempt. Facial Management Techniques enable you to control revealing the emotions you feel.

3. The Facial Feedback Hypothesis claims that facial display of an emotion can lead to physiological and psychological changes.

4. Eye movements may seek feedback, inform others to speak, signal the nature of a relationship, and compensate for increased physical distance.

5. Proxemics refers to the communicative function of space and spatial relationships. Four major proxemic distances are: (a) intimate distance, ranging from actual touching to 18 inches; (b) personal distance, ranging from 18 inches to 4 feet; (c) social distance, ranging from 4 to 12 feet; and (d) public distance, ranging from 12 to more than 25 feet.

6. Your treatment of space is influenced by such factors as status, culture, context, subject matter, sex, age, and positive or negative evaluation of the other person.

7. Territoriality refers to one's possessive reaction to an area of space or to particular objects. Markers are devices that identify a territory as ours; these include central, boundary, and ear markers.

8. Artifactual communication refers to messages that are human-made, for example, the use of color, clothing and body adornment, smell, and space decoration.

9. Touch communication (or haptics) may communicate a variety of meanings, the most important being positive affect, playfulness, control, ritual, and task-relatedness. Touch avoidance refers to our desire to avoid touching and being touched by others.

10. Paralanguage refers to the vocal but nonverbal dimension of speech. It includes rate, pitch, volume, resonance, and vocal quality, as well as pauses and hesitations. On the basis of paralanguage we make judgments about people, conversational turns, and believability.

11. Time communication (chronemics) refers to the messages communicated by our treatment of time. Cultural time focuses on how our culture defines and teaches time, and with the difficulties created by the different meanings people have for informal time terms. Psychological time focuses on time orientations, whether past, present, or future.

Throughout our discussion we covered a wide variety of communication skills. Check your ability to apply these skills. Use the following rating scale: (1) = almost always, (2) = often, (3) = sometimes, (4) = rarely, (5) = hardly ever.

_____ 1. I recognize messages communicated by body gestures and facial and eye movements.

_____ 2. I take into consideration the interaction of emotional feelings and nonverbal expressions of the emotion; each influences the other.

_____ 3. I recognize that what I perceive is only a part of the total nonverbal expression.

_____ 4. I use my eyes to seek feedback, to inform others to speak, to signal the nature of my relationship with others, and to compensate for increased physical distance.

_____ 5. I give others the space they need, for example, giving more space to those who are angry or disturbed.

_____ 6. I am sensitive to the markers (central, boundary, and ear) of others and use them to define my own territories.

_____ 7. I use artifacts to communicate the desired messages.

_____ 8. I am sensitive to the touching behaviors of others and distinguish among those touches that communicate positive emotion, playfulness, control, ritual, and task-relatedness.

_____ 9. I recognize and respect each person's touch-avoidance tendency. I am especially sensitive to cultural and gender differences in touching preferences and in touch-avoidance tendencies.

_____ 10. I vary paralinguistic features (rate, pausing, quality, tempo, and volume) to communicate my intended meanings.

_____ 11. I specify what I mean when I use informal time terms.

_____ 12. I interpret time cues from the cultural perspective of the person with whom I am interacting.

_____ 13. I balance my psychological time orientation and don't ignore the past, present, or future.

KEY WORD QUIZ

Write T for those statements that are true and F for those that are false. In addition, for those that are false, replace the boldface term with the correct term.

_____ 1. The nonverbal okay sign or the head nod that signals agreement are examples of **illustrators.**

_____ 2. Emotional expressions are called **affect displays.**

_____ 3. Facial and hand expressions that try to control the other person's speaking (for example, nonverbal movements that tell the speaker to speed up or clarify something) are known as **adaptors.**

_____ 4. The assumption that your facial expression influences your level of positive and negative physiological arousal is known as the **facial feedback hypothesis.**

_____ 5. Erving Goffman called the act of avoiding eye contact or averting your glance to help others maintain their privacy **civil inattention.**

_____ 6. The study of the way in which people use space in relating to each other and even to the layout of their towns and cities is known as **territoriality.**

_____ 7. Communication through messages of color, clothing, jewelry, and the decoration of space is known as **artificial communication.**

_____ 8. The study of communication through touch is known as **haptics.**

_____ 9. The vocal but nonverbal aspect of speech is called **paralanguage.**

_____ 10. Communication by the way in which you treat time is known as **chronemics.**

Answers: TRUE: Numbers 2, 4, 5, 8, 9, 10. FALSE: Numbers 1 (emblems), 3 (regulators), 6 (proxemics), 7 (artifactual communication).

SKILL DEVELOPMENT EXPERIENCES

6.1 Recognizing Verbal and Nonverbal Message Functions

Although verbal and nonverbal communication are presented in separate chapters, in normal communication they work together. You speak with facial expression, you express sorrow with your entire body and with your words. Six ways in which verbal and nonverbal messages interact are usually identified (Knapp & Hall, 1993; Ekman, 1965). For each function identify a specific and original example to illustrate how verbal and nonverbal messages occur together.

To accent	Nonverbal signals may highlight or emphasize some part of the verbal message, for example, smiling to emphasize your pleasure.
To complement	Nonverbal signals may reinforce or complete your verbal message as when you laugh when telling a funny story.
To contradict	You may contradict your verbal messages by, for example, winking to show you should not be taken seriously.
To regulate	Nonverbal signals may communicate your desire to control the flow of verbal

messages, for example, leaning forward to indicate your desire to speak.

To repeat	Using your fingers to echo your verbal "okay" or motioning with your hand as you say "Let's go" are examples of nonverbal signals repeating the verbal.
To substitute	Nonverbal signals may also take the place of verbal messages as when, for example, you simply nod your head to indicate agreement.

6.2 Sitting at the Company Meeting

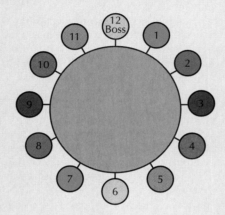

Where would you sit in each of the four situations identified below? What would be your first choice? Your second choice?

A. You want to polish the apple and ingratiate yourself with your boss.
B. You aren't prepared and want to be ignored.
C. You want to challenge your boss on a certain policy that will come up for a vote.
D. You want to be accepted as a new (but important) member of the company.

Why did you make the choices you made? Do you normally make choices based on such factors as these? What interpersonal factors—for example, the desire to talk to or the desire to get a closer look at someone—influence your day-to-day seating behavior.

6.3 Coloring Meanings

This exercise is designed to raise questions about the meanings that colors communicate and focuses on the ways in which advertisers and marketers use colors to influence our perceptions of a particular product. The color spectrum is presented with numbers from 1 to 25 to facilitate identifying the colors that you select for the objects noted below.

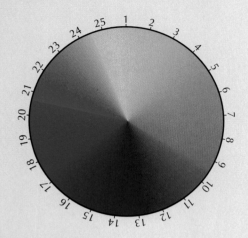

Assume that you are working for an advertising agency and that your task is to select colors for the various objects listed below. For each object select the major color as well as the secondary colors you would use in its packaging. Record these in the spaces provided by selecting the numbers corresponding to the colors of the spectrum.

Objects	Major Color	Secondary Colors
Especially rich ice cream	_____	_____
Low-calorie ice cream	_____	_____
Inexpensive puppy food	_____	_____
Packaging for up-scale jewelry store	_____	_____
An exercise machine for people over 60	_____	_____
A textbook in human communication	_____	_____

After each person has recorded his or her decisions, discuss these in small groups of five or six or with the class as a whole. You may find it helpful to consider the following:

1. What meanings did you wish to communicate for each of the objects for which you chose colors?
2. How much agreement is there among the group members that these meanings are the appropriate ones for these products?
3. How much agreement is there among group members on the colors selected?
4. How effectively do the various colors communicate the desired meanings?
5. Pool the insights of all group members and recolor the products. Are these group designs superior to those developed individually? If a number of groups are working on this project at the same time, it may be interesting to compare the final group colors for each of the products.

CHAPTER 7

Interpersonal Communication: Conversation and Conflict

CHAPTER CONCEPTS	CHAPTER GOALS After completing this chapter, you should be able to	CHAPTER SKILLS After completing this chapter, you should be able to
Conversation	1. explain the five-stage model of conversation and the suggestions for opening, maintaining, and closing a conversation	open, maintain, and close conversations effectively
Effective Conversation	2. explain the seven qualities of effective conversation	use the qualities of effective conversation as appropriate to the specific situation
Conflict	3. define *interpersonal conflict*	engage in interpersonal conflict with a realistic understanding of the myths and their potential effects
Effective Conflict Management	4. explain the suggestions for dealing with conflict productively	engage in conflict management using fair-fight strategies
Thinking Critically About Conversation and Conflict	5. explain mindfulness, flexibility, and metacommunication as skills to regulate skills	communicate with an appropriate degree of mindfulness, flexibility, and metacommunication

Interpersonal communication is communication that occurs between two persons who have a relationship between them, who are to some degree interdependent. Thus, interpersonal communication includes what takes place between a waiter and a customer, a son and his father, two people in an interview, and so on. This definition makes it almost impossible for communication between two people not to be considered interpersonal. Inevitably, some relationship between two persons exists. Even a stranger asking directions from a local resident has established a clearly defined relationship as soon as the first message is sent. Sometimes this "relational" or "dyadic" definition is extended to include small groups of persons, such as family members, groups of three or four friends, or work colleagues.

The first part of this chapter considers conversation, its stages, and the qualities that make it effective (Bochner & Kelly, 1974; Wiemann, 1977; Wiemann & Backlund, 1980; Spitzberg & Hecht, 1984; Spitzberg & Cupach, 1984, 1989; Ruben, 1988; Rubin, 1982). The second part examines interpersonal conflict, how it works, and how you can manage it for greater interpersonal effectiveness.

CONVERSATION

As shown in Figure 7.1, conversation takes place in five steps: opening, feedforward, business, feedback, and closing. Both face-to-face and computer-mediated communication can qualify as interpersonal communication. Of all the forms of Internet communication, the one closest to interpersonal communication is E-mail. In E-mail, you usually type your letter in an E-mail program and send it (along with other documents you may wish to attach) from your computer via modem to your server (the computer at your school or at some commercial organization like America Online), which relays your message through a series of computer hook-ups and eventually to the server of the person to whom you're writing. Unlike face-to-face communication, E-mail does not take place in real time. You may send your letter today but the receiver may not read it for a week and may take another week to respond.

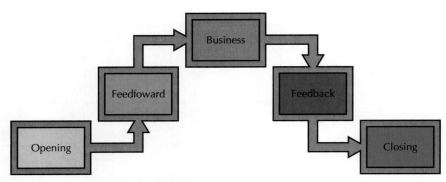

Figure 7.1 The Conversation Process

This model of the stages of conversation is best seen as a way of talking about conversation and not as the unvarying stages all conversations follow. Can you use this diagram to explain the structure of a recent conversation? How would you diagram a model of communication by E-mail?

E-mail is more like a postcard than a letter and so can be read by others along the route and, as already noted in Chapter 1, it is virtually unerasable. E-mail can also easily be forwarded to other people by anyone who has access to your files. Although this practice is considered unethical, it's unfortunately relatively common. The principle that communication is irreversible is especially important when it comes to E-mail. Don't send anything in E-mail that you wouldn't want made public.

Opening

Your first step is to open the conversation; usually you do this with some kind of greeting: "Hi," "How are you?" "Hello, I'm Joe." In face-to-face conversation, greetings can be verbal or nonverbal, but are usually both (Krivonos & Knapp, 1975; Knapp & Vangelisti, 1996). In E-mail (and in most computer communication today) the greetings are verbal with perhaps an emoticon or two thrown in. As video and sound are added to your Internet connections, these differences will be practically obliterated. Verbal greetings include, for example, verbal salutes ("Hi," "Hello"), initiation of the topic ("The reason I called . . ."), making reference to the other ("Hey, Joe, you're looking good"), and personal inquiries ("What's new?" How are you doing?"). Nonverbal greetings include waving, smiling, shaking hands, and winking (and their emoticon equivalents).

In your greeting you can accomplish several purposes (Krivonos & Knapp, 1975; Knapp & Vangelisti, 1996). For example, you can **signal a stage of access**; you can indicate that the channels of communication are open for more meaningful interaction—a good example of *phatic communion* or "small talk" opening the way for "big talk." You can also **reveal important information about the relationship between the two of you**. For example, a big smile and a warm "Hi, it's been a long time" signals that your relationship is still a friendly one. With greetings you can also **help maintain the relationship**. You see this function served between colleagues who frequently pass by each other in the workplace. This greeting-in-passing assures you that even though you do not stop and talk that you still have access to each other.

The opening of the conversation is the part that seems to cause the most anxiety or apprehension and so you may wish to pause here and take the accompanying self-test on your own apprehension in conversations.

What methods other than those described in this chapter seem to work for opening a conversation? Which openers do you especially resent? Why? How would your conversational openers differ if you wanted to establish a friendship or if you wanted to establish a romantic relationship?

Test Yourself: How Apprehensive Are You in Interpersonal Conversations?

Instructions: Although we often think of apprehension or fear of speaking in connection with public speaking, each of us has a certain degree of apprehension in all forms of communication. The following brief test is designed to measure your apprehension in interpersonal conversations.

This questionnaire consists of six statements concerning your feelings about interpersonal conversations. Indicate in the space provided the degree to which each statement applies to you by marking whether you (1) strongly agree, (2) agree, (3) are undecided, (4) disagree, or (5) strongly disagree with each statement. There are no right or wrong answers. Do not be concerned that some of the statements are similar to others. Work quickly, recording your first impression.

_____ 1. While participating in a conversation with a new acquaintance, I feel very nervous.
_____ 2. I have no fear of speaking up in conversations.
_____ 3. Ordinarily I am very tense and nervous in conversations.
_____ 4. Ordinarily I am very calm and relaxed in conversations.
_____ 5. While conversing with a new acquaintance, I feel very relaxed.
_____ 6. I'm afraid to speak up in conversations.

Thinking Critically About Conversation Apprehension

To obtain your apprehension score, do the following: start with 18 (a number chosen so that all scores can be expressed with positive numbers). To this add your scores for items 2, 4, and 5. Then, from this total, subtract your scores for items 1, 3, and 6. A score above 18 shows some degree of apprehension. Of course, conversations vary widely in the degree to which they may lead to apprehension. For which types do you experience the greatest anxiety? The least? Do others experience apprehension when talking with you? Specific suggestions for reducing apprehension are given in Chapter 13, Public Speaking Preparation and Delivery, pages 320–357.

Source: From *An Introduction to Rhetorical Communication,* 7th ed., by James C. McCroskey (Boston: Allyn and Bacon, 1997). Reprinted by permission of the author.

Feedforward

In the second step of conversation, you usually give some kind of feedforward in which you might seek to accomplish a variety of functions. One function is to **open the channels of communication,** usually with some phatic message—a message that opens the channels of communication rather than communicates any significant denotative information, for example, "Nice day, isn't it?" In E-mail this is done by the act of sending the message—it tells the other person that you want to communicate.

Another function of feedforward is to **preview future messages,** for example, "I'm afraid I have bad news for you" or "Listen to this before you make a move" or "I'll tell you all the gory details." In office memos and E-mail this function is served, in part, with headers that indicate the subject of your message, the recipients, and those who'll receive courtesy copies.

Feedforward can also help to **altercast,** to place the receiver in a specific role and request that the receiver respond to you in terms of this assumed role (Weinstein & Deutschberger, 1963; McLaughlin, 1984); for example, "But you're my best friend, you have to help me" or "As an advertising executive, what do you think of advertising directed at children?"

You can also **disclaim,** to persuade the listener to hear your message as you wish it to be heard (Hewitt & Stokes, 1975; Shapiro & Bies, 1994); for example, "Don't get me wrong, I'm not sexist" or "I didn't read the entire report, but . . ." or "Don't say anything until you hear my side." In E-mail and other forms of computer communication, you can use emoticons to indicate that you're only joking and thus disclaim any negative intent.

Business

The third step is the "business," or the substance and focus of the conversation. "Business" is a good term to use for this stage because it emphasizes that most conversations are directed at achieving some goal. You converse to fulfill one or several of the general purposes of interpersonal communication: to learn, relate, influence, play, or help (as you saw in Chapter 1). Business is conducted through an exchange of speaker and listener roles. Here you talk about the new supervisor, what happened in class, or your vacation plans. This is obviously the longest part of the conversation; both the opening and feedforward support and foreshadow this part of the conversation.

The defining feature of face-to-face conversation is that the roles of speaker and listener are exchanged frequently throughout the interaction. Usually, brief (rather than long) speaking turns characterize mutually satisfying conversations. Here is where E-mail differs greatly from most face-to-face communication. In E-mail each person sends a message without any interruptions, comments, or feedback from the receiver. Then the receiver responds. Then you respond. As you can see, E-mail better resembles the linear model of communication where either speaker or listener sends messages but never both at one time. Face-to-face conversation is, as already noted, better described with the transactional model where each person sends and receives messages simultaneously (Chapter 1). Here are just a few suggestions for sending and receiving messages in both face-to-face and computer-mediated communication.

Ask questions of clarification and extension to show that you're listening and that you're interested. Ask for opinions and ideas to draw the person into the conversation and to initiate an exchange of thoughts. Paraphrase important ideas to make sure you understand what the sender is thinking and feeling and give her or him an opportunity to correct or modify your paraphrase ("Does this mean you're going to quit your job?").

Strive for a balance between sending and receiving at least most of the time. Be sure to have good reasons if your speaking time or E-mail sending is greatly different from your listening time or your E-mail responses.

Beware of detouring, where you take a word or idea from a message and then go off on a tangent. Too many of these tangents can cause you to lose the opportunity to achieve any conversational depth. Keep the thesis or main subject of the conversation clearly in mind as you talk and as you listen.

Interruptions are possible only in face-to-face conversation; you can't interrupt someone who's writing E-mail. In face-to-face situations, it's best to avoid interruptions. Generally, interruptions that take the speaking turn away from the speaker damage a conversation by preventing each person from saying what he or she wants to say. When interruptions are excessive they may result in monologs rather than dialogs. Remember, however, that backchanneling cues you send back to the speaker do not take away the speaker's turn (Burgoon, Buller, & Woodall, 1989; Kennedy & Camden, 1988; Pearson & Spitzberg, 1990). Backchanneling cues include, for example, indicating **agreement** or disagreement through smiles or frowns, gestures of approval or disapproval, or brief comments, such as "right" or

Groucho Marx once observed, "Years ago, I tried to top everybody, but I don't anymore. I realized it was killing conversation. When you're always trying for a topper you aren't really listening. It ruins communication." What do you feel are "conversational killers?"

"never," as well as displaying **involvement** or boredom with the speaker through attentive or inattentive posture, forward or backward leaning, and focused or no eye contact. You can also give the speaker **pacing** cues, for example, to slow down by raising your hand near your ear and leaning forward or to speed up by continued nodding of your head. You can also ask for **clarification** with a puzzled facial expression, perhaps coupled with a forward lean.

Pay attention to turn-taking cues. In face-to-face conversation, look for verbal and nonverbal cues that tell you that the speaker wants to maintain or give up the turn as speaker and when a listener wants to say something (or simply remain a listener). In addition, pay attention to leave-taking cues, signals that the other person wants to end the conversation or the E-mail relationship.

The absence of gestures and facial expressions in E-mail systems makes misunderstanding more likely, so be sure to explain anything you suspect may not be clear. Use emoticons to show that you are being sarcastic or making a joke, for example. Don't be disturbed when the formalities customary in traditional letter writing are omitted in E-mail. Often E-mail is viewed more like a memo with the *to, from, subject, date,* and *courtesy copy recipients* in the preformatted heading. Still, it's important to remember, that different organizations will have different standards for what is considered acceptable E-mail style. Generally, the more formal the organization, the more likely is their E-mail style to be expected to resemble that of printed business correspondence. For example, in a formal organization emoticons would probably be avoided.

Feedback

The fourth step is the reverse of the second. Here you reflect back on the conversation to signal that as far as you're concerned the business is completed. And so you may say, for example, "So, you may want to send Jack a get well card" or "Wasn't that the dullest meeting you ever went to?"

Feedback can be looked upon in terms of five important dimensions: positive–negative, person-focused–message-focused, immediate–delayed; low monitoring–high monitoring, and critical–supportive. To give effective feedback, you need to make educated choices along each dimension (Figure 7.2).

Positive feedback (applause, smiles, head nods signifying approval, a "thank you" E-mail) tells the speaker or E-mail sender that the message is well-received and that he or she should continue communicating in the same general mode. **Negative** feedback (boos, puzzled looks, or verbal criticisms) tells the sender that something is wrong and that some adjustment needs to be made to the communication.

Feedback may be **person-focused** or **message-focused;** it may center on the person ("You're sweet," "You have a great smile") or on the message ("Can you repeat that phone number?" "Your argument is a good one"). In some situations (for example, giving criticism in a public speaking class), it's especially important to make clear that your feedback is message-focused—that you are critical of the speech's organization and not of the speaker as a person.

Positive	___:___:___:___:___:___ Negative
Person-focused	___:___:___:___:___:___ Message-focused
Immediate	___:___:___:___:___:___ Non-immediate
Low Monitoring	___:___:___:___:___:___ High Monitoring
Supportive	___:___:___:___:___:___ Critical

Figure 7.2 **Five Dimensions of Feedback**

It may be argued that, generally at least, your interpersonal relationships would be characterized by the labels on the left side of the figure. This "feedback model of relationships" would characterize close or intimate personal relationships as involving feedback that is strongly positive, person-focused, immediate, low in monitoring, and supportive. Acquaintance relationships might involve feedback somewhere in the middle of these scales. Relationships with those you dislike would involve feedback close to the right side of the scales, such as, negative, message-focused, delayed, highly monitored, and critical.

Feedback may be **immediate** or **delayed.** In interpersonal situations, feedback is most often sent immediately after the message is received. In other communication situations, however, the feedback may be delayed. Instructor evaluation questionnaires completed at the end of a course provide feedback long after the class began. When you applaud or ask questions of the public speaker or compliment the message in the previous E-mail, the feedback is also delayed. In interview situations, the feedback may come weeks afterward. In media situations, some feedback comes immediately through, for example, Nielsen ratings, while other feedback comes much later through viewing and buying patterns.

Another dimension of feedback is the variation from the spontaneous and totally honest reaction (**low-monitored** feedback) to the carefully constructed response designed to serve a specific purpose (**high-monitored** feedback). In most interpersonal situations you probably give feedback spontaneously; you allow your responses to show without any significant monitoring. At other times, however, you may be more guarded, for example, when your boss asks you what you think of the new direction the company is taking or when someone sends you an E-mail message asking for a big favor.

Critical feedback is evaluative. When you give critical feedback you judge another's performance as in, for example, evaluating a report or coaching someone learning a new skill. Feedback can also be **supportive** as when you console another, encourage the other to talk, or affirm another's self-definition.

Closing

The fifth and last step of the conversation process, the opposite of the first step, is the closing—the good-bye (Knapp, Hart, Friedrich, & Shulman, 1973; Knapp & Vangelisti, 1996). Like the opening, the closing is usually a combination of both verbal and nonverbal elements of communication. Most obviously, the closing signals the end of accessibility. Just as the opening signals access, the closing signals the intention to end access. The closing usually also signals some degree of supportiveness, for example, you express your pleasure in interacting: "Well, it was good talking with you." The closing may also summarize the interaction to offer more of a conclusion to the conversation.

Talking is like playing on the harp; there is as much in laying the hands on the strings to stop their vibration as in twanging them to bring out their music.
—*Oliver Wendell Holmes, Sr.*

Thinking About the Five Stages of Conversation

Conversation is a game of circles.

—*Ralph Waldo Emerson*

Not all conversations will be easily divided into these five steps. Often the opening and the feedforward are combined as when you see someone on campus, for example, and say "Hey, listen to this" or when in a work situation, someone says, "Well, folks, let's get the meeting going." In a similar way, the feedback and the closing might be combined: "Look, I've got to think more about this commitment, okay?"

As already noted, the business is the longest part of the conversation. The opening and the closing are usually about the same length as are the feedforward and feedback stages. When these relative lengths are severely distorted, you may feel that something is wrong. For example, when someone uses a long feedforward or too short an opening, you might suspect that what is to follow is extremely serious.

Different cultures vary the basic steps of conversation in different ways. In some cultures the openings are especially short, whereas in others the openings are elaborate, lengthy, and, in some cases, highly ritualized. It's easy in intercultural communication situations to violate another culture's conversational rules. Being overly friendly, too formal, or too forward may easily hinder the remainder of the conversation. The reasons why such violations may have significant consequences on the conversation is because you may not be aware of these rules and hence may not interpret violations as cultural differences but rather as aggressiveness, stuffiness, or pushiness—and almost immediately dislike the person and put a negative cast on future communications.

Blind and sighted people make use of the same vocal and verbal cues in managing a conversation, but the blind make little use of touch cues, postural shifts, and gestures (Sharkey & Stafford, 1990). What implications can be drawn from this finding for improving communication between blind and sighted persons?

This model may also help identify skill weaknesses and help distinguish effective and satisfying conversations from those that are ineffective and unsatisfying. Consider, for example, the following violations and how they can damage an entire conversation:

- The use of openings that are insensitive, for example, "Wow, you've gained a few pounds."
- The use of overly long feedforwards that make you wonder if the speaker will ever get to the business at hand.
- The omission of feedforward before a truly shocking message (for example, the death or illness of a friend or relative) that leads you to judge the other person as insensitive or uncaring.
- Conducting business without the normally expected greeting as when, for example, you go to a doctor who begins the conversation by saying, "Well, what's wrong?"
- The omission of feedback, which leads you to wonder if the speaker heard or read what you said.
- The omission of an appropriate closing that makes you wonder if the other person is disturbed or angry with you.

EFFECTIVE CONVERSATION

Conversation should be pleasant without scurrility, witty without affectation, free without indecency, learned without conceitedness, novel without falsehood.

—*William Shakespeare*

Recall from Chapter 4 that your listening effectiveness depends on your ability to make adjustments, for example, between empathic and objective listening. In a similar way your effectiveness in conversations depends on your ability to make adjustments along these dimensions: (1) openness, (2) empathy, (3) positiveness, (4) immediacy, (5) interaction management, (6) expressiveness, and (7) other-orientation (Figure 7.3).

As you read the discussions of these concepts, keep in mind that the most effective communicator in conversation (as you'll see later in this chapter on conflict) is one who is (1) flexible and who adapts to the individual situation, (2) mindful and aware of the situation and the available communication choices, and (3) uses metacommunication to avoid any real or potential ambiguity. (These concepts are discussed in greater detail in the section Thinking Critically About Conversation and Conflict at the end of the chapter.)

Open	___:___:___:___:___:___:___	Closed
Empathic	___:___:___:___:___:___:___	Objective
Positive	___:___:___:___:___:___:___	Negative
Immediate	___:___:___:___:___:___:___	Non-immediate
Satisfying	___:___:___:___:___:___:___	Unsatisfying
Expressive	___:___:___:___:___:___:___	Unexpressive
Other-oriented	___:___:___:___:___:___:___	Self-oriented

Figure 7.3   **The Dimensions of Interpersonal Effectiveness**

After you read this section, return to this figure and rate yourself on all seven qualities. What specific steps can you take to improve your interpersonal effectiveness?

Openness

Openness refers to your willingness to reveal information about yourself, your openness in listening to the other person, and the degree to which you "own" or acknowledge responsibility for your own feelings and thoughts. Consider the difference among these sentences:

1. Why did you say that? It was really inconsiderate.
2. Everyone thought your behavior was inconsiderate.
3. I was really disturbed when you told my father he was an old man.

Comments 1 and 2 do not show ownership of feelings. In comment 1, the speaker accuses the listener of being inconsiderate without assuming any of the responsibility for the judgment. In comment 2, the speaker assigns responsibility to the convenient, but elusive, "everyone" and again assumes none of the responsibility. Comment 3, however, is drastically different; here the speaker takes responsibility for his or her own feelings ("*I* was really disturbed").

When you own your own messages you use *I*-messages instead of *You*-messages. Instead of saying, "You make me feel so stupid when you ask what everyone else thinks but don't ask my opinion," the person who owns his or her feelings says "I feel stupid when you ask everyone else what they think but don't ask me." When you use I-messages and own your feelings and thoughts, you say in effect, "This is how *I* feel," "This is how *I* see the situation," "This is what *I* think," with the *I* always paramount. In this way you make it explicit that your feelings are the result of the interaction between what is going on in the world *outside* your self (what others say, for example) and what is going on *inside* your self (your perceptions, preconceptions, attitudes, and prejudices, for example).

Empathy

To *empathize* with someone is to feel as that person feels. When you feel empathy for another, you're are able to experience what the other is experiencing from that person's point of view. Empathy does *not* mean that you agree with what the other person says or does. You never lose your own identity or your attitudes and beliefs. To *sympathize,* on the other hand, is to feel *for* the individual—to feel sorry for the person, for example. To empathize is to feel the same feelings in the same way as the other person does. Empathy, then, enables you to understand, emotionally and intellectually, what another person is experiencing. The other half of this aspect of communication is objectivity, to remain objective and view what the speaker says and feels as an objective, totally disinterested third-party observer would.

Most people find it easier to communicate empathy in response to a person's positive statements (Heiskell & Rychiak, 1986). Perhaps you will have to exert special effort to communicate empathy for negative messages. When you experience empathy and wish to communicate it to the speaker, try the following suggestions.

Confront mixed messages that are communicated simultaneously but which contradict each other, for example, *You say that it doesn't bother you*

Why do statements such as "You make me so angry," "You make me feel stupid," and "You never want to have any fun" cause interpersonal difficulties?

Beware of people who don't know how to say "I am sorry." They are weak and frightened, and will, sometimes at the slightest provocation, fight with the desperate ferocity of a frightened animal that feels cornered.

—*Thomas Szasz*

Animal researchers have argued that some animals show empathy. For example, consider the male gorilla who watched a female try in vain to get water that collected in an automobile tire and who then secured the tire and brought it to the female. This gorilla, it has been argued, demonstrated empathy; he felt the other gorilla's thirst (Angier, 1995). Similarly, the animal who cringes when another of its species gets hurt seems also to be showing empathy. What evidence would you demand before believing that animals possess empathic abilities? What evidence would you want before believing that a relationship partner or a friend feels empathy for you?

Research shows that people pass along negative gossip more than positive gossip (Walker & Blaine, 1991). Do you find this to be true? Try to recall the last five or six gossip stories you heard. How many of these were positive? How many were negative?

but I seem to hear a lot of anger coming through. In doing so, be especially careful to avoid judgmental and evaluative (nonempathic) responses. Avoid "should" and "ought" statements that tell the other person how he or she *should* feel. For example, avoid expressions such as *don't feel so bad, don't cry, cheer up, in time you'll forget all about this,* and *you should start dating others; by next month you won't even remember her name.*

Use reinforcing comments. Let the speaker know that you understand what the speaker is saying and encourage the speaker to continue talking about this issue. For example, use comments such as *I see, I get it, I understand, yes,* and *right.*

Demonstrate interest by maintaining eye contact. Avoid scanning the room or focusing on objects or persons other than the person with whom you're interacting. Maintain physical closeness (avoid large spaces between yourself and the other person), lean toward (not away from) the other person, and communicate your interest and agreement nonverbally, with your facial expressions, head nods, and eye movements.

How empathic do you consider yourself to be? Who is the most empathic person you've ever met? How did this person communicate her or his empathic feeling?

Positiveness

In most situations you strive to increase positiveness, although we should not ignore the importance of communicating negatively. For example, if you communicated your criticism to one of your work assistants in too positive a tone, you might defeat the very purpose of your own criticism. For example, people who smile while giving criticism are believed less than those who use more negative facial expressions.

Generally, however, you want to communicate positiveness. To do so, you can state positive attitudes and you can compliment the person with

There can be no doubt that everyone spends a great deal of time gossiping. In fact, gossip seems universal among cultures (Laing, 1993) and among some it's a commonly accepted ritual (Hall, 1993). Gossip, third-party talk about another person, is an inevitable part of daily interactions. Not gossiping would eliminate one of the most frequent and enjoyable forms of communication.

In some instances, however, gossip is unethical (Bok, 1983). For example, it's unethical to reveal information that you've promised to keep secret. Although this principle may seem too obvious to even mention, it's frequently violated. For example, in a study of 133 school executives, board presidents, and superintendents, the majority received communications that violated an employee's right to confidentiality (Wilson & Bishard, 1994). When keeping the information secret may result in more harm than good (Bok offers the example of the teenager who confides a suicide plan), the information should be revealed only to those who must know it, not to the world at large. Gossip is also unethical when it invades the privacy that everyone has a right to, for example, when it concerns matters that are no one else's business and when the gossip can hurt the individuals involved. Of course, gossip is unethical when it is known to be false and is nevertheless passed on to others.

Although not easy to identify in any given instance, these conditions do provide excellent starting points for asking yourself whether or not talking about another person is ethical. Consider:

- Is it ethical to reveal information that would typically be considered private if you were not explicitly told to keep it secret?
- Under what conditions would revealing another person's secrets be ethical? Are there times when the failure to reveal such secrets would be unethical?
- You're in a conversation and observe the following: Ricky and Jose are discussing Terry. Ricky makes a number of statements about Terry that you know to be false. Is it ethical for you to say nothing? Does it matter whether these statements about Terry are positive or negative?
- Is it ethical to observe someone (without his or her knowledge) and report your observations to others? For example, would it be ethical to observe your communication professor on a date with a student or smoking marijuana and then report these observations back to your classmates?
- Is it ethical to forward someone's E-mail to third parties without the sender's permission?

[The next Ethical Issue box appears on page 214.]

whom you interact. Positiveness in attitudes also demonstrates a positive feeling for the general communication situation and makes you feel a welcomed part of the conversation. Negativeness, on the other hand, may make you feel that you're unwelcomed and you feel that communication breakdown will come soon.

Positiveness can be seen most clearly in the way you phrase statements. Consider these two sentences:

1. You look horrible in stripes.
2. You look your best, I think, in solid colors.

The first sentence is critical and will almost surely provoke an argument. The second sentence, on the other hand, expresses the speaker's thought clearly and positively and should encourage responses that are cooperative.

In communicating positiveness don't exaggerate; positive comments and compliments work best when they're realistic and not blown out of proportion. Try to be specific; instead of saying, "I liked your speech," say why you liked the speech: "Your introduction really got my attention; I especially liked the anecdote about your first day on the job." Throughout this positive exchange, own your own messages: say "I liked your report" instead of "Your report was well received."

Finally, make sure your verbal and nonverbal messages are consistent. If your comments are genuinely felt, then your verbal and nonverbal messages are likely to be consistent; if you're only pretending to be positive, your nonverbals may betray your real feelings.

Immediacy

Immediacy refers to the degree to which the speaker and listener are connected or joined. "High immediacy" refers to extreme closeness and connection, while "low immediacy" refers to distance and a lack of togetherness. The communicator who demonstrates high immediacy conveys a sense of interest and attention, a liking for and an attraction to the other person. People generally respond favorably to high immediacy.

You can communicate immediacy in many ways. Nonverbally, you can maintain appropriate eye contact, limit looking around at others, maintain a physical closeness which suggests a psychological closeness, and use a direct and open body posture by, for example, by arranging your body to keep others out of "your private conversation."

Use the other person's name, for example, say "*Joe,* what do *you* think?" instead of "What do you think?" Let the speaker know that you've heard and understood what was said and will base your feedback on it. Using questions that ask for clarification or elaboration as well as referring to the speaker's previous remarks will help achieve immediacy.

Reinforce, reward, or compliment the other person. Make use of such expressions as "I like your new outfit" or "Your comments were really to the

"Clemson here. How may I disappoint you?"

point." Smile and otherwise express that you're interested in and care about the other person and what he or she is saying.

There are, however, times when you may want to communicate a lack of immediacy, for example, in discouraging romantic advances, criticizing a subordinate, or registering a complaint. Obviously, in these situations, you would seek to avoid using the suggestions offered above.

Interaction Management

The effective communicator manages the interaction to the satisfaction of both parties. In most cases you would manage the interaction so that the other person feels ignored or on stage, and so that he or she can contribute effectively to the total communication interchange. Maintaining your role as speaker or listener and passing back and forth the opportunity to speak are interaction management skills. If one person speaks all the time while the other listens, effective conversation becomes difficult, if not impossible. Here are two suggestions for effective interactive management.

To effectively manage interaction avoid interrupting the other person; interruption signals that what you have to say is more important than what the other person is saying and puts him or her in an inferior position. The result is dissatisfaction with the conversation. Also, keep the conversation flowing and fluent to avoid long and awkward pauses that make everyone uncomfortable.

One of the best ways to look at interaction management is to take the self-test, "Are You a High Self-Monitor?" This test will help you identify personal qualities that assist the effective management of interpersonal communication situations.

Beware of allowing a tactless word, a rebuttal, a rejection to obliterate the whole sky.
—*Anaïs Nin*

Test Yourself | Are You a High Self-Monitor?

Instructions: These statements are written to elicit personal reactions to a number of different situations. No two statements are exactly alike, so consider each statement carefully before answering. If a statement is true, or mostly true, as applied to you, respond with T. If a statement is false, or not usually true, as applied to you, respond with F.

_____ 1. I find it hard to imitate the behavior of other people.
_____ 2. I guess I do put on a show to impress or entertain people.
_____ 3. I would probably make a good actor.
_____ 4. I sometimes appear to others to be experiencing deeper emotions than I actually am.
_____ 5. In a group of people, I am rarely the center of attention.
_____ 6. In different situations and with different people, I often act like very different persons.
_____ 7. I can only argue for ideas I already believe.
_____ 8. In order to get along and be liked, I tend to be what people expect me to be rather than who I really am.
_____ 9. I may deceive people by being friendly when I really dislike them.
_____ 10. I am always the person I appear to be.

Thinking Critically About Self-Monitoring Give yourself one point for each of questions 1, 5, and 7 that you answered F. Give yourself one point for each of the remaining questions that you answered T. Add up your points. If you are a good judge of yourself and scored 7 or above, you are probably a high self-monitoring individual; if you scored 3 or below, you are probably a low self-monitoring individual.

Self-Monitoring, the manipulation of the image that you present to others in your interpersonal interactions, is integrally related to interpersonal interaction management. High self-monitors carefully adjust their behaviors on the basis of feedback from others so that they produce the most desirable effect. Low self-monitors are not concerned with the image they present to others. Rather, they communicate their thoughts and feelings with no attempt to manipulate the impressions they create. Most of us lie somewhere between the two extremes.

High self-monitors are more apt to take charge of a situation, are more sensitive to the deceptive techniques of others, and are better able to detect self-monitoring or impression management techniques when used by others. High self-monitors prefer to interact with low self-monitors over whom they are able to assume positions of influence and power (Snyder, 1986). These, of course, are the extremes; most of us engage in selective self-monitoring. For example, if you go for a job interview, you are more likely to monitor your behavior than if you were talking with a group of friends.

Source: This test appeared in Mark Snyder, "The Many Me's of the Self-Monitor," *Psychology Today 13* (March 1980): 34. Copyright © 1980 by Sussex Publishers Inc. Reprinted by permission of Mark Snyder.

Expressiveness

Expressiveness refers to the degree to which you display involvement in the interaction. The expressive speaker plays the game instead of just watching it as a spectator. *Expressiveness* includes taking responsibility for your thoughts and feelings, encouraging expressiveness or openness in others, and providing direct and honest feedback.

Expressiveness also includes taking responsibility for both talking and listening and in this way is similar to interaction management. In conflict situations, discussed later in this chapter, expressiveness involves fighting actively and stating disagreement directly. It's the opposite of fighting passively, withdrawing from the encounter, or attributing responsibility to others.

When you want to communicate expressiveness, use I-messages to signal personal involvement and a willingness to share your feelings. Instead of saying "You never give me a chance to make any decisions," say "I'd like to contribute to the decisions that affect both of us." Avoid clichés and trite expressions that signal a lack of personal involvement and originality.

Vary your vocal rate, pitch, volume, and rhythm to convey involvement and interest and allow your facial muscles to reflect and echo this inner involvement. Use gestures appropriately; too few gestures may signal disinterest, while too many may communicate discomfort, uneasiness, and awkwardness.

Most of us know how to say nothing;
few of us know when.
—*Anonymous*

Because your expressiveness rewards the other person's talking, it encourages more talk. When you want to discourage a talkative person or when you want to avoid leading the speaker in any way, you may wish to limit your expressiveness.

Other-Orientation

Other-orientation is the generally desired mode of communication. It involves the ability to communicate attentiveness and interest in the other person and in what is being said. Without other-orientation each person pursues his or her own goal; cooperation and working together to achieve a common goal are absent.

Other-orientation demonstrates consideration and respect—for example, asking if it's all right to dump your troubles on someone before doing so or asking if your phone call comes at an inconvenient time before launching into your conversation. Other-orientation involves acknowledging others' feelings as legitimate: "I can understand why you're angry; I would be, too."

You can communicate other-orientation with, for example, eye contact, smiles, and head nods. Leaning toward the other person and revealing feelings and emotions through appropriate facial expressions also communicate a concern for the other person.

Focus on the person to whom you're speaking rather than focusing on yourself (avoid primping or preening, for example) or on any third person (through frequent or prolonged eye contact or body orientation).

Use "minimal responses" to encourage the other person to express himself or herself. These brief expressions encourage other people to continue talking without intruding on their thoughts and feelings or directing them to go in any particular direction. For example, *yes, I see,* or even *a-ha* or *hmm* are minimal responses that tell the other person that you're interested in learning what he or she has to say. Express agreement when appropriate. Comments such as "You're right" or "That's interesting" help to focus the interaction on the other person that encourages greater openness.

Use positive affect statements to refer to the other person and to his or her contributions to the conversation. For example, *I really enjoy talking with you* or *That was a clever way of looking at things* are positive affect statements that are often felt but rarely expressed. Ask the other person for suggestions, opinions, and clarification as appropriate. Statements such as "How do you feel about it?" or "What do you think?" will focus the communication on the other person.

There are times, of course, when you may want to be more self-oriented and self-focused. For example, in employment interview situations, the interviewee is expected to talk about himself or herself and to do more speaking than listening. Similarly, if you're being interviewed because of something you accomplished, you're expected to focus the conversation on yourself. In these situations, you would obviously not ask the interviewer for suggestions or opinions or use minimal responses to encourage the interviewer to express himself or herself. You would be positive, use focused eye contact, lean toward the other person, and so on.

What quality of interpersonal communication effectiveness most closely draws you to others? What quality is the most difficult for you to incorporate into your own interpersonal behaviors? Why?

Table 7.1 Talking with a Deaf Person*

- Get the deaf person's attention before speaking.
- Key the deaf person into the topic of discussion.
- Speak slowly and clearly, but do not yell, exaggerate, or overpronounce.
- Look directly at the deaf person when speaking.
- Do not place anything in your mouth when speaking.
- Maintain eye contact with the deaf person.
- Use the words "I" and "you."
- Avoid standing in front of a light source, such as a window or bright light. The glare and shadows created on the face make it almost impossible for the deaf person to speechread.
- First, repeat, then try to rephrase a thought if you have problems being understood, rather than repeating the same words again.
- Use pantomime, body language, and facial expression to help supplement your communication.
- Be courteous to the deaf person during conversation. If the telephone rings or someone knocks at the door, excuse yourself and tell the deaf person that you are answering the phone or responding to the knock.

* From *Tips for Communicating with Deaf People.* Reprinted by permission of the Rochester Institute of Technology, National Technical Institute for the Deaf, Division of Public Affairs, One Lomb Memorial Drive, Post Office Box 9887, Rochester, New York 14623-0887, Phone: (716)475-6824.

Not surprisingly, other orientation is especially important in communicating with a person who has a handicap such as deafness. Table 7.1 offers some useful suggestions for communicating with a deaf person.

CONFLICT

Tom wants to go to the movies and Sara wants to stay home. Tom's insisting on going to the movies interferes with Sara's staying home and Sara's determination to stay home interferes with Tom's going to the movies.

> Where there is no difference, there is only indifference.
> —*Louis Nizer*

Listening to Conflict Starters

Usually, conflicts develop over time; they begin with a word here and a disagreement there and gradually a fully developed conflict blows up in your face. Recognizing the beginnings of conflict—the first stirrings—can help you diffuse it or bring it into the open before it explodes. The art, of course, is to be able to hear these beginnings in your own speech and in that of others. So, try to listen for conflict starters. For each situation given here, rewrite the statement in a more productive form—a statement that would diffuse disagreement or difference.

Conflict "Starters"

1. You're late again. You're always late. You're so inconsiderate of my time, my interests.
2. I can't bear another weekend sitting home watching television. I'm not going to do it.
3. You think I'm fat, don't you?
4. You should have been more available when he needed us. I was always at work.
5. You shouldn't have said that. I hate when you do that.

What principles of conflict management can you derive from this experience?

[The next Listen to This box appears on page 205.]

Randy and Grace have been dating. Randy wants to get married; Grace wants to continue dating. Each couple is experiencing interpersonal conflict, a situation in which the people (Hocker & Wilmot, 1985; Folger, Poole, & Stutman, 1997):

- are interdependent; what one person does has an effect on the other person
- perceive their goals to be incompatible; if one person's goal is achieved the other's cannot be
- see each other as interfering with his or her own goal achievement

In one sentence, how would you describe your style of conflict?

Think about the issues you (and your romantic partner, your friends, your work colleagues, your family) argue about and make a list of the five or six issues that most frequently create conflict. Do this before looking at Table 7.2 or the bulleted list that follows, which represent the results of two research studies. In the first study gay, lesbian, and heterosexual couples were surveyed on the issues they argued about most; the findings are presented in Table 7.2 (Kurdek, 1994).

In another study, four conditions led up to a couple's "first big fight" (Siegert & Stamp, 1994):

- uncertainty over commitment
- jealousy
- violation of expectations
- personality differences

The types and nature of conflict can be further described by reference to the concepts of content and relationship that were developed earlier (Chapter 1).

Table 7.2 Interpersonal Conflict Issues

This table presents the rank order of the six most frequently argued about issues (1 = the most argued about). Note the striking similarity among all couples. It seems that affectional orientation has little to do with the topics people argue about. Are these topics similar to those you argue about? Are these topics similar to those your friends and colleagues argue about?

Issue	Gay (N = 75)	Lesbian (N = 51)	Heterosexual (N = 108)
Intimacy issues such as affection and sex	1	1	1
Power issues such as excessive demands or possessiveness, lack of equality in the relationship, friends, and leisure time	2	2	2
Personal flaws issues such as drinking or smoking, personal grooming, and driving style	3	3	4
Personal distance issues such as frequently being absent and school or job commitments	4	4	5
Social issues such as politics and social issues, parents, and personal values	5	5	3
Distrust issues such as previous lovers and lying	6	6	6

Differences in opinion lead to inquiry, and inquiry to truth.
—*Thomas Jefferson*

Content and Relationship Conflicts

Content conflict centers on objects, events, and persons in the world that are usually, but not always, external to the parties involved in the conflict. These include the millions of issues that we argue about every day—the value of a particular movie, what to watch on television, the fairness of the last examination or job promotion, and the way to spend our savings.

Relationship conflicts are equally numerous and include such situations as a younger brother refusing to obey his older brother, partners who each want an equal say in making vacation plans, and a mother and daughter who each want to have the final word concerning the daughter's life-style. Here conflicts do not arise as much from an external object as from relationships between individuals, with such issues as who is in charge, the equality of a primary relationship, and who has the right to establish rules of behavior.

Like many such concepts, content and relationship conflicts are easier to separate in a textbook than they are in real life, where many conflicts contain elements of both. However, it helps in understanding and in effectively managing conflict, if you can recognize those issues that pertain to content (primarily) and those that pertain to relationship (primarily).

Can you identify an interpersonal conflict that had no relationship aspects to it? Can you identify both positive and negative aspects of a specific conflict that you engaged in?

Myths About Conflict

One of the problems in dealing with interpersonal conflict is that we may be operating with false assumptions about what conflict is and what it means. For example, do you think the following are true or false?

- If two people in a relationship experience conflict, it means their relationship is in trouble.
- Conflict hurts an interpersonal relationship.
- Conflict is bad because it reveals our negative selves, for example, our pettiness, our need to control, our unreasonable expectations.

As with most things, simple answers are usually wrong. The three assumptions above may all be true or may all be false. It depends. In and of itself, conflict is neither good nor bad. Conflict is a part of every interpersonal relationship, between parents and children, brothers and sisters, friends, lovers, and co-workers. If it isn't, then the relationship is probably dull, irrelevant, or insignificant. So, it's not so much the conflict that creates a problem as the way in which you deal with the conflict. Because of this, the major portion of this chapter focuses on ways of managing conflict rather than avoiding it.

The Negatives and Positives of Conflict

Conflict can lead to both negative and positive effects. Among the potential negative effects is that it may lead to increased negative feelings for your "opponent" (who may be your best friend or lover). It may cause a depletion of energy better spent on other areas. Or, it can lead you to close yourself off from the other person, to shrink the size of your open self. When you hide your true self from an intimate, you prevent meaningful communication.

The aim of an argument or discussion should not be victory, but progress.
—*Joseph Jourbert*

What beliefs do you have about conflict? How do these beliefs influence the way you engage in conflict?

The major positive value of interpersonal conflict is that it forces you to examine a problem that you may otherwise avoid and work toward a potential solution. If productive conflict strategies are used, a stronger, healthier, and more satisfying relationship may well emerge from the encounter. The very fact that you're trying to resolve a conflict means that you feel the relationship is worth the effort—otherwise you'd walk away from such conflict. Through conflict you learn more about each other and with that knowledge comes understanding.

Cultural Context

The cultural context is important in understanding and in effectively managing conflict. Culture influences the issues that people argue about as well as what are considered appropriate or inappropriate strategies for dealing with conflict. For example, cohabiting 18-year-olds are more likely to experience conflict with their parents about their living style if they lived in the United States than if they lived in Sweden where cohabitation is much more accepted. Similarly, male infidelity is more likely to cause conflict among American couples than among southern European couples. Students from the United States are more likely to engage in conflict with another United States student than with someone from another culture. Chinese students, on the other hand, are more likely to engage in a conflict with a non-Chinese student than with a Chinese (Leung, 1988).

The types of conflicts that arise depend on the cultural orientation of the individuals involved. For example, it's likely that in collectivist cultures, such as Ecuador, Indonesia, and Korea, conflicts are more likely to center on violating collective or group norms and values. Conversely, in

If we understand others' languages, but not their culture, we can make fluent fools of ourselves.
    —William B. Gudykunst

individualist cultures, such as the United States, Canada, and Western Europe, conflicts are more likely to occur when individual norms are violated (Ting-Toomey, 1985).

The ways in which members of different cultures express conflict also differ. In Japan and China, for example, it's especially important that you not embarrass the person with whom you're in conflict, especially if that conflict occurs in public (Westwood, Tang, & Kirkbride, 1992). This face-saving principle prohibits the use of such strategies as personal rejection or verbal aggressiveness. In the United States, men and women, ideally at least, are both expected to express their desires and complaints openly and directly. Many Middle Eastern and Pacific Rim cultures would discourage women from such expressions. Rather, a more agreeable and accepting posture would be expected. Native Americans suppress interpersonal conflict by teaching, for example, sharing, noncompetitiveness, and emotional restraint (Brant, 1990).

Even within a given general culture, more specific cultures differ from each other in their methods of conflict management. African American men and women and European American men and women, for example, engage in conflict in very different ways (Kochman, 1981). The issues that cause conflict and that aggravate conflict, the conflict strategies that are expected and accepted, and the entire attitude toward conflict vary from one group to the other.

For example, African American men prefer to manage conflict with clear arguments and a focus on problem solving. African American women, however, deal with conflict by acting assertively (Collier, 1991). In another study, African American females were found to use more direct controlling strategies (for example, assuming control over the conflict and arguing persistently for their point of view) than did European American females. European American females, on the other hand, used more problem solution-oriented conflict management styles than did African American women. Interestingly, African American and European American men were very similar in their conflict management strategies: both tended to avoid or withdraw from relationship conflict. They preferred to keep quiet about their differences or downplay their significance (Ting-Toomey, 1986).

Among Mexican Americans, men prefer to achieve mutual understanding through discussing the reasons for the conflict while women focused on being supportive of the relationship. Among Anglo Americans, men preferred direct and rational argument while women preferred flexibility. These, of course, are merely examples, but the underlying principle is that techniques for dealing with interpersonal conflict will be viewed differently by different cultures.

Conflict on the Net

Even in cyberspace, you can experience conflict. On the Internet conflict occurs for the same reasons and deals with the same topics as it does in face-to-face interactions. Thus, the suggestions for dealing with conflict remain essentially the same for computer-mediated and face-to-face encounters. There is one source of conflict that is unique to cyberspace and that is the conflict created when the rules of netiquette, the rules for communicating

Are you more likely to pursue a conflict with someone from your own culture or someone from a different culture? If there is a difference, did you learn this difference from your culture?

politely over the Internet, are violated or ignored. You can avoid this source of conflict by following these rules of netiquette:

- Read the Frequently Asked Questions (FAQs). Before asking questions about the system, go to the FAQ page and see if you can find an answer to your question. Chances are that your question has probably been asked before. This way you'll put less strain on the system and will be less likely to annoy other users.
- Don't shout. WRITING IN ALL CAPS IS PERCEIVED AS SHOUTING. While it's acceptable to use caps occasionally to achieve emphasis, it's better to underline, like this, or use asterisks *like this.*
- Lurk before speaking. Lurking is reading the posted notices and conversations without contributing. In computer communication, lurking is good, not bad. Lurking educates you about the rules of a particular group and helps you avoid saying things you'd like to take back.
- Be brief. Follow the "maxim of quantity" by communicating only the information that's needed; follow the "maxim of manner" by communicating clearly, briefly, and in an organized way (Chapter 5).
- Be kind when talking to newbies; remember that you were one once yourself.
- Don't send commercial messages to those who didn't request them. Junk mail is junk mail; but on the Internet, the receiver has to waste time downloading, reading, and deleting these unwanted messages.
- Don't spam. Spamming is sending someone unsolicited mail, repeatedly sending the same mail, or posting the same message on many bulletin boards, mailing lists, or newsgroups especially when the message is irrelevant to the group's focus. Like electronic junk mail, spamming is frowned upon because it costs people money. Another reason it's viewed negatively, of course, is because it clogs the system, slowing it down for everyone and wasting everyone's time.
- Don't flame. Flaming is personally attacking another user. Personal attacks are best avoided on the Internet as they are in face-to-face conflicts. Thus, avoid flaming and participating in flame wars.
- Don't troll. Trolling is posting information you know to be false just so you can watch other people correct you. It's a waste of others' time and of the system's resources.

Before and After the Conflict

If you're to make conflict truly productive, you'll need to consider a few suggestions for preparing for the conflict and for using the conflict as a method for relational growth.

Before the Conflict Try to fight in private. In front of others, you may not be willing to be totally honest; you may feel you have to save face and therefore must win the fight at all costs. You also run the risk of incurring resentment and hostility by embarrassing your partner in front of others.

Although conflicts typically arise at the most inopportune times, you can choose the time when you will try to resolve them. Confronting your partner when she or he comes home after a hard day of work may not be the right time for resolving a conflict. Make sure you're both relatively free of other problems and ready to deal with the conflict at hand.

Know what you're fighting about. Only when you define your differences in specific terms, can you begin to understand and resolve them. Fight about problems that can be solved. Fighting about past behaviors or about family members or situations over which you have no control is usually counterproductive.

After the Conflict Learn from the conflict and from the process you went through in trying to resolve it. For example, can you identify the fight strategies that aggravated the situation? Does your partner need a cooling-off period? Do you need extra space when upset? Can you tell when minor issues are going to escalate into major arguments? Does avoidance make matters worse? What issues are particularly disturbing and likely to cause conflicts? Can these be avoided?

Keep the conflict in perspective. Be careful not to blow it out of proportion where you begin to define your relationship in terms of conflict. Avoid the tendency to see disagreement as inevitably leading to major blow-ups. Conflicts in most relationships actually occupy a very small percentage of the couple's time and yet, in their recollection, they often loom extremely large.

Attack your negative feelings. Negative feelings frequently arise because unfair fight strategies were used to undermine the other person—for example, personal rejection, manipulation, or force. Resolve surely to avoid such unfair tactics in the future, but at the same time let go of guilt and blame, for yourself and your partner. If you think it would help, discuss these feelings with your partner or even a therapist.

Increase the exchange of rewards and cherishing behaviors to demonstrate your positive feelings and that you are over the conflict. It's a good way of saying you want the relationship to survive and flourish.

EFFECTIVE CONFLICT MANAGEMENT

Throughout the process of resolving conflict, avoid the common but damaging strategies that can destroy a relationship. At the same time, consciously apply the strategies that will help resolve the conflict and even improve the relationship. Here we consider seven general strategies each of which has a destructive and a productive dimension: win–lose and win–win strategies, avoidance and fair fighting, force and talk, gunny-sacking and present focus, face-enhancing and face-detracting strategies, attack and acceptance, and verbal aggressiveness and argumentativeness.

The test of a man's or woman's breeding is how they behave in a quarrel.
—George Bernard Shaw

Win–Lose and Win–Win Strategies

In any interpersonal conflict, you have a choice. You can look for solutions in which one person wins, usually you, and the other person loses, usually the other person (win–lose solutions). Or you can look for solutions in which you and the other person both win (win–win solutions). Obviously, win–win solutions are the more desirable, at least when the conflict is interpersonal. Too often, however, we fail to even consider the possibility of win–win solutions and what they might be.

For example, let's say that I want to spend our money on a new car (my old one is unreliable) and you want to spend it on a vacation (you're exhausted and want to rest). Through conflict and its resolution, we hope to learn what each really wants. We may then be able to figure out a way for each of us to get what we want. I might accept a good used car and you might accept a less expensive vacation. Or we might buy a used car and take an inexpensive road trip. Each of these solutions will satisfy both of us—they are win–win solutions—each of us wins, and gets what we want. Additional examples of win–win strategies as they might be used in an actual problem situation are provided in Chapter 10 and Skill Development Experience 7.2 provides practice in developing win–win strategies.

Avoidance and Fighting Actively

Avoidance is physical or psychological withdrawal from the conflict situation. Sometimes it involves physical flight—you leave the scene of the conflict (walk out of the apartment or go to another part of the office). Sometimes it involves setting up a physical barrier like blasting the stereo or locking the door. Sometimes it takes the form of emotional or intellectual avoidance. In this case you leave the conflict psychologically by not dealing with any of the arguments or problems raised, much like the gentleman in the cartoon who'd rather end the discussion before it begins.

Instead of avoiding the issues, take an active role in your interpersonal conflicts. This is not to say that a cooling-off period is not at times desirable. It is to say, instead, that if you wish to resolve conflicts, you need to confront them actively.

Another part of active fighting involves taking responsibility for your thoughts and feelings. For example, when you disagree with your partner or find fault with her or his behavior, take responsibility for these feelings, use I-messages as described earlier in this chapter. For example, you can say, "I disagree with . . ." or "I don't like it when you . . . ." Avoid statements that deny your responsibility, for example, "Everybody thinks you're wrong about . . ." or "Chris thinks you shouldn't . . . ."

Force and Talk

When confronted with conflict, many people prefer not to deal with the issues but rather to emotionally or physically force their position on the other person. In either case, however, the conflict at hand is avoided and the person who "wins" is the one who exerts the most force. This technique is commonly used by warring nations, children, and even some normally sensible and mature adults. This is surely one of the most serious problems confronting relationships today, but many approach it as if it were of only minor importance or even something humorous, as in the cartoon on page 175.

More than 50% of both single and married couples reported that they had experienced physical violence in their relationship. If we add symbolic violence (for example, threatening to hit the other person or throwing something), the percentages are above 60% for singles and above 70% for marrieds (Marshall & Rose, 1987). In another study, 47% of a sample of 410 college students reported some experience with violence in a dating relationship. In most cases, the violence was reciprocal—each person

Never go to bed mad. Stay up and fight.
—*Phyllis Diller*

Why are men more likely to withdraw from a conflict than are women? What arguments can you present for or against any of these reasons (Noller, 1993): Because men have difficulty dealing with conflict? Because the culture has taught men to avoid it? Because withdrawal is an expression of power?

You cannot shake hands with a clenched fist.
—*Indira Gandhi*

"Let me finish! You always say, 'You win' before I've won!"

Modern Maturity

in the relationship used violence. In cases in which only one person was violent, the research results are conflicting. For example, Deal and Wampler (1986) found that in cases were one partner was violent, the aggressor was significantly more often the female partner. Other research, however, has found that the popular conception of men being more likely to use force than women is indeed true (DeTurck, 1987): Men are more apt than women to use violent methods to achieve compliance.

One of the most puzzling findings is that many victims of violence interpret it as a sign of love. For some reason, they see being beaten, verbally abused, or raped as a sign that their partner is fully in love with them. Many victims, in fact, accept the blame for contributing to the violence instead of blaming their partners (Gelles & Cornell, 1985; Ehrensaft & Vivian, 1996).

The only real alternative to force is talk. Instead of force, talk and listen. The qualities of openness, empathy, and positiveness, for example, discussed earlier are suitable starting points.

Why do you think so many victims interpret violence as a sign of love? What part does force or violence play in your own interpersonal relationship conflicts?

Gunnysacking and Present Focus

Gunnysacking refers to the practice of storing up grievances (as in a gunnysack, a large bag usually of burlap) so we may unload them at another time. The immediate occasion may be relatively simple (or so it might seem at first), such as someone's coming home late without calling. Instead

CHAPTER 7: Interpersonal Communication: Conversation and Conflict   **175**

"What's amazing to me is that this late in the game we _still_ have to settle our differences with rocks."

of arguing about this, the gunnysacker unloads all past grievances. The birthday you forgot 2 years ago, the time you arrived late for dinner last month, the hotel reservations you forgot to make are all noted. As you probably know from experience, when one person gunnysacks, the other person often reciprocates. As a result two people end up dumping their stored-up grievances on one another. Frequently the original problem never gets addressed. Instead, resentment and hostility escalate.

Power Perspective 7.2

Power Plays: Ignoring and Neutralizing

What do you do when confronted by power plays such as **Nobody Upstairs, You Owe Me,** or **Thought Stoppers,** as discussed on page 159 (Steiner, 1981; Steiner & Perry, 1997)? One common response is **to ignore** it and allow the other person to control the conversation and you. You might ignore this behavior out of the fear that if you object, it might start an argument. Or, you just might not see this behavior as a way of maintaining power and controlling your behavior.

Another response is **to neutralize** the power play by treating it as an isolated instance (rather than as a consistent pattern of behavior) and object to it. For example, you might say, "Please don't use my computer when I'm out of the office" or "Please don't open my mail."

Neither of these responses is necessarily bad or inappropriate; they just do not stop the behavior pattern.

[The next Power Perspective offers a way to stop the pattern and appears on page 177.]

A present focus is far more constructive. Focus your conflict on the here-and-now rather than on issues that occurred in the past (as in gunnysacking). Similarly, focus your conflict on the person with whom you're fighting, not on the person's mother, child, or friends.

Face-Enhancing and Face-Detracting Strategies

Another dimension of conflict strategies is that of face orientation. Face-detracting or face-attacking strategies involve treating the other person as incompetent, untrustworthy, or bad (Donahue & Kolt, 1992). Such attacks can vary from mildly embarrassing the other person to severely damaging his or her ego or reputation. When such attacks become extreme they may be similar to verbal aggressiveness—a tactic explained in the next section.

Face-enhancing techniques help the other person maintain a positive image, one of a person who is competent, trustworthy, and good. There is some evidence to show that even when you get what you want, for example, at bargaining, it's wise to help the other person retain positive face. This makes it less likely that future conflicts will arise (Donahue & Kolt, 1992). Not surprisingly, people are more likely to make a greater effort to support the listener's "face" if they like the listener than if they don't (Meyer, 1994).

Generally, collectivist cultures like Korea and Japan place greater emphasis on face, especially on maintaining a positive image in public. Face is generally less crucial in individualist cultures, such as the United States. Yet, there are significant exceptions that require us to qualify any such

Can you identify examples of face-detracting or face-enhancing strategies that were used during your last interpersonal conflict? Are you more likely to use one rather than the other type of strategy?

Power Perspective 7.3

Power Plays: Cooperating

In addition to responding to power plays by ignoring or neutralizing them, you can also respond cooperatively with this three-part strategy—a strategy that is more likely to stop the power play pattern (Steiner, 1981):

- Express your feelings. Tell the person that you're angry or annoyed or disturbed by his or her behavior.
- *Describe* the behavior to which you object, for example, reading your mail or trying to hug you.
- State a cooperative response. Tell the person what you want: "I want you to stop reading my mail." "I want you to stop trying to hug me."

A cooperative response to **Nobody Upstairs** might go like this: "I'm angry [*statement of feelings*] that you persist in going through my E-mail. You've done this four times this week [*description of the behavior*]. I want to keep my own mail private. If there's anything in it that concerns you, I'll let you know" [*statement of cooperative response*]. How would you respond cooperatively to the power plays **You Owe Me** and **Thought Stoppers,** following this three-part strategy?

[The next Power Perspective appears on page 207.]

Power only means the ability to have control over your life. Power implies choice.

—*Nikki Giovanni*

broad generalization. For example, in parts of China, a highly collectivist culture where face saving is extremely important, criminals are paraded publicly at rallies and humiliated before being put to death (Tyler, 1996). You could, of course, argue that the importance of face-saving in China gives this particular punishment a meaning that it could not have in more individualistic cultures.

Confirming the other person's definition of self (Chapter 5), avoiding attack and blame, and using excuses and apologies, as appropriate, are some generally useful face-enhancing strategies.

Attack and Acceptance

An attack can come in many forms. In *personal rejection,* for example, one party to a conflict withholds love and affection. He or she seeks to win the argument by getting the other person to break down in the face of this withdrawal. In withdrawing affection, the individual hopes to make the other person question his or her own self-worth. Once the other is demoralized and feels less than worthy, it's relatively easy for the "rejector" to get his or her way. The "rejector," in other words, holds out the renewal of love and affection as a reward for resolving the conflict in his or her favor.

When you attack someone by hitting below the belt, a tactic called *beltlining,* you can inflict serious injury. When you hit above the belt, however, the person is able to absorb the blow. With most interpersonal relationships, especially those of long standing, you know where the belt line is. You know, for example, that to hit Pat with the inability to have children is to hit below the belt. You know that to hit Chris with the failure to get a permanent job is to hit below the belt. Hitting below the beltline causes added problems for all persons involved. Keep blows to areas your opponent and your relationship can absorb and handle.

Express positive feelings for the other person and for your relationship. In fact, recent research shows that positiveness is a crucial factor in the survival of a relationship (Gottman, 1994). Throughout any conflict, many harsh words will probably be exchanged, later to be regretted. As you saw in Chapter 1, communication is irreversible; the words cannot be unsaid or uncommunicated, but they can be partially offset by the expression of positive statements. If you're engaged in combat with someone you love, remember that you're fighting with a loved one and express that feeling. "I love you very much, but I still don't want your mother on vacation with us. I want to be alone with you."

Verbal Aggressiveness and Argumentativeness

An especially interesting perspective on conflict has emerged from the work on verbal aggressiveness and argumentativeness (Infante & Rancer, 1982; Infante, 1988; Infante & Wigley, 1986).

Verbal aggressiveness is a method of winning an argument by inflicting psychological pain—by attacking the other person's self-concept. It's a type of disconfirmation that seeks to discredit the person's view of himself or herself and is often the talk that leads to physical force (Infante & Wigley,

A slip of the foot may be soon recovered; but that of the tongue perhaps never.

—*Thomas Fuller*

Can you identify a character in a television series who demonstrates verbal aggressiveness? One who demonstrates argumentativeness? What distinguishes these two characters? What can you do to more effectively decrease your tendencies toward verbal aggressiveness and increase them toward argumentativeness?

1986; Infante, Sabourin, Rudd, & Shannon, 1990; Infante, Riddle, Horvath, & Tumlin, 1992).

Argumentativeness, on the other hand and contrary to popular usage, refers to a quality that is productive in conflict resolution. It refers to your willingness to argue for a point of view—your tendency to speak your mind on significant issues. It's the preferred alternative to verbal aggressiveness for dealing with disagreements. Before reading about ways to increase your argumentativeness, take the following test of argumentativeness.

Which strategies (unproductive as well as productive) do you use in your own interpersonal conflicts? Which do you most resent others using? Why? Will this discussion influence you to change the way you engage in interpersonal conflict?

Test Yourself — How Argumentative Are You?

Instructions: This questionnaire contains statements about controversial issues. Indicate how often each statement is true for you personally using the following scale:

1 = almost never true
2 = rarely true
3 = occasionally true
4 = often true
5 = almost always true

_____ 1. While in an argument, I worry that the person I am arguing with will form a negative impression of me.
_____ 2. Arguing over controversial issues improves my intelligence.
_____ 3. I enjoy avoiding arguments.
_____ 4. I am energetic and enthusiastic when I argue.
_____ 5. Once I finish an argument, I promise myself that I will not get into another.
_____ 6. Arguing with a person creates more problems for me than it solves.
_____ 7. I have a pleasant, good feeling when I win a point in an argument.
_____ 8. When I finish arguing with anyone, I feel nervous and upset.
_____ 9. I enjoy a good argument over a controversial issue.
_____ 10. I get an unpleasant feeling when I realize I am about to get into an argument.
_____ 11. I enjoy defending my point of view on an issue.
_____ 12. I am happy when I keep an argument from happening.
_____ 13. I do not like to miss the opportunity to argue a controversial issue.
_____ 14. I prefer being with people who rarely disagree with me.
_____ 15. I consider an argument an exciting intellectual challenge.
_____ 16. I find myself unable to think of effective points during an argument.
_____ 17. I feel refreshed and satisfied after an argument on a controversial issue.
_____ 18. I have the ability to do well in an argument.
_____ 19. I try to avoid getting into arguments.
_____ 20. I feel excitement when I expect that a conversation I am in is leading to an argument.

Thinking Critically About Argumentativeness To compute your argumentativeness score follow these steps:

1. Add your scores on items 2, 4, 7, 9, 11, 13, 15, 17, 18, and 20.
2. Add 60 to the sum obtained in Step 1.
3. Add your scores on items 1, 3, 5, 6, 8, 10, 12, 14, 16, and 19.
4. To compute your argumentativeness score, subtract the total obtained in Step 3 from the total obtained in Step 2.

The following guidelines will help you interpret your score:

Scores between 73 and 100 indicate high argumentativeness
Scores between 56 and 72 indicate moderate argumentativeness
Scores between 20 and 55 indicate low argumentativeness

Generally, those who score high in argumentativeness have a strong tendency to state their position on controversial issues and argue against the positions of others. A high scorer sees arguing as exciting, intellectually challenging, and as an opportunity to win a kind of context.

The moderately argumentative possesses some of the qualities of the high argumentative and some of the qualities of the low argumentative. The person who scores low in argumentativeness tries to prevent arguments. This person experiences satisfaction, not from arguing, but from avoiding arguments. The low argumentative sees arguing as unpleasant and unsatisfying. Not surprisingly this person has little confidence in his or her ability to argue effectively.

The researchers who developed this test note that both high and low argumentatives may experience communication difficulties. The high argumentative, for example, may argue needlessly, too often, and too forcefully. The low argumentative, on the other hand, may avoid taking a stand even when it seems necessary. Persons scoring somewhere in the middle are probably the more interpersonally skilled and adaptable, arguing when it is necessary but avoiding the many arguments that are needless and repetitive. Does your experience support this observation?

Source: This scale was developed by Dominic Infante and Andrew Rancer and appears in Dominic Infante and Andrew Rancer, "A Conceptualization and Measure of Argumentativeness," *Journal of Personality Assessment* 46 (1982): 72–80. Copyright © 1982. Reprinted by permission of Lawrence Erlbaum Associates, Inc.

To cultivate argumentativeness and prevent it from degenerating into aggressiveness, treat disagreements as objectively as possible. Avoid assuming that because someone takes issue with your position or your interpretation, that they're attacking you as a person (Infante, 1988). Avoid attacking the other person (rather than the person's arguments) even if this would give you a tactical advantage; it will probably backfire at some later time and make your relationship more difficult. Center your arguments on issues rather than people.

Reaffirm the other person's sense of competence; compliment the other person as appropriate. Allow the other person to save face; never humiliate the other person. Avoid interrupting; allow the other person to state her or his position fully before you respond. Stress equality and the similarities that you share; stress your areas of agreement before attacking the disagreements. Throughout the conflict episode, express interest in the other person's position, attitude, and point of view. Be especially careful to avoid disconfirmation (Chapter 5).

THINKING CRITICALLY ABOUT CONVERSATION AND CONFLICT

Because each conversation and each conflict is unique, the qualities of interpersonal effectiveness cannot be applied indiscriminately. You need to know how the skills themselves should be applied. So, be mindful, flexible, and use metacommunication skills as appropriate.

Mindfulness

After you've learned a skill or rule you may have a tendency to apply it without thinking or "mindlessly," without, for example, considering the unique aspects of the situation. This is especially important when in intercultural situations, where the situation may be drastically different from your more frequently experienced encounters. For instance, after learning the skills of active listening, many will use them in response to all situations. Some of these responses will be appropriate, but others will prove inappropriate and ineffective. In interpersonal, small group, and public-speaking situations (Elmes & Gemmill, 1990) apply the skills mindfully (Langer, 1989). Several suggestions for increasing mindfulness have been offered by Langer (1989):

- Create and recreate categories. See an object, event, or person as belonging to a wide variety of categories. Avoid storing in memory an image of a person, for example, with only one specific label, since it will be difficult to recategorize it later.
- Be open to new information even if it contradicts your most firmly held stereotypes.
- Be open to different points of view. This will help you avoid the tendency to blame outside forces for your negative behaviors ("that test was unfair") and internal forces for the negative behaviors of others ("Pat didn't study," "Pat isn't very bright"). Be willing to see your own and others' behaviors from a variety of perspectives.
- Be careful of relying too heavily on first impressions; treat your first impressions as tentative—as hypotheses (Chanowitz & Langer, 1981; Langer, 1989).

Flexibility

Before reading about flexibility, take the following self-test:

Test Yourself
How Flexible Are You in Communication?

Instructions: Here are some situations that illustrate how people sometimes act when communicating with others. The first part of each situation asks you to imagine that you are in the situation. Then, a course of action is identified and you are asked to determine how much your own behavior would be like the action described in the scenario. If it is *exactly* like you, mark a 5; if it is *a lot* like you, mark a 4; if it is *somewhat* like you, mark a 3; if it is *not much* like you, mark a 2; and if it is *not at all* like you, mark a 1.

Imagine

_____ 1. Last week, as you were discussing your strained finances with your family, family members came up with several possible solutions. Even though you already decided on one solution, you decided to spend more time considering all the possibilities before making a final decision.

_____ 2. You were invited to a Halloween party and assuming it was a costume party, you dressed as a pumpkin. When you arrived at the party and found everyone else dressed in formal attire, you laughed and joked about the misunderstanding, and decided to stay and enjoy the party.

_____ 3. You have always enjoyed being with your friend Chris, but do not enjoy Chris's habit of always interrupting you. The last time you met, every time Chris interrupted you, you then interrupted Chris to teach Chris a lesson.

_____ 4. Your daily schedule is very structured and your calendar is full of appointments and commitments. When asked to make a change in your schedule, you replied that changes are impossible before even considering the change.

_____ 5. You went to a party where more than 50 people attended. You had a good time, but spent most of the evening talking to one close friend rather than meeting new people.

_____ 6. When discussing a personal problem with a group of friends, you noticed that many different solutions were offered. Although several of the solutions seemed feasible, you already had your opinion and did not listen to any of the alternative solutions.

_____ 7. You and a friend are planning a fun evening and you're dressed and ready ahead of time. You find that you are unable to do anything else until your friend arrives.

_____ 8. When you found your seat at the ball game, you realized you did not know anyone sitting nearby. However, you introduced yourself to the people sitting next to you and attempted to strike up a conversation.

_____ 9. You had lunch with your friend Chris, and Chris told you about a too-personal family problem. You quickly finished your lunch and stated that you had to leave because you had a lot to do that afternoon.

_____ 10. You were involved in a discussion about international politics with a group of acquaintances and you assumed that the members of the group were as knowledgeable as you on the topic; but, as the discussion progressed, you learned that most of the group knew little about the subject. Instead of explaining your point of view, you decided to withdraw from the discussion.

_____ 11. You and a group of friends got into a discussion about gun control and, after a while, it became obvious that your opinions differed greatly from the rest of the group. You explained your position once again, but also you agreed to respect the group's opinion.

_____ 12. You were asked to speak to a group you belong to, so you worked hard preparing a 30-minute presentation; but at the meeting, the organizer asked you to lead a question-and-answer session instead of giving your presentation. You agreed, and answered the group's questions as candidly and fully as possible.

_____ 13. You were offered a managerial position where every day you would face new tasks and challenges and a changing day-to-day routine. You decided to accept this position instead of one that has a stable daily routine.

_____ 14. You were asked to give a speech at a Chamber of Commerce breakfast. Because you did not know anyone at the breakfast and would feel uncomfortable not knowing anyone in the audience, you declined the invitation.

Thinking Critically About Flexibility

To compute your score:

1. Reverse the scoring for items 4, 5, 6, 7, 9, 10, and 14. That is, for each of these questions, substitute as follows:

   a. If you answered 5, reverse it to 1
   b. If you answered 4, reverse it to 2
   c. If you answered 3, keep it as 3
   d. If you answered 2, reverse it to 4
   e. If you answered 1, reverse it to 5

2. Add the scores for all 14 items. Be sure that you use the reversed scores for items 4, 5, 6, 7, 9, 10, and 14 instead of your original responses. Use your original scores for items 1, 2, 3, 8, 11, 12, and 13.

   In general, you can interpret your score as follows:

   - 65–70 = much more flexible than average
   - 57–64 = more flexible than average
   - 44–56 = about average
   - 37–43 = less flexible than average
   - 14–36 = much less flexible than average

Are you satisfied with your level of flexibility? What might you do to cultivate flexibility, in general, and communication flexibility, in particular?

Source: From "Development of a Communication Flexibility Measure," by Matthew M. Martin and Rebecca B. Rubin, _The Southern Communication Journal_ 59 (Winter 1994): 171–178. Reprinted by permission of the Southern States Communication Association.

As you gathered from the self-test, flexibility is the ability to respond differently depending on the specific situation, to be open to new and different alternatives, and to adapt to the situation as it unfolds. Here are a few suggestions for cultivating flexibility:

- Recall the principle of indiscrimination (Chapter 5)—no two things or situations are exactly alike. When faced with a particular problem, ask yourself what is different about this situation.
- Remember from Chapter 1 that communication always takes place in a context. Ask yourself, "What is unique about this specific context that might alter my communications?" "Will cultural differences play a role in this communication?" The physical distance you maintain between yourself and colleagues in the United States, for example, may prove too distant for Arabs and southern Europeans who may see you as cold and uninterested.
- Realize, as covered in Chapter 5, that everything is in a state of change and, therefore, responses that were appropriate yesterday may not be appropriate today. Responding protectively when your child is 5 years old might be appropriate, whereas at 18 that same response may be inappropriate. Also, recognize that sudden changes in a person's life may also exert great influence on his or her communication; the death of a lover, the knowledge of a fatal illness, the birth of a child, a promotion are just a few examples.
- Remember that everyone is different. Thus, you may openly express empathy to your American friends but may want to tone it down when expressing it to Koreans, who generally feel uncomfortable with obvious expressions of empathy (Yun, 1976).

Metacommunicational Ability

Much talk concerns people, objects, and events in the world. However, you can also talk about your talk, you can **metacommunicate** (Chapter 1). Your interpersonal effectiveness often hinges on this ability. Let's say that someone says something positive but in a negative way, for example, the person says, "At last! You've finally completed that report. Good job!" You're faced with several alternatives. Your first two alternatives are to respond to the message positively or negatively.

A third alternative, however, is to talk about the message and say something like, "I'm not sure I understand if you're complimenting or criticizing me." In this way, you may avoid lots of misunderstandings. Talking about your talk will prove an especially useful tool in intercultural situations where the chances for misunderstanding are often considerable.

Here are a few suggestions for increasing your metacommunicational effectiveness:

- Give clear feedforward. This will help the other person get a general picture of the message that will follow; it will provide a kind of schema that makes information processing and learning easier.
- Confront contradictory or inconsistent messages. At the same time, explain your own messages that may appear inconsistent to your listener.

Every difficulty slurred over will be a ghost to disturb your repose later on.
—*Chopin*

- Explain the feelings that go with the thoughts. Avoid communicating only the thinking part of your message; it will prevent listeners from appreciating the other parts of your meaning.
- Paraphrase your own complex messages. Similarly, to check on your own understanding of another's message, paraphrase what you think the other person means and ask if you're accurate.
- Ask questions. If you have doubts about another's meaning, don't assume; instead, ask.
- When you do talk about your talk, do so only to gain an understanding of the other person's thoughts and feelings. Avoid substituting talk about talk for talk about a specific problem.

SUMMARY OF CONCEPTS AND SKILLS

In this chapter we looked at the nature of interpersonal communication, especially the qualities that make for effectiveness in interpersonal communication (in general) and in interpersonal conflict.

1. The conversation process consists of at least five steps: opening, feedforward, business, feedback, and closing.
2. The qualities of interpersonal communication effectiveness are openness, empathy, positiveness, immediacy, interaction management, expressiveness, and other-orientation.
3. Interpersonal conflict is a situation in which two or a few people are interdependent, perceive their goals to be incompatible, and see each other as interfering with their own goal achievement.
4. Conflicts (in face-to-face situations and in cyberspace) can be content or relationship oriented but are usually a combination of both, can have both negative and positive benefits, and always occur within a cultural context.
5. Useful guides to fair fighting are: look for win–win strategies, fight actively, use talk instead of force, focus on the present rather than gunnysacking, use face-enhancing instead of face-detracting strategies, express acceptance instead of attacking the other person, and use your skills in argumentation, not in verbal aggressiveness.
6. In thinking critically about both interpersonal effectiveness and interpersonal conflict, do so with mindfulness, flexibility, and metacommunication as appropriate.

The skills covered in this chapter are vital to effective interpersonal interactions and relationships. Check your ability to use these skills. Use the following rating scale: (1) = almost always, (2) = often, (3) = sometimes, (4) = rarely, (5) = hardly ever.

_____ 1. I open conversations with comfort and confidence.

_____ 2. I use feedforward that is appropriate to my message and purpose.

_____ 3. I exchange roles as speaker and listener to maintain mutual conversational satisfaction.

_____ 4. I vary my feedback as appropriate on the basis of positiveness, focus (person or message), immediacy, degree of monitoring, and supportiveness.

_____ 5. I close conversations at the appropriate time and with the appropriate parting signals.

_____ 6. I practice an appropriate degree of openness.

_____ 7. I communicate empathy to others.

_____ 8. I express supportiveness.

_____ 9. I communicate positiveness in attitudes and through stroking others.

_____ 10. I express equality in my interpersonal interactions.

_____ 11. I communicate confidence in voice and bodily actions.

_____ 12. I express immediacy both verbally and nonverbally.

_____ 13. I manage interpersonal interactions to the satisfaction of both parties.

_____ 14. I self-monitor my verbal and nonverbal behaviors in order to communicate the desired impression.

_____ 15. I communicate expressiveness verbally and nonverbally.

_____ 16. I communicate other-orientation in my interactions.

17. I avoid using unproductive methods of conflict resolution.
18. I make active use of fair-fighting guides.
19. I approach communication situations with an appropriate degree of mindfulness.
20. I'm flexible in the way I communicate and adjust my communications on the basis of the unique situation.
21. I use metacommunication to clarify ambiguous meanings.

KEY WORD QUIZ

Write T for those statements that are true and F for those that are false. For those that are false replace the boldface term with the correct term.

1. The small talk that paves the way for the big talk is known as **phatic communion.**
2. Positive–negative, person-focused–message-focused, immediate–delayed, low monitoring–high monitoring, and supportive–critical are dimensions of **feedforward.**
3. To feel as another person feels is known as **sympathy.**
4. The degree to which the speaker and the listener are connected or joined is known as **interaction management.**
5. The manipulation of the image that you present to others in your interpersonal interactions is referred to as **expressiveness.**
6. The process of storing up grievances so that you may unload them at another time (usually during an interpersonal conflict) is known as **beltlining.**
7. Your willingness to defend a point of view, to speak your mind on significant issues, is called **argumentativeness.**
8. Creating and recreating categories, being open to new information and to different points of view, and not relying too heavily on first impressions are ways to achieve **flexibility.**
9. Communication about communication is called **metacommunication.**
10. Nobody upstairs, you owe me, and thought stoppers are examples of **ingratiation strategies.**

Answers: TRUE: Numbers 1, 7, 9. FALSE: Numbers 2 (**feedback**), 3 (**empathy**), 4 (**immediacy**), 5 (**interaction management**), 6 (**gunnysacking**), 8 (**mindfulness**), 10 (**power plays**).

SKILL DEVELOPMENT EXPERIENCES

7.1 Giving and Receiving Compliments

One of the most difficult forms of interpersonal communication is giving compliments gracefully and comfortably. This exercise is designed to help you gain some experience in phrasing these seemingly simple sentences. Presented below are several situations that might normally call for giving the other person a compliment. For each situation, write at least two compliments that are appropriate to the situation.

1. Your friend has just received an "A" in the history final.
   Sample response: "That's just great. You're going to have a great GPA this semester."
2. Your mother has just prepared an exceptional dinner.
3. Your kid brother tells you he hit a home run in the Little League game.
4. Your teacher gave an exceptionally interesting lecture.
5. A stranger on a train moves over so that you can sit down.
6. A colleague offers to lend you money until next payday.

Perhaps even more difficult than giving compliments is receiving them without awkwardness and uneasiness. Too often people respond to compliments in inappropriate ways that make it even more difficult for the person offering the compliment. Respond to the following compliments by (a) acknowledging the compliment and your pleasure in receiving it, and (b) thanking the person for the compliment.

1. That was a really persuasive argument you made. You really are so articulate.
   Sample response: "Thanks. I appreciate that. I worked all last night on that seemingly off-the-cuff speech."
2. You should have no trouble getting that job. You have everything they're asking for—intelligence, communication ability, and dedication.
3. You really are great at the computer.
4. I really appreciate your helping me with this term paper. You're a good friend.
5. You really deserved that A.
6. I really enjoyed this class. It was the best class I had all semester.

7.2 Generating Win–Win Solutions

To get into the habit of looking for win–win solutions, consider the following conflict situations, either alone or in groups of five or six. Try generating as many possible win–win solutions as you can for each of these 10 situations.

Give yourself 1 minute for each case. Write down all win–win solutions that you (or the group) think of; don't censor yourself or any members of the group. For purposes of this exercise, the conflict situations are identified only briefly.

1. Pat and Chris plan to take a 2-week vacation in August. Pat wants to go to the shore and relax by the water. Chris wants to go the mountains, hiking and camping.
2. Pat and Chris have recently adopted a young child. Pat thinks the child should be raised with strict rules; Chris favors an extremely permissive atmosphere.
3. Logan is an owner of an apartment building and must paint the apartments every 3 years in compliance with city laws. Because the building actually runs at a loss, due to changing real estate conditions, Logan has hired only the most inept (and least expensive) painters and uses the cheapest paint. The tenants have confronted Logan and demand better service.
4. Pat hangs around the house in underwear. Chris really hates this and they argue about it frequently.
5. Philip has recently come out as gay to his parents. He wants them to accept him and his life-style (which includes a committed relationship with another man). His parents refuse to accept him and want him to seek religious counseling to change.
6. Workers at the local accounting office want a 20% raise to bring them into line with the salaries of accountants at similar firms. The owner has repeatedly turned down their requests.

If possible, share and compare your win–win solutions with those of other individuals or groups. From this experience it should be clear that win–win solutions exist for most conflict situations but not necessarily all. Of course, some situations will allow for the easy generation of a lot more win–win solutions than others. Not all conflicts are equal.

CHAPTER 8

Interpersonal Relationships

CHAPTER CONTENTS	CHAPTER GOALS After completing this chapter, you should be able to	CHAPTER SKILLS After completing this chapter, you should be able to
Advantages and Disadvantages of Interpersonal Relationships	1. explain the advantages and disadvantages of interpersonal relationships	evaluate relationships in terms of both advantages and disadvantages
Relationship Stages	2. explain the six-stage model of interpersonal relationships	adjust your communication patterns on the basis of the desired relationship goal
Relationship Theories	3. identify the theories of interpersonal attraction, costs and rewards, and social penetration	effectively manage the factors of interpersonal attraction, the rewards and costs in relationships, and the breadth and depth of a relationship
Relationships, Culture, and Gender	4. explain the influence of culture and gender on interpersonal relationships	appreciate the influence of culture and gender on relationships
Thinking Critically About Interpersonal Relationships	5. identify popular beliefs about relationships	challenge your illogical beliefs about relationships

Think about your important interpersonal relationships. How did they develop? What stages did they pass through? Why did you develop your friendships and romantic relationships? Are your current relationships moving toward intimacy? Are they deteriorating? What makes some relationships grow and mature and others decay and die?

These are just some of the questions explored in this chapter. More specifically, we look at the advantages and disadvantages of interpersonal relationships, the stages you go through in forming relationships, the theories that try to explain why you develop the relationships you do, why some relationships last and others don't, and the influence of culture and gender.

ADVANTAGES AND DISADVANTAGES OF INTERPERSONAL RELATIONSHIPS

All relationships, whether face-to-face or online, have the power to increase or decrease your happiness and satisfaction; there are, potentially, both advantages and disadvantages to every interpersonal relationship you might form.

Advantages of Interpersonal Relationships

Since you anticipate that your relationship will bring advantages, you can look at these advantages as the reasons you develop relationships in the first place. The most general advantage of or reason for developing interpersonal relationships is to **maximize pleasures and minimize pain.** Relationships enable you to achieve this in several ways. For example, relationships help **lessen loneliness.** Close relationships assure you that someone cares and will be there when you need them. Interpersonal relationships enable you to **secure stimulation**—intellectual, physical, and emotional. Relationships help you **learn about yourself and enhance your self-esteem.** By getting to know others and comparing yourself to them, you gain self-knowledge and develop your self-concept (Chapter 2). Contact with others allows you to see yourself from different perspectives and places you in different roles, such as child or parent, colleague or supervisor, best friend or romantic partner. At the same time, healthy relationships help enhance your self-esteem. Being able to form friendships or romantic relationships makes you feel desirable and worthy. Interpersonal relationships also help **to enhance both physical and emotional health** (Goleman, 1995; Rosengren, 1993; Pennebaker, 1991). Without close interpersonal relationships you're more likely to become depressed and depression, in turn, contributes significantly to physical illness. Isolation, in fact, is one of the leading factors that contribute to mortality along with high blood pressure, high cholesterol, obesity, smoking, or lack of physical exercise (Goleman, 1995).

With the use of the Internet exploding, and the use of E-mail expanding, both for business and personal purposes, a new, slightly different interpersonal relationship has evolved: the online relationship. Participants include colleagues, superiors, and employees who E-mail back and forth within a company; suppliers, clients, and business people across the country and around the world who develop a special relationship through E-mail;

people who join chat rooms, do research on the Internet, and stay in touch with current friends through E-mail and Internet Relay Chat groups; and people and organizational members who are in touch and linked through websites. Such relationships benefit from rather unique advantages. One advantage is that on the Internet you have a better chance to make a first impression based on your inner qualities, unlike face-to-face encounters where physical appearance, especially in the beginning, tends to outweigh personality. Computer relationships are more empowering for those with "physical disabilities or disfigurements" largely because face-to-face interactions are often awkward and may end with withdrawal (Lea & Spears, 1995; Bull & Rumsey, 1988). By eliminating the physical cues, online relationships place the two people on equal footing. Online, disabled people are in more control of when and what they choose to reveal about their disability. Similarly, shut-ins and the extremely shy may find developing friendship and romantic relationships on the Internet a lot easier than in face-to-face situations.

Another advantage to some is that the socioeconomic and educational status of people on the Net is significantly higher than you're likely to find in most bars or singles clubs. Because so many people interact on the Internet, you have a better chance of meeting those who share your interests. The Internet is quickly becoming the foundation for new friendships, business–customer relationships, interest groups, clubs, organizations, and romances, perhaps even replacing the singles bars of the last few decades.

A parasocial relationship is one you see yourself having with a media personality, either real (Rosie O'Donnell) or fictional (a doctor on *ER*) (Rubin & McHugh, 1987). What do you see as the advantages and disadvantages of such relationships?

Disadvantages of Interpersonal Relationships

Unfortunately, interpersonal relationships bring potential disadvantages as well. Close relationships can put **pressure on you to reveal yourself and to expose your vulnerabilities.** While people find this to be generally worthwhile in a supportive and caring relationship, it may backfire if the relationship deteriorates and the knowledge of any personal weaknesses is used against you. Furthermore, some people find little satisfaction in self-disclosure and in exposing vulnerabilities. Friendships or romances often involve **increased obligations.** In close relationships these obligations involve time, money, or emotional energy. Your time is no longer entirely your own (Buchholz, 1998). If your money is pooled (as it is in many close relationships), then your financial successes have to be shared as do your partner's loses. Emotional obligations in a close relationship can be trying and exhausting. To be emotionally responsive and sensitive is not always easy. When one person becomes ill, the psychological and physical pressures of caretaking increase sometimes to the point of breakdown. Involvement in close relationships can **increase isolation** and result in the abandonment of other relationships, for example, someone you like but your partner can't stand. Sometimes it's simply a matter of time and energy; relationships take a lot of both and you simply have less to give to these less intimate relationships.

Once entered into, a relationship may prove **difficult to get out of.** In some cultures, for example, religious pressures may prevent married couples from separating. If children are part of the relationship, it may be emotionally difficult to exit. In addition, if a lot of money is involved,

No person is your friend who demands your silence, or denies your right to grow.

—*Alice Walker*

> Whenever I date a guy, I think, is this the man I want my children to spend their weekends with?
>
> —*Rita Rudner*

dissolving a relationship can often mean giving up the fortune you've spent your life accumulating. Of course, your partner may **break your heart.** Your partner may leave you—against all your pleading and promises. Not surprisingly, your hurt will be in proportion to how much you care and need your partner. The person who cares a lot is hurt a lot, while the person who cares little is hurt little; it's one of life's little ironies (see the Power Perspective on page 208).

Online relationships also have unique disadvantages. To many people, not seeing what their communication partner looks like would be a disadvantage. Unless you exchange photographs or meet face-to-face you won't know what the person looks like. Even if photographs are exchanged, you can't be certain that they are of the person or that they were taken recently. In addition, you can't hear their voices—which, as you've seen in Chapter 6, communicate a great deal of information. Of course, you can always add an occasional telephone call to give you this added information or upgrade your computer system to include voice and video.

Online, people can present a false self with little chance of detection. For example, minors may present themselves as adults to access sites limited to adults and adults may present themselves as children to lure children into illegal sexual communications and even arrange face-to-face meetings. Similarly, you can present yourself as rich when you're poor, as mature when you're immature, and as serious and committed when you're not. Because so many people create false identities online, especially in the beginning of their relationships, the transition from online to face-to-face interaction is often difficult.

All relationships will bring both advantages and disadvantages; in an imperfect world, that's to be expected. What specific advantages and disadvantages do you currently experience from your social and professional relationships?

Another potential disadvantage—although some might argue is actually an advantage—is that computer interactions may become all-consuming and may eventually take the place of face-to-face relationships.

What do you think of online relationships? What do you think of people who maintain long-term online relationships but who never talk on the telephone, exchange photographs, or actually meet face-to-face?

RELATIONSHIP STAGES

Friendship, love, and, in fact, all relationships, develop gradually over time and pass through a number of stages. The six-stage model presented in Figure 8.1 describes the stages in developing relationships: contact, involvement, intimacy, deterioration, repair, and dissolution. Each of these stages has an early and a late phase.

This figure also indicates movement within the process with the three types of arrows. The **exit arrows** indicate that each stage offers the opportunity to exit the relationship. After saying hello, you can say good-bye and exit. The vertical or **movement arrows** between stages indicate that you can move to another stage in the relationship, to a more intense stage (from involvement to intimacy) or to a less intense one (from intimacy to deterioration). You can also go back to a previously established stage. For example, you may have established an intimate relationship with someone but don't

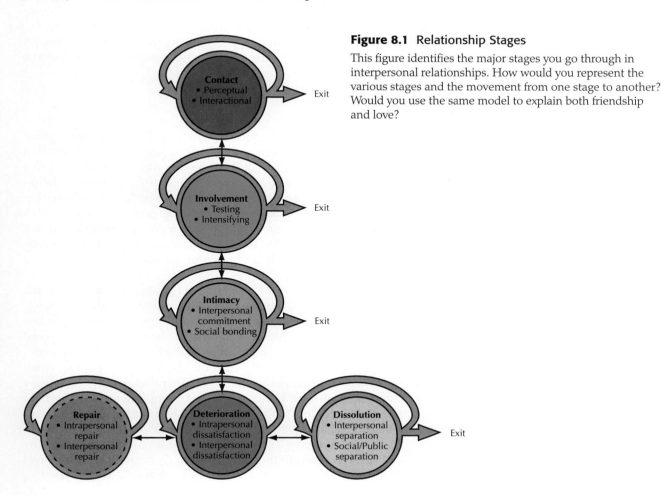

Figure 8.1 Relationship Stages

This figure identifies the major stages you go through in interpersonal relationships. How would you represent the various stages and the movement from one stage to another? Would you use the same model to explain both friendship and love?

want to maintain it at that level. You want it to be less intense. So you may go back to the involvement stage and reestablish the relationship at that more comfortable level (Masheter & Harris, 1986). The **self-reflexive arrows**—the arrows that loop back to the beginning of the same level or stage—signify that any relationship may become stabilized at any point. You may, for example, maintain a relationship at the intimate level without its deteriorating or returning to the less intense stage of involvement. Or you might remain at the "Hello, how are you?" stage—the contact stage— without ever getting further involved.

Movement through the stages is usually a gradual process; you don't jump from contact to involvement to intimacy. Rather, you progress a few degrees at a time. Yet there are leaps that often occur throughout the relationship process (Graham, 1997). For example, during the involvement stage of a romantic relationship, the first kiss or the first sexual encounter requires a leap. It requires a change in the kind of communication and in the kind of intimacy experienced by the two people. Before you take such leaps, you probably first test the waters. Before the first kiss, for example, you may hold each other, look longingly into each other's eyes, and perhaps caress each other's face. You might do this (in part) to discover if the leap—the kiss, for example—will be met with a favorable response. No one wants rejection—especially of romantic advances. These major jumps or "turning points" provide an interesting perspective on how relationships develop. Table 8.1 presents the five most frequently reported turning points in romantic relationships among college students (Baxter & Bullis, 1986).

Contact

A relationship may be seen as beginning when you first make **perceptual contact:** you see, hear, and perhaps even smell the other person. According to some researchers (Zunin, 1972), it's during this stage—within the first 4 minutes of interaction—that you decide whether or not to pursue the relationship. At this stage, physical appearance is especially important because this is what is seen most quickly. Yet, personality traits such as friendliness, warmth, openness, and dynamism are also revealed at this stage. If you decide you like the individual and want to pursue the relationship, you proceed to the later phase, **interactional contact,** where you would begin to communicate.

The initial conversation takes place in this phase. In addition to the conversation openers discussed in Chapter 7, three types of "opening lines" can be identified (Kleinke, 1986). *Cute–flippant* openers are humorous, indirect, and ambiguous as to whether or not the person opening the conversation really wants an extended encounter. Examples include: "Is that really your hair?" "I bet the cherry jubilee isn't as sweet as you are." *Innocuous* openers are highly ambiguous as to whether they are made to just anyone or, in fact, designed to initiate an extended encounter. Examples include: "What do you think of the band?" "I haven't been here before. What's good on the menu?" and "Could you show me how to work this machine?" *Direct* openers clearly demonstrate the speaker's interest in meeting the other person. Examples include: "I feel a little embarrassed about this, but I'd like to meet you." "Would you like

What is the best opening line you have ever heard? What is the worst? What makes one great and another terrible?

I feel that the moment a date happens that it is a social encounter. And the question of sex needs to be negotiated from the first moment on.
—Camille Paglia

Table 8.1 Turning Points in Romantic Relationships

Can you think of similar turning points in your own relationships? What turning points were most important to you? If you are in a close relationship now, ask your partner to identify the five most important turning points as he or she sees them and see if they match your own. This table is based on research by Baxter and Bullis (1986).

Turning Point	Examples
Getting-to-know time	The first meeting, the time spent together studying, the first date
Quality time that enables the couple to appreciate one another and their relationship	Meeting the family or getting away together
Physical separation	Separations due to vacations or trips (not to breakups)
External competition	The presence of a new or old rival and other demands that compete for relationship time
Reunion	Getting back together after physical separation

to have a drink after work?" and "Since we're both eating alone, would you like to join me?"

According to Kleinke (1986), the most preferred opening lines by both men and women are generally those that are direct or innocuous. The least preferred lines by both men and women are those that are cute–flippant; women dislike these openers even more than men.

Involvement

In this stage people explore each others' interests and look for common ground. Here you experiment and try to learn more about each other. At the initial phase of involvement a kind of **testing** goes on. You want to see if your initial judgment—made perhaps at the contact stage—proves correct. You try to get to know the other person by asking about his or her work, interests, and goals. If you're committed to getting to know the other person further, you might continue your interaction to the later phase by **intensifying** your involvement. If this is to be a romantic relationship, then you might begin to date. If it is to be a friendship, you might share your mutual interests, for example, by going to the movies or to a sporting event. Here you begin to see each other as unique individuals.

Throughout the relationship process, but especially during the involvement and early stages of intimacy, you test your partner; you try to find out how your partner feels about the relationship. These are commonly used testing strategies (Bell & Buerkel-Rothfuss, 1990; Baxter & Wilmot, 1984):

- Directness: You ask your partner directly how he or she feels or you disclose to encourage your partner to also disclose.
- Endurance: You subject your partner to various negative behaviors (for example, behaving badly or making inconvenient requests), assuming that if your partner endures them, he or she is serious about the relationship.

The opening lines discussed here were studied in the context of romantic relationships. Do these three types of opening lines have counterparts in the business world?

THE CHRONICLE OF HIGHER EDUCATION   MISCHA RICHTER AND HARALD BAKKEN

"Haven't we met in a previous Web page?"

Does this cartoon fall clearly into one of the three categories of opening lines: cute–flippant, innocuous, and direct? How would you classify this opening?

- Public presentation: For example, you might introduce your partner as your "boyfriend" or "girlfriend" and see how your partner responds.
- Separation: Separating yourself physically to see how the other person responds; if your partner calls, then you know that he or she is interested in the relationship.
- Third party: You might question mutual friends as to your partner's feelings and intentions.

Intimacy

True intimacy is a positive force only if it is a combining of strengths and energies with other mature persons for the continued growth of each.
—*Leo F. Buscaglia*

The intimacy stage usually divides itself quite neatly into two phases: an **interpersonal commitment** phase, in which you commit yourselves to each other in a private way, and a **social bonding** phase, in which the commitment is made public—perhaps to family and friends, perhaps to the public at large through formal announcements. By the end of this stage, you've become a unit, an identifiable pair, in your own mind as well as in the eyes of your social group.

Of course, not everyone strives for intimacy (Bartholomew, 1990). Some, although they may consciously desire intimacy, so fear its consequences that they avoid it. Others dismiss intimacy, denying their need for more and deeper interpersonal contact. To some people relational intimacy is extremely risky. To others, it involves little significant risk. For example, how closely do the following statements match your attitudes?

- It is dangerous to get really close to people.
- I'm afraid to get really close to someone because I might get hurt.
- I find it difficult to trust other people.
- The most important thing to consider in a relationship is whether I might get hurt.

We can only learn to love by loving.
—*Iris Murdock*

People who agree with these statements (and other similar ones), which come from research on risk in intimacy (Pilkington & Richardson, 1988), perceive a great risk in intimacy. Such people, it has been found, have fewer close friends, are less likely to be involved in a romantic relationship, have less trust in others, have a low level of dating assertiveness, and are generally less sociable than those who see intimacy as involving little risk.

In the popular mind, the intimacy stage is the stage of falling in love. This is the time you "become lovers" and commit yourselves to being romantic partners. It's important to note, however, that *love* means very different things to different people. To illustrate this important concept, take the following love test, "What Kind of Lover Are You?"

> If you have ever loved, been loved, or wanted to be in love, you have had to face a frustrating fact: different people can mean different things by that simple phrase "I love you."
>
> —*John Alan Lee*

Test Yourself: What Kind of Lover Are You?

Instructions: Respond to each of the following statements with T (if you believe the statement to be a generally accurate representation of your attitudes about love) or F (if you believe the statement does not adequately represent your attitudes about love).

_____ 1. My lover and I have the right physical "chemistry" between us.

_____ 2. I feel that my lover and I were meant for each other.

_____ 3. My lover and I really understand each other.

_____ 4. I believe that what my lover doesn't know about me won't hurt him or her.

_____ 5. My lover would get upset if he or she knew of some of the things I've done with other people.

_____ 6. When my lover gets too dependent on me, I want to back off a little.

_____ 7. I expect to always be friends with my lover.

_____ 8. Our love is really a deep friendship, not a mysterious, mystical emotion.

_____ 9. Our love relationship is the most satisfying because it developed from a good friendship.

_____ 10. In choosing my lover, I believed it was best to love someone with a similar background.

_____ 11. An important factor in choosing a partner is whether or not he or she would be a good parent.

_____ 12. One consideration in choosing my lover was how he or she would reflect on my career.

_____ 13. Sometimes I get so excited about being in love with my lover that I can't sleep.

_____ 14. When my lover doesn't pay attention to me, I feel sick all over.

_____ 15. I cannot relax if I suspect that my lover is with someone else.

_____ 16. I would rather suffer myself than let my lover suffer.

_____ 17. When my lover gets angry with me, I still love him or her fully and unconditionally.

_____ 18. I would endure all things for the sake of my lover.

Thinking Critically About Your Love Style This scale is designed to enable you to identify those styles that best reflect your own beliefs about love. The statements refer to the six types of love that we discuss in the Special Interest Box. "True" answers represent your agreement and "false" answers represent your disagreement with the type of love to which the statements refer.

Statements 1–3 are characteristic of the eros lover. If you answered "true" to these statements, you have a strong eros component to your love style. If you answered "false," you have a weak eros component. The eros lover seeks beauty and sensuality and focuses on physical attractiveness, sometimes to the exclusion of qualities we might consider more important and more lasting. The erotic lover has an idealized image of beauty that is unattainable in reality. Consequently, the erotic lover often feels unfulfilled.

Statements 4–6 refer to ludus love, a love that seeks entertainment and excitement and sees love as fun, a game. To the ludic lover, love is not to be taken too seriously; emotions are to be held in check lest they get out of hand and make trouble. The ludic lover retains a partner only so long as the partner is interesting and amusing. When the partner is no longer interesting enough, it is time to change.

Statements 7–9 refer to storge love, a love that is peaceful and tranquil. Like ludus, storge lacks passion and intensity. Storgic lovers do not set out to find lovers but to establish a companion-like relationship with someone they know and can share interests and activities. Storgic love is a gradual process of unfolding thoughts and feelings and is sometimes difficult to separate from friendship.

Statements 10–12 refer to pragma love, a love that seeks the practical and traditional and wants compatibility and a relationship in which important needs and desires will be satisfied. The pragma lover is concerned with the social qualifications of a potential mate even more than personal qualities; family and background are extremely important to the pragma lover, who relies not so much on feelings as on logic.

Statements 13–15 refer to manic love, an obsessive love that needs to give and to receive constant attention and affection. When this is not given or when an expression of increased commitment is not returned, such reactions as depression, jealousy, and self-doubt are often experienced and can lead to the extreme lows characteristic of the manic lover.

Statements 16–18 refer to agapic love, a compassionate and selfless love. The agapic lover loves the stranger on the road and the annoying neighbor. Jesus, Buddha, and Gandhi practiced and preached this unqualified, spiritual love, a love that is offered without concern for personal reward or gain, without any expectation that the love will be returned or reciprocated.

Do your scores seem accurate reflections of what you think about love?

Source: This scale comes from Hendrick and Hendrick (1990) and is reprinted by permission of Select Press Publications. It is based on the work of Lee (1976) as is our discussion of the six types of love.

Deterioration

Relational deterioration, the weakening of bonds that hold people together, may be sudden or gradual. Sometimes a relationship rule (for example, the rule of fidelity) is broken and the relationship ends almost immediately. At other times, displeasures grow over time and the relationship dies gradually (Davis, 1973).

The first phase of relationship deterioration is usually **intrapersonal dissatisfaction:** You begin to feel that this relationship may not be as important or as satisfying as you had previously thought. If this intrapersonal dissatisfaction continues, you may pass into the second phase, **interpersonal deterioration.** In this phase you withdraw and grow further and further apart. You share less of your free time with your partner and conflicts may become more and more common and their resolution increasingly difficult.

The Causes of Relationship Deterioration

The causes of relationship deterioration are many. One obvious cause is that the reasons for establishing the relationship have diminished. For instance, when loneliness is no longer lessened, the relationship may suffer. If stimulation weakens, one or both parties may begin to look elsewhere for stimulation. When attractiveness fades, an important reason for establishing the relationship in the first place may be lost. We know, for example, that when relationships break up, it is the more attractive partner who initiates the break up (Blumstein & Schwartz, 1983).

Changes in one or both parties may contribute to relational deterioration. Psychological changes, such as the development of different intellectual interests, or incompatible attitudes may create problems as may behavioral changes, such as preoccupation with business or schooling.

When the quality of sexual relationships is poor, partners may seek satisfaction outside the primary relationship. Research on the effects of this is clear: Extrarelational affairs contribute significantly to breakups for all couples, whether married or cohabiting, heterosexual or homosexual. Even "open relationships"—ones based on sexual freedom outside the primary relationship—experience these problems and, in fact, are more likely to break up than the traditional "closed" relationship (Blumstein & Schwartz, 1983).

Because most people are unable to separate work problems from their relationships, unhappiness with work often leads to difficulties in relationships and is often associated with relationship breakup (Blumstein & Schwartz, 1983). This is equally true for heterosexual and homosexual couples.

Finally, in surveys of problems among couples, financial difficulties are almost always in the top three. Money is important in relationships largely because of its close connection with power; the one who earns more money has more power to control the relationship. Money also creates problems because men and women view it differently. To many men, money is power. To many women, it is security and independence (Blumstein & Schwartz, 1984). Conflicts over how to spend the money can easily result from such different perceptions.

Communication in Relationship Deterioration

People in the deterioration stage of a relationship often communicate in unique ways. The way you communicate during deterioration is, in part, a response to the deterioration and, in part, a cause of the deterioration.

Withdrawal is probably the easiest pattern to observe in a deteriorating relationship. When people are close emotionally, they can occupy

Can you describe one of your own relationships—a friendship or a love relationship—in terms of the six-stage model? What stage provided the greatest satisfaction?

Why do you think the more attractive partner is the one who initiates the breakup? What other factors might account for who leaves a relationship first?

Communication is to a relationship what breathing is to maintaining life.
—*Virginia Satir*

Why do you think self-disclosure declines during relationship deterioration?

close physical quarters, but when they are growing apart, they need greater private space. They literally move away from each other. Other nonverbal signs include the failure to engage in eye contact, even to look at each other generally, to smile, and to touch each other (Miller & Parks, 1982). Verbally, withdrawal entails less talking and especially less listening. Not surprisingly, couples in the deterioration stage also curtail their self-disclosures.

Relational deterioration often brings an increase in negative evaluations and a decrease in positive evaluations of the other person. Where once you praised the other's behaviors, talents, or ideas, you now find fault with the same qualities. Compliments, once given frequently and sincerely, are now rare. Positive stroking is minimal.

Deception also increases as relationships break down. Sometimes this involves direct and clear-cut lies; at other times the lies are exaggerations or omissions.

Repair

The repair stage is optional and so is indicated by a broken circle in Figure 8.1. Some relational partners may pause during deterioration and try to repair their relationship. Others, however, may progress—without stopping—to dissolution.

The first phase of repair is **intrapersonal repair** in which you would analyze what went wrong and consider ways of resolving your differences. You might at this stage consider changing your behaviors or perhaps changing your expectations. Should you decide that you want to repair the relationship, you might discuss this with your partner at the **interpersonal repair** phase. Here you might discuss the problems in the relationship, the corrections you would want to see, and perhaps what you would be willing to do and what you would want the other person to do.

You have a wide variety of strategies that can help you improve your relationship. Here are six that conveniently spell the word R-E-P-A-I-R:

William Lederer (1984) suggests that partners make lists of cherishing behaviors (small behaviors that are easily and quickly done, for example, a kiss, a call to say hello, a compliment) they each wish to receive and then exchange the lists. Each person then performs the cherishing behaviors desired by the partner. What advantages do you see to this technique? Any disadvantages?

- *Recognize* the problem. Your first step is to identify the problem; specify what is wrong with your present relationship and the specific changes you feel would be needed to improve it. Exchange perspectives with your partner, empathically and with an open mind. Try to see the problem from your partner's point of view and to have your partner see it from yours.
- *Engage* in productive conflict resolution. Look back at Chapter 7 for some additional tools for resolving conflict effectively. For example, also try to be descriptive when discussing grievances, being especially careful to avoid such troublesome terms as *always* and *never*. Also, own your own feelings and thoughts; use I-messages and take responsibility for your feelings instead of blaming your partner.
- *Pose* possible solutions. After the problem is identified, discuss possible solutions—ways to lessen or eliminate the difficulty. Look for win–win solutions instead of win–lose solutions. With win–lose solutions, resentment and hostility are likely to fester.

- *A*ffirm each other. Any strategy of relationship repair should incorporate increasing supportiveness and positive evaluations. For example, it's been found that couples who are happily married engage in greater positive behavior exchange; they communicate more agreement, approval, and positive effect than unhappily married couples (Dindia & Fitzpatrick, 1985). Clearly, these behaviors result from the positive feelings these spouses have for each other. However, these expressions also help to increase the positive regard that each person has for his or her partner.
- *I*ntegrate solutions into normal behavior. Often solutions that are reached after an argument are followed for only a very short time; then the couple goes back to their previous unproductive behavior patterns. Instead, these solutions need to become a part of your normal behavior.
- *R*isk. There is no gain without risk-taking. This holds equally true for relationship repair. Incorporate risk-taking into your repair strategy, risk being supportive—without the certainty of reciprocity; risk rejection—make the first move toward conciliation. In short, risk change; be willing to adapt and take on new responsibilities.

The discussion of relationship repair focused on repairing close relationships, such as a friendship or love relationship. How applicable are the suggestions for repair to, say, the business context, for example, restoring a relationship between a disenchanted customer and small retail store owner or between an employee and employer?

And the trouble is, if you don't risk anything, you risk even more.
—*Erica Jong*

Dissolution

The dissolution stage, involves cutting the bonds that tie you together. In the beginning it usually takes the form of **interpersonal separation,** where you might move into your own apartments and begin to lead separate lives. If the separation works better than the original relationship, you enter the phase of **social** or **public separation** where you'd avoid each other and return to a "single" status.

The reasons for the dissolution of relationships are many. Sometimes there is simply not enough to hold the couple together. Sometimes there are problems that can't be resolved. Sometimes the costs are too high and the rewards too few, or the relationship is recognized as destructive with escape the only logical alternative. Regardless of the specific reason, it is difficult to deal with relationship breakups; invariably they cause stress (Simpson, 1987; Frazier & Cook, 1993).

Given both the inevitability that some relationships will break up and the significant effects such breakups will have on you, here are some steps you can take to ease the pain during this difficult time. These suggestions apply to the termination of any type of relationship—a friendship or love affair, through death, separation, or breakup.

Break the Loneliness–Depression Cycle   The two most common feelings following the end of a relationship are loneliness and depression. These feelings are significant, so treat them seriously. Depression, for example, often leads to serious physical illness. In most cases, fortunately, loneliness and depression are temporary. The loneliness and depression that follow a breakup are generally linked to this specific situation and will fade when your perception of the situation changes. But when depression does last, is especially deep, or disturbs your normal functioning, it's time to seek professional help.

Take Time Out   Resist the temptation to jump into a new relationship while you still have strong feelings and before a new one can be assessed with some objectivity. At the same time, resist swearing off all relationships. Neither extreme works well. Take time out for yourself. Renew your relationship with yourself. If you were in a long-term relationship, you probably saw yourself as part of a team, as part of a couple. Now get to know yourself as a unique individual, standing alone at present but fully capable of entering a meaningful relationship in the future.

Bolster Self-Esteem   When relationships fail you're likely to experience a decline in self-esteem. This seems especially true for those who did *not* initiate the breakup (Collins & Clark, 1989). You may feel guilty for having caused the breakup or inadequate for not holding on to the relationship. You may feel rejected, unwanted, and unloved. Your task is to regain the positive self-image needed to function effectively. Try the suggestions for bolstering self-esteem offered in the Listen to This box in Chapter 2 (see page 40). Recognize, too, that having been in a relationship that failed—even if you view yourself as the main cause of the breakup— does not mean that *you are a failure.* Neither does it mean that you cannot succeed in a new and different relationship. It does mean that something went wrong with this particular relationship. And (ideally) it was a failure from which you have learned something important about yourself and about your relationship behavior.

Remove or Avoid Uncomfortable Symbols   After any breakup, there are many reminders—photographs, gifts, and letters, for example. These symbols will bring back uncomfortable memories. Resist the temptation to throw these out. Instead, remove them and give them to a friend to hold or put them in a closet where you won't see them. If possible, avoid places you frequented together. In fact, research shows that the more vivid your memory of a broken love affair—a memory greatly aided by these relationship symbols—the greater your depression is likely to be (Harvey, Flanary, & Morgan, 1986). After you've achieved some emotional distance, you can go back and enjoy these as reminders of the good times you had with your former partner.

Seek Support   Many people feel they should bear their burdens alone. Men, in particular, have been taught that this is the only "masculine" way to handle things. However, seeking the support of others is one of the best antidotes to the unhappiness caused when a relationship ends. Tell your friends and family of your situation—in only general terms, if you prefer— and make it clear that you want support. Seek out people who are positive and nurturing. Avoid negative people who will paint the world in even darker tones or blame you for what happened. Make the distinction between seeking support and seeking advice. If you feel you need advice, consult a professional.

After all, my erstwhile dear, my no longer cherished, need we say it was not love, just because it perished?
—*Edna St. Vincent Millay*

Avoid Repeating Negative Patterns Many people repeat their mistakes. They enter future relationships with the same blinders, faulty preconceptions, and unrealistic expectations with which they entered earlier ones. Instead, use the knowledge gained from your failed relationships to avoid repeating the same patterns. At the same time, don't see vestiges of the old in every relationship. Use past relationships and experiences as guides, not filters.

Maintenance in Relationships

Although we illustrated the relationship stages through dissolution, most people in long-term, serious relationships try hard not to reach this point. The most obvious reason for maintaining a relationship is **emotional attachment,** that is, both partners like or love each other and want to preserve their relationship. Their needs are being satisfied in the current relationship and so they see little need for exploring alternative relationships. In some cases, these needs are predominantly for love and mutual caring, but in other cases, the needs being met may not be quite so positive. For example, one individual may maintain a relationship because it provides a means of exercising control over another, while another might continue the relationship because it provides ego gratification.

Another important reason for maintaining the relationship is that you have a strong **commitment** toward each other and toward the relationship (Knapp & Taylor, 1994; Kurdek, 1995). Not surprisingly, people in satisfying relationships have greater feelings of commitment to each other than do those in less satisfying relationships. This is true for couples in the United States and in Taiwan and may suggest that commitment is a cultural universal (Lin & Rusbult, 1995).

Often the relationship involves neither great love nor great need satisfaction but is maintained for reasons of **convenience,** something the man in the cartoon on page 204 seems to be looking for. Perhaps the partners may jointly own a business or socialize with a circle of mutual friends who are important to them. In these cases it may be more convenient to stay together than to break up and go through the difficulties involved in finding another person for a relationship or business partner, housemate, or social escort.

When **children** are involved, even a souring relationship is often maintained. Children are sometimes brought into the world to save a relationship. In some cases they do. The parents stay together because they feel, rightly or wrongly, that it is in the best interests of the children. In other cases, the children provide a socially acceptable excuse to mask the real reason—convenience, financial advantage, a fear of being alone, and so on. In childless relationships, both parties can be more independent and can make life choices based more on individual needs and wants. These individuals, therefore, are less likely to remain in relationships they find unpleasant or uncomfortable.

Fear motivates many couples to stay together. The individuals may fear the outside world; they may fear being alone and of facing others as "singles." As a result they may feel that their current relationship is a better alternative. Sometimes the fear may be of social criticism and of what others

> Falling out of love is very enlightening; for a short while you see the world with new eyes.
> —*Iris Murdoch*

Commitment can be divided into three types (Johnson, 1991; Knapp & Taylor, 1994): "Want to" commitment is based on your positive feelings for the other person; "ought to" commitment is based on your sense of moral obligation, for example, you made a promise to stay together; and "have to" commitment is based on your belief that you have no acceptable alternative. What implications do each of these types of commitment have for relationship development and deterioration?

*"Don't you understand? I love you! I need you!
I want to spend the rest of my vacation with you!"*

will think of them if the relationship ends. Sometimes the fear concerns the consequences of violating some religious or parental tenet that tells you to stay together, no matter what happens.

Financial advantages motivate many couples to stick it out. Divorces and separations are emotionally and financially expensive. Some people fear a breakup that may cost them half their wealth or even more. Depending on where the individuals live and their preferred life-styles, being single can be expensive. The cost of living in Boston, Tokyo, Paris, and many other cities is almost prohibitive for single people. Many couples stay together to avoid facing additional economic problems.

Another reason for the preservation of many relationships is **inertia,** the tendency for a body at rest to remain at rest and a body in motion to remain in motion. Many people just go along with what they've grown accustomed to without even thinking of changing their relationship status; such change seems too much trouble.

Still another factor in relationship maintenance is **communication.** In one research study, four communication patterns were identified as contributing to relationship maintenance (Gao, 1991).

Openness. The willingness to maintain open and honest communication.

Involvement. A strong sense of being a pair, a couple; a lot of time put into the relationship.

Shared meanings. Mutual understanding of each other's nonverbal communication messages.

Relationship assessment. Both individuals see the relationship and its future in similar and mutually compatible ways.

Listening to Stage Talk

Learning to listen for stage-talk messages—messages that express a desire to move the relationship in a particular way or to maintain it at a particular stage—will help you understand and manage your own interpersonal relationships, whether business or personal. Over the next few days listen carefully to all stage-talk messages. Listen to those messages referring to your own relationships as well as those messages that friends or co-workers disclose to you about their relationships. Collect these messages and classify them into the following categories.

1. **Contact messages** that express a desire for contact: *Hi, my name is Joe.*
2. **Closeness messages** that express a desire to increased closeness, involvement, or intimacy: *I'd like to see you more often.*
3. **Maintenance messages** that express a desire to stabilize the relationship at one stage: *Let's stay friends for now. I'm afraid to get more involved at this point in my life.*
4. **Distancing messages** that express a desire to distance oneself from a relationship. *I think we should spend a few weeks apart.*

5. **Repair messages** that express a desire to repair the relationship: *Let's discuss this issue again, this time in a more constructive way. I didn't mean to be hurt your feelings.*
6. **Dissolution messages** that express a desire to break up or dissolve the existing relationship: *Look, it's just not working out as we planned; let's each go our own way.*

Share these collected messages with others in small groups or with the class as a whole. Consider, for example: (1) What types of messages are used to indicate the six different desires noted above? (2) Do people give reasons for their desire to move from one stage to another or to stabilize their relationship? If so, what types of reasons do they give? (3) Do men and women talk about relationship stages in the same way? In different ways? (4) Do you observe cultural differences? Do members of different cultures talk about relationships in the same way?

[The next Listen to This box appears on page 238.]

More generally we might say that the communication patterns that contribute to successful relationship maintenance are those covered in Chapter 7 that promote effective conversation, such as openness, empathy, positiveness, immediacy, interaction management, expressiveness, and other orientation—performed mindfully, flexibly, and with metacommunication when necessary. Additional communication skills, such as appropriate self-disclosure, active listening, and confirmation, complete a rather comprehensive list of communication tools useful for maintaining a relationship.

> Since there is rarely any lasting advantage of ignorance about compatibility, open communication is essential to developing healthy relationships.
> —*Michael J. Beatty*

RELATIONSHIP THEORIES

Why do you develop the relationships you do? Why are you attracted to certain people but not to others? Why do you dissolve the relationships you end? Why do you maintain the friendships and romantic relationships you do? Here are a few theories that try to answer these questions.

Interpersonal Attraction

A theory of interpersonal attraction holds that you're attracted to others because of four factors: (1) you find them attractive (both physically and in terms of personality), (2) they're close or nearby, (3) they're reinforcing, and (4) they're similar to you.

If you're like most people, you're attracted to people you find physically attractive and who have a pleasing personality. Further, you probably attribute positive qualities to those you find attractive and negative qualities to those you find unattractive.

People are attracted to those who are physically close to them. For example, you become friends with and form romantic relationships with those you come into contact most often: people from your neighborhood, classes, or work groups. The more you interact with someone, the more likely you are to become attracted to them when your initial contact with them was positive (or neutral). But if your initial interaction with the person was unpleasant, repeated contact will not increase attraction but will actually decrease it. Proximity works only if the initial interaction is favorable or neutral.

People are also attracted to those who reward or reinforce them (socially as with compliments or praise, or materially as with gifts or a promotion). The opposite is also true; you become attracted to those you reward; you come to like people for whom you do favors. Perhaps there is a need to justify going out of your way for someone and to convince yourself that the person is likable and worth the effort.

People are also attracted to those who are similar to them, to people who look, act, think, and have attitudes and preferences much like they do. Similarity in attitudes is especially important and has been found to be important in such diverse cultures as the United States, India, Japan, and Mexico (Hatfield & Rapson, 1992). Not surprisingly, people who are similar in attitudes grow more attracted to each other over time, while people who are dissimilar in attitudes grow less attracted to each other (Neimeyer & Mitchell, 1988; Honeycutt, 1986). Marriages between people with many dissimilarities are more likely to end in divorce than marriages between people who are very much alike (Blumstein & Schwartz, 1983). Attitudinal similarity, in fact, is even more important than cultural similarity (Kim, 1991).

As long as these attractiveness factors remain, the interpersonal attraction and the relationship built on them is likely to be maintained. When attractiveness fades, the relationship may deteriorate. Thus, for example, when away from each other for long periods of time (and the factor of proximity is no longer present), the relationship may deteriorate. Absence, research tells us, does not make the heart grow fonder; it makes the heart forget (eventually). Similarly, as physical attractiveness fades (in the eyes of the other person), the relationship may be in trouble.

Rewards and Costs

Social exchange theory claims that you develop relationships that you think will provide more rewards than costs (Thibaut & Kelley, 1959; Kelley & Thibaut, 1978). The general assumption is that you develop (and

---

What constitutes a pleasing personality to you? Can you identify five or six specific qualities?

Of all the girls that are so smart
There's none like pretty Sally:
She is the darling of my heart,
And lives in our alley.

—*Henry Carey*

The matching hypothesis predicts that we date and mate those who are similar to us in physical attractiveness. Do you find this generally true? What comes to your mind when you see couples who differ greatly in physical attractiveness? Do you think that there must be "compensating factors"—for example, that the less attractive person is rich or has prestige or power?

Beauty can't amuse you, but brainwork—reading, writing, thinking—can.

—*Helen Gurley Brown*

Power Perspective 8.1

Reward and Coercive Power

You have **reward power** over a person if you have the ability to give that person rewards—either material (money, promotions, jewelry) or social (love, friendship, respect). Conversely, you have **coercive power** if you have the ability to remove rewards from that person or to administer punishments. Usually, the two go hand in hand; if you have one type of power, you also have the other. A good example is parents who may grant as well as deny privileges to their children.

Reward power increases attractiveness; we like those who have the power to reward us and who do, in fact, give us rewards. Coercive power, on the other hand, decreases attractiveness; we dislike those who have the power to punish us and who threaten us with punishment, whether they actually follow through or not. Thus, as a parent, manager, teacher, or group leader, you'll be better liked and more persuasive if you reward people for their desirable behaviors rather than punish them for undesirable behaviors.

[The next Power Perspective appears on page 208.]

will maintain) relationships in which your rewards are greater than your costs. Rewards are those things that fulfill your needs for security: social approval, love, financial gain, status, sex, and so on. Rewards also involve some cost or "payback." In order to acquire the reward of financial gain, for example, you must take a job and thus give up some freedom (a cost). Using this basic model, the theory puts into perspective our tendency to seek gain or reward while incurring the least cost (punishment or loss).

Equity theory builds on social exchange theory and claims that not only do you seek to establish relationships in which rewards exceed costs, but that you experience relationship satisfaction when there is equity in the distribution of rewards and costs (Berscheid & Walster, 1978; Hatfield & Traupman, 1981). That is, not only do you want your rewards to be greater than your costs, you also want your rewards and your partner's rewards to be proportional to the costs each pays. Thus, if you pay the larger share of the costs (for example, work longer hours or do most of the household chores), you expect to receive the larger share of the rewards. In this situation you would be relatively happy. On the other hand, you would be unhappy if you paid the larger share of the costs and your partner derived an equal or larger share of the rewards (for example, lived in equal comfort or had more free time).

Most people will at times regret their relationships when the costs jump or the rewards fall significantly. As long as rewards exceed costs (according to social exchange theory) and as long as costs and rewards are distributed in proportion to the costs paid into the relationship (according to equity theory), your relationship is likely to be maintained. If the costs begin to exceed the rewards and there is an alternative relationship that offers

Can you identify at least five rewards you derive from any one of your close relationships? Can you identify five costs of this same relationship? Do the rewards exceed the costs?

How equitable are your relationships? Do you give more than you get? Do you get more than you give? If there is inequity, how does it affect the relationship?

a better ratio of rewards to costs, the original relationship is likely to deteriorate and dissolve and this alternative relationship is likely to be pursued. According to equity theory, the relationship is likely to be maintained if the costs and rewards are distributed in proportion to the costs paid into the relationship and is likely to deteriorate if the person paying the greater share of the costs does not receive the greater share of the rewards.

Social Penetration

Remember only this of our hopeless
    love
That never till Time is done
Will the fire of the heart and the fire of
    the mind be one.
            —Edith Sitwell

Social penetration theory focuses not on why relationships develop or deteriorate but rather describes relationships in varying degrees of involvement; it focuses on the number of topics that people talk about and their degree of "personalness" (Altman & Taylor, 1973). The *breadth* of a relationship refers to the number of topics you and your partner talk about. The *depth* of a relationship refers to the degree to which you penetrate the inner personality—the core of your individuality.

We can represent an individual as a circle and divide that circle into various parts. These parts represent the different topics you might discuss with someone or breadth. Further, visualize the circle and its parts as consisting of concentric inner circles, rather like an onion. These represent the different levels of communication, or the depth (Figure 8.2). The circles illustrate eight topic areas (A through H) and five levels of intimacy (represented by the concentric circles).

How would you describe the relationship between yourself and your best friend, using the concepts of breadth and depth?

In its initial stage a relationship is usually narrow (you discuss few topics) and shallow (you discuss the topics only superficially). As a relationship becomes more intimate, you increase both breadth and depth. When a relationship begins to deteriorate, the breadth and depth will, in many ways, reverse themselves in a process called *depenetration*. For example, while ending a relationship, you might cut out certain topics from

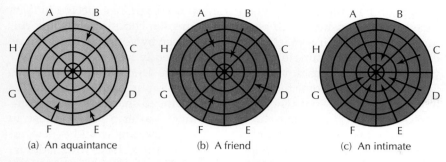

(a) An acquaintance   (b) A friend   (c) An intimate

Figure 8.2 Social Penetration with an Acquaintance (a), a Friend (b), and an Intimate (c).

Note that in circle (a) only three topics are discussed. Two are penetrated only to the first level and one to the second level. In this type of interaction, the individuals talk about three topic areas and discuss these at rather superficial levels. This is the type of relationship you might have with an acquaintance. Circle (b) represents a more intense relationship. It is both broader and deeper. This is the type of relationship you might have with a friend. Circle (c) represents a still more intense relationship. There is considerable breadth and depth. This is the type of relationship you might have with a lover, a parent, or a sibling.

your interpersonal communications. At the same time you might discuss the remaining topics in less depth. You would, for example, reduce the level of your self-disclosures and reveal less of your innermost feelings.

This reversal does not always work, of course. In some instances of relational deterioration, both the breadth and the depth of interaction increase. For example, when two people split up and each is finally free from an oppressive relationship, they may—although usually only after a period of time—begin to discuss problems and feelings they never would have discussed when they were together. In fact, they may become extremely close friends and come to like each other more than when they were a couple. In these cases, the breadth and depth of their relationship may well increase rather than decrease (Baxter, 1983).

RELATIONSHIPS, CULTURE, AND GENDER

As illustrated throughout this chapter and this text, communication is heavily influenced by both culture and gender. Interpersonal relationships are no exception. Although we've paused periodically to note specific cultural and gender differences, it's helpful now that we've covered interpersonal relationship stages and theories to bring the influence of culture and gender together and to look at these two factors in detail.

Relationships and Culture

The research and theory discussed throughout this chapter derive, in great part, from research conducted in the United States and on heterosexual couples. Therefore, this research and the corresponding theory reflect the way most heterosexual relationships are viewed in the United States. For example, we assume in the model of relationships that you voluntarily choose to pursue certain relationships and not others. This is certainly true

Using any of the insights presented in this section, how would you describe the interpersonal communication and the interpersonal relationships of one couple in a television situation comedy or drama?

In 1967—after 9 years of trials and appeals—the United States Supreme Court forbade any state laws against interracial marriage (Crohn, 1995). How would you describe the state of interracial romantic relationships today? What obstacles do such relationships face? What advantages do they offer?

What meaning do you get from the Nigerian proverb: "Hold a true friend with both hands"?

in most of the United States where, for example, you're expected to form romantic relationships with people of your own choosing. In some cultures, however, your romantic partner is chosen by your parents. In some parts of India, for example, children are frequently wed as early as 6 or 7 years old. In some cases, your husband or wife is chosen to solidify two families or to bring some financial advantage to your family or village. It's interesting to note that when people in arranged marriages were compared with people in self-chosen marriages—after 5 years—those in arranged marriages, contrary to what most Americans would expect, indicated a greater intensity of love (Gupta & Singh, 1982; Moghaddam, Taylor, & Wright, 1993).

In the United States, researchers study and textbook authors write about dissolving relationships and how to manage your life after a relationship breaks up. In the United States you have the right to exit an undesirable relationship. However, that is not true in every culture. In some cultures, you simply cannot dissolve a relationship once it is formed or once there are children. In the practice of Roman Catholicism, once people are validly married, they are considered to be always married and cannot dissolve that relationship.

A similar assumption of choice is seen in the research and theory on friendships. In most of the United States, interpersonal friendships are drawn from a relatively large pool. Out of all the people you come into regular contact with, you choose relatively few of these as friends. With the help of the Internet, the number of friends you can have increases enormously as does the range from which these friends can be chosen. In rural areas and in small villages throughout the world, however, you would have very few choices. The two or three other children your age become your friends probably for life; there is no real choice because these are the only possible friends you could make.

Some cultures consider sexual relationships to be undesirable outside of a formally sanctioned marriage whereas others consider it a normal part of relationships and view chastity as undesirable. Intercultural researchers Elaine Hatfield and Richard Rapson (1996, p. 36) recall a meeting of the International Academy of Sex Research where colleagues from Sweden and the United States were discussing ways of preventing AIDS. When members from the United States suggested teaching abstinence as a way of preventing AIDS, Swedish members asked, "How will teenagers ever learn to become loving, considerate sexual partners if they don't practice?" "The silence that greeted the question," note Hatfield and Rapson, "was the sound of two cultures clashing."

A cultural bias is also seen in the research on maintenance. It is assumed that relationships should be permanent or at least long-lasting. Consequently, it's assumed that people want to keep relationships together and will exert considerable energy to maintain them. Because of this bias, there is little research that has studied how to move effortlessly from one intimate relationship to another or that advises you how to do this more effectively and efficiently.

Even the consideration of dissolution as an important phase of interpersonal relationships implies that this is a possible option. However, in other cultures, relationships—such as marriage—are considered permanent and cannot be dissolved if things begin to go wrong, or even if things go very wrong. More important in such cultures are such issues as how do you maintain a relationship that has problems, how can you live with an unpleasant relationship, and how can you repair a relationship that is troubled (Moghaddam, Taylor, & Wright, 1993).

Culture influences heterosexual relationships by assigning different roles to men and to women. In the United States, men and women are supposed to be equal, at least that is the stated ideal. As a result, both men and women can initiate relationships and both men and women can dissolve them. Both men and women are expected to derive satisfaction from their interpersonal relationships and when that satisfaction is not present, either may seek to exit the relationship. In Iran, on the other hand, only the man has the right to dissolve a marriage without giving reasons.

In some cultures, gay and lesbian relationships are accepted and in others condemned. In some states in the United States and in many other countries "domestic partnerships" may be registered and this grants gay men, lesbians, and, in some instances, unmarried heterosexuals, rights that were formerly reserved only for married couples, for example, health insurance benefits and the right to make decisions when one member is incapacitated. In Norway, Iceland, Sweden, and Denmark, same-sex relationships are legally sanctioned in much the same way as are heterosexual marriages. In Afghanistan, if two men walk in public holding hands they can be stoned to death (Ventura, 1998).

In cultures that emphasize continuity from one generation to the next and where being like your ancestors are evaluated positively—as in China—interpersonal relationships are likely to be long-lasting and permanent. However, in cultures where change is seen as positive and being old-fashioned as negative—as in, for example, the Scandanavian countries or even the United States—interpersonal relationships are likely to be more temporary (Moghaddam, Taylor, & Wright, 1993). Here the rewards for long-term relationships and the punishments for broken relationships will be significantly less.

Notice the cultural bias in equity theory, which is consistent with the capitalistic orientation of Western culture, where each person is paid, for example, according to his or her contributions. The more you contribute to the organization or the relationship, the more rewards you should get out of it. In other cultures, a principle of equality or need might operate. Under the equality principle, each person receives an equal amount of rewards, regardless of his or her individual contributions. Under the need principle, each person reaps rewards according to his or her individual need (Moghaddam, Taylor, & Wright, 1993). In the United States, equity is found to be highly correlated with relationship satisfaction and with relationship endurance (Schafer & Keith, 1980), but in Europe equity seems to be unrelated to satisfaction or endurance (Lujansky & Mikula, 1983).

In one study, students in the United States and India were asked to read scenarios in which a bonus was to be divided between a worker who had contributed a great deal to the company but who was economically well-off and a worker who contributed much less but who was poor. The

In some cases unmarried heterosexuals are prohibited from securing domestic partnerships and their benefits on the theory that they can, if they were really in a committed relationship, get married. How do you feel about this?

Table 8.2 Equity and Cultural Differences

What basis would you use in giving out the bonus? What influenced you to make the decision you did?

Method for Allocating Bonus	Subjects from United States (%)	Subjects from India (%)
Equity	49	16
Equality	34	32
Need	16	51

participants were offered the following choices: to distribute the bonus to the workers equitably (on the basis of contribution), equally, or in terms of need (Berman, Murphy-Berman, & Singh, 1985; Moghaddam, Taylor, & Wright, 1993). As you can see from the results given in Table 8.2, culture influences what people think is fair. In Korea, students allocated resources on the basis of equity only when they did not expect to interact with the co-worker in the future (Han & Park, 1995). And in Brazil students allocated resources on the basis of equity only if the primary goal of the work was economic; if the goal was to foster interpersonal relationships, for example, they allocated resources on the basis of equality or need (Assmar & Rodriques, 1994).

Relationships and Gender

Interpersonal relationship research has addressed gender differences in both friendship and love. Here we consider just some of the ways in which men and women are different in their friendship and love behaviors.

Gender Differences in Friendship   Perhaps the best-documented finding—already noted in our discussion of self-disclosure—is that women self-disclose more than do men (for example, Dolgin, Meyer, & Schwartz, 1991). This difference holds throughout male and female friendships. Male friends self-disclose less often and with less intimate details than female friends do. Men generally do not view intimacy as a necessary quality of their friendships (Hart, 1990).

Women engage in significantly more affectional behaviors with their friends than do males (Hays, 1989). This difference, Hays notes, may account for the greater difficulty men experience in initiating and maintaining close friendships. Communication, in all its forms and functions, seems a much more important dimension of women's friendships.

When women and men were asked to evaluate their friendships, women rated their same-sex friendships higher in general quality, intimacy, enjoyment, and nurturance than did men (Sapadin, 1988). Men, in contrast, rated their opposite-sex friendships higher in quality, enjoyment, and nurturance than did women. Both men and women rated their opposite-sex friendships similarly in intimacy. These differences may be due, in part, to our society's suspicion of male friendships; as a result, a man may be reluctant to admit to having close relationship bonds with another man.

Friendship researchers warn that even when we find differences, the reasons for them are not always clear (Blieszner & Adams, 1992). An interesting example is the finding that middle-aged men have more friends than middle-aged women and that women have more intimate friendships (Fischer & Oliker, 1983). But why is this so? Do men have more friends because they are friendlier than women? Because they have more opportunities to develop such friendships? Do women have more intimate friends because they have more opportunities to pursue such friendships? Because they have a greater psychological capacity for intimacy? What do you think?

Men's friendships are often built around shared activities—attending a ball game, playing cards, working on a project at the office. Women's friendships, on the other hand, are built more around a sharing of feelings, support, and "personalism." Similarity in academic major, in status, in willingness to protect one's friend in uncomfortable situations, and even in proficiency in playing Password were significantly related to the relationship closeness of male–male friends but not of female–female or female–male friends (Griffin & Sparks, 1990). Perhaps, then, similarity is more important in male friendships than in female or mixed-sex friendships.

Gender Differences in Love   In the United States, the differences between men and women in love are considered great. In poetry, novels, the mass media, and even in cartoons as so aptly illustrated in *Cathy*, women and men are depicted as acting very differently when falling in love, being in love, and ending a love relationship. Women are portrayed as emotional, while men are portrayed as logical. Women are supposed to love intensely; men are supposed to love with detachment.

Women and men seem to experience love to a similar degree (Rubin, 1973). However, women indicate greater love than men do for their same-sex friends. This may reflect a real difference between the sexes, or it may be a function of the greater social restrictions on men. A man is not supposed to admit his love for another man. Women are permitted greater freedom to communicate their love for other women.

Men and women also differ in the types of love they prefer (Hendrick et al., 1984). For example, on a love self-test similar to the one presented earlier, men have been found to score higher on erotic and ludic love, whereas women score higher on manic, pragmatic, and storgic love. No difference has been found for agapic love.

Man's love is of man's life a thing apart,
'Tis woman's whole existence.
—*Lord Byron*

Love enters a man through his eyes; a woman through her ears.
—*Polish proverb*

Women report having their first romantic experiences earlier than men. The median age of first infatuation for women is 13 and for men is 13.6; the median age for first time in love for women is 17.1 and for men is 17.6 (Kirkpatrick & Caplow, 1945; Hendrick et al., 1984).

Another gender difference frequently noted is that of romanticism. Men were found to place more emphasis on romance than women (Kirkpatrick & Caplow, 1945). For example, when college students were asked the question posed in the photo caption on page 215, approximately two-thirds of the men responded no, which seems to indicate that a high percentage were concerned with love and romance. However, less than one-third of the women responded no. Further, when men and women were surveyed concerning their view on love—whether it's basically realistic or romantic—it was found that married women had a more realistic and less romantic conception of love than did married men (Knapp & Vangelisti, 1996).

More recent research confirms the view that men are more romantic. For example, researchers have found that "men are more likely than women to believe in love at first sight, in love as the basis for marriage and for overcoming obstacles, and to believe that their partner and relationship will be

Ethical Issue

Censoring Messages and Interactions

Throughout your life, the messages you receive are censored. When you were young, your parents may have censored certain television programs, magazines, and movies—perhaps even music—that they thought inappropriate, usually because they were either too sexually explicit or too violent. Moderators of computer mailing lists and IRC groups may also censor messages and may, in fact, ban certain members from participating in the group if your messages are considered inappropriate or destructive to the group.

In addition, relationships are often censored. When you were young, your parents may have encouraged you to play with certain children and not to play with others. Sometimes these decisions were based on the character of the other children. Sometimes they may have been based on the racial, religious, or national background of your would-be friends. Today, the most obvious instances where interactions are prevented are those concerning romantic relationships between interracial and homosexual couples. These prohibitions prevent certain people from interacting in the manner in which they choose. Interracial cou-

ples run into difficulty finding housing, employment, and, most significantly, acceptance into a community. Gay men and lesbians encounter the same difficulties.

Consider the following situations:

- Do interracial couples experience difficulties in your community, workplace, and school? Do you believe that interracial relationships should be encouraged? Discouraged?
- What are the ethical implications of the laws preventing gays and lesbians from marrying? What arguments can you think of for preventing gays and lesbians from marrying? For allowing gays and lesbians to marry?
- What would you do if your best friend or romantic partner broke the law, for example, sold cocaine to children or committed child abuse? Would you turn this person into the police or would you try to help this person while protecting him or her? What are the ethical obligations of friendship? Of love?

[The next Ethical Issue box appears on page 231.]

Men and women from different cultures were asked: "If a man (woman) has all the other qualities you desired, would you marry this person if you were not in love with him (her)? The results varied greatly from one culture to another (Levine, Sato, Hashimoto, & Verma, 1994). For example, 50.4% of the respondents from Pakistan, 49% from India, and 18.8% from Thailand responded "yes" to this question. At the other extreme, only 2.3% from Japan, 3.5% from the United States, and 4.3% from Brazil said "yes." How would you answer this question? What factors influenced your answer?

perfect" (Sprecher & Metts, 1989). This difference seems to increase as the romantic relationship develops: men become more romantic and women less romantic over time (Fengler, 1974).

One further gender difference may be noted and that is differences between men and women in breaking up a relationship (Blumstein & Schwartz, 1983; cf. Janus & Janus, 1993). Popular myth would have us believe that love affairs most often break up as a result of the man's outside affair. However, this myth is not supported by research. When surveyed as to the reason for breaking up, only 15% of the men indicated that it was their interest in another partner, whereas 32% of the women noted this as a cause of the breakup. These findings are consistent with their partners' perceptions as well: 30% of the men (but only 15% of the women) noted that their partner's interest in another person was the reason for the breakup.

In their reactions to broken romantic affairs, women and men exhibit both similarities and differences. For example, the tendency for women and men to recall only pleasant memories and to revisit places with past associations was about equal. However, men engage in more dreaming about the lost partner and in more daydreaming as a reaction to the breakup than did women.

THINKING CRITICALLY ABOUT INTERPERSONAL RELATIONSHIPS

What you believe about relationships will influence just about every aspect of your relationships that you can imagine: the kinds of relationships you seek, your expectations concerning rewards, and the costs you find reasonable in a relationship. They will influence how you communicate and what you do within your relationship. Here is a brief test designed to help you identify your beliefs and to consider some of the consequences of these beliefs.

Occasionally, thinking is an end in itself, but usually the purpose of thinking is to choose or design a course of action.

—*Edward deBono*

Test Yourself

Beliefs About Your Relationships

Instructions: For each of the following statements, select the number (1–7) of the category that best fits how much you agree or disagree. Enter that number on the line next to each statement.

7 = agree completely
6 = agree a good deal
5 = agree somewhat
4 = neither agree nor disagree
3 = disagree somewhat
2 = disagree a good deal
1 = disagree completely

_____ 1. If a person has any questions about the relationship, then it means there is something wrong with it.
_____ 2. If my partner truly loved me, we would not have any quarrels.
_____ 3. If my partner really cared, he or she would always feel affection for me.
_____ 4. If my partner gets angry at me or is critical in public, this indicates he or she doesn't really love me.
_____ 5. My partner should know what is important to me without my having to tell him or her.
_____ 6. If I have to ask for something that I really want, it spoils it.
_____ 7. If my partner really cared, he or she would do what I ask.
_____ 8. A good relationship should not have any problems.
_____ 9. If people really love each other, they should not have to work on their relationship.
_____ 10. If my partner does something that upsets me, I think it is because he or she deliberately wants to hurt me.
_____ 11. When my partner disagrees with me in public, I think it is a sign that he or she doesn't care for me very much.
_____ 12. If my partner contradicts me, I think that he or she doesn't have much respect for me.
_____ 13. If my partner hurts my feelings, I think that it is because he or she is mean.
_____ 14. My partner always tries to get his or her own way.
_____ 15. My partner doesn't listen to what I have to say.

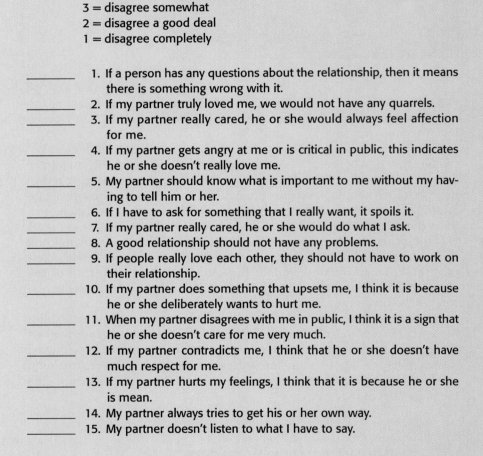

Thinking Critically About Relationship Beliefs Aaron Beck, one of the leading theorists in cognitive therapy and the author of the popular *Love Is Never Enough,* claims that all of these beliefs are unrealistic and may well create problems in your interpersonal relationships. The test was developed to help people identify potential sources of difficulty for relationship development and maintenance. The more statements that you indicated you believe in, the more unrealistic your expectations are.

Do you agree with Beck that these beliefs are unrealistic and that they will cause problems? Which belief is the most dangerous to the development and maintenance of an interpersonal relationship? Review the list—individually or in small groups—and identify with hypothetical or real examples why each belief is unrealistic (or realistic).

Source: This test was taken from Aaron Beck, *Love Is Never Enough* (New York: Harper and Row, 1988), pp. 67–68. Beck notes that this test was adapted in part from the Relationship Belief Inventory of N. Epstein, J. L. Pretzer, and B. Fleming, "The Role of Cognitive Appraisal in Self-Reports of Marital Communication," *Behavior Therapy* 18 (1987): 51–69. Reprinted by permission of HarperCollins Publishers, Inc.

SUMMARY OF CONCEPTS AND SKILLS

In this chapter we explored interpersonal relationships—their nature, development, maintenance, deterioration, and repair. We also examined several theories that explain what happens in interpersonal relationships.

1. Both face-to-face and online relationships have advantages (for example, they lessen loneliness and enhance your self-esteem) and disadvantages (for example, they involve increased obligations and may increase isolation).
2. Relationships are established in stages. The following six stages should be recognized: contact, involvement, intimacy, deterioration, repair, and dissolution. Each of these stages can be further broken down into an early and a later phase.
3. Love is perhaps the most important form of intimacy; several types of love were identified: eros, ludus, storge, pragma, mania, and agape.
4. Among the major causes of relationship deterioration are: a lessening of the reasons for establishing the relationship, changes in the parties, sexual difficulties, work, and financial problems.
5. Interpersonal attraction depends on personality and physical attractiveness, proximity, reinforcement, and similarity.
6. In social exchange theory, relationships are considered in terms of exchanging rewards and costs. Rewards are things we enjoy and want. Costs are unpleasant things we try to avoid.
7. Equity theory concerns the rewards people get in proportion to the costs they expended. Relationships that are perceived to be equitable are found to be more stable than relationships in which members perceive inequities to exist.

8. Social penetration theory describes relationships in breadth (the number of topics talked about) and depth (the degree of "personalness" or intimacy to which the topics are pursued). The theory holds that as relationships develop, the breadth and depth increase. When a relationship deteriorates, the breadth and depth will often (but not always) decrease, a process referred to as depenetration.
9. Relationships of all kinds and in all their aspects are heavily influenced by culture. Similarly, the theories that explain relationships and the topics research focuses on are also heavily influenced by culture.
10. Gender differences in both friendship and love are often considerable and influence the ways in which these relationships are viewed and the communication that takes place within them.

Check your competence in using these skills for effective relationship development. Use the following rating scale: (1) = almost always, (2) = often, (3) = sometimes, (4) = rarely, (5) = hardly ever.

_____ 1. I understand that relationships involve both advantages and disadvantages.
_____ 2. I adjust my communication patterns on the basis of the relationship's intimacy.
_____ 3. I can identify changes in communication patterns that may signal relationship deterioration.
_____ 4. I can use the accepted repair strategies to heal an ailing relationship, for example, reversing negative communication patterns, using cherishing behaviors, and adopting a positive action program.
_____ 5. I can apply to my own relationships such communication skills as identifying relational mes-

sages, exchanging perspectives due to differences in punctuation, empathic and supportive understanding, and eliminating unfair fight strategies.

_____ 6. I can effectively manage physical proximity, reinforcement, and emphasizing similarities as ways to increase interpersonal attractiveness.

_____ 7. I can identify and, to some extent, control the rewards and costs of my relationships.

_____ 8. I can appreciate the other person's perception of relationship equity and can modify my own behavior to make the relationship more productive and satisfying.

_____ 9. I increase the breadth and depth of a relationship gradually.

_____ 10. I understand relationships as cultural institutions.

_____ 11. I take gender differences into consideration in trying to understand friendship and love relationships.

KEY WORD QUIZ

Write T for those statements that are true and F for those that are false. In addition, for those that are false, replace the boldface term with the correct term.

_____ 1. The lover who focuses on beauty and physical attractiveness, sometimes to the exclusion of qualities we might consider more important and more lasting, is the **agapic lover.**

_____ 2. The love that is compassionate, egoless, and self-giving is **storge.**

_____ 3. The theory that explains relationships in terms of costs and rewards is known as **social exchange theory.**

_____ 4. The theory which claims that people are satisfied in their relationships when the costs and rewards are distributed in proportion to what the parties put into the relationship is known as **social penetration.**

_____ 5. The concepts of breadth (the number of topics talked about) and depth (the degree of personalness to which topics are pursued) are central to the theory of **equity.**

_____ 6. Social approval, financial gain, sex, and status are examples of relationship **rewards.**

_____ 7. The relationship stage of interpersonal commitment and social bonding is **involvement.**

_____ 8. The power base that is the opposite of reward power and that actually decreases interpersonal attractiveness is **coercive power.**

_____ 9. The theory of interpersonal relationships that holds that we establish relationships with those who are physically close to us, to those who are similar to us, and to those who reinforce or reward us is known as **interpersonal attraction.**

_____ 10. The prediction that you will date and mate those who are similar to you in physical attractiveness is known as **the principle of less interest.**

Answers. TRUE: Numbers 3, 6, 8, 9. FALSE: Numbers 1 (erotic lover), 2 (agape), 4 (equity theory), 5 (social penetration), 7 (intimacy), 10 (matching hypothesis).

SKILL DEVELOPMENT EXPERIENCES

8.1 Seeking Affinity

Here are 10 affinity-seeking strategies—the techniques we use to get others to like us (Bell & Daly, 1984). Select one of the following situations and indicate—with reference to specific communication behaviors—how you might use any three of the strategies to achieve your goal. In the definitions, the term "Other" is used as shorthand for "other person or persons."

Situations
1. You're at an employment interview and want the interviewer to like you.
2. You are introduced to Chris and would like to get to know Chris better and perhaps go on a date.
3. You have just started a new job and want your co-workers to like you.
4. You just opened a small business in a new neighborhood. You want the people in the area to like you and buy in your store.

Affinity-Seeking Strategies
1. Stimulate and encourage Other to talk about himself or herself; reinforce disclosures and contributions of Other.
2. Ensure that activities with Other are enjoyable and positive.
3. Include Other in your social activities and groupings.
4. Communicate interest in Other.
5. Engage in self-disclosure with Other.
6. Appear to Other as an interesting person to get to know.
7. Appear as one who is able to administer rewards to Other for associating with you.
8. Show respect for Other and help Other to feel positively about himself or herself.
9. Show that you share significant attitudes and values with Other.
10. Communicate supportiveness for Other's thoughts and feelings.

8.2 Understanding Men and Women

This exercise is designed to increase your awareness of matters that may prevent meaningful interpersonal communication between the sexes. It should also stimulate dialog among class members.

The women and men are separated with one group going into another classroom. Each group's task is to write on the blackboard all the things that they dislike having the other sex think, believe, do, or say about them, in general—and that prevent meaningful interpersonal communication from taking place. After this is done, the groups should change rooms so the men can discuss what the women have written and the women discuss what the men have written. After satisfactory discussion, the groups should get together in the original room. Discussion might center on the following questions.

1. Were there any surprises?
2. Were there any disagreements? That is, did members of one sex write anything that members of the other sex argued they do not believe, think, do, or say?
3. How do you suppose the ideas about the other sex got started?
4. Is there any reliable evidence in support of the beliefs of the men about the women or the women about the men?
5. What is the basis for the dislikes? Why was each statement written on the blackboard?
6. What kind of education or training program (if any) do you feel is needed to eliminate these problems?
7. In what specific ways do these beliefs, thoughts, actions, and statements prevent meaningful interpersonal communication?
8. How do you feel now that these matters have been discussed?

CHAPTER 9

Interviewing

CHAPTER CONTENTS	CHAPTER GOALS After completing this chapter, you should be able to	CHAPTER SKILLS After completing this chapter, you should be able to
Interviewing Defined	1. define the different types of interviewing	use a variety of interview structures effectively
The Information Interview	2. describe the principles for conducting an information interview	follow the basic guidelines in conducting informative interviews
The Employment Interview	3. explain the principles for effective employment interviewing	follow the basic suggestions in real employment interviews
Thinking Critically About the Lawfulness of Interview Questions	4. explain the types of questions that are unlawful	recognize and effectively respond to unlawful questions

You'll no doubt find yourself in a wide variety of interviewing situations throughout your social and professional life. As you'll see throughout this chapter, your effectiveness—whether as interviewer or interviewee—in this form of communication will prove crucial in helping you achieve many of your goals. Interviewing includes a wide range of communication situations:

- A supervisor evaluates a trainee.
- A salesperson tries to sell a client a new car.
- A teacher advises a student about graduate schools.
- A counselor talks with a family about their communication problems.
- A recent graduate applies to Microsoft for a job in the product development division.
- A building owner questions a potential apartment renter.
- A lawyer examines a witness during a trial.
- An employer discusses some of the reasons for terminating a contract with a consultant.
- A boss offers a performance review to an employee and invites the employee's feedback.

INTERVIEWING DEFINED

Interviewing is a form of interpersonal communication in which two people interact most often face-to-face, largely through a question-and-answer format to achieve specific goals. While interviews usually involve two people, some involve more. At job fairs, for example, where many people apply for the same few jobs, interviewers may talk with several persons at once. Similarly, counseling interviewers frequently involve entire families, groups of co-workers, or other related individuals.

Although most interviewing is done face-to-face, much interviewing is now taking place via computer—through E-mail (Chapter 7) and on Internet Relay Chat groups (Chapter 10). For example, you can use E-mail or IRC groups to conduct an informative interview with people living in different parts of the world. The Internet enables employers to interview candidates in different parts of the world all for the price of a few local phone calls. Of course, it enables candidates to explore employment opportunities from their own desks. With advanced hardware and software enabling audio and video exchanges over the Internet, the computer-mediated interview will very closely resemble the traditional face-to-face situation.

The interview is different from other forms of communication because it proceeds through questions and answers. Both parties in the interview can ask and answer questions, but most often the interviewer asks and the interviewee answers. The specific goals of the interview guide and structure its content and format. In an employment interview, for example, the interviewer's goal is to find an applicant who can fulfill the tasks of the position. The interviewee's goal is to get the job, if it seems desirable.

Interviews vary from relatively informal talks that resemble everyday conversations to those with rigidly prescribed questions in a set order. Select the interview structure that best fits your specific purpose, or combine

---

What role does interviewing play in your interpersonal relationships, for example, as you move from contact, through involvement, to intimacy (see Chapter 8)?

In the hands of a skilled practitioner [the interview] is like a sharp knife that can cut away all the fat of irrelevant detail to get to the meat of the subject.

—*Jack Gratus*

the various types to create a new interview structure tailored to your needs (Hambrick, 1991):

- The **informal interview** resembles conversation; the general theme is chosen in advance but the specific questions arise from the context. This type of interview is especially useful for obtaining information informally.
- The **guided interview** deals with topics chosen in advance. The specific questions and wordings, however, are guided by the ongoing interaction. It's useful in assuring maximum flexibility and responsiveness to the dynamics of the situation. The interviews on television talk shows are good examples of this format.
- The **standard open interview** relies on open-ended questions with their order selected in advance. It's useful when standardization is needed, for example, when interviewing several candidates for the same job.
- The **quantitative interview** uses questions that guide responses into pre-established categories. For example, questions may contain multiple choice responses that the interviewee would select from or may ask for a number from 1 to 10 to indicate an interviewee's level of agreement. It's useful when large amounts of information (which can be put into categories) are to be collected and statistically analyzed, for example, in a marketing survey of customer satisfaction.

How would you prepare a short interview guide to study one of the following questions: (1) Why do students select the elective courses they do? (2) Why do people become teachers (or law enforcement officers or health care workers)? (3) Why do people watch the television shows they watch?

We can also distinguish the different types of interviews by the goals of the interviewer and interviewee. Some of the most important interviews are persuasion, appraisal, exit, counseling, information, and employment. You'll probably come into contact most often with information and employment interviews so these are covered in detail. The discussion of the information interview focuses on the role of the interviewer and the employment interview discussion, on the role of the interviewee, roles you're most likely to experience now and in the near future. Of course, the principles for effective information and employment interviews will also prove useful for other types of interviews.

The Persuasion Interview

The goal of the **persuasion interview** is to change a person's attitudes, beliefs, or behaviors. One way in which this is accomplished is for the interviewer to ask questions that will lead to the desired conclusion. For example, if you go into a showroom to buy a new car, the salesperson may ask you questions that are obviously and favorably answered by the car he or she wants to sell, for example, "Is safety an important factor?" or "Do you want to save a bundle?" Another way is for the salesperson to become the interviewee, explaining the superiority of this car above all others in answer to your questions about mileage, safety features, and finance terms.

All interviews contain elements of both information and persuasion. When, for example, a guest appears on *The Tonight Show* and talks about a new movie, information is communicated. There is also persuasion; the performer is trying to persuade the audience to see the movie.

Do you agree with interviewing researchers, Stewart and Cash (1988) when they write: "The persuasive interview has a unique advantage over the public speaker and the mass persuader (radio, television, newspaper). The interviewer can tailor a persuasive effort to fit a particular person, at a particular time, in a particular place"?

The Appraisal Interview

In the evaluation or **appraisal interview,** the interviewee's job performance is assessed by his or her supervisor, management, or colleagues on the work team. The general aim is to communicate what the interviewee is doing well, offer praise and encouragement, as well as to identify what needs improvement, the reasons for this, and to develop a plan to improve performance. These interviews are important because they help all members of an organization see how their performances match the expectations of those making promotion and firing decisions. These interviews also help teach employees the norms and rules of the organizational culture; they spell out what it takes to succeed in the company.

The Exit Interview

The **exit interview** is used widely by organizations in the United States and throughout the world. When an employee leaves a company voluntarily, it's important for management to know why. All organizations compete for superior employees; if an organization is losing them, it must discover why, to prevent others from leaving. This type of interview also provides a method for making the departure as pleasant and efficient as possible for both employee and employer, something the executive in the accompanying cartoon has apparently not learned.

The Counseling Interview

Counseling interviews provide guidance. The goal is to help the person deal more effectively with problems involving work, friends or lovers, or just the hassles of daily living. For the interview to be of any value, the interviewer must learn about the person's habits, problems, self-perceptions, goals, and so on. With this information, the counselor tries to persuade the person to alter certain aspects of his or her thinking or behaving. The counselor may try to persuade you, for example, to listen more attentively to relationship messages or to devote more time to your class work.

A prudent question is one-half of wisdom.

—*Francis Bacon*

"*Marissa, have we a lovely parting gift for Mr. Griswold?*"

THE INFORMATION INTERVIEW

In the **information interview,** the interviewer tries to learn something about the interviewee, usually a person of some reputation and accomplishment. The interviewer asks the interviewee a series of questions designed to elicit his or her views, beliefs, insights, perspectives, predictions, life history, and so on. Examples of the information interview are those published in popular magazines and newspapers. The television interviews conducted by Conan O'Brien, Rosie O'Donnell, Larry King, and Diane Sawyer as well as many of those conducted by lawyers during a trial are all information interviews. Each aims to gather specific information from someone who supposedly knows something others do not.

Information interviews are commonly used to gather information about a specific career field and to evaluate employment opportunities. Let's say that you're conducting an interview to get information about the available job opportunities, and the preparation you would need to get into desktop publishing. Here are a few guidelines for conducting such an information-gathering interview.

> The scientist is not a person who gives the right answers, he's one who asks the right questions.
> —*Claude Levi-Strauss*

Secure an Appointment

In selecting a person to interview, you might, for example, look through your college catalog for a desktop publishing course and interview the instructor, or you might call a local publishing company and ask for the person in charge of desktop publishing. Try to learn something about the person before the interview. For example, has the instructor written a book or articles about the field? Look at the book catalog, at indexes to periodicals, and at relevant websites.

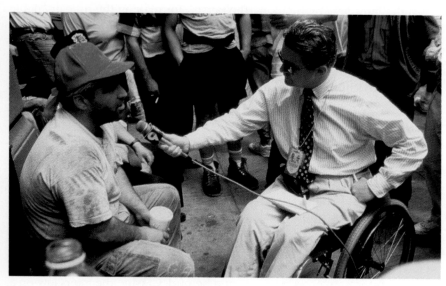

How would you evaluate the effectiveness of one of the popular television interviewers, for example, Rosie O'Donnell, Oprah Winfrey, Jay Leno, Larry King, Charlie Rose, or Geraldo Rivera?

Call or send a letter to request an interview and to identify the purpose of your request. For example, you might say: "I'm considering a career in desktop publishing and I'd appreciate an interview with you to learn more about the business and your company. The interview should take about 20 to 30 minutes." By stating up front a limited time for the interview, you make the interviewee know that it will not take too long. Since you're asking the favor of the interviewee's time, it's best to be available at her or his convenience. Indicate flexibility on your part, for example, "What time is good for you? I'm available any day next week after 12 noon."

If you find it necessary to conduct the interview by phone, call to set up a time for a future call. For example, you might say: "I'm interested in a career in desktop publishing and I would like to interview you about job opportunities. If you agree, I can call you back at a time that's convenient for you." In this way, you don't run the risk of interrupting the interviewee's busy day and asking the person to hold still for an interview.

Prepare Your Questions

Preparing questions in advance will ensure using the time available to your best advantage. Of course, as the interview progresses, you may think of other questions and you should pursue these as well. A prepared list of questions that can be altered as the interview progresses will help you obtain efficiently the information you need.

Use open-ended questions that give the interviewee room to discuss the issues you want to raise. Instead of asking a question that asks for only a simple "yes" or "no" such as "Do you have academic training in desktop publishing?" ask open-ended questions that allow the person greater freedom to elaborate, such as "Can you tell me about your background in this field?"

Establish Rapport with the Interviewee

Open the interview by thanking the person for making the time available and again stating your interest in the field and the opportunity to learn more about it. Many people receive numerous requests and it helps to remind the person of your specific purpose. You might say something like: "I really appreciate your making time for this interview. As I mentioned, I'm interested in learning about job opportunities in desktop publishing and learning about your experience in this area will help a great deal."

Ask Permission to Tape the Interview

Generally, it's a good idea to tape record the interview. It will ensure accuracy and will also allow you to concentrate on the interviewee rather than on note-taking. However, always ask for permission first. Even if the interview is being conducted by phone, ask permission if you intend to tape the conversation.

Close and Follow Up the Interview

At the end of the interview, thank the person for making the time available, for being informative, cooperative, and helpful. Closing the interview on a positive note makes it easier to secure a second interview should you need it. Within the next 2 or 3 days, follow up the interview with a brief note of

If you could interview anyone in the world, who would it be? What questions would you ask?

To question a wise person is the beginning of wisdom.

—*German proverb*

How would you analyze the interviewing style of one of the popular television talk show hosts: Larry King, Jay Leno, or Oprah Winfrey?

thanks. You might express your appreciation for the person's time, your enjoyment in speaking with the person, and your accomplishing your goal of getting the information you needed. A sample letter might look like this:

---

123 Walnut Street, Apt 3C
New York, New York 10038-1525
May 30, 1999

Ms. Anita Brice
Brice Publishers, Inc.
17 Michigan Avenue, Suite 233
Chicago, Illinois 60600-2345

Dear Ms. Brice:

It was a pleasure meeting you on Tuesday. Thank you for taking the time to talk to me. I greatly appreciate your sharing your knowledge of the online publishing industry, as well as your insights into the future of this business.

I now have a much more complete understanding of the field, as well as Brice Publishing's position in the industry. Understanding your background and experience has given me a clear idea of the kinds of skills I'll need to develop in order to succeed in this growing industry.

Again, thank you for your time and your willingness to share your expertise. I wish you continued success.

Sincerely,
Wayne Ing
Wayne Ing

THE EMPLOYMENT INTERVIEW

Perhaps of most immediate concern to college students, although significant for all working people, is the employment, or selection, interview. In such an interview, a great deal of information and persuasion will be exchanged. The interviewer will learn about you, your work experience, college record, interests, talents—and, if clever enough, some of your weaknesses and liabilities. You will be informed about the nature of the company and the position for which you are interviewing, its benefits, its advantages—and, if you are clever enough, some of its disadvantages and problems.

For a variety of reasons—because this interview is so crucial in determining your future and because it's a relatively infrequent and unfamiliar experience—you may experience apprehension. You may, therefore, want to take the accompanying test to examine your apprehension in this situation.

Prepare Yourself

Before going into a job interview, do your homework. Interviewing counselor Marci Taub (1997) suggests that this homework consists of researching four areas: the field, the position, the company, and current events.

Self-confidence is the first requisite to great undertakings.
—*Samuel Johnson*

Power Perspective 9.1

Power, Confidence, and Verbal Messages

The appearance of confidence communicates power. Here are some suggestions for communicating confidence with particular reference to the interview situation. The principles, however, apply to all forms of human communication:

- Control your emotions. If you let your emotions take over, you'll have lost your power and, with that, the appearance of confidence.
- Admit your mistakes. A confident person is one who can admit mistakes without worrying about what others think.
- Take the initiative in introducing yourself and specific topics of conversation. These behaviors communicate your ability to control a social situation.
- Don't ask for agreement by using tag questions ("That was appropriate, don't you think?") or turn declarative sentences into questions with a rising intonation ("I'll arrive at nine?"). Asking for agreement communicates a lack of confidence.
- Use open-ended questions to involve the other person in the interaction and signal your personal attention to the person with "you" statements ("What do you think?" "How do you feel about this?").

[The next Power Perspective appears on page 235.]

Visit one of the websites noted in this chapter and locate a job that you think might be appropriate for yourself or for someone in the class. What do you see as the advantages and disadvantages of job searching on the Web?

First, research the career field you're entering and its current trends. With this information you'll be able to demonstrate that you're up-to-date and committed to the area you want this company to pay you to work in.

Second, research the specific position you're applying for so you'll be able to show how your skills and talents mesh with the position. A good way to do this is to visit the company's website. Most large corporations and, increasingly, many small firms, maintain websites and frequently include detailed job descriptions. Prepare yourself to demonstrate your ability to perform each of the tasks noted in the job description. The photo of The Monster Board and caption (see page 230) will give you a good starting place in searching websites to learn about jobs and specific companies and even improve your résumé.

Third, research the company or organization—its history, mission, and current directions. If it's a publishing company, familiarize yourself with their books and software products. If it's an advertising agency, familiarize yourself with their major clients and major advertising campaigns. A good way to do this is to call and ask the company to send you any company brochures, newsletters, or perhaps a quarterly or annual report. Visiting their website will not only provide you with lots of useful information about the company but it will show the interviewer that you make use of the latest technology. With extensive knowledge of the company, you'll be better able to show your interest and focus on this specific company.

Fourth, research what is going on in the world, in general, and in the business world, in particular. This will help you to demonstrate your breadth of knowledge and that you're a knowledgeable individual who

How Apprehensive Are You in Employment Interviews?

Instructions: This questionnaire is composed of five questions concerning your feelings about communicating in the job interview setting. In the spaces provided, indicate the degree to which each statement adequately describes your feelings about the employment interview. Use the following scale: (1) strongly agree, (2) agree, (3) are undecided, (4) disagree, or (5) strongly disagree.

_____ 1. While participating in a job interview with a potential employer, I am not nervous.

_____ 2. Ordinarily, I am very tense and nervous in job interviews.

_____ 3. I have no fear of speaking up in job interviews.

_____ 4. I'm afraid to speak up in job interviews.

_____ 5. Ordinarily, I am very calm and relaxed in job interviews.

In computing your score, follow these steps:

1. Reverse your scores for items 2 and 4 as follows

if you said	reverse it to
1	5
2	4
3	3
4	2
5	1

2. Add the scores from all 5 items; be sure to use the reverse scores for items 2 and 4 and the original scores for 1, 3, and 5.

Thinking Critically About Apprehension in the Job Interview The higher your score, the greater your apprehension. Since this test is still under development, specific meanings for specific scores are not possible. A score of 25 (the highest possible score) would indicate an extremely apprehensive individual while a score of 5 (the lowest possible score) would indicate an extremely unapprehensive individual. How does your score compare with those of your peers? What score do you think would ensure optimum performance at the job interview?

Your apprehension will probably differ somewhat depending on the type of job interview, your responsibilities, the need and desire you have for the job, and so on. What factors would make you especially apprehensive? Do these answers give you clues as to how to lessen your apprehension?

People demonstrating apprehension during a job interview will be perceived less positively than would those demonstrating confidence and composure. How might you learn to better display confidence? Suggestions for reducing your apprehension are provided in Chapter 13.

Source: This test was developed by Joe Ayres, Debbie M. Ayres, and Diane Sharp (1993). A Progress Report on the Development of an Instrument to Measure Communication Apprehension in Employment Interviews. *Communication Research Reports* 10, 87–94. Copyright 1993.

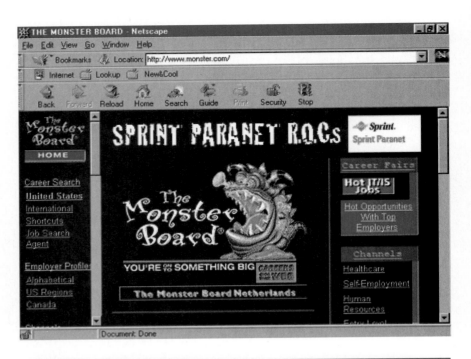

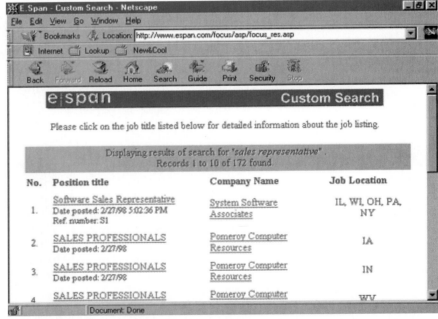

Employment Websites. The first screen presents a website (http://www.monster.com) that lists some 50,000 jobs you can access by keyword, location, or industry; it's just one of the many websites that are useful for finding jobs. Take a look at a few others, for example: http://www.adamsonline.com—discussion groups about jobs and career opportunities; http://www.careermosaic.com—lists thousands of jobs; and http://www.espan.com—gives more than 10,000 job listings and profiles of employers (Heenehan, 1997). The second screen is from this last website when asked to search for jobs as a "sales representative." Notice that the search pulled up 172 jobs; the photo just gives the first few. Jandt and Nemnich (1995) provide an excellent guide to using the Internet to find a job. Try accessing one of these websites or some similar website.

Ethical Issue

Questions and Answers

Another way of looking at questions is in terms of the ethical obligations to respond honestly, an issue that is relevant to questions in all communication situations, not only the interview. Consider each of the following questions that others might ask of you; all are questions asking for information that you're presumed to have. For each question there are extenuating circumstances that may militate against your responding fully or even truthfully (these are noted under the "Thought" you're thinking as you consider your answer). How do you respond?

Question [An interviewer asks] You seem a bit old for this type of job. How old are you?

Thought *I am old for this job but I need it anyway. I don't want to turn the interviewer off because I really need this job. Yet, I don't want to reveal my age either.*

Question [A friend asks your opinion] How do I look?

Thought *You look terrible but I don't want to hurt your feelings.*

Question [A 15-year-old asks] Was I adopted? Who are my real parents?

Thought *Yes, you were adopted but I fear that you will look for your biological parents and will be hurt when you find that they're drug dealers and murderers.*

Question [A relationship partner of 20 years asks] Did you have any affairs since we've been together?

Thought *Yes, but I don't want to say anything because the affairs were insignificant (none are ongoing) and will only create problems for the one important relationship in my life.*

Question [A potential romantic partner asks] What's your HIV status?

Thought *I've never been tested, but now is not the time to talk about this. I'll practice safe-sex so as not to endanger my partner.*

What general ethical principle(s) did you use in developing your responses?

[The next Ethical Issue box appears on page 255.]

continues to learn. Reading a good newspaper daily or a news magazine weekly should help you in mastering current events.

With the employment interview, both you and the company are trying to fill a need. You want a job that will help build your career and the company wants an effective employee who will be an asset to the company. View the interview as an opportunity to engage in a joint effort to each gain something beneficial. If you approach the interview in this cooperative frame of mind, you're much less likely to become defensive, which, in turn, will make you a more appealing potential colleague.

The most important element you can prepare is your résumé. The résumé is a summary of essential information about your experience, education, and abilities. Often, a job applicant may respond to a job listing and submit a résumé. If the employer thinks the applicant's résumé is promising, the candidate is asked in for an interview. Because of the importance of the résumé and its close association with the interview, a sample one-page résumé and some guidelines to assist you in preparing your own are provided on pages 232–233. A variety of computer programs are available to help you in preparing your résumé; most offer an extensive array of templates that you fill in (or customize if you wish) with your specific data. You can also post your résumé on the Net by

Can you use one of the search engines (for example, Infoseek, Yahoo!, or AltaVista) and locate a website that will prove useful to someone looking for a job? How do you locate it? What types of information does it contain?

```
┌─────────────────────────────────────────────────────────────┐
│                        Ramona Morales                         │
│  ①         57-12 Horace Harding Expressway #15D               │
│                      Corona, NY 11368                         │
│                       (718) 583-0005                          │
│                    rmorales@ifindit.com                       │
```

② Objective To secure a position with a college textbook publisher in marketing and sales

③ Employment Experience

Bookstore Assistant, Queens College Bookstore
1998–present

- Maintained shelf stock
- Managed inventory data base
- Placed orders with textbook publishers
- Assisted with front desk operations including client interaction, operating cash register, typing, and filing

Front Desk Employee, Queens College Library
1989–1995

- Responsible for periodical library
- Checked books in and out at front desk
- Acted as liaison for interlibrary loan books
- Offered general information about college library, the online catalog system, interlibrary loan, and the Internet terminals

Retail sales and management, luggage department, Macy's Department Store, Queens Center

④ Education

Queens College, BA expected 1999

Major: Communication (Emphasis on interpersonal communication and public relations)

Minor: Marketing

12 Credits in Computer Science

LaGuardia Community College, AA, 1997

Major: Business

⑤ Activities

- Vice President, Debate Club, Queens College, 1998–1999
- Member, Championship Debate Team, Eastern Division, 1997–1999
- Literacy Volunteer for Spanish-speaking grade school students in English at PS 150, 1995
- Class Treasurer, LaGuardia Community College, 1996–1997
- Member, Young Business Person's Association

Skills and Competencies

- Apple Macintosh (MS Word, MacWrite)
- IBM (Word, WordPerfect)
- Working knowledge of Microsoft Excel, and Lotus 1-2-3
- Knowledge of HTML language inventory software
- Bilingual in English and Spanish, capable in French
- Excellent interpersonal and public speaking skills

⑥ References Available upon request

⑦

1. Your name, address, phone and fax number (if you have one), and E-mail address are generally centered at the top of the resume.

2. For some people, employment objectives may be more general than indicated here, for example, "to secure a management trainee position with an international investment bank." If you do have more specific objectives, put them down. Don't imply that you'll take just anything, but also don't appear too specific or demanding.

3. List work experience in chronological order, beginning with your latest position and work back. Depending on your work experience, you may have to pare down what you write. Or, you may have little or nothing to write, so you will have to search through your employment history for some relevant experience. Often the dates of the various positions are included. If you have little or no paid work experience or huge gaps in employment history due, for example, to time off raising a family, include volunteer work or other unpaid work that requires skills important to the job, for example, coordinator of a little league team or treasurer of the PTA.

4. Provide more information than simply your educational degree. For example, include your major and your minor and perhaps sequences of courses in communication or management or some other field that will further establish your suitability for the job. List honors or awards if they are relevant to your educational or job experience. If the awards are primarily educational (for example, Dean's list), list them under the Education heading; if job-related, list them under the Work Experience heading.

5. Highlight your special skills and competencies. Do you have some foreign language ability? Do you have experience with business or statistical software? If you do, put it down. Such competencies are relevant to many jobs.

6. Some interview experts recommend you include on your résumé the names of references, people who can attest to your ability and character. If you do this, then include these names with addresses, phone numbers, and E-mail address at the end of the résumé under a heading labeled "References." Usually, however, you mention in your cover letter that references are available on request.

7. Make sure your résumé creates the impression you want to make. Typographical errors, incorrect spelling, poorly spaced headings and entries, and generally sloppy work will make a negative impression.

E-mailing it to **occ-resumes@msen.com.** It will remain here for 90 days for virtually anyone to see.

Prepare Answers and Questions

It's often helpful to anticipate the questions you'll be asked. If the interview is at all important to you, you'll probably think about it for some time. If you rehearse the interview's predicted course, you're likely to walk into the interview feeling much more in control of the situation. Try also to predict

"Well, this is a reassuring note, Mr. Bonwell: 'No dolphins were killed in the preparation of this résumé.'"

Figure out what your most magnificent qualities are and make them indispensable to the people you want to work with. Notice that I didn't say "work for."
—*Linda Bloodworth Thomason*

the questions you'll be asked. Table 9.1 identifies some of the frequently asked questions you may wish to consider.

When answering questions be specific and be prepared to give specific examples that testify as to your abilities—from your work, school, or extracurricular activities (Taub, 1997). For example, if the interviewer asks you to identify your best quality, an *ineffective* response would be to give an abstract answer such as "I'm an effective communicator and I enjoy it." A more preferred response would be to say: "I'm an effective communicator; I led focus groups and brainstorming sessions, and I represented my department several times at general meetings. All turned out successfully and I really enjoyed the experience as well and, I'm pleased to say, I got an 'A' in my public speaking class."

In responding, emphasize your positive qualities (you're dependable, creative, and team-oriented, for example). At the same time, emphasize your knowledge and skills (you can speak Chinese, lead work groups, or use QuarkXPress, for example).

Even though the interviewer will ask most of the questions, you'll also want to ask questions. In addition to rehearsing some answers to predicted questions, think of some open-ended questions that will reveal the information you need.

Make an Effective Presentation of Self

Arrive on time—in interview situations, this means 10 to 15 minutes early. This will allow you time to relax, get accustomed to the general surroundings, and perhaps fill out any required forms. It also gives you a cushion should something delay you on the way.

Résumé Power

In writing your résumé, use verbs that communicate power. Here are some suggestions from résumé expert Tim Haft (1997): Use verbs that demonstrate

management skills: directed, formed, governed, instituted, managed, produced

organizational skills: coordinated, implemented, installed, planned, prepared

communication skills: conducted, demonstrated, explained, instructed, lectured, reported

research skills: analyzed, audited, documented, evaluated, researched, tested

creativity: authored, conceived, created, designed, devised, originated

[The next Power Perspective appears on page 237.]

Table 9.1 Common Interview Questions

Think about the questions you're likely to be asked and how you'll answer them. This table presents a list of questions commonly asked in employment interviews organized around the major topics on the résumé and draws from a variety of interviewing experts (Stewart & Cash, 1984; Skopec, 1986; Sincoff & Goyer, 1984; Zima, 1983; Seidman, 1991). Jandt and Nemnich (1995) provide suggestions specifically for Internet interviews. You may find it helpful to rehearse using this list before going into the interview.

Question Areas	Examples	Suggestions
Questions about objectives and career goals	Why did you decide to work in this field? What made you apply to Datacomm? If you took a job with us, where do you see yourself in 5 years? What benefits do you want to get out of this job? What are your salary requirements?	Be positive (and as specific as you can be) about the company. Demonstrate your knowledge of the company. Take a long-range view; no firm wants to hire someone who will be looking for another job in six months. Be prepared to state a salary range that you're seeking.
Questions about employment	Tell me about your previous work experience. What did you do exactly? Did you enjoy working at Happy Publications? Why did you leave? How does this previous experience relate to the work you'd be doing here at Datacomm? What kinds of problems did you encounter at your last position? How did you solve them?	Again, be positive; never knock a previous job. If you do, the interviewer will think you may be criticizing them in the near future. Especially avoid criticizing specific people with whom you worked. When asked about problems be ready to present a specific case with your positive and constructive solution.
Questions about education	What do you think of the education you got at Queens College? Has it prepared you for a career at Datacomm? Why did you major in communication? What kinds of courses did you take? What courses did you like the most? Did you do an internship? What were your responsibilities?	Be positive about your educational experience. Try to relate your educational experience to the job for which you're interviewing. Demonstrate competence but, at the same time, the willingness to continue your education (either formally or informally).
Questions about skills	I see here you have a speaking and writing knowledge of Spanish. Could you talk with someone on the phone in Spanish or write letters in Spanish to our customers? Do you know any other languages? How much do you know about computers?	Before going into the interview, review your competencies. Explain your skills in as much detail as needed to establish their relevance to the job and your own specific competencies.

If you want to succeed, you'd better look as if you mean business.
—*Jeanne Holm*

Why is your attitude going into a job interview so important to your eventual success or failure?

A great number of jobs are won or lost solely on physical appearance, so also give attention to physical preparation. Dress in a way that shows you care enough about the interview to make a good impression. At the same time, dress comfortably so that you're not fidgeting throughout the interview. Perhaps the most specific advice that can be given is to avoid extremes—in hairstyles, makeup, jewelry, and perfumes or colognes. Remember that "casual Friday," popular at many organizations, does not apply to people interviewing for jobs. If in doubt, it's probably best to err on the side of formality: Wear the tie, high heels (but not too high), dress or skirt; avoid sneakers and jeans.

Be sure you know the name of the company, the job title, and the interviewer's name. Although you will have much on your mind, the interviewer's name is not one of the things you can afford to forget or mispronounce.

Bring with you the appropriate materials, whatever they may be. At the very least, bring a pen, an extra copy or two of your résumé, and, if appropriate, a business card. If you're applying for a job in which you have experience, you might bring samples of your previous work.

In presenting yourself, try not to be too casual or too formal. When there is doubt, choose increased formality. Slouching back in the chair, smoking, and chewing gum or candy are obvious behaviors to avoid when you're trying to impress an interviewer.

Acknowledge Cultural Rules and Customs

Each culture—and each organization is much like a culture—has its own rules for communicating (Burna, 1991; Ruben, 1985; Spitzberg, 1991). These rules—whether in the interview situation or in friendly conversation—prescribe appropriate and inappropriate behavior, rewards and punishments, and what will help you get the job and what won't. For example, the general advice given in Table 9.2 (under "positiveness") on page 239 is to emphasize your positive qualities, to highlight your abilities and positive

"This is fine, general, but how are your typing skills?"

Joseph Farris © 1997 from the *New Yorker* Collection. All Rights Reserved.

236   PART II: The Contexts of Human Communication

qualities, and to minimize any negative characteristics or failings. However, in some cultures—especially collectivist cultures such as China, Korea, and Japan—interviewees are expected to show modesty (Copeland & Griggs, 1985). Should you stress your own competencies too much, you may be seen as arrogant, brash, and unfit to work in an organization where teamwork and cooperation are emphasized.

In collectivist cultures, great deference is to be shown to the interviewer who represents the company. If you don't treat the interviewer with great respect, you may appear as disrespecting the entire company. On the other hand, in individualist cultures, such as the United States, too much deference may make you appear unassertive, unsure of yourself, and unable to assume a position of authority.

Demonstrate Effective Interpersonal Communication

Throughout the interview, be certain to demonstrate the interpersonal communication skills covered throughout this book. Table 9.2 shows seven characteristics of interpersonal effectiveness specifically applied to the interview situation.

Follow Up

Much as you would write a thank-you note to the person you interviewed for information, you would also follow up the employment interview with a thank-you note to the interviewer. In this brief, professional letter thank the interviewer for his or her time and consideration and reiterate your interest in the company. You might also use this letter as an opportunity to resell yourself—to mention qualities you possess and wish to emphasize, but may have been too modest or too nervous to discuss at the time.

When they ask about hobbies, you must tell them the only hobbies you enjoy are active ones. . . . You participate in sports, particularly status sports such as golf or tennis. You're not an observer, you're an active participant.
—*John T. Molloy*

What would be your three greatest strengths as a job applicant in your chosen profession? How would you go about communicating these to the interviewer during your first interview?

Some positions ask for a reference list, people the employer can contact who could comment as to your suitability for the position. Who would you include on your reference list? Why are they appropriate for such a list? What (ideally) would each person say about you?

Power Perspective 9.3

Power, Confidence, and Nonverbal Messages

Here are a few suggestions for communicating power and confidence nonverbally:

- Avoid excessive movements, especially self-touching. Tapping a pencil, crossing and uncrossing your legs in rapid succession, or touching your face or hair all communicate a lack of social confidence.
- Maintain eye contact. People who maintain eye contact are judged to be more at ease and unafraid to engage in meaningful interaction.
- Allow your facial expressions to reflect your feelings. Smile, for example, to signal positive reactions (but not too much or too often or you'll look nervous or insincere).
- Avoid vocalized pauses—the *-ers* and *-ahs*—that often punctuate conversations.
- Maintain reasonably close distances between yourself and those with whom you interact. Avoid violating expected conversational distances.

[The next Power Perspective appears on page 256.]

Listening for Question Type

In addition to listening to the question content, listen to the type of question asked. Part of the art of successful interviewing is to respond with answers that are appropriate to the question type. **Open questions** give you considerable freedom in your responses whereas **closed questions** impose greater limits. At times there is almost unlimited latitude in what may constitute an answer, for example, "What are you goals?" "Why do you want to work at Peabody and Peabody?" At the opposite extreme are closed questions that require only a "yes" or "no" answer, for example, "Are you willing to relocate to San Francisco?" "Have you used Java?" Between these extremes are short-answer questions—those that are relatively closed and to which you have only limited freedom in responding, for example, "What would you do as manager here?" "What computer skills do you have?"

Primary questions introduce a topic and **follow-up questions** ask for elaboration on what was just said. Too many primary questions and not enough follow-up questions often signal a lack of interest and perhaps a failure to listen. When a topic is introduced you expect interviewers to ask follow-up questions. When they don't, you may feel that they're not interested in what you're saying or aren't really listening. A balance between primary and follow-up questions, determined in large part by the situation and by your own communication goals, yields the most effective interviews.

Direct questions require you to respond very specifically; **indirect questions** allow greater freedom in how you answer. This aspect of questions will vary greatly from one culture to another. In the United States, be prepared for rather direct questions, whether you're being interviewed for information or for a job. In Japan, on the other hand, the interviewee is expected to reveal himself or herself despite the indirectness of the questions. Similarly, cultures vary in what they consider appropriate directness in speaking of one's accomplishments, for example, in a job interview. In many Asian cultures, the interviewee is expected to appear modest and unassuming and to allow his or her competencies to emerge indirectly during the interview. In the United States, on the other hand, you're expected to state your competencies without undue modesty.

Neutral questions and their opposites, **biased questions**, refer to the extent to which the question specifies the answer the interviewer wants or expects. Neutral questions don't specify any answer as more appropriate than any other, for example, "How did you feel about managing your own desktop publishing company?" Biased, or loaded questions indicate clearly the particular answer the interviewer expects or wants, for example, "And you're willing to relocate, are you?" An interviewer who asks too many biased questions will not learn about the interviewee's talents or experiences, but only about the interviewee's ability to give the desired answer. As an interviewee, pay special attention to any biases in the question. When your responses are not what the interviewer expects, consider explaining why you're responding as you are.

[The next Listen to This box appears on page 254.]

THINKING CRITICALLY ABOUT THE LAWFULNESS OF INTERVIEW QUESTIONS

Through the Equal Employment Opportunity Commission, the federal government has classified some questions as unlawful. These are federal guidelines and therefore apply in all 50 states; individual states, however, may have added further restrictions. You may find it interesting to take the following self-test (constructed with the help of Stewart & Cash, 1984, and Zincoff & Goyer, 1984) to see whether you can identify those questions that are lawful and those that are not.

'Tis not every question that deserves an answer.

—*Thomas Fuller*

Instructions: For each question write L (Lawful) if you think the question is legal for an interviewer to ask in an employment interview and U (Unlawful) if you think the question is illegal. For each question you consider unlawful, indicate why you think it is so classified.

_____ 1. Are you married, Tom?
_____ 2. When did you graduate from high school, Mary?
_____ 3. Do you have a picture so I can attach it to your résumé?
_____ 4. Will you need to be near a mosque (church, synagogue)?
_____ 5. I see you taught courses in "gay and lesbian studies." Are you gay?
_____ 6. Is Chinese your native language?
_____ 7. Will you have difficulty getting a baby-sitter?
_____ 8. I notice that you walk with a limp. Is this a permanent injury?
_____ 9. Where were you born?
_____ 10. Have you ever been arrested for a crime?

Thinking Critically About the Legality of Employment Interview Questions All 10 questions are unlawful. Review the questions and try to identify the general principles of the illegality of employment interview questions. Think about how you would respond to each question if you were asked this in an actual job interview.

Table 9.2 Some Dos and Don'ts for Communicating in the Interview

These dos and don'ts are organized around the seven qualities of effective interpersonal communication discussed in Chapter 7. What other dos and don'ts would you suggest job interviewees observe?

Characteristic	Do	Don't
Openness	Answer questions as fully as appropriate. Give enough detail to answer the question.	Give one-word answers that may signal a lack of interest or knowledge or, at the other extreme, ramble or go off on tangents.
Empathy	See the questions from the interviewer's point of view. Focus your eye contact and orient your body toward the interviewer. Lean forward as appropriate.	Focus your attention away from the interviewer or the interview situation.
Positiveness	Emphasize your positive qualities and your interest in the position and in the company.	Criticize yourself or emphasize your negative qualities. Criticize your previous employer or your education.
Immediacy	Connect yourself with the interviewer throughout the interview by, for example, using the interviewer's name, focusing clearly on the interviewer's remarks, and expressing responsibility for your thoughts and feelings.	Distance yourself from the interviewer, forget the interviewer's name (or mispronounce it), or fail to respond directly to the interviewer's questions.
Interaction management	Ensure the interviewer's satisfaction by being positive, complimentary, and generally cooperative.	Appear defensive, cocky, lacking in assertiveness, extremely introverted, or overly aggressive.
Expressiveness	Let your nonverbal behaviors (especially facial expression and vocal variety) reflect your verbal messages and your general enthusiasm.	Fidget, move about excessively, or use self-adaptors, self-touching gestures that communicate a lack of confidence and comfort. Talk in a monotone or look bored or unenthusiastic.
Other-orientation	Focus on and express interest in the interviewer and in the company. Express agreement and ask for clarification as appropriate.	Argue or engage in unnecessary criticism.

Dress codes are a part of many organizations' culture. In many organizations you're expected to follow the dress code, for example, conservative, dark business suits for both women and men. If you dress in ways that contradict this code—even in an early interview—it may make you appear an unlikely candidate to join this particular organizational culture. What is the dress code for teachers at your college? For the administration?

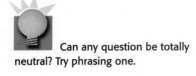

Can any question be totally neutral? Try phrasing one.

Recognizing Unlawful Questions

Some of the more important areas about which unlawful questions are frequently asked concern age, marital status, race, religion, nationality, physical condition, and arrest and criminal records. For example, it's legal to ask applicants whether they meet the legal age requirements for the job and could provide proof of that. But it's unlawful to ask their exact age, even in indirect ways as illustrated in question 2 in the self-test. It's unlawful to ask about a person's marital status (question 1) or about family matters that are unrelated to the job (question 7). An interviewer may ask you, however, to identify a close relative or guardian if you're a minor, or any relative who currently works for the company.

Questions concerning your race (questions 3 and 6), religion (question 4), national origin (question 9), affectional orientation (question 5), age (question 2), handicaps unrelated to job performance (question 8), or even arrest record (question 10) are unlawful, as are questions that get at this same information in oblique ways. For example, requiring a picture may be a way of discriminating against an applicant on the basis of sex, race, and age.

Thus, for example, the interviewer may ask you what languages you are fluent in but may not ask what your native language is (question 6), what language you speak at home, or what language your parents speak. The interviewer may ask you if you if are in this country legally but may not ask if you were born in this country or area naturalized citizen (question 9).

The interviewer may inquire into your physical condition only insofar as the job is concerned. For example, the interviewer may ask, "Do you have any physical problems that might prevent you from fulfilling your responsibilities at this job?" The interviewer may not ask about physical disabilities that are not job related (question 8). The interviewer may ask you if you have been convicted of a felony but not if you've been arrested (question 10).

These are merely examples of some of the lawful and unlawful questions that may be asked during an interview. Note that even the questions used as examples here might be lawful in specific situations. The test to apply is simple: is the information related to your ability to perform the job? Such questions are referred to as BFOQ—bona fide occupational qualification—questions. Once you've discovered what questions are unlawful, consider how to deal with them.

Dealing with Unlawful Questions

One strategy is to deal with such questions by answering the part you do not object to and omitting any information you do not want to give. For example, if you're asked the unlawful question concerning what language is spoken at home, you may respond with a statement such as "I have some language facility in German and Italian," without specifying a direct answer to the question. If you're asked to list all the organizations of which you are a member (an unlawful question in many states, since it's often a way of getting at political affiliation, religion, nationality, and various other areas), you might respond by saying something like: "The organizations I belong to that are relevant to this job are the International Communication Association and the National Communication Association."

The things most people want to know are usually none of their business.
—*George Bernard Shaw*

He must be very ignorant for he answers every question he is asked.
—*Voltaire*

Can you identify possible legitimate reasons for asking each of the questions given in the self-test on the lawfulness of questions? Do you agree that certain questions should be considered illegal in a job interview? What types of questions do you think should be considered illegal?

Occasionally, it [a biased or leading question] is used to test whether the interviewee has the courage to disagree, and how the interviewee handles pressure.

—Sam Deep and Lyle Sussman

Generally, this type of response is preferable to the one that immediately tells the interviewer he or she is asking an unlawful question. In many cases, the interviewer may not even be aware of the legality of various questions and may have no intention of trying to get at information you're not obliged to give.

On the other hand, recognize that in many employment interviews, the unwritten intention is to keep certain people out, whether it's people who are older or those of a particular, affectional orientation, nationality, religion, and so on. If you're confronted by questions that are unlawful and that you do not want to answer, and if the gentle method described above does not work and your interviewer persists—saying, for example, "Is German the language spoken at home?" or "What other organizations have you belonged to?"—you might counter by saying that such information is irrelevant to the interview and to the position you're seeking. Again, be courteous but firm. Say something like "This position doesn't call for any particular language skill and so it doesn't matter what language is spoken in my home." Or you might say, "The organizations I mentioned are the only relevant ones; whatever other organizations I belong to will certainly not interfere with my ability to perform this job."

If the interviewer still persists—and it's doubtful that many would after these rather clear and direct responses—you might note that these questions are unlawful and that you're not going to answer them.

SUMMARY OF CONCEPTS AND SKILLS

In this chapter we looked at the unique form of interpersonal communication that relies essentially on a question-and-answer format—the interview. We considered the types of interviews and focused on the principles for the information gathering and the employment interviews. The types of questions used in interviews (and their potential illegality) were identified.

1. Interviewing is a form of interpersonal communication in which two persons interact largely through a question-and-answer format to achieve specific goals.
2. Six types of interviewing are the persuasive interview, the appraisal interview, the exit interview, the counseling interview, the information interview, and the employment interview.
3. In the information interview the following guides should prove useful: select the person you want to interview, secure an appointment, prepare your questions, establish rapport with the interviewer, ask permission to tape the interview, ask open-ended questions, and follow-up the interview.
4. In the employment interview, prepare yourself. Predict answers to questions, make an effective presentation of yourself, acknowledge cultural rules of customs, demonstrate effective interpersonal communication skills, and follow up the interview with a brief thank you letter.
5. Questions may be indexed in terms of open–closed, primary–follow up, direct–indirect, and neutral–biased. The type of question asked will influence the usefulness of the information obtained.

6. Interviewees should familiarize themselves with possible unlawful questions and develop strategies to deal with them.

Throughout this chapter, we stressed the skills of interviewing. Check your ability to apply these skills. Use the following scale: (1) = almost always, (2) = often, (3) = sometimes, (4) = rarely, (5) = hardly ever.

_____ 1. I follow the basic guidelines in conducting informative interviews.

_____ 2. Before the interview, I prepare myself intellectually and physically; establish my objectives as clearly as I can; and prepare answers to predicted questions.

_____ 3. During the interview, I make an effective presentation of myself and demonstrate effective interpersonal communication skills.

_____ 4. After the interview, I mentally review the interview and follow it up with a letter.

_____ 5. I can frame and respond appropriately to questions varying in terms of openness–closedness, primary–follow up, direct–indirect, and neutral–biased.

_____ 6. I can recognize and respond appropriately to unlawful questions.

KEY WORD QUIZ

Write T for those statements that are true and F for those that are false. For those that are false replace the boldface term with the correct term.

_____ 1. A particular form of interpersonal communication in which two persons interact, largely through a question-and-answer format to achieve specific goals is called **interviewing.**

_____ 2. The type of interview in which topics are chosen in advance, but specific questions and wordings are chosen on the basis of the ongoing interaction and that is especially useful in assuring maximum flexibility and responsiveness to the dynamics of the situation is known as the **quantitative interview.**

_____ 3. Widely used in organizations to discover why workers leave their employ is known as the **appraisal interview.**

_____ 4. The degree of freedom the interviewee has to respond, both in content and form, depends on the **formality of the questions.**

_____ 5. Questions that do not reveal the answer the interviewer is looking for are known as **neutral questions.**

_____ 6. The test to apply to discover if interview questions are legal or illegal is to ask if the questions refer in some way to your ability to perform the job; such legal, job-related questions are known as **BFOQ (bona fide occupational qualification) questions.**

_____ 7. The type of interview that assesses a worker's performance by management or by more experienced colleagues is known as the **counseling interview.**

_____ 8. The interview that seeks to change an individual's attitudes, beliefs, or behaviors is known as the **persuasive interview.**

_____ 9. The interviews by Jay Leno on the *Tonight Show* or by Ted Koppel on *Nightline* are often designed to persuade you to think in a particular way or to do something, but on the surface are **information interviews.**

_____ 10. A written summary of essential information about your experience, goals, and abilities—essential to most employment interviews—is a **résumé.**

Answers: TRUE: Numbers 1, 5, 6, 8, 9, 10. FALSE: Numbers 2 (guided interview), 3 (exit interview), 4 (openness of the questions), 7 (appraisal interview).

SKILL DEVELOPMENT EXPERIENCES

9.1 Responding to Unlawful Questions

This exercise is designed to raise some of the unlawful questions that you don't have to answer, and provide you with some practice in developing responses that protect your privacy while maintaining a positive relationship with the interviewer. In the self-test, "Can you identify unlawful questions?" ten questions were presented. Assume that you did not want to answer the questions, how would you respond to each of them? One useful procedure is to write your responses and then compare them with those of other students, either in groups or with the class as a whole. Or form two-person groups and role-play the interviewer–interviewee situation. To make this realistic, the person playing the interviewer should press for an answer, while the interviewee should continue to avoid answering, yet respond positively and cordially. You'll discover this is not always easy; tempers often flare in this type of interaction.

9.2 Experiencing and Analyzing Interviews

Form three-person groups, preferably among persons who do not know each other well or who have had relatively little interaction. One person should be designated the interviewer, another the interviewee, and the third the interview analyst. The interview analyst should choose one of the following situations:

1. An interview for the position of camp counselor for children with disabilities.
2. An interview for a part in a new Broadway musical.
3. A therapy interview to focus on communication problems in relating to superiors.
4. A teacher–student interview in which the teacher is trying to discover why the course taught last semester was such a dismal failure.
5. An interview between the Chair of the Communication Department and a candidate for the position of instructor of Human Communication.

After the situation is chosen, the interviewer should interview the interviewee for approximately 10 minutes. The analyst should observe but not interfere in any way. After the interview is over, the analyst should offer a detailed analysis, considering each of the following:

1. What happened during the interview (essentially a description of the interaction)?
2. What was well handled?
3. What went wrong? What aspects of the interview were not handled as effectively as they might have been?
4. What could have been done to make the interview more effective?

The analysts for each interview may then report their major findings to the class as a whole. A list of "common faults" or "suggestions for improving interviews" may then be developed by the instructor or group leader.

CHAPTER 10

Small Groups

CHAPTER CONTENTS	CHAPTER GOALS After completing this chapter, you should be able to	CHAPTER SKILLS After completing this chapter, you should be able to
The Small Group	1. define *small group* and *small group communication*	recognize the norms of the groups in which you function and take these into consideration when interacting
The Idea-Generation Group	2. explain the purpose of brainstorming and its four rules	brainstorm effectively
Information Sharing Groups	3. describe the educational or learning group and the focus group	employ organizational structure in educational or learning groups
Problem-Solving Groups	4. explain the phases of problem solving and the use of problem-solving groups at work	participate effectively in a wide variety of problem-solving groups
Thinking Critically About Small Groups	5. explain the critical thinking guidelines and techniques for small group communication	think critically in groups and use the six thinking hats technique to evaluate problems and solutions

How many groups are you a member of? Why do you belong to these groups? What needs do these groups satisfy?

Consider the number of groups to which you belong. The family is the most obvious example, but you may also be a member of a team, a class, a club, an organization, a sorority or fraternity, a collection of friends, and, perhaps, a band or theater group. Some of your most important and satisfying communications probably take place in small groups like these. In this chapter we look at the nature and characteristics of small groups and examine three types of small groups.

THE SMALL GROUP

A **small group** is a relatively small number of individuals who share a common purpose and follow similar organizing rules. It's a collection of individuals, few enough in number that all may communicate with relative ease as both senders and receivers. Generally, a small group consists of approximately 5 to 12 people; if the group is much larger than 12, communication becomes difficult.

To constitute a group, members must share a common purpose. This does not mean that all members must have exactly the same purpose, but there must be some similarity in their reasons for interacting.

Groups operate by following certain organizing rules. Sometimes these rules are extremely rigid—as in groups operating under parliamentary procedure, where comments must follow prescribed rules. At other times, the rules are more loosely defined, as in a social gathering. Even here, however, there are rules, for example, two people do not speak at the same time, a member's comments or questions are responded to, not ignored, and so on.

A group is best defined as a dynamic whole based on inter-dependence rather than on similarity.
—Kurt Lewin

Small Group Stages

As in conversation (Chapter 7), there are five stages in small group interaction: opening, feedforward, business, feedback, and closing. The **opening** period is usually a getting-acquainted time where members introduce themselves and engage in phatic communion ("How was your weekend?" "Does anyone want coffee?"). After this preliminary get-together, there is usually some **feedforward,** some attempt to identify what needs to be done, who will do it, and so on. In a more formal group, the agenda (which is a perfect example of feedforward) might be reviewed and the tasks of the group meeting identified. The **business** portion is the actual discussion of the tasks—the problem solving, the sharing of information, or whatever goal the group needs to achieve. At the **feedback** stage, the group might reflect on what it has done and perhaps what remains to be done. Some groups may even evaluate their performance at this stage. At the **closing** stage the group members again return to their focus on individuals and will perhaps exchange closing comments—"It was good seeing you," or "Let's get together again next week."

Note that the group focus shifts from people to task and then back again to people. Although different groups will naturally follow different patterns, a fairly typical pattern would look like Figure 10.1 (see page 248). For example, a work group that gathers to solve a problem is likely to spend a great

Society in its full sense . . . is never an entity separable from the individuals who compose it.
—*Ruth Benedict*

What organizing rules does your family use? What rules do you use with your close friends? What are the rules for you and your business associates? What happens when these rules are broken?

deal more time focused on the task, whereas an informal social group, say two or three couples who get together for dinner, will spend more time focused on people concerns. Similarly, the amount of time spent on the opening or business or closing, for example, will vary with the type of group and with the purposes the group wants to accomplish.

Small Group Formats

Small groups serve their functions in a variety of formats. Among the most popular are the round table, panel, symposium, and symposium-forum.

In the **round-table** format, group members arrange themselves in a circular or semicircular pattern. They share information or try to solve a problem without any set pattern of who speaks when. Group interaction is informal and members contribute to the discussion as they see fit. A leader or moderator may, for example, try to keep the discussion focused on the topic or encourage the more reticent members to contribute.

The **panel** format is similar to the round table. Here participating group members are "experts." Like the round-table format, members' remarks are informal and there is no set pattern for who speaks when. One difference

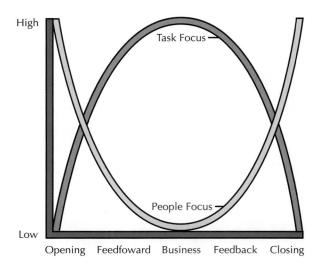

Figure 10.1 Small Group Stages and the Focus on Task and People

Do the groups to which you belong follow these five stages when interacting? How do these groups divide their focus between people and task?

is that the panel is observed by an audience whose members may interject comments or ask questions. Many television talk shows, such as *Jerry Springer* and *The Oprah Winfrey Show*, use this format.

The **symposium** consists of a series of prepared presentations much like public speeches. All speeches address different aspects of a single topic. The leader of a symposium introduces the speakers, provides transitions from one speaker to another, and may provide periodic summaries.

The **symposium-forum** consists of two parts: a symposium of prepared speeches and a forum consisting largely of questions and comments from the audience and responses from the symposium speakers. The symposium leader introduces the speakers and moderates the question-and-answer session.

These four formats, illustrated in Figure 10.2, are general patterns that may describe a wide variety of groups. Within each type, there will naturally be considerable variation. For example, in the symposium-forum there is no set pattern for how much time will be spent on the symposium part and how much time will be spent on the forum part. Similarly, combinations may be used. Thus, for example, group members may each present a position paper (basically a symposium) and then participate in a round-table discussion.

Small Group Channels

Small groups use a wide variety of channels. Often, of course, they take place face-to-face. This is the type of group that probably comes to mind when you think of group interaction. Especially today, much small group interaction takes place online. Online groups are proliferating and are becoming part of people's experiences throughout the world. They're important personally and socially, as well as professionally. Two major online groups may be noted here: the mailing list group and the Internet Relay Chat (IRC) group.

Mailing List Groups   The mailing list group consists of a group of people interested in a particular topic who communicate with each other through E-mail. Generally, you subscribe to a list and communicate with all other members by addressing your mail to the group E-mail address. Any message

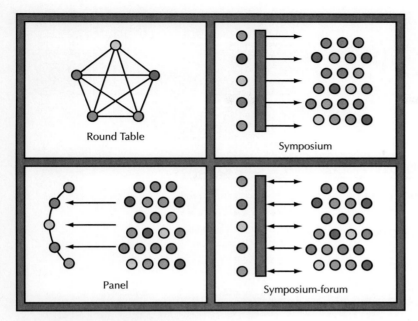

Figure 10.2 Small Group Formats

With how many of these group formats have you had experience?

you send to this address will be sent to each member who subscribes to the list. Your message is sent to all members at the same time; there are no asides to the person sitting next to you (as in face-to-face groups).

The first website noted on page 250 will provide you with a list of 1500 mailing lists categorized by topic. The screen beneath it shows one of the mailing lists that turned up in a request to search for mailing lists in "communication." Another useful site is http://www.liszt.com, which contains more than 60,000 lists. A list of frequently asked questions and mailing list addresses can be found at http://www.cis.ohio-state.edu/hypertext/faq/usenet/mail/mailing-lists/top.html. Of course you could also go to one of the search engines (Yahoo!, Infoseek, or Excite, for example) and search for "mailing lists." To locate a mailing list on your next speech topic, you might E-mail your request to listserv@listserv.net. Send the message: **list public-speaking-topic,** for example, **list United Nations.**

Communication through mailing lists does not take place in real time. It's like regular E-mail; you may send your message today but it may not be read until next week and you may not get an answer for another week. Much of the spontaneity created by real-time communication is lost here. You may, for example, be very enthusiastic about a topic when you send your E-mail, but practically forget it by the time someone responds.

Internet Relay Chat Groups   Internet Relay Chat (IRC) groups have proliferated across the Internet. These groups enable members to communicate with each other in real time in discussion groups called "channels." At any one time, there may be perhaps 4000 channels, so your chances of finding a topic you're interested in is fairly high.

> There is somebody wiser than any of us, and that is everybody.
> —*Napoleon Bonaparte*

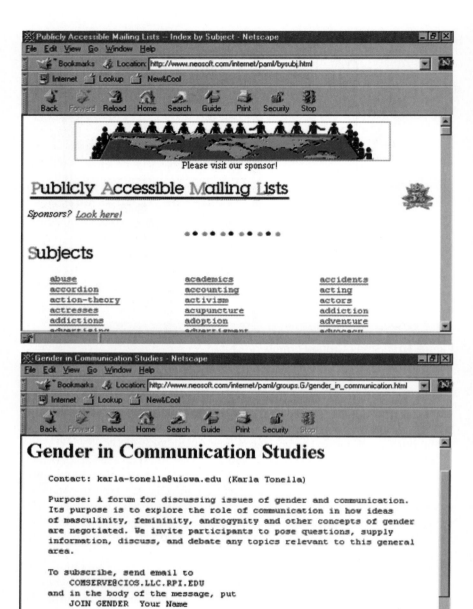

How many mailing lists can you find that might be appropriate to your next research topic?

Unlike mailing lists, IRC communication takes place in real time; you see a member's message as it's being sent—there is virtually no delay. Like mailing lists and face-to-face conversation, the purposes of IRCs vary from communication that simply maintains connection with others (what many would call "idle chatter" or phatic communion) to extremely significant, for example, IRCs were used to gather information on military activities during the

Persian Gulf war and to provide an information database during the California earthquake in 1994 (Estabrook, 1997).

Communication on an IRC resembles the conversation you would observe at a large party. The total number of guests divide up into small groups varying from two and up and each discusses its own topic or version of the general topic. For example, in an IRC about food, ten people may be discussing food calories, eight people may be discussing restaurant food preparation, and two people may be discussing the basic food groups all on this one channel dealing with food. Although you may be communicating in one primary group (say, dealing with restaurant food), you also have your eye trained to pick up something particularly interesting in another group (much as you do at a party). IRCs also notify you when someone new comes into the group and when someone leaves. IRCs, like mailing lists, have the great advantage that they enable you to communicate with people you would otherwise never meet and interact with. Because IRCs are international, they provide excellent exposure to other cultures, other ideas, and other ways of communicating.

IRCs, unlike E-mail, also allow you to "whisper"—to communicate with just one other person without giving access to your message to other participants. In this situation, IRCs resemble interpersonal rather than small group communication.

Log on to one of the IRC game channels (for example, #boggle or #chaos). How might one of these games serve to illustrate or teach a principle of communication?

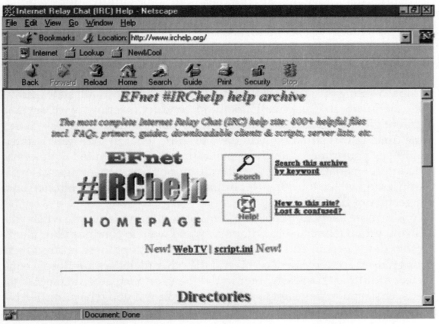

This screen illustrates how easy it is to get help in learning about IRCs. When in doubt there is almost always a help screen somewhere as there is for almost any online task. To learn more about IRCs try: http://www.kei.com/irc.html, http://ftp.acsu.buffalo.edu/irc/www/ircdocs.html, or http://www.irchelp.org/. Log onto an international IRC channel (for example, #brazil, #finland, #italia, #polska). What can you learn about intercultural communication from just lurking on this channel? Do you feel that intercultural communication differences are more or less pronounced on the Internet than in face-to-face situations?

What other differences can you identify between face-to-face groups and groups on the Internet?

Group norms define the limits within which behavior is deemed acceptable or appropriate. They establish the group basis for controlling behavior, and set the standards by which individual behavior is judged.
—*Charles S. Palazzolo*

What norms govern your class in human communication? What norms govern your family? Do you have any difficulty with these norms?

"High communication apprehensives," note Richmond and McCroskey (1992), "typically attempt to avoid small group communication or to sit rather quietly in a group if they must be present." Do you observe this tendency in yourself or in others? As a group member, how might you help reduce this apprehension?

In face-to-face group communication you're expected to contribute to the ongoing discussion. In IRCs you can simply observe; in fact, you're encouraged to lurk—to observe the group's interaction before you say anything yourself. In this way, you'll learn the customs of the group and not violate any of its rules or norms.

Small Group Culture

Many groups—especially long-standing ones—develop a distinctive culture with their own **norms**: rules or standards identifying which behaviors are considered appropriate (for example, willingness to take on added tasks or directing conflict toward issues rather than toward people) and which are considered inappropriate (for example, coming late or not contributing actively). Sometimes these rules for appropriate behavior are explicitly stated in a company contract or policy: all members must attend department meetings. Sometimes the rules are implicit: group members should be well-groomed. Regardless of whether norms are spelled out or not, they are powerful regulators of members' behaviors.

Norms may apply to individual members as well as to the group as a whole and, of course, will differ from one group to another (Axtell, 1990, 1993). For example, in the United States, men and women in business are expected to interact when making business decisions as well as when socializing. In Muslim and Buddhist societies, however, there are religious restrictions that prevent mixing the sexes. In some cultures (for example, the United States, Bangladesh, Australia, Germany, Finland, and Hong Kong) punctuality for business meetings is very important. But, in others (for example, Morocco, Italy, Brazil, Zambia, Ireland, and Panama) punctuality is less important and being late is no great insult and, in some situations, is even expected. In the United States, and in much of Asia and Europe, meetings are held between two groups. In many Gulf states, however, the business executive is likely to conduct meetings with several different groups—sometimes dealing with totally different issues—at the same time. In this situation, you have to share what in the United States would be "your time" with these other groups. In the United States very little interpersonal touching goes on during business meetings; in Arab countries, however, touching (for example, hand holding) is common and is a gesture of friendship.

You're more likely to accept the norms of your group's culture when you feel your group membership is important and want to continue your membership in the group. You're also more likely to accept these norms when your group is cohesive, when you and the other members are closely connected, are attracted to each other, and depend on each other to meet your needs. Last, you're more apt to accept these norms if you'd be punished by negative reactions or exclusion from the group for violating them (Napier & Gershenfeld, 1989).

Small Group Apprehension

Just as you have some apprehension in interpersonal conversations (Chapter 7), so probably do you experience apprehension to some degree in group discussions. Because small groups vary so widely, you're likely to experience different degrees of apprehension depending on the nature of the specific group. Work groups, for example, may cause greater apprehension than groups of friends. Interacting with superiors is also likely to generate greater apprehension than meeting with peers or subordinates. Similarly, the degree of familiarity you have with the group members and the extent to which you see yourself as a part of the group (as opposed to an outsider) will also influence your apprehension. You may wish at this point to take the accompanying apprehension test.

Test Yourself | How Apprehensive Are You in Group Discussions?

Instructions: This brief test is designed to measure your apprehension in small group communication situations. This questionnaire consists of 6 statements concerning your feelings about communication in group discussions. Indicate the degree to which each statement applies to you by marking whether you (1) strongly agree, (2) agree, (3) are undecided, (4) disagree, or (5) strongly disagree with each statement. There are no right or wrong answers. Do not be concerned that some of the statements are similar. Work quickly, recording your first impression.

_____ 1. I dislike participating in group discussions.
_____ 2. Generally, I am comfortable while participating in group discussions.
_____ 3. I am tense and nervous while participating in group discussions.
_____ 4. I like to get involved in group discussions.
_____ 5. Engaging in a group discussion with new people makes me tense and nervous.
_____ 6. I am calm and relaxed while participating in group discussions.

Thinking Critically About Small Group Apprehension

To obtain your apprehension for group discussion score use the following formula: 18 plus scores for items 2, 4, and 6 minus scores for items 1, 3, and 5. Scores above 18 show some degree of apprehension.

What kinds of groups generate the most apprehension for you? Can you identify the major characteristics of these high apprehension groups? How do these differ from groups generating little apprehension? What other factors might influence your small group apprehension? Suggestions for reducing apprehension are given in Chapter 13.

Source: From *An Introduction to Rhetorical Communication,* 7th ed., by James C. McCrosky. Copyright ©1997 by Allyn and Bacon. Reprinted by permission.

THE IDEA-GENERATION GROUP

Many small groups are established to generate ideas or "brainstorm"—a technique for analyzing a problem by generating as many ideas as possible (Osborn, 1957; Beebe & Masterson, 1997). While brainstorming can also be useful when you're trying to generate ideas by yourself—ideas for speeches or term papers, ideas for a fun vacation, or ways to make money—it is more typically seen in small group settings. Organizations

Much as you can communicate power and authority with words and nonverbal expression (see Power Perspectives in Chapters 5 and 6), you also communicate power through listening, a topic with obvious relevance to the small group setting where communication as power really comes to the fore. After all, throughout your listening, you're communicating messages to others and these messages comment in some way on your power. To communicate power through listening:

Respond visibly but in moderation. An occasional nod of agreement or a facial expression that says "that's interesting" are usually sufficient. Responding with too little or too much reaction is likely to be perceived as powerless. Too little response says you aren't listening and too much response says you aren't listening critically. Use backchanneling cues—head nods and minimal vocal responses that say you're listening.

Much as you would avoid adaptors while speaking, avoid them also while listening. *Adaptors,* playing with your hair or a pencil or drawing pictures on a styrofoam cup, signal that you're uncomfortable and, hence, that you lack power. These body movements show you to be more concerned with yourself than with the speaker. The lack of adaptors, on the other hand, makes you appear in control of the situation and comfortable in the role of listener.

Maintain an open posture. When around a table or in an audience resist covering your face, chest, or stomach with your hands. This type of posture is often interpreted as indicating defensiveness and may, therefore, communicate a feeling of vulnerability and hence powerlessness.

Avoid interrupting the speaker. The reason is simple: not interrupting is one of the rules of business communication that powerful people follow and powerless people don't. Completing the speaker's thought (or what you think is the speaker's thought) has a similar powerless effect.

Take modest notes when appropriate. Taking too many notes may communicate a lack of ability to distinguish between what is and what is not important. Taking too few notes may communicate a lack of interest or unwillingness to deal with the material.

You can also signal power through "visual dominance behavior" (Exline, Ellyson, & Long, 1975). For example, the average speaker maintains a high level of eye contact while listening and a lower level while speaking. When you want to signal dominance, you can reverse this pattern. You might, for example, maintain a high level of eye contact while talking but a much lower level while listening.

[The next Listen to This box appears on page 281.]

Studies find that persons high in communication apprehension are generally less effective in idea-generation groups than are those low in apprehension (Jablin, 1981; Comadena, 1984; Cragan & Wright, 1990). Do you find this true from your own experience? Why do you think this is so?

have come to embrace brainstorming because it lessens group members' inhibitions and encourages all participants to exercise their creativity. It also fosters cooperative team work; members soon learn that their own ideas and creativity are sparked by the contributions of others. The technique builds member pride and ownership in the final solution or product or service since all members contribute to it.

Brainstorming occurs in two phases. The first is the brainstorming period proper; the second is the evaluation period. The procedures are simple. A problem is selected; the "problem" may be almost anything that is amenable to many possible solutions or ideas, for example, how to devise an effective advertising campaign, how to recruit new members to the organization, or how to market a new product. Before the actual session, group members are informed of the problem so they can think about the topic. When the group meets, each person contributes as many ideas as he

Secrets

This dialogue focuses on the ethics of revealing secrets.

Frank: father
Laura: mother
Barbara: daughter
Jeff: son

Jeff: Listen, everyone. Kim told me something today that I want to tell you. I promised her I wouldn't tell anyone but I just have to tell you.

Laura: Well, maybe you shouldn't. I mean, if you promised Kim maybe you shouldn't tell us.

Jeff: No, no, I really want to—I have to.

Frank: Your mother's right. If you promised to keep a secret, then keep it. You'll be the better person for it.

Jeff: Well, if you all promise to keep it a secret, it'll be okay.

Would it be wrong for Jeff to reveal the secret? Would your answer depend on the kind of secret? If so, what would you have to know about the secret to answer this question? What would you answer if:

- Kim broke up with her boyfriend yesterday for the third time this month (and they are both 14 years old)?
- Kim, 17 years old, plans to commit suicide?
- Kim is heavily into drugs?
- Kim was 4 and Jeff was 5? Kim was 4 and Jeff was 32? Kim and Jeff were both 19?
- If the family members kept the secret confidential?

When is it ethical to reveal another's secrets? When is it unethical?

[The next Ethical Issue box appears on page 273.]

---

or she can think of. Often companies use chalkboards or easels with note paper to record all the ideas. If ideas are to be recorded on tape, a tape recorder is set up (and tested) at the beginning of the session. During this idea-generating session, members follow four rules.

- No evaluation is permitted at this stage. All ideas are recorded for the group to see (or hear later). Any evaluation—whether verbal or nonverbal—is criticized by the leader or members. By prohibiting evaluation, group members will more likely participate freely.
- Quantity of ideas is the goal. The more ideas that are generated, the more likely a useful solution will be found.
- Combinations and extensions of ideas are encouraged. While members may not criticize a particular idea, they may extend or combine it. The value of a particular idea may well be in the way it stimulates other ideas.
- Freewheeling (developing as wild an idea as possible) is desired. A wild idea can be easily tempered, but it's not so easy to elaborate on a simple or conservative idea.

At times, the brainstorming session may slow down with members failing to contribute new ideas. At this point, the moderator may step in to encourage members with statements such as:

> The best way to have a good idea is to have a lot of ideas.
> —*Linus Pauling*

Power Perspective 10.1

Power is the great aphrodisiac.
—*Henry Kissinger*

Gaining Compliance

One way to exert power is to use *compliance-gaining strategies*—tactics that influence others to do what you want them to do. Although effective, these strategies are not necessarily ethical. In fact, as you read these, consider the ethical implications. Here are a few such strategies (Marwell & Schmitt, 1967; Miller & Parks, 1982).

1. **Liking.** Be helpful and friendly in order to get the person in a good mood so that he or she will be more likely to comply with your request. For example, after treating a coworker to lunch, you might say *I'd really like to be elected chair of the new personnel committee; I'm hoping I can count on your support.*
2. **Promise.** Promise to reward the person if he or she complies with your request: *With me on the personnel committee, you'll have a great chance at promotion.*
3. **Positive self-feelings.** Show that the person will feel better by complying with your request or will feel worse by not complying (**negative self-feelings**): *You'll feel a lot better after the divorce.* Or, *You'll hate yourself if you don't give me this divorce.*
4. **Moral appeals.** Argue that the person should comply because it's the moral thing to do. *Ethical people just don't stand in the way of another person's freedom and sanity.*

[The next Power Perspective appears on page 263.]

Of what value might brainstorming be to you in your academic life? In your personal and professional life?

- "Let's try to get a few more ideas before we close this session."
- "Can we piggyback any other ideas or extensions on the suggestion to . . . ."
- "Here's what we have so far. As I read the list of contributed suggestions, additional ideas may come to mind."
- "Here's an aspect we haven't focused on. . . . Does this stimulate any ideas?"

After all the ideas are generated—a period that lasts about 15 to 20 minutes—the entire list is evaluated by the group. Unworkable ones are crossed off the list; those showing promise are retained and evaluated. During this phase, criticism is allowed.

INFORMATION-SHARING GROUPS

The purpose of information-sharing groups is to acquire new information or skills through sharing knowledge. In most information-sharing groups, all members have something to teach and something to learn, for example, a group of students sharing information to prepare for an examination. In others, the interaction takes place because some have information and some do not, for example, a discussion between patients and health care professionals.

Educational or Learning Groups

Members may follow a variety of discussion patterns (Christensen, 1983). For example, a historical topic (such as the development of free speech or equal rights) might be developed chronologically, with the discussion progressing from the past into the present and perhaps predicting the future. Issues in developmental psychology, such as, a child's language development or physical maturity, might also be discussed chronologically. Other topics lend themselves to spatial development. For example, the development of the United States might take a spatial pattern—from east to west—or a chronological pattern—from 1776 to the present. Other suitable patterns, depending on the topic and the group's needs, might be causes and effects, problems and solutions, or structures and functions.

Perhaps the most popular is the topical pattern. A group might discuss the legal profession by itemizing and discussing each of its major functions. A corporation's structure might be considered in terms of its major divisions. As can be appreciated, each of these topics may be further systematized by, for example, listing the legal profession's functions in terms of importance or complexity and ordering the corporation's major structures in terms of decision-making power.

The wisest mind has something yet to learn.

—*George Santayana*

Have you ever participated in an educational or learning group? Was it effective? How might it have been more effective?

Focus Groups

A special type of learning group is the focus group, a kind of indepth interview of a small group. The aim here is to discover what people think about an issue or product, for example, "What do teachers of communication think are today's significant ethical issues? What do young executives earning more than $100,000 think of buying a foreign luxury car?"

In the focus group the leader tries to discover the beliefs, attitudes, thoughts, and feelings that participants have, so as to better guide decisions on, for example, developing a code of ethics or constructing advertisements for luxury cars. It's the leader's task to prod members to analyze their thoughts and feelings on a deeper level and to react to or elaborate on the thoughts and feelings of others in the group.

For example, in one study the researcher tried "to collect supplementary data on the perceptions graduates have of the Department of Communication at ABC University" (Lederman, 1990). Two major research questions, taken directly from Lederman's study, motivated this focus group:

- What do graduates of the program perceive is the educational effectiveness of their major at ABC?
- What would they want implemented in the program as it exists today?

Group participants then discussed their perceptions that were organized around the following questions (Lederman, 1990):

- The first issue to discuss is what the program was like when you were a major in the department. Let's begin by going around the table and making introductions. Will you tell me your name, when you graduated from ABC, what you're doing now, and what the program was like when you were here, as you remember it?
- Based on what you remember of the program and what you have used from your major since graduating, what kinds of changes, if any, would you suggest?

PROBLEM-SOLVING GROUPS

A problem-solving group meets to solve a particular problem or to reach a decision on some issue. In a sense, this is the most demanding kind of group because it requires not only a knowledge of small group communication techniques, but also a thorough knowledge of the particular problem on the part of all members. For the most successful outcome, it usually demands faithful adherence to a set of procedural rules.

At times, the problem-solving group members may all come from the same area or department; all may be sales representatives or all may be health professionals. At other times, the group members consist of what has come to be called an "integrated work team," which consists of members from different areas of the organization who have related goals and who must work together to accomplish these goals (Hill, 1997). For example, a publishing company work team might consist of persons from the editorial, design, advertising, production, and marketing departments.

The Problem-Solving Sequence

The problem-solving approach discussed here identifies six steps and owes its formulation to philosopher John Dewey's insights into how people think (see Figure 10.3). These steps are designed to make problem solving more efficient and effective.

Define and Analyze the Problem In many instances the nature of the problem is clearly specified. For example, a work team might discuss how to package the new CD-ROMs for Valentine's Day. In other instances, the problem may be vague, and it's up to the group to define it in more specific terms. Thus, for example, the general problem may be poor campus communications. However, such a vague and general topic is difficult to tackle in a problem-solving discussion. So, for purposes of discussion, a group might be more specific and focus on improving the college website.

Define the problem as an open-ended question ("How can we improve the college website?") rather than as a statement ("The website needs to be improved") or a yes/no question ("Does the website need improvement?"). The open-ended question allows greater freedom of exploration.

Limit the problem to a manageable area for discussion. A question such as "How can we improve communication at the college?" is too broad and general. It would be more effective to limit the problem by focusing on one

A problem well stated is a problem half solved.

—*Charles F. Kettering*

The mere formulation of a problem is often far more essential than its solution, which may be a matter of mathematical or experimental skill. To raise new questions, new possibilities, to regard old problems from a new angle requires creative imagination and marks real advance in science.

—*Albert Einstein*

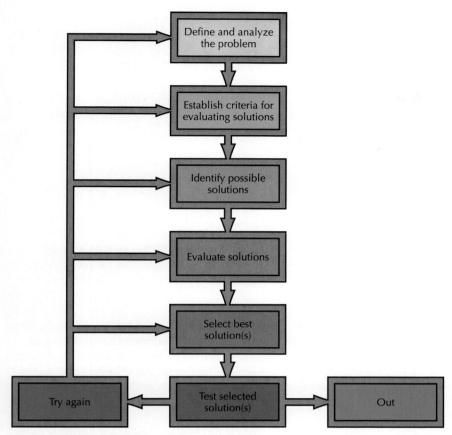

Figure 10.3 The Problem-Solving Sequence

While most small group theorists would advise you to follow the problem-solving pattern as presented here, others would alter it somewhat. For example, some would advise you to identify possible solutions first and then consider the criteria for evaluating them (Brilhart & Galanes, 1992). The advantage of this approach is that you're likely to generate more creative solutions, since you will not be restricted by standards of evaluation. The disadvantage is that you might spend a great deal of time generating very impractical solutions that would never meet the standards you will eventually propose.

Is this problem-solving sequence also appropriate for resolving interpersonal conflicts? Can you trace an example through this sequence?

subdivision of the college, for example, the student newspaper, student–faculty relationships, registration, examination scheduling, student advisory services, or the website.

Establish Criteria for Evaluating Solutions   Decide how you'll evaluate the solutions, before proposing any of them. Identify the standards or criteria you'll use in evaluating the solutions or in preferring one solution over another. Generally, problem-solving groups consider two types of criteria: practical and value criteria. As an example of practical criteria, you might decide that the solutions must not increase the budget or that they must lead to a 10% increase in website visits.

What type of criteria would an advertising agency use in evaluating a campaign to sell soap? A university in evaluating a new multicultural curriculum? Parents in evaluating a preschool for their children?

"You know what your problem is? You don't know what your problem is ... That's what your problem is!!"

© Rick Stromoski

The value criteria are more difficult to identify. For example, value criteria might state that the website information must not violate anyone's right to privacy or that it must provide a forum for all members of the college community.

Identify Possible Solutions   Identify as many solutions as possible. At this stage focus on *quantity* rather than *quality*. Brainstorming may be particularly useful at this point. Solutions to the website improvement problem might include incorporating reviews of faculty publications, student evaluations of specific courses, reviews of restaurants in the campus area, outlines for new courses, and employment information.

Evaluate Solutions   After all solutions have been proposed, evaluate each. For example, will incorporating reviews of area restaurants meet the criteria? Would it increase the budget, for example? Would posting grades violate students' rights to privacy? Each potential solution should be matched against the evaluating criteria.

Select the Best Solution(s)   Select the best solution and put it into operation. Let's assume that reviews of faculty publications and outlines for new courses best meet the criteria for evaluating solutions. The group might then incorporate these two new items into the website.

Groups use different decision-making methods in deciding, for example, which solution to accept. The method to be used should naturally be stated at the outset of the group discussion. The three main ones are:

- In **decision by authority,** group members voice their feelings and opinions, but the leader, boss, or CEO makes the final decision. This method has the advantage of being efficient and of giving greater importance to the suggestions of the more experienced members. The great disadvantage is that members may feel that their contributions have too little influence and may decline to participate with real enthusiasm.
- Under **majority rule** the group agrees to abide by the majority decision and may vote on various issues as the group searches to solve its problem. Like decision by authority, this method is efficient. A

How do the groups of which you're a member reach their decisions? Are you a member of a group that reaches decisions by authority, by majority rule, or by consensus?

disadvantage is that it may lead the group to limit discussion by calling for a vote once a majority has agreed. Also, members not voting with the majority may feel disenfranchised and left out.

- In some groups decisions are reached through **consensus.** In some situations consensus means unanimous agreement. For example, a criminal jury must reach a unanimous decision to convict or acquit a defendant. In most business groups consensus means that members agree that they can live with the solution. They agree that they can do whatever the solution requires (Kelly, 1994). Consensus is especially helpful when the group wants the satisfaction and commitment of each member to the decision and to the decision-making process as a whole (DeStephen & Hirokawa, 1988; Rothwell, 1992). Consensus obviously takes the longest amount of time of any of the decision-making methods and can lead to a great deal of inefficiency, especially if members wish to prolong the discussion process needlessly or selfishly.

What decision-making method is used in your family? What decision-making method is used in most of your college classes? Are you satisfied with either of these?

Note that these decision-making methods may be used at any point in the problem-solving sequence. For example, the vice president may decide what problem to study (decision by authority) or the members may vote on what criteria the solution should meet (decision by majority vote).

Test Selected Solution(s)   After putting the solution(s) into operation, test their effectiveness. The group might, for example, poll the students or college employees about the new website. Or the group might analyze the number of visits to the website to see if the number of visits increased the desired 10%. If these solutions prove ineffective, return to a previous stage and repeat that part of the process. Often this involves selecting other solutions to test. However, it may also mean going even further back in the process, for example, to a reanalysis of the problem, an identification of other solutions, or a restatement of criteria.

Problem Solving at Work

The problem-solving sequence discussed here is used widely in business in a variety of different types of groups. Here are three groups popular in business that rely largely on problem solving: the nominal group technique, the Delphi technique, and quality circles.

The Nominal Group Technique   The **nominal group technique** is a method of problem solving that uses limited discussion and confidential voting to obtain a group decision. It's especially helpful when some members may be reluctant to voice their opinions in a regular problem-solving group or when the issue is controversial or sensitive. With this technique, each member contributes equally and each contribution is treated equally. Another advantage of this technique is that it can be accomplished in a relatively short period of time. The nominal group technique can be divided into seven steps (Kelly, 1994):

1. The problem is defined and clarified for all members.
2. Each member writes down (without discussion or consultation with others) his or her ideas on or possible solutions to the problem.
3. Each member—in sequence—states one idea from his or her list that is recorded on a board or flip chart so everyone can see it. This process is repeated until all suggestions are stated and recorded.
4. Each suggestion is clarified (without debate). Ideally, each suggestion should be given equal time.
5. Each member rank orders the suggestions.
6. The rankings of the members are combined to get a group ranking, which is then written on the board.
7. Clarification, discussion, and possible reordering may follow.

The highest ranking solution might then be selected to be tested or perhaps several high-ranking solutions may be put into operation.

The Delphi Method   In the **Delphi method,** a group of experts is established but there is no interaction among them; instead they communicate by repeatedly responding to questionnaires (Tersine & Riggs, 1980; Kelly, 1994). The method is especially useful when you want to involve people who are geographically distant from each other, when you want all members to act a part of the solution and to uphold it, and when you want to minimize the effects of dominant members or even of peer pressure. The method is best explained as a series of steps (Kelly, 1994).

1. The problem is defined (for example, "How can we improve intradepartmental communication?"). What each member is expected

Some problems are so complex that you have to be highly intelligent and well informed just to be undecided about them.

—*Laurence J. Peter*

to do is specified (for example, each member should contribute five ideas on this specific question).

2. Each member then contributes anonymously his or her ideas in writing. This stage used to be completed through questionnaires sent through traditional mail, but is now more frequently done through E-mail, which greatly increases the speed with which this entire process can be accomplished.

3. The ideas of all members are combined, written up, and distributed to all members who may be asked to, for example, select the three or four best ideas from this composite list.

4. Members then select the three or four best ideas and submit these.

5. From these responses another list is produced and distributed to all members who may be asked to select the one or two best ideas.

6. Members then select the one or two best ideas and these are submitted.

7. From these responses, another list is produced and distributed to all members. The process may be repeated any number of times, but usually three rounds are sufficient for achieving a fair degree of agreement.

8. The "final" solutions are identified and are communicated to all members.

Quality Circles **Quality circles** are groups of workers (usually from about 6 to 12) whose task is to investigate and make recommendations for improving the quality of some organizational function. The

---

Power Perspective 10.2

Resisting Compliance

How do you respond when someone asks you to do something you don't want to do, for example, borrow a report you wrote so they can (basically) copy it and present it as their own. Here are four ways of resisting compliance (O'Hair, Cody, & O'Hair, 1991):

Refuse directly by saying "no." ("I don't lend out my work.")

Justify your refusal by citing possible consequences of compliance or noncompliance. For example, you might cite a negative consequence if you complied ("I'm afraid you'd get caught") or a positive consequence of not complying ("You'll learn a lot from writing this report; it's a really important job skill to learn").

Resist by offering a compromise ("I'll let you read my report but not copy it") or by offering to help the person in some other way ("If you write a first draft, I'll go over it for you").

Resist by manipulating the image of the person making the request. For example, you might picture the person as unreasonable and say: "You know this material much better than I do; you can easily do a much better report yourself."

[The next Power Perspective appears on page 276.]

Power never takes a back step—only in the face of more power.

—Malcolm X

members are drawn from the workers whose area is being studied. Thus, for example, if the problem is to improve advertising on the Internet, then the quality circle membership would be drawn from the advertising and computer departments. Generally, the motivation for establishing quality circles is economic; the company's aim is to improve quality and profitability. Another related goal is to improve worker morale. Because quality circles involve workers in decision making, workers may feel empowered and more essential to the organization (Gorden & Nevins, 1993).

The basic idea is that people who work on similar tasks will be better able to improve their departments or jobs by pooling their insights and working through problems they share. The quality circle style of problem solving is often considered one of the major reasons for the success of Japanese businesses where it's widely used (Gorden & Nevins, 1993).

Quality circle members investigate problems using any methods they feel might be helpful, for example, face-to-face problem-solving groups, nominal groups, delphi methods. Usually, the group then reports its findings and its suggestions to those who can do something about them. In some cases, however, the quality circle members may implement their solutions without approval from upper management levels.

THINKING CRITICALLY ABOUT SMALL GROUPS

In approaching the study of small groups and your own participation in groups, keep the following in mind:

- The skills of small group communication are largely, in general, the skills of leadership. Look at this material and these skills as guides to improving your own leadership skills, a topic covered more specifically in the next chapter.
- Small groups are usually more effective in solving problems than are individuals working alone. Creative solutions emerge from a combination of thoughts. Therefore, approach small group situations with flexibility. Come to the small group with ideas and information but resist coming with firmly formulated conclusions.
- Small groups work best when each person remains true to her or his own beliefs, rather than accepting solutions or ideas because others have done so. At the same time, small groups work best when we each see ourselves as part of the group and subordinate our own preferences for the well-being and effectiveness of the group.

The Six Critical Thinking Hats Technique

Critical thinking pioneer Edward deBono (1987) suggests we use six "thinking" hats to define and analyze problems. This technique is a useful adjunct to the problem-solving sequence discussed earlier. With each hat you look at the problem from a different perspective. The technique provides a convenient and interesting way to explore a problem from a variety of different angles.

- The **fact hat** focuses on the data—the facts and figures that bear on the problem. For example, What are the relevant data on the website? How can I get more information on the website's history? How much does it cost to construct and maintain? Can we include advertising?
- The **feeling hat** focuses on your feelings, emotions, and intuitions concerning the problem. How do you feel about the website and about making major changes?
- The **negative argument hat** asks you to become the devil's advocate. Why might this proposal fail? What are the problems with publishing outlines and reviews of courses? What is the worst-case scenario?
- The **positive benefits hat** asks you to look at the upside. What are the opportunities that this new format will open up? What benefits will publishing outlines and reviews of courses provide for the students? What is the best-case scenario?
- The **creative new idea hat** focuses on new ways of looking at the problem and can be easily combined with brainstorming techniques (discussed earlier in this chapter). What other ways can you look at this problem? What other functions can a website serve? Can the website serve the nonacademic community as well?
- The **control of thinking hat** helps you analyze what you've done and are doing. It asks that you reflect on your own thinking processes and synthesize the results. Have you adequately defined the problem? Are you focusing too much on insignificant issues? Have you given enough attention to the possible negative effects?

Never, never rest contented with any circle of ideas, but always be certain that a wider one is still possible.
—*Richard Jefferies*

Why is the six thinking hats technique useful in critical thinking? In what specific situations can this technique have practical value?

SUMMARY OF CONCEPTS AND SKILLS

In this chapter we provided an overview of the small group's nature, the ways in which some major groups (idea generation, information sharing, and problem solving) work, and the popular small group formats.

1. A small group is a collection of individuals, few enough for all members to communicate with relative ease as both senders and receivers. The members are related by some common purpose and have some degree of organization or structure.
2. Small groups generally follow the five stages of conversation: opening, feedforward, business, feedback, closing.
3. Four popular small group formats are the round table, the panel, the symposium, and the symposium–forum.
4. Small groups develop norms—rules or standards of behavior—that are heavily influenced by the larger culture of which the groups are a part.
5. Two popular Internet groups are the mailing list group and the IRC group, both are changing the way we think about small group communication.

6. The idea-generation or brainstorming group attempts to generate as many ideas as possible by emphasizing the avoiding of critical evaluation and encouraging quantity, combinations and extensions, and freewheeling.
7. Information-sharing groups (for example, the educational or learning group or the focus group) attempt to acquire new information or skill through a mutual sharing of knowledge or insight.
8. The problem-solving group attempts to solve a particular problem or at least reach a decision that may be a preface to solving the problem and may do so through decision by authority, majority rule, or consensus.
9. The six steps in the problem-solving approach are: define and analyze the problem, establish criteria for evaluating solutions, identify possible solutions, evaluate solutions, select best solution(s), and test solution(s).
10. Three problem-solving groups popular in business today are the nominal technique, the Delphi technique, and quality circles.
11. A useful technique in analyzing problems is the critical thinking hats technique in which you approach

a problem in terms of facts, feelings, negative arguments, positive benefits, creative ideas, and overall analysis.

The skills covered in this chapter focus on our ability to effectively use the various types of small groups. Check your ability to apply these skills. Use the following scale: (1) = almost always, (2) = often, (3) = sometimes, (4) = rarely, (5) = hardly ever.

_____ 1. I actively seek to discover the norms of the groups in which I function and take these norms into consideration when interacting in the group.

_____ 2. I can communicate in mailing list and IRC groups.

_____ 3. I follow the general rules when brainstorming: I avoid negative criticism, strive for quantity, combine and extend the contributions of others, and contribute as wild an idea as I can.

_____ 4. I appropriately restimulate a brainstorming group that has lost its steam.

_____ 5. I employ organizational structure in educational or learning groups.

_____ 6. I follow the six steps when in group problem-solving situations: define and analyze the problem, establish the criteria for evaluating solutions, identify possible solutions, evaluate solutions, select the best solution(s), and test selected solution(s).

_____ 7. I can make use of such techniques as the nominal group, the delphi method, and quality circles.

_____ 8. I use the critical thinking hats technique and think about problems in terms of facts, feelings, negative arguments, positive benefits, creative ideas, and overall analysis.

KEY WORD QUIZ

Write T for those statements that are true and F for those that are false. For those that are false, replace the boldface term with the correct term.

_____ 1. No evaluation, an emphasis on quantity, combinations and extensions, and freewheeling are desired characteristics of the **problem-solving group.**

_____ 2. An in-depth interview of a small group to discover what people think about an issue or product is known as a **learning group.**

_____ 3. Defining and analyzing the problem, establishing criteria for evaluating solutions, identi-

fying possible solutions, evaluating solutions, selecting the best solutions, and testing the selected solutions are stages in the **consciousness-raising group.**

_____ 4. An Internet group that allows you to communicate in real time is the **mailing list group.**

_____ 5. A number of people working on a problem together who submit solutions in writing and who don't talk directly with one another is known as a **focus group.**

_____ 6. Groups of workers whose task it is to improve working conditions or productivity are known as **quality circles.**

_____ 7. When a group reaches a decision that all members agree with and feel they can live with, the decision is said to be by **consensus.**

_____ 8. A general discussion, largely of questions and answers from the audience directed at group members, is known as a **symposium.**

_____ 9. Authority, majority rule, and consensus are types of **decision-making methods.**

_____ 10. The type of group in which a pool of experts interacts, not interpersonally, but by repeatedly responding to questionnaires, is known as the **Delphi group.**

Answers: TRUE 6, 7, 9, 10. FALSE 1 (brainstorming group), 2 (focus group), 3 (problem-solving group), 4 (Internet Relay Chat group), 5 (nominal group), 7 (symposium), 8 (forum).

SKILL DEVELOPMENT EXPERIENCES

10.1 Brainstorming

Together with a small group or with the class as a whole, sit in a circle and brainstorm one of the topics identified in Skill Development Experience 10.2: Solving Problems in Groups. Be sure to appoint someone to write down all the contributions or use a tape recorder. After this brainstorming session, consider these questions:

1. Did any members give negative criticism (even nonverbally)?
2. Did any members hesitate to contribute really wild ideas? Why?
3. Was it necessary to restimulate the group members at any point? Did this help?
4. Did possible solutions emerge in the brainstorming session that were not considered by members of the problem-solving group?

10.2 Solving Problems in Groups

Together with four, five, or six others, form a problem-solving group and discuss one of the following questions:

- What should we do about the homeless?
- What should we do to improve employee morale?
- What should we do to better prepare ourselves for the job market?
- How can we improve student–faculty communication?
- What should be the college's responsibility concerning students and faculty with AIDS?

Before beginning the discussion, each member should prepare a discussion outline, answering the following questions:

1. What is the problem? How long has it existed? What caused it? What are the effects of the problem?
2. What are some possible solutions?
3. What are the advantages and disadvantages of each of these possible solutions?
4. What solution seems best (in light of the advantages and disadvantages)?
5. How might you test this solution?

CHAPTER 11

Members and Leaders in Group Communication

CHAPTER CONTENTS	CHAPTER GOALS After completing this chapter, you should be able to	CHAPTER SKILLS After completing this chapter, you should be able to
Members in Small Group Communication	1. identify the three major types of member roles and the guidelines for member participation	participate in small groups with a group orientation, serving group task and group building and maintenance roles, and avoiding dysfunctional (individual) roles
Leaders in Small Group Communication	2. describe the styles and functions of leadership	adjust your leadership style to the task at hand and the needs of group members
Membership, Leadership, and Culture	3. explain the role of culture in group membership and leadership	communicate in groups with cultural awareness and sensitivity
Thinking Critically About Groupthink	4. define *groupthink* and identify its major symptoms	recognize and combat groupthink tendencies

This chapter continues our exploration of small group communication and focuses on both membership and leadership in the small group. Here we consider the roles members serve, the styles and functions of leadership, and the influence of culture on small group interaction.

MEMBERS IN SMALL GROUP COMMUNICATION

Each of us serves many roles, patterns of behaviors that we customarily serve and that we're expected to serve by others. Javier, for example, is a part-time college student, father, bookkeeper, bowling team captain, and sometime poet. That is, he acts as a student—attends class, reads textbooks, takes exams, and does the things we expect of college students. Similarly, he performs those behaviors associated with fathers, bookkeepers, and so on. In a similar way, you develop ways of behaving when participating in small groups. Here are some roles that were developed from analyses of face-to-face groups, but you'll notice the same roles performed in online groups as well. With an understanding of these roles as a foundation, guidelines for participating effectively in small groups are then offered.

Member Roles

Kenneth Benne and Paul Sheats (1948) proposed a classification of members' roles in small group communication that still provides the best overview of this important topic (Lumsden & Lumsden, 1993; Beebe & Masterson, 1994). They divide members' roles into three general classes: group task roles, group building and maintenance roles, and individual roles. These roles are, of course, frequently performed by leaders as well.

Group Task Roles   Group task roles help the group focus on achieving its goals. Effective group members serve several roles, although some people do lock into a few specific roles. Usually, this single focus is counterproductive—it's better for the roles to be spread more evenly among the members and for the roles to be alternated frequently. Some examples of these roles include:

> Do not wait for leaders; do it alone, person to person.
>
> —*Mother Teresa*

- **the information seeker or giver and the opinion seeker or giver** asks for or gives facts and opinions, seeks clarification of issues being discussed, presents facts and opinions to group members
- **the evaluator–critic** evaluates the group's decisions, questions the logic or practicality of the suggestions, and thus provides the group with both positive and negative feedback
- **the procedural technician or recorder** takes care of the various mechanical duties such as distributing group materials and arranging the seating; writes down the group's activities, suggestions, and decisions; and serves as the group's memory

Group Building and Maintenance Roles   No group can be task-oriented at all times. Group members have varied interpersonal relationships and these need to be nourished if the group is to function effectively. Group members need to be satisfied if they're to be productive. Group building and maintenance roles serve these relationship needs. Examples include:

- **the encourager, harmonizer** provides members with positive reinforcement through social approval or praise for their ideas; mediates the various differences between group members
- **the compromiser** tries to resolve conflict between his or her ideas and those of others and offers compromises
- **the follower** goes along with members, passively accepts the ideas of others, and functions more as an audience than as an active member

Individual Roles The group task roles and group building and maintenance roles just considered are productive roles; they help the group achieve its goal, and are group-oriented. Individual roles, on the other hand, are counterproductive. They hinder the group from achieving its goal and are individual rather than group-oriented. Such roles, often termed dysfunctional, hinder the group's effectiveness in both productivity and personal satisfaction. Examples of such roles include:

- **the aggressor or blocker** expresses negative evaluation of members and attacks the group, is generally disagreeable, and opposes other members or their suggestions regardless of their merit
- **the recognition seeker and self-confessor** try to focus attention on themselves, boast about their accomplishments rather than the task at hand, and express their own feelings rather than focusing on the group
- **the dominator** tries to run the group or members, by pulling rank, flattering members, or acting the role of boss

A popular individual role born on the Internet (and introduced in Chapter 7) is **trolling,** the practice of posting messages that you know are false just so you can watch the group members correct you. This type of behavior wastes time and energy and diverts the group from its primary objective.

What general types of roles do you most often play in small groups (task, building and maintenance, or individual roles)? Within this general category, what more specific roles do you regularly play? What specific behaviors do you display that correspond to these roles?

Member Participation

Here are several guidelines to help make your participation in small group communication more effective and enjoyable.

Be Group- or Team-Oriented When participating in a small group you serve as a member of a team. You share a common goal with the other group members and your participation is valuable to the extent that it advances this shared goal. In a team situation you need to pool your talents, knowledge, and insights to promote the best possible solution for the group. While this solution benefits greatly from the participation and co-operation of all group members, group orientation does not suggest that you abandon your individuality, personal values, or beliefs for the group's sake. Individuality with a group orientation is *most* effective. This group orientation is also seen in one of the rules of netiquette, which holds that you should not protest the subject of, say, a mailing list or an IRC group. If you don't wish to be group-oriented and discuss what the group is discussing, you're expected to unsubscribe from the mailing list or withdraw from the group.

Center Conflict on Issues When people interact, conflict is inevitable; it's a natural part of the give and take of ideas. Recognize that conflict is a natural part of the small group process that often promotes a better outcome (Kushner, 1996). To manage it effectively, however, it must be centered on issues rather than on personalities. When group members disagree, it must be clear that the disagreement is with the ideas expressed and not with the person who expressed them. Similarly, when you find someone disagreeing with you, try not to take it personally or react emotionally. Rather, view the disagreement as an opportunity to discuss issues from an alternative point of view. In the language of the Internet, don't flame—don't attack the person—and don't contribute to flame wars by flame baiting, saying things that will further incite the personal attacks.

Be Critically Open-Minded When members join a group with their minds already made up, the small group process degenerates into a series of debates in which each person argues for his or her position. In this situation, the group goals are neglected and the group process breaks down. To avoid this, come to the group with information that will contribute to the discussion and the group goal. Don't decide on a solution or draw conclusions before discussing it with the group. Advance solutions and conclusions tentatively rather than with certainty. Be willing to accept other people's suggestions as well as revise your own in light of the discussion. Be willing to subject all suggestions—even your own—to critical analysis and evaluation. Listen openly but critically to comments of all members (including yourself).

Ensure Understanding Make sure all participants understand your ideas and information. If something is worth saying, it's worth making it clear. When in doubt, ask: "Is that clear?" "Did I explain that clearly?" Make sure, too, that you fully understand other members' contributions, especially before you disagree with them. In fact, it's often wise to preface any expression of disagreement with some kind of paraphrase to ensure you really are in disagreement. For example, you might say "If I understand you correctly, you feel that marketing should bear sole responsibility for updating the product database." After waiting for the response, you would state your thoughts.

LEADERS IN SMALL GROUP COMMUNICATION

In many small groups, one person serves as leader. In other groups, leadership is shared by several people. In some groups, a person may be appointed or serve as leader because she or he holds the highest position

Leadership appears to be the art of getting others to want to do something you are convinced should be done.

—*Vance Packard*

Ethical Issue — Means and Ends

A long-standing debate in ethics focuses on means and ends. Do the ends justify the means? Is it ethical for a group to do things that would normally be considered unethical, for example, writing deliberately misleading advertising, if the end you hoped to achieve was a worthy one, like keeping children from using drugs? Those taking an objective position (see Ethical Issue box, Chapter 2) would argue that the ends do not justify the means, that the lie, for example, is always wrong regardless of the specific situation. Those taking a subjective position would argue that, at times, the end would justify the means and at times it wouldn't; it would depend on the specific means and ends in question.

You'll probably make at least some of your communication decisions—whether in groups, in public, or with one or two other people—on the basis of a means–ends analysis. How would you respond to each of these situations?

1. To lie about your past to your romantic partner to preserve peace and stability in the relationship?
2. Exaggerate your skills and experience in a job interview to get the job you need to support your family?
3. To misrepresent yourself on an Internet group to spice things up?
4. To work on an advertising team writing an ad using only emotional and credibility appeals (nothing logical about it) to get children to buy expensive sneakers? To get teens to avoid potentially dangerous sexual practices?
5. To make up statistics to support your point of view in a public speech because you know that what you're advocating will benefit the audience?

[The next Ethical Issue box appears on page 305.]

within the company or hierarchy. In other groups, the leader emerges as the group proceeds in fulfilling its functions or may be voted as leader by the group members. In any case the role of the leader is vital to the well-being and effectiveness of the group. Even in leaderless groups, where all members are equal, leadership functions must still be served.

Approaches to Leadership

Not surprisingly, leadership has been the focus of considerable attention from researchers who have identified a number of approaches. Looking at a few of these approaches will give you a better idea of the varied ways in which leadership may be viewed and a better grasp on what leadership is and how it may be achieved.

The **traits approach** views the leader as the one who possesses those characteristics (or traits) that contribute to leadership. This approach is valuable for stressing the characteristics that often (but not always) distinguish leaders from nonleaders. The problem with the traits approach is that these qualities often vary with the group situation, with the members, and with the culture in which the leader functions. Thus, for some groups a youthful, energetic, humorous leader might be effective (for example, a new computer game development group), whereas, for other groups, an older, more experienced and serious leader might be effective (for example, a medical diagnosis team). Nevertheless, research does find that there

Reason and judgment are the qualities of a leader.

—Tacitus

Leadership is action, not position.
—Donald H. McGannon

Learn to lead in a nourishing manner.
Learn to lead without being
    possessive.
Learn to be helpful without taking
    the credit.
Learn to lead without coercion.
—John Heider

It's found that the person with the highest rate of participation in a group is the one most likely to be chosen leader (Muller, Salas, & Driskell, 1989). Do you find this to be true of the groups in which you have participated? Why do you suppose this relationship exists?

are certain traits that are more frequently associated with leadership than others. These include intelligence, self-confidence, determination, integrity, and sociability (Northouse, 1997).

The **transformational approach** claims that the leader is the one who elevates the group's members, enabling them not only to accomplish the group task but to also emerge as more empowered individuals. At the center of the transformational approach is the concept of charisma, that quality of an individual that makes us believe or want to follow him or her. Mahatma Gandhi, Martin Luther King, Jr., and John F. Kennedy are often cited as examples of transformational leaders. These leaders were role models of what they asked of their members, were seen as extremely competent and able, and articulated moral goals, for example (Northouse, 1997). We return to this concept of charisma and to these qualities in our discussion of credibility in Chapter 15.

The **situational approach** holds that the leader adjusts his or her focus between task accomplishment and member satisfaction on the basis of the specific group situation. The general idea of situational leadership is that although both task and people are significant concerns, each situation will call for a different combination. Some situations call for a high focus on task issues but will need little people encouragement (for example, a group of scientists researching a cure for AIDS). On the other hand, a group of recovering alcoholics might require leadership that stresses the members' emotional needs. The situational approach stresses a flexibility in leadership style according to the specific situation. Just as you adjust your conversational style on the basis of the specific situation, so must you adjust your leadership style on the basis of the task to be accomplished and the needs of the group members.

How would you define yourself-as-leader using: (1) the traits perspective, (2) the functional perspective, and (3) the situational perspective?

At this point, you should find it interesting to analyze your own views on and style of leadership by taking the accompanying self-test: What Kind of Leader Are You?

Test Yourself What Kind of Leader Are You?

Instructions: Respond by indicating YES if the statement is a generally accurate description of your leadership style and NO if it's not.

_____ 1. I would speak as a representative of the group.
_____ 2. I would settle conflicts when they occur in the group.
_____ 3. I would be reluctant to allow the others freedom of action.
_____ 4. I would decide what should be done and how it should be done.
_____ 5. I would refuse to explain my actions when questioned.
_____ 6. I would allow members complete freedom in their work.
_____ 7. I would permit the others to use their own judgment in solving problems.
_____ 8. I would let the others do their work as they think best.
_____ 9. I would allow the others a high degree of initiative.
_____ 10. I would permit the group to set its own pace.

Thinking Critically About Leadership Style These questions come from an extensive leadership test and should help you focus on some ways a leader can accomplish a task and ensure member satisfaction. Questions 1–5 are phrased so a leader concerned with completing the group's task would answer YES. Questions 6–10 are phrased so a leader concerned with ensuring that the group members are satisfied would answer YES. Think about your own style of leadership. Do you adjust your style on the basis of the group or do you have one style that you use in all situations? Consider, too, the styles of leadership that you respond to best.

Source: "T-P Leadership Questionnaire: An Assessment of Style," from J. W. Pfeiffer and J. E. Jones, *Structured Experiences for Human Relations Training.* Copyright by the American Educational Research Association. Reprinted by permission of the publisher.

Styles of Leadership

In addition to looking at the major approaches to leadership, we can also look at leadership's three major styles: laissez-faire, democratic, and authoritarian (Shaw, 1981; Bennis & Nanus, 1985).

Laissez-Faire Leader Laissez-faire comes from the French and means literally "allow to do." Applied to group communication, it refers to a leadership style in which the leader takes no (or very little) initiative in directing or suggesting courses of action. Rather, the leader allows the group to develop and progress on its own, even allowing it to make its own mistakes. This leader gives up or denies any real authority. The laissez-faire

In a social group at a friend's house, any leadership other than laissez-faire would be difficult to tolerate. In what other situations would laissez-faire leadership be appropriate?

leader answers questions or provides relevant information, but only when asked, and gives little if any reinforcement to group members. At the same time, since this type of leader does not evaluate or criticize members, laissez-faire leadership is nonthreatening.

Democratic Leader The democratic leader provides direction, but allows the group to develop and progress the way members wish. This leader encourages members to determine goals and procedures and stimulates members' self-direction and self-actualization. Unlike the laissez-faire leader, the democratic leader reinforces members and contributes suggestions. This leader always allows the group to make its own decisions.

Authoritarian Leader The authoritarian leader is the opposite of the laissez-faire leader. This leader determines the group's policies, assigns tasks to members, and makes decisions without getting agreement from, or even consulting, with members. Communication goes to and from the leader, but rarely from member to member. The authoritarian leader assumes the greatest responsibility for the group's progress and does not welcome interference from members.

The moderator of an Internet group (for example, a mailing list or an IRC channnel) is a kind of group leader. For example, a person usually sets

When all members are about equal in their knowledge of the topic or when the members are very concerned with their individual rights, the democratic leader seems the most appropriate. In what other situations might democratic leadership be appropriate?

When time and efficiency are critical or when group members continue to lack motivation despite repeated democratic efforts, authoritarian leadership may be the most effective. In what other situations might authoritarian leadership be appropriate?

up a mailing list, serves as leader for a time, and then lets it operate as an automated system. IRC groups also have "channel operators" who are like leaders; these too are usually the ones who established the group. The moderator (who may be a person or a computer program) may also serve as a filter or gatekeeper who allows certain messages to go through and others to not go through. Much like a supervisor in an organization, the Internet group moderator may on occasion decide to exclude a particular member from further group participation, usually for violating the rules of the particular Internet group. Most Internet group moderators are laissez-faire leaders; they usually don't intrude in the group's ongoing interaction.

Functions of Leadership

With the various views of leadership in mind, especially the situational theory with its concern for both task and people, we can look at some of the major functions leaders serve. These functions are not exclusively the leader's; often they may be served by group members. Nevertheless, when there's a specific leader, she or he is expected to perform them.

Prepare Members and Start Interaction   Groups form gradually and often need to be eased into meaningful discussion. The leader needs to prepare members for the small group interaction as well as for the discussion of a specific issue or problem. Don't expect diverse members to work together cohesively to solve a problem without first becoming familiar with each other. Similarly, if members are to discuss a specific problem, a proper briefing may be necessary. Perhaps materials need to be distributed before the actual discussion, or perhaps members need to read certain materials or view a particular film or television show. Whatever the preparations, the leader should organize and coordinate them. Once the members are assembled the leader may need to stimulate the members to interact.

Maintain Effective Interaction   Even after the group has begun to interact, the leader should monitor the members' effective interaction. When the discussion begins to drag, the leader should step in and motivate the

Power Perspective 11.2

Legitimate Power

You have **legitimate power** over another when this person believes you have a right—by virtue of your position (for example, you're the appointed group leader)—to influence or control his or her behavior. Legitimate power usually comes from the roles people occupy. Teachers have legitimate power and this is doubly true for religious teachers. Parents have legitimate power over their children. Employers, judges, managers, doctors, and police officers are others who may hold legitimate power. What these people share is that they occupy positions of leadership.

[The next Power Perspective appears on page 282.]

Be willing to make decisions. That's the most important quality in a good leader. Don't fall victim to what I call the "ready-aim-aim-aim-aim syndrome." You must be willing to fire.
—T. Boone Pickens

group: "Do we have any additional comments on the proposal to eliminate required courses?" "What do those of you who are members of the college curriculum committee think about the proposal?" The leader also needs to ensure that all members have an opportunity to express themselves.

Guide Members Through the Agreed-Upon Agenda   The leader may keep the discussion on track by asking relevant questions, periodically summarizing the discussions, or by offering a transition from one issue to the next. This often involves following the tasks to be accomplished by the group as outlined in the meeting agenda and efficiently managing the amount of time allotted for each event.

Ensure Member Satisfaction   Members have different psychological needs and wants, and many people enter groups because of them. Even though a group may, for example, deal with political issues, members may have come together more for psychological than for political reasons. If a group is to be effective, it must achieve the group goal (in this case, political) without denying the psychological purposes or goals that motivates many of the members to come together. One way to meet these needs is for the leader to allow digressions and personal comments, assuming they are not too frequent or overly long. Another way is to be supportive and reinforcing.

Depending on the specific members, special adjustments may have to be made to accommodate those with handicaps. One such group that is often ignored in discussions of leadership functions is those with hearing problems. Table 11.1 offers some suggestions.

Encourage Ongoing Evaluation and Improvement   All groups encounter obstacles as they try to solve a problem, reach a decision, or generate ideas. No group is totally effective. All groups have room for improvement. To improve, the group must focus on itself. Along with trying to solve some external problem, it must try to solve its own internal problems, for example, personal conflicts, failure of members to meet on time, or members

> Leadership is a serving relationship that has the effect of facilitating human development.
> —*William Arthur Ward*

"The kids want to know what's next on the agenda."

Table 11.1 Facilitating Small Group Communication with Deaf People*

- Seat the deaf person to his or her best advantage. This usually means a seat near the speaker, so that the deaf person can see the speaker's lips.
- Provide new vocabulary in advance. If new vocabulary cannot be presented in advance, write the terms on paper, a chalkboard, or an overhead projector, if possible.
- Avoid unnecessary pace and speaking when writing on a chalkboard. It is difficult to speechread a person in motion, and impossible to speechread one whose back is turned.
- Use visual aids if possible.
- Make sure the deaf person doesn't miss vital information. Write out any changes in meeting times, special assignments, additional instructions, etc.
- Slow down the pace of communication slightly to facilitate understanding.
- Repeat questions and statements made from the back of the room and point to the person who's speaking.
- Allow full participation by the deaf person in the discussion. It is difficult for deaf persons to participate in group discussions because they are not sure when speakers have finished. The group leader or teacher should recognize the deaf person from time to time to allow full participation by that person.
- Use hands-on experience whenever possible in training situations.
- Use an interpreter in a large group setting.
- Use a notetaker when possible to record information. It is difficult for many deaf persons to pay attention to a speaker and take notes simultaneously.

* From *Tips for Communicating with Deaf People*. Reprinted by permission of the Rochester Institute of Technology, National Technical Institute for the Deaf, Division of Public Affairs, One Lomb Memorial Drive, Post Office Box 9887, Rochester, New York 14623-0887, Phone: (716)475-6824.

who come unprepared. When leaders notice some serious group failing, she or he needs to address this, perhaps posing this very issue (say, member lateness) as a problem to be solved.

Manage Conflict   As in interpersonal relationships, conflict is a part of small group interaction. It is a function of leadership to deal effectively with it. Small group communication researchers distinguish between procedural and people conflicts and offer a wide variety of conflict management strategies (Patton, Giffin, & Patton, 1989; Folger, Poole, & Stutman, 1997; Kindler, 1996).

Procedural and People Conflicts   **Procedural conflicts** involve disagreements over who is in charge (who is the leader or who should be the leader), what the agenda or task of the group should be, and how the group should conduct its business. The best way to deal with procedural problems is to prevent them from occurring in the first place by establishing, early in the group's interaction, who is to serve as leader and what the agenda should be. If procedural problems arise after these agreements are reached, members or the leader can refer the conflicting participants to the group's earlier decisions. When members disagree or become dissatisfied with these early decisions, they may become negative or antagonistic and cease to participate in the discussion. When this happens (or if members want to change procedures), a brief discussion on the procedures can be held. The important point to realize is that the procedural conflicts should be dealt with as procedural conflicts and should not be allowed to escalate into something else.

Attila the Hun, the Mongol leader who ruled throughout much of Asia in the fifth century, identified these qualities of effective leaders: empathy, courage, accountability, dependability, credibility, stewardship, loyalty, desire, emotional stamina, physical stamina, decisiveness, anticipation, timing, competitiveness, self-confidence, responsibility, and tenacity (Roberts, 1987). What other qualities might you add to this list?

Most people, research finds, prefer to follow leaders who use task cues (maintain eye contact, sit at the head of the table, use a relatively rapid speech rate, speak fluently, and gesture appropriately) rather than those who use dominance cues (speak in a loud and angry voice, point fingers, maintain rigid posture, use forceful gestures, and lower their eyebrows) (Driskell, Olmstead, & Salas, 1993). Group members will also see people who use task cues as more competent and more likable than those who use dominance cues. Can you see this difference operating in your work environment or among your friends?

People conflicts can occur when one member dominates the group, when several members battle for control, or when some members refuse to participate. The leader should try to secure the commitment of all members and to get all to see that the progress of the group depends on everyone's contributions. At times, it may be necessary to redirect the focus of the group to concentrate on people needs, on satisfying members' needs for group approval, for periodic rewards, or for encouragement.

People conflicts are also created when people rather than ideas are attacked. The leader needs to ensure that attacks and disagreements are clearly focused on ideas not people. If a personal attack does begin, the leader should step in to refocus the difference onto the idea and away from the person.

Conflict Management Strategies for Small Groups   The conflict management strategies presented in Chapter 7 are also applicable to the small group situation. In addition, here are four principles that have special relevance to the small group situation (Kindler, 1996):

- Preserve the dignity and respect of all members. Assume, for example, that each person's disagreement is legitimate and stems from a genuine concern for the good of the group. Therefore, treat disagreements kindly; even if someone attacks you personally, it's generally wise not to respond in kind but to redirect the criticism to the issues at hand.

- Listen empathically. See the perspectives of the other members, and try to feel what they're feeling without making any critical judgments. Try to ask yourself, why these people see the situation differently from the way you see it.
- Seek out and emphasize common ground. Even in the midst of disagreement, there are areas of common interest, common beliefs, and common aims. Find these and build on them.
- Value diversity and differences. Creative solutions often emerge from conflicting perspectives. Don't gloss over differences, but explore them for the valuable information they can give you.

MEMBERSHIP, LEADERSHIP, AND CULTURE

Most of the research and theory on small group communication, membership, and leadership has been conducted in universities in the United States

Listening to Complaints

Complaints—whether in an interpersonal, small group, or organizational situation—are essential sources of feedback. If you wish to keep this channel of vital information open, try listening to complaints positively. These suggestions will help greatly to prevent or reduce conflict.

1. Let the person know you're open to complaints, that you view them as helpful sources of information, and that you're listening. Welcome complaints; they're essential for improvement in a group as well as in a relationship or an organization. Be careful that you don't fall into the trap of seeing someone who voices a complaint as someone to avoid.
2. Make sure you understand both the thoughts and the feelings that go with the complaint. Listen to both the complaint about the inadequate copying facilities and to the frustration that the worker feels when he or she has to turn in work that looks unprofessional. Express not only your concern about the inadequate facilities but also your understanding of the frustration this person is feeling.

3. Respect confidentiality. Let the person know that the complaint will be treated in strict confidence or that it will be revealed only to those he or she wishes.
4. Ask the person what he or she would like you to do about the complaint. Sometimes, all a person wants is for someone to hear the complaint and to appreciate its legitimacy. Other times, the complaint is presented for you to do something specific. Before you assume that you know what the person really wants, ask. The very act of asking is a further affirmation that you welcome complaints and that you value the person's bringing this to your attention.
5. Thank the person for voicing the complaint and assure him or her of your intention to follow up on the complaint: "Thanks, Joe, for bringing this to my attention. I hear so little about what goes on in the mailroom and I really have to know if we're to raise the quality of our service. We have a section manager's meeting on Monday, and I'll bring up your concerns then. And I'll keep you posted on what happens."

[The next Listen to This box appears on page 297.]

Power Perspective 11.3

Empowering Others

An important function of leadership (though not limited to leadership positions) is to empower others, to help others (say, group members, your relational partner, co-workers, employees, other students, or siblings) to gain increased power over themselves and their environment. Here are a few ways to empower others:

- Raise the person's self-esteem. Compliment. Resist fault-finding.
- Share skills and share decision-making power and authority.
- Be constructively critical. React honestly to suggestions from all group members.
- Encourage growth in all forms—academic, relational, and professional. This growth and empowerment of the other person enhances your own growth and power.

[The next Power Perspective appears on page 312.]

> The purpose of getting power is to be able to give it away.
>
> —*Aneurin Bevan*

> A life isn't significant except for its impact on other lives.
>
> —*Jackie Robinson*

and reflects American culture. For example, in the United States—and in individualistic cultures generally—the individual group member is extremely important. In collectivist cultures, the individual is less important; the group is more dominant. In Japan, for example, "individual fulfillment of self is attained through finding and maintaining one's place within the group" (Cathcart & Cathcart, 1985, p. 191). In the United States, individual fulfillment of self is attained by the individual and through his or her own efforts, not by the group.

It's often thought that because group membership and group identity are so important in collectivist cultures that it's the group that makes important decisions. Actually this does not seem to be the case. In fact, in a study of 48 Japanese organizations (highly collectivist) participating in decision-making groups, the members weren't given decision-making power. So, although members are encouraged to contribute ideas, the decision-making power is reserved for the CEO and for managers higher up the organizational ladder (Brennan, 1991).

In the discussion of member roles earlier in this chapter, an entire category was devoted to individual roles, roles that individuals play to satisfy individual rather than group goals. In collectivist cultures, these roles would probably not even be mentioned simply because they wouldn't be acted out often enough to deserve extended discussion. In many collectivist cultures, the group orientation is too pervasive for individuals to violate it by acting as the blocker, the recognition seeker, or dominator, for example.

One obvious consequence of this difference can be seen when a group member commits a serious error, for example, when a team member submits the wrong advertising copy to the media. In a group governed by individualistic norms, that member is likely to be singled out, reprimanded, and perhaps fired. Further, the leader or supervisor is likely to distance himself or herself from this member for fear that this error will reflect negatively on his or her leadership. In a more collectivist culture, this error is more likely to be seen as a group mistake. The individual is unlikely to be singled out—especially not in public—and the leader is likely to bear part of the blame. The same is true when one member comes up with a great idea. In individualistic cultures, that person is likely to be singled out for praise and rewards. In a collectivist culture, it's the group that gets recognized and rewarded for the idea.

In a similar way, each culture maintains its own belief system that influences group members' behavior. For example, members of many Asian cultures, influenced by Confucian principles, believe that "the protruding nail gets pounded down" and are, therefore, not likely to voice disagreement with the majority of the group. Americans, on the other hand, influenced by the belief that "the squeaky wheel gets the grease," are more likely to voice disagreement or to act in ways different from other group members in order to get what they want (Hofstede, 1997).

Each culture also has its own rules of preferred and expected leadership style. In the United States, the general and expected style for a group leader is democratic. Our political leaders are elected by a democratic process; similarly, CEOs are elected by the shareholders of a corporation. In other situations, of course, leaders are chosen by those in authority. The president of the company will normally decide who will supervise and who will be supervised. Even in this situation, however, the supervisor is expected to behave democratically—to listen to the ideas of the members, to take their views into consideration when decisions are to be made, to keep them informed of corporate developments, and to not discriminate on the basis of sex, race, or affectional orientation. Also, we expect that leaders will be changed fairly regularly, much as we change political leaders, on a regular basis. In other cultures, leaders are chosen by right of birth. They are not elected nor are they expected to behave democratically. Similarly, their tenure as leaders is usually extremely long and may, in fact, last their entire lives and then be passed on to their children. In other cases, leaders may be chosen by the military dictator.

The important point to realize is that both membership and leadership behavior are influenced by culture. Consequently, when in a group with members of different cultures, consider the differences in both membership and leadership style that individuals bring with them. For example, a member who plays individual roles may be tolerated in many groups in the United States and in some may even be thought amusing and different. That same member playing the same roles in a group with a more collectivist orientation is likely to be much more negatively evaluated. Multicultural groups may find it helpful to discuss the views they have of group membership and leadership and what constitutes comfortable interaction for them.

Leadership is not manifested by coercion.

—*Margaret Chase Smith*

How does the cultural background of members influence the small group communication that takes place in your class? On the job?

"On second thought, don't correct me if I'm wrong."

THINKING CRITICALLY ABOUT GROUPTHINK

An especially insightful perspective on thinking critically in the small group situation is provided by the concept of groupthink. **Groupthink** is a way of thinking that people use when agreement among members becomes extremely important. So important is agreement among members that it tends to shut out realistic and logical analysis of a problem or of possible alternatives (Janis, 1983; Park, 1990; Mullen, Tara, Salas, & Driskell, 1994). The term itself is meant to signal a "deterioration of mental efficiency, reality testing, and moral judgment that results from in-group pressures (Janis, 1983, p. 9).

Many specific behaviors of group members can lead to groupthink. A simple example is presented in the accompanying cartoon—the unwillingness to invite disagreement and a re-examination of the issue. One of the most significant occurs when the group limits its discussion to only a few alternative solutions. Another occurs when the group does not re-examine its decisions despite indications of possible dangers. Still another happens when the group spends little time discussing why certain initial alternatives were rejected. For example, if the group rejected a certain alternative because it was too costly, members will devote little time, if any, to examine possible ways to reduce the cost.

In groupthink, members are extremely selective in the information they consider seriously. While facts and opinions contrary to the group's position are generally ignored, those that support the group's position are readily and uncritically accepted. The following symptoms should help you recognize groupthink in groups you observe or participate in:

If everyone is thinking alike, then somebody isn't thinking.
—*George S. Patton*

- Group members think the group and its members are invulnerable.
- Members create rationalizations to avoid dealing with warnings or threats.
- Members believe their group is moral.
- Those opposed to the group are perceived in simplistic, stereotyped ways.
- Group pressure is applied to any member who expresses doubts or questions the group's arguments or proposals.
- Members censor their own doubts.
- Group members believe all are in unanimous agreement, whether this is stated or not.
- Group members emerge whose function it is to guard the information that gets to other members, especially when it may create diversity of opinion.

> Think wrongly, if you please, but in all cases think for yourself.
> —*Doris Lessing*

SUMMARY OF CONCEPTS AND SKILLS

In this chapter we looked at membership and leadership in the small group. We examined the roles of members—some productive and some counterproductive—groupthink, and leadership.

1. A popular classification of small group member roles divides them into three types: group task roles, group building and maintenance roles, and individual roles.
2. Among the group task roles are information seeker or giver, opinion seeker or giver, evaluator-critic, and procedural technician or recorder; among the group building and maintenance roles are: encourager/harmonizer, compromiser, and follower; among the individual (dysfunctional) roles are: aggressor/blocker, recognition seeker/self-confessor, and dominator.
3. Member participation should be group-oriented, center conflict on issues, be critically open-minded, and ensure understanding.
4. Three approaches to leadership are especially helpful in understanding the varied nature of leadership: the traits approach identifies the characteristics such as as intelligence and self-confidence that contribute to leadership; the transformational approach focuses on leaders as people who raise the performance of group members and also empower them; the situational approach views leadership as varying its focus between accomplishing the task and serving the member's social and emotional needs, depending on the specific group and the unique situation.
5. Three major leadership styles are laissez-faire, democratic, and authoritarian.
6. Among the leader's task functions are to prepare members and start the group interaction, maintain effective interaction, guide members through the agreed-upon agenda, ensure member satisfaction, encourage ongoing evaluation and improvement, prepare members for the discussion, and manage conflict.
7. Group membership and leadership attitudes and behaviors are likely to be heavily influenced by culture.
8. Groupthink is a way of thinking that occurs when group members are overly concerned with securing agreement that it discourages critical thinking and the exploration of alternative ways of doing things.

The skills identified in this discussion center on increasing your ability to function more effectively as small group member and leader. Check your ability to use these skills. Use the following rating scale: (1) = almost always, (2) = often, (3) = sometimes, (4) = rarely, (5) = hardly ever.

_____ 1. I avoid playing the popular but dysfunctional individual roles in a small group: aggressor, blocker, recognition seeker, self-confessor, or dominator.

_____ 2. In participating in a small group, I am group-, rather than individual-, oriented, center the conflict on issues rather than on personalities, am critically open-minded, and make sure that my meanings and the meanings of others are clearly understood.

_____ 3. I adjust my leadership style to the task at hand and on the needs of group members.

_____ 4. As a small group leader, I start group interaction, maintain effective interaction throughout the discussion, keep members on track, ensure member satisfaction, encourage ongoing evaluation and improvement, and prepare members for the discussion as necessary.

_____ 5. I recognize and appreciate the cultural differences that people have toward group membership and leadership.

6. I recognize the symptoms of groupthink and actively counter my own groupthinking tendencies as well as those evidenced in the group.

KEY WORD QUIZ

Write T for those statements that are true and F for those that are false. For those that are false, replace the boldface term with the correct term.

_____ 1. Information seeker, evaluator-critic, and procedural technician are examples of **group building and maintenance roles.**

_____ 2. Encourager, compromiser, and follower are examples of **group task roles.**

_____ 3. Aggressor/blocker, recognition seeker/self-confessor, and dominator are examples of **functional roles.**

_____ 4. Social emotional positive, social emotional negative, attempted answers, and questions are the four major categories used in **interaction process analysis.**

_____ 5. The leadership style in which the leader takes no initiative in directing or suggesting courses of action is known as **democratic.**

_____ 6. The leadership style in which the leader determines the group's agenda and decisions is known as **laissez-faire.**

_____ 7. The group (rather than the individual) is likely to be given greater emphasis in **individualist cultures.**

_____ 8. The way of thinking that group members engage in when agreement becomes all important and overrides logical and realistic analysis is known as **groupthink.**

_____ 9. Maintaining eye contact, sitting at the head of the table, using a relatively rapid speech rate, speaking fluently, and gesturing appropriately are examples of **task cues.**

_____ 10. Group problems such as members competing for leadership positions or having a lack of clarity about their functions or short-circuiting the process of analyzing the problem are examples of **personality conflicts.**

Answers: TRUE: 4, 8, 9. FALSE: 1 (group task roles), 2 (group building and maintenance roles), 3 (dysfunctional or individual roles), 5 (laissez-faire leader), 6 (authoritarian), 7 (collectivist cultures), 10 (procedural conflicts).

11.1 Dealing with Small Group Complaints and Potential Conflicts

You're the leader of a work team consisting of members from each of the major departments in your company. For each of the following complaints explain: (1) what you would say and (2) what objective your response is designed to achieve.

1. Reducing costs is an impossible task; we're wasting our time here. Costs have gone up; there's no way we can reduce costs. Period. The end.

2. Look, we've been at this for 2 hours and I still haven't heard anything about accounting which is my department. I really don't know why I'm here. How can the accounting department help reduce costs?

3. You're calling these meetings much too often and much too early to suit us. We'd like fewer meetings scheduled for late in the day.

4. That's not fair. Why do I always have to take the minutes of these meetings. Can't we have a real secretary in here?

5. There's a good reason why I don't contribute to the discussion. I don't contribute because no one listens to what I say.

11.2 Lost on the Moon

This exercise is often used to illustrate the differences between individual and group decision making, almost always demonstrating that group decisions are much more effective and efficient than individual decisions. Of course, this is something that most people know intellectually, but this exercise dramatizes it for students in an interesting and provocative way.

The class is given the list of fifteen items noted below. Each person is to visualize himself or herself as a member of a space crew stranded on the moon. Their ship is damaged and they must travel 200 miles to return to the mother ship. The fifteen items have been salvaged from the crashed ship and their task is to rank the items in terms of their value in assisting them to return to the mother ship. Use number 1 for the most important item, number 2 for the next most important, and so on to 15 for the least important item.

After completing the rankings, form groups of five or six and construct a group ranking. After this is complete, correct answers and reasons should be given to students (see *Instructor's Manual*). They should then compute their individual error scores and the error score of the group decisions.

The computations are made as follows: For each incorrect item, the student subtracts his or her score from the correct score, regardless of sign. This is the error score for that item. He or she does this for all 15 items and totals the error points. This is the total error score. The same procedure is followed for computing the group error score. A high error score (say, between 56 and 112) means that the student's or group's decisions were not very good ones; a low error score (say, between 0 and 45) means that the decisions were good ones or, more correctly, were similar to those responses supplied by NASA. Almost without exception the group score will be better than the individual scores.

_____ box of matches
_____ food concentrate
_____ 50 feet of nylon rope
_____ parachute silk
_____ solar-powered portable heating unit
_____ 2 .45-caliber pistols
_____ 1 case dehydrated milk
_____ 2 100-pound tanks of oxygen
_____ stellar map (of moon's constellation)
_____ self-inflating life raft
_____ magnetic compass
_____ 5 gallons of water
_____ signal flares
_____ first-aid kit containing injection needles
_____ solar-powered FM receiver-transmitter

Source: From Jay Hall, "Decisions, Decisions, Decisions,"*Psychology Today* 5, 51–54, 86, 88. Copyright © 1971 by Sussex Publishers, Inc. Reprinted by permission.

CHAPTER 12

Preparing Speeches

AFTER READING THIS CHAPTER, YOU SHOULD BE ABLE TO:

- Understand and apply the principles of outlining and the organizational development of speeches.
- Describe and use techniques for analyzing an audience.
- Identify and locate a variety of supporting materials.
- Feel competent to create and present a speech in public.
- Have a commitment to communicating with your listeners.
- Create an acceptable, formal speech outline.

As you begin preparing a public presentation, you need to consider many factors—yourself, your listeners, your topic, the occasion, the setting, the amount of time you will have, the purpose, and perhaps many other things. Central to any message, however, is that it be clear. If you fail to have clarity, your message is likely to be misunderstood. The foundation of clarity is organization, and good organization will help you to accomplish all of your other goals. After learning about organization, you will learn how to analyze your listeners so that your message can be adapted to them. Different types of supporting materials and how to find them are also covered in this chapter. But as was mentioned above, organizing your message is the starting point. Two approaches to help you with organization will be discussed: outlining principles and organizational development in speeches.

OUTLINING PRINCIPLES

This section is intended as a review of the outlining principles and techniques that you have been studying for many years in language arts classes. You are probably familiar with the major symbols that are used to organize an outline: Roman numerals, capital letters, Arabic numbers, lowercase letters, numbers in parentheses, and letters in parentheses. This system is universally used in the composition of both written and oral discourse. These symbols have been developed over many years as a way to keep ideas in order, in terms of both sequence and relationship. Speaking well involves much more than just talking clearly. A coherent message is one that is carefully constructed and pays attention to techniques of organization from the very beginning. When you have selected a particular type of speech and the appropriate thesis to go with it, an outline will provide you with a complete structure to guide you in constructing a speech.

General Outlines

The outline format lends itself to a variety of purposes, and you can also select from among several patterns of development in speeches, all of which fit into the same general outline structure. A simple outline that can

Critical Thinking in Communication

The Logical Structure of Outlines

One of the things you will notice about an outline is that it is logical. If you can look at items and put them in a logical sequence of relationships to each other, you will be able to create an organized speech. The linking together of superior, coordinate, and subordinate ideas can help you to move from large subjects to specific, supporting materials. It helps to cluster ideas or examples because the items in these clusters will form the subdivisions for your speech outline. Look for main ideas (superior position in the outline) and for supporting details or explanations (subordinate position in the outline) that fit logically under the main ideas.

be used in virtually any public-speaking situation has five main parts. Each of these parts is defined briefly, and then some rules and guidelines for creating an outline are presented.

Sample Outline A five-part speech outline looks like this:

I. **Introduction.** About 10 percent of your time can be spent on the introduction. A brief story, an interesting example or statistic, or a startling statement, quotation, or illustration can work well as an introduction.

II. **Thesis sentence.** This item represents the main idea of your entire speech. It also expresses the central purpose of your speech.

III. **Body of the speech.** About 85 percent of your time will be spent on the body of the speech. A preview of the main ideas in the body of the speech can be a good transition from the thesis sentence to the body itself. The body of the speech usually has between two and five main subsections. This example has four main subdivisions.
   A. First main subdivision
       1. Supporting material for A
       2. Supporting material for A
   B. Second main subdivision
       1. Supporting material for B
       2. Supporting material for B
       3. Supporting material for B
   C. Third main subdivision
       1. Supporting material for C
       2. Supporting material for C
   D. Fourth main subdivision
       1. Supporting material for D
       2. Supporting material for D
       3. Supporting material for D

IV. **Conclusion.** About 2 to 5 percent of your time will be used for the conclusion. A brief review of A, B, C, and D; the thesis sentence; and the introduction.

V. **Sources/bibliography/references.** You may list sources alphabetically by author or in footnote order—the order in which they appear in your speech. This section is not read aloud during your speech, but you may cite a specific source at the point in the speech when you are presenting information from that source.
   A. First source, listed in a standard format.
   B. Second source.
   C. Third source.

Introduction and Thesis The outline format presented here shows how you can link your ideas together. Each part has a function that relates to every other part. The *introduction* is where you capture the audience's attention so that your listeners will be ready to focus on your thesis sentence. You can take these moments—about 10 percent of your total time for a short speech—to become comfortable with the situation and to let your audience become accustomed to looking at you and hearing your voice. You can also set the mood you want for your presentation. Will it be humorous or serious? Let your listeners clearly understand your mood from the beginning.

The *thesis sentence* is the main idea of your entire speech, but should you start with it? Often, the audience is not quite focused on you; and if you begin by saying, "Today, my speech is on . . . ," they might miss your main idea. In addition, your listeners will be disappointed by such an unimaginative and uninteresting opening. Do not get to your thesis sentence until after the introduction. Then make it simple and to the point. Everything else in the presentation is controlled by your thesis sentence. The introduction must lead up to it, and the body explains and supports it. The thesis sentence is the most important—but smallest—part of your speech.

Body and Supporting Materials　　The *body* is where the speech takes shape and where 85 percent or so of your time will be spent. The body clarifies, explains, extends, defends, and supports your thesis sentence. Usually, the explanation of your thesis sentence can be broken down into two to five main subsections or subdivisions. Later in this chapter, you will see some examples of how to divide the body into logical patterns. For now, notice how each subsection has specific supporting materials under it.

Supporting materials are the specific items that you use to illustrate or prove your point. They may be examples, statistics, short stories, illustrations, quotations, visual aids, or statements. Supporting materials can include personal experiences; case histories; results of opinion polls, research studies, or experiments; and materials from songs, literature, or poetry. One way to enrich your presentation is to use a variety of supporting materials. Each of these is explained in more detail later in the chapter.

Conclusion　　The fourth subsection of the outline is the *conclusion*, which is a short review of the main subsections of the body (but not the specific supporting materials), the thesis sentence, and a reference to the opening material that you used in the introduction. The conclusion should be brief—about half as long as your introduction—and it should tell your listeners that you have come to a close.

Sources　　Finally, you need a list of your sources—Part V in the sample outline. Sources can be a standard bibliography, a list of references, or footnotes such as you add to the end of a term paper. You need to credit the sources of your material to avoid a charge of plagiarism. **Plagiarism** means using someone else's ideas or words without giving that person credit. It is dishonest—a form of academic and intellectual theft—and a serious crime in any field. Certainly, you need to use and probably depend on other people's work and ideas to create your own. By giving those sources credit, you acknowledge their contribution to your effort. In fact, you build your own credibility by making listeners aware of all the experts you have consulted. So for many reasons, make certain that you properly credit all work that is not your own.

There are several ways to acknowledge this credit. The Modern Language Association (MLA) format is the format that most colleges use. The MLA is a national group of English teachers, scholars, and others who are interested in the field of English. They publish the *MLA Handbook for Writers of Research Papers,* which presents standard ways to cite sources for everything, from books to interviews. Citations usually begin with the author's name, last name first, then the title of the article or book, then the name of the larger work if the material is only one section of it, then the publisher, city, date, and perhaps the page numbers. This is the format you have probably been using on every paper you have written since junior high school. For this book, the citation would look like this:

> Zeuschner, Raymond. *Communicating Today.* 2nd ed. Boston: Allyn and Bacon, 1997.

If you were using an article from a magazine or a journal, it would look like this:

> Rubin, Rebecca B. "Assessing Speaking and Listening Competence at the College Level: The Communication Competence Assessment Instrument." *Communication Education* 31 (January 1983): 19–33.

There are minor variations on these forms, but the important information is consistent throughout. You need to give listeners and readers enough information that they can easily locate the source. Although following the form makes your bibliography look correct, what is really important is that you credit all your sources in a clear and consistent way.

Subordination and Grouping

There are rules to keep in mind as you create any outline for any message. Outlines have a logical construction, and the simple rules of subordination and grouping can help you to create a logical structure to your own outline. Always remember that your ideas exist in *relationship* to each other, with the more abstract or general main ideas listed flush left and the smaller, detailed, supporting ideas indented to the right. The rule of subordination tells you whether something should be labeled with a Roman numeral or a capital letter—that is, whether the item is a main idea or a supporting detail.

The rule of grouping tells you that all related ideas need to be in the same group. If a supporting detail relates directly to subdivision X, it needs to be in X's group. If it's not related to X, then it belongs to Y's group or Z's group. If it is not related to any of these, it belongs in yet another group or in a different outline.

Sample Outlines. The rule of grouping says that there must be a direct link among all the items in the group. At the beginning, it might look like this:

I. Main idea X
    A. First subordinate idea related to X
    B. Second subordinate idea related to X
II. Main idea Y
    A. First subordinate idea related to Y
    B. Second subordinate idea related to Y
    C. Third subordinate idea related to Y
    D. Fourth subordinate idea related to Y

III. Main idea Z
    A. First subordinate idea related to Z
    B. Second subordinate idea related to Z

The rules of subordination could continue further under X—A and B; or under Y—A, B, C, and D; or under Z—A and B, as follows:

I. Main idea X
    A. First subordinate idea related to X
    B. Second subordinate idea related to X
        1. Supporting material related to B
        2. Second supporting material related to B
II. Main idea Y
    A. First subordinate idea related to Y
    B. Second subordinate idea related to Y
    C. Third subordinate idea related to Y
        1. First supporting material related to C
        2. Second supporting material related to C
    D. Fourth subordinate idea related to Y
III. Main idea Z
    A. First subordinate idea related to Z
    B. Second subordinate idea related to Z

When an item is indented below another item, it must be related to the item directly above and must be of less importance, or subordinate to it. Thus you can see the main principle of outlining at work: *Keep the relationship in order.* The most important, comprehensive ideas are flush left. Less important ideas, examples, illustrations, or research results that *support* the important ideas are indented. All similar or coordinate ideas must be in the same group.

Let us put these principles into a real-word outline format. Look at the two examples below and determine which one follows these principles correctly and which does not.

Example A
I. Television shows and entertainment
    A. TV and music
        1. MTV
        2. *Great Performances*
    B. TV and comedy
        1. *Seinfeld*
        2. *Murphy Brown*
        3. *Home Improvement*
    C. Sports programs on TV
        1. *Monday Night Football*
        2. Olympic games
II. Television shows and information
    A. News programs
        1. *The News Hour with Jim Lehrer*
        2. *Nightline*
        3. CNN—all-news format

B. Special series
1. *Nova*
2. Jacques Cousteau specials
3. *National Geographic* specials
   a. "Voyage of Columbus"
   b. "World of Antarctica"

Example B
  I. TV has comedy.
    A. Television entertains us.
    B. *Seinfeld*
    C. *Murphy Brown*
    D. *Home Improvement*
  II. Television news informs us.
    A. Sports programs such as *Monday Night Football*
    B. Olympics every four years
    C. *The News Hour with Jim Lehrer*
 III. *Nova* and other PBS specials
    A. *The News Hour with Jim Lehrer*
    B. Jacques Cousteau specials
      a. Other specials are *National Geographic*
      b. The "Voyage of Columbus" and "Antarctica"
    C. *Nightline* is another good show.
    D. Specials and sports
      1. MTV has specials.

Even a quick glance will show that Example B is a hodgepodge of disorganization. Not only do the ideas not follow the principle of subordination, but the rule of grouping is also disobeyed, since many of the ideas do not belong together. Items related to sports are listed under both II and III, and there does not appear to be any system at work. Which are the main ideas and which are subordinate? Go back to Example A and see that the more ab-

Improving Competency

Practicing Subordination

Try looking at any system of organization and see how these relationships are present. For example, look at the college you are attending. If you think of the entire school as your main idea, then what would constitute A, B, and C? Perhaps you would put the words *Academic Affairs* as A, and then put *Student Activities as B. Facilities Operations* might be C, and perhaps D would be Fiscal Affairs. You could then take each one of those areas and begin listing Arabic numbers under them, so that academic departments become 1, 2, 3, 4, and so on under A. The various student clubs and activities would be listed with Arabic numbers under B. Try filling out such an outline for your job, church, club, family, team, or city government, and you will see how patterns of organization are present in every aspect of our lives. Learning and applying the principles of outlining can help you to see, understand, and use the patterns that operate in our daily affairs.

stract concepts—the ones that are comprehensive or "bigger"—are to the left while the specific examples are indented to the right.

Note that Example A is a clear illustration of the principles of outlining: The main ideas are flush left, symbols are used consistently, there is one single idea per item, and all items in one group are related to each other and to the main idea above them. Although both examples follow the rules for indenting, in Example B one area has reversed the use of numbers and letters. Can you find the error? If you identified III, B as the problem and said that the a and b should really be 1 and 2, you understand how to use these principles. That example brings us to the next step in preparing a good outline: the consistent use of proper symbols.

Symbols

In preparing an outline for your speeches, use the *standard outline symbol system*. Remember to do the following: (1) Start with capital Roman numerals; (2) alternate between numbers and letters; (3) indent so that all capital letters are the same distance from the left-hand margin and all similar numbers are indented and aligned with each other. The following example illustrates these guidelines:

I. _____
   A. _____
   B. _____
      1. _____
      2. _____
      3. _____
   C. _____
II. _____
   A. _____
      1. _____
      2. _____
      3. _____
   B. _____
   C. _____
   D. _____
      1. _____
      2. _____
         a. _____
         b. _____
      3. _____
   E. _____
      1. _____
         a. _____
         b. _____
         c. _____
      2. _____
III. _____
   A. _____
   B. _____

Technology in Communication

Software Outlines

The importance of outlining can be measured by the development of software packages to help students and people in business develop outlines. Many of these packages have a template format that puts ideas into a format, automatically using the next correct symbol and providing the proper indentation. As you make internal changes and substitutions, the program then automatically renumbers the subsequent material. However, responsibility for what goes into the outline still lies with the writer.

Notice how each subsection is indented so that the relationship is clearly expressed. Superior ideas contain subordinate materials. Coordinate ideas are equally placed and are of equal importance. Thus E is superior to E.1 and E.2 but is subordinate to II. Which items are coordinate with E? If you said A, B, C, and D, you have the right idea. What do you know about the material to be listed under II. D. 2. b? You should be able to say that b is a specific supporting idea or fact that is similar to a in degree of importance and that they are both linked to 2, which is a subordinate idea under D, which in turn is a main category under the major concept II. If that little b does not relate back through its series of links, then it belongs somewhere else. If b is more than a very specific idea, then it probably needs to be upgraded to a number or perhaps to a capital letter. For most of your speeches, you will probably be able to express your ideas and their relationships by using just this level of detail and nothing more detailed. You may even stop at the Arabic numbers in a key idea outline.

Efficiency of Expression

Your main ideas should be expressed as simple, single ideas. You may use a full sentence or key words. Whichever you choose or your instructor assigns, be consistent throughout your preparation. Do not mix sentences and single words or phrases in the same outline. Keep each line focused on one single idea. This guideline will help you decide to which group or cluster a particular item belongs. Try to avoid the use of the word *and* in your sentences or key ideas. That word may indicate that you have two ideas in one item. For example:

Wrong
I. It's hard to raise guide dogs because of the time and attention and the strain it puts on the owners when you have to give them up.
   A. They take a lot of time away from other activities, and you need training to give them proper attention.
   B. It is difficult to give them up after you've raised them, so be prepared.

Instead, try being concise and simple:

Right
    I. Raising guide dogs can be a difficult task.
       A. You need lots of time.
       B. You need special training.
       C. You need to be prepared to give them away.

The second example correctly identifies three distinct areas of difficulty and keeps the sentences brief.

Outlining can be of real assistance to you in your speech preparation. If you remember the five major parts, you can put your thoughts in order and visualize the relationships among the parts. All parts connect to the thesis sentence.

In addition to the overall organization of an outline, there are a variety of ways to focus on the body of the speech and put it into a pattern.

ORGANIZATIONAL PATTERNS

As you can probably sense, a good speech does not just come out of someone's mouth on the spur of the moment. Many excellent speakers *appear* smooth and spontaneous as a result of spending many hours thinking about their speech, researching ideas and supporting materials, trying out a variety of ways to organize it, and practicing until they are confident and comfortable. If you are going to achieve your purpose with your presentation, you should think carefully about your ideas and how each is related to the others. Examine your thesis sentence, and decide whether there are ways to break it down into a few subordinate ideas. For example, some topics can be thought of in terms of a sequence of steps or stages, each following the previous one in a logical or systematic order. Another common-sense pattern is to arrange subordinate ideas according to particular topics or divisions among the ideas. Finally, in persuasive communication, you may wish to put the body of your speech into a motivational pattern to move your listeners to agreement or action. Let us take a look at each of these **organizational development patterns.**

Sequential Patterns

If your topic has an obvious, step-by-step order, or involves a series of ideas or events that move in a certain logical progression, you are dealing with sequence, or the *sequential pattern*. There are four major sequential patterns: time, space, size, and importance. The *time sequence pattern* is often called *chronological*, which means that you organize the A-B-C-D sections of the body of your presentation according to the relationship your ideas have, or have had, over time.

For example, it you are discussing an event in the past—an event leading up to World War I or the chronological events of your vacation trip—you start with the earliest events and finish with the most recent events. Many speakers find the past-present-future time pattern a convenient way to discuss items. If you use it, you'll find that the A-B-C parts of the outline are ready made for you. In the A section, you will cluster the information about the topic's history and about the events that led up to the current situation. The B section will describe what is happening now. In the C section, you can

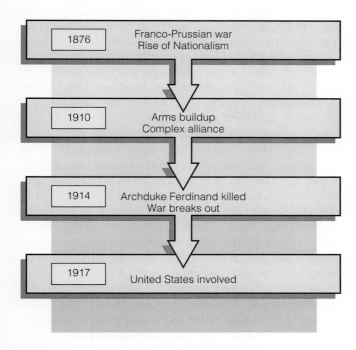

A chronological pattern is appropriate for historical topics.

speculate on what will be coming in the future This pattern is popular because both the speaker and the audience can follow it and remember it with ease.

Another use of the time sequence pattern is found in the process, or how-to, speech. Follow the steps above until you have completed your description of the process. Are you building a house? Preparing lasagna? Producing a play? The time sequence pattern may be perfect for your presentation.

A related pattern that could work for some of the above topics involves *space*. For example, if your vacation started in Miami and you then went to Atlanta, then to New Orleans, and back to Miami, these events are con-

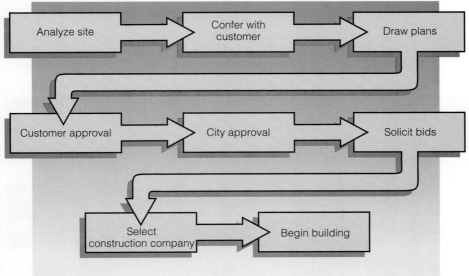

A sequence is a pattern of related steps.

nected geographically—that is, in space—as well as in time. The *spatial sequence pattern* is easy to see in an outline that explains things that exist in the material world. For example, you could give a speech about the Hawaiian Islands from the perspective of time—early volcanic activity, the settling by Polynesians, the kingdom era, European arrivals, annexation to the United States, and statehood. Or you could discuss the fact that the island start at Midway Island and end with the island of Hawaii. Your outline could also start with Midway Island and end with Hawaii. You could give a talk about your campus, starting at one end and moving in a spatial relationship from one building or section of campus to the next one that a person would come to if he or she were walking. Of course, you could also talk about the buildings according to the order in which they were built and then go back to chronological order. Do you want to discuss the solar system? Start with the sun and work your way out from there—chronologically *and* spatially.

The *size sequence pattern* is the third pattern, and it works well for certain topics. For example, your solar system speech may start with the sun, then move to Jupiter as the next largest, then Neptune, and so on until you got to Pluto, the smallest planet. Or you could reverse the order: Start with the smallest and move on to the largest. A speech on types of hawks, for example, might start with smallest species, continue to the middle-size birds, and end with a discussion about the largest member of the hawk family.

Finally, an *importance sequence pattern* could be used to discuss topics that make a judgment or use criteria to evaluate ideas. If you were running a political campaign, you might start your speech with a time pattern, or if you had only a few minutes to explain a complex idea, you could put the body of your speech into the order of importance of the items it contains. You could say, "The most important thing to do is . . ." and then, "The next most important thing is . . ." and then, "Finally, if you have the time or resources, consider. . . ." In this way, your listeners will grasp the relative importance of each item.

As you can tell from these examples, a speech can be logically arranged in a number of ways, all of which make some sequential sense. Your task is to select from among the sequential patterns and find the one that best suits you, your approach to the topic, your purpose, your research, your time frame, and your audience.

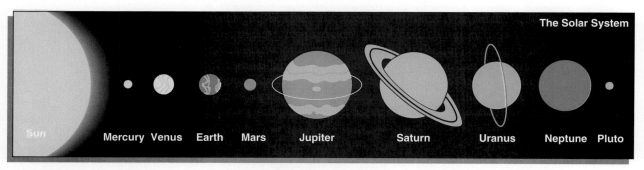

A visual aid can show objects related in size and space.

Topical Patterns

If your ideas do not fit the sequence format very well, you might try this group of patterns to provide a framework for the body of your speech. Topical patterns are based on the way we think about ideas or topics when we try to break them down or cluster them into logical divisions. This pattern is called the topical pattern because the subtopics of the thesis seem to flow naturally and logically from the subject of the thesis. The breakdown of the main ideas into subordinate ideas stems not from the relationship of those ideas in time or space, but from the logical way they can be put together.

One of the most popular topical patterns is one that shows the relationship of cause and effect. This pattern asserts that event X was the cause of event Y. For example, the Hawaiian Islands were formed by a series of volcanic eruptions, so you could give a speech about the series of events that caused the islands to form. The factors that caused the earthquakes could be the subject of a cause–effect topical pattern. This can be a tricky pattern. One of the most common logical fallacies occurs because many things are related only in time, but we make the faulty assumption that they also have a causal relationship. This fallacy is called *ergo propter hoc* (Latin meaning "After this, therefore because of this") or just the *post hoc* fallacy.

There is a similar pattern—a correlation—that sometimes looks like a cause–effect pattern but is not. For example, the failure to wear a seat belt is correlated with high death rates in motor vehicle accidents. The lack of a seat belt does not *cause* the accident, nor does it *cause* death. Smashing through a windshield or hitting the pavement with great force may cause death. However, the lack of a seat belt is connected, or *correlated*, with an increase in death rates in automobile accidents. Sometimes, correlation studies do show that one event *might* cause another. For example, all the studies of rates of cancer in smokers suggest that smokers have a much greater chance of getting lung cancer than nonsmokers. However, the fact that some people smoke and do not get lung cancer keeps this relationship from being, strictly speaking, a cause–effect relationship and places it in the category of a correlation. If you constantly miss class, will you get a low grade on the tests? Quite probably you will, but it is not certain that you will. However, it can be demonstrated that as a group, students who skip class frequently have lower grades than students who attend class regularly. You *might* be an exception; for example, if U.S. history is your hobby, you might be able to miss your U.S. history class and still do well on the tests. On the other hand, regular attendance correlates highly with high grades.

Parallel to the cause—effect pattern is the *problem–solution* pattern. In this pattern, the A section of the outline presents a particular problem, such as air pollution. The B section follows, with ideas and suggestions for solving the problem. You will find the problem–solution format useful in giving persuasive speeches. Many policy decisions are made through problem–solution approaches. Watch television commercials, and you will see dozens of problem–solution presentations in an hour: "Do you have gray hair? Just use Young Forever Hair Cream." "How can you get rid of roaches in your kitchen? Easy, just buy Roach Bomb Spray!" "Are you tired of corruption in government? Vote for Zeuschner!" Examples of this format are everywhere.

Motivational Patterns

There are many explicitly persuasive patterns that speakers have used for centuries, and they belong in the motivational pattern group. Although each of the patterns previously discussed could probably be used to organize the body of a persuasive speech, motivational patterns have that application as their goal. One of the most widely used motivational patterns is called the motivated sequence. It was developed by speech teacher Alan H. Monroe over sixty years ago and has been popular ever since (Gronbeck, 1995). The five parts of this pattern are as follows:

1. *Attention:* Capture the attention of the audience and focus it on the topic.
2. *Need:* Present the problem so that the audience sees it as one that needs solving.
3. *Satisfaction:* Present the solution to the problem.
4. *Visualization:* Stimulate the audience's imagination by having them think about the consequences of either adopting or not adopting the solution.
5. *Action:* Get your listeners to take some specific step to put the solution into operation.

Although Monroe and his later collaborators used this five-part process to describe many types of speeches, its effectiveness is seen most clearly when the speaker asks the audience to take some action to solve the problem. In this format, your speech outline would have four parts to the body because step one, attention, would already be on your outline as I. *Introduction*, in the format presented earlier. Then, under III. *Body of the Speech,* you would list A as the need step, B as satisfaction, C for visualization, and D for action.

You can also motivate your listeners by using a *benefits* pattern, a pattern that describes all the good things they will gain if they adopt your thesis. Or you might take the opposite view and show them the costs they would incur if they took another course of action. Or you might combine the two into

The Story of Communication

Alan H. Monroe

Alan H. Monroe was one of the important figures in the development of the field of speech communication. His textbook Principles and Types of Speech was published in 1935. It included materials he had tested for nearly a decade in his own classes and in collaboration with scholars in psychology and business. He developed his organizational format largely on the basis of formats used in sales presentations. In 1940, while at Purdue University, he was president of the national Speech Communication Association. He continued to teach and influence an entire generation of teachers and scholars in the field with his use of social science approaches to a field then dominated by traditional rhetorical perspectives. Speech communication today continues to draw from a blend of the social sciences and the humanities, psychology and rhetoric. Professor Monroe died in 1975.

a cost–benefits pattern showing how much your suggestion costs and how much the alternatives would cost. Then you could compare the two on the basis of probable benefits.

From these organizational patterns—sequential, topical, and motivational—you can create the body of your speech so that it flows together in a logical order that makes sense to you and your listeners. Your presentations will be clear and will have the impact that you intended on your audience. When your main topic and its subordinate ideas are related in terms of size or time, you will probably use a sequential pattern. If the relationship is more like a grouping or cluster, you may want a topical pattern. Finally if you are trying to get your audience to do something, look to a motivational pattern to organize the body of your speech.

Each of these patterns is designed to help two parties in a communication transaction: you and your audience. To create a message that has both clarity and impact, you need to select a pattern that will enhance it. Communication in this setting takes place only if the audience gets the message that you intended, so make your message clear and strong by taking some time to think about the pattern that will best help you do that.

ANALYZING YOUR LISTENERS

A great deal was said in Chapter 3 about active listening from a receiver's point of view. In Chapter 7, you read about yourself as a processor of information. Now put those two ideas together, but see yourself as the *sender* of a message to a group of individuals who will try to listen to what you have to say. When you focus on the audience, you can begin the steps of **audience analysis.**

Aristotle's book Rhetoric devoted large sections to advice about how to approach a topic if older people or younger people were the audience. His reasoning was based on the values, attitudes, and beliefs that people bring with them when they are listening to a speaker. Values, attitudes, and beliefs as they relate to you personally are discussed in Chapter 7. Now it is time to think about how those aspects of your listeners might affect the way you create and deliver your presentation. The attitudes of your audience will affect their ability to listen. If they are in a good mood; if they like you, the speaker; and if they feel involved and connected to the topic, it will be easier for you to deliver your message (Lumsden and Lumsden, 1996).

Values are the social principles, goals, and standards that members of your audience have in common. Their values determine the overall guidelines for their life patterns, and they are generally few in number. If you are speaking to a college group, you can guess that they value education. A group of owners of small businesses probably value hard work and independence. These values provide the framework or foundation for their feelings and attitudes.

Several major **value systems** in our society have been identified that can help you to adapt your message to your listeners. For example, the Protestant–Puritan–Peasant system is known for its emphasis on hard work, family, religion, and education. Incidentally, these values are held by many more people than those who come from those three backgrounds. Jews, Catholics, Buddhists, and very wealthy people all may also hold these fundamental

Audience analysis helps you to adapt your speech to the values and concerns of your listeners.

values. Another type of value system is the progressive value system, which stresses newness, invention, development, and exploration. On the other hand, some people hold primarily to the transcendental value system, which places an emphasis on spiritual feelings, intuition, and getting away from materialistic ties. Some researchers have identified Native American value systems, Mormon value systems, and specific corporate value structures (Reike and Sillars, 1983). The important thing to remember is that your listeners will apply whatever seems to them to be a relevant value, attitude, or belief to the message they hear—your message. Therefore when you function as the primary sender of a message, you need to consider how to connect your values to those of the audience. Consider the people listening to you and how they will react to your message.

To speak effectively to your audience, you need to gather information about it and the situation in which you will be speaking. Recall that in earlier chapters, you learned about communication as an interactive process—a transaction between senders and receivers.

Analyzing the Occasion

When you consider your listeners, think about why they want to hear your speech. What event or purpose brings them together? Think about the degree of formality of the **occasion**. If the speech is a classroom assignment, then one style of dress and presentation is appropriate. If it is a formal contest or the presentation of an award, a different mode of dress and style of presentation are called for. You may be giving a speech welcoming an important visitor to your business or school. Be aware that different occasions call for different norms of behavior. The joke that you have for the classroom may not be the right one to tell at a religious meeting in a temple or church. Formal approaches may work at a business presentation in the

Diversity in Communication

Understanding Audience Diversity

Audiences come in all sizes and shapes, and that diversity challenges you to adapt appropriately to your listeners. Their age, gender, ethnic background, and other demographic factors can guide you to become a speaker who connects with the specific group of listeners you face. Be careful, however, of stereotyping. One student began her speech by saying, "Ladies, would you like to save money on your dresses, blouses, and skirts? I know I would, and I do by sewing many of my own clothes, so today I'll tell you about some simple sewing techniques you can use to make your own clothes or keep the ones you buy in good repair." Fourteen of the twenty-five people in the class were males. Does this mean that she picked the wrong topic? If you said yes, then you, too, are stereotyping. Are there good reasons why men should know some basic elements of clothing construction, maintenance, and repair? It seems to me that everyone could profit from this knowledge. In another class, a young man began his speech by telling "us guys" about automotive tune-ups and oil changes. Does this mean that women have nothing useful to learn about automobile maintenance and repair? Often, it is not the topic, but *what we choose to do with the topic* that adapts it to the diverse audiences who are likely to hear it. Even if you are one of only a few African Americans in a class, there are lots of reasons why your classmates should hear about the concerns and perspectives of your group. Likewise, age differences, gender, culture, and background can all be linked to members of a diverse audience as long as you take care to be inclusive, not exclusive. Find the common connections, concerns, interests or motivations, and build on those in the development decisions you make as you create your speech.

main conference room of a major corporate headquarters but not at an outdoor pep rally.

Many of you reading this advice probably think that it is unnecessary and that you would certainly adapt appropriately. You would be surprised at the number of people who forget to do so. Speakers who fail to consider the different demands of various occasions fail to reach their audience. If you violate listeners' expectations associated with the occasion, they will stop paying careful attention to your message. In addition, you also need to think about the setting—that is, where you will be presenting your message.

Analyzing the Environment

One of the most important environmental factors in your presentation is location. **Location factors** include the size of the setting. Will you be speaking in a small conference room or a large auditorium? Indoors or outdoors? Although this consideration usually relates to the probable size of the audience, it is not always the case. For example, you may be outside, but speaking to only twenty or thirty people. What if you are scheduled for a large convention hall or auditorium, and only thirty or forty people show up? You might consider stepping down from the platform, asking the audience to move to the first few rows, and increasing your interaction with them. You should also think about where to stand, where to put your chart or overhead projector, or even whether to use a chart if it is not visible to everyone in the audience. Other elements such as poor lighting, distracting views, windows, possible noise, drafts, and heating and air-conditioning vents must all be considered so that you can adjust your plans to the location or, if necessary, change the location.

Once you have become aware of your listeners' values, the occasion or context for your speech, and the setting in which you will give your presentation, you need to consider ways to support your message so that it is clear, relevant, and interesting. The way to do this is to add good supporting materials to a well-constructed outline.

USING SUPPORTING MATERIALS

Suppose that you have identified a topic that is suitable—for you, the occasion, the audience, and the setting. Suppose that you have put together a tentative outline, complete with major parts and two, three, or four major subdivisions. The next step is to find support for each of those subdivisions. You can provide interest and substance for your main ideas by including specific information about them. The following section presents the types of information to look for, and the next section helps you to find some specific materials. There are three classes of information that can support your ideas: verbal, numerical, and visual (Zeuschner, 1994).

Verbal Supporting Materials

Specific pieces of information that can be conveyed only in words are called *verbal supporting materials*. You already use these supports every day whenever you try to explain or describe something to someone else. When you tell your friends on Monday morning that you had a great weekend, then tell them about the football game and party on Saturday, and finally give them details about the picnic on Sunday, you are using verbal supporting materials to amplify or describe your thesis—that is, that the weekend was great. In your speeches, you will probably use short stories or anecdotes, definitions, descriptions, examples, and quotations as verbal supporting materials.

Short stories are sometimes called *anecdotes* and can be an excellent way to support your ideas. If you can tell a vivid, clever, funny, or moving story, your audience will have a chance to identify with the story and remember your point. A good story for a speech should meet several criteria. It must clearly illustrate the point you wish to make, be complete so that your audience will understand the plot, and be appropriate to the situation. Do not tell a series of complex stories to an audience that is unfamiliar with your subject. Personal experiences are one type of story that, if used carefully, can both clarify ideas and show your connection with, or your interest or expertise in, the topic.

Keep off-color jokes out of a speech to a formal audience. Stories that are offensive because they mock gender, race, or age are sure to backfire. Your story must also be concise so that it does not take up too much time. If the story runs on, you risk having your audience forget the point. Remember that a story should not dominate the point, but support it. Look at the outline again, and notice that supporting materials are listed as 1 or 2, not A or B. This placement tells you that they are subordinate to the idea they support.

Definitions are sometimes very easy to find. Go to your dictionary and look up a term or concept. Sometimes you will find an encyclopedia or one of your textbooks to be helpful. If you cite your sources for your audience when you present a definition, you will give it greater impact. Definitions are good supports because they usually come from a professional source. They are also short and clearly written. Of course, you can always create your own definition and thereby possibly add an element of humor to a speech.

Descriptions are a combination of definitions and examples. When describing an object, an event, or even a feeling, you have to give your listeners only relevant, specific, information so that they can picture what you are describing. If you tell them that the Empire State Building is really very big, you are not being very descriptive. However, if you describe the number of floors it has, to what distance you can see from the top, and how many tons of steel and building materials it took to build it, you are approaching a good description.

By using the elements of *comparison and contrast,* you can describe something in terms of its relationship to something else. If your listeners are in Chicago, then comparing the Empire State Building to the Sears Tower will help them to understand their comparable sizes. A miniature pony can be described as being similar in size to a golden retriever. The texture of a mango can be compared to that of a peach. Descriptions like these will help to enrich your speech and make it interesting for your audience. If you go into a point-by-point comparison, you are probably drawing an analogy. These extended comparisons often have a poetic or figurative element. You may recall from your English classes the uses of metaphor and simile as forms of comparison that are rich in expression and vivid in content. Each of these forms—analogy, metaphor, and simile—can be usefully included in your supporting materials.

Examples are detailed, specific instances of an event, idea, activity, and so on. If you have a story that is not long enough to have a plot, it is probably an example. You should provide enough detail in your examples that the audience can appreciate and understand both your example and how it relates to the main idea it supports. If you are urging your classroom listeners to visit the campus counseling center, you can tell them the following:

> Many services are available at the center. For example, you can get free aptitude testing and other testing for career guidance. They offer career-planning small groups and interest workshops all year. If you need someone to talk to about personal problems, they can help you immediately with someone on staff. Or they can refer you to a trained professional in many areas, including health. They can even help you select a graduate school. These are just a few examples of the free services that are available at the counseling center.

Quotations allow you to use someone else's direct words to support your ideas. You may think of quotations as being the lofty or clever words of famous people. Go beyond that framework, and think about quoting a newspaper article, a poem, a line from a song, even your grandmother or your next-door neighbor. Quote the words of great authors or well-known speakers, but you can also quote many others to support your ideas as long as the quotations are clearly relevant to the topic and capture your listeners' attention. Make certain to credit your quotation when you present it. Giving the source of your quotation *before* you present it helps the audience to focus its attention and realize that a shift in voice is coming up. Sometimes, and for a surprise effect, you may want to wait until after the quotation to give the source. A favorite example of this surprise strategy is a quotation about how young people these days are unruly, hard to teach, impolite, and academically ill prepared. Then tell your listeners that the author of the statement is Socrates, speaking nearly 2,400 years ago! Usually, however, you will increase audience attention if you present your source first.

As you have seen, verbal supporting materials are an excellent way to define, clarify, and add impact to your presentation. However, there are times when they do not fit the content or purpose of your main ideas. Another form of supporting materials may be just what you need—numbers.

Statistical Supporting Materials

When you collect several single examples into a unit of measure, you are using numbers. You would not talk about each baseball hit by a major-league player; you would give only his average. You cannot enumerate every donation to the local blood bank, so you say the following:

> Last year, our local blood bank collected over 1,200 pints of blood. That comes out to less than four pints a day. The need for blood transfusions was well over six per day. Clearly, we are failing to provide this blood bank with sufficient funds.

Since you cannot detail all the examples of needed transfusions, you collect them into a statistical support—"six per day." You might select one powerful story to bring the statistical support "six per day" to life for your class, but the sheer volume of many examples will force you to collect material into numerical units. Although not as colorful as stories, statistics can often have a significant impact on your audience if you use them wisely. Since numbers are not as easily remembered as stories and examples are, your impact will be stronger if you use only a few numbers during a speech.

Any time that you use numbers to show relationships, you are in the area of statistics. In the blood bank example, if you had mentioned only the 1,200 pints of blood collected by the local blood bank, your listeners would not have been able to relate to anything meaningful. However, when you applied that number to both a daily donation rate and a daily need rate, you were discussing the relationship of those numbers to each other. In other words, you were using statistics, thereby increasing the impact of your message on your listeners.

You are probably familiar with such basic statistical concepts as rounding off, averages, trends, and percentages. These concepts will be familiar to your audience as well, so you should feel free to use them. If you are trained in more complex statistics and think that your audience would benefit from information about standard deviation, margin of error, or correlation coefficients, include that information as well. But do not assume, because you know what these concepts mean, that your listeners will as well. For most purposes, basic statistical relationships will tell your audience what it needs

Comparing three objects is easy with a proportional visual aid.

to know to understand your point. Remember to be accurate, clear, up to date, interesting, and relevant.

Visual Supporting Materials

Effective, total communication involves more than the sound channel; it includes the sense of sight as well. If you supplement the words you speak and the numbers you present with supporting materials that can be seen, you will increase the interest and clarity of your presentation for your audience. Using **visual aids** to support your ideas gives your listeners more ways in which to receive and understand your message, thus increasing your chances of success in transmitting your message. Using visual supporting materials also gives you an opportunity to add variety to your speech and to give your audience a break from listening to words.

As with any supporting material, make certain that your visual aids are linked to your ideas by placing them on the outline as a level 1 or 2 item. They should support, clarify, emphasize, define, or explain an idea better than words alone could possibly do. Sometimes, you might find an excellent photograph or object that has little to do with your main idea. Do not make the mistake of trying to use it. Make your visual supporting materials both relevant and uniquely valuable to your speech. For example, if you try to explain the beauty of the Grand Canyon without using a visual aid, you are probably making a mistake. If you want to explain the checks and balances of the federal government and show as your only visual aid a photograph of the White House, a drawing of George Washington, or a map of Washington, D.C., you are also making a poor choice.

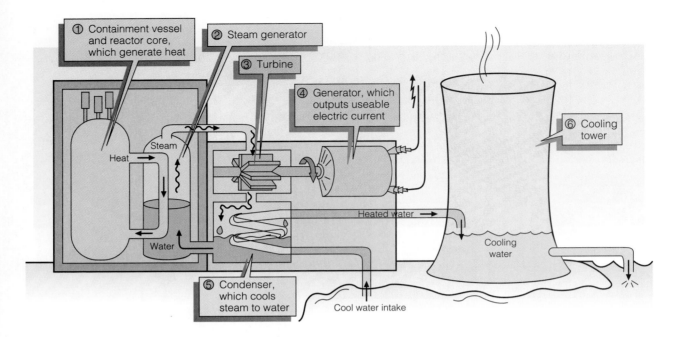

A schematic visual aid can help to explain how a complex process works.

There are several types of useful visual aids: pictures, maps, diagrams, objects, and models. You can also combine numbers and visual aids into graphs and charts.

Pictures and Maps   Pictures and photographs are the most popular visual aids. You can use anything that will illustrate an item in your speech—a photo of your car, of the Eiffel Tower, of your pet calf, or of your apartment building. If professional photographs or pictures are not available, do not be afraid to make one yourself. You do not have to be an artist to create a reasonably clear line drawing or sketch. If it's the right size, is clearly drawn, and supports your idea well, do not worry about its aesthetic merit.

A picture can indeed be worth a thousand words. Try showing a photograph of the Yosemite Valley to an audience and then try matching it with a verbal description. Color, size, shape, scale, and setting are almost always easier to show than to tell about. How would you begin to describe the color purple when there are dozens of shades of purple? Bring in a sample of the shade you want to describe, and your description will be clear instantly. A description that is long, labored, and obscure in words can be quick, direct, and clear in a visual aid. Keep your visual supporting materials simple. Use them for one major item or theme at a time. Make sure that people at the back of the room can see them. Make them interesting and colorful. Do all of these things, and you will have effective visual supports,

Maps, too, can be useful and effective. If you buy a professional map from a bookstore, it will be neat and clearly drawn. However, it might be too small or overly detailed for your presentation, so you could try drawing one

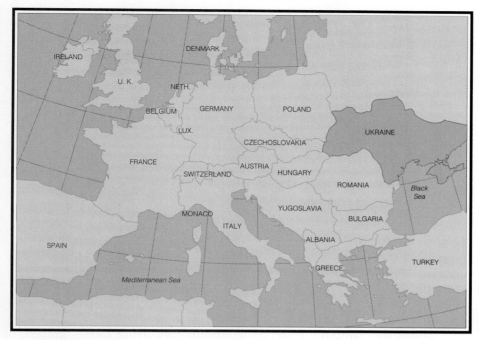

A map is an excellent way to explain location.

yourself. Keep it neat and simple, and follow the suggestions for size, clarity, and color that were previously discussed.

The location of Ukraine may be too difficult to explain, but a map segment of Europe and the former Soviet Union, with Ukraine shown in a bright color, could be very helpful to your audience. If you want to give the audience directions to your favorite eating spot, you can draw the directions on a large poster board, using a city map as your guide. A good map shows details and relationships more clearly and precisely than you can with words alone.

Objects and Models   Objects and models can also help you clarify your ideas if you can find any that are large enough to be seen by an audience. Do not ever bring a small object to class or to any other setting and say, "I hope everyone can see this." *Hope?* You should *know* whether it is large enough because you were supposed to have checked it beforehand. Even worse is the speaker who says, "I'm sorry most of you can't see this." This statement tells your listeners that you know they cannot see the object, but you had decided to use it anyway. Make certain that your object or model will be useful to your listeners so that they can experience it as support for your ideas. If it is not a good support, find something else to use. Show the types of rope used in sailing, or bring in three different kinds of bicycle helmets, or make a three-foot tall scale model of the Empire State Building or the Eiffel Tower. Do not let yourself be caught in the position of not knowing whether your object or model is providing the support for your listeners that it should. Go to the back of the room before your speech, turn around, look at your object, and see for yourself whether or not it can be seen from a distance.

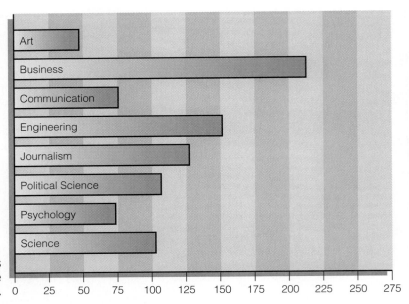

Bar graphs can help listeners to visualize comparative sizes or amounts.

Charts and Graphs Combining supports by using charts, graphs, or diagrams can also be an effective way to supplement your communication. You could create a chart showing the steps of a process, or the relationship of rising costs to declining profits. Graphs are an especially good way to show relationships among numbers. You might make some simple bar graphs to communicate the relative quantities of several numbers or amounts. Use different colors for different items, and your audience will be able to find them easily as you discuss them. A line graph can show trends over time, such as tuition levels over the past twenty years at your school, the price of automobiles, or population changes. If time is an important part of your idea, then a line graph would be a good supporting material to use for that idea. You might wish to show proportions of parts of a thing compared to the whole thing. In that case, use a pie graph. It can easily communicate that kind of relationship to your audience. A pie graph or chart illustrates the parts of a whole, and the relative sizes of all the parts equal the whole. Whether it is the distribution of your monthly expenses, the size of each department in a business, or the amount of calories in each part of a balanced meal, a good-size pie chart, with clear lines and a variety of colors, can do a great deal to support your idea.

In short, make sure that all of your visual aids are large enough to be seen; are easily made, handled, and presented; and are simple to operate. You probably should avoid electrical or mechanical devices that are subject to failure. Make certain that your visual aid is appropriate to both the audience and the setting. If you collect venomous snakes as a hobby and would like to bring them to your presentation on snakes, don't do it. Substitute a photograph for the real thing, and make your point that way. In the same vein, bringing in guns may be illegal, but diagrams of guns are not. If you are discussing drought and famine, you might be tempted to bring in pictures of dying or dead children to emphasize your thesis, but most people in your audience would be overwhelmed by such photographs and would probably stop paying attention to you. A student recently brought to class detailed photographs of an abortion in process to convince her listeners to oppose the procedure. The entire class avoided looking at her material, and two students left the room. So be careful about the appropriateness of your visual supports.

Time is also a factor. Does your visual aid take ten or fifteen minutes to set up and then dismantle? Be aware of the time limits you will have to cope with in any setting. Remember, your visual aid is just like any other type of supporting material. It is a support for a subordinate idea. It is a third-level event and should be allotted only that proportion of time in your presentation.

Finally, passing around small objects or handouts to the audience can be distracting. It is better to enlarge one object so that everyone can see it at the same time, you can control the time that it goes out of sight, and there will be no distractions in the audience while you are speaking. If the members of the audience really have to have something, hand it out to them at the end of the speech or presentation.

If you follow these guidelines, you can give a speech that has good supporting materials. The key to success here is to make sure the materials are appropriate and to lend them variety so that you can explain your ideas to your listeners in several different ways. Just how many of which type of support should you use? It all depends on you, your topic, your audience, and the situation. You can be sure, however, that a speech with a variety of supporting materials will go over better with an audience than a speech that is dominated by just one single type of material. Keep variety in mind as you look for supporting materials. Where do you look for these supports? The next section will answer that question.

RESEARCHING YOUR IDEAS

Finding interesting and stimulating supporting materials is one of the best reasons to do research for your speech. As you learn more about your subject through research, you add depth and interest to your presentation. Sometimes, you may be speaking about a personal experience—your trip from Miami to Atlanta to New Orleans. That does not exempt you from doing research. If you limit your speech to saying, "Well, then I went . . ." and "After that I went . . ." you will fail to provide both depth and variety for your listeners. Find out about the history of some of the places you visited. Quote from *Gone With the Wind*, get a map of the three areas from an auto club, use statistics about the populations of those cities. That type of supporting material will rescue your speech from being a self-centered, monotonous travelogue and turn it into a speech that is of keen interest to your listeners. Your presentation will be made more interesting by your personal touches, but they do not and cannot replace outside supporting materials culled from solid research.

So how and where do you find supporting materials? You can start with yourself, then talk to other people, and then research the print and nonprint resources available to you.

Finding and Recording Information

You will have to do some exploration to find all the supports that were discussed earlier—short stories, statistics, visual aids, definitions, descriptions, comparisons, and contrasts. Once you have found this information, you must record it so that you can both remember it and properly credit it in your speech. How much information should you gather? A good rule of thumb is that you should collect two or three times as much information as you have time for in your speech. For example, if you have a four- to six-minute speech, you should collect about fifteen minutes worth of supporting materials. That way you can go through your stack of stories, examples, statistics, and so on, and select the best ones for each subordinate idea. Evaluate each item for interest, clarity, and variety, and choose only the items that give your presentation the most value. Otherwise, if you have only four minutes' worth of material, you will have to use it. It may be good, bad, weak, strong, clear, or unclear. It doesn't matter; you are stuck with it. So give yourself an opportunity to choose.

Using Personal Resources

Think of yourself as an expert in experiences—your experiences. You have visited different places, taken classes in many subjects, had hobbies and jobs, and read a small mountain of books and magazines. All of these experiences make you a resource. Consider the cartoons you have clipped out, the books you have read, or your photographs of favorite stars, sports figures, or favorite vacations spots. Think about the variety of life experiences you have had, and use them as a starting point for gathering your supporting material.

Next, talk to some of the people you know. *Interviews* are an excellent way to gather quotations, and you have friends and associates who can lend their expertise to your speech if you ask them to do so. Your campus is filled with experts on hundreds of subjects, and most of your faculty members enjoy talking to students about their specialties. Most of the time, the main reason that students go to see teachers is to complain about a grade or ask about an assignment that the teacher thought had already been explained. What a pleasure it is for your teachers to have an intellectual discussion with someone who wants to know about their expertise. Remember to make an appointment and to prepare your questions in advance, as described in the section on interviews in Chapter 9.

Using Library Resources

Print resources are probably what you thought about immediately when you first read about doing research. Books, magazines, newspapers, and other printed material are some of the best sources of supporting materials. The best place to find these items is, of course, a library; and learning how to use a library can be a great advantage to your college career as well as to your speech preparation.

Books are an easy and plentiful source of information. Keep track of what you read so that you can list it properly in your bibliography. Small 3" × 5" or 4" × 6" index cards are useful for this purpose. You can write on them the important bibliographic information found on the copyright page of the

Interviewing people allows you to share their life experiences.

book and still have plenty of room to note important information such as statistics, facts, or direct quotations. The library may have a card catalogue—a large set of file drawers containing cards—that lists the books that are available. These cards are filed in three separate ways: by subject, by title, and by the author's last name. Many libraries have electronic catalogues that organize their listings in the same way—by author, title, and subject. When you begin your research, it may be a good idea to browse through the listings of either types of catalogue to get an idea of the holdings. Remember, books are always somewhat out of date, since they take at least a year and sometimes two to get from the author to the library. If an author has spent a year or more doing research, the information in the book may be at least two, and sometimes four or more, years old. For many items, this time gap will not matter, but if you plan to talk about current world events, unemployment rates, the cost of automobiles, or stock prices, books are not adequate. You will need current sources.

Newspapers and magazines can give you that information. Libraries subscribe to dozens of newspapers and magazines from all over the world. Magazines such as *Time, Newsweek,* and *U.S. News and World Report* are all well established and provide weekly coverage of important events. Of course, each has a particular perspective; nevertheless, they are well known for their accuracy. Other magazines may have a special interest, a particular political point of view, or a perspective from a different culture or country, all of which can give your speech both comprehensiveness and depth. Consult the *Readers' Guide to Periodical Literature* to locate the specific magazines that have the information you seek.

The library is a treasure house of information for every speaker.

In addition, libraries collect booklets, documents, pamphlets, and flyers published on a variety of very specific topics. College libraries also collect professional journals in every subject taught on campus, and they can be a source of sophisticated and highly specialized information. Check the library's vertical file or the publication *Facts on File* for short articles about current research in a variety of fields. You might even call organizations that are related to your topic and request some of their publications. Most organizations are happy to share their information and they usually enjoy helping students. Community action groups, local government, and utility companies are more places where you can get interesting print materials.

Nonprint resources are increasingly important in a world of computers and electronic information processing. Traditional sources such as films, tapes, and records have been augmented by compact discs, videotapes, electronic data banks, CD-ROMs, and on-line services. If you are going to discuss the speeches of former Presidents, you will get much more information about the topic from films and videotapes than if you simply read transcripts of the speeches. A speech on Native American literature would be somewhat impoverished unless you took the time to listen to some recordings of tribal storytellers. If you want to give something unique and memorable to your listeners, you need to look beyond ordinary sources of information. Most libraries have extensive indexes of nonprint resources including catalogues, references, and microfilm readers.

Using electronic databases with a computer will help you to combine this electronic format with traditional print media. Since these resources are on-line, they may be updated frequently, even as often as daily, so they become a rich resource of current information. Your library or your own on-line service provider may give you access to *InfoTrac,* which includes several thousand separate periodicals. Its *Expanded Academic Index* would be an excellent place to start your search. You can also try *Magazine Index Plus* as well as the *New York Times* and the *Wall Street Journal,* which are probably available via your computer connection. Web browser programs and search engines make using the Internet a useful part of you research. One further labor-saving advantage to your computer search is to hook up to a printer; the printout will give you properly recorded information to include in your speech bibliography (Grice and Skinner, 1995).

You can also collect supporting materials from television and radio. Did you recently watch a good program, see an important news broadcast, or listen to a great song? Write them down so they will be available to you for your speeches in the future. The average American household watches seven hours of television a day, so you have an opportunity to do research while you are being entertained. News broadcasts, documentaries, weather reports, sports programs, comedy series, and special programs are all potential sources for an example, a great story, a funny description, a bold analogy, or a key fact. Intelligent and focused television viewing can produce excellent supporting materials.

Synthesizing Your Material

Once you have gathered your information, it is time to reconsider the basic speech outline discussed earlier in this chapter. To construct a speech that meets the goals of clarity and impact, you need to support your thesis, and the main divisions of that thesis, with materials that are lively, specific, colorful, memorable, relevant, and convincing. Your goal is to communicate a worthwhile message to your audience members so that they will both understand and remember what you said. The better the supporting materials you use, the more likely it is that your intended results can be achieved.

Consult your stack of index cards, and sort them into groups according to the divisions of the body of your speech (A, B, C, and so on). Some items may not be appropriate, in which case you can either adjust your ideas or put the items aside. A great story that does not fit in one place often can be used in another. The introduction of a speech, for example, is often a story, so that is a way to create an introduction from the materials you have already gathered. If you have twice as much material as you need, you can review your speech outline, checking all items for interest, variety, and impact, and keeping only the very best ones.

SUMMARY

Preparing speeches is like doing a term paper. You need to organize your speech by preparing an outline. You have to think about who your listeners will be and adapt your ideas to that audience. Then you must present your information clearly and in a way that will show your audience that it is relevant to them. If you do not address the needs, concerns, and values of your listeners, you will be speaking only to yourself. The best way to prepare a presentation that is both clear and relevant is to assess your audience accurately, then engage in the research of supporting materials to which you feel it will respond. Verbal supporting materials are the most commonly used, and they can be augmented with simple statistics and compelling visual aids.

The use of supporting material should follow some common-sense guidelines. The next chapter deals with this issue by showing you how to put your preparation into practice so that you meet your goals.

KEY TERMS

outlining, p. 290
introduction, p. 291
thesis sentence, p. 292
body of the speech, p. 292
conclusion, p. 292
sources/bibliography/references, p. 292
supporting materials, p. 292
plagiarism, p. 292
organizational development patterns, p. 298
motivated sequence, p. 302
audience analysis, p. 303
value systems, p. 303
occasion, p. 304
location factors, p. 305
visual aids, p. 309
print resources, p. 314
nonprint resources, p. 316

EXERCISES

1. Watch a frequently appearing commercial on television. Watch it several times so that you can verify your observations. Determine what pattern of organization is used in the commercial. You can probably identify a chronological or cause–effect pattern fairly easily. Are there any others? Bring a list of three or four differently organized commercials to class, and compare them with those observed by your classmates. Did anyone use the same commercial but classify it as having a different pattern from yours? Why might this happen?

2. Create five areas of a speech are included. Now use the same topic and thesis sentence, but organize the body of the outline into a different format. Which one works better? Why?

3. Buy a packet of 4″ × 6″ note cards, and have them with you when you go to the library, watch television, and attend classes, lectures, or speeches. On these cards, write specific items you might use in a speech or presentation as they occur or happen to you. For example, you might record an interesting anecdote, some compelling statistics, or a vivid example. Even if you are not planning to speak on the same subject as your example or statistic, you will find that items can often be transferred from one presentation to another. These cards will also help you to build a reserve of information in case you are asked to give an impromptu speech.

4. Substitute a visual support for a verbal one. Can you show something better than you can tell it? Now do the reverse. Take something you think would make a good visual aid, and put the content into words. Is this item easier to say than it is to show? These tests can be done any time that you use supporting materials. Do them mentally to see whether an item should be a verbal or a visual support.

REFERENCES

Grice, George L., and John F. Skinner. *Mastering Public Speaking.* Boston: Allyn and Bacon, 1995.

Gronbeck, Bruce E., R. E. McKerrow, A. H. Monroe, and D. Ehninger. *Principles and Types of Speech Communication.* 12th ed. New York: HarperCollins, 1995.

Lumsden, Gay, and Donald Lumsden. *Communicating with Credibility and Confidence.* Belmont: Wadsworth, 1996.

Reike, Richard, and Malcolm Sillars. *Argumentation and the Decision-Making Process.* Glenview: Scott, Foresman, 1983.

Zeuschner, R. B. *Effective Public Speaking.* Dubuque: Kendall-Hunt, 1994.

CHAPTER 13

Presenting Speeches

AFTER READING THIS CHAPTER, YOU SHOULD BE ABLE TO:

- Know the four types of speech presentation styles, the causes of speech apprehension, and the standards for presenting and evaluating speeches.
- Feel ready to give speeches to your classmates and other listeners.
- Have control over your nervous energy.
- Uphold ethical standards in communication.
- Present an effective speech, and evaluate it and other speeches you hear.

When you have done your research, gathered your supporting materials, put them in order, and developed your visual aids, you will be ready to start practicing your presentation. No matter how much effort you put into research, outline construction, revision of your thesis sentence, and organization of the body of your speech, without an effective presentation your speech is not likely to have its desired effect. It is true that you must begin with substantial information on a worthwhile topic. But once your preparation is in place, it is time to make sure that your presentation does justice to all your preparatory work.

As noted several times earlier in this book, your presentation should clarify your ideas and give them impact. Speech delivery involves coordinating your voice and your body in a way that makes your message come alive for your audience. This chapter presents you with several optional styles to use when delivering a speech, suggests ways to deal with the speech anxiety you probably will feel, and enhances your verbal and nonverbal presentation skills. Finally, you learn about standards for evaluating speeches—your own as well as those you hear in class, in the community, and in the media. Let us begin with the four styles of presenting speeches.

TYPES OF PRESENTATIONS

For as long as there have been speakers, essentially four different types of **presentation styles** have been available: memorized, with a manuscript, extemporaneous, and impromptu. Your speech will fall into one of these styles of delivery every time you speak. Depending on the time and place, one type will be more appropriate than the others. Yet each one will be the right one at some particular time. The appropriateness, strengths, and weaknesses of each type will help you decide when to use and when to avoid a particular style. Your instructor may assign you one style for your classroom presentations; but outside of the class, you will need to select the one you believe is most appropriate.

Memorized

A **memorized** presentation follows a word-for-word preparation. This process, although time-consuming and tiring, gives you the advantage of speaking without notes, of including every detail exactly as you had planned, and of knowing precisely how long your speech will last. In a formal setting, and when you need only a few minutes to express your thoughts, this style of presentation may be just right. However, this style has one major drawback: You might forget parts of your speech. The pressure that public communication can put on you may result in your forgetting a line or a word. If you memorize the way most people do, you depend on one line following another, like the links of a chain. Each sentence ties you to the next. If you blank out on one sentence or word, you might forget not only that line, but all the lines that follow. If this happens, then all the benefits of memorization evaporate, along with the lost lines. You are now unable to speak. Now you need your notes, your timing is off, and you may skip ideas or materials on which you worked very hard.

Unfortunately, many beginning speakers think that they *must* memorize to make a good impression. The more concerned and worried they are, the more they are tempted to control every second and every syllable of their presentation. Their very anxiety is their worst enemy. They forget their speech, and the disaster that they had nightmares about actually happens—caused by their own overpreparation. Memorized speeches are usually best left to very experienced speakers.

Another disadvantage of memorization is that all but the very best speakers tend to sound mechanical, stilted, and uninvolved when speaking from memory. Instead of establishing genuine rapport with their audiences, speakers who memorize often look and sound like robots, reciting lines with no direct connection to their listeners. If the audience does respond with some feedback, these speakers cannot adapt or respond to the audience, and communication interaction fails. The use of memory for most people is probably manageable if it is limited to very short speeches, such as a thank you or a brief introduction in a very formal setting. Memorization probably will not be appropriate for most of the classroom speeches you give or for most of the presentations you will give throughout your lifetime.

Manuscript

A speaker who delivers a speech from a **manuscript** usually writes out or types the speech word for word and then presents the speech by reading the manuscript. In the best manuscript delivery, speakers spend about 10 to 20 percent of their time looking down at the script and 80 to 90 percent of the time looking at the audience to establish eye contact and direct interaction. The speaker must always focus on the audience and not on the manuscript. The advantage of speaking from a manuscript is that you have no fear of forgetting. In addition, you have control over what you say, and your timing will be very accurate.

When you attend major events—graduations, dedications, presidential addresses, public ceremonies, or religious services—you will usually see a manuscript delivery. Often, the delivery is very good, but sometimes it is not. One reason that people use manuscripts is to lend an elevated tone to the event by using highly polished vocabulary and sentence structure. With this kind of preparation, they can be sure that they will make no mistakes. Generally, a manuscript speaker does not sound as mechanical as a memorized speaker, but a manuscript can still create a barrier to good eye contact, and it does not allow for much adjustment to audience feedback. Reading from a manuscript lacks both spontaneity and immediacy and runs the risk of making the speaker sound flat, recycled, stale, or not directly related to the listeners. Manuscript presentation is usually found in longer presentations—beyond eight or ten minutes—and when the ceremony itself or the accuracy of the information is the most important consideration.

Extemporaneous

An **extemporaneous** speech is the type you will give most often—both in the classroom and later in life. To deliver a good extemporaneous speech, you have to prepare and practice, but you must stop short of memorizing the words of your presentation or writing them out in sentences. Good ex-

The more formal the setting, the more likely you'll use a manuscript.

temporaneous speakers will carefully prepare a key idea or key word outline. The speakers then memorize the outline but allow the exact words of the body to emerge spontaneously. They practice out loud many times; and although the speech is very similar each time, it is never exactly the same. Moreover, they do not attempt to achieve exactness. If a phrase or a sentence reverses itself from one time to the next, that is permissible, as long as the point of the topic or idea is clearly made each time.

The advantages of an outline to you as a speaker are many. Using an outline gives you a comprehensive plan, helps you to be comfortable with the materials, and ensures that you will have the results of your research and organization readily at hand. An outline also allows you to practice sufficiently that you will know the length of your presentation. Finally, using an outline gives you the flexibility to be spontaneous and direct and to adapt to your audience immediately. You can remain conversational, thereby increasing audience attention and rapport, and you can create a directness in your approach that helps to give an impact to your ideas. In virtually every situation, audiences prefer extemporaneous speeches, and they rate the speakers who give such speeches very highly.

There are, of course, some potential disadvantages to this type of presentation. You do not have exactness in your wording or your timing. You need to smooth out your phrasing; and some speakers, especially if they are working in a second language, may not be as adept at spontaneity as others. However, because it is such an appropriate type of presentation for so many settings, it is important for you to develop skills in extemporaneous speaking.

Impromptu

When you deliver a speech on only a few moments' notice, you are engaging in **impromptu** speaking. You may find yourself at a meeting and decide to speak about the issue under consideration. In your career, you may suddenly be asked by a visiting team to explain your section of the company. In class, you may be called on to provide a lengthy explanation of a point or a defense of a position. At a business conference, someone may have heard of your creative work and may ask you to stand up and explain your latest project to a group or an assembly.

In each of these situations, you have not prepared an outline or rehearsed your presentation. However, it is a mistake to call impromptu speeches unprepared speeches. In a very real sense, you are prepared, and in many ways. First, notice that no one is ever asked to speak about something unless there is a reason or expectation that the person can do so. In class, you should know the material. In a meeting, you are there because of your interest. A career setting will find you explaining things that are directly related to that carrier. So you do have some research and some supporting materials that are with you always and everywhere: your experience, background, and knowledge. Moreover, this class and others have given you some preparation for organizing those experiences into a coherent speech. If you are asked five years from now to give an impromptu speech about something, you will already know that your speech should have an introduction, a clear thesis sentence, and a body organized into some pattern that has from two to five main divisions that relate to the thesis. You know right now that you need a quick review for the conclusion and supporting materials that are vivid, specific, and varied. You may not know it, but you are already writing your future impromptu speeches. When the time comes, you will need only a few moments to jot down some notes so that you can quickly create a basic outline, fill in spaces, and be ready to give your speech. All of your earlier speeches will have given you practice in modulating your voice, making eye contact, creating transitions, and using good body language, so those skills will also be with you everywhere you go.

The advantages of being able to deliver an impromptu speech will make your ideas more compelling than those of people who do not know how to make such speeches. Impromptu speeches are immediately adaptable to the situation and the audience, and they make it possible for the speaker to respond directly to any feedback from the audience. On the other hand, you may not remember to organize an outline, or your supporting materials might not be as strong or as varied as you would like. Your timing and phrasing might be off. Being a good impromptu speaker is a real challenge, but it is one that can be personally gratifying for the person who does it well.

Improving Competency

Honing Your Presentation Skills

As you speak in your classes, on the job, or in your community, try applying the four different types of presentations. You might read notes in one setting and make an impromptu speech in another. You could memorize a short presentation or try the extemporaneous method. By being aware of the four different types of delivery, and by putting them into practice, you will expand your range of abilities. What is more, you can start today.

The four types of presentation can be selected and evaluated according to the circumstances of your speech. No matter which type you select, you will most likely have one experience each and every time you present a speech: some nervousness.

DEALING WITH APPREHENSION

As mentioned in Chapter 2, the mere thought of giving a speech is enough to produce apprehension in most people (Richmond and McCroskey, 1995). This reaction is common and normal. The symptoms—tension, "butter-flies," sweaty palms, tight and shallow breathing, and a lump in the throat—are felt by everyone. These symptoms are the standard physiological reactions to fear and stress. Like many other fears, this one can be managed and reduced.

It is important to know that any nervousness you have is natural and that with preparation, you can respond to it so that it no longer hinders you when you are doing a presentation. You read about the source and effects of speech **apprehension** in Chapter 2, in which several approaches to the problem in general were recommended.

Apprehension may flow from one or more of three areas: excessive activation of your physical responses, inappropriate cognitive processing of the situation, or inadequate communication skills (Richmond and McCroskey, 1995). In this chapter, some very practical, specific suggestions are made that you can use when it is your turn to speak. Most people have a strong desire to appear competent in the eyes of others, and giving a speech puts a person in the spotlight. If you have never had any training in giving speeches, you might be afraid of making mistakes and appearing to lack competence. If you have never learned how to drive a car, you should keep out of the driver's seat. However, once you take a driver-training course and gain a little experience, you still won't be an expert driver, but driving should no longer

Give yourself the gift of practice.

be such a formidable experience that you avoid it altogether. In the same way, preparing and presenting a speech, when that task is approached with some knowledge and experience, can develop your competence and your confidence.

The bottom line is: To appear credible, you should *be* credible. Many of the ways to become credible have already been covered—select a substantial and worthwhile topic, give it the clear organization and preparation it deserves, provide yourself with significant supporting materials, and select a presentation type that is appropriate for both you and the situation. The last task of your preparation is to practice; and while you practice your speech aloud, you can also practice some physiological and psychological exercises that can assist you in your *total* preparation.

Physiological Preparation

If you have excess energy, you can learn to use your physiology to spend some of that energy. As you sit awaiting your turn to speak, you will probably experience your greatest anxiety. There are several physical exercises that you can practice ahead of time that will help train your muscles to relax. If you practice **physiological preparation** now, and again as you practice the spoken part of your speech, you will have some excellent tools to help overcome the negative effects of your natural tension.

Correct Breathing   First of all, the best and proven method of helping you counter excess tension involves your breathing. In ancient cultures that taught us yoga and in modern Lamaze childbirth methods, correct breathing is at the heart of controlling and channeling energy. The importance of breath control is seen in sports, singing, exercise, acting, childbirth, and public speaking. These techniques can help you to gain control over your apprehension and ease the task of presenting your ideas to others. These breathing techniques are easy to learn and easy to apply.

The basic exercise is to breathe slowly and regularly from your diaphragm. The diaphragm is a large muscular tissue located beneath your lungs, just below the rib cage. As you push this muscle down, you create a vacuum in your lungs. Air rushes in from outside to equalize the pressure, and you inhale. Although this description sounds like a fairly involved way to describe something that you do without thinking, you do need to think about it when an anxiety reaction interferes with your presentation. To give you greater strength with which to face your "danger," the anxiety response tenses up your midsection, which in turn forces you to breathe in a shallow manner and with only the upper lungs. Singers and actors exercise to increase their lung power because they know they can support a stronger voice with full lungs. Like you, they need to overcome the effects of tension, so they practice deep breathing and continue with it when their physiology tries to make them breathe with only the top part of the lungs. Learning to feel your diaphragm and monitor its movement can help you to attack immediately one of the prime causes of continuing tension: incorrect breathing. Incidentally, your solar plexus, the place where you feel "butterflies," is at the base of the diaphragm; and by slowing down your breathing, you can chase the butterflies away as well.

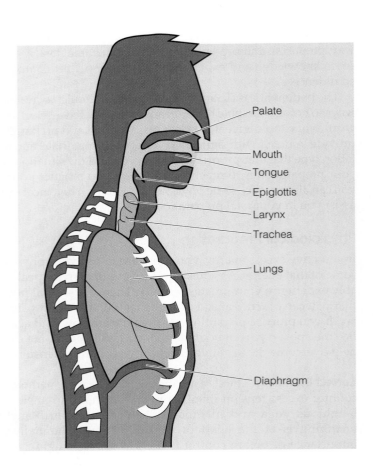

The diaphragm is at the base of the lungs and supports the rest of sound production.

Yoga teachers point out that when you relax the center of your body, a calming feeling spreads from there throughout the rest of your body. By breathing regularly and slowly, in and out, while you practice your speech, you will be creating an automatic reminder to do the same kind of breathing while you are waiting for your turn to speak. By so doing, you will supply your brain with oxygen, keep your butterflies under control, and begin to calm your entire body. You can practice slow, regular, and deep breathing while you are practicing your speech.

Muscle Relaxation Another physical exercise that you can practice and then do while waiting for your turn to speak, is a tensing and relaxing of various muscles. Locate the calf muscle on your right leg. Now, keeping your thigh muscle relaxed, tense just the calf muscle. This exercise is not easy, but try to make the calf muscle tight. Hold it for a count of ten, then relax. During this exercise, you should be breathing slowly. Now switch legs, and repeat the exercise. Try the same exercise with the thigh muscles. Continue to breathe slowly. Now try tensing your forearm but leaving your biceps relaxed. Breathe slowly.

You can do these exercises very subtly so that even if you are doing them on stage in front of an audience, no one will be aware of what you are doing. In fact, what you will be doing is using up some energy—skimming off some of the tension so that your muscles will be more relaxed. You will still have plenty of energy to give a dynamic presentation, but you will not have the shaky knees or the quivering hands of speakers who tense up and then hold onto that tension. You might try the exercise at home with any combination of muscles. Try selective tensing, hold for five deep breaths, then relax. Airline passengers are often taught these and similar isometric exercises as a way of avoiding fatigue.

If you are not on stage but in a somewhat private setting, you can try shrugging your shoulders and rotating them forward and then backward. Another helpful exercise for reducing tension is to lower your head slowly until your chin rests on your chest. Then slowly rotate up one side, then down again, and slowly up the other side. A good, long yawn can help to relax the throat. You can even yawn on stage if you remember to keep your mouth closed. Try it now. Can you feel the stretch of your larynx? That stretch will relax your voice.

As you do the breathing exercises and the muscle tensing and relaxing exercises, remember that you are in control. If you practice these exercises often, doing them in a slow and regular pattern, you can build your confidence. You will, of course, feel the direct, physical benefits immediately. When you go to your presentation, remember to start your deep breathing as you approach your destination. Start your muscle tensing and relaxing as soon as you reach your seat. Getting in control of your physical reactions is a direct way to meet the challenge your physiology presents to you when you are under stress. Incidentally, many people use these techniques in many different kinds of situations: taking a test, being interviewed, meeting a special person's parents, trying out for a team, or doing an audition for a show. When

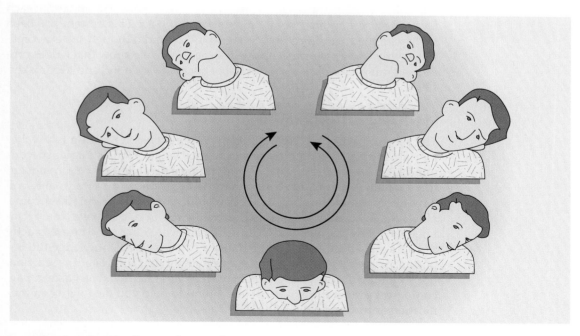

A gentle, slow head roll can relax tension.

The Story of Communication

Creative Visualization

A few years ago, the Public Broadcasting Service television stations ran a feature that described a basketball training camp experiment. The researchers divided students at the camp into three groups, and they were tested on their free-throw ability. The first group was thanked for its participation, sent home, and told to come back in a month. The second group was given four hours a day of instruction for four weeks and practice in free-throw technique. The third group was taken to a classroom, shown a film on perfect free-throw technique, and given instruction on positive visualization and self-imagery. For a month, these students sat in a quiet room for twenty minutes a day and imagined themselves shooting perfect free-throws. At the end of the month, the first group had a 10 percent decrease in average free-throw ability. The second group had a 23 percent increase in free-throws. The third group had a 21 percent increase in free-throw ability. Although visualization was not as good as the actual practice, the third group did improve significantly. This experiment indicates the power of visualization.

you are in a situation in which you begin to feel the flight-or-fight reaction, counteract it immediately with the physiological responses described.

In some cases, the extremes of physiological reaction can be reduced effectively by a six-step process known as systematic desensitization (Wolpe, 1958). This process takes extremely anxious individuals through a series of imagined anxiety-producing situations and, combined with deep muscle relaxation training, moves from low to high stress levels. The anxiety at each level must be mastered before moving to the next. This system has been widely applied (Hoffman and Sprague, 1982); and although the exact reason(s) why it works are not conclusively accepted, we know that it does produce significant improvement for many people (Richmond and McCroskey, 1995).

Psychological Preparation

The second part of the communication apprehension reaction is psychological. Your mind is the place where the danger signals begin, so your mind is where you can work on countermeasures. Remember, in most of these situations, you *should* feel that the occasion is important, and you have every right to be concerned about your presentation and its outcome. However, in an effort not just to control the reaction, but to eliminate it altogether, many people wind themselves up even tighter and create exactly the opposite effect from the one that was intended. Acknowledge the importance of what you are doing, but remember that control of the reaction, not its elimination, is your goal. There are several steps you can take in **psychological preparation** to enlist your mind to help you deal with communication apprehension.

Familiarity   Become familiar with the situation. This means that you need to follow up on your analysis of the setting. If you take that advice, you are already well on your way to having a good frame of mind rather than an anxious frame of mind.

People dislike what is unfamiliar, so getting to know your setting is a big step toward psychological control. Your efforts to become familiar with your listeners—their backgrounds, values, and listening goals—will also help you to know what the situation calls for and how to prepare for it. As you become more familiar with the speaking environment and your intended audience, you will have fewer uncertainties and greater confidence.

Involvement   Be involved in your topic. This step helps you to focus on your topic and its importance to your listeners and therefore to be less focused on *yourself*. Select a topic that you care about. After you have expended energy on research and preparation, you will develop a psychological investment in the topic. As the ideas in your presentation gain greater importance, your ego becomes less important. If you have a strong desire to communicate to your audience about something you find worthwhile and substantial, you will replace concern for your appearance or your nervousness with concern for your message. If you are genuinely involved in your ideas, your involvement and commitment to those ideas will show in your preparation, practice, and presentation. For that reason, you need to avoid a topic picked out of a magazine the night before the presentation or recycled from a friend. Create a sincere message, and your sincerity will be evident.

Concern   Show concern for your audience. After you have selected a good topic, take the time to demonstrate that you also care about your listeners. Do you have a sincere desire to communicate with them? Have you considered their reasons for being in the audience? Have you approached the topic from their point of view? By responding to these questions, you place the attention on your ideas and your audience, not on you. Center yourself on your listeners, and relate your speech to *them*. In that way, your psychological commitment is to the ideas in your presentation and to the receivers to whom you send those ideas, not to your own personal concerns. The message happens in collaboration with the audience or not at all. Review Chapter 11 to gain a deeper appreciation of your listeners. Remember that you are speaking not to a mirror but to real people. If you keep your listeners uppermost in your mind, you will have less time to become overly concerned with yourself. And don't forget to smile.

Imaging   Imagine yourself as a strong speaker. Do you recall the discussion about how powerful self-concept messages can be? Use that knowledge to help you create an ideal speaker in your mind—in other words, you. See yourself doing a good job. Imagine smiles on the faces of your listeners. Visualize your speech going smoothly and ending at just the right time and in just the right way. Many people dwell on negative thoughts when they are feeling apprehensive. They invest large amounts of psychological capital in all the awful things they fear might happen. As

Positive visualization helps you to reach your goals.

you learned in interpersonal communication, your internal messages are very powerful, but they are under your control. When you find your internal messages drifting toward negative thoughts, replace those thoughts with positive visualizations. Imagine yourself as a calm, energetic, and dynamic person who thinks and speaks clearly. Imagine your audience's reactions as being positive—nods of agreement, smiles at your ideas, and applause at the end of your presentation. Keep this image in your mind when you practice, while you wait your turn to speak, and during your presentation. Positive visualization works for sports teams and is exactly what is meant by getting "psyched up" for an event. If you mentally predict success, it is more likely to come your way.

You know enough about public speaking by now to realize that the best way for physiological and psychological preparation to work is for them to work together. The mind and the body are a team, not independent entities. When you *concentrate* on your breathing, you will forget to get butterflies. In other words, the human mind concentrates best on only one thing at a time. When you create a positive mental image, your physical energy is channeled into that image, and both your mind and your body help you to realize it. Teamwork between physical exercises and psychological responses can give you the focus and confidence you need to make the image a reality. You will find that you are able to control your public-speaking energy. You can then direct that energy into making yourself a skilled public speaker.

EFFECTIVE PUBLIC SPEAKING SKILLS

Once your preparation is strong and solid, you can pay attention to the presentation itself. The success of your delivery will depend on how effectively you use your voice and body to deliver your message with clarity and impact. There are five elements of **vocal delivery,** and we begin with a discussion of those elements. Next, we look at how to use posture, movement, and gestures to enhance your message.

Verbal Skills

Volume is obviously the first element of good vocal delivery because your listeners must be able to hear you, at the very least. Speak loudly enough to be heard by every person in your audience. You may need to use a microphone if the room is especially large, so test the microphone for sound level and feedback—in advance if possible—and then practice using it. In a classroom or business conference room, a microphone is not only inappropriate, it is unnecessary. For the majority of your speeches, you will be in front of a small or medium-size group, and you will speak with a voice supported by good breathing from your deep-breathing routine.

You can find out whether the volume of your voice is adequate by practicing in the room in which you are going to speak and by having someone tell you how you sound. When you are actually giving your presentation, you can carefully observe your listeners as they relax and seem comfortable, or as they strain and lean forward to hear what you are saying. Keep in mind, however, that a room full of people absorbs sound, so do not practice in an empty room.

Another important thing to remember about volume is to have variety in the sound of your voice. You can emphasize ideas by varying your volume, but do not be misguided into thinking that *loud* means important. Although we often raise our volume to emphasize an important idea, we also drop the volume very low to show the same thing. At a wedding, for example, the bride and groom speak at a very low volume when they say some of the most important words they will ever utter. Variety means to speak louder and then softer; it is the change in volume that alerts listeners that a change is taking place in the message.

*Articulation and pronunciation a*re also important to your vocal delivery in terms of being understood by your listeners and building your credibility. The way you make your sounds should be clear, and your pronunciation should be within acceptable ranges for your audience.

Articulation is the clear production of sounds so that they are crisp and distinct. It means involving your muscles and vocal structures so that these tools can be used to produce the sounds clearly and audibly. To develop clear articulation, you need to be able to hear yourself. Although that sounds like an easy task, it is actually somewhat difficult, at least at first. You are so used to the sound of your own voice that you might not be objective about the sounds you produce. Use a tape recorder. Then listen to your voice with a sensitive ear. You may want to use a dictionary pronunciation guide at first. It will give you the standard, correct pronunciation of any words about which you are uncertain. Be especially sensitive to the final consonants t and d. They are frequently ignored by many people. Sometimes middle syllables get altered, as when people say things like "fas'nating" instead of "fascinating." Some people add syllables to words, as when someone says "orientate," when the correct word is *orient,* or "orientated" instead of the word *oriented*. As you work on developing sensitive self-feedback, your articulation can become improved.

Sometimes people worry about pronunciation. Pronunciation is the use of clearly articulated sounds in any given word. You might try using a dictionary pronunciation guide at first; it will tell you how educated speakers of Mainstream English pronounce the word.

Your pronunciation can affect your credibility. Many listeners associate a level of competence with a certain pronunciation. Sometimes, if you have a strong regional accent, you might want to modify it when your audience is from a different region. In a well-known example, former President Kennedy was speaking to a group of ministers in Houston, far from his native Boston. In a recording of that speech, you can hear Kennedy modify at times his New England pronunciation of "Americur" to "America."

In many ways, once a word has been clearly articulated, most regional and ethnic differences in pronunciation can be perfectly acceptable, depending on the listeners. If you have a regional color to your speech, there is no need to be overly concerned as long as your audience can follow you easily and respond to you credibly. Follow the generally accepted standards of educated people in your audience. Sometimes an accent can add interest or uniqueness to your presentation, and it may be a genuine part of you that you wish to retain, even when you are not dealing with listeners from the same cultural or regional background. Can your present listeners understand you? Does your credibility remain high? If so, don't feel that you must eliminate every trace of your background accent.

However, some accents do create an unfavorable impression if they are associated with substandard speech. Saying "gist" for the word *just* is an example of pronunciation that is often associated with a lack of education. Again, your dictionary can help you with problems like this one, and it may even list several pronunciations for the same word. By following the standards of educated people in your community, you can be both faithful to your background and understood by your listeners.

Pitch is simply the musical note that your voice makes when it issues a sound. You may have a high soprano voice, or you may be a deep bass. In any case, your voice has a range that is comfortable, and you have a typical pitch at which you usually speak. When you are tense, there is a tendency to speak a note or two higher than your typical pitch. A closed-mouth yawn can help get you back to normal. If you feel that your pitch is too high in general, you can develop a lower voice by relaxing your throat and learning to speak in a lower, relaxed tone. In a private setting, you might try to tilt your head back slightly and slowly gargle air by letting your vocal bands relax and "flap" on the airstream. Lower tones also carry better than higher ones, so speaking in a low tone that is still within your normal range can help your voice to project farther out into the room.

Variety in pitch is also important. When you raise your pitch slightly at the end of an interrogative sentence, you are telling your listeners that your sentence is a question. You can also use the range of your voice to create interest and emphasis. A tape recorder can assist you in developing good variety in the pitch of your voice. Use it to learn how to enhance your message or to see what areas you need to work on if your voice seems to be stuck in a limited monotone.

Your *rate* of speech refers to how fast or slowly you speak. You have probably heard speakers who speed along so fast that you cannot follow them and others who seem to drag on for so long that it takes them forever to get to the point. As is true for the other elements of vocal presentation, variety can be a key ingredient to your success as a speaker. Going fast sometimes and then slowing down add interest in general to your speech, and you can also use this technique to emphasize key ideas for your audience.

A very important aspect of your rate of speech is silence. Pause at key places to emphasize an idea. For example, if you have an important word coming up, pause just before you say it to set up your listeners. During the pause, gaze around the room at your audience to heighten the expectation. "And the winner is . . . !" is a perfect example of the use of a pause before a key idea to create an impact. After you have presented an important idea, you may want to pause to give the audience a moment to absorb or think about what you have just said. Try going through your speech to discover the impact that a well-chosen pause might have on your message.

The final element, tone, is the most difficult to vary. This aspect of your voice is also called *quality,* or *timbre*. The tone of your voice refers to those qualities that are unique in your resonance and sound production. When Jim calls on the phone, you can distinguish his voice from Walt's voice. When a clarinet plays a note, you can tell that it is not a violin even if it is playing the exact same note. The instruments may be played at the same volume, rate, and pitch, but their tone is what distinguishes each instrument. Brothers or sisters may sound very much alike because they share many genes and have been raised in a similar environment. Therefore their vocal production and patterns may also be very similar.

It is difficult to provide variety in your tone of voice; and unless your voice is at one extreme or another of the tonal scale, it is probably not very important to do so. However, if your voice is excessively nasal or so breathy that people think you are trying to imitate a movie star, you may wish to work on altering your tone production.

When is a person's tone of voice excessive? When your audience pays more attention to the tone of your voice than to your ideas, you are probably a candidate for tone modification. You can alter a nasal voice by learning how to close off the nasal passages and open your mouth and throat more. You can reduce a breathy voice by using less air in your vocal production and by forcing that air through a slightly smaller opening. Of course, you can have fun playing around with your tone production, and that may be one way to discover some tonal variety that you can use to your advantage in your presentation. If your tone production gets severely in the way of clear communication with your listeners, you may need some sessions with a qualified speech therapist to develop some new habits of sound production.

All of these aspects of good vocal delivery are designed to bring clarity and emphasis to your message. The use of volume, diction, pitch, rate, and tone can be enhanced by appropriate variety. You can increase your ability to discover and use this variety by careful self-monitoring, especially through tape-recorded practice.

Nonverbal Skills

Studies of speech communication have found that the use of both voice and body are very important in giving a speech. In one experiment, a trained actor presented a speech to several different audiences. Although the speech was the same on each occasion, in one half of the sessions he stood perfectly still and simply gave his speech. In the other half, he took a few steps from time to time and used a few arm, hand, and head movements. The responses to the speech were markedly different. The second group of listeners thought that the speaker was more intelligent than the first group did. They also thought that he was better looking and taller than the first group did. What is most important, though, is that after a month, the second group *remembered the content* better than the first group did. Clearly, nonverbal communication, when it complements a verbal message appropriately, can make that message more effective. Physical communication delivery has four major aspects: appearance, posture, movements, and facial expressions.

Appearance is the first thing your audience will notice about you, even in a classroom setting. It is said, "You never get a second chance to make a first impression." That first impression is always made by your appearance, and it can affect the way listeners will receive your complete message. An easy way to be guided regarding your appearance is to ask yourself what is generally expected or worn in similar circumstances. Is your speech a classroom speech? Are you going to be interviewed for a job or a scholarship? Will you be doing a reading at a religious service, or are you going to be a commencement speaker? Each of these settings probably has a standard of dress and grooming that is appropriate to it. Why should you be concerned with such a seemingly superficial concept as appearance? For the same reason that you would be concerned about your voice or a visual aid. If receivers pay more attention to those factors than they do to your message, they will miss the point of your communication. All the choices you make should enhance and highlight the content of your message. The great fashion designer and perfume manufacturer Coco Chanel was reputed to have said, "If they remember the dress and not the woman, they have remembered the wrong thing." On the days that you present a speech in class, you need not wear a business suit. But you can dress at the better end of the spectrum of what people normally wear to class. Caring about your appearance is one way to demonstrate care and respect for your topic, your ideas, your listeners, and yourself.

Posture refers to your overall, general stance, or how you hold yourself when speaking. Usually, listeners expect speakers to stand up straight, not slouch, lean on the lectern, or drape themselves across a chair or table. Your posture need not be stiff and formal, but it should communicate alertness and energy. Posture also includes the way you position your body. You should turn from one side to another while speaking and eventually face all parts of the room. In this way, you can vary your posture in a comfortable, useful way.

Movements are the many shifts, turns, and gestures you make while you still maintain a consistent posture. Appropriate movement that assists in the clear transmission of your message is not only desirable, it is essential. Some speakers seem to be in constant movement, which can be distracting to the audience. But your standing perfectly still can be boring to the audience. Somewhere in between the two extremes is a level of movement that suits you and will enhance your communication effectiveness. Speakers who engage in a moderate number of movements and gestures are rated by au-

Technology in Communication

Honest Feedback

Videotaping your practices may be one way to get some direct feedback on your use of gestures, postures, and vocal variety. The widespread availability of videocameras and players makes this tool one to which you probably have easy access. Each year, the cost of these cameras and players comes down, and the quality and capabilities of the equipment go up. Technological advances will allow you to see yourself in slow motion, freeze the action, or fast-forward to get an exaggerated picture of yourself. About ten years ago, I began the practice of videotaping my students' speeches and letting them view the tape later, one at a time. Since that time, their abilities to present oral communication have improved beyond the levels my students used to reach. Take advantage of this technology, and use it to provide accurate feedback.

diences as being more credible than those who do not move very much or those who are in almost constant motion. If you are showing your listeners a picture or a chart, you may need to move so that they can all see it properly.

Smaller movements are called *gestures* and include everything from slight hand movements and head nods to the expansive and descriptive shaping of space with your arms or perhaps your entire body. Most people think of gestures as hand movements because they are the most common and most noticeable. You could, of course, lift your foot and point with your toe, but most people do not. Are you wondering what to do with your hands? Most people seem uncomfortable just letting them hang at their sides. Some people try clasping their hands behind their back, shoving them into their pockets, or folding them in front of the lower chest. These options severely restrict the opportunity to reinforce and complement your ideas with appropriate gestures. They may also have the effect of holding onto tension. Gestures are best used when they are natural and spontaneous—just the way you would use them if you were sitting in your living room or at a lunch table talking with friends. A relaxed, natural animation helps the audience connect with the speaker and creates a friendly rapport. Videotaping your practice sessions is one way to get some direct feedback on your use of gestures.

Facial expressions include a raised eyebrow, a smile, a wink, a frown, or wide-eyed surprise. Research suggests that the face is the most powerful, nonverbal communicator because of the hundreds of possible combinations of facial expressions you can make with your facial muscles. You are also capable of recognizing and giving meaning to these combinations. Make certain that the message your face sends is consistent with the message of your speech. Have a friend watch your presentation or, better yet, arrange to have it videotaped. Then check it for clear and communicative facial expressions.

Eye contact is an important element in communication. Having good eye contact means that you look at your listeners almost all of the time, establishing a direct link between yourself and individual members of the audience. Many students find this contact difficult to establish and maintain.

The Emperor and the Messenger

In Kyoto, Japan, the imperial palace has a reception hall where messengers used to bring news and information to the emperor. A lowly messenger could not speak directly to the emperor, so three floor levels were built into the room. The messenger would kneel at the first level and present the message to the shogun, or intermediary, who sat at the second level, about ten feet away. The intermediary would then turn to the emperor, who sat at the third level, also about ten feet away, and repeat the message. The emperor probably heard every word the messenger said, since he was barely twenty feet away. Nevertheless, cultural communication norms had to be observed. Consequently the emperor showed no reaction, not even to terrible news, until the intermediary repeated it to him. The same process was reversed if the emperor had a return message. First he told it to the intermediary, who then told it to the messenger. The messenger, of course, could give no indication that he had heard a single word spoken by the emperor.

Some are reluctant to use eye contact because they start thinking about the person they are looking at instead of the idea they are speaking about. Other speakers may come from a culture or tradition in which direct eye contact is considered rude. In traditional Asian and African families, it is often a sign of respect to look away from the person whom you are addressing. Some families maintain these cultural norms through many generations. However, the mainstream American social norm is to establish direct eye contact with the audience when you are in a public-speaking situation.

It is difficult to think about your speech and simultaneously gaze around the room, looking at all the members of your audience. One common problem for classroom speakers is that they will find a friendly face and present most or all of the speech to that one person. Speakers are usually unaware that they are doing this. The best thing to do is to glance slowly around the room, looking directly at each person for only a brief moment, then move on to the next person. Although some members of the audience may not be looking back at you at that precise moment, most of them will be, and you will make them feel included. You can also be reading their expressions and postures for feedback as you look around. Do you see some puzzled looks? Maybe you should explain your idea from a different angle. Do some people seem bored? Tell a lively story, change the volume of your voice, or make a dynamic movement. Eye contact makes the audience feel connected to the speaker and the speech. This connection is called *rapport,* and it is a strong factor in getting your message across. One way to create and maintain rapport is through direct, but passing, eye contact while speaking.

Verbal and nonverbal presentation skills are important because together, they carry your complete message to your listeners. Good delivery enhances, but cannot replace, good content. The best speakers have both; they begin with a worthwhile message and then give it a good presentation. Each speaker will have some personal variations on the general suggestions presented here, so you can still demonstrate your individuality while working within this framework.

EVALUATING PUBLIC SPEECHES

Every time you give a speech in class or a presentation in public, you will be evaluated. You won't always get a written grade for your outline or your speech, but you can be sure that people will be forming evaluations of you and your message. Because evaluation is integral to any communication event, it is appropriate to look at how people judge the communication they receive. One way to evaluate speeches is to judge them according to three standards for evaluating speeches: presentation, audience adaptation, and ethics.

Standards of Presentation

Included in this criterion are the preparation and speaking skills you exhibit in your speech. When you listen to others speak, and when they listen to you, the following aspects of your speech become important to the process of evaluation.

The *significance of the topic* means that the topic itself must be worth the time and effort that you invest in preparing it. It must also be important enough to warrant your audience's attention. The topic should inspire new insights and perspectives in the listeners. It should not be trivial or superficial. The ideas you express should address what you assume to be the best aspects of your audience.

Enhance, illustrate, and focus your topic with adequate and appropriate *supporting materials.* The research sources and factual basis for the speech should be solid and very clearly presented. The supporting materials should contain material of real substance. A quick look at one issue of *Time* magazine is not adequate to support a speech on changing our policies in the Middle East. Moreover, personal experience should not be considered more than a place to begin. Even a presentation on your trip to the Grand Canyon

Critical Thinking in Communication

Critical Message Reception

One of the positive aspects of being a critical thinker is that you automatically become a critical consumer of information. This ability is called on when you evaluate advertising, marketing, and other information that you receive. For example, you can evaluate the speeches you hear in class or the advertising you see on television. As you read and gather information in support of your messages, keep in mind what you learned from evaluating the messages of others. You need to select from among many choices and options. Critical thinking helps you to compare your options and choose the best ones for the time, place, and circumstances of your communication. In short, applying critical-thinking skills will help you to listen more carefully to others and select more carefully for yourself.

could include some statistics about the canyon, a quotation from John Wesley Powell (the first explorer to travel the entire canyon by boat), a reference to a Havasupai legend, and a published interview with a ranger stationed there. Finally, the material must be appropriate for the maturity level of the audience, as well as for the setting, the occasion, and the time limits.

For clarity of *organization,* your outline is the basic guideline. Do you have clear and distinct subordinate ideas? Is the thesis clearly stated? Are there clear transitions that link each major item together in a cohesive body? Remember, the body must have its own internal logic. Use one of the patterns suggested in the previous chapter to create a complete and comprehensive outline.

Choice and fluency of language involve two aspect of your delivery that go hand in hand. One is the level and vividness of your chosen vocabulary. Do you select words that both communicate and create interest? Are you using too abstract a vocabulary? Do you talk down to, or talk at, your listeners? Fluency concerns the ease with which your words flow. Do they flow smoothly, and are they presented in a tone and at a rate to which your audience can respond?

The final standard—*delivery,* use of voice and body—is what many people think of when they discuss presentation. Many beginning speakers focus almost exclusively on these aspects of their presentation. But these criteria represent only one of the five areas of evaluation. On the other hand, you do need to speak loudly and clearly and use movement, gestures, facial expressions, and eye contact to enhance your message.

Evaluating speeches according to these five standards will probably be sufficient for most presentations. However, if presentations were judged only by these standards, the judges would be lacking in terms of two very important, additional criteria: the adaptation of the speech to the audience and the adherence of the speaker to ethical standards of communication.

Adaptation to the Audience

This standard means that any presentation should demonstrate the sender's clear attempts to make the content of the speech apply to the *particular* group that is listening to it. Such things as level of interest, complexity of ideas, clarity of sentence structure, and type of visual aids are included in this standard. References to the immediate listeners—to their values and to their reasons for being present—are also included in this standard. In short, the question to be answered in evaluating presentations according to this standard is: What is the value of the information to the audience?

Standards of Ethics

An **ethical communication** must meet several tests. It must be honest; that is, you cannot lie to your listeners. You must make certain that what you purport to be true is in fact true. Some speakers depend on the statements of others. Then, when the statements turn out to be erroneous or faulty, they blame their sources. The responsibility for the content of a speech rests clearly and solely with the speaker. If the speaker depends on others' faulty research, it is the speaker who bears the fault. That is why it is so important to do wide-ranging research. Any unusual or inconsistent information will become noticeable to you when no other source confirms it.

Sometimes a speaker will invent a story to illustrate an idea. This type of invention is fine, as long as the speaker makes it clear to the listeners that the story is only a hypothetical support. Speakers usually let the audience know that they are only telling a story when they say things like, "Let's imagine for a moment . . . ," or "Suppose that this happened to you . . . ," or "I once heard a story about a man who . . ." These phrases say very clearly that the information the audience is about to hear is fictional. Then you can be as creative as you wish. Otherwise, if you give your listeners the impression that what you are saying is true, it had better be true.

A second aspect of ethical communication follows from the first. That is, you must credit your sources. If you follow the five-part outline suggested in Chapter 11, you will include a bibliography in your own outline to document your research and give credit to the ideas that are not your own. But what about your audience? Since the spoken part of your presentation ends with the fourth section, the conclusion, you do not actually read your bibliography to your listeners. The way to include your citations is to work them into the flow of your speech. Instead of saying, "There were nearly 50,000 deaths on the highway last year due to drunk drivers," you might say, "According to the National Safety Council in their September report this year, there were nearly 50,000 deaths on the highway last year." This is a good citation, and it makes a strong impact. The audience will listen more carefully if you cite a respected authority. You do not need to include the complete citation, with page numbers, city of publication, and so on, but a reference to the source alone is sufficient to meet the ethical requirement so that your listeners know where you got the information.

A third area of ethical consideration relates to the way in which the audience is capable of using the information. The meaning of this statement can be shown in the following analogy: A high-power sales pitch for a set of expensive books is appropriate for a consumer who can afford them and who can benefit from them. A family that is struggling to pay the rent each month or has limited language skills would probably benefit from a gift of used books and information about free courses to improve their language skills. It would be unethical to try to pressure this family into a purchase. An ethical salesperson would give the first family a lively sales presentation and give the second family a list of resources where they might find free reading material, and language training.

Another way to evaluate the ethics of a message is according to its completeness. Not only must your message be true, supported, cited, and of value to the listeners, it must not deliberately leave out vital information. If a speaker tells you about a cure for cancer and fails to mention that it has been investigated and rejected by the American Medical Association, the speaker is being dishonest by giving you incomplete information.

To summarize, the hallmark of ethical speakers is that their speeches are truthful, complete, fair, and well documented. Anything less would be judged as not meeting the minimum standards of communication ethics.

IMPROVING PUBLIC COMMUNICATION COMPETENCY

There are four distinct ways to improve your competency as a public speaker. If you have ever admired speakers who exhibit excellent speaking abilities, you know that the first thing you notice about them is their **confidence.** The way to look confident is to *be* confident, and confidence can be achieved by following these steps (Zeuschner, 1994).

Know your subject well. If you have a comfortable feeling about your topic, you are well on your way to becoming a confident speaker. Of course, you need to select a topic that interests you or about which you already know something. Then you must spend time to develop your knowledge and interest in the subject. If you consult many sources, if you interview or find published interviews of experts, and if you have personal connections to the topic, you will enjoy the confidence that comes from knowing your subject well.

Know your speech materials. Once you have gathered and reviewed your material, you should feel that you have selected a comprehensive variety of the best information available to you. Go through the research you have collected, and check it for variety, interest, and impact and for how up-to-date the information is. Have you tested your ideas for their relevance to the audience, the situation, and the time limits? Have you chosen an interesting story or quotation for your introduction? Do your visual supporting materials meet the tests of clarity and impact? If so, you can feel secure with your materials.

Know your outline. This step requires that you fully understand and use the principles of outlining. Are all five parts of your outline distinctly labeled? Are the five parts clearly related to the thesis and to each other? Make certain that the body of the speech helps to explain, clarify, define, or defend the thesis and that it is broken into two, three, four, or five main subdivisions based on a logical pattern. Try using a few different patterns until you are sure that you have the most appropriate one for you, your topic, and your audience. If your outline stands up under careful analysis and alternative outlines do not work as well, you can have confidence that you have selected the correct outline for your material. As you know, good organization is the foundation of good communication.

Finally, *practice*—and practice again. The best method for developing competency is, and always will be, practice. But it works only if you are practicing correctly. Go over your presentation enough times so that you know that you know your speech. Say the words aloud six, eight, or ten times, until you can enunciate them clearly and naturally. Do not force yourself to repeat a sentence over and over or to work toward perfection in your recitation. Try to achieve a comfortable ease. It is the flow of your ideas that should be smooth. Your transitions should link one idea to the next. If you develop a direct, extemporaneous style, your speech will have slight variations each time you present it, yet the ideas will remain essentially the same. Knowing that you have the ability to present your speech comfortably will give you the confidence that is characteristic of a competent public speaker.

You can see how developing these areas increases your communication repertoire, giving you standards and criteria by which you can make appropriate selections from that repertoire. Practice in these activities and skills will allow you to enhance your implementation. Finally, the systems for evaluation presented above complete the competency cycle.

SUMMARY

You probably understand by now that you have control over your ability to become a competent speaker. In other words, this competency is not something you have, but is something that you *develop* through effort. First, you need to develop a repertoire of delivery styles and types, of organizational patterns, of research strategies, of supporting materials, and of presentational skills so that you can quickly and readily select the ones that are appropriate for you, your audience, your topic, and the occasion. Your selection of a subject that is both important and interesting to you and your audience is the next step. Then you can implement your choices with materials that support, clarify, and give impact to your topic. Furthermore, you will become more confident if you know that you have created an outline that follows specific guidelines for good organization and addresses the major sections of the outline format. Next, good speakers work at controlling excess energy, which is common to everyone. Not to be neglected in giving good speeches is the feedback from your teachers, friends, and even yourself with which you can evaluate both your own development as a speaker and that of others. Finally, you will gain a good deal of confidence if you give yourself sufficient time to practice your presentation until you know that you can deliver the ideas contained in your presentation with comfort and ease.

If you follow the steps suggested in this and other chapters, you will become like the vast majority of good speakers—a bit nervous on the inside, but also ready, willing, prepared, able, and confident when you appear before your audience.

KEY TERMS

presentation styles, p. 320
memorized, p. 320
manuscript, p. 321
extemporaneous, p. 321
impromptu, p. 322
speech apprehension, p. 324
physiological preparation, p. 325
psychological preparation, p. 328
vocal delivery, p. 331
appearance, p. 334

posture, p. 334
movements, p. 334
facial expressions, p. 335
standards for evaluating speeches, p. 337
ethical communication, p. 338
confidence, p. 340

EXERCISES

1. Describe specific examples of presentations that you have recently seen in which each of the four types of presentation was used appropriately by a speaker. For each example, describe the circumstances that made one type of presentation more appropriate than another. Can you think of a recent experience you had in which the speaker used an inappropriate style? What factors made the style seem wrong for the situation?

2. As you watch a sports program on television, identify some of the relaxation techniques used by the athletes that are similar to the ones you can use before a speech. Jot down some examples to share with the class. Look for deep breathing, head and neck movements, tensing and relaxing muscles, and eyes closed in concentration or visualization.

3. The next time that you are about to take a test, try the breathing exercises and the exercises in tensing and relaxing the muscles described in this chapter. Evaluate the effectiveness of the exercises after the test. Try to teach the exercises to someone else. Ask that person to apply them in a tense situation. Find out later whether the exercises help to relieve the tension.

4. Listen to a speech on campus or in the community, and conduct an evaluation of the speech, just as your instructor does for your speeches in class. Rate the speaker according to the five criteria presented in this chapter. Some elements of a presentation are easier to rate than others. Why? Share your evaluation with the class in an evaluation session.

5. Pair off with a member of the class and become that person's speech buddy. Agree to listen to your classmate's practice sessions in exchange for your classmate's doing the same for you. Then practice—and practice again.

REFERENCES

Hoffman, J., and J. Sprague. "A Survey of Reticence and Communication Apprehension Treatment Programs at U.S. Colleges and Universities." *Communication Education* 31 (1982), 185.

Richmond, V., and J. C. McCroskey. *Communication: Apprehension, Avoidance and Effectiveness.* Scottsdale: Gorsuch Scarisbrick, 1995.

Wolpe, J. *Psychological Inhibition by Reciprocal Inhibition.* Stanford: Stanford University Press, 1958.

Zeuschner, R. B. *Effective Public Speaking.* Dubuque: Kendall-Hunt, 1994.

CHAPTER 14

Informing Others

AFTER READING THIS CHAPTER, YOU SHOULD BE ABLE TO:

* Understand the purposes of informative speeches, and be able to use different types and patterns.
* Apply the standards that are used to evaluate informative speeches.
* Be confident and willing to create your own informative speeches.
* Present a short speech of definition, demonstration, or exposition.
* Follow the steps for improving your informative speaking competency.

One of the most common types of presentation or speech is one that informs the listeners. The speaker may be telling about a place or an event, describing a person or a process, or shedding light on an invention or a hobby. When your listeners' goal is to gain information, you are probably giving an informative presentation. The goal of an informative speech is to leave your audience with more information than it had before your speech. Your listeners should walk away saying, "That was really interesting. I never knew that before!"

The key to their understanding an informative speech, or any speech, is the thesis sentence. When the thesis sentence states, "The microchip was developed in four distinct steps," listeners can tell that they are about to hear an informative speech. The body will probably be divided into four subdivisions, and it will most likely follow a chronological pattern of development. If your thesis sentence states, "Yellowstone is a great place to visit," your audience will again probably hear an informative speech, but this time it may follow a topical pattern. On the other hand, if you say to your audience, "There are four reasons why you should vote for Smith," you are making a persuasive speech.

The difference between an informative and a persuasive thesis sentence is that the first talks about a thing or an event as the subject of the sentence, while the second makes the listener the subject. The word **should** indicates persuasion. When you say, "I'm going to inform you why you should give blood," you are about to give a persuasive speech. On the other hand, the goal of informative speeches is to convey information, and to do so clearly and accurately. The report on the speaking style of Sojourner Truth that appeared in an earlier chapter was an informative presentation, as would be for example, a demonstration of pottery making.

When you are in a job setting, you may need to train a new group of employees, explain how a piece of equipment works, or clarify a new plan for or-

Diversity in Communication

Informative Styles

In some cultures, it is rude to be direct when asking for action or compliance. For example, an Asian speaker may present what appears to be neutral information to Europeans, yet it is really an indirect way of seeking compliance. Some writers believe that in the United States, some women's use of politeness in communication may seem to men to have informative functions. Some messages that women present in the form of questions may, in reality, be softened or polite forms of persuasion. For example, a woman who says, "Do you think it's time to go yet?" might not be looking for a "yes" or "no" response but instead be trying to influence the other party to hurry or to leave (Lakoff, 1979, 1990; Hoar, 1988).

By contrast, an American male might ask his female companion, "Do you want to make dinner tonight?" in an attempt to find out whether she has already planned a menu or whether he should go ahead with the one he planned. She might reply, "Okay, I will," treating the question as a request to make dinner even though she had not planned to and expressing compliance to the perceived request (Tannen, 1994).

ganizing the work area. Your community life is also filled with informative presentations, such as the town meeting at which the new water plan is presented, or the city council meeting at which a person comes to explain the operations of a neighborhood crime watch.

The next section describes three ways of looking at informative presentations. Some applications of the patterns of organization covered in the previous chapter follow. The chapter concludes with a description of ways in which to evaluate your informative presentation and improve your competency as an informative speaker.

TYPES AND PURPOSES OF INFORMATIVE SPEAKING

There are different ways to categorize informative speeches, but the three following general categories are the most frequently used: speeches of definition, of demonstration, and of exposition. The differences among them are not great; in fact, you may notice a good deal of overlap.

Speeches of Definition

This type of informative presentation requires you to present an idea that is unfamiliar to your audience and tell them about it so that they understand something new. You need to divide the topic into logical units, describe the parts or aspects or history of the concept, and give your listeners enough detail that they fully comprehend the idea. Speeches of **definition** may be short and can be combined with others as a first step in a longer process. For example, you may be a member of a panel that is discussing an issue before an audience. The first speaker usually gives a speech of definition by defining the problem, describing the background, or clarifying the vocabulary or terms to be used in the rest of the discussion.

Defining ideas or concepts is not an easy task, and a good speech of definition is concrete, rather than abstract; is specific, not general; and uses multiple approaches to making the idea clear. There are several steps that you can follow to create a good definition of an idea or concept for your audience. These steps can become the body of your speech.

You might first turn to a dictionary for help and present your listeners with the definition(s) you find there. One way to work in some variety here is to use a variety of dictionaries. There are many specialized dictionaries, and even the popular, general ones may have slightly different, interesting ways to define the same term. You might begin with *Webster's New Collegiate Dictionary,* then turn to the *Oxford Dictionary of the English Language.* Suppose you were talking about issues concerning the freedom of speech, and you wanted to explain the concept of libel. A general description would be adequate for a start, but do not stop there. You could then turn to *Black's Law Dictionary* or *Ballentine's Law Dictionary.* You might find citations on the Lexus electronic search system to cases or rulings in the area of libel containing statements that you could include in your definition.

A next step might be to discuss the origin of the term *libel.* In that case, you would present the etymology of the word, which means that you would discuss its origins, roots, history, or development. Because much of the English

The Story of Communication

The Evolution of Modern English

If you lived in London in the year 1065, you would be speaking a form of Old German called Anglo-Saxon, and you might still be speaking a similar language today if William of Normandy had failed in his attack on England in 1066. William and his conquering armies spoke Old French, which was derived from Latin. As was true of most conquerors, the Normans took all the good jobs—king, duke, and baron—and left to the Saxons the occupations of servant and peasant.

The official language of England for about the next 400 years was French, and modern English grew out of a blending of Saxon syntax and French vocabulary. During those years, a great deal of tension and strife was associated with the two languages. The tales of Robin Hood, for example, pit the oppressed Saxons as represented by the Merry Men against Norman officials as symbolized by the Sheriff of Nottingham.

In England today, there are still strong associations with family names from the two cultures as well as the pronunciations used by different social classes and in different geographical locations. The United States, of course, also has linguistic stereotypes, as seen in a variety of regional accents or dialects. In other countries, especially those having a conquered minority, language differences, as a reflection of deep-seated nationalism, can cause persecution, punishment, and even war. The strife in many parts of the former Soviet Union and Yugoslavia is due to interethnic tensions and the desire of a national or ethnic group to have autonomy, including its own language. It took our English-language ancestors about 400 years to blend their languages, and the story of communication is still being written when it comes to languages.

---

language is derived from Latin and Greek—via the French of William the Conqueror—you may find yourself describing an ancient root for your audience, taking it apart, and delineating its meanings. If you are dealing with an idea or concept such as socialism, you could also research the origins, history, and evolution of the socialist movement.

One of the best ways to define any idea, word, or concept is by example. An example is a form of supporting material, so a speech of definition requires several clear, specific instances to help the members of the audience understand your point. If they are familiar with your examples, and if your examples are precise and clear, you will have made your subject understandable to them. For example, when telling your listeners about types of dogs—spaniels, retrievers, shepherds, and so on—make certain you provide an example or two of each so that your audience will see that a cocker and a springer are examples of spaniels, that a golden and a Labrador are types of retrievers, and that the Australian, German, and collie are examples of the shepherd group. Examples will make your presentation come alive.

If you tell your audience what something is not, you are defining by negation. For example, you might say to your listeners,

"Let's talk about transportation for a minute. No, I'm not talking about fancy luxury cars. I'm not talking about all-terrain vehicles, nor am I interested in high-performance, two-passenger sporty models. I want to focus your attention on the economy transportation car."

By eliminating some factors from your definition, you focus the attention of your audience on the definition of your topic. The problem with using this pattern for an entire speech is that you spend too much time on the areas in which you are *not* interested. This pattern can be useful if, for the sake of variety, you work it into a larger, positive speech of definition.

Finally, you can define something by providing additional words about it. This type of definition is called *rhetorical* and uses synonyms, rephrasing, or context to add clarity to your definition. For example, if you use a word that is unfamiliar to your listeners, you might give them some synonyms to help them understand the word's meaning. "The family was distraught—anxious, distressed, upset, and frantic—when their child got lost." Not only has your rhetorical technique helped anyone who did not know the meaning of the word *distraught,* but you have also reinforced the feeling and meaning of the term. Context refers to the setting, situation, or circumstances that may affect the meaning of a word. For example, the word *spare* in the context of bowling is very different from the word spare in the context of auto repair. A *citation* may be very desirable when it is from the Red Cross, very undesirable when it is from a police officer, who has stopped your car, but desirable when it is from the Chief of Police for valor.

These approaches to speeches of definition can be used together; and by using several forms for your ideas, you can be reasonably assured that your audience will understand your definition. A combination of approaches will also help you to create interest through variety. As noted above, a speech of definition can function as the first part of a longer speech. The definition clarifies your idea, then the rest of the speech explains its details. For example, if your topic is nuclear energy, step one of your presentation might be to define the words *fission* and *fusion*, giving your listeners several approaches to definition to clarify these important terms.

Speeches of Demonstration

One popular informative speech, both in class and in your career, is the "how-to" presentation, or the speech of demonstration. Whenever you show your listeners a process or illustrate or teach them how to do something, you are giving a speech of **demonstration**. When you teach someone how to assemble a model, stand on a surfboard, play the guitar, perform CPR or *t'ai chi,* or even breathe deeply as a relaxation exercise, the demonstration speech is the form you will probably use. We learn most of our skills from watching others and then trying to imitate them. We watch someone riding a bicycle, and we attempt to copy the technique. Cooking lessons, carpentry, calf roping, and calligraphy can be taught with a good demonstration.

There are several ways to create and present a strong demonstration. First, break the process down into smaller units that follow a logical order. A complex gymnastic routine will be easy to understand if each move is taken one at a time. The most intricate pattern—music, lace, dances,

The speech of demonstration is often fun and lively.

macramé, computer programs—can be made clear if its structure is identified and divided into smaller units.

Next, arrange the units in logical order. Determine the appropriate sequence for your topic and group the basic steps into that order. You will probably build from the simple to the complex. For example, when you talk about model airplanes, you might begin by demonstrating assembly of the fuselage, then the wings, and then the supporting struts.

Third, be sure that each step of the demonstration is connected by a clear **transition**. You must show your listeners how the links of your chain are joined together. Watch a cooking show or a demonstration of carpentry or plumbing on television. Each step of the process is clearly linked to the previous one. Professional demonstrators know that showing these connections is the best way to teach someone who does not understand a process enough that they can comprehend it clearly. In class, you might demonstrate a hobby or craft, an experimental procedure, or a design sequence. In a career setting, you may be asked to show others in your workplace how to do a certain procedure or how to accomplish a specific task. For example, you could be a training technician, showing others how to run a blueprint or loading machine or how to operate a computer terminal or a spreadsheet program. In many jobs, you will be called on to make a formal presentation to a group demonstrating one of your company's important procedures.

A significant part of any demonstration presentation usually involves visual aids. Recall that in Chapter 11, several guidelines were presented for the effective use of visual supporting materials. It would be wise to review those guidelines before preparing a speech of demonstration. Even if you know your topic very well, your audience does not, and competent speakers approach a demonstration not from their own expert perspective, but from the point of view of their listeners. Remember to present your demonstration so that everyone in the audience can see it and at a pace that they can follow.

The parts or steps of a demonstration function in your speech outline at the same level as a chart, map, diagram, or photograph. A demonstration is another form of visual aid and should be indicated as such on your outline.

Technology in Communication

Computer Aids

One of the interesting developments in the speech of demonstration is how demonstrations have become more electronically generated. Using an interactive laptop computer and a CD-ROM unit, many presenters now include computer graphics as part of their demonstrations. A lecture on Shakespeare's plays can now include a projected outline of the plot and a diagram of the relationship of the characters, followed by an actual video clip of a production to demonstrate these elements in action.

The guidelines for those visual materials are the same as those for your demonstration. If you have access to a videocamera, it will be beneficial for you to videotape your demonstration first, then watch it from the perspective of an audience member.

Speeches of Exposition

While these speeches certainly may include elements of definition and perhaps of demonstration, they go beyond the limits of these forms to include additional explanation and are somewhat more complex in their subject matter and supporting materials.

If you are trying to explain surfing to your listeners, you might begin with some historical references to the Polynesians. Then you might show a diagram or photograph of a surfboard, demonstrate how to position your feet or hold your body, and then relate some personal experiences or stories about surfing competitions. The purpose of this speech goes beyond definition or demonstration, although it includes elements of both. The goal of a speech of **exposition** is to explain completely some event, idea, or process. These speeches are most successful when you select a topic that is of interest to your audience and when you use a variety of vivid supporting materials.

When you make a **topic selection** for a speech of exposition, keep in mind that the information must be complete. Although you can never say everything about any topic, you can anticipate the major elements that listeners need to know and those that they will most likely want to know. Keeping your thesis sentence to a relatively narrow idea can help you to explore it in depth.

For example, investing in the stock market is too complex a topic for a five-minute speech. But you can divide this general topic and select one aspect of it—municipal bonds or how to invest on a college student's budget. These smaller topics will make it possible for you to present a complete explanation, whereas the general topic will not. In short, your goal of creating understanding can be attained by keeping your topic clearly and narrowly focused and by applying the guidelines discussed in earlier chapters for organizing and supporting speeches.

The speech of exposition may be the most frequently used presentation, so you should be thinking of ways to use definition and demonstration in combination to create a more effective speech. For example, you may wish to make the definition of your topic A in the body of your outline. You could then take some of the methods of definition described above and make those A.1, A.2, and A.3. For the B heading, you might develop a demonstration and show some aspect of your topic. These items become B.1, B.2, and so on. The supporting materials in this section would be mostly visual—maps, photographs, and actual demonstrations. You could then finish the speech with a C heading, which might cover developing the relevance of the topic to your audience and making connections between your explanation of the topic and the experiences or values of your audience. The supporting materials for C.1, C.2, and so on might consist of stories, examples, verbal illustrations, comparisons, contrasts, and perhaps a few more defining examples or even some additional visual aids.

To summarize, the informative speech is one of the most important and most frequent speaking experiences you will encounter. Both in class and on the job, you will need to explain ideas, interests, abilities, and duties—either your own or someone else's. Knowing how to prepare a complete explanation, enhanced by definitions and demonstrations, will enable you to present a well-prepared, clear expository speech.

PATTERNS OF INFORMATIVE SPEAKING

As you know, the goal of an informative speech is to convey information, so the presentation pattern that you select should help the audience to understand your material. This section traces the step-by-step development of an informative speech so that you can see how to construct such a speech yourself. The first three steps are (1) select your topic, (2) compose your thesis sentence, and (3) develop your supporting materials.

Selecting your topic means to review the possible areas you could talk about, judging them on their suitability to the allotted time, to the informative purpose, to the audience, and to you. The topic is usually a general idea that meets the following criteria: It is something you know about and that interests you, something that you can adapt to your listeners' interest and relevance, something you feel comfortable talking about, and something about which there is sufficient, *available* information for you to develop a substantial and worthwhile message. If the topic is too broad in scope, select a subdivision.

Next, compose your thesis sentence. The key to creating a clear thesis sentence is to make it focused, simple, and comprehensive. Your entire speech is guided by your thesis sentence, so it is worth some time and effort to phrase it well. Suppose you have selected investing as your topic, and now it is time to narrow down this general idea. You consider your allotted time and the fact that the audience is composed of people who know very little about sophisticated investment strategies. You know that they have some knowledge of the stock market, and you guess that they would probably like to learn more about this aspect of investment. You create several tentative phrasings and finally settle on this one: "Stock market mutual funds are an easy way for people to begin investing."

Now you can turn to a consideration of an appropriate outline format and begin constructing your speech. Since you are not going to give a speech on

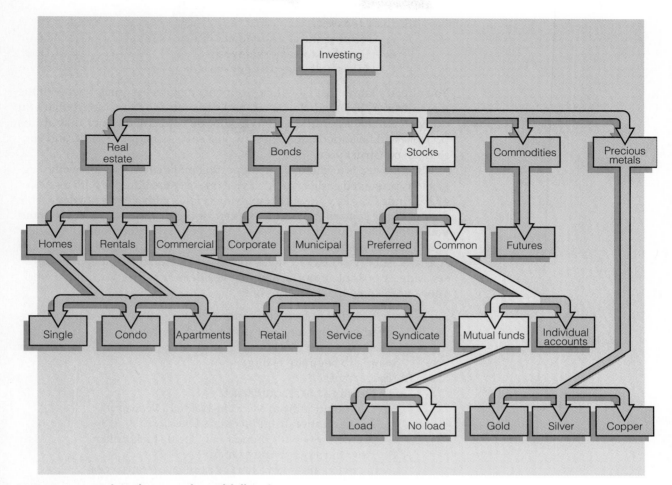

Narrow your topic, select a path, and follow it.

the history of the stock market or the location of various parts of the stock exchange building, you reject both the chronological and spatial patterns and select a topical format instead. Your outline begins to take shape and looks like the following outline:

   I. Introduction
  II. *(thesis sentence)* Stock market mutual funds are an easy way for
      people to begin investing.
 III. *(body [preview])*
    A. Defining the stock market

Starting with these two items, you can then create a few more major subdivisions:

   I. Introduction
  II. *(thesis sentence)* Stock market mutual funds are an easy way for
      people to begin investing.

III. *(body [preview])*
   A. Defining the stock market
   B. How the stock market works
   C. How small investors get started

You already know that IV will be your conclusions—a quick review of the main ideas A, B, and C, the thesis, and your introduction. Notice that you do not yet have an introduction. Do not be concerned about that at this point. It will be added later. For now, just save some space for it, and continue to construct your speech.

   The next step is to gather your supporting materials. If you follow the suggestions presented earlier, you will visit one or more libraries with a stack of 4" ¥ 6" index cards, you will arrange interviews with a few knowledgeable persons, and you will take an inventory of the books and materials about your topic that you already possess. After you have accumulated a variety of supporting materials, it is time to sort them into groups according to the A, B, or C subdivisions. Any items that do not fit into those categories can be set aside. A possible introduction may reside in that pile. With some work, your outline now looks like this one:

    I. *(introduction)* Short story about parents who started a small investment fund for children's college education.
   II. *(thesis sentence)* Stock market mutual funds are an easy way for people to begin investing.
  III. *(body [preview])*
    A. Defining the stock market
      1. Quotation from *Merriam-Webster Dictionary*
      2. Description from *Investor's Encyclopedia*
      3. Interview with Brenda Hill, local stockbroker
    B. How the stock market works
      1. Visual aid—flowchart of purchase/transaction
      2. Statistics on quantity of daily transactions
      3. Quotation from *Everybody's Business* (textbook)
      4. Graph of Dow Jones averages—ten-year trends
    C. How small investors get started
      1. Types of investments—examples
      2. Yield projection statistics
      3. How college students can benefit
      4. Quotation from Ramon Arguello, investment counselor in town
  IV. *(conclusion)* Brief review of A, B, C, thesis sentence, and introduction
   V. Bibliography
      1. Source #1
      2. Source #2
      3. Source #3
      4. and so on

   Notice that this outline is simple. It states the key ideas and avoids any extraneous items. It does not elaborate on each item but simply indicates it. It provides variety in the supporting materials by beginning with a story and including a definition, three quotations, two statistics, two visual aids, and some examples and descriptions. The speaker makes an effort in the outline to relate to a college audience, so this outline is probably for a speech in a beginning speech class.

Notice that the idea for the speech came out of an abstract and unwieldy topic—investing—and narrowed it down so that it could be discussed in an informative way in five to seven minutes. Notice also that it relies on specific supporting materials to clarify the meaning of the subdivisions of the body. You could take the same topic, and even the same thesis sentence, and create an entirely different speech. You might select another pattern or choose from your store of supporting materials seven or eight alternative items. The preceding example is only that—one example. How you would develop a similar topic depends on your personal perspective, creativity, and associations.

In general, an informative speech can follow a variety of organizational formats, and you should try out a few of them to get a feel for each type. An informative speech does not usually follow a problem–solution or motivational sequence. You are more likely to use a chronological, spatial, or topical pattern in your presentation, as was shown in the example.

This review was designed to take you through the process of creating an informative speech. Try to follow the same steps as you create your own informative presentations. Remember that the basis for good communication is good organization, and the key-word outline is a good way to achieve that organization. Once you have your outline in order, consider it a preliminary draft of your speech. You can always change it, and it is much easier to change an outline than a manuscript. If you find new material that you think is better than the material you selected, just eliminate the old and insert the new. If you change your thinking about the subject, feel free to change the outline—that is, to rework the order, substitute new supporting materials for old ones, add or delete information, or make any other modifications you

Critical Thinking in Communication

Structuring the Informative Speech

Notice how your skills in examining ideas in a sequence can be used to help you select an organizational framework. The post hoc fallacy is the one you should keep in mind while arranging your main ideas. The post hoc fallacy means thinking that an event that follows another event must therefore be its result. Do the items that make up your topic follow a logical pattern in time, space or structure? If they do, then your ability to apply inductive or deductive reasoning can help you to decide which pattern is most appropriate for your particular speech. Listeners like logic, too. If you create an organizational pattern that flows smoothly, your audience's critical-thinking abilities will be stimulated and will, in turn help your listeners to discover and remember your main ideas. When the time comes to present your speech, the clear pattern that you have organized will help you to remember the correct sequence of items, and it will help the audience to make the transitions from idea to idea with you. Critical thinking applications play an important part in your entire communication.

like. One of the best resources at your disposal can be time. If you give yourself enough time to create your outline, then put it away for a day or two, and then come back to it, you will gain some perspective on it, and maybe some fresh ideas will help you to improve it. Last-minute preparers do not give themselves this gift, and their speeches are weaker for it.

Once you have gone through your revision to a point at which you are satisfied, it is time to begin practicing your presentation. Select a presentation style—probably extemporaneous—and copy your outline either on a single sheet of paper or on a few (three to seven) note cards. *Limit your notes to the outline format you have already prepared.* Many beginning speakers fall short at this point, and they attempt to write out their presentation on note cards, word for word. Unless the occasion calls for a manuscript speech, limit your notes to your outline. Then put into practice the ideas and guidelines from Chapter 12 to help you achieve clarity and impact in your speech.

EVALUATING INFORMATIVE SPEECHES

In addition to the criteria for evaluating speeches outlined in Chapter 12, you can examine your informative speech from three points of view: (1) the goals involved when you are a listener, (2) the goals you would have as a speech critic, and (3) the larger goals you have as a consumer.

Goals as a Listener

As a listener, you will be seeking particular information from speakers. You will want them to make their ideas clear so that you can understand the point of the presentation. You should be able to restate the speaker's thesis sentence in your own words. You should also be able to recall the main ideas that developed the thesis, and you will often be able to remember some of the more significant supporting materials that the speaker used. Now the people who listen to your speeches should be able to do the same. They will evaluate your presentation according to how easy it was for them to accomplish their listening goals. If you put yourself in their place as you create your speech, you will be able to double-check yourself in advance. Any adjustments that you make from the listener's perspective will help to give your speech greater clarity.

Goals as a Critic

To be a good speech critic, you need to keep in mind the evaluation criteria presented in Chapter 12: the standards of presentation, ethics, and audience adaptation. Although each of these areas measures a different aspect of the speech, all must be considered in order to carry out a complete evaluation of the quality of the speech. Most untrained audiences tend to focus on only a few of the presentation skills of the speaker—voice, eye contact, appearance, smoothness of delivery. More insightful critics will balance their perceptions of those areas with an attention to organization, support, honesty, completeness, and value to the listeners. That is why your instructor may emphasize certain areas that at first may not seem that important to you or your classmates. Your teacher has been trained to keep all of these factors in mind and to balance them while forming a critique of the speaker and of the speech. The critical feedback that you get from a teacher may be in oral or written form or a combination of the two. Very often, a teacher will focus the oral critique on the positive aspects of the speech and save any commentary on weaknesses or areas needing improvement for a written critique. The major factors that a speech critic will keep in mind are the topic, audience adaptation, form or pattern, organization, time allocation, clarity, transitions, use of supporting materials, use of language, and delivery. Notice that for a speech critic, delivery is only one of several areas to be evaluated.

There are ways to combine all aspects of a speech into a coherent evaluation. For reasons of efficiency, the evaluation criteria are often clustered on an evaluation form. Evaluation forms cover major principles of public speaking and allow critics to be specific in their criticism. A professional critique will cover these same areas, although it will probably be in narrative form and many extend to a dozen or more pages. The professional speech communication journals often publish exceptionally well-done pieces of criticism

---

Student Name _____

Topic _____ Date _____

SPEECH EVALUATION
Dr. Zeuschner

Scale: (0-5 points possible per item)

   0 = *Missing or done incorrectly*
  1-2 = *Meets minimum requirements for university–level work*
  3-4 = *Fulfills requirements above university minimum level*
   5 = *Substantially beyond expectation for university minimum*

Outline: Overall impression, coherence, form, clarity, neatness   _____

Topic: Appropriately adapted to audience, substantial   _____

Introduction: Clear, compelling, commanding attention, interesting, relevent, sufficient length   _____

Thesis Sentence: To the point, simple, single sentence   _____

Transitions: Clear relationship of ideas, smooth flow   _____

Body: Logical order, organization, cover the necessary points   _____

Support: Quality of supports, evidence, substance   _____
         Variety, impact of supports (incl. visual aid, if used)   _____

Reasoning: Connections and conclusions clearly warranted   _____

Ending: Clear, simple review of major ideas, thesis, introduction   _____

Bibliography: Sources listed clearly at end of outline   _____
         Substantial consultation evident   _____
         Sources utilized in flow of speech   _____

Communicative Skills: Vocal quality, nonverbal   _____
         Direct presentation, non-dependence on notes _____
                            TOTAL _____

                       (possible 75)

Evaluation: 30-40 points = Average
             45-50 points = Excellent
             55+   points = Outstanding

SPEECH CRITICISM FORM

Critic: _____ Speaker: _____

Speech subject: _____

Date of Rehearsal: _____ Place of Rehearsal: _____

Time Spent: _____
Significance of topic and value of ideas:

Adequacy and appropriateness of supporting materials:

Clarity of organization:

Adaptation of content to audience:

Choice and fluency of language:

Use of voice and body in delivery:

Either one of these evaluations forms will help to guide feedback and critique.

as a way of offering insights into the communication processes of notable speakers. In any case, the two forms shown here differ in areas of emphasis, the second one allowing for more free commentary from the critic. You may use these guides when you are criticizing other speakers or as a tool for self-evaluation. You could also create your own, or perhaps your class has one that everyone can use.

The main value that being a good critic will have for you lies in your ability to tell others and yourself about the *specific* strengths and weaknesses of a speech so that the speech can be improved. Critiques help you specifically to become a better speaker by pinpointing areas where you are already competent or where you demonstrate skillful application. They also help by pointing out to you areas where your speaking skills could be improved. By observing the strengths of others, you learn what techniques are effective and worthy of emulation. By noting the weaknesses of other speakers, you identify speaking behaviors to avoid. In other words, if you can be a good critic of others' speeches, you should be able to look at your own messages more carefully and use your critical insight to improve them.

Goals as a Consumer of Information

Because you consume information daily and in large doses, it pays to be selective about the messages to which you give your time and attention and those that you can reliably dismiss as being of poor quality. One of your lifelong functions will be that of a **consumer of information** in our information society. You will continue to receive messages constantly; and to some degree, you have already developed a system for evaluating them.

Many people do not evaluate the messages that come their way very carefully but simply accept or reject them on the basis of some automatic response pattern that they have developed. Young children, for example, seem to accept messages uncritically. As teenagers, people typically begin to reject many messages, especially those from parents or other authority figures.

Improving Competency

The Value of Honest Feedback

One of the best ways to improve your competency as a speaker is to use the power of intrapersonal communication. As you recall, the messages you send yourself about yourself are quite capable of motivating and influencing you. How can you give yourself honest feedback about your speaking abilities? Technology can aid you through the use of a videocamera. Try checking one out from your school if you do not have one readily available. Did you find a speech buddy yet? If not, then this is an excellent opportunity to look for one. Have your buddy videotape you, and do the same for your buddy. Then, after you have heard your buddy's comments and suggestions, play back the tape of your speech and look at it in light of the critique. Then try being a critic for yourself, and find out whether it helps to pay attention to the internal monitoring that is your own personal feedback. We are usually our own most severe critics, so be gentle with yourself, but be honest.

Again, this type of rejection may be automatic, based solely on a rejection of authority rather than on an evaluation of the message.

As you go through a typical day, you will be bombarded by informative messages from newspapers, magazines, television, friends, neighbors, teachers, and others. As you evaluate messages in the public domain, remember to look at three areas: their application to you, the trustworthiness of the source, and their demonstration of good communication principles.

Application to you means that any message has some value if you can use it. For example, as you listen to the news, look for connections that you can make to your own circumstances. A broadcast on earthquake preparedness in the area in which you live will connect to your need to prepare your living quarters. At the other extreme, the broadcast may be lengthy, sensational, and attention-getting yet not have any real value for you. Have you ever seen the way some television stations cover a gruesome train wreck? They interview survivors who are frightened and in shock. They ask family members of the fatalities, "How do you feel?" and in general exploit the sensational aspects of the story. This kind of information probably has little value for most listeners except to appeal to their emotions with pictures of other peoples' tragedies. A critical evaluator would ask, "How does this apply to me?" Your answer to this question will give you insight into what the source is trying to accomplish and how well it is reaching its goals. If your listening goals are not being met, you can question the value of continued listening.

A source that is trustworthy merits your attention more than one that is not. Trustworthiness includes having a record and reputation for furnishing truthful information, carrying out reliable reporting, conducting conscientious research, and having supplied previous information that was substantial and related to the interests of the intended audience. If the person or source has a long-standing and well-earned reputation for being accurate, you can use that credibility as an evaluative criterion. *The New York Times*, for example, has a long-standing record for being truthful and accurate in the stories it publishes. Network news broadcasts on radio and television also make substantial efforts to be accurate in their reporting. You probably have friends whom you can reliably trust to give you accurate information because they have always done so in the past. You probably can think of leaders in your community—in clubs, religious organizations, and business or political affairs—who have established reputations for accuracy, so you also view them as trustworthy sources of information.

However, if you do not have the source's record, how can you evaluate the trustworthiness of the source? That question can be answered by the third measure of public communication criticism: use of good communication principles.

Good communication principles include all the factors you have been studying in this section, especially the use of the supporting materials. Does the speaker use outside research and cite it during the presentation? Or does the speaker depend solely on self-reports, unnamed experts, or undocumented studies? Does the speaker supply names, dates, titles of publications, and qualifications of authorities cited? Is there any support at all? You may hear someone say, "A recent survey shows conclusively that. . . ." While that statement may very well turn out to a trustworthy support, without a spe-

Informative speaking means presenting information clearly.

cific citation you have no way to judge its credibility. On the other hand, if the speaker says, "A Gallup poll published last week in Time magazine shows conclusively that . . . ," you have a basis for evaluating that support. If the speaker said, "A poll of several neighbors published in a mimeographed flyer proved conclusively that . . . ," you would have another basis for evaluating the information. Check the citations offered.

In addition to verifying the supporting materials, you could use one of the speech evaluation forms and check for good use of other principles. Is the message well organized? Is the thesis clearly stated? How does the message apply to you? You probably will not be carrying a copy of these forms around with you for the rest of your life, so you will need to make a permanent copy in your mind of the major principles involved. You will always remember this system if you apply it regularly—by being a critic of others' speeches and of your own presentations. Just as you are a careful consumer of automobiles, stereo equipment, clothing, appliances, and food products, can you become a careful consumer of information. You want value for your money when it comes to purchasing products, so demand value for your time when listening to information presented in the public forum.

In summation, you can apply your evaluation skills as a listener in the classroom or career setting, as a critic looking for specific strengths or weaknesses, or as an everyday consumer. Each of these roles can, in turn, help you to create better messages. When you listen to a presentation with an open, critical mind, you can then become an objective critic of your own work. While perfection is not a reasonable goal, improvement certainly is. Give yourself praise when you do a good job, and always seek to improve a worthy effort so that it meets the requirements of clarity, substance, and impact.

IMPROVING INFORMATIVE SPEAKING COMPETENCY

The four elements of communication competency—repertoire, selection, implementation, and evaluation—have been implicit in the discussions throughout this chapter. Your repertoire of choices is now expanded by knowing the several approaches that are available to you when you prepare an informative presentation. Guidelines for choosing one or another are now well established, as are the areas to keep in mind in applying any of those choices. Finally, you are now familiar with some detailed methods for evaluating communication choices made by yourself and others.

Among the most important ways for you to improve your communication skills is to learn to make your meaning clear. Be concerned with your choice of words. Review the material on verbal communication if you like, and apply the suggestions given there to the preparation of your informative speech. Keep your vocabulary at a level that is appropriate for the listeners. Think about what they are likely to know already, and what they probably do not yet know, about your topic. Being concrete and specific will help you to achieve clarity. Watch your use of pronouns (she, he, it, they) and be specific when possible—Adele Jones, Robert Gomez, Sandy Point State Park on Highway 41, or Mayor Settle.

Enliven your specific references with vivid descriptions. Color, size, shape, comparison, and contrast will help your audience to create a memorable mental image from your words. "Then I returned home" can be transformed into "After the fire died down, I raced home to tell everyone else about it, but arrived out of breath and too exhausted to speak for several minutes." The latter statement is, to say the least, more interesting, vivid, and memorable for your listeners.

Try to balance your use of exciting language with an effort to be concise. Being concise means to express your thoughts with efficiency, avoiding extra words that do not add information to your ideas. Keep your presentation simple. Your listeners cannot reread your previous sentences as they can in a written essay. If your sentences stretch out and become complex, compound, and lengthy, apply the principle of conciseness in the selection and implementation of your language choices. Check your language use for economy and brevity.

Clear transitions also help an audience to follow your ideas. Connector sentences such as "First we will examine the causes of the war" help your listeners prepare to hear that particular part of your presentation. After each major section, you should link your ideas together with a transition sentence such as "Now that we have looked at the causes of the war, let us examine its effect on the people in the region." This sentence lets your listeners know that you are finished with one major section and are moving to the next one. Of course, you could also say, "Next, the war's effects," but this sentence only announces the change, it does not link the two ideas, nor does it help the audience to move smoothly from one idea to the next. Again, the audience cannot reread what you have just said. Oral style differs from written style in that it requires clear and frequent transitions.

One method to help the audience listen is related to the transition and is called a preview. On the sample outlines you may have noticed the following: "III. *(body [preview])*." As you begin the main part of your speech, it is useful to let the audience know how you will divide the topics stated in your thesis sentence. By giving listeners a preview, you enable them to identify your information by category. Your listeners will prepare themselves mentally to receive three or four units of information from you. Your organizational pattern will also be made clear in advance, and you will have provided a helpful, overall orientation to your presentation. "To explain the effects of the Vietnam war, I will first discuss the causes of the war, then describe some of the effects it has had on the people of the area, and finally talk about several of the major impacts it has had in the United States." This short preview gives your audience a clear pattern of your speech and will help them to pay attention to what you are about to say.

Similar to a preview is an internal summary. When you take a moment in the middle of your speech to summarize the major ideas up to that point, you are doing an **internal summary.** If your speech is longer than eight or ten minutes or contains a very complex sequence of ideas, an occasional internal summary can help your listeners to understand and remember your speech. If you are giving a short, impromptu speech, an internal summary benefits both you and the audience because it gives you a moment to think about where your speech will go next.

Transitions, previews, reviews, and summaries are all methods of improving your informative speaking abilities. If you make frequent use of them, your speech will flow smoothly, and its meaning will be clear. These techniques will help you to remember each section of your speech as you pause mentally and use a transition or a summary to prepare for the next section of your presentation. Get into the habit of employing these tools; they can help you to develop into an effective, informative speaker. If you are not sure when to use them, it is better to have them on hand anyway than to risk leaving them out and losing your audience as you move from one idea to the next. Competent speakers always have these tools in their repertoire of skills. They practice which ones to use and when, and they also regularly evaluate the effectiveness of these methods in their speeches.

SUMMARY

Informative speaking consists of speeches that define, demonstrate, or explain. These three styles can be mixed successfully in a single presentation, yet the goal remains the same: to leave the listeners with a greater understanding of the topic than they had before the presentation. A successful informative presentation has that goal as its main focus.

Methods for organizing informative presentations and for evaluating those presentations were also presented in this chapter. Competency can also be increased by using good supporting materials for interest and clarity and by working on verbal skills, using transitions, being concise, and including previews and summaries.

When evaluating informative speeches, remember to concentrate on the value of the message to the listener, whether you are the listener or the listener is *your audience.* Adopt the perspective of a critic or a day-to-day consumer to help you make that judgment. Apply the principles of good communication to any messages that you send or receive. Informative speaking is a common experience in both classroom and career settings. Being a receiver of information is a lifelong role, so learning to become expert at it is worthwhile. This chapter was designed to start you on that path.

KEY TERMS

definition, p. 345
demonstration, p. 347
transition, p. 348
exposition, p. 349
topic selection, p. 349
speech critic, p. 354
consumer of information, p. 356
internal summary, p. 360

EXERCISES

1. Imagine that you have been asked to present a speech of definition to your class. What topic could you choose that would be informative to them? What resources would you gather to support it?

How would you organize it? Go through the same questions for a speech to demonstrate and a speech of exposition. Has your teacher assigned one of these for you to present next week?

2. Although many televised speeches are designed to be persuasive, some may be informative. Do news broadcasters follow the patterns of organization presented in this chapter? Watch the network news for three consecutive nights, and keep track of which patterns occur most frequently. What about the nature specials or biographies that you see on television? What patterns do they use? Compare your examples with those of other students in class.

3. As you prepare your informative speech, try at least two different organizing patterns for the same topic. Select the one that "feels" better, and try to explain why it seems to work and the other does not.

4. Seek out a public speaker on your campus, and attend the presentation in person. Keep track of the outline, the pattern of organization, the supporting materials, and the style of presentation. How would you rate this person? What did the speaker do that you would like to emulate in your own presentations? Did the speaker do anything that you think should be avoided?

REFERENCES

Hoar, Nancy. "Genderlect, Powerlect and Politeness." *Women and Communicative Power.* Annandale: Speech Communication Association, 1988.

Lakoff, Robin. "Stylistic Strategies within a Grammar of Style." *Language, Sex and Gender.* Ed. J. Orasanu, M. Slater, and L. L. Adler. New York: Annals of the New York Academy of Sciences, 1979.

Lakoff, R. T. *Talking Power.* New York: Basic Books, 1990.

Tannen, Deborah. *Talking* 9 to 5. New York: Morrow, 1994.

CHAPTER 15

Persuading Others

AFTER READING THIS CHAPTER, YOU SHOULD BE ABLE TO:

* Identify the main components of value systems and explain how attitudes change.
* Describe a variety of persuasive speeches and the ways in which they are developed, supported, and presented.
* Present your ideas to influence others.
* Believe that you have something substantial to say and feel confident to say it.
* Develop and present a persuasive speech to your classmates.
* Evaluate and critique the persuasive messages of others.

When you think of the great speakers of the past, you are probably thinking of the great **persuasive** speakers. The speakers who are remembered are those who influenced the events around them. Ancient Greek orations, many of which are still available for us to read today, were often persuasive discourses about the great issues of the day. Collections of these orations feature both pro and con speeches about a single subject.

From the ancient Greek orations to the Iroquois addresses in the Long House, to the abolitionists and suffragettes, to the President's most recent State of the Union speech, public speeches have dealt persuasively with the great issues of their time. Many of these orators often spoke at great length—from thirty minutes to several hours. These speakers followed the guidelines for effective speaking for their time, and many of those guidelines are still appropriate today. Your **persuasive speeches** will join a several-hundred-year-old tradition of carefully prepared communication about significant, contemporary issues. Those many years have produced proven ideas and insights regarding the way people react to messages that are intended to influence them and how a speaker—in this case, you—can take advantage of those insights to produce a message that can successfully persuade your audience to think, feel, or act in a particular way. In addition to the wisdom passed down by a long, rhetorical tradition, modern psychology has provided useful knowledge about how to influence the minds and emotions of other people.

We begin with a definition of persuasion, then follow with an examination of three categories of persuasive messages. A discussion of how we form and modify our attitudes is followed by a description of four types of persuasive speaking. The chapter also presents information on supporting materials, organization, and persuasive language and presentation styles. Finally, we look at ways to evaluate and improve persuasive speaking.

A DEFINITION OF PERSUASION

A message that influences the opinions, attitudes or actions of the receiver is a persuasive message. The definition of a persuasive speech includes the process used to create a message that is intended to influence the listener. Whenever you try to convince someone to eat at your favorite restaurant, vote for your preferred candidate, attend a particular religious service, or buy a compact disc by your favorite group, you are dealing with persuasion. Although each of these messages has influence on the audience as a goal, there are three categories of persuasion that are usually identified by the type of influence they address.

FACTS, VALUES, AND POLICIES

Typically, you can create a persuasive speech about one of three main types of concerns. These concerns, or questions, are related to facts, values, and policies.

Facts are usually the concern of historical and legal persuasion. Did Lincoln issue the Emancipation Proclamation for political reasons? Was John Doe murdered? Was Amelia Earhart a spy? Does that newspaper article libel my reputation? These are questions or propositions of fact.

Diversity in Communication

The Evolution of Acceptance

It might seem strange to you, but the ability of ordinary citizens to speak in public on important issues is a relatively new concept. Even in the early history of our country, only white males could participate in important meetings, either as advocates or antagonists. In the late 1800s, women seldom attended meetings, much less spoke at them. At some of the early women's Suffrage conferences, men ran the entire meeting, and at issue was whether to allow such people as Susan B. Anthony or Elizabeth Cady Stanton to speak. Sometimes these women had to sit in a separate section of the auditorium, screened off with a curtain. Even more interesting is the case of Sojouner Truth, a former slave who for years faced the double barrier of being African American and female before finally gaining a large and strong audience of listeners—mostly white males.

Diversity has only recently come to advertising. Before 1960, virtually no people of African, Latino, or Asian ancestry appeared in any television commercials. In 1968, S. I. Hayakawa speculated that it would be revolutionary to include all types of people in commercials, since the companies behind those ads depend on high credibility to make their sales. In some ways, the current increase in the diversity of people in television commercials demonstrates their inclusion in society as a whole.

Values are deeply held beliefs that direct our lives. Do we support public education? Is honesty the best policy? Does a promise of lifelong commitment mean the same thing as marriage? Values represent the area in which some of the most intense and personally involving persuasion takes place.

Finally, questions of **policy** are those that ask what should be done. Should we spend our vacation touring the coast on bicycle, visiting Disney World, or helping to rebuild grandmother's house? Should we take a vacation at all? Should we vote for Candidate X? Should we vote? These actions are the subject of speeches that discuss policies.

Each of these concerns—fact, value, and policy—can be discussed in the same speech. If an education bond issue is to be successful, its proponents need to convince you of the facts, relate the facts to your values to motivate you, and finally, persuade you to act. A political candidate and the makers of a new brand of detergent both follow the same steps in their efforts to persuade you. However, most persuasive speeches are categorized by their ultimate goal, even if they touch on other, ancillary goals or concerns along the way.

To be successful in your attempts at persuasion, you need to address the motivations of your listeners. These motivators are the values and attitudes that are shared by large groups of people. Let us begin with a quick review of those values and attitudes.

Value Systems

In Chapter 7, values and attitudes were presented in relation to self-concept. You probably recall that values comprise a person's primary orientation toward life—the principles by which a person's actions are guided. Your value system provides you with a general orientation to life situations. Values tend to remain stable and are less likely to change than are attitudes or beliefs. If they do change, they will probably change very slowly. Therefore values are difficult things to change in a persuasive speech, especially if the speech is a short one. Short speeches are typically given in classrooms, in brief presentations by political candidates, or in television commercials. Instead, these persuaders use the existing values of the audience as a basis for creating a persuasive message. In that way the message can concentrate on an attitude—a smaller unit of belief that is more easily modified if listeners perceive the core value from which it stems to be the same as the core value that is implicit in the message. For example, two candidates for office assume that their listeners value education, so they try to persuade their audience that one of them will do a better job of supporting education.

The question of which candidate will better implement your value system leads to a consideration of attitude toward the two office seekers. If you believe that one will do a better job of acting on your values than the other, your attitude toward that person will be more positive than your attitude toward the other.

ATTITUDE CHANGE THEORY

How do attitudes form? More important in the context of persuasive speeches, how are they changed? These questions are the subject of research by communication scholars who study **attitude change theory.**

Early studies of persuasion and influence included a definition of the concept of attitude. As you know, attitudes are based on values and more specific applications of those values to the events in the world around you. A simple definition provided by researchers in the 1930s is still valid today and is useful in learning more about persuasive speaking. An attitude can be defined as "primarily a way of being 'set' toward or against certain things" (Murphy et al., 1937).

Because attitudes are internal and cannot be seen directly, we rely on reports about attitudes to tell us what they are. These reports may be simple, such as responses to questions and other verbal or nonverbal expressions of them. For example, a person might say, "I don't like Senator Jones's record on educational issues. I think I'll vote for Smith instead." Answers to a questionnaire about likes and dislikes in general and responses to a public opinion poll are also expressions of attitudes.

Attitudes may come from many sources, and many people, especially in the field of psychology, have tried to explain both the development of attitudes and attitude change theory.

Early Approaches

The period before World War II saw the development of several approaches to the study of attitudes. The early work on attitudes followed the work of Pavlov and his experiments in operant conditioning in which dogs were trained to salivate when they heard a bell ring. The sound of the bell had

Sojourner Truth, an illiterate slave, overcame many attitudinal barriers and became a powerful orator.

previously been associated with food, and so the bell became a *conditioned stimulus* for the dogs.

Psychologists then applied Pavlov's findings to humans and speculated that our attitudes might be a result of some repeated association, or conditioning. A similar theory was formulated by B. F. Skinner; but instead of forcing an association to create a conditioned response, a reward was provided every time a correct response was given. Although the work was initially done with rats—teaching them to press a lever to get a food pellet—these findings in *behavior modification* were applied to human behavior. For example, if you expressed a particular opinion as a child and your parents said, "My, what a wonderful child!" or made some other positive response, you may have been reinforced in that opinion. A third approach was taken by Hull, who theorized that both habit and drive worked together to create reinforcement. **Habits** are repeated behaviors; **drives** are needs, such as the need for food, shelter, and the avoidance of pain or injury. As we respond to these needs, we develop predispositions for behaving or believing in certain ways (Hilgard and Bower, 1966).

During World War II, a great deal of attention was focused on the extensive use of propaganda through the use of mass media. Films became a weapon of psychological warfare, and all the countries participating in the war made propaganda films for use in their own countries. They also produced other films for export to persuade people in other countries to be on their side.

The use of training films by the U.S. Army allowed for extensive testing of various types of persuasive messages on the attitudes of soldiers, largely because thousands of them were available to be tested in a fairly controlled setting. Much of this work was connected with Yale psychologist Carl Hovland. His studies concluded that most of the early army training films had

Technology in Communication

Digitizing Images

With the improvement of sophisticated photograph development techniques, alterations in pictures became possible. Thus with airbrush techniques, some advertisers would insert hidden messages in their ads, messages that were intended to reinforce the persuasive impact of the ad. The development of digitized sound and images now let us remove, insert, or otherwise alter features of the message. On a home computer, you can change someone's eye color pixel by pixel and give your Uncle Fred's new digitized likeness glowing magenta pupils, one orange tooth, or extra ears. "Seeing is believing" is probably on its way out as a truism because of our digitized technology.

little effect on soldiers' attitudes. The government then wanted to discover what kind of messages would produce a predictable change of attitude. Hovland found that sometimes an attitude would change after a period of time. This delayed reaction was called the *sleeper effect*. He also noticed differences in attitude change between the presentation of a message that gave only one side of an issue and that of a message that gave mostly one side and a little of the opposing side as well. The researchers discovered that one-sided messages had a positive effect on audiences who already held the particular attitude, but two-sided messages had an effect on people who were initially unfavorable to the message (Hovland et al., 1949).

Later, Hovland and others who were influenced by his work continued to study how attitudes are affected by source credibility and by fear appeals. Briefly, **source credibility** theory says that receivers of information are more likely to be influenced by a source that they find to be credible. Most studies show that immediately after a presentation, audiences are more influenced by highly credible speakers than by speakers who are not so credible. But because of the sleeper effect, the influence of both high- and low-credibility sources begins to even out as time passes.

What constitutes high credibility? Researchers have identified four elements associated with credibility: expertise, dynamism, trustworthiness, and goodwill. These factors exist in the minds of the audience as beliefs. In other words, it is important to your credibility that the audience *believe* that you are an expert, that you are trustworthy, that you have goodwill toward them, and that you are energetic. Sad to say, the phenomenon of source credibility explains why people are taken in by con artists every day. Since we do not have a good, dependable, or absolute way to determine the existence of these qualities in other people, we depend on unreliable criteria such as appearance or whatever people tell us about themselves. Genuine tests of credibility require a little more investigation. These tests were covered in Chapter 12 in the discussion of criteria that are used to evaluate public speeches and in the discussion of ethics and communication.

Source credibility is not a modern concept in persuasive speaking. Early Greek and then Roman rhetoricians wrote extensively about how the speakers of their day could persuade others, and prime among their concerns was source credibility—called *ethos*. **Ethos** is usually translated to mean the speaker's character, and you can see the root of the word ethics in that term. Good ethos probably blends together what we call *expertise, trustworthiness,* and *goodwill*. When you talk about someone's reputation, you are probably referring to those qualities as well. Far from being an abstract and intangible idea, a good reputation is a very important characteristic for anyone to possess. It either opens up or closes off the potential for communication, depending on the quality of the reputation.

Advertisers depend on creating and using a positive reputation. That is why they hire easily recognizable people who already have a positive reputation to appear in their advertisements. They put actors, sports figures, and celebrities in their ads, having paid them enormous sums of money, hoping that you will be influenced sufficiently by their reputation to transfer it to the product being sold or that the ads will at least catch your attention. Automobile ads constantly tell you how high the product was rated in consumer satisfaction polls or how low it was rated in surveys of automobile repair costs. Lawsuits are filed over defamation of character because a person's reputation, character, or ethos can be demonstrated to have monetary value.

Later, we will discuss how you can develop credibility with your listeners to persuade them. If you want to affect their attitudes, keep in mind that source credibility is a major factor in bringing about that change. Another factor that was extensively studied was the use of fear as a persuader.

Fear Appeals

You probably remember seeing films in driver education classes showing the results of terrible accidents. Perhaps your dentist's office has photographs of rotten teeth, bleeding gums, or deformed jaws on the walls of the waiting room. These are obvious **fear appeals.** Do they work?

In a classic study conducted by Janis and Feshbach, fear appeals were used to create better dental hygiene. Building on the work of Hovland, these researchers knew that an attitude could be modified more easily if the subjects of the study were psychologically aroused during the presentation of the persuasive message (Hovland et al., 1953). The subjects, students at a large high school, attended a mild, medium, or strong fear-related lecture on tooth decay. In general, the most improvement in dental hygiene occurred in subjects who had been exposed to the mild fear appeal. The least effective approach turned out to be the strong fear appeal.

Additional research showed that two-sided messages were stronger in their positive effect on receivers' resistance to later persuasive efforts (Lumsdaine and Janis, 1953). Therefore if you want your audience to resist rebuttals to your presentation by other speakers, you should probably present some of the other side's arguments during your presentation. Another line of research showed that the strength of the fear appeal must be realistically related to the change that is desired. For example, a very simple action, such as brushing your teeth, may be seen as being too simple a way to prevent horrible disfigurement. One strong point of these studies was that the measured attitude change was not just a change of answers on a questionnaire, but an actual change in behavior. Another strong point was that attitude changes seemed to be long-lasting.

In an effort to account for the variations in the results of studies of fear appeals, researchers later identified three factors that work together to make fear appeals change attitudes (Rogers, 1975). These factors are (1) the amount of harmfulness of an event, (2) the likelihood of the event happening to the listener, and (3) how well the action being recommended is likely to work. For example, if a problem does not seem to be very significant or harmful, it is unlikely to cause fear. On the other hand, if the degree of harm seems overly exaggerated, the audience will dismiss the problem. Or an audience may agree that the problem being discussed is bad but feel that it does not apply to them. It is therefore unlikely that they will feel involved enough to modify an existing attitude or behavior. Finally, an audience may find that the problem presented is indeed terrible and believe that there is a chance it will happen to them, yet they do not adopt the solution or action.

It appears that all three elements must be relevant to the audience for fear appeals to work. The current national effort to stop the spread of AIDS is an excellent example of how these elements are used. Almost everyone is convinced that AIDS leads to death, in fact, that it is a direct cause of death. There is no need to concentrate on the first element of fear appeals—harmfulness. It is toward the second element that much of the persuasive effort against AIDS is being directed—that it can happen to anyone. At first this statement was not believed by most people. AIDS was associated with members of the gay community, or perhaps with Haitians, or with a few recipients of blood transfusions, or with drug addicts who share needles. The death of movie star Rock Hudson and the persuasive speaking of Elizabeth Taylor helped to increase discussion and attention related to the disease, but not until basketball great Earvin "Magic" Johnson became infected with the HIV virus were many Americans able to accept the second factor of this appeal to fear—the disease was spreading beyond the groups originally associated with it. The third factor—the effectiveness of the solution to the problem—is still the center of much debate about safe sex, abstinence, or totally monogamous relationships. How have people's attitudes and behavior been affected by persuasive and informative speeches about AIDS? Public opinion and private practices are monitored constantly by health officials, and some positive changes in both opinions and actions are being reported.

If you take a course in persuasion, political communication, or mass media, you are likely to study in detail the work of the investigators named here and many others. Modern psychological investigation has provided extensive information about attitudes and how they are changed. For now, these few elements of attitude change theory can at least help you to think about the messages that you receive daily from advertisers, as well as the messages that you create when you try to persuade others.

TYPES OF PERSUASIVE SPEECHES

There are several ways to approach the various persuasive speaking situations that you may encounter. Four general categories of speech seem to cover most of them. They are (1) speeches to convince, (2) speeches to actuate, (3) speeches to reinforce or inspire, and (4) debates and public argumentation.

Speeches to Convince

When the primary audience reaction that the speaker is trying to obtain concerns the listeners' opinions, then it is likely that the speech that is being given is a speech to convince. No direct action is required of the listeners; their attitude will be the focus of attention. For example, if a speaker tells you that Franklin Roosevelt was wrong to try to increase the size of the Supreme Court, that Sara Teasdale is a better poet than Emily Dickinson, that abortion is wrong, or that more money should be spent on the space program, you are dealing with a speaker who is trying to convince you of something. Once again, very little, if any, action is required. Later on, you may form your opinion of Roosevelt as a President, buy Dickinson's collected works, put a bumper sticker on your car opposing abortion, or vote for a candidate on the basis of that person's position on supporting funding for NASA. Nevertheless, the immediate goal of the presentation is not to create a sleeper effect in terms of action, but to modify your attitude.

Speakers can certainly discuss controversial issues; and while historical issues do not have any action implications, other issues may. An audience may be convinced that abortion is wrong and then feel justified in asking the speaker, "So, what do you want me to *do* about it?" You may be convinced that NASA needs more money, and it seems logical to ask the speaker-advocate, "How can I help get NASA more funding?" Those questions about action are what change speeches to convince into the next type of speech: speeches to actuate.

Speeches to Actuate

Getting people to do what you want them to do is sometimes difficult. You first need to convince them that the action you propose is the right one for them. The next step, taking action, is the goal of the speech to actuate. Nearly all advertising is geared toward action. It does the Superclean Dishwasher Company little good if you are convinced that the product is good but you do not actually buy it. Advertising can be direct or very subtle, but the intention is clear: to motivate the receivers of the information to engage in some sort of action. On the job, you may hear a speech about getting better safety behavior from employees or more productivity. Clearly, these are persuasive speeches that are designed to actuate. On campus and in your community, you regularly get persuasive messages asking you to vote for a certain issue or candidate. The key word in a speech to actuate is usually should. You should work harder, you *should* vote for Joanne, and you should buy a Superclean Dishwasher.

Speeches to Reinforce or Inspire

These speeches are commonly given to audiences that are already leaning in a favorable direction. A sermon is a good example of such a speech. People seldom come to a religious service to be converted. They usually attend because they already share the religious beliefs of the speaker, and the sermon simply reinforces those beliefs and builds enthusiasm in the congregation. Many public speakers try to make their listeners feel more enthusiastic for one reason or another. One such example is that of the team coach talking before a game. The coach does not need to make the team

Martin Luther King, Jr.'s inspiring speech "I Have a Dream" reinforced the values of the listeners.

want to win, but the coach must energize the players so that they will try harder to win. Speakers at most public ceremonies, such as dedications, awards ceremonies, or graduations, use the inspirational model. The speaker's goal in each of these situations is to remind the audience of the values or commitments its members already hold or once held and then get them to become rededicated or reinforced in those values. These speeches are usually filled with inspirational stories, examples, and testimonies and often appeal more to the emotions of the listeners than to their logic. Audiences, of course, bring their expectations of these inspirational elements with them to the occasion, and good inspirational speakers, being sensitive to these anticipations, tailor their speeches accordingly. A graduation is not the time for a speaker to announce support for a presidential candidate or to push the sale of a favorite sports car. One of the most famous speeches of our era, Martin Luther King, Jr.'s "I Have a Dream," is a stunning speech of inspiration. The thousands of people who marched with Dr. King to the Lincoln Memorial in 1963 already supported the cause of civil rights. They were tired and sometimes impatient, so he reinforced their original commitment with the power of his voice and his words.

Debates and Public Argumentation

A special type of persuasive speaking occurs when two people speak—one for and one against the same issue. These forums, usually called **debates,** feature the opportunity to hear opposing views from supporters of both sides. A public forum can be held on a question of fact, value, or policy. Although it is possible to have more than two sides, interactions featuring multiple positions are usually less satisfying to an audience because of the necessity of keeping fine distinctions among the advocates in mind. For example, every four years, during presidential elections, you may see a televised "debate" with five, six, or seven candidates, each of whom is vying for the party's nomination. Although these forums may be useful for gaining superficial impressions of the candidates, they are less debates than showcases. In fact, the national Speech Communication Association now refers to these events, even when just two people are speaking, as joint appearances by the candidates, not as debates.

Public argumentation can be an important part of community involvement and civic awareness. Presentations can include meetings of the city council or board of supervisors, commissions and government hearings, and programs sponsored by local interest groups. Republican and Democratic party organizations are found in most communities, and other groups, such as environmental action associations, religious organizations, other political parties, civil rights leagues, and many others hold public meetings to address issues and questions of importance to them. These meetings, in addition to being a rich source of information about particular topics, continue the long U.S. tradition of freedom of expression.

One thing that all of the speakers in these speaking situations have in common is a desire to motivate the audience. To get people to agree with them, they need to organize and support their ideas in a way that goes beyond what is required of the informative speaker. On the other hand, both the supporting materials and the organizational patterns used by speakers in public argumentation can be adapted to the persuasive setting.

Developing Motivating Supporting Materials

From before the time of Aristotle, speakers have been concerned with finding the most effective way to reach others with their message. Aristotle called these methods *proofs* and divided them into three main categories: personal proof, which he called *ethos;* emotional proof, known as *pathos;* and logical proof, or *logos.* These categories still represent useful ways of analyzing speeches of persuasion.

Ethos

Ethos, or personal proof, was included in the earlier discussion of source credibility. To create an impact on your listeners, you must tap the four elements of expertise, trustworthiness, dynamism, and goodwill that are within you. You can show yourself to be an expert by actually being one. That means that you can pick topics about which you already know a good deal or about which you can do extensive research. Furthermore, you should have a personal connection to the topic to show the audience that you have both knowledge of, and a genuine concern for, the topic. During the speech, reveal that you have done extensive research and can quote objective sources and established experts. You want your listeners to credit you with having the competence to be an expert on the topic. Politicians who visit a disaster site or travel to other countries to get first-hand experience are seeking ethos, or personal proof.

Second, your audience is more likely to be persuaded by your speech if they think you are trustworthy. Once again, the best way to appear trustworthy is to *be* trustworthy. The reputation for honesty and truthfulness that you earned in the past will greatly enhance your credibility with your current audience. As was discussed earlier, professional persuaders in advertising and politics constantly try to give their clients either the appearance or the substance of honesty. Your classmates will have an impression of you from previous communication interactions; and in a formal setting, someone will probably introduce you and will mention your trustworthiness in the past.

Dynamism, the third element of ethos, is the one that is most directly under your immediate control. Audiences generally respond favorably to speakers who are lively, energetic, and upbeat—if, of course, these behaviors are appropriate to the topic and situation. Voice, posture, gesture, and movement—all can contribute to an impression of dynamism. You may need to adjust your delivery style to the size of the room, the audience, and the space available, but an interesting presentation will keep an audience interested. The delivery skills discussed in Chapter 12 did not come from some abstract idea about an ideal speaker. They are grounded in research confirming that a good delivery style makes audiences more attentive and receptive to the content of your speech. In persuasive speaking, a delivery that communicates sincerity and dedication to the topic will be received by the audience as part of the persuasive message. More information about persuasive delivery styles follows in this chapter.

Goodwill, the fourth element of ethos, requires that you tailor your message to the needs and for the benefit of your listeners. If you have their best interests at heart, they are likely to be responsive to your speech. You can also demonstrate goodwill as you give your presentation. Are you pleasant? Do you observe social courtesy and everyday norms of behavior? Do you communicate positive regard for your audience? All of these factors will help to create a climate of goodwill during your persuasive message. The advertising that you see on television features warm, family scenes at a fast-food restaurant, a young person calling home to mom, or a major oil company showing how it cares for the animals and plants in the environment. All are attempts to secure the viewer's goodwill.

In addition to developing your credibility through these methods, you can add persuasive force to your messages by using the other two types of proof that Aristotle identified: emotion and logic.

Pathos

Emotion, or **pathos,** helps your listeners to become involved or aroused. Attitude change theory states that getting the listener to identify with or have feeling for the topic creates a persuasive communication climate. Arousing and using your listeners' feelings can be a highly effective way to get them to pay attention to what you are saying and may also motivate many of them to do what you ask. Consider magazine ads that ask you to send money to help poor children. They may show a picture of a sad-eyed child dressed in ragged clothes, and you may feel a response of sympathy. On television, you may see film footage of people in desperate condition in programs that are designed to raise money for worldwide hunger relief. These are examples of emotional proof. However, do not think that sadness and pity are the only emotions that you can use persuasively. Any human emotion can help you get your audience involved in your thesis. Persuaders often used humor, fear, and pride. How do persuaders get you to buy their brand of toothpaste or mouthwash? Fear is usually the motivator. What awful fate awaits you if you have bad breath or dull teeth? Sometimes a funny story or example will make the audience feel good about the topic. Humor, then, can be a persuasive tool, and so can poking fun at something. Political cartoons are an example of using humor to persuade.

Research shows that emotional proof, or pathos, can be very strong in helping to persuade others. Research also indicates that emotion is best used when it is combined with solid reasoning so that your listeners both feel and understand your message. One of the best ways to get emotional support into your persuasive messages is to use compelling stories or examples. Remember, they must be short enough to simply illustrate one or two ideas in your speech. You could include a moving or humorous personal experience, a touching example, a humorous anecdote, or a compelling description of an event that relates to your thesis. Some communicators use emotional proof to the exclusion of any other. This technique is effective only in the short run and with an audience that does not respond thoughtfully to messages. The best use of emotion in persuasive speaking is in conjunction with other forms that also help to make the topic memorable and motivating. Most listeners, especially as their level of education and sophistication increases, demand the inclusion of factual information and a logical interpretation of that information before they make any important commitments.

Logos

Emotional supports are powerful, but they must be used with care and only to heighten interest or command attention. They must not replace other forms of proof. **Logos** was Aristotle's term for logic, or reason. While logic certainly includes making connections from a set of facts and drawing logical conclusions from those facts, as used here the term also includes the entire range of logical supporting materials and the reasoning process that brings them together. (See the Critical Thinking in Communication box on the next page.)

Recall that inductive reasoning asks you to find supporting materials that are typical. When you create persuasive messages, select supporting materials that meet this logical test. Have you chosen examples that are representative of other examples that are readily available? Or did you select examples that represent only one side of the issue? If so, you not only violated the rules of induction, you also ignored the psychological research that found that it is more effective to introduce arguments for both sides of an is-

Logical Constructs in the Persuasive Speech

In the chapter on critical thinking, you learned about deduction and induction as logical forms of reasoning. The tests of both truth and validity were used to examine sequences and conclusions. The same processes now apply to material in this chapter as you examine both the facts used in persuasion and the processes used to link those facts together to reach a conclusion. Suggestions drawn from Chapter 4 can now help you to apply those logical elements to your persuasive speaking and listening.

sue rather than one side alone. Good induction also takes into consideration the effects of time and requires that you select supporting materials that are recent. Finally, your supports must be *sufficient* if they are going to help you prove your point.

Applying deductive principles to the selection and use of persuasive supporting materials can be accomplished in several ways. You can adopt a deductive organization for the body of your speech by first presenting and then supporting a general principle in the same way that you would lead off with a major premise in a deductive syllogism. Next, the middle part of the speech, the body of the speech, would develop related concepts in the same way that you would phrase minor premises. Finally, a conclusion would constitute the final section of the body of the speech in the same way that a syllogism ends with a conclusion.

You may wish to make causal claims during your speech. Causal claims link events by stating that one event (cause) made another event happen (result). The major shortcomings of causal reasoning involve the fallacies of hasty generalization, whereby a conclusion is drawn too quickly from insufficient support, and of post hoc, whereby a statement is in error because it assumes that if one event follows another in time, the first event must be the cause of the second. As an educated persuader, use the principles of critical thinking to help you avoid these reasoning pitfalls. These elements of formal reasoning are a good place to start, but you might also make use of informal types of critical thinking to augment your use of logos.

Informal Reasoning

The best way to recall the earlier discussion of informal reasoning is to think about the Toulmin system presented in Chapter 4. Toulmin examined the reasoning process as people use it to help them reach conclusions. He noted that we take some information (grounds) and connect it to a conclusion (claim) by means of some principle (the warrant). For example, several of your friends like Nana's Ice Cream (grounds), so you conclude that it is probably a good place to go after a movie (claim) because your friends' judgments on such matters are usually right (warrant). In your persuasive speech, you will probably offer grounds to support your claims. In so doing, make certain that you examine the warrants that are operating. For example, if nobody knows your friends or, worse, your friends are known but not trusted, then your grounds will not be connected to your claim in the minds of your audience. Persuasion, and all communication for that matter, happens as a transaction between senders and receivers. Failure on the part of many would-be persuaders to consider the warrants *of the audience* has meant failure to persuade altogether.

Consider your own firmly held core values, such as your religious, moral, ethical, or political values. Others who hold different but also firmly held values are unlikely to be persuaded by your warrants. As illustrated by attitude change theory, you must appeal to the audience on the basis of *their* values, because it is within a person's value system that warrants often develop.

Why do different people reach different claims or conclusions, when presented with the same data? Members of a jury often differ, even after hearing the same information. The famous O. J. Simpson trial demonstrated that listeners from various backgrounds interpreted the same information very differently (Lacayo, 1995). Why? The answer is that they apply different *warrants,* or principles, to their reasoning processes. Make certain that when you develop persuasive messages, you examine the warrants that are operating in your own reasoning processes and assumptions.

For your persuasive message to be effective, you also need to select supporting materials from the items your research has produced. You should have a variety of resources at your disposal, including statistics, short stories, quotations, examples, visual aids, and illustrations. Use the ideas contained in ethos, pathos, and logos to help you select the best and most appropriate materials from the many possible supports. Choose those that will most probably motivate your listeners. A review of the principles of audience analysis in Chapter 11 can also help you to make a connection between your supporting materials and your listeners. A good rule of thumb is to create variety in your supporting materials, both in their probable effect on your listeners and in their type. For example, avoid using too many statistics, quotations, or personal anecdotes. At the same time, make certain that you appeal at one time or another during your speech to your listeners' sense of logic, their emotions, and their impression of your credibility. How much logic? How much emotion? How much credibility? It all depends, as in any speech, on you, your topic, the audience, the occasion, the time limits, and the circumstances. You can be sure, however, that the best speakers include each of these areas in their speeches.

DEVELOPING PERSUASIVE ORGANIZATION

Although you could certainly use any of the organizational patterns discussed earlier to prepare a persuasive speech, those patterns lack the advantage of being specifically designed to persuade. There are several ways to outline your persuasive message, building a case for your thesis and taking your listeners from one idea to the next, creating a strong, motivational speech. First, we look at some logical patterns based on what you already know about critical thinking. Then we examine a special method of preparing persuasive speeches that has been used and tested for over fifty years, called the motivated sequence.

Logical Patterns

Perhaps the most common way to organize a persuasive message is to use the problem–solution pattern. This **logical pattern** outlines a problem or problems in a certain area and then urges the listeners to adopt a particular solution. The body of the speech has only two major divisions: A. Problems, followed by B. Solutions. This pattern is easy for a speaker to use and for an audience to follow. The only real difficulties that this pattern involves is that the problem may not be significant or the solution offered may not be practical, may cost too much, or may not solve the problem. Make certain that you use the principles of cause-and-effect reasoning when preparing a problem–solution speech. In addition, test for fallacies of *non sequitur*, especially the *post hoc* fallacy.

If you use a problem–solution format, your outline will look like this:

    I. Introduction *(a compelling story related to problem X)*
   II. Thesis sentence *(You should solve problem X.)*
  III. Body *(preview)*
      A. Identify the problem
        1. Supporting material that defines it
        2. Supporting material that shows its significance
        3. Supporting material that shows its extent
        4. Supporting material that applies to listeners
      B. Solution to the problem
        1. Proposed action step
        2. Justification for the proposed action
        3. Probable consequences or benefits of the proposed action
   IV. Conclusion (brief review of A, B, thesis sentence, and introduction)
    V. Sources/bibliography

This type of presentation is commonly used in groups, committees, civic organizations, councils, and clubs and even among roommates. You sense a problem and propose a solution. Everything from cleaning the city streets to cleaning the bathroom that you share with roommates can be organized into a problem–solution format. It is quite clear and direct.

A format that is related to problem–solution is the cause–effect format. If you wanted to convince someone that there is a logical relationship between a sun tan and skin cancer, you would use a cause–effect organizational format. This format resembles the problem–solution format in many ways. The first step in both is the same. However, if you were to consider a historical question—the causes of World War I, for example—you would see that no solution is included in your format. Instead, you would be trying to establish causal links between events. Your logical reasoning would have to be clear, compelling, and free of fallacies for your audience to be convinced of your thesis. Your organizational pattern would look like the problem–solution one, but it would not have a solution or an action step.

Motivated Sequence

Perhaps the most widely studied organizational pattern is the one developed by Alan H. Monroe over sixty years ago (Monroe, 1935). The reason that it has gained such popularity is because it works! Its parts are similar to outline sections you have already studied, but their arrangement is such that it helps to lead your listeners to the desired conclusion. The five steps of the motivated sequence are (1) attention, (2) need, (3) satisfaction, (4) visualization, and (5) action.

The *attention* step is similar to the introduction of any speech outline. Here is where you capture the interest of your listeners and turn it into concern for your topic. To establish a *need*, you indicate a problem that should be solved. The need step can involve a fact—understanding an event or solving a mystery; or a value—reevaluating a position on evolution or on safe sex; or a policy—electing a person to office, buying a particular car, or supporting national health insurance.

Once you have the attention of the audience and have addressed the need involved in your thesis, you move directly to showing your audience the solution—that is, the *satisfaction* step. This step may be fairly short and is often a restatement of your thesis. This is when you ask your listeners to change their minds or take some action. The next step is *visualization,* and here is where you can be somewhat imaginative. Try to get your audience to *see* the consequences of your solution, to *imagine* the benefits they will get if they adopt your thesis. You can also indicate the negative effects of *not* choosing your thesis: the bad things that will happen if they do not adopt your idea. Some speakers do try to introduce both positive and negative visualizations in this step, thereby creating a comparison–contrast form of supporting material.

Finally, you request of your listeners a specific *action.* It is usually a directly focused form of your satisfaction step and may be designed to be inspirational or motivational. "So when you go to the polls tomorrow, remember to put an X next to Jane Doe's name!"

If you were preparing a standard outline for a speech and wanted to put your ideas into a motivated sequence pattern, your quick outline would look like this one:

   I. Attention step *(introduction: story, example)*
  II. Thesis sentence
 III. Body *(preview)*
     A. Need step *(problems, difficulty)*
        1. Supporting material #1
        2. Supporting material #2
        3. Supporting material #3
        4. Additional supporting materials

    B. Satisfaction step
       1. Support for your solution
       2. Details of your plan or idea
    C. Visualization step
       1. Support for the positive effects of your idea
       2. Support for the negative consequences of rejecting the idea
    D. Action
       1. Description of steps to take
       2. Support for acting on the idea
 IV. Conclusion *(brief review of A, B, C, D, thesis sentence, and attention step.)*
  V. Sources/bibliography

By using a persuasive format to organize your speech, combining that outline with strong and appropriate supporting materials, and motivating your listeners through your credibility, the strength and logic of your reasoning, and your appeal to their emotions will create an influential presentation (Gronbeck et al., 1995)

DEVELOPING PERSUASIVE LANGUAGE

Getting people to do what you advocate is a difficult process, but you can improve your chances of success if you put some time and effort into increasing the impact of your language choices. Most effective speakers select their words very carefully.

As in your informative speeches, you want your **persuasive language** to be clear and memorable. One way to create a response in your listeners is to excite their imagination. When you use the motivated sequence in your organizational plan, you will engage their imaginations directly during the visualization step, but you can tap into their imaginative processes throughout a speech using imagery.

Imagery

There are several ways in which language can help you create images or scenes in the minds of your audience. Chapter 6 presents ways in which language affects our thoughts and imagination. One powerful way is by analogy, which is a form of comparison. Analogies are usually divided into two types: figurative and literal. A figurative analogy is the more imaginative because it takes two things that are not alike in the real sense and uses comparison to make one of them more colorful and memorable. A literal analogy takes two real things and compares them. For example, an easy chair is like a recliner in many real ways, and your college is very much like my college in many real ways.

Examples of figurative analogies are much easier to think of just because they are so colorful and memorable. When people speak of our country as a ship of state and compare the President to a captain, they are using figurative analogy to express an idea about how our country is governed or should be governed. Of course, the President is also very different from a captain in many ways, but as with other analogies, there is a point to be made. A company may be compared to a bicycle, with each element of the corporation connected somehow to some part of the bicycle, or a family may be compared to a tree, or a community to a beehive, or the object of your affection "to a summer's day."

You probably recall that the type of comparison that uses the word *like* is a simile and that other comparisons are called *metaphors*. Long, extended, story-length comparisons are labeled *allegories,* and many of our religious teachings come to us in the form of *parables,* another form of metaphor. Each time you see these types of supporting materials, you are helping your message become clear and memorable to your audiences. In the field of communication, recent attention has focused on the use of stories as a way to help researchers and scholars understand how people receive, organize, remember, and respond to communication (Fisher, 1984, 1985).

As a persuader, take advantage of this knowledge and of the tools described here to help you make your ideas memorable and effective. Research conducted at Michigan State University demonstrated that speeches that used analogies had a greater persuasive effect on their listeners than did those that did not use analogies (McCroskey and Combs, 1969).

Colorful and judicious use of adjectives and adverbs can also enhance your speech and the willingness of your audience to get involved in your ideas. Creative use of description to create images can make your ideas live on in your listeners' minds. You might simply describe someone as being tall, or you could elaborate, saying that he "was a giant of a man, towering over the heads of everyone else in the room." The first description does not create a scene in your listeners' minds, whereas the second one creates a vivid image immediately.

Adjectives and adverbs are the descriptors in our language. They can, of course, also help to describe the image that your audience is forming about you and your ideas. Your audience is judgmental and can label you as being outgoing and upbeat or a talkative, overbearing loudmouth. The subject of the description could be the same person, but the imagery creates a very different picture. Did the soccer player walk away from the field slowly, or did she "drag herself along, one aching step at a time, until she finally sank into a heap at the sidelines"? Use the power of language to make your message memorable with images that will remain in your listeners' minds long after you have stopped speaking.

Impact

Another way to create and use persuasive language is to give impact to your message through emphasis, humor, and personal references.

Emphasis means that you alert your audience to important ideas as they emerge by using transitions. A transition might be worded as follows: "This next idea will save you hundreds of dollars on your car repair bills." Notice how the transition calls attention to an important point. The statement "This problem is not limited to our cities, but can be found right here on campus" emphasizes the application of your ideas directly to your immediate audience. Of course, you must limit your use of emphasis, or everything will seem really important. When that happens, your speech never varies from a high pitch, creating a situation that becomes very stressful for the audience.

Humor is another way to give your ideas impact. You may recall that pathos included the use of humor as a persuasive technique. The test of humor, as of all other supporting materials, is that it must be appropriate to the situation. A persuasive speech is often about controversial ideas, and while humor can help the audience relax to receive your message, you must be careful not to offend your listeners and turn them against your thesis. Good humor based on wit, surprise, intelligence, and goodwill can enhance your credibility. On the other hand, if your humor is based on sarcasm, vulgar or off-color material, or mean satire, you can damage or destroy the impact of your message. Sarcasm is usually perceived as pettiness, and vulgarity may offend your listeners. Satire is very hard to do well and may confuse your audience about your real message. Good persuasion does not demean, offend, or confuse your listeners.

Finally, personal references command attention and make a connection between you and your material that the audience can appreciate. Your first-hand experience with a topic can be worked into your presentation so that it enhances your expertise. The story of your sunburn can be a dramatic support for your speech on sunscreens. Your experience of driving a friend to the hospital after he had drunk too much will give impact to your speech on alcohol abuse. These supports can be powerful, so it is wise not to overdo them. The speech should not turn into a monologue about the great tragedies in your life, or you will risk losing your listeners. The topic must remain relevant to your *receivers* throughout your presentation; and if your personal references are directed to a significant idea in your speech, they can add impact to that relevance.

DEVELOPING PERSUASIVE PRESENTATIONS

Your delivery should match your thesis. You should speak about significant, relevant, important issues; and your presentation should reflect these purposes. Do not hesitate to communicate to your listeners that you find the material you are speaking about to be very important. In comparison to your delivery when you give an informative speech, your delivery of a persuasive speech will probably be more serious, formal, and dynamic; will include a greater range of voice variety; and will make use of more pauses. You need not become theatrical, nor employ dramatic gestures, but you should truly reflect the importance of your ideas in a way that is appropriate to the audience and the situation. Watch yourself practice on videotape to get a feeling for the persuasive impact your presentation is making. Is there anything more that you can do to increase your effectiveness? Do you need to tone down your presentation because it is too jarring? Is your speaking rate too fast for your audience to follow as you tell an important and touching story? Are you making use of pauses so that your listeners can get a sense of drama before you present a key idea? Do you sound cheery, upbeat, and bright during your speech on child abuse? Do not forget the test of appropriateness: Do you and your presentation fit the room, the topic, and the audience?

In addition to vocal considerations in speeches of persuasion, keep in mind nonverbal elements. Gestures and facial expressions must be consistent with the ideas expressed. If your movements are too grandiose or if your facial expression is inappropriate, your listeners will be distracted from your thesis and instead will concentrate on your nonverbal behaviors.

Humor and energy contribute to persuasive presentations.

The impact on the audience should come from your idea, not from your delivery of the idea.

Good organization, supporting materials, and variety in type and function of supports, combined with a presentation on a substantial and worthwhile topic, will create a successful persuasive message. Your speech will gain polish when you add persuasive language and a persuasive delivery.

ADAPTING PERSUASIVE SPEECHES TO YOUR AUDIENCE

Now that you have a variety of persuasive tools from which to select as you prepare your speech, you need to think about the different conditions you may face as you analyze your listeners. Four distinct types of audiences may be present: supportive, interested, apathetic, and hostile.

If you know that your listeners are already likely to be in support of your thesis, then you can treat your speech as one to inspire or reinforce. You may need to give them some of the most recent information so that they feel confident that they are current, and you may find your use of pathos to be important to reenergize their efforts. Perhaps a reminder of some direct action steps that they need to take will finish your presentation.

Suppose your research into your audience reveals that they are interested in the topic but undecided on the issue. You can then compose your presentation to include strong evidence, paying careful attention to expert testimony and statistical supporting materials if appropriate. These people are likely to have some idea of opposing arguments, so take advantage of the attitude change theory research that advises you to include some mention of opposing arguments and a rebuttal to those arguments.

A third condition you may face is apathetic listeners—they are not yet interested and do not care about your issue. Sometimes apathy can be traced to lack of knowledge, so you would spend a significant portion of your time developing the problem. In your outline, main section A in the body should have sufficient supporting materials to show the extent of the problem *and* how that problem directly affects your listeners. If your audience is apathetic because the issue really does not apply to them, seek another topic; you would be violating one of the principles of ethical speaking if you tried to persuade an audience to act on an issue of no importance to them.

Finally, you may face a hostile audience—they are already opposed to your position. Rather than give up, you may be able to reach them if you first spend time developing common ground with these listeners. Using Burke's terminology, seek their *identification* with you and your perspective. Demonstrate the qualities of goodwill and trustworthiness. Once you have created a common ground, proceed with your expertise to connect their interests, concerns, and values with your position.

If you take time to do a considered audience analysis, you stand a better chance of reaching your desired goal in persuasion. Of course, you may face an audience that includes a mixture of all these types, so you may need to combine approaches. Since the hostile group may quit listening first, you might want to begin with common ground materials and end with your reinforcement and inspirational elements. Attention to these considerations will help you to be evaluated positive by your various listeners.

EVALUATING PERSUASIVE SPEECHES

As is true for informative speeches, you can evaluate persuasive speeches from the three perspectives of a listener, a critic, and a consumer. Compared to an informative speech, there are more things to listen to and listen for in a speech of persuasion. Consequently, there are more things to evaluate in persuasive speaking.

Listening Goals

When listening to any speech, the listener evaluates the organization, relevance of the topic, main ideas, and supporting materials. When the speech is persuasive, the listener must also be very demanding in evaluating the logic that is used to connect all of these elements into a motivating message.

As a listener, first try to decide whether the speech is aimed at convincing, inspiring, or moving you to action. Listen carefully for the thesis, because it might not be stated overtly but might merely be implied, as in the case of most advertising and political presentations. A listener should always be concerned about the value of the proposed action *for the listener.* You can be certain that presenters sense some value in the proposed action for themselves, but what motivates them to want you to join in? It may be their care and concern for your welfare, that their favorite cause needs more supporters, or that they stand to gain personally or financially from your support. A critical listener uses active listening skills in this situation to sort out ideas, discover the thesis, evaluate information, check the quality of supporting materials, and follow the development of the main ideas to determine whether sections build on each other in a logical manner.

Since persuasive speeches usually involve values and attitudes and are often about controversial subjects, it may be difficult for you to concentrate on your active listening skills. Suppose the speaker is talking about abortion, gun control, the death penalty, college tuition, nuclear power, or any one of a dozen other topics about which people have strong opinions. If the speaker takes a position that is different from yours, you will have to try hard to keep listening with an open mind. It will be difficult to withhold a quick judgment and avoid preparing a rebuttal mentally while the speaker is still talking. It would seem that when you need the skills of active listening the most, you are the least able to use them. Therefore an important listening goal in persuasion presentations is to be very attentive to your own reactions. Suppose that the speaker has selected a controversial topic and the view that is expressed in the speech is exactly like your own. Again, active listening will be difficult because you may spend your listening time cheering the speaker along mentally and forget to activate your listening skills.

You may not be able to be a successful listener every time you listen to a persuasive message, but the *effort* to do so can still help you to evaluate persuasive messages, as both a critic and a consumer. You will be better prepared for both of those roles if your listening practice has been complete and careful.

Critical Goals

As you can see from the items discussed in the section on listening goals, you as a listener need a complete set of criteria to function as a competent critic of any message. The evaluation criteria that are presented in Chapter 12 can help to make you an effective critic of persuasive speeches. Evaluate the speaker's methods, supporting materials, audience elements, and presentation. Examine the logical, emotional, and personal forms of proof that are used in the message, and be especially concerned with the speaker's adaptation (or lack thereof) to a particular audience. Has the speaker taken care to apply the ideas, costs, and benefits of the message to this particular group of listeners? Are the supporting materials directly related to the interests of this group?

Take a close look at how the speaker uses language, transitions, interest, and delivery skills. Can you comprehend the vocabulary? Is it offensive? Does it move you? Does the speech follow a sensible and appropriate pattern that you can identify? The critique forms used in class can help you begin to organize your criticism. Later, you will want to come back to the list of items you use to criticize other presentations and apply them to your own messages.

Criticism involves more than just picking out the flaws and successes of others. The goals of a critic are to explain why and how a presenter does certain things but not others in their speeches, evaluate the success or failure of the presenter's choices, and suggest alternatives.

In any message, there are probably areas of excellence and areas that are in need of improvement. As a critic, you should try to carry out an objective evaluation, using the criteria for judging good speeches in a way that is independent of your personal opinions or biases. For example, you may be opposed to handgun controls but still able to judge a speech that advocates such controls as being well organized and convincingly presented. You can agree or disagree with a thesis and like or dislike a speech. It is challenging to give positive criticism to a speech when you oppose its thesis. It is also a challenge to admit that a speech supporting your favorite cause was not very well presented. However, a critic must be able to do exactly that if such a judgment is warranted by applying objective criteria. However, this does not mean that critics can never express their opinions. Opinions are the topic of the next section on being an effective consumer of persuasive messages.

Consumer Goals

The best consumers hold an informed opinion that they develop by listening carefully, completely, and critically to the great volume of information with which they are bombarded every day. If you have learned how to be an active listener and an objective critic, you are in an excellent position to draw reasonable conclusions and take wise and sensible actions. You will be able to base your decisions on complete information and good judgment. Some people form opinions on the basis of surface impressions or a quick response. As a trained communicator, you can avoid making superficial responses to advertisements and instead seek out complete and reliable points of view. Persuasive speakers will ask you for your time, your money, or your personal support. To be an effective consumer, you should think very carefully before parting with any of those things. Before you consider such a major commitment, evaluate very carefully any persuasive messages, especially those from advertising and politics, for the value they can give you. Professional persuaders have the job of getting you to part with something. Make certain that your job is to be a professional consumer, and insist that presenters, including yourself, maintain high standards of clarity, support, ethics, and honesty in the information that they design to influence you and others.

IMPROVING PERSUASIVE COMMUNICATION COMPETENCY

Unfortunately, there are few controls over the kind and type of persuasive messages to which you are exposed every day, so you must become a competent source for controlling the quality of these messages. Being personally competent at persuasion will be valuable to you for the rest of your life as you listen to, react to, and send out persuasive communication.

The first step toward persuasive communication competency is to be aware of the principles and techniques of persuasion. By studying how people can and do change attitudes, you can enlarge your own repertoire of communicative options. Attitude change theory, combined with the wisdom inherited from classical rhetoric and modern presentation techniques, have given you sophisticated, technical skills as well as an appreciation and knowledge of human behavior. This combination of knowledge, choices, and skills enhances your basic competency.

Next, using guidelines reflected by the choices that are available to you, select a topic from among your options. Construct a message based on your analysis of the topic, yourself, the audience, and the occasion. Continue working on your speech until you have constructed a solid piece of communication. The selections you make from among your choices of supporting materials are important because they underscore your personal credibility. Logical reasoning and providing for audience involvement add even more credibility to your presentation. Keep in mind that you have a variety of patterns to use for the organization of your speech, so select one that you think is appropriate for both you and your subject.

Once you have made all of the selections mentioned above, it is time to implement these choices in your actual presentation. Practice giving your speech by using appropriate delivery skills, increasing the impact of your vocabulary, viewing yourself on videotape, and having someone listen to and react to your practice sessions. Be sure to follow the guidelines for time allotment as well.

If you work conscientiously on these guidelines and recommendations, your presentations not only will implement and increase your knowledge about persuasion, but you will also be ready to judge the outcome of your efforts in an evaluation.

Evaluation means that you carry out some self-evaluation as your own best critic. Using the criteria for judging persuasive messages, review your presentation to see how well it measures up to those standards. Did you focus on your own concerns or those of your listeners? Did you select a topic that was significant to them, as well as to you? Were your supporting materials substantial, relevant, recent, well researched, and credited to their sources? Were you able to introduce variety into both the forms of support and their function to establish credibility, logic, and emotional proof? You should have presented a message that is rich in content, clear in meaning, and challenging to the intellect of your audience. Did you do that?

Another way to be evaluated is through the responses of your listeners. Did the audience react favorably? Did you get some direct feedback, either from your listeners or from your instructor? Take into account the evaluation of others, and add it to your own evaluative perceptions to obtain a full, balanced evaluation.

SUMMARY

Your attitudes and values give direction to the way you live your life. The development or changing of listeners' attitudes and the ability to influence their actions are at the heart of persuasion. The theories about how these changes come about are important to know to gain a full understanding of ourselves as communicators—both senders and receivers of messages.

The variety of persuasive messages—speeches to convince, to reinforce, or to move to action—all have a similar goal: to influence the audience. You can choose claims or questions of fact, value, or policy when selecting your topic. As you plan a persuasive message, you must pay careful attention to the types of supporting materials that you select. Apply the principles of critical thinking in choosing evidence to substantiate your main ideas. Does your evidence enhance your personal credibility, demonstrate logical connections, and provide an emotional link between your audience and your topic?

When you are ready to organize your outline, look at different patterns, such as the problem–solution or the motivated sequence patterns. Try organizing your information in a variety of ways until you find one that seems to work best for you, your audience, the setting, and the time allotted for your speech.

Use the ideas discussed above for creating an impact through an enhanced use of language and delivery skills.

You can create and maintain listener attention and interest if you apply those suggestions. Follow the steps that you know very well by now of selecting a topic, creating a thesis sentence, organizing the body, selecting effective supporting materials, and creating an interesting introduction and conclusion. These steps parallel the process for preparing an informative speech, but their content and their logical interconnection are specifically directed to the goal of motivating your listeners.

You have also learned how to evaluate a persuasive speech from the perspective of a listener, a critic, and a consumer. Finally, you have seen how you can use those evaluation techniques and apply them to improve your own competency as a persuasive communicator.

KEY WORDS

persuasive speeches, p. 364
facts, p. 364
values, p. 365
policy, p. 365
value system, p. 366
attitude change theory, p. 366
habits, p. 367
drives, p. 367
source credibility, p. 368
ethos, p. 369, 373
fear appeals, p. 369
debates, p. 372
public argumentation, p. 373
pathos, p. 374
logos, p. 375
logical pattern, p. 378
persuasive language, p. 380

REFERENCES

1. Watch television for one uninterrupted hour to collect data on the types of persuasive appeals that are used in advertising. Collect examples of the following appeals: fear, humor, and pity. Can you identify other appeals? Then make a note of the different values on which television commercials are based. Prepare a three- to five-page report about your hour-long observation and share it with the class.
2. If persuasive speech presentations are given in your class, take critical notes on one of them. Then present a brief critique to the class, based on your evaluation of the speaker's choice of topic as well as the organization, supports, and delivery.
3. Bring several magazine ads to class, and describe how ethos, pathos, and logos operate in magazine advertising. Do some ads always have only one kind of appeal, whereas others use a different appeal? What do you think accounts for these differences?
4. The next time you observe a persuasive speaker in person, notice the adaptations that the speaker employs or misses. For example, does the speaker make reference to the specific situation—time, audience, and location? Is the vocabulary that he or she uses appropriate to the audience? What other specific adaptations do you notice?
5. Present a six- to eight-minute long persuasive speech to your class following the guidelines presented in this chapter.

REFERENCES

Fisher, Walter. "Narration as a Human Communication Paradigm: The Case of Public Moral Argument." *Communication Monographs* 51 (1984), 1.

Fisher, Walter. "The Narrative Paradigm: An Elaboration." *Communication Monographs* 52 (1985), 347.

Gronbeck, B., K. German, D. Ehninger, and A. Monroe. *Principles and Types of Speech Communication.* 12th ed. New York: HarperCollins, 1995.

Hilgard, E. R., and G. H. Bower. *Theories of Learning.* Englewood Cliffs: Prentice-Hall, 1966.

Hovland, C. I., I. L. Janis, and H. H. Kelley. *Communication and Persuasion.* New Haven: Yale University Press, 1953.

Hovland, C. I., A. R. Lumsdaine, and E. D. Sheffield. *Experiments on Mass Communication.* Princeton: Princeton University Press, 1949.

Lacayo, Richard. "An Ugly End to It All." *Time,* 9 Oct. 1995: 30–37.

Lumsdaine, A., and I. Janis. "Resistance to 'Counterpropaganda' Produced by One-Sided and Two-Sided 'Propaganda' Presentations." *Public Opinion Quarterly* 17 (1953).

McCroskey, J. C., and W. H. Combs. "The Effects of the Use of Analogy on Attitude Change and Source Credibility." *Journal of Communication* 19 (1969), 333.

Monroe, Alan H. *Principles and Types of Speech.* Chicago: Scott, Foresman, 1935.

Murphy, G., L. B. Murphy, and T. M. Newcomb. *Experimental Social Psychology.* New York: Harper & Row, 1937.

Rogers, R. W. "A Protection Motivation Theory of Fear Appeals and Attitude Change." *Journal of Psychology,* 91 (1975).

Employment Interviewing: Preparing for Your Future

THIS APPENDIX WILL HELP YOU:

- Use the Internet to help you prepare for the interview, research organizations, locate job openings, and get a job.
- Describe the qualities that employers seek in applicants.
- Develop a résumé that will make a good impression on prospective employers.
- Research a company to determine its background, products, location, and future.
- Conduct yourself effectively in an employment interview.

Bill, who is graduating in May, is looking for a public relations position with a major corporation. He has called Mr. Muller, the personnel director of S & S Enterprises, to discuss his chances of being hired by that firm.

Liz is looking for an internship in marketing in order to get some experience before she goes into the real job hunt. She has contacted several different marketing firms through her university internship office and is ready to be interviewed.

Sam needs to make a few dollars in order to make it through college. He decides to get a part-time job and is scheduled to interview with a local clothing store.

The students in these examples will participate in interviews that will affect the rest of their lives. In this appendix, we will look at the employment interview—what you as a job hunter can expect to encounter and how you can prepare to make the best impression.

PREPARING FOR JOB HUNTING

The purpose of this book is to help you with the following skills: speaking, organizing, critical thinking, researching, persuading, informing, listening, discussing, making decisions, solving problems, and using nonverbal and verbal communication. Another purpose is to help you develop your leadership and interpersonal skills. After you have completed this course, it will then be up to you to continue developing each skill throughout your education and your lifetime. Because employment interviews are among the most important interpersonal communication events of your life, we have devoted this appendix to them.

Most of you taking this course are probably just beginning your college education. Whether you are a recent high school graduate or someone who has returned to school after pursuing other interests, the following pages on employment interviews will give you important information that will aid

Making Connections   Thinking About Your Future

Refer back to the opening scenario, and think about what each person must be able to demonstrate in order to land a job. SKILLS! That one word means a lot to your future. The recurring theme among the experts we surveyed is an emphasis on skills and competencies, rather than on completing specific studies.

Your major alone may not make a decisive difference in your future, but the skills you master and the way you communicate them to others can carry you through a lifetime of careers.

1. What is the message in the above statements?
2. What advice would you give to Bill, Liz, and Sam as they prepare themselves for their interviews?

J. Meyers, "The Ideal Job Candidate," Collegiate Employment Institute Letter, 15 July 1989, 6; Ford's Insider: Continuing Series of College Newspaper Supplements (Knoxville, Tenn.: 13–30 Corporation, 1980), 14.

you in preparing for your future after graduation. Although graduation and hunting for a full-time job may seem far away, your preparation for them should begin now. You can begin by attending your university or community's career day programs. Such programs bring together undergraduates, graduate students, and alumni with employers from government, private enterprise, and nonprofit organizations. It is a time for everyone—even freshmen—to find out what organizations are looking for in potential employees. Don't wait until you are a senior to begin research.

CAREER RESEARCH ON THE INTERNET

One of the most valuable tools available in preparing for the employment interview is the Internet. The Internet, via the World Wide Web, will allow you to research every aspect of the employment interview. For example, you can learn on the Internet how to prepare for the interview, write a résumé, create an electronic résumé, research organizations, find job opportunities, find out what questions are commonly asked in interviews, and even get advice on what to wear to an interview. Most colleges and universities have a career and placement center that you can visit in person or contact through their homepage. The career or placement center's home page can be an extremely valuable source of information. The University of Nebraska's (UNL) Career Services Center, for example, has one of the most up-to-date homepages on the Internet (see Figure A.1). Its Internet ad-

Figure A.1 A Sample Career Services Home Page

This figure illustrates the information provided to students by university and college career services and placement offices.

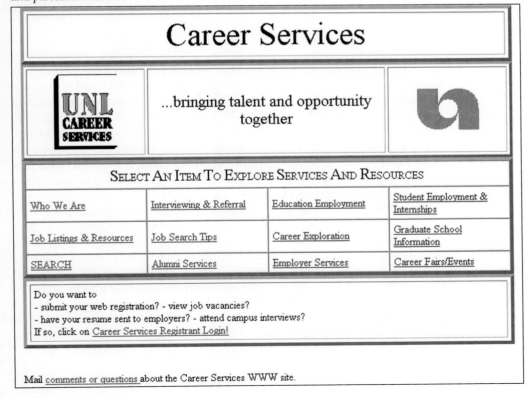

Your Personal Headhunter

In quest of the perfect job? Here are seven Web sites with personal search agents:

CareerBuilder
http://www.careerbuilder.com
   Jobs: 3,000–5,000
   Employers: 200, including Sallie Mae, Southwestern Bell, Taco Bell

CareerSite
http://www.careersite.com
   Jobs: 5,000–7,000
   Employers: 400, including AT&T, Booz Allen Hamilton, CIGNA Insurance, Ford

IntelliMatch
http://intellimatch.com
   Jobs: 2,500
   Employers: 2,500, including AT&T, Hewlett-Packard, Microsoft, National Semiconductor

CareerMart
http://www.careermart.com
   Jobs: 5,000
   Employers: 500, including IBM, Philips, Burger King

E. Span
http://www.espan.com
   Jobs: 15,000
   Employers: 1,000, including Caterpillar, Compaq, IBM, Lotus, MCI, Microsoft, Texas Instruments, Westinghouse

The Monster Board
http://www.monsterboard.com
   Jobs: 25,000
   Employers: 25,000, including CVS, Compaq, IBM, Intel, McDonald's, Price Waterhouse

4Work.com
http://www.4work.com
   Jobs: 6,000
   Employers: 1,735, including Blockbuster, Norell, United Way

M. Mannix, "Putting the Net to Work: Can Search Agents Make Sense of Job-Hunt Banks?" *U.S. News & World Report*, 27 October 1997, 94.

dress is *http://www.unl.edu/careers/csc.html* and provides information pertaining to almost every aspect related to careers and the employment interview. You can click any of the boxed items to explore services and resources. For example, the Job Search Tips box will lead to information on how to search for a job on the Internet, job search strategies, résumé tips and a sample résumé, how to write application letters and sample application letters, who to get as references, how to create a portfolio, information on organizations, and interviewing tips. The Internet is an incredibly valuable tool in preparing for your future career.

You should check with your college or university's career and placement center for its Internet address. You can also locate a search engine—a program that searches for and retrieves information on the Internet. Yahoo (*http://search.yahoo.com*) or Webcrawler (*http://webcrawler.com*) for example, are two of the most popular search engines. Once you are on either Yahoo or Webcrawler, type in the word job or employment. You will find a vast array of information at your finger tips. Yahoo has seventy-one categories related to jobs and over forty-five hundred listings; Webcrawler offers twenty-seven thousand listings related to jobs.

CHOOSING A CAREER

Choosing a career may be the most important decision you will ever make. An estimated ten thousand days of your lifetime are at stake—that's about how much time the average person spends on the job. According to some experts, there are a minimum of forty-two thousand career options for college students to choose from. The October 27, 1997, issue of *U.S. News & World Report* describes the twenty hot job tracks for the future. Each year *U.S. News & World Report* publishes an issue on careers—a must-see resource for every college student.

Studying the following pages will not guarantee you the perfect job after graduation, but it should help improve your chances of getting it. Approximately 150 million employment interviews are conducted in the United States each year. To compete successfully for available jobs requires planning and preparation—now, rather than at the last minute.

In order to learn firsthand what corporations are looking for today when they hire a college graduate, Bill Seiler interviewed Gary Danek, an account executive at Proctor and Gamble, a Fortune 500 corporation (visit P&G's home page for career information and a variety of information pertaining to P&G—*http://www.pg.com/*). Danek and Seiler spoke for the first time in the fall of 1991, again in November 1993, and most recently on December 29, 1997. Danek has been with Proctor and Gamble for over thirty-two years and has interviewed hundreds of college students. Here are some excepts from these three discussions:

Dr. S.: What advice would you give to first- or second-year students to help them prepare for an employment interview after they have graduated?

Mr. D.: I would suggest students, besides getting good grades, should participate in as many activities as time will allow. Activities are important because they help to create much more rounded individuals and shows that they are interested in working with others. I also suggest that students try to get into some leadership positions whenever possible. Students must be able to demonstrate they have the ability to take charge of things and influence others, which I believe is critical to success. The key here is that students get involved in activities. I realize that some students must work full- or part-time, but even then, they should do more than just put time in on the job. It is through leadership roles that I believe students can demonstrate their leadership and decision-making potential.

I also highly recommend that students, whenever possible, take both oral and written communication courses because in order to succeed students must be able to communicate effectively with others.

Students need to be able to demonstrate that they can set specific goals that can be measured within a particular time frame. I emphasize that the goal should not simply be getting a college degree because I feel that should be everyone's goal who enters college. We also look at the quantity and quality of the student's experiences beyond going to classes.

Dr. S.: Mr. Danek, could you elaborate on or provide some examples of specific goals that a student might give that could be measured within a time frame?

Mr. D.: Yes. For example, a student may work for a school newspaper and be responsible for getting businesses to buy advertising space in the paper. The job might require the student to get ten ads per semester. The student sets her goal to get fifteen ads. Here the student has taken initiative and set her own goal. Naturally, anything above the ten required is going beyond the newspaper's expectation. By setting realistic goals and accomplishing them, this applicant is showing that she is motivated. She is also demonstrating that she can influence people by getting them to buy ads in the school paper. Accomplishing her goal shows us some very important behaviors that our company looks for in potential employees: goal setting, going beyond what everyone else is expected to accomplish, and an ability to influence others in order to reach her goal.

Dr. S.: What are the specific criteria or qualities you look for in those you hire?

Mr. D.: The selection criteria my company uses are based upon the same factors they use for job performance reviews. For example, initiative and follow-through, leadership, thinking and problem solving, communication, working effectively with others, creativity and innovation, and priority setting are important skills.

Dr. S.: Which of these criteria do you believe to be the most important?

Mr. D.: (with no hesitation) Communication. This is the most important because without effective communication a person would not be able to meet all the other criteria.

Dr. S.: How would you describe the typical initial interview?

Mr. D.: The first interview often takes place on campus and lasts about twenty to thirty minutes. In this interview we are mainly interested in learning if applicants have the qualities and skills necessary for success with our company.

Dr. S.: What are some of the typical questions you might ask to determine if applicants you are interviewing have the qualities and skills you are looking for?

Mr. D.: In order to determine if applicants have *initiative and follow-through qualities*, I would, for example, ask them to provide a situation where they had to overcome major obstacles in order to achieve the objective.

For leadership, I might ask applicants to discuss a time when they stepped into a situation, took charge, mustered support, and brought about results. Or I might ask applicants to tell about a time when they wanted to accomplish something significant that wouldn't have happened if it had not been for their ability to make it happen.

For *thinking and problem solving,* I ask applicants to tell about a time when they had to analyze facts quickly, define the key issues, and develop a plan that produced results. Or I might ask applicants to tell about a complex problem they had solved, and, if they had to do the activity over again, how they would do it differently.

For *communication* (selling or motivating, listening and speaking), I might ask applicants to tell about a situation where they had to be persuasive and sell their idea to someone else. Or, about a time when they had to present a proposal to a person in authority and if they were able to do this successfully.

For *working effectively with others* (teamwork), I might ask: "Can you give me an example which would show you've been able to develop and maintain productive relations with others, even though they may have different points of view?" Or I'd ask about a time when they were able to motivate others to get the desired results they wanted.

For *creativity and innovation* (improving productivity, using resources), I might ask applicants to tell about a situation in which they were able to find a new and better way of doing something significant—or to describe a time when they were able to come up with a new idea that was the key to the success of some activity or project.

Finally, for *priority setting,* I might ask applicants tell about a time when they had to balance many competing priorities and did so successfully, or about a time when they had to pick out the most important things in some activity and make sure those got done.

Dr. S.: How important is the résumé?

Mr. D.: Very important! It should be done neatly and should clearly state the applicants work experiences as well as the activities they have participated in while in school.

Dr. S.: What are some of the major reasons for rejecting an applicant?

Mr. D.: Usually it is because the applicant hasn't met any of the selection criteria, lacks organizational skills, cannot communicate effectively, or lacks self-confidence.

Dr. S.: What questions should an applicant avoid asking during the first interview?

Mr. D. An applicant should not ask about salary, how many hours will I work, how many sick days are there, is there an expense account, or how much vacation time is offered.

These questions indicate the person is not interested in working, but in what they can get from the job or how they can get out of work.

Dr. S.: What are appropriate questions to ask?

Mr. D.: What is the typical day like for a person who has this job, how do you get people to do what you want, are there opportunities for training or additional schooling, why is the company moving into this market, and so on. All of these questions indicate an interest in the company and the job.

Dr. S.: What specifically are you looking for in an applicant?

Mr. D.: A person who can juggle many balls at one time and do it well. That is, we need individuals who are able to address many issues and deal with a variety of people and do it successfully.

As you can see, there is a great deal that you can do to prepare yourself for the employment interview. Whether you are a first-year student or a graduating senior, it is important that you start preparing today for the interview.

Dr. Larry Routh, (email address: lrouth@unlinfo.unl.edu) director of career services at the University of Nebraska–Lincoln, suggests that students get as much experience in team building and working in teams as possible. Companies are no longer looking exclusively for people with supervisory skills as much as they are looking for individuals who can work with others. Dr. Routh said, "Hiring people who are team players is important to many companies that have downsized and have fewer management positions because they are much more team oriented." One company recruiter asks students the following question: "When you work as a part of a team, what unique role do you play?" One senior student answered the question by indicating that she brought the group back to task by clarifying concepts and relating the ideas to the objective. Dr. Routh suggested his strength when working on a team was his ability to brainstorm ideas. Dr. Routh's strength is quite different from the senior student's, but both are important to team success.

What is your role when working with others? Is it leading, organizing, brainstorming, or something else? You need to know what your strengths are.

Internships are also important. Dr. Routh suggests that students should get involved in internships that are related to the jobs they will seek after graduation. He says that students who can say that they have done the job or similar work will have a better chance at getting a job than those with no experience.

QUALITIES EMPLOYERS SEEK

Demographics of our nation's workplace are changing rapidly as we move into the twenty-first century. Women now make up 50 percent of the workforce, and there has been significant growth in Hispanic and Asian populations as well. In addition, people are living longer and working longer. What does this mean to you? No one knows for sure, but many of you will be facing increased competition with larger numbers of applicants for fewer jobs. Many organizations are reducing the range of jobs they offer by cutting back the number of management positions. Thus, advancement positions in many organizations are going to be fewer and much more difficult to get. In the past, college graduates who started on the ground floor of an organization were almost guaranteed that working hard would move them up the organizational ladder to higher management positions (of course, this has been less true for women). The higher management jobs are now fewer in number, and those that are available are very competitive.

The typical company employee of the 1960s and 1970s stayed with the same company for twenty, thirty, or forty years. Career changes during this period might number two or three. Today, however, a typical college graduate can expect to change jobs from five to seven times. Managers of organizations are rethinking how and whom they are going to hire. Employers consider how a potential employee might fit in the organizational culture and concentrate on hiring someone not for a specific position, but for the organization in general.

Many employers are looking for these qualities in prospective employees today:

1. You must not only have specific job skills but be able to handle rapid change and periods of job ambiguity.
2. You must have computer literacy that enables you to enter, extract, and input data in common computer systems.
3. You must have a global perspective and understand other cultures.
4. You must have interpersonal skills both to secure a position and to move up within an organization.

Almost every career requires skills such as writing, speaking, reading, listening, decision making, researching, reasoning, creativity, persuasion, leadership, interpersonal communication, and organization. In addition, a number of characteristics may be important for specific jobs: achievement, aggressiveness, ambition, dependability, discipline, honesty, initiative, motivation, people orientation, persistence, responsibility, self-confidence, sensitivity, sincerity, tenacity, and tough-mindedness. The way you acquire these skills and behaviors is, to a great extent, up to you. Without them, no matter how bright and knowledgeable you may be, landing a job will be extremely difficult, if not impossible. The most likely way to obtain these skills and behaviors is through courses, reading, internships, part-time or full-time employment, extracurricular activities, and participation in communication functions. Acquiring most of them requires training and practice under a qualified instructor.

Knowing what an employer is looking for in a potential employee can help an applicant prepare for an interview. Most employers that we have talked with emphasize the ability to communicate. Can the applicants speak clearly? Can they articulate what kind of person they believe themselves to be? In what kinds of work situations do they perform well? What are their strengths and weaknesses? Employers want to know about the personal qualities of the individual, so they ask questions to draw him or her out and reveal whether the applicant has a sense of himself or herself. They look for an ability to verbalize an idea in clear, simple, understandable language.

They also look for the ability to listen attentively and then to be able to respond to an idea or thought that has been presented to them.

They also look for creativity. Is the applicant spontaneous? Some recruiters will ask "off the wall" questions just to see if this "throws" an applicant. How does an applicant respond in these tough situations? Can the applicant be creative with his or her answers? This is very important to most employers, because in business situations with customers, employees often have to respond to sudden changes and unfamiliar problems. Employers need to know whether an applicant can handle such situations.

What employers look for most are personal qualities—assertiveness, self-motivation, drive, ambition, and a competitive instinct. Applicants should be high achievers and want to work hard. Employers say they can usually tell about these qualities from how the person presents himself or herself and from reviewing the activities he or she has engaged in. Much of this information can be found right on the job application and résumé.

PREPARATION FOR AN INTERVIEW

Preparation for a job interview takes planning and some thought about what will be expected of you as an applicant. Initial job interviews average only twenty to thirty minutes in length—a short time in comparison to the time you've spent earning a college degree. Yet, these are probably the most important minutes you will spend in determining your job future. You would be surprised to learn how many applicants fail to plan adequately. Instead, they enter the interview saying essentially, "Here I am. Now what?" This gives the impression that they are indifferent—an impression that is seldom dispelled in the course of the interview. Ensuring that an impression of indifference isn't left with the employer is up to you. Make sure that you are prepared and that you present a positive picture of yourself.

Writing a Résumé

A **résumé** (sometimes referred to as a vita) is a written document that briefly and accurately describes an individual's personal, educational, and professional qualifications and experiences. A well-written résumé increases a person's chances of making a good impression. A poorly written résumé can seriously jeopardize a person's chances, even though he or she may be well qualified. The résumé should clearly detail the experiences the applicant has had and demonstrate that he or she is an individual who

THE WIZARD OF ID   Brant parker and Johnny hart

Résumés reflect who you are and your qualifications for the job. Employers want to know a person's qualifications and the résumé, if done concisely and accurately, is an invaluable tool for creating a favorable impression.

By permission of Johnny Hart and Creators Syndicate, Inc.

takes action. For example, an assertive person might say, "I can do these things" and "I decided on this course of action," whereas a more passive person might say, "These are the experiences I have had." Employers are looking for people who demonstrate that they can do things and get them done.

Many companies are now requesting that résumés be written so they can be scanned and placed into a computer database. This means that résumés must include key words that describe your competencies and skills. The employer is then able quickly and efficiently to search thousands of résumés for certain key words that describe and narrow down a long list of potentially qualified applicants for a specific job. So that a résumé can be scanned, it must be typed neatly on high-quality white bond paper. You cannot use boldface type, underlining, or bullets if a résumé is to be scanned. See some of the following Internet sites for additional help for preparing an electronic résumé: *http://www.dbm.com/jobguide/eresume.html* (UNL's Career Service Center), *http://www.resumix.com/resume_tips.html* (preparing the ideal scannable resume), *http://www.occ.com/occ/JLK/HowTo-EResume.html* (Joyce Lain Kennedy, "How to Write an Electronic Resume"). Many helpful books are available on this subject at your library, as well: Joyce Kennedy and Thomas Morrow, *Electronic Résumé Revolution: Creating a Winning Résumé for the New World of Job Seeking,* second edition (New York: Wiley, 1995), or Peter D. Weddle, *Electronic Résumés for the New Job Market* (Manassas Park, Va.: Impact Publications, 1995). Some applicants have their résumés reproduced at a local print shop or create it on a word processor to obtain a professional look.

There are two kinds of résumés: the standard data sheet used by most placement and employment services (see Figure A.2) and the self-prepared or personal résumé. The personal résumé may highlight work experience (see Figure A.3) or skills (see Figure A.4 on page 454). In addition, many companies also require applicants to complete an application form, which requests personal data (name, address, phone number, social security number, citizenship, and may ask if you have ever been convicted of a felony), job interests (position desired, data available, and salary desired), educational training (high school, college, or graduate school), references (name, occupation, phone number, and address), employment history (name, address, dates of employment, salary, position held, and reason for leaving), and possibly voluntary information (sex, race, or ethnic identification; military service record, if you are a veteran or disabled veteran; whether you have a disability).

A résumé is an extremely powerful form of communication. Because it represents an applicant, it must be accurate, complete, and neat. The contents and layouts of résumés vary as widely as the number of individuals who apply for jobs. A general rule, and the safest, it *to keep it simple, limit it to one or two pages, and list items within each section beginning with the most current one.* Employers are busy and do not have time to read lengthy, involved reports.

Most résumés include the following sections: introductory information, career objective, educational training, work experiences, extracurricular activities, and references. The *introductory information* section should include the applicant's name, address, and phone number. As an applicant, you are

Figure A.2 Standard Data Sheet

This figure illustrates a standard data sheet form that is used by many career placement centers. The form itself may vary, but the information requested is usually the same.

Personal Data Form

Name _____

           Last   First   Middle   Social Security Number

Present Mailing Address _____

           Street / Box City   State   Zip   (Area Code) Phone Number

Permanent Address _____

           Street / Box City   State   Zip   (Area Code) Phone Number

Career Objective_____

	University	Major	Degree	Date
Education				

Areas of Concentration and/or Certification _____

_____

Percent of College Expenses Earned by: Working _____ Scholarships _____ Other _____

                  (Specify)

Citizen _____ Non-Citizen _____ Type of Visa _____

	Position (Include Student Teaching Experience if Applicable) Acquired Skills Dates Employer/Organization
Experience	

Location Preferences: Flexible _____ Restricted _____ Location _____

Activities, Honors, and Other Information:

I hereby authorize the CPPC to release this data sheet and related information including references, to any and all prospective employers and/or institutions of higher learning.

_____   _____

                 Signature   Date

not required to provide information that might be discriminatory. This includes your age, sex, marital status, race, religion, and other data as set forth by the Title VII Equal Employment Opportunity Act of 1972 and other affirmative action laws. The inclusion of such facts in a résumé is up to the applicant, but it is generally advised that they be omitted.

Figure A.3 Self-Prepared or Personal Résumé Emphasizing Work Experience

This figure illustrates a résumé that is used by many students. The résumé layout is fairly standard, but may vary depending on the work experiences of the individual.

Jo Ann Doe
712 Garfield Street, Apt.2-A
Lincoln, Nebraska 68508
402/484-9797

OBJECTIVE

An administrative assistant position in a federal, state, or city government agency where I can utilize my public relations skills.

EXPERIENCE

Assistant Campaign Manager: Senator Jack Kay, Lincoln, Nebraska (July 1992–November 1994).

Responsible for directing and coordinating all public activities.

Arranged and scheduled personal appearances, debates, and media releases.

Purchased, designed, and supervised the development of campaign materials.

Recruited, trained, and supervised community volunteer groups.

Supervised a staff of 16 community volunteers.

Staff Assistant as an Intern: United Volunteer Agency, Lincoln, Nebraska (December 1991–June 1992).

Responsible for communicating the scope of Agency programs to Lincoln area businesses and community groups.

Prepared Agency filmstrips, brochures, and news releases.

Conducted public relations information sessions.

Legislative Assistant: Nebraska Legislative Session, Lincoln, Nebraska (June 1990–December 1991).

Responsible for the collection, compilation, and release of information briefs and legislative action profiles to public news media.

Typed and edited legislative bills.

EDUCATION

The University of Nebraska, Lincoln, Nebraska (1990–1994)
Bachelor of Arts Degree. Speech Communication and Journalism.
Grade Point Average: 3.75/4.00.

EDUCATIONAL HIGHLIGHTS

Outstanding Senior Award, Creative Writing Award. Speech Club Secretary, Phi Delta Kappa Vice-President.

Related Course Work

Public Relations and Publicity	Survey of Mass Media
Social Political	CommunicationInterviewing
Public Speaking	Advertising Principles
Federal Grant Development	Public Opinion

Available: Immediately

References: Upon request

Figure A.4 Self-Prepared or Personal Résumé Emphasizing Skills

This figure illustrates a résumé that emphasizes a person's skills. The résumé layout is fairly standard, but may vary depending upon the work experiences and skills of the individual.

Adapted from *Introducing Résumé Expert Computer Software for Writing Your Résumé*, Kansas City, Mo.: Business Technology, 1990, 31.

Robert L. Smith
1525 East Center Street
Los Angeles, California 90008
213/674-9797

OBJECTIVE	To help a retail company provide high customer satisfaction while managing merchandise efficiently in an entry level management position.
SKILLS	• Resolved customer problems in retail merchandising • Organized product floor for customer convenience • Experienced in dealing with wholesalers • Organized and maintained inventories • College courses in management, personnel, finance, statistics, and marketing
EDUCATION	University of Southern California, Los Angeles, California Bachelor of Science Degree Business, May 1991, Management
HONORS	Academic Scholarships, Delta Mu Delta (Business Honorary)
ACTIVITIES and MEMBERSHIPS	President of Delta Mu Delta; Student Senator; Youth Leader of 30 member church youth group.
EXPERIENCE **February 89–Present**	B. C. PRINTING, Los Angeles *Graphic Arts–Delivery Person* • Mastered all aspects of pre-press operations • Effectively dealt with and resolved conflicts • Oversaw various camera procedures including working with numerous types of film and preparing press plates
January 88–89	QUALITY PRESS, INC., Los Angeles *Internship Graphic Arts–Delivery Person* • Demonstrated ability to serve and communicate with customers in a diverse office supply operation • Organized and maintained product floor and inventory
Additional **Information**	Paid 100% of college expenses Worked to support wife and child while attending college Computer training includes Basic, Cobol, Assembler, and Pascal
Available	Immediately
References	Available on request

The employment interview is a key communication event for most people for which the applicant should be prepared to discuss goals and skills and be able to clearly answer questions pertaining to why he or she will be right for the job.

Many placement-service directors recommend that a brief *career objective* be stated on the résumé immediately following the introductory information. The objective should be as specific as possible. For example:

My long-term objective is to become a public relations director in either a major corporation or agency. My immediate goal is to obtain experience in sales, advertising, or marketing related to that long-term objective.

Such a statement can help a potential employer understand the applicant's goals and to assess whether those goals relate to a particular job opening or company.

In the *educational training* section of the résumé, the applicant should list colleges and universities attended, degrees conferred, dates of degrees, majors, minors, and special major subjects. Scholarships should be listed, and some statement about grade achievement may be included, although it is not required.

The *work experience* section should include all paid and unpaid jobs held, the dates they were held, and their locations. If the applicant has held numerous part-time jobs, only a few of the most important, most recent, and most relevant jobs should be listed. Other job experience can always be discussed at the interview, if it is appropriate to do so.

In the *extracurricular activities,* section the applicant should list all offices held, all social and professional organizations that he or she was involved in, and any athletic participation. This section demonstrates the applicant's outside interests, well-roundedness, and social, leadership, and organizational skills. Such information is less important for experienced or older applicants who have demonstrated similar skills in other areas.

The *reference* section should simply state that the applicant will provide references upon request. In preparation, you might make a list of persons who are familiar with your work experience and professors in your major field or with whom you have taken several courses. Even though you may not be planning to apply for a job now, it is wise to get to know your pro-

Make a written list of at least three people who could write a letter of recommendation for you. Do not include relatives or friends. After each name on your list, answer the following questions:

1. Why do you believe this person would be an appropriate reference for you?
2. What does this person know about you, your competencies, and your ability to succeed?

Share your completed list of references and information with your teacher, a career councilor, or a person who could advise you as to the appropriateness of your choices.

fessors and to make sure that they get to know you. Find an appropriate time (office hours, perhaps) and reason (discussion of a paper or an assignment) to visit with your professors so they become acquainted with you. Most professors enjoy meeting with their students. Use common sense, and don't overstay your visits. Professors will find it easier to write a letter of recommendation for you, and the letter will be more personal and believable if they know who you are.

Never put a person's name on a reference list unless you have his or her permission to do so. When asking individuals to write references for you, be prepared to hand them a copy of your résumé and to tell them what kind of job you are seeking. Contacting people to write letters of recommendation should be done as professionally and efficiently as possible. Remember that you are requesting someone to take time to help you. Since most people enjoy helping others, you should never be afraid to ask for a reference.

After you write your résumé, proofread it carefully for errors and omissions. Then ask a counselor in the career and placement office or a professor to suggest improvements. If you follow these simple steps, your completed résumé should be acceptable.

Searching the Job Market

Getting a job requires motivation, energy, hard work, and preparation. Even an applicant with superb qualifications faces tremendous competition for the best positions. According to placement service records, the average applicant spends only about three to ten hours a week searching for employment, but the person who is highly motivated will treat the search as if it was a job itself. The more time a person spends searching, the sooner and more likely he or she will be hired.

Newspaper want ads, professional magazines, placement services, former teachers, and people working in jobs you are interested in can all be good sources of job leads. However, the most productive approach to locating jobs is networking. **Networking** is the systematic contacting of people who can provide information about available jobs or who can offer jobs. Relatives, friends, classmates, colleagues, and people at social and professional gatherings are all potential sources of information. If someone does not know of

Making Connections Thinking About Your Career

Twenty years from now, the typical American worker will have changed jobs four times and careers twice and will be employed in an occupation that does not exist today.

Jeffrey Hallet, Worklife Visions, 1990

1. What does this quotation tell you about your employment search?
2. How does the quotation make you feel? How can you be prepared to face possible career transitions in the future?

any job openings himself or herself, ask if he or she knows of anyone who might. Then contact the person. In this way, your network expands from one person to another, and you gain information from each new contact. The more people you know, the better your chances of being interviewed and the greater your opportunity for employment.

Researching the Company

Before arriving for an interview, you should know the full name of the company; background information on the company's history; where its head-quarters, plants, offices, or stores are located; what its products or services are; and what its economic growth has been and how its future prospects look. Such knowledge demonstrates your initiative and interest to the interviewer and can serve as a springboard for discussion (see Table A.1). This also shows you have an interest in the company, rather than giving the impression you're "settling" for whatever job you can find.

An applicant can find out about almost any business or professional organization by writing for its annual report or for recruiting materials and by looking through some of the following publications. Such resources are available in libraries and placement offices.

Dun and Bradstreet's Reference Book contains a virtually complete listing of all types of business organizations, arranged geographically and coded as to product or service. Included is an evaluation of each firm's reliability.

MacRea's Blue Book consists of four volumes listing the names and addresses of companies classified by product and trade name. Included in the listing are the locations of branches and the capital rating of the company.

Moody's manuals are individual volumes on banking and finance, manufacturing (domestic and foreign), public utilities, and transportation.

Standard and Poor's Corporation Records lists thousands of leading business firms, their products, number of employees, and names and positions of key employees.

Thomas' Register of American Manufacturers, consisting of seven volumes plus an index, contains detailed information on leading manufacturing or-

Table A.1 Key Facts to Know About an Organization

Statistics	Position of company in its industry or field
	Location of corporate headquarters and other facilities
	Size of organization
Financial stability	Bond ratings
	Growth in sales and profits
	View of stock analysis
Growth plans	New plants, stores, offices
Research and development, product development, and manufacturing	Investments for the future
	Emerging products and services
	Uses of new technologies
	Chief Competitors
Marketing and distribution methods	In-house sales force
	Advertising methods
	Service centers
	Computerized communication with customers
Employee benefits	Wealth-building benefit plans
	Tuition reimbursement
	Pension plan
Quality of work factors	Continuing training
	Relocation policies
	Health programs
	Child care
	Promotion from within
	Performance reviews
	Product discounts

Adapted from "Researching an Organization," pamphlet printed by Placement Service, University of Nebraska, Lincoln, Nebraska, 1993

ganizations throughout the country. Names and addresses of companies are listed under product headings and are classified by state and city.

Careers in Business lists companies interested in hiring business and liberal arts graduates. Included in the listings are the name of the person to contact, type of business, size, and the majors from which they normally hire.

There are also specialized directories:

Standard Directory of Advertising Agencies lists four thousand leading advertising agencies in the United States with key executives, major accounts, and geographical index.

Polks Bank Directory lists names, addresses, and directors of banks.

American Register of Importers and Exporters lists thirty thousand importers and exporters classified by product, with names of executives.

Management Consulting lists twenty-six hundred consulting firms arranged by type and location, with principals' and officers' names.

Handbook of Independent Marketing/Advertising Services lists two hundred consulting firms in marketing, advertising, packaging, media, and new products fields.

PR Blue Book lists public relations consulting firms with owners' names plus five thousand public relations directors of major organizations.

1. Select a major private or public organization that you would consider working for.
2. Using the Internet, find its Web site and write a brief one-page report about the company. Include the types of information listed in Table A.1.

If you do not have access to the Internet, use your library or career and placement office to locate the information about the organization.

Developing Questions to Ask the Interviewer

In preparation for your meeting, think about possible questions to ask the interviewer. Sometimes an interviewer may choose to say little or to stop talking altogether, in which case it becomes your responsibility to carry the conversation by asking questions and continuing to emphasize your qualifications for the job. Whether or not the interviewer stops talking, you should have a list of questions to ask. This does not mean coming to the interview with a written list of questions, but it does mean coming prepared to ask questions such as these: What are the duties and responsibilities of the job? Does the company provide training programs? How much traveling is involved in the job? What's the next step up from the starting position? Would I be able to continue my education?

How to Dress for an Interview

Your primary goal in dressing for an interview is to feel great about the way you look while projecting an image that matches the requirements of the job and the company.

Go for perfection. Wear professionally pressed clothing in natural fabrics. Spend even more than you can afford on your interview clothes. But, don't make a fashion statement. Conservative is the password. The interview is usually not the time to make a personal statement of nonconformity or disagreement with society's concept of professional image.

THE INTERVIEW

Much of the responsibility for a successful interview rests with the interviewer, but this doesn't mean that you can merely relax and let things happen. On the contrary, research suggests that most interviewers develop a strong opinion about a job applicant in the first thirty seconds. If you do poorly at the opening, your chances of getting the job are slim, no matter how brilliantly you handle the rest of the interview. It may seem unfair or superficial, but people do judge others on the basis of first impressions, and such impressions can be long-lasting. By all means be on time for the interview.

Frequently Asked Questions

One expert states that most applicants make two devastating mistakes when they are being questioned. First, they fail to listen to the question, and they answer a question that was not asked or give superfluous information. Second, they attempt to answer questions with virtually no preparation. Lack of preparation will reduce the chances of success for even skillful communicators. You should always take a moment to think about your answer before you respond to each question unless it is something that you have already thought through.

Here are some of the most common questions interviewers ask and some possible responses to them.

1. *"What can you tell me about yourself?"* This is not an invitation to give your life history. The interviewer is looking for clues about your character, qualifications, ambitions, and motivations. The following is a good example of a positive response. "In high school I was involved in competitive sports and I always tried to improve in each sport I participated in. As a college student, I worked in a clothing store part-time and found that I could sell things easily. The sale was important, but for me, it was even more important to make sure that the customer was satisfied. It wasn't long before customers came back to the store and specifically asked for me to help them. I'm very competitive and it means a lot to me to be the best."

2. *"Why do you want to work for us?"* This is an obvious question and, if you have done research on the company, you should be able to give a good reason. Organize your reasons into several short sentences that clearly spell out your interest. "You are a leader in the field of electronics. Your company is a Fortune 500 company. Your management is very progressive."

3. *"Why should I hire you?"* Once again, you should not be long-winded, but you should provide a summary of your qualifications. Be positive, and show that you are capable of doing the job. "Based on the internships that I have participated in and the related part-time experiences I have had, I can do the job."

4. *"How do you feel about your progress to date?"* Never apologize for what you have done. "I think I did well in school. In fact, in a number of courses I received the highest exam scores in the class." "As an intern for the X Company, I received some of the highest evaluations that had been given in years." "Considering that I played on the university's volleyball team and worked part-time, I think you'll agree that I accomplished quite a bit during my four years in school."

5. *"What would you like to be doing five years from now?"* Know what you can realistically accomplish. You can find out by talking to others about what they accomplished in their first five years with a particular company. "I hope to be the best I can be at my job, and because many in this line of work are promoted to area manager, I am planning on that also."

6. *"What is your greatest weakness?"* You cannot avoid this question by saying that you do not have any; everyone has weaknesses. The best approach is to admit your weakness, but show that you are working on it and have a plan to overcome it. If possible, cite a weakness that will work to the company's advantage. "I'm not very good at detail work, but I have been working on it and I've improved dramatically over the past several years." "I'm such a perfectionist that I won't stop until a report is written just right."

7. *"What is your greatest strength?"* This is a real opportunity to "toot your own horn." Do not brag or get too egotistical, but let the employer know that you believe in yourself and that you know your strengths. "I feel that my strongest asset is my ability to stick to things to get them done. I feel a real sense of accomplishment when I finish a job and it turns out just as I'd planned. I've set some high goals for myself. For example, I want to graduate with highest distinction. And even though I had a slow start in my freshman year, I made up for it by doing an honor's thesis."

8. *"What goals have you set, and how did you meet them?"* This question examines your ability to plan ahead and meet your plan with specific actions. "Last year, during a magazine drive to raise money for our band trip, I set my goal at raising 20 percent more than I had the year before. I knew the drive was going to begin in September, so I started contacting people in August. I asked each of my customers from last year to give me the name of one or two new people who might also buy a magazine. I not only met my goal, but I also was the top salesperson on the drive."

If an interviewer was to ask you any of these eight frequently asked questions, do you know how you would answer them? The key is to understand why a question is being asked. Remember the purpose of the employment interview is to hire the best-qualified person for the job. The more often you can demonstrate through your responses to questions that you are the best qualified, the more likely you will be to get the job offer.

No matter what question you are asked, answer it honestly and succinctly. Most interviewers are looking for positive statements, well-expressed ideas, persuasiveness, and clear thinking under pressure.

If you are asked a question that violates the affirmative action laws, you can decline to answer. You might say, "I'm sorry, but I don't find that question relevant to the position being offered and it is against affirmative action laws to ask it." You may simply ask the interviewer why he or she is asking you that question. Make sure that you are tactful, but be firm in letting the interviewer know that he or she is doing something illegal.

Other Considerations

As a job applicant, you are expected to show good judgment and common sense about appearance, assertiveness, being on time, and being at the right place. Always maintain eye contact with the interviewer. Show that you are confident by looking straight at the speaker. Eye contact may not get you the job, but lack of eye contact can reduce your chances dramatically.

Most interviewers greet the applicant with a handshake. Make sure that your clasp is firm. Being jittery about the interview can result in cold, clammy hands, which create a negative impression. Therefore, try to make sure your hands are warm and dry. If not possible, the firm handshake will show more confidence.

When the interviewer asks you to sit down, if you have a choice, take the chair beside the desk rather than the one in front. This helps to eliminate any barriers between you and the interviewer and also makes you a little more equal, for which the interviewer will unconsciously respect you.

Before leaving, try to find out exactly what action will follow the interview and when it will happen. Shake hands as you say goodbye, and thank the interviewer for spending time with you. If you plan ahead and follow these simple suggestions, you should be able to avoid any serious problems.

FACTORS LEADING TO REJECTION

Rejection is difficult for all of us to accept, but you should never give up. Being rejected by employers eight or nine times before receiving a job offer is not unusual in the present job market.

Employers from numerous companies were asked, "What negative factors most often lead to the rejection of an applicant?" Here are their responses in order of frequency:

1. Negative personality or poor impression—more specifically, lack of motivation, ambition, maturity, aggressiveness, or enthusiasm
2. Inability to communicate; poor communication skills
3. Lack of competence; inadequate training
4. Low grades; poor grades in major field
5. Lack of specific goals
6. Unrealistic expectations
7. Lack of interest in type of work
8. Unwillingness to travel or relocate
9. Poor preparation for the interview
10. Lack of experience.

You must realize that rejection or not receiving a job offer has a lot to do with the number of people seeking jobs and the number of jobs available. You can of course enhance your chances of getting job offers by being prepared and presenting yourself in a positive and energetic way.

FACTORS LEADING TO JOB OFFERS

An applicant that is well-rounded and has good grades, some relevant work experience, a variety of extracurricular activities, an all-around pleasant personality, and effective written and oral communication skills is more likely to get job offers than those who do not possess these qualities, according to Jason Meyers of *Collegiate Employment Institute Newsletter*. Meyers says, "Sounds too good to be true? Perhaps it is, but a candidate who strives to attain these qualities and who comes across as a hard-working, mature individual should have a promising career outlook."

A research study, cited by Meyers in his article, asked recruiters to describe what they believed to be the qualities of a well-rounded individual. They listed maturity, ability to be part of a team, good work ethic, good decision-making skills, superior work habits, and good judgment. Another study cited by Meyers found that the most popular characteristics that recruiters sought in job applicants fit two categories: (1) quantifiable characteristics, such as grade-point average, education, and work experience, and (2) interpersonal characteristics, such as communication skills, personality, and career and management skills. The study suggests that a balance of the quantifiable characteristics and interpersonal characteristics is what makes an ideal job candidate.

It seems that those who are well-prepared, have effective communication skills, are mature, motivated, hard-working, team players, and can make good decisions will always be in demand. You must ask yourself how you match up to these qualities now and try to improve in those areas in which you are not as strong. You must also be able to demonstrate that you actually possess these qualities through the actions you have taken.

SUMMARY

Choosing a career is one of the most important decisions a person can make, and a successful job interview is a crucial step in achieving that end. Planning and preparation are critical to a successful employment interview. Applicants must know their strengths and weaknesses and be able to communicate effectively with the interviewer. Getting a job requires motivation, energy, hard work, and research, plus knowing where to look and whom to contact in order to obtain the necessary information.

An effective résumé (a written document that briefly describes a person's personal, educational, and professional qualifications and experiences) can pave the way for a productive interview. In judging a résumé, employers look for thoughtfulness, creativity, accuracy, and neatness. The two most common kinds of résumés are the standard data sheet used by most placement and employment services and the self-prepared résumé. Both formats summarize basic information about the applicant's career objective, educational training, work experience, extracurricular activities, and references.

Searching the job market requires motivation, energy, hard work, and preparation. Sources for job openings include newspaper want ads, professional magazines, placement services, former teachers, and friends or others who work in companies that have jobs that interest you. *Networking* is the systematic contacting of people who can provide information about available jobs or who can offer jobs. The more people you know, the better your chances of employment.

Before an interview, an applicant should find out about a company's background, location, products or services, growth, and prospects for the future. Using such information, the applicant can prepare possible questions to ask the interviewer.

Applicants must create a strong positive impression from the moment they meet the interviewer. They should prepare responses to commonly asked questions, show confidence, maintain eye contact with the interviewer, give a firm handshake, and sit, if given a choice, in the chair at the side of the desk or table rather than in front.

Job applicants who prepare carefully and present themselves well can avoid some of the most common reasons for rejection.

From *Communication: Making Connections: Making Connections, Fourth Edition*, by William J. Seiler and Milissa L. Beall, copyright © 1999 by Allyn & Bacon, pgs. 442–463.

GROUPS

Table Appendix B.1 Individual versus Group Decision Making

Tasks are best left to individuals when	*Tasks are best left to individuals when*
1. the decision is simple and its rationale is apparent to all members;	1. the decision is complex and needs an innovative, creative solution;
2. a single individual clearly has the expertise to make the decision, and that individual is trusted by the group;	2. the resources of the entire group are needed;
3. time pressures are great and it is difficult to get group members together;	3. there is adequate time for group members to meet;
4. implementing a decision does not necessitate the committed action of all group members	4. full commitment of all group member is needed to get the job done;
5. little risk is involved;	5. a good solution is risky;
6. there is substantial agreement within the group.	6. the possibility for disagreement or misunderstanding exists unless members talk about the problem.

From *Thinking Through Communication: An Introduction to the Study of Human Communication, Second Edition,* by Sarah Trenholm, Copyright © 1999, 1995 by Allyn & Bacon, pg. 195.

Table Appendix B.2 Factors Related to Group Productivity

Factors That Increase Group Productivity
- Members have a variety of different skills and knowledge.
- Everyone is committed to group goals.• There is individual accountability.
- All members have an opportunity to contribute.
- Members have critical skills.
- There is an atmosphere of positive interdependence.

Factors That Decrease Group Productivilty
- The group is too large to adequately use all members' resources.
- Members feel their individual efforts don't make a difference.
- There is a perception that others are taking a free ride.
- Members lack commitment to the group.
- There is too great a desire for unanimity.
- Members have hidden agendas or conflicting goals.

From *Thinking Through Communication: An Introduction to the Study of Human Communication, Second Edition,* by Sarah Trenholm, Copyright © 1999, 1995 by Allyn & Bacon, pg. 196.

Table Appendix B.3 Task and Maintenance Roles

Task Roles

Role	Description
Initiator Contributor	Suggests new ideas to group or offers new way of regarding group problem
Information Seeker	Asks for clarification of suggestions and for information and facts pertinent to problem
Opinion Seeker	Asks for clarification of values associated with group problem or with decision suggestions
Information Giver	Offers facts or generalizations or relates experiences relevant to group problem
Opinion Giver	States beliefs or opinions pertinent to group problem or to decision suggestions
Elaborator	Thinks of examples, offers rationales, or works out details of previous suggestions
Coordinator	Pulls together ideas and suggestions and coordinates work of various subgroups
Orienter	Summarizes what has occurred or asks questions about the path the group will take
Evaluator-Critic	Develops standards for group functioning and compares group performance to standards
Energizer	Prods group to action and stimulates greater levels of group activity
Procedural Technician	Expedites group movement by taking on routine task
Recorder	Writes down suggestions, records decisions, and takes minutes

Maintenance Roles

Role	Description
Encourager	Accepts and praises others' contributions
Harmonizer	Relieves tension and mediates disagreements
Compromiser	Seeks to find solution for conflict that involves own ideas
Gatekeeper-Expediter	Keeps communication channels open and facilitates others participation
Standard Setter	Expresses maintenance standards or applies standards to group process
Group Observer	Observes group process and offers feedback about maintenance procedures
Follower	Accepts ideas of group and serves as audience

Adapted from "Functional Roles of Group Members," by Kenneth Benne and Paul Sheats, 1948, *Journal of Social Issues, 4*, pp. 41–49.

Table Appendix B.4 Negative Roles

Role	Description
Dominator	Refuses to allow others to express their opinions and dominates discussion
Blocker	Prolongs or stops decision making by footdragging and nitpicking
SelfConfessor	Distracts group by disclosing personal problems and by using group for personal therapy
Help Seeker	Constantly expresses own inadequacy and asks group for sympath and compliments
Recognition Seeker	Spends time boasting about own accomplishments in order to be center of attention
Special-Interest Pleader	Manipulates group in interests of some other group; has hidden agenda
Playboy or Playgirl	Fails to take group seriously; spends time playing around and mocks serious behavior
Joker or Clown	Uses humor and horseplay to divert group from task

Reprinted by permission from pages 116–117 of *Communication in Small Group Discussions: A Case Study Approach* by lohn F. Cragan and David W. Wright; Copyright © 1980 by West Publishing Company. Al1 rights reserved.

Table Appendix B.5 Steps in the Standard Agenda

STEP 1   Problem Identification
Group members clarify the problem, often by specifying the difference between a present state of affairs and a desired state of affairs. Problems should be concrete, clear, and solvable.

STEP 2   Problem Analysis
Group members collect information about the problem, identifying factors that are causing the problem and factors that may help in solving the problem.

STEP 3   Criteria Selection
Group members decide on the characteristics of a valid solution prior to discussing specific solutions.

STEP 4   Solution Generation
Group members generate as many solution alternatives as possible.

STEP 5   Solution Evaluation and Seiection
Group members use previously selected criteria to evaluate each solution. The solution hat best meets evaluation criteria is chosen.

STEP 6   Solution Implementation
Group members follow through by putting the solution into effect.

From *Thinking Through Communication: An Introduction to the Study of Human Communication, Second Edition,* by Sarah Trenholm, Copyright © 1999, 1995 by Allyn & Bacon, pg. 214.

Preparing Visual Aids for Presentations

no matter what career path you pursue after you graduate from college, chances are that sooner or later you will be asked to give a work-related presentation in front of an audience. Typically, the oral reports and public relations speeches described in the section "Public Speaking in the Workplace" in Chapter 18 rely more heavily upon visual support than do traditional speeches. This Appendix is designed to help you prepare the materials you need for such presentations. It supplements the information on Visual Aids in Chapter 14, introducing more specific planning and design techniques for creating effective graphics.

We will begin with a discussion of storyboarding, a visual planning technique used widely in advertising and other industries. Storyboarding encourages speaking to treat visual aids as an integral part of a presentation rather than as an afterthought. Next we will introduce you to basic principles of layout and design that will help you produce attractive visuals in any medium, touching upon considerations such as choosing typefaces, point sizes and colors. Finally, we will provide a brief introduction to using graphic software, including the popular PowerPoint™ program. For users who can apply basic design principles, these programs make it easy to produce polished, professional-looking presentations for a wide variety of audiences and settings.

STORYBOARDING

Storyboarding is a planning technique that combines words and pictures to create an outline. Each page in the storyboard focuses on the support for a single point, described in sentences, phrases, or key words, and then illustrated with rough sketches of visuals. The verbal support might include facts, statistics, anecdotes, quotes, references to sources, or transition statements to move your presentation from one point to the next.

Experienced public speakers may use storyboards as a substitute for a detailed formal outline when they are preparing a presentation. But until you have logged in hours of successful public presentations, you should probably consider storyboarding as a way to coordinate your visual ideas with your words. Either begin with a storyboard and then construct a more polished outline, or begin with a preparation outline and then transform it into a storyboard.

To get a sense of how storyboarding might work for you, imagine that you have been asked by your supervisor to prepare a 20-minute public relations presentation for a town planning committee on a proposed addition to your company's building. There was some resistance when the company announced its plans, so you know you must make your presentation persuasive. First, consider your audience and fine tune your persuasive objective. Then you can make a list of the main points you'd like to cover, knowing that each one will become a page of your storyboard:

1. Over the years, Nortco has established strong bonds with the community;
2. Nortco's expansion will increase economic benefits to the community;
3. Nortco's addition has been carefully planned and thoughtfully designed to create minimal disturbance during the construction phase and to beautify and enhance the surrounding neighborhood.

Storyboard #1—
Town Planning Presentation

Point: Over the years, Nortco has established strong bonds with the community.

Support:

- Employs 150 local workers with combined annual wages of 3,750,000.
- Sponsors local organizations with donations totalling more than $500K annually.
- Scholarships totalling more than $300K annually.
- Summer music series, winter festival, Run-for-Fun Fest.
- Key player in the fight against airport development.

Transition: Now let's see how we plan to sustain and increase this community commitment with the planned expansion.

OR

Storyboard #2—
Town Planning Presentation

Point: Nortco's expansion will increase economic benefits to the community.

Support:

- New facility will extend 50 more skilled job opportunities to the community.
- The increase in workers will mean growth in revenues for local retailers.
- The expansion will also increase tax revenues for the town.
- Nortco is planning a PR campaign in conjunction with the expansion that will boost the town's images and attract more businesses.

Transition: By now you're probably wondering what the new facility will look like.

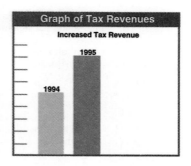

Figures C1
Storyboards for a Persuasive Presentation

Once you have your main points, you can begin creating your storyboards. Divide a piece of paper into two columns and label it "Storyboard #1." In the left column, write the main idea, then notes about supporting points, as shown in Figure C1.

Next, as shown in Figure C1, sketch the visuals you plan to include in the right column. Don't worry if you are not a fabulous artist. These sketches are placeholders for the finished visual aids that you will learn to prepare later in this Appendix.

When you do your sketches, be conservative about the number of visuals you plan. Select key supporting points to illustrate with a few memorable words or images. No matter what medium you plan to use, you should give your audience enough time to absorb what you place in front of their eyes and to listen carefully to your verbal information before they must shift their attention to another image.

Converting a simple main point and support outline like the ones in our sample storyboards into a more formal outline is a relatively simple task. Figure C2 shows an outline mode from the storyboard for the second main point listed above.

DESIGNING YOUR VISUAL AIDS

After you do your storyboard and select an appropriate graphic medium for your audience, topic, and setting, you can begin designing your visual

Figure C2 Translating a Storyboard into a Formal Outline

Town Planning Presentation Outline

Purpose: To persuade the audience that they should support Nortco's expansion.

I. Over the years, Nortco has established strong bonds with the community.
  A. Nortco employs 150 local workers with combined annual wages $3,7500,000
  B. Nortco sponsors local organizations with donations totaling more than $500K annually
  C. Nortco's endowed scholarships total more than $300K annually :
  D. Nortco sponsors community events:
    1. music series
    2. winter festival
    3. Run-for-Fun Fest
  E. Nortco has been a key player in the fight against airport development

II. Nortco's expansion will increase economic benefits to the community.
  A. The new facility will extend 50 more skilled job opportunities to the community
    1. 15 will be managerial positions paying $30K plus
    2. 25 will be administrative paying $15K plus
    3. The remainder will be clerical and maintenance paying 12K plus
  B. The increase in workers will mean growth in revenues for local retailer!
    1. Restaurants, dry cleaners, shoe repairs, clothing and gift shops, etc., will get more robust lunch-hour and after-five trade
    2. A higher overall wage base will result in higher spending across all local retail categories
  C. The expansion will also increase tax revenues for the town
    1. Overall projections show a $50K plus increase in annual taxes over 5 years
    2. Employees will also purchase and upgrade homes, boosting the re base
  D. Nortco is planning a regional PR campaign in conjunction with the expansion that will boost the town's image and attract more business
    1. There is promised coverage from local newspapers, cable TV, and radio
    2. We are placing articles in regional business publications and planning a regional marketing/advertising campaign
    3. Governor and state officials are coming for the ribbon-cutting ceremony

aids. Even if you are paying a professional to execute graphics from your rough sketches, it is helpful to know the basic principles that govern good design so that you can specify what you want in the final product. The strategies below apply to graphic preparation in any medium. Keeping these in mind as you design will enable you to produce visual aids that are attractive, instructive, and memorable.

Keep Your Graphics Simple

Presentation graphics should be simple and uncluttered. This principle, introduced in Chapter 14, bears repeating. As you begin to work with sophisticated layout and design tools, you may be tempted to load up your graphics with fancy fonts, clip art, and outlandish colors. Resist that temptation. Such visuals can quickly become hard to read and distracting. Instead of supporting your presentation, they will actually confuse your audience and detract from your message.

Remember that your visual aids are meant to clarify and amplify, not merely decorate, your presentation. Each element in your visual aid should serve a clear and specific purpose that is appropriate to your audience, topic, and setting. A decorative background using clip art of a desert island, for example (see Figure C3), would not be appropriate for an instructional presentation on how to surf the Internet. However colorful and attention-getting it might be, the background would not relate to the subject matter, so it would do nothing to enhance your audience's understanding of cyberspace.

Include a Manageable Amount of Information

Your visual aids should enhance your message, not deliver it for you. The text on each visual should convey a sufficient amount of information to tell your audience what you think is most important, but your speech should fill in the blanks. Each visual aid should also make sense on its own. The slide in Figure C4, for example, does not provide enough information to

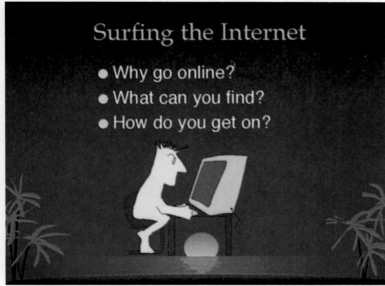

Figure C3 An Inappropriate Use of Clip Art

Figure C4 Not Enough Information

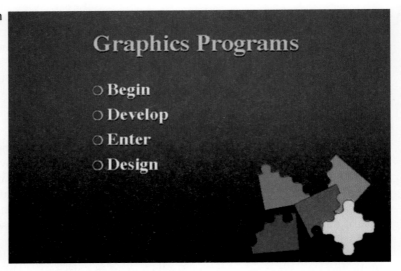

give audience members much of a handle on the topic. They might grasp that the presentation will be about how to develop graphics programs and that it will cover four steps. But it does not have enough specific information for readers to understand the nature of those steps.

In contrast, the slide in Figure C5 is overloaded with information; the key words in each step are obscured by the extra words that surround them. Slides like these create interference during a presentation. Instead of focusing on the speaker's words, audience members have to struggle to read and absorb this information, which makes them stop listening. In addition, audience members who take notes have a tendency to write down whatever appears on the screen. If there are too many words for them to jot down quickly, they tune out and concentrate on writing.

The slide in Figure C6 achieves a happy medium; each step is stated succinctly so that the key words receive proper emphasis; readers can easily fol-

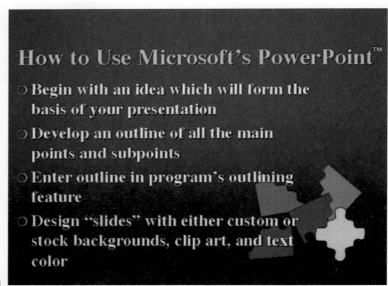

Figure C5 Too Much Information

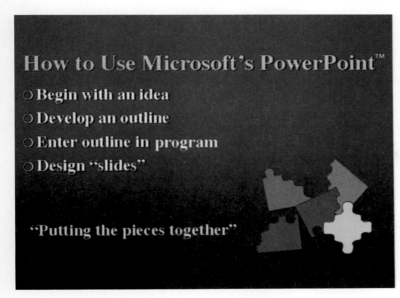

low along and listen without distraction as the speaker provides more verbal information about each step. Note-takers can use the key words as headings, and then fill in as they listen. In addition, note that the caption "putting the pieces together" explains why the puzzle art is in the slide; it serves as a visual metaphor for the PowerPoint™ design process.

Group Related Elements into Visual Units

By grouping related points, you can help your audience grasp key concepts and understand relationships as you convey information. In Figure C7, for example, it is immediately obvious that the elements on the left relate to text concerns, whereas those grouped on the right relate to visual concerns. As the text in the figure states, grouping points frees up space. This space, in turn, highlights the text blocks and also provides a resting place for the eye.

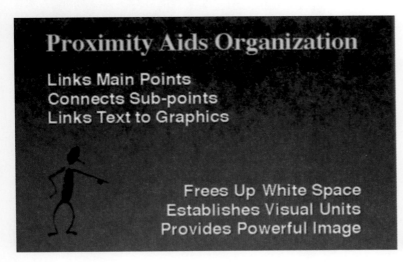

Figure C7 Use of Grouping and Alignment

The alignment you choose for your type and images also affects the open space on the page and directs the reader's gaze. Alignment can be flush left (initial letters line up at the left margin), flush right (final letters line up at the right margin), or centered. Centered alignment is often effective for titles, but cen-body text can look ragged and disorderly. As Figure C7 shows, a flush left alignment (top text grouping) or flush right alignment (bottom text grouping) makes the text look crisp and allows the eye to flow easily from point to point.

Repeat Elements to Unify Your Presentation

If you are designing a series of graphics, try to repeat a word, symbol, style, or font to convey a sense of unity in your presentation. Figure C8 shows a number of ways you can accomplish this repetition, such as choosing a different symbol to use instead of a bullet, a consistent color scheme, or consistent spacing. Repetition can be boring, so you may want to vary your visuals a bit more than the ones shown here, but keep in mind that consistency will help your audience process and remember complex information.

Vary Your Typefaces and Point Sizes Judiciously

Today's personal computers offer thousands of options for designers when it comes to choosing typefaces and varying the size of the type. It is easy to get carried away by all of the possibilities, but if you combine typefaces carelessly, you will soon discover that your choices will conflict instead of

Figure C8 Options for Designing with Repetitive Elements

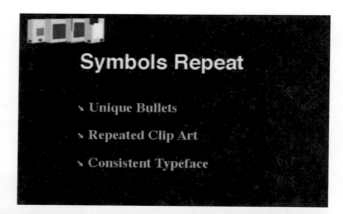

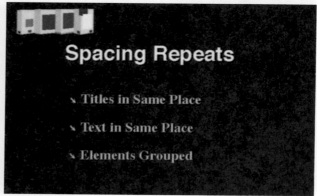

complementing one another. The strategies below should help you avoid conflict in your designs.

Choosing a Typeface

A single typeface includes a collection of all upper and lowercase letters, numbers, symbols, and punctuation which have a consistent structure and form. Each typeface has a name. It may also have variations that have an identical structure but a different form. The difference between structure and form is illustrated in Figure C9. Each of the lines in the box is a variation of the typeface Arial. The letters for each variation have the same structure. They have a vertical orientation, the transitions between their vertical and horizontal lines are smooth, and the lines that make up the letters do not vary much in thickness. The form for each variation, however, is quite different. If we consider Arial as the standard form, then Arial Black is a stronger, bolder, thicker variation. Arial Narrow is reduced on the horizontal scale and, as the name implies, it looks narrower. The differences in the form give each variation its own personality, conveying a heavier more solid feeling, or a lighter, more delicate feeling.

Designers usually divide typefaces into four different types of fonts: serif, sans serif, script, and what we will call decorative. Serif fonts are those like the one you are reading. They have little lines at the tops and bottoms of the letters (serifs) which are a remnant of the finishing strokes on letters when they were handwritten. San serif fonts do not have extra lines, and all the lines in the letters are of uniform thickness. Serif fonts are easier to read for longer passages because the serifs guide the eye from one letter to the next. Script fonts mimic handwriting, but they are far more precise and uniform. They can be very fancy and complicated. They can also be hard to read, so be cautious about using them in your visual aids. Finally, there are ornamental fonts. Decorative fonts are designed not so much to be easily read, but to convey a feeling or tone. The letters in decorative fonts may look like trains, flowers, small people, cow spots, bobby pins, strange symbols, and even playing cards. Use these fonts sparingly, for emphasis. Figure C10 shows a few examples of each font type. Notice how much easier it is to read some of them than others.

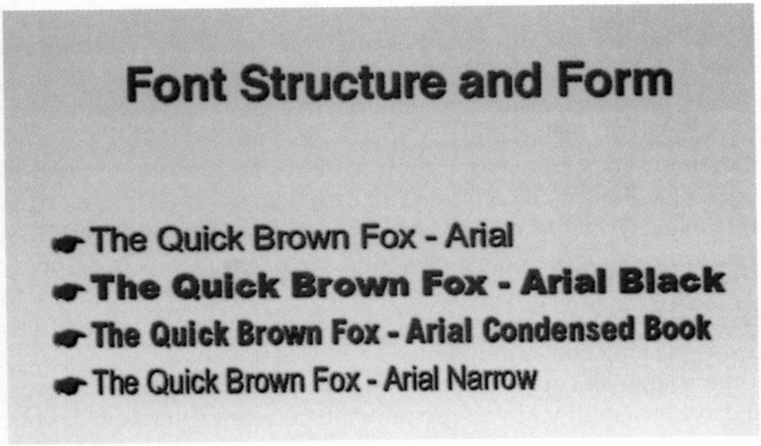

Figure C9 Variations of a Typeface

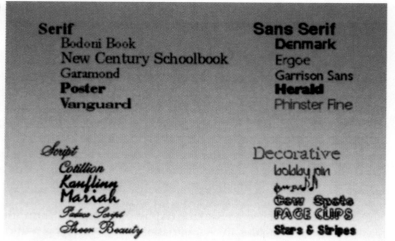

Most designers agree that you should not use more than two typefaces on a single visual aid and that they should be from two different font categories. The most common combination is a sans serif font for a title and a serif font for a subtitle or text. This choice is driven by considerations of readability and clarity. A sans serif font is clean and clear; it can convey a feeling of strength as long as there is not too much text. Serif fonts are more readable, so they are a better choice for body text or subtitles. Of course, designers do sometimes violate these guidelines to achieve special effects. There is no law that says you cannot use a serif font in a title and a sans serif font in the text. Just be sure that your audience will be able to read and understand your message.

Choosing Type Sizes

You also need to think about readability when you decide what sizes of type to use for the various elements in your graphics. Of course, all of your type must be big enough to be seen by people in the back row of your audience. How big is big enough? The people at Microsoft who designed the templates for the PowerPoint™ graphics presentation program have specified general guidelines for visual aids. They recommend 44 point type for titles, 32 point type for subtitles or text if there is no subtitle, and 28 point type if there is a subtitle. These are somewhat larger point sizes than you might have seen elsewhere, but they reason that it is better to be too big than too small. The minimum point sizes you should consider for visuals other than slides are 36 point for titles, 24 point for subtitles, and 18 point for text. For slides, you could go somewhat smaller, since projection enlarges the image. You might use 24 point for titles, 18 point for subtitles, and 14 point for text. Figure C11 shows how these points look in print.

In any medium, avoid using all upper case letters for emphasis. except in short titles. Longer stretches of text in all caps is hard to read, because our eyes are used to seeing contrasting letter sizes. When we read, we not only recognize the shapes of individual letters, but also the shapes of words. When you drive on a highway, you can probably recognize the sign for your

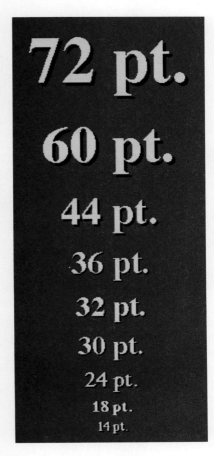

Figure C11 A Range of Point Sizes

exit far before you are close enough to make out the individual letters because you recognize the shape of the words.

USE COLOR TO CREATE A MOOD AND SUSTAIN ATTENTION

Graphic design people have long known that warm colors (oranges, reds) appear to come forward and have an exciting effect, whereas cool colors (greens, blues) seem to recede and have a more calming effect. So when you choose colors, think about how you want your audience to react to your visual aid. Your topic, setting, personality, and purpose should influence your choice of colors. For example, if you are in a business setting, you might use cool colors to convey news which is not particularly good and warm colors to convey news that is. In the first instance you might want to calm your listeners, and in the second you might want to excite them.

It is also important to choose colors for backgrounds and text or graphics that contrast with one another but do not conflict. Figure C12 provides examples of an effective and ineffective color combination. The use of purple against a blue background is not effective because both colors are dark and the purple does not stand out from the background.

Figure C12 Effective and Ineffective Color Combinations

Be cautious about using green and red combinations in your visual aids. Some of your audience members may have a type of color blindness that makes these two colors indistinguishable from one another. Moreover, even for those without red-green color blindness, this combination is not effective. As you can see in Figure C13, the red type against the green background is difficult to read. The colors are not harmonious and do not contrast effectively, and the text and graph are hard on the eyes. For those with red- green color blindness, Figure C13 would appear to be an almost solid box with few or no distinctive features.

If your visual aids will be overheads, you should consider dark text on a light background. You might use black, dark blue, or dark red text that would stand out crisply from a white, light gray, or light yellow background.

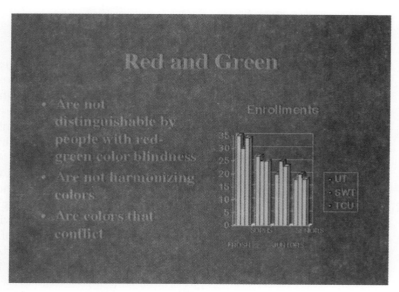

Figure C13 Red-Green Color Combinations Are Not Effective

Each color would be distinctive and would provide excellent contrast for high readability. If your visual aids will be computer generated and projected using 35 millimeter slides, an LCD, or other projection system, light text on a dark background will produce better results. Yellow and white text on black, dark blue, or dark green backgrounds will provide the contrast you will need for an attention-getting presentation. Attractive and harmonious color combinations will get and hold your listeners' attentions longer than combinations which are neither. Don't use too many colors. Two different colors of text on one background color should be sufficient. To unify your presentation, consider using the same color for all of your backgrounds, then vary the complementary colors you use for the text. For example, if you choose a dark green for your background color, you could use white, yellow, and a very light gray for text. Save your most dramatic color contrasts for the most important point.

Using Black and White Effectively

If your budget or lack of equipment limits your color choice to black and white, you can still use contrast to create attractive graphics. By choosing contrasting typefaces, spacing text widely or more compactly, using larger or smaller text, and using both bold and normal text, you can create differences in textual color. The different groups of text in Figure C14 contrast dramatically with one another and show the interesting "coloring" that you can achieve with black and white.

USING POWERPOINT™ AND OTHER GRAPHICS PROGRAMS

So far, this Appendix has attempted to suggest guidelines for the production of effective and visually appealing graphics. You have learned guidelines for layout and design, selecting fonts and type size, and the use of

Bodoni Black
Along with close spacing, bolding, and large type size appears dense and heavy.

Fifth Avenue
Along with wide spacing, bolding, and smaller type size appears lighter and airier.

Relief-Serif
Along with wide spacing, no bolding, and smaller type size appears even lighter and less substantial.

Figure C14 Using Contrasts to Create "Color" with Black and White color. Although these guidelines are very useful, it may be difficult for you to translate them into effective graphics unless you have the proper equipment.

One of the best tools for producing graphics today is a graphics presentation program like PowerPoint™ by Microsoft, Persuasion by Adobe, or Freelance Graphics by Lotus. These programs can assist you in making extremely professional looking visual aids, including transparencies, 35 millimeter slides, handouts, and even posters. You can also show the visual aids you produce with these programs right on a computer screen to show a small audience (6–12) or project them onto a large screen using a projection system. These programs allow you to adapt your designs to suit a wide variety of settings without actually redoing them each time.

Although you need to have some computer skills to use these programs, the skills you need are really quite basic. If you are reasonably adept at word processing, for example, then using a graphics presentation program should not be very difficult. In fact, most of the programs make the learning relatively easy and provide professionally designed templates to guide your efforts. Using these templates, you can input your text in outline form, and the program will automatically format it into a presentation. The real strength of these programs, then, is that they make getting started a simple matter. As you become more expert, you can alter, improve, adapt, and refine your presentations to a greater extent.

There are many powerful and user-friendly graphics presentation programs available for use on both Windows© and Macintosh© computers. PowerPoint™ is the industry leader, and you will probably encounter it when you enter the business world, so we have chosen it for our demonstration. Let's now walk through a visual display preparation using Power-Point™ to see how this programs works. We will work from the outline of the speech on the proposed Nortco addition that we developed earlier (see page A-15).Keep in mind that we will cover only a few basic functions of this powerful, versatile program.

WALKTHROUGH: PREPARING A VISUAL DISPLAY WITH POWERPOINT™

After we load the PowerPoint™ program into our computer and double-click on the PowerPoint™ icon on our desktop, we see a screen that looks like Figure C15. Notice that we have several choices. The "Auto Content Wizard" would guide us through the design and layout process by asking specific questions about our presentation. The "wizard" would simply plug the information we give it into an appropriate presentation format. "Pick a Look Wizard" formats the screen to fit the type of presentation we're giving. For example, if we're giving a computer-generated slide show, the "Pick a Look Wizard" will automatically create a slide with dark backgrounds and light text. Or, if we are creating transparencies, it will create slides with light backgrounds and dark text. The "Template" option would offer us a variety of presentation formats and designs from which to choose. To start from scratch and create an original presentation format, we would choose "Blank Presentation." Finally, if we wanted to access a

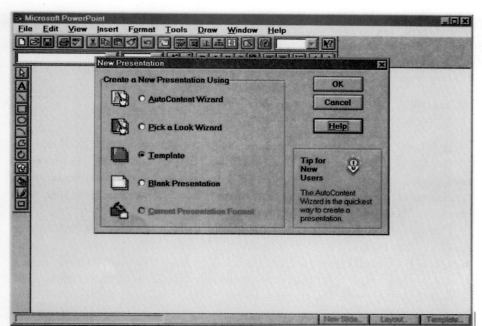

Figure C15 PowerPoint™ Main Menu (Screen shot reprinted with permission from Microsoft Corporation.)

format we had previously created, we would click on "Current Presentation Format."

For now we will just open a template. So we click on the Template button and then the OK button. Next we see a menu screen which looks like Figure C16. The center box tells us that we are in the PowerPoint™ templates slideshow directory. The left box provides the name of 55* templates available to us. We can preview each template by clicking on it once and seeing

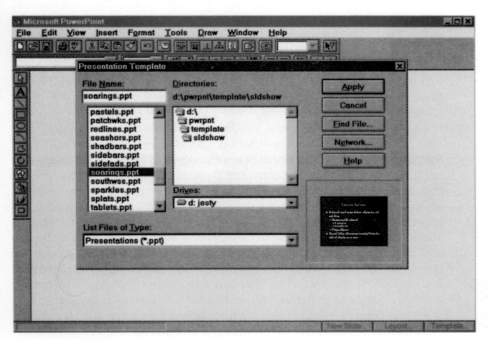

Figure C16 PowerPoint™ Template Menu (Screen shot reprinted with permission from Microsoft Corporation.)

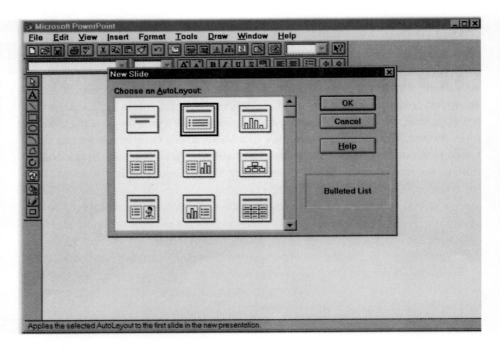

it in the preview box on the lower right. When we find one we like, we simply highlight it and click on the "Apply" button. You can see that we have chosen the template "soarings.ppt" and it is highlighted in the preview box.

Having selected a template for the color and background design of our presentation and clicked "Apply," we are presented with the AutoLayout menu screen (Figure C17). We have a choice of twenty-one AutoLayouts for our text and graphics. No matter which template we had chosen, we would still see these same choices for layouts. The templates determine the style and colors for the background and text; the AutoLayout menu allows us to choose the design and layout of the text and graphics on the template. We'll choose the second layout from the left at the top. It will provide us with a title and a bulleted text box. When we click on the "OK" button, Power-Point™ will combine our template and layout choices and display the results (Figure C18).

Now we have more choices. We can do what the template suggests and click anywhere in either box to enter our text. However, since we have saved the outline we created from our Nortco storyboard in our word processing application, we can use the copy and paste functions to insert our outline here. First, we select an option from one of the five small option boxes at the lower left corner of the template slide. We click on the second box from the left which displays the skeleton of an outline. The computer then gives us a blank screen onto which we can either type a new outline or paste the one we have already saved. To paste in our Nortco outline, we first open up the word processing file where our outline is saved. Then we select all of the text, copy it, and exit the file. When the blank PowerPoint™ outline screen reappears, we can paste in the text. PowerPoint™ will then give us a screen that looks like Figure C19. Note that we have edited the outline a bit for an oral presentation, paring down the number of words in each item. Finally, we can

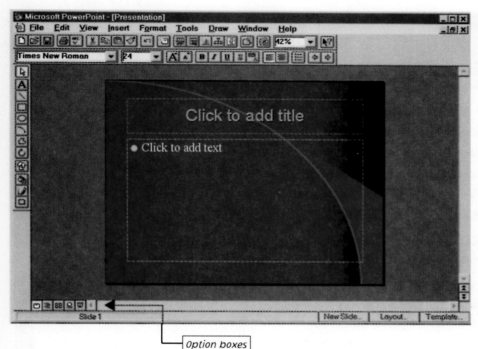

tell PowerPoint™ to transfer the outline to the "soaring" template we chose earlier.

We click on the far left icon at the bottom of the screen to get to the slide screen. PowerPoint™ places our first main point and its supporting sub-points on the first slide (Figure C20), and produces slides for all of the remaining points in the outline.

Once we have completed this step, we are ready to show the visual displays on the computer screen for a small number of people, project them onto a large screen using a projection system, or print them as a series of transparencies, notes, slides, or handouts.

Note that these visual displays follow the design principles we learned in this Appendix: the text color contrasts well with the background color but is complementary; the text is left justified and spaced in a way that suggests a relationship among the elements; there is enough but not too much information; the background and bullets are repetitive elements that tie the slides together; the title is a 44 point sans serif font and the body text is a 32 point serif font for greater readability; and we have avoided using reds and greens. PowerPoint™ made it easy for us, because these design principles are built into the templates.

We have briefly described the ease with which you can develop an effective presentation in PowerPoint™, but you should know that most computer graphics programs are extremely powerful and can produce very sophisticated results.

For example, if you were giving a PowerPoint™ presentation in which you needed to display a graph, you could either create it within Power-Point™ or import the graph from another program. PowerPoint™ would au-

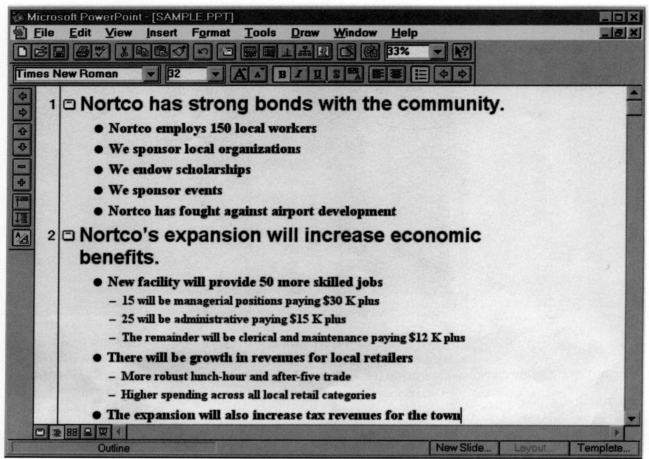

Figure C19 PowerPoint™ Outline Screen (Screen shot reprinted with permission from Microsoft Corporation.)

tomatically alter the colors to match your color scheme. In addition, Power-Point™ can also import images that you have entered in your computer using a scanning device. So if you were giving the speech in our earlier Nortco example, you could take a picture of the finish line at the Run-For-Fun, digitize it using your scanner, and then import it into your presentation. Some programs are also capable of producing a quick series of images that look like animation, integrating sound clips, and even displaying short film clips to make your presentations even more exciting and attention-grabbing. For more details, see the user's manual of the program you are using to see how it can help you prepare the kinds of presentations that are becoming an increasingly important requirement for many careers.

The suggestions in this Appendix about storyboarding, layout and design, and using graphics software provide only a glimpse of the thousands of available options for producing effective graphics. We encourage you to experiment with different techniques, programs, and visual elements before you are up against a tight deadline for a course or workplace presentation. Then, when you have a specific task to complete, you will have the facility

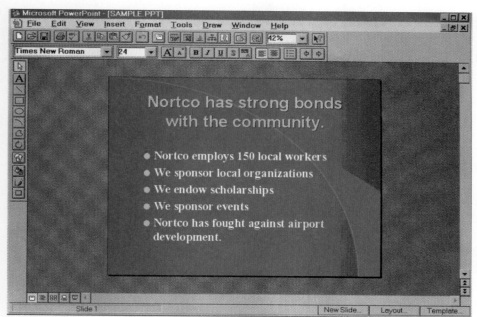

Figure C20 PowerPoint™ Final Screen (Screen shot reprinted with permission from Microsoft Corporation.)

to produce efficiently the kinds of visual aids that are appropriate for your particular audience, topic and setting.

> From *Public Speaking: An Audience-Centered Approach, Third Edition,* by Steven A. Beebe and Susan J. Beebe, Copyright © 1997, 1994, 1991 by Allyn & Bacon, pgs. A-14 to A-28.

GRAPHS

Speakers integrate **graphs** into their presentations in an effort to help their listeners better understand statistical data. Well-designed graphic formats can help speakers communicate statistical information, illustrate trends, and vivify patterns. Among the graphs most commonly used by speakers are line graphs, bar graphs, pie graphs, and pictographs.

Speakers rely on **line graphs** to help them show trends over time. Figure C21 is one such graph used by a student in a speech on abortion. The speaker chose the graph to support her contention that abortions are on the decline.

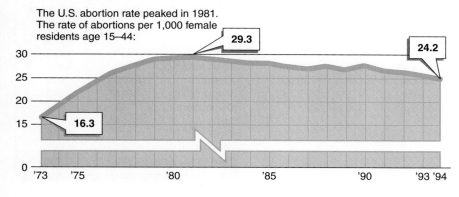

Figure C21

Referring to the graph the speaker said:

As you can see from the graph derived from information in the August 8, 1996, issue of *USA Today* abortions have declined from the peak year of 1981.

By incorporating these words, the speaker helped her listeners interpret the graph. By describing the course revealed by the statistical data, she was able to substantiate the apparent trend.

A line graph can also be used to make comparisons by adding two or more lines to it. In Figure C22 comparisons are made between the percentages of Hispanics, African Americans, and Asians in Bergen and Passaic counties in New Jersey. The lines are color coded for clarity.

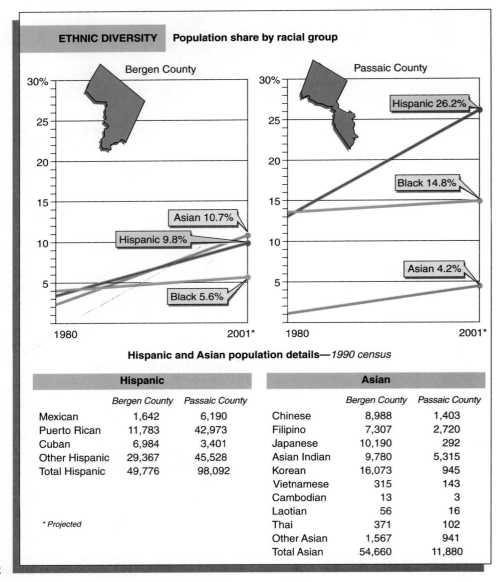

Figure C22

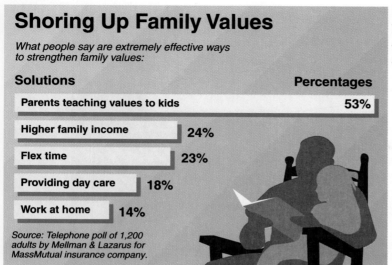

Shoring Up Family Values

What people say are extremely effective ways to strengthen family values:

Solutions	Percentages
Parents teaching values to kids	53%
Higher family income	24%
Flex time	23%
Providing day care	18%
Work at home	14%

Source: Telephone poll of 1,200 adults by Mellman & Lazarus for MassMutual insurance company.

Figure C23

Bar graphs enable speakers to compare and/or contrast two or more items or groups.

The **bar graph,** like the line graph, is useful for comparing or contrasting two or more items or groups. Figure C23 is a bar graph that shows opinions on the strengthening of family values.

Figure C24 is another color-coded bar graph, this one used in a speech on telecommuters (a term meaning employees who work outside of the company office) to show the growth in the number of people who work in their own homes.

By referring to each bar of the graph the speaker made his case that there has been and probably will continue to be a steady increase in the number of people who work at home. "In total," the speaker noted, referring to the graph, "39 million Americans or 31.4 percent of the adult work force labor in a home office at least part time. The largest segment, 12.1 million, consists mainly of the self-employed."

U.S. Home Office Work Style Trends

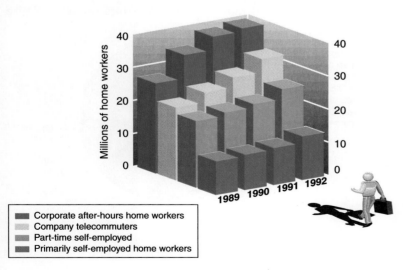

Corporate after-hours home workers
Company telecommuters
Part-time self-employed
Primarily self-employed home workers

Figure C24

When color coded, bar graphs facilitate comprehension.

Figure C25

Bar graphs can show growth over time.

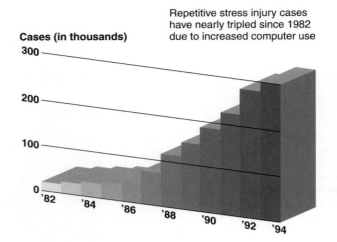

Cases (in thousands)

Repetitive stress injury cases have nearly tripled since 1982 due to increased computer use

Similarly, the bar graph in Figure C25 was used by a speaker advocating that stricter measures be taken to prevent repetitive stress injuries. The graph dramatically illustrates the rise in repetitive stress injuries due to increased computer use.

Bar graphs can be either horizontal or vertical. But even while varying in length, the bars should be kept the same width. When prepared properly the bar graph is usually easy for the uninitiated to read and interpret. While speakers could transmit the statistical information contained in bar graphs verbally, referring to the bar graphs helps make those data more meaningful and dramatic for receivers.

In contrast to line and bar graphs, **pie graphs** are good for illustrating either percentages of a whole or distribution patterns. Also referred to as circle graphs, pie graphs indicate and dramatize the size of a subject's parts relative to each other and to the whole. Ideally, for purposes of clarity, pie graphs should contain from two to five "slices" or divisions, and should be clearly labeled. Pie graphs are the simplest way of graphically representing percentages available to a speaker. Figure C26 shows a pie graph used by a speaker discussing the types of radio stations Hispanics listen to. Notice

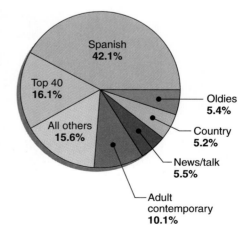

Hispanics 12 years old and up listen to radio an average 25 hours 15 minutes a week – more than the U.S. average of 22 hours. Types of stations Hispanics listen to:

Figure C26

Simple pie graphs speed comprehension.

that the graph contains seven main divisions. Any more cuts in the pie would have made the graph too cluttered.

Pictographs include pictorial representations of the graph's subject. For example, the graphs in Figure C27, describing the number of women in politics compared to men and when people consult financial planners, appear somewhat less formal than bar graphs and thus may be even more interesting for receivers.

Whatever types of graphs you use, keep in mind the following guidelines.

- Keep the graph as simple as possible. Graph overload—too many graphs or too much information on a single graph—contributes to information overload and can overwhelm receivers.

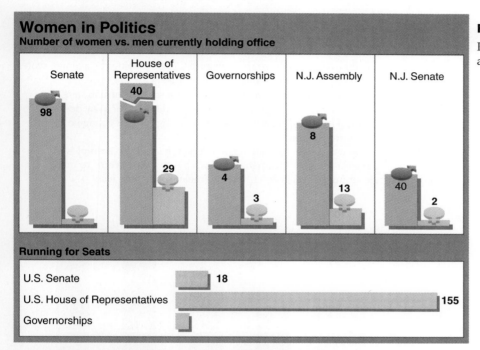

Figure C27

Pictographs are less formal and add interest.

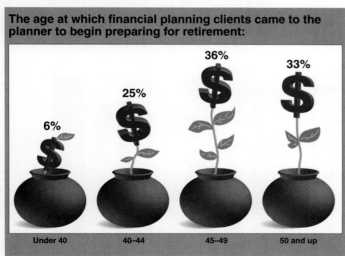

- Help receivers with the interpretation process. Don't assume they will read the graph the way you expect them to read it.
- Make sure the graph is large enough for the audience to see everything written on it. Poor graph visibility decreases speaker intelligibility. Clear graphs facilitate clear speech.

CHARTS, DRAWINGS, AND MAPS

Speakers use **charts** to help them compress or summarize large amounts of information. By enabling listeners to organize their own thoughts and fol-

Speaking of Critical Thinking

Evaluating What You See

Consider this: Is there more to the graph in Figure C28 displaying the average scores of four English classes on an achievement test than meets the eye?

While the graph pictured in Figure C29 shows the same information as the previous graph, why are we led to perceive the results differently? Why does showing the bars full length instead of cut short as in Figure C28 change our impression of the information?

Speakers who use visual aids can derive a lesson from these examples. A speaker should never present information in such a way that it seems to mean one thing but on closer inspection is determined to mean something else.

Figure C28

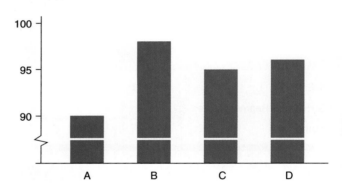

Figure C29

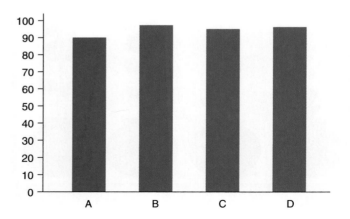

Vanilla
25.2%

Chocolate
8.8%

Neapolitan
6.1%

Strawberry
5.1%

Peach
4.5%

Cookie
Dough

Apple

Cheesecake

Brownie

Caramel
combinations

**Top-selling
flavors**

**Fast-growing
flavors**

**Share of ice
cream sales
(in dollar terms)**

**Recently
introduced flavors
whose sales grew
most**

low your speech's progress, charts also simplify note taking and facilitate retention. The most commonly used is a word chart like the one pictured in Figure C30.

To vivify the information in a chart and give it more eye appeal, the speaker can use a drawing that enhances key words, as shown in Figure C31.

The chart is also particularly useful for speakers who want to discuss a process, an organization schema, channels of communication, or chains of command as Figure C32 exemplifies. Most commonly displayed on a

Food Guide Pyramid

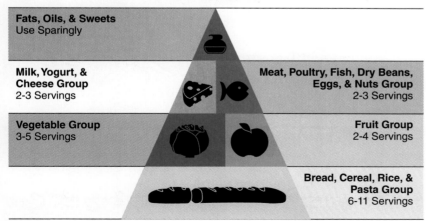

Fats, Oils, & Sweets
Use Sparingly

**Milk, Yogurt, &
Cheese Group**
2-3 Servings

**Meat, Poultry, Fish, Dry Beans,
Eggs, & Nuts Group**
2-3 Servings

Vegetable Group
3-5 Servings

Fruit Group
2-4 Servings

**Bread, Cereal, Rice, &
Pasta Group**
6-11 Servings

Figure C31

Drawings or sketches enhance the meaning of key words.

Figure C32

Organizational charts reveal chains of command.

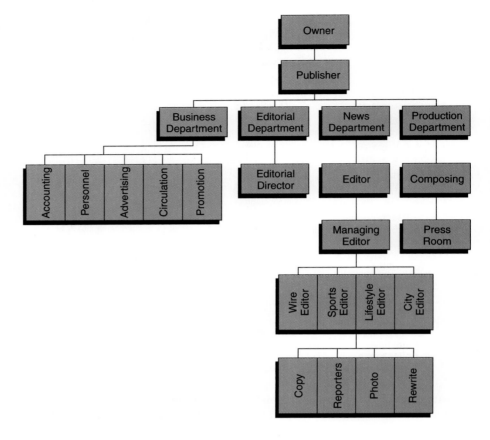

flipchart, a poster, or an overhead projector, charts are versatile and adaptable speech aids.

Like charts, **drawings and maps** can also be customized by the speaker to help him or her illustrate specific speech points. Drawings and maps help translate complex information into a visual format that receivers usually

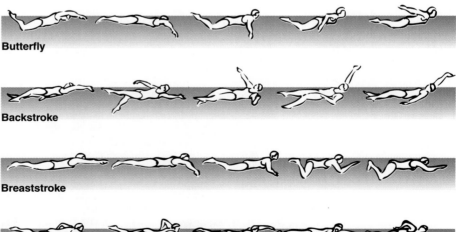

Butterfly

Backstroke

Breaststroke

Figure C33

Drawings facilitate the sharing of key message aspects.

Freestyle   Olympic record: 200-meter, 2:12.59; 400-meter, 4:36.29

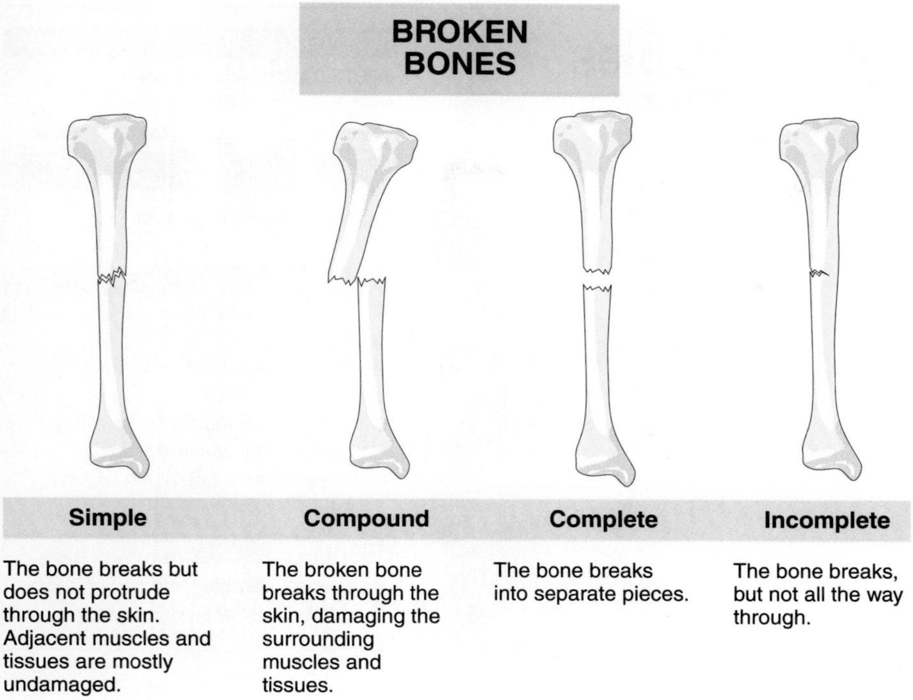

BROKEN BONES

Simple	Compound	Complete	Incomplete
The bone breaks but does not protrude through the skin. Adjacent muscles and tissues are mostly undamaged.	The broken bone breaks through the skin, damaging the surrounding muscles and tissues.	The bone breaks into separate pieces.	The bone breaks, but not all the way through.

Figure C34

Drawings can help the audience to understand the technical points of a speaker's message.

grasp more readily. A speaker who sought to compare and contrast different swim strokes used the drawing depicted in Figure C33 to facilitate her task. This visual made it easier for the speaker to refer to and explain each swimmer's arm and leg movements in turn. Initially, only that portion of the drawing the speaker was referring to was visible to the audience; remaining sections were covered until mentioned by the speaker.

The drawings in Figure C34 enabled the speaker to accurately describe the differences between four kinds of broken bones: simple fractures, compound fractures, complete fractures, and incomplete fractures, just as the drawing in Figure C35 on page 444 made it easier for the speaker to explain how rabies spreads.

Maps also make versatile visual aids. One speaker used the map in Figure C36 on page 444 as visual support when delivering a speech on tornadoes. As you can see, the U.S. Plains states, which consume a key portion of the visual aid, are a prime tornado target.

Although you do not need to be an artist, drawings and maps should be prepared in advance, not produced on the spur of the moment. Attempting to generate them while your audience is watching can consume valuable speaking time, cause audience members to lose patience with you, produce art that is less than suitable for use, and obscure rather than clarify the points you hope to convey. Whether you make your own drawings and maps, have someone make them for you, or use some that were published previously, the feature you are going to discuss should be easy to see.

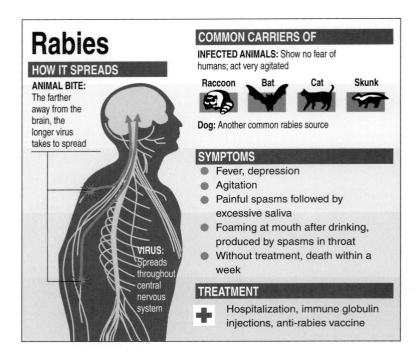

SLIDES, VIDEOTAPES, AND
OVERHEAD TRANSPARENCIES

Requiring more preparation time and the use of special equipment, **slides,
videotapes,** and **overhead transparencies,** are used extensively in business
and professional settings. Each of these visual aids can help make a speech
more dynamic, involving, and exciting for receivers. Because they allow a
speaker to custom design more sophisticated examples of visual support,
they can be extremely effective tools to use with today's media-wise
audiences.

Though these visual aids do require that speakers familiarize themselves
with more complicated equipment and usually necessitate more money for

Figure C36

Maps can show movement
as well as location.

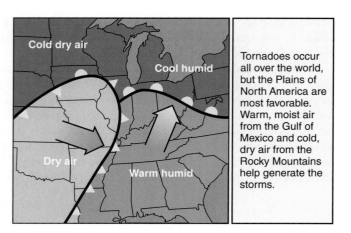

preparation and more time for rehearsal and set-up, the vividness and reinforcement these visuals provide is difficult to beat. Still, they should not be used unless the presenter or an assistant is well versed in their use and adept at coordinating the presentation with the showing of the visuals.

From *Public Speaking in the Age of Diversity, Second Edition,* by Teri Kwal Gamble and Michael W. Gamble, Copyright © 1998, 1994 by Allyn & Bacon, pgs. 299–309.

STRATEGIES FOR USING VISUAL AIDS

Before the Speech

Determine the Information to be Presented Visually Sections of a presentation that are complex or detailed may be particularly appropriate for visualization. Be careful, however, not to use too many visual aids. The premium in a speech is on the spoken word. Multimedia presentations can be exciting; they may also be extremely difficult to coordinate. Handling too many charts and posters quickly becomes cumbersome and distracting.

Select the Type of Visual Aid Best Suited to Your Resources and Speech The visual aid you select will be influenced by the information you need to present, the amount of preparation time you have, your technical expertise at producing the visual aid, and the cost involved. If preparing quality visual aids to illustrate your speech will take more time, money, or expertise than you have, you are probably better off without them. A visual aid that calls attention to its poor production is a handicap, no matter how important the information it contains.

Ensure Easy Viewing by All Audience Members A speaker addressing an audience of 500 would not want to use a videotaped presentation displayed on a single television or computer monitor. A bar graph on posterboard should be visible to more than just the first four rows of the audience. If possible, practice with your visual aids in the room where you will speak. Position the visual aid and then sit in the seat of your farthest possible audience member. (In an auditorium, make it the back row; people will not move forward unless forced to.) If you can read your visual aid from that distance, it is sufficient in size. If you cannot, you must either enlarge the visual aid or eliminate it.

Make Sure That the Visual Aid Communicates the Information Clearly Simplicity should be your guiding principle in constructing your visual aid. Michael Talman, a graphics design consultant, compares a graphic in a presentation to "going by a highway billboard at 55 miles per hour. Its effectiveness can be judged by how quickly the viewer sees and understands its message." Too much information may clutter or confuse. For example, speakers sometimes construct posters in technicolor to make them lively and interesting. But, remember that the purpose of visual aids is to inform, not to impress, the audience. You may use red to indicate a budget deficit, but, as a rule, black or dark blue on white is the most visually distinct color combination for graphics.

Construct a Visual Aid That is Professional in Appearance In the business and professional world, a hand-lettered poster, no matter how neatly done, is inappropriate. Professionals understand the importance of a good impression. How can you as a student on a limited budget make a professional-looking graphic without spending a fortune? Many print shops have word processors and printers with many different-sized fonts for your use for about $10 an hour. If you have access to a computer and are familiar with a computer graphics program that meets your needs, by all means use it. If you can't use a computer and doubt your freehand skills, hiring an art student to draw and letter a visual aid you have designed is another alternative.

If you throw together a chart or graph the night before your speech, that is exactly what it will look like. Your hastily prepared work will undermine an image of careful and thorough preparation.

Practice Using Your Visual Aid A conscientious speaker will spend hours preparing a speech; visual aids are a part of that presentation. Just as you rehearse the words of your speech, you should rehearse referring to your visual aid, uncovering and covering charts, advancing slides, and writing on overhead transparencies. In short, if you plan to use visual aids, learn how *before* your speech; no audience will be impressed by how much you learn during the course of your presentation.

Arrange for Safe Transportation of Your Visual Aids Visual aids worth using are worth transporting safely. The laptop computer you've bought or borrowed needs obvious care. Posterboards should be protected from

Strategies for Using Visual Aids

Before the Speech

1. Determine the information to be presented visually.
2. Select the type of visual aid best suited to your resources and speech.
3. Ensure easy viewing by all audience members.
4. Make sure that the visual aid communicates the information clearly.
5. Construct a visual aid that is professional in appearance.
6. Practice using your visual aid.
7. Arrange for safe transportation of your visual aids.
8. Carry back-up supplies with you.
9. Properly position the visual aid.

During the Speech

1. Reveal the visual aid only when you are ready for it.
2. Talk to your audience—not to the visual aid.
3. Refer to the visual aid.
4. Keep your visual aid in view until the audience understands your point.
5. Conceal the visual aid after you have made your point.
6. Use handouts with caution.

Q: What visual aids did you decide would work best for your speech? Did they present any special problems or concerns?

A: I used two types of visual aids in my speech: a diagram and an object. I felt pretty good about them. I knew the simple diagram was clearly drawn and would be easy to see. I knew the ship in a bottle would be harder for people in the back to see clearly, so I thought I would hold it and walk closer to the audience when I talked about it. The only nervousness I really had was about picking up the bottle, for fear I would drop it in front of everyone. It may sound silly, but I was concerned about sweaty palms and that glass bottle.

Note: The material in Speaker's Journal refers to Daniel Sarvis's speech, "A Ship in a Bottle," which appears in the Appendix.

moisture and bending. Cover your visual aid with plastic to protect it from a freak rainstorm or that flying Frisbee you encounter just before speech class. Do not roll up paper or posterboard charts, carrying them to different classes or leaving them in a car trunk throughout the day, and then expect them to lay flat when you speak. You will have a cylinder, not an effective visual aid.

Carry Back-up Supplies with You An exciting and informative presentation can be ruined when a projector bulb blows as you are preparing to speak. Make an inventory of equipment you may need, such as extension cords, bulbs, and batteries, and then take them with you.

Properly Position the Visual Aid Arrive at the place where you will give your speech *before* the audience arrives. Position your visual aid in the most desirable location. Make sure that the maximum number of people will see it and that nothing obstructs the audience's view. If you are not the first speaker, have your visual aid and equipment conveniently located so that you can set up quickly and with little disruption.

During the Speech

Reveal the Visual Aid Only When You Are Ready for It A visual aid is designed to attract attention and convey information. If it is visible at the beginning of the speech, the audience may focus on it rather than on what you are saying. Your visual aid should be seen only when you are ready to discuss the point it illustrates.

With an aid on posterboard, cover it with a blank posterboard or turn the blank side to the audience. At the appropriate time, expose the visual aid. If you are using projections, have someone cued to turn the lights off and the projector on at the appropriate time.

Occasionally, a speaker will stop speaking, uncover a visual aid, and then continue. This is where rehearsal can really help you. You want to avoid creating unnecessary breaks in the flow of your speech. With practice you will be able to keep talking as you uncover your visual aid.

Talk to Your Audience—Not to the Visual Aid Remember, eye contact is a speaker's most important nonverbal tool. Sustained visual interaction with your audience keeps their attention on you and allows you to monitor their feedback regarding your speech. Turning your back to your listeners undermines your impact. For this reason, use prepared graphics rather than a blackboard.

Refer to the Visual Aid Speakers sometimes stand at the lectern using their notes or reading their manuscript, relatively far from their visual aid. This creates two lines of vision and can confuse your audience. It may also give the impression that you must rely on your notes since you do not fully understand what the visual aid conveys.

Other speakers carry their notes with them as they move to the visual aid, referring to them as they point out key concepts. This is cumbersome, and again reinforces the image of a speaker unsure of what he or she wants to say.

A well-constructed visual aid should be used as a set of notes. The key ideas represented on the aid should trigger the explanation you will provide. You should not need to refer to anything else as you discuss the point your visual aid illustrates. When you practice using your visual aid, use your aid as your notes.

If you use a metal, wooden, or light beam pointer to refer to the visual aid, have it easily accessible, use it only when pointing to the visual aid, and set it down immediately after you are finished with it. Too many speakers pick up a pen to use when referring to their visual aid and end up playing with the pen during the rest of the speech.

Finally, point to your visual aid with the hand closer to it. This keeps your body open and makes communication physically more direct with your audience.

Keep Your Visual Aid in View Until the Audience Understands Your Point Remember that you are more familiar with your speech than is your audience. Too often, a speaker hurries through an explanation and covers or removes the visual aid before the audience fully comprehends its significance or the point being made. Just as you should not reveal your visual aid too soon, do not cover it up too quickly. You will have invested time and effort in preparing the visual aid. Give your audience the time necessary to digest the information it conveys. As you discuss and describe the visual aid, check your audience response. Many will likely signal their understanding of the visual aid by nodding their heads or changing their posture.

Conceal the Visual Aid After You Have Made Your Point Once you proceed to the next section of your speech, you do not want the audience to continue thinking about the visual aid. If the aid is an object or posterboard, cover it. If you are using projections, turn off the projector and turn on the room lights.

Use Handouts with Caution Of all the forms of visual aids, the handout may be the most troublesome. If you distribute handouts before your remarks, the audience is already ahead of you. Passing out information during a presentation can be distracting, especially if you stop talking as you do so. In addition, the rustling of paper can distract the speaker and other audience members. Disseminating material after the presentation eliminates distractions but does not allow the listener to refer to the printed information as you are explaining it. In general, then, use handouts in a public speech only if that is the best way to clarify and give impact to your ideas.

You will encounter some speaking situations, such as the business presentation, that not only benefit from but may also demand handout material. Those audiences are often decision-making groups. During an especially technical presentation, they may need to take notes. Afterward, they may need to study the information presented. Handouts provide a record of the presenter's remarks and supplementary information the speaker did not have time to explain.

Visual aids—objects, graphics, projections, and handouts—can make your speech more effective. By seeing as well as hearing your message, the audience becomes more involved with your speech and more responsive to your appeals.

From *Mastering Public Speaking, Third Edition,* by George L. Grice and John F. Skinner, Copyright © 1998, 1995, 1993 by Allyn & Bacon, pgs. 300–303.

Glossary of Human Communication Concepts and Skills

A word is dead
When it is said
Some say
I say it just begins to live.
—EMILY DICKINSON

Listed here are definitions of the technical terms of human communication—the words that are peculiar or unique to this discipline—and, where appropriate, the corresponding skills. These definitions and statements of skills should make new or difficult terms a bit easier to understand and should help to place the skill in context. The statements of skills appear in italics. All boldface terms within the definitions appear as separate entries in the glossary.

Abstraction. A general concept derived from a class of objects; a part representation of some whole.

Abstraction process. The process by which a general concept is derived from specifics; the process by which some (never all) characteristics of an object, person, or event are perceived by the senses or included in some term, phrase, or sentence.

Accent. The stress or emphasis placed on a syllable when pronounced.

Acculturation. The processes by which a person's culture is modified or changed through contact with or exposure to another culture.

Active listening. A process of putting together into some meaningful whole the listener's understanding of the speaker's total message—the verbal and the nonverbal, the content and the feelings. *Listen actively by paraphrasing the speaker's meanings, expressing an understanding of the speaker's feelings, and asking questions to check the accuracy of your understanding of the speaker.*

Adaptors. Nonverbal behaviors that satisfy some personal need and usually occur without awareness, for example, scratching to relieve an itch or moistening your lips to relieve the dry feeling. Three types of adaptors are often distinguished: **self-adaptors, alter-adaptors,** and **object-adaptors.** *Generally, avoid adaptors (especially self-adaptors); they interfere with effective communication and may be taken as a sign of your discomfort or anxiety.*

Adjustment (principle of). The principle of verbal interaction that claims that communication takes place only to the extent that the parties communicating share the same system of signals. *Expand the common areas between you and significant others; learn each other's system of communication signals and meanings in order to increase understanding and interpersonal communication effectiveness.*

Affect displays. Movements of the facial area that convey emotional meaning—for example, anger, fear, and surprise.

Affinity-seeking strategies. Behaviors designed to increase our interpersonal attractiveness. *Use the various affinity-seeking strategies (for example, listening, openness, and dynamism), as appropriate to the interpersonal relationship and the situation, to increase your own interpersonal attractiveness.*

Affirmation. The communication of support and approval. *Use affirmation to express your supportiveness and to raise esteem.*

Agenda. A list of the items that a small group must deal with in the order in which they should be covered.

Agenda-setting. A persuasive technique in which the speaker argues that XYZ is the issue and that all others are unimportant.

Aggressiveness. *See* **verbal aggressiveness.**

Allness. The assumption that all can be known or is known about a given person, issue, object, or event. *End statements with an implicit "etc." ("et cetera") to indicate that more could be known and said; avoid allness terms and statements.*

Alter-adaptors. Body movements you make in response to your current interactions, for example, crossing your arms over your chest when someone unpleasant approaches or moving closer to someone you like.

Altercasting. Placing the listener in a specific role for a specific purpose and asking that the listener approach the question or problem from the perspective of this specific role.

Ambiguity. The condition in which a message may be interpreted as having more than one meaning.

Analogy, reasoning from. A type of reasoning in which you compare like things and conclude that since they are alike in so many respects that they are also alike in some previously unknown respect.

Apology. A type of excuse in which you acknowledge responsibility for the behavior, generally ask forgiveness, and claim that this will not happen again.

Appraisal interview. A type of **interview** in which the interviewee's performance is assessed by management or by more experienced colleagues.

Apprehension. *See* **communication apprehension.**

Arbitrariness. The feature of human language that reflects the absence of a real or inherent relationship between the form of a word and its meaning. If we do not know anything of a particular language, we cannot examine the form of a word and thereby discover its meaning.

Argot. The language (largely **cant** and **jargon**) of a particular class, generally an underworld, or criminal class, which is difficult and sometimes impossible for outsiders to understand.

Argument. Evidence (for example, facts or statistics) and a conclusion drawn from the evidence.

Argumentativeness. A willingness to argue for a point of view, to speak one's mind. *Cultivate your argumentativeness, your willingness to argue for what you believe by, for example, treating disagreements as objectively as possible, reaffirming the other, stressing equality, expressing interest in the other's position, and allowing the other person to save face.* Distinguished from **verbal aggressiveness.**

Articulation. The physiological movements of the speech organs as they modify and interrupt the air stream emitted from the lungs.

Artifactual communication. Communication that takes place through the wearing and arrangement of various artifacts—for example, clothing, jewelry, buttons, or the furniture in your house and its arrangement.

Assertiveness. A willingness to stand up for one's rights but with a respect for the rights of others. *Increase assertiveness (if desired) by analyzing the assertive and nonassertive behaviors of others, analyzing your own behaviors in terms of assertiveness, recording your behaviors, rehearsing assertive behaviors, and acting assertively in appropriate situations. Secure feedback from others for further guidance in increasing assertiveness.*

Assimilation. A process of distortion in which messages are reconstructed to conform to our own attitudes, prejudices, needs, and values.

Attack. A persuasive technique that involves accusing another person (usually an opponent) of some serious wrongdoing so that the issue under discussion never gets examined.

Attention. The process of responding to a stimulus or stimuli; usually some consciousness of responding is implied.

Attitude. A predisposition to respond for or against an object, person, or position.

Attraction. The state or process by which one individual is drawn to another, by having a highly positive evaluation of that other person.

Attraction theory. A theory holding that we form relationships on the basis of our attraction for another person.

Attractiveness. The degree to which a person is perceived to be physically attractive and to possess a pleasing personality.

Attribution. A process through which we attempt to understand the behaviors of others (as well as our own), particularly the reasons or motivations for these behaviors.

Attribution theory. A theory concerned with the processes involved in attributing causation or motivation to a person's behavior. *In attempting to identify the motivation for behaviors, examine consensus, consistency, distinctiveness, and controllability. Generally, low consensus, high consistency, low distinctiveness, and high controllability identify internally motivated behavior; high consensus, low consistency, high distinctiveness, and low controllability identify externally motivated behavior.*

Audience participation principle. A principle of persuasion stating that persuasion is achieved more effectively when the audience participates actively.

Authoritarian leader. A group leader who determines the group policies or makes decisions without consulting or securing agreement from group members.

Avoidance. An unproductive **conflict** strategy in which a person takes mental or physical flight from the actual conflict.

Back-channeling cues. Listener responses to a speaker that do not ask for the speaking role. *Respond to back-channeling cues as appropriate to the conversation. Use back-channeling cues to let the speaker know you are listening.*

Bandwagon. A persuasive technique by which the speaker tries to gain compliance by saying that everyone is doing it and urges you to jump on the bandwagon.

Barriers to communication. Those factors (physical or psychological) that prevent or hinder effective communication. *Applying the skills of human communication covered throughout this text will help reduce the existing barriers and prevent others from arising.*

Behavioral synchrony. The similarity in the behavior, usually nonverbal, of two persons. Generally, it is taken as an index of mutual liking.

Belief. Confidence in the existence or truth of something; conviction. *Weigh both verbal and nonverbal messages before making believability judgments; increase your own sensitivity to nonverbal (and verbal) deception cues—for example, too little movement, long pauses, slow speech, increased speech errors, mouth guard, nose touching, eye rubbing, or the use of few words, especially monosyllabic answers. Use such cues to formulate hypotheses rather than conclusions concerning deception.*

Beltlining. An unproductive **conflict** strategy in which one hits at the level at which the other person cannot withstand the blow. *Avoid it.*

Blame. An unproductive **conflict** strategy in which we attribute the cause of the conflict to the other person or devote our energies to discovering who is the cause and avoid talking about the issues causing the conflict. *Avoid using blame to win an argument, especially with those with whom you're in close relationships.*

Boundary marker. A marker that sets boundaries that divide one person's territory from another's—for example, a fence.

Brainstorming. A technique for generating ideas either alone or, more usually, in a small group. *In brainstorming avoid evaluating contributions, strive for quantity, combine and extend your own or the ideas of others, and try really wild ideas.*

Breadth. The number of topics about which individuals in a relationship communicate.

Cant. The conversational language of a special group (usually, a lower social-class group), generally understood only by members of that group.

Card stacking. A persuasive technique in which the speaker selects only the evidence and arguments that build a case and omits or distorts any contradictory evidence.

Causes and effects, reasoning from. A form of reasoning in which you conclude that certain effects are due to specific causes or that specific causes produce certain effects.

Censorship. Legal restriction imposed on one's right to produce, distribute, or receive various communications.

Central marker. A marker or item that is placed in a territory to reserve it for a specific person—for example, the sweater thrown over a library chair to signal that the chair is taken.

Certainty. An attitude of closed-mindedness that creates a defensiveness among communication participants; opposed to **provisionalism.**

Channel. The vehicle or medium through which signals are sent.

Character. One of the qualities of **credibility;** the individual's honesty and basic nature; moral qualities. *In establishing character stress your fairness, your concern for enduring values, and your similarity with the audience.*

Charisma. One of the qualities of **credibility;** the individual's dynamism or forcefulness. *In establishing charisma demonstrate positiveness, act assertively, and express enthusiasm.*

Cherishing behaviors. Small behaviors we enjoy receiving from others, especially from our relational partner—for example, a kiss, a smile, or being given flowers.

Chronemics. The study of the communicative nature of time—the way you treat time and use it to communicate. Two general areas of chronemics are cultural and psychological time.

Civil inattention. Polite ignoring of others so as not to invade their privacy.

Cliché. An overused expression that has lost its novelty and part of its meaning, and that calls attention to itself because of its overuse; "tall, dark, and handsome" as a description of a man is a cliché. *Avoid clichés in all forms of communication.*

Closed-mindedness. An unwillingness to receive certain communication messages.

Code. A set of symbols used to translate a message from one form to another.

Coercive power. Power dependent on one's ability to punish or to remove rewards from another person.

Cognitive restructuring. A theory for substituting logical and realistic beliefs for unrealistic ones and used in reducing communication apprehension and in raising self-esteem.

Cohesiveness. The property of togetherness. Applied to group communication situations, it refers to the mutual attractiveness among members; a measure of the extent to which individual members of a group work together as a group.

Collective orientation. A cultural orientation in which the group's rather than the individual's goals and preferences are given greater importance. Opposed to **individual orientation.**

Collectivist culture. A culture in which the group's goals rather than the individual's are given greater importance and where, for example, benevolence, tradition, and conformity are given special emphasis. Opposed to **individualistic culture.**

Communication. (1) The process or act of communicating; (2) the actual message or messages sent and received; (3) the study of the processes involved in the sending and receiving of messages. (The term **communicology** is suggested for the third definition.)

Communication accommodation theory. The theory holding that speakers adjust their speaking style to their listeners to gain social approval and achieve greater communication effectiveness.

Communication apprehension. Fear or anxiety over communicating and may be "trait apprehension"—a fear of communication generally, regardless of the specific situation—or state apprehension—a fear that is specific to a given communication situation. *Manage your own communication apprehension by reversing the potential causes of apprehension, try performance visualization, systematically desensitize yourself, and use the skills and techniques for dealing with apprehension.*

Communication competence. A knowledge of the rules and skills of communication and is often used to refer to the qualities that make for effectiveness in communication.

Communication network. The pathways of messages; the organizational structure through which messages are sent and received.

Communicology. The study of communication, particularly the subsection concerned with human communication.

Competence. One of the qualities of **credibility,** which encompasses a person's ability and knowledge. *In establishing your competence tell your listeners of your special experience or training, cite a variety of research sources, and stress the particular competencies of your sources.*

Complementarity. A principle of **attraction,** stating that one is attracted by qualities one does not possess or one wishes to possess and to people who are opposite or different from oneself; opposed to **similarity.** *Identify the characteristics that you do not find in yourself but admire in others and that, therefore, might be important in influencing your perception of another person.*

Complementary relationship. A relationship in which the behavior of one person serves as the stimulus for the complementary behavior of the other; in complementary relationships, behavioral differences are maximized.

Compliance-gaining strategies. Behaviors that are directed toward gaining the agreement of others; behaviors designed to persuade others to do as we wish. *Use the various compliance-gaining strategies to increase your own persuasive power.*

Compliance-resisting strategies. Behaviors directed at resisting the persuasive attempts of others. *Use such strategies as identity management, nonnegotiation, negotiation, and justification as appropriate in resisting compliance.*

Confidence. A quality of interpersonal effectiveness; a comfortable, at-ease feeling in interpersonal communication situations. *Communicate a feeling of being comfortable and at ease with the interaction through appropriate verbal and nonverbal signals.*

Confirmation. A communication pattern that acknowledges another person's presence and also indicates an acceptance of this person, this person's definition of self, and the relationship as defined or viewed by this other person; opposed to **disconfirmation.** *Avoid those verbal and nonverbal behaviors that disconfirm another person. Substitute confirming behaviors, those that acknowledge the presence and the contributions of the other person.*

Conflict. An extreme form of competition in which a person attempts to bring a rival to surrender; a situation in which one person's behaviors are directed at preventing something or at interfering with or harming another individual. *See also* **interpersonal conflict.**

Congruence. A condition in which both verbal and nonverbal behaviors reinforce each other.

Connotation. The feeling or emotional aspect of meaning, generally viewed as consisting of the evaluative (for example, good–bad), potency (strong–weak), and activity (fast–slow) dimensions; the associations of a term; *see also* **denotation.**

Consensus. A principle of attribution through which we attempt to establish whether other people react or behave in the same way as the person on whom we are now focusing. If the person is acting in accordance with the general consensus, then we seek reasons for the behavior outside the individual; if the person is not acting in accordance with the general consensus, then we seek reasons that are internal to the individual.

Consistency. A perceptual process that influences us to maintain balance among our perceptions; a process that makes us tend to see what we expect to see and to be uncomfortable when our perceptions run contrary to our expectations. *Recognize the human tendency to seek and to see consistency even where it does not exist—to see our friends as all positive and our enemies as all negative, for example.*

Contact. The first stage of an interpersonal relationship in which perceptual and interactional contact occurs.

Contamination. A form of territorial encroachment that renders another's territory impure.

Content and relationship dimensions. A principle of communication that messages refer both to content (the world external to both speaker and listener) and to the relationship existing between the individuals who are interacting.

Context of communication. The physical, psychological, social, and temporal environment in which communication takes place. *Assess the context in which messages are communicated and interpret that communication behavior accordingly; avoid seeing messages as independent of context.*

Controllability. One of the factors considered in judging whether or not a person is responsible for his or her behavior. If the person was in control, then you judge that he or she was responsible. *See* **attribution theory.**

Conversation. Two-person communication usually possessing an opening, feedforward, a business stage, feedback, and a closing.

Conversational maxims. Principles that are followed in conversation to ensure that the goal of the conversation is achieved. *Discover, try not to violate, and, if appropriate, follow the conversational maxims of the culture in which you are communicating.*

Conversational turns. The process of exchanging the speaker and listener roles during conversation. *Become sensitive to and respond appropriately to conversational turn cues, such as turn-maintaining, turn-yielding, turn-requesting, and turn-denying cues.*

Cooperation. An interpersonal process by which individuals work together for a common end; the pooling of efforts to produce a mutually desired outcome.

Cooperation (principle of). An implicit agreement between speaker and listener to cooperate in trying to understand what each is communicating.

Counseling interview. A type of **interview** in which the interviewer tries to learn about the interviewee in an attempt to provide some form of guidance, advice, or insight.

Credibility. The degree to which a receiver perceives the speaker to be believable; **competence, character,** and **charisma** (dynamism) are its major dimensions.

Critical thinking. The process of logically evaluating reasons and evidence and reaching a judgment on the basis of this analysis.

Critical thinking-hats technique. A technique developed by Edward deBono in which a problem or issue is viewed from six distinct perspectives.

Criticism. The reasoned judgment of some work; although often equated with fault finding, criticism can involve both positive or negative evaluations.

Cultural display. Signs that communicate ones cultural identification, for example, clothing or religious jewelry.

Cultural time. The meanings given to time communication by a particular culture.

Culture. The relatively specialized lifestyle of a group of people—consisting of their values, beliefs, artifacts, ways of behaving, and ways of communicating—that is passed on from one generation to the next.

Culture shock. The psychological reaction one experiences at being placed in a culture very different from one's own or from what one is used to.

Color communication. The meanings that different cultures communicate. *Use colors (in clothing and in room decor, for example) to convey desired meanings and recognize the cultural meanings that different colors have.*

Conversational management. The ways in which a conversation is conducted. *Respond to conversational turn cues from the other person, and use conversational cues to signal your own desire to exchange (or maintain) speaker or listener roles.*

Cultural rules. Rules that are specific to a given cultural group. *Respond to messages according to the cultural rules of the sender; avoid interpreting the messages of others exclusively through the perspective of your own culture in order to prevent misinterpretation of the intended meanings.*

Date. An **extensional** device used to emphasize the notion of constant change and symbolized by a subscript: for example, John Smith$_{1986}$ is not John Smith$_{1996}$.

Deception cues. Verbal or nonverbal cues that reveal the person is lying.

Decoder. Something that takes a message in one form (for example, sound waves) and translates it into another form (for example, nerve impulses) from which meaning can be formulated (for example, in vocal–auditory communication). In human communication, the decoder is the auditory mechanism; in electronic communication, the decoder is, for example, the telephone earpiece. Decoding is the process of extracting a message from a code—for example, translating speech sounds into nerve impulses. *See also* **encoder.**

Decoding. The process of extracting a message from a code—for example, translating speech sounds into nerve impulses. *See also* **encoding.**

Defensiveness. An attitude of an individual or an atmosphere in a group characterized by threats, fear, and domination; messages evidencing evaluation, control, strategy, neutrality, superiority, and certainty are assumed to lead to defensiveness; opposed to **supportiveness.**

Delayed reactions. Reactions that are consciously delayed while a situation is analyzed.

Delphi method. A type of problem-solving group in which questionnaires are used to poll members (who don't interact among themselves) on several occasions so as to arrive at a group decision on, for example, the most important problems a company faces or activities a group might undertake.

Democratic leader. A group leader who stimulates self-direction and self-actualization of the group members.

Denial. One of the obstacles to the expression of emotion; the process by which we deny our emotions to ourselves or to others.

Denotation. Referential meaning; the objective or descriptive meaning of a word. *See also* **connotation**.

Depenetration. A reversal of penetration; a condition in which the **breadth** and **depth** of a relationship decrease. See **social penetration theory**.

Depth. The degree to which the inner personality—the inner core of an individual—is penetrated in interpersonal interaction.

Deterioration. A stage in an interpersonal relationship in which the bonds holding the individuals together are weakened.

Determinism (principle of). The principle of verbal interaction that holds that all verbalizations are to some extent purposeful—that there is a reason for every verbalization.

Dialog. A form of **communication** in which each person is both speaker and listener; communication characterized by involvement, concern, and respect for the other person; opposed to **monolog**.

Dialogic conversation. Treat conversation as a dialogue rather than a monologue; show concern for the other person, and for the relationship between you, with other-orientation.

Direct speech. Speech in which the speakers intentions are stated clearly and directly. *Use direct speech, for example, in making requests or in responding to others (1) to encourage compromise, (2) to acknowledge responsibility for your own feelings and desires, and (3) to state your own desires honestly so as to encourage honesty, openness, and supportiveness in others.*

Disclaimer. Statement that asks the listener to receive what the speaker says as intended without its reflecting negatively on the image of the speaker. *Avoid using disclaimers that may not be accepted by your listeners; they may raise the very doubts you wish to put to rest. Consider using disclaimers when you think your future messages might offend your listeners.*

Disconfirmation. The process by which one ignores or denies the right of the individual even to define himself or herself; opposed to **confirmation**.

Dissolution. The breaking of the bonds holding an interpersonal relationship together. *In dealing with the end of a relationship consider: (1) breaking the loneliness–depression cycle, (2) taking time out to get to know yourself as an individual, (3) bolstering your self-esteem, (4) removing or avoiding uncomfortable symbols that may remind you of your past relationship and may make you uncomfortable, (5) seeking the support of friends and relatives, and (6) avoiding the repetition of negative patterns.*

Dyadic communication. Two-person communication.

Dyadic consciousness. An awareness of an interpersonal relationship or pairing of two individuals; distinguished from situations in which two individuals are together but do not perceive themselves as being a unit or twosome.

Dyadic effect. The process by which one person in a dyad imitates the behavior of the other person, usually used to refer to the tendency of one person's self-disclosures to prompt the other to also self-disclose. *Be responsive to the dyadic effect; if it is not operating, consider why.*

Ear marker. A marker that identifies an item as belonging to a specific person—for example, a nameplate on a desk or initials on an attaché case.

Effect. The outcome or consequence of an action or behavior; communication is assumed always to have some effect.

Emblems. Nonverbal behaviors that directly translate words or phrases—for example, the signs for "okay" and "peace."

Emotion. The feelings we have—for example, our feelings of guilt, anger, or sorrow.

Empathy. The feeling of another person's feeling; feeling or perceiving something as does another person. *Increase empathic understanding by sharing experiences, role-playing, and seeing the world from his or her perspective. Express this empathic understanding verbally and nonverbally.*

Employment interview. A type of **interview** in which the interviewee is questioned to ascertain his or her suitability for a particular job. *In interviewing for a job: prepare yourself, prepare answers and questions, make an effective presentation of self, acknowledge cultural rules and customs, demonstrate effective interpersonal communication, and follow up the interview.*

Encoder. Something that takes a message in one form (for example, nerve impulses) and translates it into another form (for example, sound waves). In human communication, the encoder is the speaking mechanism; in electronic communication, the encoder is, for example, the telephone mouthpiece. Encoding is the process of putting a message into a code—for example, translating nerve impulses into speech sounds. *See also* **decoder**.

Encoding. The process of putting a message into a code—for example, translating nerve impulses into speech sounds. *See also* **decoding**.

Enculturation. The process by which culture is transmitted from one generation to another.

E-prime. A form of the language that omits the verb "to be" except when used as an auxiliary or in statements of existence. Designed to eliminate the tendency toward **projection**.

Equality. An attitude that recognizes that each individual in a communication interaction is equal, that no one is superior to any other; encourages supportiveness; opposed to **superiority**. *Talk neither down nor up to others but communicate as an equal to increase interpersonal satisfaction and efficiency; share the speaking and the listening; recognize that all parties in communication have something to contribute.*

Equilibrium theory. A theory of proxemics holding that intimacy and physical closeness are positively related; as relationship becomes more intimate, the individuals will use shorter distances between them.

Equity theory. A theory claiming that we experience relational satisfaction when there is an equal distribution of rewards and costs between the two persons in the relationship.

Etc. (et cetera). An **extensional device** used to emphasize the notion of infinite complexity; because one can never know all about anything, any statement about the world or an event must end with an explicit or implicit "etc." *Use the implicit or explicit "etc." to remind yourself and others that there is more to be known and more to be said.*

Ethics. The branch of philosophy that deals with the rightness or wrongness of actions; the study of moral values.

Ethnocentrism. The tendency to see others and their behaviors through our own cultural filters, often as distortions of our own behaviors; the tendency to evaluate the values and beliefs of one's own culture more positively than those of another culture.

Euphemism. A polite word or phrase used to substitute for some taboo or otherwise offensive term.

Excluding talk. Talk about a subject or in a vocabulary that only certain people understand, often in the presence of someone who does not belong to this group and therefore does not understand; use of terms unique to a specific culture as if they were universal.

Excuse. An explanation designed to lessen the negative consequences of something done or said. *Avoid excessive excuse-making. Too many excuses may backfire and create image problems for the excuse-maker.*

Exit interview. A type of **interview** in which employees and management discuss the reasons for the employee's leaving the corporation.

Expectancy violations theory. A theory of proxemics holding that people have a certain expectancy for space relationships. When that is violated (for example, a person stands too close to you or a romantic partner maintains abnormally large distances from you), the relationship comes into clearer focus and you wonder why this "normal distance" is being violated.

Experiential limitation. The limit of an individual's ability to communicate, as set by the nature and extent of that individual's experiences.

Expert power. Power dependent on a person's expertise or knowledge; knowledge gives an individual expert power.

Expressiveness. A quality of interpersonal effectiveness; genuine involvement in speaking and listening, conveyed verbally and nonverbally. *Communicate involvement and interest by providing appropriate feedback, assuming responsibility for your thoughts and feelings and your role as speaker and listener, and using variety and flexibility in voice and bodily action.*

Extemporaneous speech. A speech that is thoroughly prepared and organized in detail and in which certain aspects of style are predetermined.

Extensional devices. Linguistic devices proposed by Alfred Korzybski to keep language a more accurate means for talking about the world. The extensional devices include **etc., date,** and **index** (the working devices) and the **hyphen** and **quotes** (the safety devices).

Extensional orientation. A point of view in which the primary consideration is given to the world of experience and only secondary consideration is given to labels. *See also* **intensional orientation.**

Face saving. Maintaining a positive public self-image in the minds of others.

Facial feedback hypothesis. The hypothesis or theory that your facial expressions can produce physiological and emotional effects.

Facial management techniques. Techniques used to mask certain emotions and to emphasize others, for example, intensifying your expression of happiness to make a friend feel good about a promotion.

Fact-inference confusion. A misevaluation in which one makes an inference, regards it as a fact, and acts upon it as if it were a fact.

Distinguish facts from inferences; respond to inferences as inferences and not as facts.

Factual statement. A statement made by the observer after observation and limited to what is observed. *See also* **inferential statement.**

Family. A group of people who consider themselves related and connected to one another and where the actions of one have consequences for others.

Fear appeal. The appeal to fear to persuade an individual or group of individuals to believe or to act in a certain way.

Feedback. Information that is given back to the source. Feedback may come from the source's own messages (as when we hear what we are saying) or from the receiver(s) in the form of applause, yawning, puzzled looks, questions, letters to the editor of a newspaper, increased or decreased subscriptions to a magazine, and so forth. *Give clear feedback to others, and respond to other's feedback, either through corrective measures or by continuing current performance, to increase communication efficiency and satisfaction. See also* **negative feedback; positive feedback.**

Feedforward. Information that is sent prior to the regular messages telling the listener something about what is to follow. *When appropriate, preface your messages in order to open the channels of communication, to preview the messages to be sent, to disclaim, and to altercast. In your use of feedforward, be brief, use feedforward sparingly, and follow through on your feedforward promises. Also, be sure to respond to the feedforward as well as the content messages of others.*

Field of experience. The sum total of an individual's experiences, which influences his or her ability to communicate. In some views of communication, two people can communicate only to the extent that their fields of experience overlap.

Flexibility. The ability to adjust communication strategies on the basis of the unique situation. *Apply the principles of interpersonal communication with flexibility; remember that each situation calls for somewhat different skills.*

Focus group. A group designed to explore the feelings and attitudes of its individuals and which usually follows a question and answer format.

Force. An unproductive **conflict** strategy in which one attempts to win an argument by physical force or threats of force. *Avoid it.*

Forum. A small group format in which members of the group answer questions from the audience; often follows a symposium.

Free information. Information that is revealed implicitly and that may be used as a basis for opening or pursuing conversations.

Friendship. An interpersonal relationship between two persons that is mutually productive, established and maintained through perceived mutual free choice, and characterized by mutual positive regard. *Adjust your verbal and nonverbal communication as appropriate to the stages of your various friendships. Learn the rules that govern your friendships; follow them or risk damaging the relationship.*

Fundamental attribution error. The tendency to attribute a person's behavior to the kind of person he or she is (to the person's personality, perhaps) and to not give sufficient importance to the situation the person is in.

Game. A simulation of some situation with rules governing the behaviors of the participants and with some payoff for winning;

in transactional analysis, "game" refers to a series of ulterior transactions that lead to a payoff; the term also refers to a basically dishonest kind of transaction in which participants hide their true feelings.

General semantics. The study of the relationships among language, thought, and behavior.

Glittering generality. The opposite of **name calling**, which occurs when the speaker tries to gain your acceptance of an idea by associating it with things you value highly.

Gossip. Communication about someone not present, some third party, usually about matters that are private to this third party. *Avoid gossip that breaches confidentiality, is known to be false, and is unnecessarily invasive.*

Granfalloon. The tendency of people to see themselves as constituting a cohesive and like-minded group because they are given a label.

Grapevine. The informal lines through which messages in an organization may travel; these informal lines resemble the physical grapevine, with its unpredictable pattern of branches.

Group. A collection of individuals related to each other with some common purpose and with some structure among them.

Group norm. Rules or expectations of appropriate behavior for a member of the group.

Groupthink. A tendency observed in some groups in which agreement among members becomes more important than the exploration of the issues at hand.

Gunnysacking. An unproductive **conflict** strategy of storing up grievances—as if in a gunnysack—and holding them in readiness to dump on the person with whom one is in conflict. *Avoid it.*

Halo effect. The tendency to generalize an individual's virtue or expertise from one area to another.

Haptics. Technical term for the study of touch communication.

Heterosexist language. Language that assumes all people are heterosexual and thereby denigrates lesbians and gay men. *Avoid it.*

High-context culture. A culture in which much of the information in communication is in the context or in the person rather than explicitly coded in the verbal messages. **Collectivist cultures** are generally high context. Opposed to **low-context** culture.

Home-field advantage. The increased power that comes from being in your own territory.

Home territories. Territories for which individuals have a sense of intimacy and over which they exercise control—for example, a professor's office.

Hyphen. An **extensional device** used to illustrate that what may be separated verbally may not be separable on the event level or on the nonverbal level; although one may talk about body and mind as if they were separable, in reality they are better referred to as body–mind.

Idea-generation group. A group whose purpose is to generate ideas; see **brainstorming.**

Illustrators. Nonverbal behaviors that accompany and literally illustrate the verbal messages—for example, upward movements that accompany the verbalization "It's up there."

I-messages. Messages in which the speaker accepts responsibility for personal thoughts and behaviors; messages in which the speaker's point of view is stated explicitly; opposed to **you-messages.** *Use I-messages to take responsibility for your thoughts and behaviors.*

Immediacy. A quality of interpersonal effectiveness; a sense of contact and togetherness; a feeling of interest and liking for the other person. *Communicate immediacy through appropriate word choice, feedback, eye contact, body posture, and physical closeness.*

Implicit personality theory. A theory of personality that each individual maintains, complete with rules or systems, through which others are perceived. *Be conscious of your implicit personality theories; avoid drawing firm conclusions about other people on the basis of these theories.*

Impromptu speech. A speech given without any explicit prior preparation.

Inclusion principle. In verbal interaction, the principle that all members should be a part of (included in) the interaction. *Include everyone present in the interaction (both verbally and nonverbally) so you do not exclude or offend others or fail to profit from their contributions.*

Inclusive talk. Communication that includes all people; communication that does not exclude certain groups, for example, women, lesbians and gays, or members of certain races or nationalities.

Index. An **extensional device** used to emphasize the notion of nonidentity (no two things are the same) and symbolized by a subscript—for example, politician$_1$ is not politician$_2$.

Indirect speech. Speech that may hide the speaker's true intentions or that may be used to make requests and observations indirectly. *Use direct speech, for example, (1) to express a desire without insulting or offending anyone, (2) to ask for compliments in a socially acceptable manner, and (3) to disagree without being disagreeable.*

Indiscrimination. A misevaluation caused by categorizing people, events, or objects into a particular class and responding to them only as members of the class; a failure to recognize that each individual is unique; a failure to apply the **index.** *Index your terms and statements to emphasize that each person and event is unique; avoid treating all individuals the same way because they are covered by the same label or term.*

Individualistic culture. A culture in which the individual's rather than the group's goals and preferences are given greater importance. Opposed to **collectivist cultures.**

Individual orientation. A cultural orientation in which the individual's rather than the group's goals and preferences are given greater importance. Opposed to **collective orientation.**

Inevitability. A principle of communication referring to the fact that communication cannot be avoided; all behavior in an interactional setting is communication. *Because all behavior in an interactional situation communicates, seek out nonobvious messages and meanings.*

Inferential statement. A statement that can be made by anyone, is not limited to what is observed, and can be made at any time; see also **factual statement.**

Informal time terms. Terms that describe approximate rather than exact time, for example, "soon," "early," and "in a while." *Recognize that informal time terms are often the cause of interpersonal difficulties. When misunderstanding is likely, use more precise terms.*

Information. That which reduces uncertainty.

Information overload. A condition in which the amount of information is too great to be dealt with effectively or the number or complexity of messages is so great that the individual or organization is not able to deal with them.

Information power. Power dependent on one's information and one's ability to communicate logically and persuasively. Also called "persuasion power."

Informative interview. A type of **interview** in which the interviewer asks the interviewee, usually a person of some reputation and accomplishment, questions designed to elicit his or her views, predictions, and perspectives on specific topics. *In interviewing for information: secure an appointment, prepare your questions, establish rapport with the interviewer, ask permission to tape the interview, and close and follow up the interview.*

Inoculation principle. A principle stating that persuasion will be more difficult to achieve when beliefs and attitudes that have already been challenged previously are attacked, because the individual has built up defenses against such attacks in a manner similar to inoculation. *In persuading an audience inoculated against your position, be content with small gains; trying to reverse an inoculated audience in one speech is probably unrealistic.*

Insulation. A reaction to **territorial encroachment** in which you erect some sort of barrier between yourself and the invaders.

Intensional orientation. A point of view in which primary consideration is given to the way things are labeled and only secondary consideration (if any) to the world of experience. *Respond first to things; avoid responding to labels as if they were things; do not let labels distort your perception of the world. See also* **extensional orientation.**

Interaction management. A quality of interpersonal effectiveness; the control of interaction to the satisfaction of both parties; managing conversational turns, fluency, and message consistency. *Manage the interaction to the satisfaction of both parties by sharing the roles of speaker and listener, avoiding long and awkward silences, and being consistent in your verbal and nonverbal messages.*

Interaction process analysis. A content analysis method that classifies messages into four general categories: social emotional positive, social emotional negative, attempted answers, and questions.

Intercultural communication. Communication that takes place between persons of different cultures or persons who have different cultural beliefs, values, or ways of behaving.

Interpersonal communication. Communication between two persons or among a small group of persons and distinguished from public or mass communication; communication of a personal nature and distinguished from impersonal communication; communication between or among intimates or those involved in a close relationship; often, intrapersonal, dyadic, and small group communication in general.

Interpersonal conflict. A conflict or disagreement between two persons. *To fight more productively: look for win–win strategies, fight actively, use talk instead of force, focus on the present rather than gunnysacking, use face-enhancing instead of face-detracting strategies, express acceptance instead of attacking the other person, and use your skills in argumentation, not in verbal aggressiveness.*

Interpersonal perception. The perception of people; the processes through which we interpret and evaluate people and their behavior. *Increase the accuracy of your interpersonal perceptions by checking your perceptions, subjecting your perceptions to critical thinking,* reducing uncertainty, and becoming aware of cultural differences and influences on perception.

Interview. A particular form of interpersonal communication in which two persons interact largely by question-and-answer format for the purpose of achieving specific goals. Also see the specific types of interviews: **appraisal interview, counseling interview, employment interview, exit interview, information interview,** and **persuasion interview.**

Intimacy. The closest interpersonal relationship; usually used to denote a close primary relationship.

Intimacy claims. Obligations incurred by virtue of being in a close and intimate relationship. *Reduce the intensity of intimacy claims when things get rough; give each other space as appropriate.*

Intimate distance. The closest proxemic distance, ranging from touching to 18 inches. *See also* **proxemics.**

Intrapersonal communication. Communication with oneself.

Invasion. The unwarranted entrance into another's territory that changes the meaning of the territory. *See* **territorial encroachment.**

Involvement stage. That stage in an interpersonal relationship that normally follows contact in which the individuals get to know each other better and explore the potential for greater intimacy.

Irreversibility. A principle of communication holding that communication cannot be reversed; once something has been communicated, it cannot be uncommunicated. *Avoid saying things (for example, in anger) or making commitments that you may wish to retract (but will not be able to) in order to prevent resentment and ill feeling.*

Jargon. The technical language of any specialized group, often a professional class that is unintelligible to individuals not belonging to the group; "shop talk."

Johari window. A diagram of the four selves (**open, blind, hidden,** and **unknown**) that illustrates the different kinds of information in each self.

Kinesics. The study of the communicative dimensions of facial and bodily movements.

Laissez-faire leader. A group leader who allows the group to develop and progress or make mistakes on its own.

Lateral communication. Communication among equals—for example, manager to manager, worker to worker.

Leadership. That quality by which one individual directs or influences the thoughts and/or the behaviors of others. *See* **laissez-faire leader, democratic leader,** and **authoritarian leader.**

Leave-taking cues. Verbal and nonverbal cues that indicate a desire to terminate a conversation. *Increase your sensitivity to leave-taking cues; pick up on the leave-taking cues of others, and communicate such cues tactfully so as not to insult or offend others.*

Legitimate power. Power dependent on the belief that a person has a right, by virtue of position, to influence or control another's behavior.

Leveling. A process of message distortion in which a message is repeated but the number of details is reduced, some details are omitted entirely, and some details lose their complexity.

Level of abstraction. The relative distance of a term or statement from the actual perception; a low-order abstraction would be a description of the perception, whereas a high-order abstraction would consist of inferences about descriptions of a perception.

Listening. An active process of receiving messages sent orally; this process consists of five stages: receiving, understanding, remembering, evaluating, and responding. *Adjust your listening perspective, as the situation warrants, between judgmental and nonjudgmental, surface and depth, and empathic and objective listening. Listen actively when appropriate.*

Logic. The science of reasoning; the study of the principles governing the analysis of inference making.

Looking-glass self. The self-concept that results from the image of yourself that others reveal to you.

Loving. An interpersonal process in which one feels a closeness, a caring, a warmth, and an excitement for another person.

Low-context culture. A culture in which most of the information in communication is explicitly stated in the verbal messages. **Individualistic cultures** are usually low-context cultures. Opposed to **high-context culture.**

Magnitude of change principle. A principle of persuasion stating that the greater and more important the change desired by the speaker, the more difficult its achievement will be.

Maintenance. A stage of relationship stability at which the relationship does not progress or deteriorate significantly; a continuation as opposed to a dissolution of a relationship.

Maintenance strategies. Specific behaviors designed to preserve an interpersonal relationship. *Use appropriate maintenance strategies (for example, openness, sharing joint activities, and acting positively) to preserve a valued relationship. See also* **repair strategies.**

Manipulation. An unproductive **conflict** strategy that avoids open conflict; instead, attempts are made to divert the conflict by being especially charming and getting the other person into a noncombative frame of mind. *Avoid it.*

Manuscript speech. A speech designed to be read verbatim from a script.

Markers. Devices that signify that a certain territory belongs to a particular person. Become sensitive to the markers (central, boundary, and ear) of others, and learn to use these markers to define your own territories and to communicate the desired impression. *See also* **boundary marker, central marker,** and **earmarker.**

Mass communication. Communication addressed to an extremely large audience, mediated by audio and/or visual transmitters, and processed by gatekeepers before transmission.

Matching hypothesis. An assumption that we date and mate with people who are similar to ourselves—who match us—in physical attractiveness.

Meaningfulness. A perception principle that refers to your assumption that people's behavior is sensible, stems from some logical antecedent, and is consequently meaningful rather than meaningless.

Mere exposure hypothesis. The theory that repeated or prolonged exposure to a stimulus may result in a change in attitude toward the stimulus object, generally in the direction of increased positiveness.

Message. Any signal or combination of signals that serves as a **stimulus** for a receiver.

Metacommunication. Communication about communication. *Metacommunicate to ensure understanding of the other person's thoughts and feelings: give clear feedforward, explain feelings as well as thoughts, paraphrase your own complex thoughts, and ask questions.*

Metalanguage. Language used to talk about language.

Metamessage. A message that makes reference to another message, for example, the statements "Did I make myself clear?" or "That's a lie" refer to other messages and are therefore considered metamessages. *Use metamessages to clarify your understanding of what another thinks and feels.*

Metaskills. Skills for regulating more specific skills, for example, the skills of interpersonal communication such as openness and empathy must be regulated by the metaskills of flexibility, mindfulness, and metacommunication.

Mindfulness and mindlessness. States of relative awareness. In a mindful state, we are aware of the logic and rationality of our behaviors and the logical connections existing among elements. In a mindless state, we are unaware of this logic and rationality. *Apply the principles of interpersonal communication mindfully rather than mindlessly. Increase mindfulness by creating and re-creating categories, being open to new information and points of view, and being careful of relying too heavily on first impressions.*

Mixed message. A message that contradicts itself; a message that asks for two different (often incompatible) responses. Avoid emitting mixed messages by focusing clearly on your purposes when communicating and by increasing conscious control over your verbal and nonverbal behaviors. *Detect mixed messages in other people's communications and respond to them as appropriate. Avoid sending mixed messages—they make you appear unsure and unfocused.*

Model. A representation of an object or process.

Monochronic time orientation. A view of time in which things are done sequentially; one thing is scheduled at a time. Opposed to **polychronic time orientation.**

Monolog. A form of **communication** in which one person speaks and the other listens; there is no real interaction among participants. *Avoid it, at least generally.* Opposed to **dialog.**

Motivated sequence. An organizational pattern for arranging the information in a discourse to motivate an audience to respond positively to one's purpose.

Name calling. A persuasive technique in which the speaker gives an idea a derogatory name.

Negative feedback. Feedback that serves a corrective function by informing the source that his or her message is not being received in the way intended. Negative feedback serves to redirect the source's behavior. Looks of boredom, shouts of disagreement, letters critical of newspaper policy, and teacher's instructions on how better to approach a problem would be examples of negative feedback. *See* **positive feedback.**

Neutrality. A response pattern lacking in personal involvement; encourages defensiveness; opposed to **empathy.**

Noise. Anything that interferes with a person's receiving a message as the source intended the message to be received. Noise is present in a communication system to the extent that the message received is not the message sent. *Combat the effects of physical, semantic, and psychological noise by eliminating or lessening the sources* of physical noise, securing agreement on meanings, and interacting with an open mind in order to increase communication accuracy.

Nominal group. A collection of individuals who record their thoughts and opinions, which are then distributed to others. Without direct interaction, the thoughts and opinions are gradually pared down until a manageable list (of solutions or decisions) is produced. When this occurs, the nominal group (a group in name only) may restructure itself into a problem-solving group that analyzes the final list.

Nonallness. An attitude or point of view in which it is recognized that one can never know all about anything and that what we know, say, or hear is only a part of what there is to know, say, or hear.

Nondirective language. Language that does not direct or focus our attention on certain aspects; neutral language. *Use nondirective language when you wish to encourage others to talk without moving them in any specific direction.*

Nonnegotiation. An unproductive **conflict** strategy in which the individual refuses to discuss the conflict or to listen to the other person.

Nonverbal communication. Communication without words; communication by means of space, gestures, facial expressions, touching, vocal variation, and silence, for example.

Nonverbal dominance. Nonverbal behavior that allows one person to achieve psychological dominance over another. *Resist (as sender and receiver) nonverbal expressions of dominance when they are inappropriate—for example, when they are sexist.*

Norm. *See* **group norm.**

Object-adaptors. Movements that involve your manipulation of some object, for example, punching holes in or drawing on the styrofoam coffee cup, clicking a ballpoint pen, or chewing on a pencil. *Avoid them; they generally communicate discomfort and a lack of control over the communication situation.*

Object language. Language used to communicate about objects, events, and relations in the world; the structure of the object language is described in a **metalanguage**; the display of physical objects—for example, flower arranging and the colors of the clothes we wear.

Olfactory communication. Communication by smell.

Openness. A quality of interpersonal effectiveness encompassing (1) a willingness to interact openly with others, to self-disclose as appropriate; (2) a willingness to react honestly to incoming stimuli; and (3) a willingness to own one's feelings and thoughts.

Oral style. The style of spoken discourse that, when compared with written style, consists of shorter, simpler, and more familiar words; more qualification, self-reference terms, allness terms, verbs and adverbs; and more concrete terms and terms indicative of consciousness of projection—for example, "as I see it."

Other-orientation. A quality of interpersonal effectiveness involving attentiveness, interest, and concern for the other person. *Convey concern for and interest in the other person by means of empathic responses, appropriate feedback, and attentive listening responses.*

Other talk. Talk about the listener or some third party.

Owning feelings. The process by which you take responsibility for your own feelings instead of attributing them to others. *Use I-messages to express ownership and to acknowledge responsibility for your own thoughts and feelings.*

Packaging. *See* **reinforcement.**

Panel or round table. A small group format in which participants are arranged in a circular pattern and speak without any set pattern.

Paralanguage. The vocal (but nonverbal) aspect of speech. Paralanguage consists of voice qualities (for example, pitch range, resonance, tempo), vocal characterizers (laughing or crying, yelling or whispering), vocal qualifiers (intensity, pitch height), and vocal segregates ("uh-uh," meaning "no," or "sh" meaning "silence"). *Vary paralinguistic elements, such as rate, volume, and stress, to add variety and emphasis to your communications, and be responsive to the meanings communicated by others' paralanguage.*

Parasocial relationship. Relationships between a real and an imagined or fictional character, usually used to refer to relationships between a viewer and a fictional character in a television show.

Pauses. Silent periods in the normally fluent stream of speech. Pauses are of two major types: filled pauses (interruptions in speech that are filled with such vocalizations as "er "or "um") and unfilled pauses (silences of unusually long duration).

Perception. The process of becoming aware of objects and events from the senses. *See* **interpersonal perception.**

Perception checking. The process of verifying your understanding of some message or situation or feeling to reduce uncertainty. *Use perception checking to get more information about your impressions: (1) describe what you see or hear and what you think is happening, and (2) ask whether this is correct or in error.*

Perceptual accentuation. A process that leads you to see what you expect to see and what you want to see—for example, seeing people you like as better looking and smarter than people you do not like. *Be aware of the influence your own needs, wants, and expectations have on your perceptions. Recognize that what you perceive is a function both of what exists in reality and what is going on inside your own head.*

Personal distance. The second-closest proxemic distance, ranging from 18 inches to 4 feet. *See also* **proxemics.**

Personal rejection. An unproductive **conflict** strategy in which the individual withholds love and affection and seeks to win the argument by getting the other person to break down under this withdrawal.

Persuasion. The process of influencing attitudes and behavior.

Persuasive interview. A type of **interview** in which the interviewer attempts to change the interviewee's attitudes or behavior.

Phatic communication. Communication that is primarily social; communication designed to open the channels of communication rather than to communicate something about the external world; "Hello" and "How are you?" in everyday interaction are examples.

Pitch. The highness or lowness of the vocal tone.

Plain folks. A persuasive strategy in when the speaker identifies himself or herself and the proposal with the audience.

Polarization. A form of fallacious reasoning by which only two extremes are considered; also referred to as "black-or-white" and "either-or" thinking or two-valued orientation. *Use middle terms and qualifiers when describing the world; avoid talking in terms of polar opposites (black and white, good and bad) in order to describe reality more accurately.*

Polychronic time orientation. A view of time in which several things may be scheduled or engaged in at the same time. Opposed to **monochronic time orientation.**

Positive feedback. Feedback that supports or reinforces the continuation of behavior along the same lines in which it is already proceeding—for example, applause during a speech.

Positiveness. A characteristic of effective communication involving positive attitudes toward oneself and toward the interpersonal interaction. Also used to refer to complimenting another and expressing acceptance and approval. *Verbally and nonverbally communicate a positive attitude toward yourself, others, and the situation with smiles, positive facial expressions, attentive gestures, positive verbal expressions, and the elimination or reduction of negative appraisals.*

Power. The ability to control the behaviors of others.

Power communication. Communicate power through forceful speech, avoidance of weak modifiers and excessive body movement, and demonstration of your knowledge, preparation, and organization in the matters at hand.

Power play. A consistent pattern of behavior in which one person tries to control the behavior of another. *Identify the power plays people use on you and respond to these power plays so as to stop them. Use an effective management strategy such as "cooperation," by, for example, expressing your feelings, describing the behavior you object to, and stating a cooperative response.*

Pragmatic implication. An assumption that seems logical but is not necessarily true. *Identify your own pragmatic implications, distinguishing these from logical implications (those that are necessarily true), and recognize that memory often confuses the two. In recalling situations and events, ask yourself whether your conclusions are based on pragmatic or logical implications.*

Premature self-disclosures. Disclosures that are made before the relationship has developed sufficiently. *Resist too intimate or too negative self-disclosures early in the development of a relationship.*

Primacy effect. The condition by which what comes first exerts greater influence than what comes later. *See also* **recency effect.**

Primacy and recency. Primacy refers to giving more credence to that which occurs first; recency refers to giving more credence to that which occurs last (that is, most recently). *Resist the normal tendency for first impressions to leave lasting impressions and to color both what we see later and the conclusions we draw. Take the time and effort to revise your impressions of others on the basis of new information. Be at your very best in first encounters because others may well be operating with a primacy bias.*

Primary relationship. The relationship between two people that they consider their most (or one of their most) important, for example, the relationship between spouses or domestic partners.

Primary territory. Areas that one can consider one's exclusive preserve—for example, one's room or office.

Problem-solving group. A group whose primary task is to solve a problem, but more often to reach a decision.

Problem-solving sequence. A logical step-by-step process for solving a problem frequently used by groups and consisting of defining and analyzing the problem, establishing criteria for evaluating solutions, identifying possible solutions, evaluating solutions, selecting the best solution, and testing the selected solutions.

Process. Ongoing activity; communication is referred to as a process to emphasize that it is always changing, always in motion.

Productivity. The feature of language that makes possible the creation and understanding of novel utterances. With human language we can talk about matters that have never been talked about before, and we can understand utterances we have never heard before. Also referred to as **openness.**

Progressive differentiation. A relational problem caused by the exaggeration or intensification of differences or similarities between individuals.

Projection. A psychological process whereby we attribute characteristics or feelings of our own to others; often used to refer to the process whereby we attribute our own faults to others.

Pronunciation. The production of syllables or words according to some accepted standard, as presented, for example, in a dictionary.

Protection theory. A theory of proxemics referring to the fact that people establish a body-buffer zone to protect themselves from unwanted closeness, touching, or attack.

Provisionalism. An attitude of open-mindedness that leads to the creation of supportiveness; opposed to **certainty.**

Proxemic distances. The spatial distances that are maintained in communication and social interaction. *Adjust spatial (proxemic) distances as appropriate to the specific interaction; avoid distances that are too far, too close, or otherwise inappropriate, as they might falsely convey, for example, aloofness or aggression.*

Proxemics. The study of the communicative function of space; the study of how people unconsciously structure their space—the distance between people in their interactions, the organization of space in homes and offices, and even the design of cities.

Proximity. As a principle of perception, the tendency to perceive people or events that are physically close as belonging together or representing some unit; physical closeness; one of the qualities influencing **interpersonal attraction.** *Use physical proximity to increase interpersonal attractiveness.*

Psychological time. The importance you place on past, pres-ent, or future time. *Recognize the significance of your own time orientation to your ultimate success, and make whatever adjustments you think desirable.*

Public communication. Communication in which the source is one person and the receiver is an audience of many persons.

Public distance. The longest proxemic distance, ranging from 12 to more than 25 feet.

Public territory. Areas that are open to all people—for example, restaurants or parks.

Punctuation of communication. The breaking up of continuous communication sequences into short sequences with identifiable beginnings and endings or stimuli and responses. *To increase empathy and mutual understanding, see the sequence of events punctuated from perspectives other than your own.*

Punishment. Noxious or aversive stimulation.

Pupillometrics. The study of communication through changes in the size of the pupils of the eyes. *Detect pupil dilation and constriction, and formulate hypotheses (not conclusions) concerning their possible meanings.*

Purr words. Highly positive words that express the speaker's feelings rather than refer to any objective reality; opposite of **snarl words**.

Quotes. An **extensional device** to emphasize that a word or phrase is being used in a special sense and should therefore be given special attention.

Racist language. Language that denigrates or is derogatory toward members of a particular race. *Avoid racist language so as not to offend or alienate others or reinforce stereotypes.*

Rate. The speed with which you speak, generally measured in words per minute.

Receiver. Any person or thing that takes in messages. Receivers may be individuals listening to or reading a message, a group of persons hearing a speech, a scattered television audience, or machines that store information.

Recency effect. The condition in which what comes last (that is, most recently) exerts greater influence than what comes first. *See also* **primacy effect.**

Redundancy. The quality of a message that makes it totally predictable and therefore lacking in information. A message of zero redundancy would be completely unpredictable; a message of 100% redundancy would be completely predictable. All human languages contain some degree of built-in redundancy, generally estimated to be about 50%.

Referent power. Power dependent on one's desire to identify with or be like another person.

Reflexiveness. The feature of human language that makes it possible for that language to be used to refer to itself; that is, we can talk about our talk and create a **metalanguage**—a language for talking about language.

Regulators. Nonverbal behaviors that regulate, monitor, or control the communications of another person.

Reinforcement theory. A theory of behavior that when applied to relationships would hold (essentially) that relationships develop because they are rewarding and end because they are punishing. *Reinforce others as a way to increase interpersonal attractiveness and general interpersonal satisfaction.*

Rejection. A response to an individual that rejects or denies the validity of that individual's self-view.

Relational communication. Communication between or among intimates or those in close relationships; used by some theorists as synonymous with **interpersonal communication**.

Relationship deterioration. The stage of a relationship during which the connecting bonds between the partners weaken and the partners begin drifting apart.

Relationship development. The stages of relationships during which you move closer to intimacy; in the model of relationships presented here, relationship development includes the contact and the involvement stages.

Relationship dialectics theory. A theory that describes relationships along a series of opposites representing competing desires or motivations, such as the desire for autonomy and the desire to belong to someone, for novelty and predictability, and for closedness and openness.

Relationship maintenance. The processes by which you attempt to keep the relationship stable.

Relationship messages. Messages that comment on the relationship between the speakers rather than on matters external to them. *Recognize and respond to relationship as well as content messages in order to ensure a more complete understanding of the messages intended.*

Relationship repair. Attempts to reverse the process of **relationship deterioration**. *To repair a relationship: recognize the problem, engage in productive conflict resolution, pose possible solutions, affirm each other, integrate solutions into normal behavior, and take risks.*

Response. Any overt or covert behavior.

Reward power. Power dependent on one's ability to reward another person.

Rigid complementarity. The inability to break away from the complementary type of relationship that was once appropriate but is no longer.

Role. The part an individual plays in a group; an individual's function or expected behavior.

Rules theory. A theory that describes relationships as interactions governed by a series of rules that a couple agrees to follow. When the rules are followed, the relationship is maintained and when they are broken, the relationship experiences difficulty.

Secondary territory. Areas that do not belong to a particular person but have been occupied by that person and are therefore associated with her or him—for example, the seat you normally take in class.

Selective exposure (principle of). A principle of persuasion that states that listeners actively seek out information that supports their opinions and actively avoid information that contradicts their existing opinions, beliefs, attitudes, and values.

Self-acceptance. Being satisfied with ourselves, our virtues and vices, and our abilities and limitations.

Self-adaptors. Movements that usually satisfy a physical need, especially to make you more comfortable, for example, scratching your head to relieve an itch, moistening your lips because they feel dry, or pushing your hair out of your eyes. *Because these often communicate your nervousness or discomfort, they are best avoided.*

Self-attribution. A process through which we seek to account for and understand the reasons and motivations for our own behaviors.

Self-awareness. The degree to which a person knows himself or herself. *Increase self-awareness by asking yourself about yourself and listening to others; actively seek information about yourself from others by carefully observing their interactions with you and by asking relevant questions. See yourself from different perspectives (see your different selves), and increase your open self.*

Self-concept. An individual's self-evaluation; an individual's self-appraisal.

Self-disclosure. The process of revealing something about ourselves to another, usually used to refer to information that would normally be kept hidden. *Self-disclose when the motivation is to improve the relationship, when the context and the relationship are appropriate for the self-disclosure, when there is an opportunity for open and honest responses, when the self-disclosures will be clear and direct, when there are appropriate reciprocal disclosures, and when you have exam-*

ined and are willing to risk the possible burdens that self-disclosure might entail. Self-disclose selectively; regulate your self-disclosures as appropriate to the context, topic, audience, and potential rewards and risks to secure the maximum advantage and reduce the possibility of negative effects. In responding to the disclosures of others, demonstrate the skills of effective listening, express support for the discloser (but resist evaluation), reinforce the disclosing behavior, keep the disclosures confidential, and avoid using the disclosures against the person.

Self-esteem. The value you place on yourself; your self-evaluation; usually used to refer to the positive value placed on oneself. *Increase your self-esteem by attacking self-destructive statements and engage in self-affirmation.*

Self-fulfilling prophecy. The situation in which we make a prediction or prophecy and fulfill it ourselves—for example, expecting a class to be boring and then fulfilling this expectation by perceiving it as boring. *Avoid fulfilling your own negative prophecies and seeing only what you want to see. Be especially careful to examine your perceptions when they conform too closely to your expectations; check to make sure that you are seeing what exists in real life, not just in your expectations or predictions.*

Self-monitoring. The manipulation of the image one presents to others in interpersonal interactions so as to give the most favorable impression of oneself. *Monitor your verbal and nonverbal behavior as appropriate to communicate the desired impression.*

Self-serving bias. A bias that operates in the self-attribution process and leads us to take credit for the positive consequences and to deny responsibility for the negative consequences of our behaviors. *In examining the causes of your own behavior, beware of the tendency to attribute negative behaviors to external factors and positive behaviors to internal factors. In self-examinations, ask whether and how the self-serving bias might be operating.*

Self-talk. Talk about oneself. *Balance talk about yourself with talk about the other; avoid excessive self-talk or extreme avoidance of self-talk to encourage equal sharing and interpersonal satisfaction.*

Semantics. The area of language study concerned with meaning.

Sexist language. Language derogatory to one sex, usually women. *Whether man or woman, avoid sexist language—for example, terms that presume maleness as the norm ("policeman" or "mailman") or terms that may be considered insulting or demeaning.*

Sexual harassment. Unsolicited and unwanted sexual messages. *If confronted with sexual harassment, consider talking to the harasser, collecting evidence, using appropriate channels within the organization, or filing a complaint. Avoid any indication of sexual harassment by beginning with the assumption that others at work are not interested in sexual advances and stories; listen for negative reactions to any sexually explicit discussions, and avoid behaviors you think might prove offensive.*

Shyness. The condition of discomfort and uneasiness in interpersonal situations.

Sign, reasoning from. A form of reasoning in which the presence of certain signs (clues) are interpreted as leading to a particular conclusion.

Signal and noise (relativity of). The principle of verbal interaction that holds that what is signal (meaningful) and what is noise (interference) is relative to the communication analyst, the participants, and the context.

Signal reaction. A conditioned response to a signal; a response to some signal that is immediate rather than delayed.

Silence. The absence of vocal communication; often misunderstood to refer to the absence of any and all communication. Silence is often used to communicate feelings or to prevent communication about certain topics. *Interpret silences of others through their culturally determined rules rather than your own.*

Similarity. A principle of **attraction** holding that one is attracted to qualities similar to those possessed by oneself and to people who are similar to oneself; opposed to **complementarity.**

Slang. The language used by special groups that is not considered proper by the general society; language made up of the **argot, cant,** and **jargon** of various groups and known by the general public.

Small group communication. Communication among a collection of individuals, small enough in number that all members may interact with relative ease as both senders and receivers, the members being related to each other by some common purpose and with some degree of organization or structure.

Snarl words. Highly negative words that express the feelings of the speaker rather than refer to any objective reality; opposite to **purr words.**

Social comparison processes. The processes by which you compare yourself (for example, your abilities, opinions, and values) with others and then assess and evaluate yourself; one of the sources of **self-concept.**

Social distance. The third **proxemic** distance, ranging from 4 to 12 feet; the distance at which business is usually conducted.

Social exchange theory. A theory hypothesizing that we develop relationships in which our rewards or profits will be greater than our costs and that we avoid or terminate relationships in which the costs exceed the rewards.

Social penetration theory. A theory concerned with relationship development from the superficial to the intimate levels and from few to many areas of interpersonal interaction.

Source. Any person or thing that creates messages. A source may be an individual speaking, writing, or gesturing or a computer sending an error message.

Spatial distance. Use spatial distance to signal the type of relationship you are in: intimate, personal, social, or public. Let your spatial relationships reflect your interpersonal relationships.

Specific instances, reasoning from. A form of reasoning in which several specific instances are examined and then a conclusion about the whole is formed.

Speech. Messages utilizing a vocal–auditory channel.

Speech rate. Use variations in rate to increase communication efficiency and persuasiveness as appropriate.

Spontaneity. The communication pattern in which one verbalizes what one is thinking without attempting to develop strategies for control; encourages **supportiveness;** opposed to **strategy.**

Stability. The principle of perception that refers to the fact that our perceptions of things and of people are relatively consistent with our previous perceptions.

Static evaluation. An orientation that fails to recognize that the world is characterized by constant change; an attitude that sees people and events as fixed rather than as constantly changing. *Date your statements to emphasize constant change; avoid the tendency to think of and describe things as static and unchanging.*

Status. The relative level one occupies in a hierarchy; status always involves a comparison, and thus one's status is only relative to the status of another.

Stereotype. In communication, a fixed impression of a group of people through which we then perceive specific individuals; stereotypes are most often negative but may also be positive. *Avoid stereotyping others; instead, see and respond to each individual as a unique individual.*

Stimulus. Any external or internal change that impinges on or arouses an organism.

Stimulus–response models of communication. Models of communication that assume that the process of communication is linear, beginning with a stimulus that then leads to a response.

Subjectivity. The principle of perception that refers to the fact that one's perceptions are not objective but are influenced by one's wants and needs and one's expectations and predictions.

Supportiveness. An attitude of an individual or an atmo-sphere in a group that is characterized by openness, absence of fear, and a genuine feeling of equality. *Exhibit supportiveness to others by being descriptive rather than evaluative, spontaneous rather than strategic, and provisional rather than certain.*

Symmetrical relationship. A relation between two or more persons in which one person's behavior serves as a stimulus for the same type of behavior in the other person(s). Examples of such relationships include those in which anger in one person encourages or serves as a stimulus for anger in another person or in which a critical comment by the person leads the other person to respond in like manner.

Symposium. A small group format in which each member of the group delivers a relatively prepared talk on some aspect of the topic. Often combined with a **forum.**

Systematic desensitization. A theory and technique for dealing with a variety of fears (such as communication apprehension) in which you gradually desensitize yourself to behaviors you wish to eliminate.

Taboo. Forbidden; culturally censored. Taboo language is language that is frowned upon by "polite society." Topics and specific words may be considered taboo—for example, death, sex, certain forms of illness, and various words denoting sexual activities and excretory functions. *Avoid taboo expressions so that others do not make negative evaluations; substitute more socially acceptable expressions or euphemisms where and when appropriate.*

Temporal communication. The messages that one's time orientation and treatment of time communicates.

Territoriality. A possessive or ownership reaction to an area of space or to particular objects. *Establish and maintain territory nonverbally by marking or otherwise indicating temporary or permanent ownership. Become sensitive to the territorial behavior of others.*

Testimonial. A persuasive technique in which the speaker uses the authority or image of some positively evaluated person to gain your approval or of some negatively evaluated person to gain your rejection.

Theory. A general statement or principle applicable to a number of related phenomena.

Thesis. The main assertion of a message—for example, the theme of a public speech.

Touch avoidance. The tendency to avoid touching and being touched by others. *Recognize that some people may prefer to avoid touching and being touched. Avoid drawing too many conclusions about people from the way they treat interpersonal touching.*

Touch communication. Communication through tactile means. *Use touch when appropriate to express positive effect, playfulness, control, and ritualistic meanings and to serve task-related functions. Avoid touching that is unwelcomed or that may be considered inappropriate.*

Transactional. Characterizing the relationship among elements whereby each influences and is influenced by each other element; communication is a transactional process because no element is independent of any other element.

Transfer. A persuasive technique in which a speaker associates an idea with something you respect to gain your approval or with something you dislike to gain your rejection.

Uncertainty reduction strategies. Passive, active, and interactive ways of increasing your accuracy in interpersonal perception. *Use all three as ways of reducing your uncertainty about others.*

Uncertainty reduction theory. The theory holding that as relationships develop, uncertainty is reduced; relationship development is seen as a process of reducing uncertainty about one another.

Universal of interpersonal communication. A feature of communication common to all interpersonal communication acts.

Unknown self. That part of the self that contains information about the self that is unknown to oneself and to others, but that is inferred to exist on the basis of various projective tests, slips of the tongue, dream analyses, and the like.

Upward communication. Communication in which the messages originate from the lower levels of an organization or hierarchy and are sent to upper levels—for example, line worker to management.

Value. Relative worth of an object; a quality that makes something desirable or undesirable; ideals or customs about which we have emotional responses, whether positive or negative.

Verbal aggressiveness. A method of winning an argument by attacking the other person's **self-concept.** *Avoid inflicting psychological pain on the other person to win an argument.* Often considered opposed to **argumentativeness.**

Violation. Unwarranted use of another's territory. See **territorial encroachment.**

Visual dominance. The use of your eyes to maintain a superior or dominant position, for example, when making an especially important point, you might look intently at the other person. *Use visual dominance behavior when you wish to emphasize certain messages.*

Voice qualities. Aspects of **paralanguage**—specifically, pitch range, vocal lip control, glottis control, pitch control, articulation control, rhythm control, resonance, and tempo.

Volume. The relative loudness of the voice.

Withdrawal. (1) A reaction to territorial encroachment in which we leave the territory. (2) A tendency to close oneself off from conflicts rather than confront the issues.

You-messages. Messages in which the speaker denies responsibility for his or her own thoughts and behaviors; messages that attribute the speaker's perception to another person; messages of blame; opposed to **I-messages.**

Bibliography

*It is the vice of scholars to suppose
that there is no knowledge in the world but that of books.
Do you avoid it, I conjure you; and thereby save yourself the pain and mortification
that must otherwise ensue from finding out your mistake continually!*
—WILLIAM HAZLITT

Akinnaso, F. Niyi. (1982). On the differences between spoken and written language. *Language and Speech 25 (Part 2)*, 97–125.

Albas, Daniel C., & Albas, Cheryl A. (1989). Meaning in context: The impact of eye contact and perception of threat on proximity. *Journal of Social Psychology 129*, 525–531.

Albas, Daniel C., McCluskey, Ken W., & Albas, Cheryl A. (1976). Perception of the emotional content of speech: A comparison of two Canadian groups. *Journal of Cross Cultural Psychology 7*, 481–490.

Albert, Rosita, & Nelson, Gayle L. (1993). Hispanic/Anglo American differences in attributions to paralinguistic behavior. *International Journal of Intercultural Relations 17*, 19–40.

Albrecht, Karl. (1980). *Brain power: Learn to improve your thinking skills.* Englewood Cliffs, NJ: Prentice-Hall Spectrum.

Alessandra, Tony. (1986). How to listen effectively. *Speaking of success* [Videotape Series]. San Diego, CA: Levitz Sommer Productions.

Alexander, Susan, & Baker, Keith. (1992). Some ethical issues in applied social psychology: The case of bilingual education and self-esteem. *Journal of Applied Social Psychology 22*, 1741–1757.

Altman, Irwin, & Taylor, Dalmas. (1973). *Social penetration: The development of interpersonal relationships.* New York: Holt, Rinehart and Winston.

Andersen, Peter A., & Leibowitz, Ken. (1978). The development and nature of the construct of touch avoidance. *Environmental Psychology and Nonverbal Behavior 3*, 89–106.

Angier, Natalie. (1995, May 9). Scientists mull role of empathy in man and beast. *The New York Times*, pp. C1, C6.

Argyle, Michael. (1988). *Bodily communication* (2nd ed.). New York: Methuen & Co.

Argyle, Michael, & Henderson, M. (1985). *The anatomy of relationships: And the rules and skills needed to manage them successfully.* London: Heinemann.

Argyle, Michael, & Ingham, R. (1972). Gaze, mutual gaze and distance. *Semiotica 1*, 32–49.

Aronson, Elliot, Wilson, Timothy D., & Akert, Robin M. (1997). *Social psychology: The heart and the mind* (2nd ed.). New York: Longman.

Asch, Solomon. (1946). Forming impressions of personality. *Journal of Abnormal and Social Psychology 41*, 258–290.

Assmar, Eveline Mria Leal, & Rodriques, Aroldo. (1994). The value base of distributed justice: Testing Deutsch's hypotheses in a different culture. *Revista Interamericana de Psicologia 28*, 1–11.

Aune, R. Kelly, & Kikuchi, Toshiyuki. (1993). Effects of language intensity similarity on perceptions of credibility, relational attributions, and persuasion. *Journal of Language and Social Psychology 12*, 224–238.

Axtell, Roger. (1993). *Do's and taboos around the world* (3rd ed.). New York: Wiley.

Axtell, Roger E. (1990). *Do's and taboos of hosting international visitors.* New York: Wiley.

Axtell, Roger E. (1991). *Do's and taboos of public speaking: How to get those butterflies flying in formation.* New York: Wiley.

Ayres, Joe. (1986). Perceptions of speaking ability: An explanation for stage fright. *Communication Education 35*, 275–287.

Ayres, Joe, Ayres, Debbie M., & Sharp, Diane. (1993). A progress report on the development of an instrument to measure communication apprehension in employment interviews. *Communication Research Reports 10*, 87–94.

Ayres, Joe, & Hopf, Tim. (1993). *Coping with speech anxiety.* Norwood, NJ: Ablex Publishing Company.

Ayres, Joe, & Hopf, Tim. (1995). An assessment of the role of communication apprehension in communicating with the terminally ill. *Communication Research Reports 12*, 227–234.

Barker, Larry L. (1990). *Communication* (5th ed.). Englewood Cliffs, NJ: Prentice-Hall.

Barker, Larry, Edwards, R., Gaines, C., Gladney, K., & Holley, F. (1980). An investigation of proportional time spent in various communication activities by college students. *Journal of Applied Communication Research 8*, 101–109.

Barna, LaRay M. (1988). Stumbling blocks in intercultural communication. In Larry A. Samovar & Richard E. Porter (Eds.), *Intercultural communication: A reader* (5th ed., pp. 322–330). Belmont, CA: Wadsworth.

Barnlund, Dean C. (1970). A transactional model of communication. In *Language behavior: A book of readings in communication* (compiled by J. Akin, A. Goldberg, G. Myers, and J. Stewart). The Hague: Mouton.

Barnlund, Dean C. (1975). Communicative styles in two cultures: Japan and the United States. In A. Kendon, R. M. Harris, & M. R. Key (Eds.), *Organization of behavior in face-to-face interaction.* The Hague: Mouton.

Barnlund, Dean C. (1989). *Communicative styles of Japanese and Americans: Images and realities.* Belmont, CA: Wadsworth.

Bartholomew, Kim. (1990). Avoidance of intimacy: An attachment perspective. *Journal of Social and Personal Relationships 7*, 147–178.

Basso, K. H. (1972). To give up on words: Silence in Apache culture. In Pier Paolo Giglioli (Ed.), *Language and social context.* New York: Penguin.

Bavelas, Janet Beavin. (1990). Can one not communicate? Behaving and communicating: A reply to Motley. *Western Journal of Speech Communication 54,* 593–602.

Baxter, Leslie A. (1983). Relationship disengagement: An examination of the reversal hypothesis. *Western Journal of Speech Communication 47,* 85–98.

Baxter, Leslie A., & Bullis, C. (1986). Turning points in developing romantic relationships. *Human Communication Research 12,* 469–493.

Baxter, Leslie A., & Wilmot, William, W. (1984). "Secret tests": Social strategies for acquiring information about the state of the relationship. *Human Communication Research 11,* 171–201.

Beatty, Michael J. (1988). Situational and predispositional correlates of public speaking anxiety. *Communication Education 37,* 28–39.

Beck, A. T. (1988). *Love is never enough.* New York: Harper & Row.

Beebe, Steven A., & Masterson, John T. (1997). *Communicating in small groups: Principles and practices* (5th ed.). Glenview, IL: Scott, Foresman.

Beier, Ernst. (1974). How we send emotional messages. *Psychology Today 8,* 53–56.

Bell, Robert A., & Buerkel-Rothfuss, Nancy L. (1990). S(he) loves me, s(he) loves me not: Predictors of relational information-seeking in courtship and beyond. *Communication Quarterly 38,* 64–82.

Bell, Robert A., & Daly, John A. (1984). The affinity-seeking function of communication. *Communication Monographs 51,* 91–115.

Benne, Kenneth D., & Sheats, Paul. (1948). Functional roles of group members. *Journal of Social Issues 4,* 41–49.

Bennis, Warren, & Nanus, Burt. (1985). *Leaders: The strategies for taking charge.* New York: Harper & Row.

Berg, John H., & Archer, Richard L. (1983). The disclosure–liking relationship. *Human Communication Research 10,* 269–281.

Berger, Charles R., & Bradac, James J. (1982). *Language and social knowlege: Uncertainty in interpersonal relations.* London: Edward Arnold.

Berger, Charles R., & Calabrese, Richard J. (1975). Some explorations in initial interaction and beyond: Toward a theory of interpersonal communication. *Human Communication Research 1,* 99–112.

Berman, J. J., Murphy-Berman, V., & Singh, P. (1985). Cross-cultural similarities and differences in perceptions of fairness. *Journal of Cross-Cultural Psychology 16,* 55–67.

Bernstein, W. M., Stephan, W. G., & Davis, M. H. (1979). Explaining attributions for achievement: A path analytic approach. *Journal of Personality and Social Psychology 37,* 1810–1821.

Berscheid, Ellen, & Hatfield Walster, Elaine. (1978). *Interpersonal attraction* (2nd ed.). Reading, MA: Addison-Wesley.

Blieszner, Rosemary, & Adams, Rebecca G. (1992). *Adult friendship.* Newbury Park, CA: Sage.

Blumstein, Philip, & Schwartz, Pepper. (1983). *American couples: Money, work, sex.* New York: Morrow.

Bochner, Arthur. (1984). The functions of human communication in interpersonal bonding. In Carroll C. Arnold & John Waite Bowers (Eds.), *Handbook of rhetorical and communication theory.* Boston: Allyn and Bacon.

Bochner, Arthur, & Kelly, Clifford. (1974). Interpersonal competence: Rationale, philosophy, and implementation of a conceptual framework. *Communication Education 23,* 279–301.

Bochner, Stephen, & Hesketh, Beryl. (1994). Power distance, individualism/collectivism, and job-related attitudes in a culturally diverse work group. *Journal of Cross Cultural Psychology 25,* 233–257.

Bok, Sissela. (1978). *Lying: Moral choice in public and private life.* New York: Pantheon.

Bok, Sissela. (1983). *Secrets.* New York: Vintage Books.

Borden, George A. (1991). *Cultural orientation: An approach to understanding intercultural communication.* Englewood Cliffs, NJ: Prentice-Hall.

Bourland, D. David, Jr. (1965–66). A linguistic note: Writing in E-prime. *General Semantics Bulletin 32–33,* 111–114.

Bourland, D. David, Jr., & Johnston, Paul Dennithorne, eds. (1998). *E-prime III! A third anthology.* Concord, CA: International Society for General Semantics.

Bransford, John D., & Stein, Barry S. (1993). *The ideal problem solver* (2nd ed.). New York: W. H. Freeman.

Brant, Clare C. (1990). Native ethics and rules of behavior. *Canadian Journal of Psychiatry 35,* 534–539.

Bravo, Ellen, & Cassedy, Ellen. (1992). *The 9 to 5 guide to combating sexual harassment.* New York: Wiley.

Brennan, Maire. (1991). Mismanagement and quality circles: How middle managers influence direct participation. *Employee Relations 13,* 22–32.

Brilhart, John, & Galanes, Gloria. (1992). *Effective group discussion* (7th ed.). Dubuque, IA: Brown & Benchmark.

Brody, Jane E. (1994, March 21). Notions of beauty transcend culture, new study suggests. *The New York Times,* p. A-14.

Brody, Jane F. (1991, April 28). How to foster self-esteem. *The New York Times Magazine, 15,* 26–27.

Brown, P., & Levinson, S. C. (1987). *Politeness: Some universals of language usage.* Cambridge: Cambridge University Press.

Brown, Penelope. (1980). How and why are women more polite: Some evidence from a Mayan community. In Sally McConnell-Ginet, Ruth Borker, & Mellie Furman (Eds.), *Women and language in literature and society* (pp. 111–136). New York: Praeger.

Brownell, Judi. (1987). Listening: The toughest management skill. *Cornell Hotel and Restaurant Administration Quarterly 27,* 64–71.

Bruneau, Tom. (1985). The time dimension in intercultural communication. In Larry A. Samovar & Richard E. Porter (Eds.), *Intercultural communication: A reader* (4th ed., pp. 280–289). Belmont, CA: Wadsworth.

Bruneau, Tom. (1990). Chronemics: The study of time in human interaction. In Joseph A. DeVito & Michael L. Hecht (Eds.), *The nonverbal communication reader* (pp. 301–311). Prospect Heights, IL: Waveland Press.

Buchholz, Ester. (1998). The call of solitude. *Psychology Today 31,* 50–54, 80, 82.

Bull, R., & Ramsey, N. (1988). *The social psychology of facial appearance.* New York: Springer-Verlag.

Buller, David B., & Aune, R. Kelly. (1992). The effects of speech rate similarity on compliance: Application of communication accommodation Theory. *Western Journal of Communication 56,* 37–53.

Buller, David B., LePoire, Beth A., Aune, Kelly, & Eloy, Sylvie. (1992). Social perceptions as mediators of the effect of speech rate similarity on compliance. *Human Communication Research 19*, 286–311.

Burgoon, Judee K., Buller, David B., & Woodall, W. Gill (1995). *Nonverbal communication: The unspoken dialogue* (2nd ed.). New York: McGraw-Hill.

Burgoon, Judee K., & Hale, Jerold L. (1988). Nonverbal expectancy violations: Model elaboration and application to immediacy behaviors. *Communication Monographs 55*, 58–79.

Butler, Pamela E. (1981). *Talking to yourself: Learning the language of self-support.* New York: Harper & Row.

Cappella, Joseph N. (1993). The facial feedback hypothesis in human interaction: Review and speculation. *Journal of Language and Social Psychology 12*, 13–29.

Cathcart, Dolores, & Cathcart, Robert. (1985). Japanese social experience and concept of groups. In Larry A. Samovar & Richard E. Porter (Eds.), *Intercultural communication: A reader* (4th ed., pp. 190–197). Belmont, CA: Wadsworth.

Chanowitz, B., & Langer, E. (1981). Premature cognitive commitment. *Journal of Personality and Social Psychology 41*, 1051–1063.

Chen, Guo Ming (1992). *Differences in self-disclosure patterns among Americans versus Chinese: A comparative study.* Paper presented at the annual meeting of the Eastern Communication Association, Portland, ME.

Cialdini, Robert T. (1984). *Influence: How and why people agree to things.* New York: Morrow, 1984.

Cialdini, Robert T., & Ascani, K. (1976). Test of a concession procedure for inducing verbal, behavioral, and further compliance with a request to give blood. *Journal of Applied Psychology 61*, 295–300.

Clark, Herbert. (1974). The power of positive speaking. *Psychology Today 8*, 102, 108–111.

Cline, M. G. (1956). The influence of social context on the perception of faces. *Journal of Personality 2*, 142–185.

Coates, J., & Cameron, D. (1989). *Women, men, and language: Studies in language and linguistics.* London: Longman.

Collier, Mary Jane. (1991). Conflict competence within African, Mexican, and Anglo American friendships. In Stell Ting-Toomey and Felipe Korzenny (Eds.), *Cross-cultural interpersonal communication* (pp. 132–154). Newbury Park, CA: Sage.

Collins, James E., & Clark, Leslie F. (1989). Responsibility and rumination: The trouble with understanding the dissolution of a relationship. *Social Cognition 7*, 152–173.

Comadena, Mark E. (1984). Brainstorming groups: Ambiguity tolerance, communication apprehension, task attraction, and individual productivity. *Small Group Behavior 15*, 251–254.

Cook, Mark. (1971). *Interpersonal perception.* Baltimore: Penguin.

Cooley, Charles Horton. (1922). *Human nature and the social order* (Rev. ed.). New York: Scribner's.

Cragan, John F., & Wright, David W. (1990). Small group communication research of the 1980s: A synthesis and critique. *Communication Studies 41*, 212–236.

Crohn, Joel. (1995). *Mixed matches.* New York: Fawcett.

Davis, Murray S. (1973). *Intimate relations.* New York: Free Press.

Davitz, Joel R. (Ed.). (1964). *The communication of emotional meaning.* New York: McGraw-Hill.

Deal, James E., & Smith Wampler, Karen. (1986). Dating violence: The primacy of previous experience. *Journal of Social and Personal Relationships 3*, 457–471.

deBono, Edward. (1976). *Teaching thinking.* New York: Penguin.

deBono, Edward. (1987). *The six thinking hats.* New York: Penguin.

DeJong, W. (1979). An examination of self perception mediation of the foot-in-the door effect. *Journal of Personality and Social Psychology 37*, 2221–2239.

Derlega, Valerian J., Winstead, Barbara, Wong, Paul T. P., & Hunter, Susan. (1985). Gender effects in an initial encounter: A case where men exceed women in disclosure. *Journal of Social and Personal Relationships 2*, 25–44.

DeStephen, R., Hirokawa, R. (1988). Small group consensus: Stability of group support of the decision, task process, and group relationships. *Small Group Behavior 19*, 227–239.

DeTurck, Mark A. (1987). When communication fails: Physical aggression as a compliance-gaining strategy. *Communication Monographs 54*, 106–112.

DeVito, Joseph A. (1965). Comprehension factors in oral and written discourse of skilled communicators. *Communication Monographs 32*, 124–128.

DeVito, Joseph A. (1976). Relative ease in comprehending Yes/No questions. In Jane Blankenship & Herman G. Stelzner (Eds.), *Rhetoric and communication* (pp. 143–154). Urbana: University of Illinois Press.

DeVito, Joseph A. (1981). *The psychology of speech and language: An introduction to psycholinguistics.* Washington, DC: University Press of America.

DeVito, Joseph A. (1989). *The nonverbal communication workbook.* Prospect Heights, IL: Waveland Press.

DeVito, Joseph A. (1996). *Messages: Building interpersonal communication skills* (3rd ed.). New York: Longman.

DeVito, Joseph A., & Hecht Michael L. (Eds.). (1990). *The Nonverbal Communication Reader.* Prospect Heights, IL: Waveland Press.

Diener, E., & Walbom, M. (1976). Effects of self-awareness on antinormative behavior. *Journal of Research in Personality 10*, 107–111.

Dindia, Kathryn, & Fitzpatrick, Mary Anne. (1985). Marital communication: Three approaches compared. In Steve Duck & Daniel Perlman (Eds.), *Understanding personal relationships: An interdisciplinary approach* (pp. 137–158). Newbury Park, CA: Sage.

Dodd, Carley H. (1995) *Dynamics of intercultural Communication.* Dubuque, IA: Wm. C. Brown.

Dolgin, Kim, G., Meyer, Leslie, & Schwartz, Janet. (1991). Effects of gender, target's gender, topic, and Self-Esteem on Disclosure to Best and Midling Friends. *Sex Roles 25*, 311–329.

Donahue, William A., with Kolt, Robert. (1992). *Managing interpersonal conflict.* Thousand Oaks, CA: Sage.

Dosey, M., & Meisels, M. (1969). Personal space and self-protection. *Journal of Personality and Social Psychology 38*, 959–965.

Dresser, Norine. (1996). *Multicultural manners: New rules of etiquette for a changing society.* New York: Wiley.

Dreyfuss, Henry. (1971). *Symbol sourcebook*. New York: Mc-Graw-Hill.

Driskell, James, Olmstead, Beckett, & Salas, Eduardo. (1993). Task cues, dominance cues, and influence in task groups. *Journal of Applied Psychology 78*, 51–60.

Eden, Dov. (1992). Leadership and expectations: Pygmalion effects and other self-fulfilling prophecies in organizations. *Leadership Quarterly 3*, 271–305.

Ehrenhaus, Peter. (1988). Silence and symbolic expression. *Communication Monographs 55*, 41–57.

Ehrensaft, Miriam K., & Vivian, Dina. (1996). Spouses' reasons for not reporting existing marital aggression as a marital problem. *Journal of Family Psychology 10*, 443–453.

Ekman, Paul. (1965). Communication through nonverbal behavior: A source of information about an interpersonal relationship. In S. S. Tomkins & C. E. Izard (Eds.), *Affect, cognition and personality*. New York: Springer.

Ekman, Paul. (1985). *Telling lies: Clues to deceit in the marketplace, politics, and marriage*. New York: W. W. Norton.

Ekman, Paul, & Friesen, Wallace V. (1969). The repertoire of nonverbal behavior: Categories, origins, usage, and coding. *Semiotica 1*, 49–98.

Ekman, Paul, Friesen, Wallace V., & Ellsworth, Phoebe. (1972). *Emotion in the human face: Guidelines for research and an integration of findings*. New York: Pergamon Press.

Ellis, Albert. (1988). *How to stubbornly refuse to make yourself miserable about anything, yes anything*. Secaucus, NJ: Lyle Stuart.

Ellis, Albert, & Harper, Robert A. (1975). *A new guide to rational living*. Hollywood, CA: Wilshire Books.

Elmes, Michael B., & Gemmill, Gary. (1990). The psychodynamics of mindlessness and dissent in small groups. *Small Group Research 21*, 28–44.

Estabrook, Noel. (1997). *Teach yourself the Internet in 24 hours*. Indianapolis, IN: Sams Publishing.

Esten, Geri, & Willmott, Lynn. (1993). Double-bind messages: The effects of attitude towards disability on therapy. *Women and Therapy 14*, 29–41.

Exline, R. V., Ellyson, S. L., & Long, B. (1975). Visual behavior as an aspect of power role relationships. In P. Pliner, L. Krames, & T. Alloway (Eds.), *Nonverbal communication of aggression*. New York: Plenum.

Fengler, A. P. (1974). Romantic love in courtship: Divergent paths of male and female students. *Journal of Comparative Family Studies*, 134–139.

Feraco, Frank J. (1997). *Vital Speeches of the Day 64*, 157–160.

Festinger, Leon. (1954). A theory of social comparison processes. *Human Relations 7*, 117–140.

Field, R. H. G. (1989). The self-fulfilling prophecy leader: Achieving the metharme effect. *Journal of Management Studies 26*, 151–175.

Fischer, C. S., & Oliker, S. J. (1983). A research note on friendship, gender, and the life cycle. *Social Forces 62*, 124–133.

Folger, Joseph P., Poole, Marshall Scott, & Stutman, Randall K. (1997). *Working through conflict: A communication perspective* (3rd ed.). New York: Longman.

Fraser, Bruce. (1990). Perspectives on politeness. *Journal of Pragmatics 14*, 219–236.

Frazier, P. A., & Cook, S. W. (1993). Correlates of distress following heterosexual relationship dissolution. *Journal of Social and Personal Relationships 10*, 55–67.

Freedman, J., & Fraser, S. (1966). Compliance without pressure: The foot-in-the door technique. *Journal of Personality and Social Psychology 4*, 195–202.

Furlow, F. Bryant. (1996). The smell of love. *Psychology Today*, 38–45.

Furnham, Adrian, & Bitar, Nadine. (1993). The stereotyped portrayal of men and women in British television advertisements. *Sex Roles 29*, 297–310.

Galvin, Kathleen, & Brommel, Bernard J. (1996). *Family communication: Cohesion and change* (4th ed.). New York: Longman.

Gelles, R., & Cornell, C. (1985). *Intimate violence in families*. Newbury Park, CA: Sage.

Giles, Howard, Mulac, Anthony., Bradac, James J., & Johnson, Patricia. (1987). Speech accommodation theory: The first decade and beyond. In Margaret L. McLaughlin (Ed.), *Communication yearbook 10* (pp. 13–48). Thousand Oaks, CA: Sage.

Glucksberg, Sam, & Danks, Joseph H. (1975). *Experimental psycholinguistics: An introduction*. Hillsdale, NJ: Lawrence Erlbaum.

Goffman, Erving. (1967). *Interaction ritual: Essays on face-to-face behavior*. New York: Pantheon.

Goleman, Daniel. (1992, Oct. 27). Voters assailed by unfair persuasion. *The New York Times*, pp. C1, C8.

Goleman, Daniel. (1995a). *Emotional intelligence*. New York: Bantam.

Goleman, Daniel. (1995b). For man and beast, language of love shares many traits. *The New York Times*, pp. C1, C9.

Gonzalez, Alexander, & Zimbardo Philip G. (1985). Time in perspective. *Psychology Today 19*, 20–26.

Goodwin, Robin, & Lee, Iona. (1994). Taboo topics among Chinese and English friends: A cross-cultural comparison. *Journal of Cross Cultural Psychology 25*, 325–338.

Gorden, William I., & Nevins, Randi J. (1993). *We mean business: Building communication competence in business and professions*. New York: HarperCollins.

Gordon, Thomas. (1975). *P.E.T.: Parent effectiveness training*. New York: New American Library.

Goss, Blaine, Thompson, M., & Olds, S. (1978). Behavioral support for systematic desensitization for communication apprehension. *Human Communication Research 4*, 158–163.

Gottman, John. (1994). What makes marriage work? *Psychology Today 27*, 38–43, 68.

Graham, Elizabeth E. (1997). Turning points and commitment in post-divorce relationships. *Communication Monographs 64*, 350–368.

Graham, Jean Ann, & Argyle, M. (1975). The effects of different patterns of gaze combined with different facial expressions on impression formation. *Journal of Movement Studies 1*, 178–182.

Graham, Jean Ann, Bitti, Pio Ricci, & Argyle, M. (1975). A cross-cultural study of the communication of emotion by facial and gestural cues. *Journal of Human Movement Studies 1*, 68–77.

Griffin, Em, & Sparks, Glenn G. (1990). Friends forever: A longitudinal exploration of intimacy in same-sex friends and platonic pairs. *Journal of Social and Personal Relationships 7*, 29–46.

Gu, Yueguo. (1997). Polite phenomena in modern Chinese. *Journal of Pragmatics 14*, 237–257.

Gudykunst, W. B. (Ed.). (1983). *Intercultural communication theory: Current perspectives.* Newbury Park, CA: Sage.

Gudykunst, W. B. (1991). *Bridging differences: Effective intergroup communication.* Newbury Park, CA: Sage.

Gudykunst, W. B., & Kim, Y. Y. (1984). *Communicating with strangers: An approach to intercultural communication.* New York: Random House.

Gudykunst, W. B., & Kim, Y. Y. (Eds.). (1992). *Readings on communication with strangers: An approach to intercultural communication.* New York: McGraw-Hill.

Gudykunst, W., & Nishida, T. (1984). Individual and cultural influence on uncertainty reduction. *Communication Monographs 51,* 23–36.

Gudykunst, W., Yang, S. & Nishida, T. (1985). A cross-cultural test of uncertainty reduction theory: Comparisons of acquaintance, friend, and dating relationships in Japan, Korea, and the United States. *Human Communication Research 11,* 407–454.

Gupta, U., & Singh, P. (1982). Exploratory studies in love and liking and types of marriages. *Indian Journal of Applied Psychology 19,* 92–97.

Haga, Yasushi. (1988). Traits de langage et caractere Japonais. *Cahiers de Sociologie Economique et Culturelle 9,* 105–109.

Hall, Edward T. (1959). *The silent language.* Garden City, NY: Doubleday.

Hall, Edward T. (1966). *The hidden dimension.* Garden City, NY: Doubleday.

Hall, Edward T. (1976). *Beyond culture.* Garden City, NY: Anchor Press.

Hall, Edward T., & Reed Hall, Mildred. (1987). *Hidden differences: Doing business with the Japanese.* New York: Anchor Books/Doubleday.

Hall, J. (1971). Decisions, decisions, decisions. *Psychology Today 5,* 51–54, 86, 88.

Hall, J. A. (1984). *Nonverbal sex differences.* Baltimore, MD: Johns Hopkins University Press.

Hall, Joan Kelly. (1993). Tengo una bomba: The paralinguistic and linguistic conventions of the oral practice Chismeando. *Research on Language and Social Interaction 26,* 55–83.

Hambrick, Ralph S. (1991). *The management skills builder: Self-Directed learning strategies for career development.* New York: Praeger.

Han, Gyuseog, & Park, Bongsoon. (1995). Children's choice in conflict: Application of the theory of individualism-collectivism. *Journal of Cross-Cultural Psychology 26,* 298–313.

Haney, William. (1973). *Communication and organizational behavior: text and cases* (3rd ed.). Homewood, IL: Irwin.

Hart, Fiona (1990). The construction of masculinity in men's friendships: Misogyny, heterosexuality, and homophobia. *Resources for Feminist Research 19,* 60–67.

Harvey, John H., Flanary, Rodney, & Morgan, Melinda. (1986). Vivid memories of vivid loves gone by. *Journal of Social and Personal Relationships 3,* 359–373.

Hatfield, Elaine, & Rapson, Richard L. (1992). Similarity and attraction in close relationships. *Communication Monographs 59,* 209–212.

Hatfield, Elaine, & Rapson, Richard L. (1996). *Love and sex: Cross cultural perspectives.* Boston: Allyn and Bacon.

Hatfield, Elaine, & Traupman, Jane. (1981). Intimate relationships: A perspective from equity theory. In Steve Duck & Robin Gilmour (Eds.), *Personal relationships. 1: Studying personal relationships* (pp. 165–178). New York: Academic Press.

Hays, Robert B. (1989). The day-to-day functioning of close versus casual friendships. *Journal of Social and Personal Relationships 6,* 21–37.

Hecht, Michael L., Collier, Mary Jane, & Ribeau, Sidney, (1993). *African American communication: Ethnic identify and cultural interpretation.* Thousand Oaks, CA: Sage.

Heenehan, Meg. (1997). *Networking.* New York: Random House.

Heinrich, Robert, et al. (1983). *Instructional media: The new technologies of instruction.* New York: Wiley.

Heiskell, Thomas L., & Rychiak, Joseph F. (1986). The therapeutic relationship: Inexperienced therapists' affective preference and empathic communication. *Journal of Social and Personal Relationships 3,* 267–274.

Hendrick, Clyde, & Hendrick, Susan. (1990). A relationship-specific version of the love attitudes scale. In J. W. Heulip (Ed.), Handbook of replication research in the behavioral and social sciences [Special Issue]. *Journal of Social Behavior and Personality 5,* 239–254.

Hendrick, Clyde, Hendrick, Susan, Foote, Franklin H., & Slapion-Foote, Michelle J. (1984). Do men and women love differently? *Journal of Social and Personal Relationships 1,* 177–195.

Henley, Nancy M. (1977). *Body politics: Power, sex, and nonverbal communication.* Englewood Cliffs, NJ: Prentice-Hall.

Hess, Ekhard H. (1975). *The tell-tale eye.* New York: Van Nostrand Reinhold.

Hess, Ursula, Kappas, Arvid, McHugo, Gregory J., Lanzetta, John T. (1992, May). The facilitative effect of facial expression of the self-generation of emotion. *International Journal of Psychophysiology 12,* 251–265.

Hewitt, John, & Stokes, Randall (1975). Disclaimers. *American Sociological Review 40,* 1–11.

Hickson, Mark L., & Stacks, Don W. (1989). *NVC: Nonverbal communication: Studies and applications* (2nd ed.). Dubuque, IA: Wm. C. Brown.

Hill, Susan E. Kogler. (1997). Team leadership theory. In Peter G. Northouse, *Leadership: Theory and practice* (pp. 159–183). Thousand Oaks, CA: Sage.

Hocker, Joyce L., & Wilmot, William W. (1985). *Interpersonal conflict* (2nd ed.). Dubuque, IA: Wm. C. Brown.

Hofstede, Geert. (1997). *Cultures and organizations: Software of the mind.* New York: McGraw-Hill.

Hoft, Nancy L. (1995). *International technical communication: How to export information about high technology.* New York: Wiley.

Holmes, Janet (1995). *Women, men and politeness.* New York: Longman.

Honeycutt, James. (1986). A model of marital functioning based on an attraction paradigm and social penetration dimensions. *Journal of Marriage and the Family 48,* 51–59.

Infante, Dominic A. (1988). *Arguing constructively.* Prospect Heights, IL: Waveland Press.

Infante, Dominic A., Riddle, Bruce L., Horvath, Cary L., & Tumlin, S. A. (1992). Verbal aggressiveness: Messages and reasons. *Communication Quarterly 40,* 116–126.

Infante, Dominic A., Sabourin, T. C., Rudd, J. E., & Shannon, E. A. (1990). Verbal aggression in violent and nonviolent marital disputes. *Communication Quarterly 38,* 361–371.

Infante, Dominic, & Rancer, Andrew. (1982). A conceptualization and measure of argumentativeness. *Journal of Personality Assessment 46*, 72–80.

Infante, Dominic, & Wigley, C. J. (1986). Verbal aggressiveness: An interpersonal model and measure. *Communication Monographs 53*, 61–69.

Insel, Paul M., & Jacobson, Lenore F. (Eds.). (1975). *What do you expect? An inquiry into self-fulfilling prophecies.* Menlo Park, CA: Cummings.

Jablin, Fred M. (1981). Cultivating imagination: Factors that enhance and inhibit creativity in brainstorming groups. *Human Communication Research 7*, 245–258.

Jaksa, James A., & Pritchard, Michael S. (1994). *Communication ethics: Methods of analysis* (2nd ed.). Belmont, CA: Wadsworth.

James, David L. (1995). *The executive guide to Asia-Pacific communications.* New York: Kodansha International.

Jamieson, Kathleen Hall, & Kohrs Campbell, Karlyn. (1996). *The interplay of influence* (4th ed.). Belmont, CA: Wadsworth.

Jandt, Fred E. (1995). *Intercultural communication.* Thousand Oaks, CA: Sage.

Jandt, Fred E., & Nemnich, Mary B. (1995). *Using the Internet in your job search.* Indianapolis, IN: Jist Works.

Janis, Irving. (1983). *Victims of group thinking: A psychological study of foreign policy decisions and fiascoes* (2nd Rev. ed.). Boston: Houghton Mifflin.

Janus, Samuel S., & Janus, Cynthia L. (1993). *The Janus report on sexual behavior.* New York: Wiley.

Jaworski, Adam. (1993). *The power of silence: Social and pragmatic perspectives.* Newbury Park, CA: Sage.

Johannesen, Richard L. (1990). *Ethics in human communication* (3rd ed.). Prospect Heights, IL: Waveland Press.

Johnson, C. E. (1987). An introduction to powerful and powerless talk in the classroom. *Communication Education 36*, 167–172.

Johnson, Geneva B. (1991). *Vital speeches of the day 57*, 393–398.

Johnson, Geri M. (1992). Subordinate perceptions of superior's communication competence and task attraction related to superior's use of compliance-gaining tactics. *Western Journal of Communication 56*, 54–67.

Johnson, M. P. (1991). Commitment to personal relationships. In W. H. Jones & D. Perlman (Eds.), *Advances in personal relationships* (Vol. 3, pp. 117–143). London: Jessica Kingsley.

Jones, E. E., & Pittman, T. S. (1982). Toward a general theory of strategic self-presentation. In J. Suls (Ed.), *Psychological perspectives on the self* (Vol. 1, pp. 231–262). Hillsdale, NJ: Lawrence Erlbaum.

Jones, E. E. (1990). *Interpersonal perception.* New York: W. H. Freeman.

Jones, Stanley, & Yarbrough, A. Elaine. (1985). A naturalistic study of the meanings of touch. *Communication Monographs 52*, 19–56.

Joseph, James A. (1997). *Vital speeches of the day 64*, 133–135.

Jourard, Sidney M. (1968). *Disclosing man to himself.* New York: Van Nostrand Reinhold.

Jourard, Sidney M. (1971a). *Self-disclosure.* New York: Wiley.

Jourard, Sidney M. (1971b). *The transparent self* (Rev. ed.). New York: Van Nostrand Reinhold.

Kanner, Bernice. (1989, April 3). Color schemes. *New York Magazine*, 22–23.

Kelley, H. H., & Thibaut, J. W. (1978). *Interpersonal relations: A theory of interdependence.* New York: Wiley/Interscience.

Kelly, P. Keith (1994). *Team decision-making techniques.* Irvine, CA: Richard Chang Associates.

Kemp, Jerrold E., & Dayton, Deane K. (1985). *Planning and producing instructional media* (5th ed.). New York: Harper & Row.

Kennedy, C. W., & Camden, C. T. (1988). A new look at interruptions. *Western Journal of Speech Communication 47*, 45–58.

Keshavarz, Mohammad Hossein. (1988). Forms of address in post-revolutionary Iranian Persian. A sociolinguistic analysis. *Language in Society 17*, 565–575.

Kesselman-Turkel, Judi, & Peterson, Franklynn. (1982). *Note-taking made easy.* Chicago: Contemporary Books.

Keyes, Ralph. (1980). *The height of your life.* New York: Warner Books.

Kim, Hyun J. (1991). Influence of language and similarity on initial intercultural attraction. In Stella Ting-Toomey & Felipe Korzenny (Eds.), *Cross-cultural interpersonal communication* (pp. 213–229). Newbury Park, CA: Sage.

Kindler, Herbert S. (1996). Managing disagreement constructively (Rev. ed.). Menlo Park, CA: Crisp Publications.

King, Robert, & DiMichael, Eleanor. (1992). *Voice and diction.* Prospect Heights, IL: Waveland Press.

Kirkpatrick, C., & Caplow, T. (1945). Courtship in a group of Minnesota students. *American Journal of Sociology 51*, 114–125.

Kleinfeld, N. R. (1992, October 25). The smell of money. *The New York Times*, Section 9, pp. 1, 8.

Kleinke, Chris L. (1986). *Meeting and understanding people.* New York: W. H. Freeman.

Knapp, Mark L. (1984). *Interpersonal communication and human relationships.* Boston: Allyn and Bacon.

Knapp, Mark L., & Vangelisti, Anita. (1996). *Interpersonal communication and human relationships* (3rd ed.). Boston: Allyn and Bacon.

Knapp, Mark L., & Hall, Judith. (1997). *Nonverbal communication in human interaction* (4th ed.). Fort Worth, TX: Harcourt Brace Jovanovich.

Knapp, Mark L., Hart, Roderick P., Friedrich, Gustav W., & Shulman, Gary M. (1973). The rhetoric of goodbye: Verbal and nonverbal correlates of human leave-taking. *Communication Monographs 40*, 182–198.

Knapp, Mark L., & Taylor, Eric H. (1994). Commitment and its communication in romantic relationships. In Ann L. Weber & John H. Harvey (Eds.), *Perspectives on close relationships* (pp. 153–175). Boston: Allyn and Bacon.

Kochman, Thomas. (1981). *Black and white: Styles in conflict.* Chicago: University of Chicago Press.

Komarovsky, M. (1964). *Blue collar marriage.* New York: Random House.

Korzybski, A. (1933). *Science and sanity.* Lakeville, CT: The International Non-Aristotelian Library.

Kramarae, Cheris. (1974a). Folklinguistics. *Psychology Today 8*, 82–85.

Kramarae, Cheris. (1974b). Stereotypes of women's speech: The word from cartoons. *Journal of Popular Culture 8*, 624–630.

Kramarae, Cheris. (1977). Perceptions of female and male speech. *Language and Speech 20*, 151–161.

Kramarae, Cheris. (1981). *Women and men speaking.* Rowley, MA: Newbury House.

Krivonos, P. D., & Knapp, M. L. (1975). Initiating communication: What do you say when you say hello? *Central States Speech Journal 26,* 115–125.

Kurdek, Lawrence A. (1994). Areas of conflict for gay, lesbian, and heterosexual couples: What couples argue about influences relationship satisfaction. *Journal of Marriage and the Family 56,* 923–934.

Kurdek, Lawrence A. (1995). Developmental changes in relationship quality in gay and lesbian cohabiting couples. *Developmental Psychology 31,* 86–93.

Kushner, Remigia. (1996). Some ways of looking at conflict. *NASSP Bulletin 80,* 104–108.

Laing, Milli. (1993). Gossip: Does it play a role in the socialization of nurses. *Journal of Nursing Scholarship 25,* 37–43.

Laing, Ronald D., Phillipson, H., & Lee, A. Russell. (1966). *Interpersonal perception.* New York: Springer.

Lamm, Kathryn. (1993). *10,000 ideas for term papers, projects, reports and speeches* (3rd ed.). New York: Prentice-Hall [ARCO].

Langer, Ellen J. (1989). *Mindfulness.* Reading, MA: Addison-Wesley.

Lanzetta, J. T., Cartwright-Smith, J., & Kleck, R. E. (1976). Effects of nonverbal dissimulations on emotional experience and autonomic arousal. *Journal of Personality and Social Psychology 33,* 354–370.

Larsen, Randy J., Kasimatis, Margaret, & Frey, Kurt. (1992). Facilitating the furrowed brow: An unobtrusive test of the facial feedback hypothesis applied to unpleasant affect. *Cognition and Emotion 6,* 321–338.

Lea, Martin, & Russell Spears (1995). Love at first byte? Building personal relationships over computer networks. In Julia T. Wood & Steve Duck (Ed.), *Under-studied relationships: Off the beaten track* (pp. 197–233). Thousand Oaks, CA: Sage.

Leathers, Dale G. (1997). *Successful nonverbal communication: Principles and applications* (3rd ed.). Boston, MA: Allyn and Bacon.

Lederer, William J. (1984). *Creating a good relationship.* New York: W. W. Norton.

Lederman, Linda. (1990). Assessing educational effectiveness: The focus group interview as a technique for data collection. *Communication Education 39,* 117–127.

Lee, Alfred McClung, & Lee, Elizabeth Briant. (1972). *The fine art of propaganda.* San Francisco, CA: International Society for General Semantics.

Lee, Alfred McClung, & Lee, Elizabeth Briant. (1995). The iconography of propaganda analysis. *ETC.: A Review of General Semantics 52,* 13–17.

Lee, Fiona. (1993). Being polite and keeping MUM: How bad news is communicated in organizational hierarchies. *Journal of Applied Social Psychology 23,* 1124–1149.

Lee, John Alan. (1976). *The colors of love.* New York: Bantam.

Leung, Kwok. (1988, March). Some determinants of conflict avoidance. *Journal of Cross Cultural Psychology 19,* 125–136.

Lever, Janet. (1995). The 1995 advocate survey of sexuality and relationships: The women, lesbian sex survey. *The Advocate 687/688,* 22–30.

Levine, Robert. (1997). *A geography of time: The temporal misadventures of a social psychologist.* New York: Basic Books.

Lewis, David. (1989). *The secret language of success.* New York: Carroll and Graf.

Lin, Yuan-Huei W., & Rusbult, Caryl E. (1995). Commitment to dating relationships and cross-sex friendships in America and China. *Journal of Social and Personal Relationships 12,* 7–26.

Littlejohn, Stephen W. (1996). *Theories of human communication* (5th ed.). Belmont, CA: Wadsworth.

Lujansky, H., & Mikula, G. (1983). Can equity theory explain the quality and stability of romantic relationships? *British Journal of Social Psychology 22,* 101–112.

Lukens, J. (1978). Ethnocentric speech. *Ethnic Groups 2,* 35–53.

Lumsden, Gay, & Lumsden, Donald. (1993). *Communicating in groups and teams.* Belmont, CA: Wadsworth.

Lustig, Myron, W., & Koester, Jolene (1996). *Intercultural competence: Interpersonal communication across cultures* (2nd ed.). New York: HarperCollins, 1993.

Ma, Karen. (1996). *The modern Madame Butterfly: Fantasy and reality in Japanese cross-cultural relationships.* Rutland, VT: Charles E. Tuttle.

Ma, Ringo. (1992). The role of unofficial intermediaries in interpersonal conflicts in the Chinese culture. *Communication Quarterly 40,* 269–278.

MacLachlan, James. (1979). What people really think of fast talkers. *Psychology Today 13,* 113–117.

Malandro, Loretta A., Barker, Larry, & Barker, Deborah Ann (1989). *Nonverbal Communication* (2nd ed.). New York: Random House.

Manes, Joan, & Wolfson, Nessa. (1981). The compliment formula. In Florian Coulmas (Ed.), *Conversational routine* (pp. 115–132). The Hague: Mouton.

Mao, LuMing Robert (1994). Beyond politeness theory: "Face" Revisited and Renewed. *Journal of Pragmatics 21,* 451–486.

Marshall, Evan. (1983). *Eye language: Understanding the eloquent eye.* New York: New Trend.

Marshall, Linda L., & Rose, Patricia. (1987). Gender, stress and violence in the adult relationships of a sample of college students. *Journal of Social and Personal Relationships 4,* 299–316.

Martin, Matthew M., & Anderson, Carolyn M. (1995). Roommate similarity: Are roommates who are similar in their communication traits more satisfied? *Communication Research Reports 12,* 46–52.

Marwell, G., & Schmitt, David R. (1967). Dimensions of compliance-gaining behavior: An empirical analysis. *Sociometry 39,* 350–364.

Masheter, Carol, & Harris, Linda M. (1986). From divorce to friendship: A study of dialectic relationship development. *Journal of Social and Personal Relationships 3,* 177–189.

Matsumoto, David. (1991). Cultural influences on facial expressions of emotion. *Southern Communication Journal 56,* 128–137.

Matsumoto, David, & Kudoh, T. (1993). American-Japanese Cultural Differences in Attributions of Personality Based on Smiles. *Journal of Nonverbal Behavior 17,* 231–243.

Maynard, Harry E. (1963). How to become a better premise detective. *Public Relations Journal 19,* 20–22.

McCroskey, James C. (1997). *An introduction to rhetorical communication* (7th ed.). Englewood Cliffs, NJ: Prentice-Hall.

McCroskey, James C., & Wheeless, Lawrence. (1976). *Introduction to human communication*. Boston: Allyn & Bacon.

McGill, Michael E. (1985). *The McGill report on male intimacy*. New York: Harper & Row.

McLaughlin, Margaret L. (1984). *Conversation: How talk is organized*. Newbury Park, CA: Sage.

McLoyd, Vonnie, & Wilson, Leon. (1992). Telling them like it is: The role of economic and environmental factors in single mothers' discussions with their children. *American Journal of Community Psychology 20*, 419–444.

Mehrabian, Albert. (1976). *Public places and private spaces*. New York: Basic Books.

Merton, Robert K. (1957). *Social theory and social structure*. New York: Free Press.

Meyer, Janet R. (1994). Effect of situational features on the likelihood of addressing face needs in requests. *Southern Communication Journal 59*, 240–254.

Midooka, Kiyoski.(1990). Charactersitics of Japanese style communication. *Media Culture and Society 12*, 47–49.

Miller, Gerald R., & Parks, Malcolm R. (1982). Communication in dissolving relationships. In Steve Duck (Ed.), *Personal relationships. 4: Dissolving personal relationships*. New York: Academic Press.

Mir, Montserrat. (1993). *Direct requests can also be polite*. Paper presented at the annual meeting of the International Conference on Pragmatics and Language Learning, Champaign, IL.

Moghaddam, Fathali M., Taylor, Donald M., & Wright, Stephen C. (1993). *Social psychology in cross-cultural perspective*. New York: W. H. Freeman.

Molloy, John.(1981). *Molloy's live for success*. New York: Bantam.

Montagu, Ashley. (1971). *Touching: The human significance of the skin*. New York: Harper & Row.

Morris, Desmond. (1977). *Manwatching: A field guide to human behavior*. New York: Abrams.

Mullen, Brian, Salas, Edwardo, & Driskell, James. (1989). Salience, motivation, and artifact as contributions to the relation between participation rate and leadership. *Journal of Experimental Social Psychology 25*, 545–559.

Naifeh, Steven, & White Smith, Gregory. (1984). *Why can't men open up? Overcoming men's fear of intimacy*. New York: Clarkson N. Potter.

Napier, Rodney W., & Gershenfeld, Matti K. (1989). *Groups: Theory and experience* (4th ed.). Boston: Houghton Mifflin.

Neimeyer, Robert A., & Mitchell, Kelly A. (1988). Similarity and attraction: A longitudinal study. *Journal of Social and Personal Relationships 5*, 131–148.

Nelson, Paul, & Pearson, Judy. (1996). *Confidence in public speaking* (6th ed.). Dubuque, IA: Brown & Benchmark.

Neugarten, Bernice. (1979). Time, age, and the life cycle. *American Journal of Psychiatry 136*, 887–894.

Ng, Sik Hung, & Bradac, James J. (1993). *Power in langauge: Verbal communication and social influence*. Newbury Park, CA: Sage.

Noble, Barbara Presley. (1994). The gender wars: Talking peace. *The New York Times* (August 14), p. 21.

Noller, Patricia. (1993). Gender and emotional communication in marriage: Different cultures or differential social power? Special Issue: Emotional Communication, Culture, and Power. *Journal of Language and Social Psychology 12*, 132–152.

Northouse, Peter G. (1997). *Leadership: Theory and practice*. Thousand Oaks, CA: Sage.

Oberg, Kalervo.(1960). Cultural shock: Adjustment to new cultural Environments. *Practical Anthropology 7*, 177–182.

O'Hair, Henry D., Cody, Michael J., & McLaughlin, Margaret L. (1981). Prepared lies, spontaneous lies, machiavellianism, and nonverbal communication. *Human Communication Research 7*, 325–339.

O'Hair, Mary John, Cody, Michael J., & O'Hair, Dan. (1991). The impact of situational dimensions on compliance-resisting strategies: A comparison of methods. *Communication Quarterly 39*, 226–240.

Osborn, Alex. (1957). *Applied imagination* (Rev. ed.). New York: Scribners.

Osborn, Michael, & Osborn, Suzanne. (1997). *Speaking in public* (4th ed.). Boston, MA: Houghton Mifflin.

Park, Won Woo. (1990). A review of research on groupthink. *Journal of Behavioral Decision Making 3*, 229–245.

Patton, Bobby R., Giffin, Kim, & Nyquist Patton, Eleanor. (1989). *Decision-making group interaction* (3rd ed.). New York: HarperCollins.

Pearson, Judy C. (1980). Sex roles and self-disclosure. *Psychological Reports 47*, 640.

Pearson, Judy C. (1993). *Communication in the family* (2nd ed.). New York: Harper & Row.

Pearson, Judy C., & Spitzberg, B. H. (1990). *Interpersonal communication: Concepts, components, and contexts* (2nd ed.). Dubuque, IA: Wm. C. Brown.

Pearson, Judy C., West, Richard, & Turner, Lynn H. (1995). *Gender and communication* (3rd ed.). Dubuque, IA: Wm. C. Brown.

Penfield, Joyce. (Ed.). (1987). *Women and language in transition*. Albany, NY: State University of New York Press.

Pennebaker, James W. (1991). *Opening up: The healing power of confiding in others*. New York: Morrow.

Petrocelli, William, & Kate Repa, Barbara. (1992). *Sexual harassment on the job*. Berkeley, CA: Nolo Press.

Piot, Charles D. (1993). Secrecy, ambiguity, and the everyday in Kabre culture. *American Anthropologist 95*, 353–370.

Pittenger, Robert E., Hockett, Charles F., & Danehy, John J. (1960). *The first five minutes*. Ithaca, NY: Paul Martineau.

Porter, R. H., & Moore, J. D. (1981). Human kin recognition by olfactory cues. *Physiology and Behavior 27*, 493–495.

Pratkanis, Anthony, Aronson, Elliot. (1991). *Age of propaganda: The everyday use and abuse of persuasion*. New York: W. H. Freeman.

Rankin, Paul. (1929). *Listening ability*. Proceedings of the Ohio State Educational Conference's Ninth Annual Session.

Rich, Andrea L. (1974). *Interracial communication*. New York: Harper & Row.

Richards, I. A. (1951). Communication between men: The meaning of language. In Heinz von Foerster (Ed.), *Cybernetics, Transactions of the Eighth Conference*.

Richmond, Virginia P., & McCroskey, James C. (1998). *Communication: Apprehension, avoidance, and effectiveness* (5th ed.). Needham Heights, MA: Allyn and Bacon.

Riggio, Ronald E. (1987). *The charisma quotient*. New York: Dodd, Mead.

Roberts, Wes. (1987). *Leadership secrets of Attila the Hun.* New York: Warner.

Rockefeller, David.(1985). *Vital speeches of the day 51* (September 15).

Rogers, Carl. (1970). *Carl Rogers on encounter groups.* New York: Harrow Books.

Rosenfeld, Lawrence. (1979). Self-disclosure avoidance: Why I am afraid to tell you who I am. *Communication Monographs 46,* 63–74.

Rosengren, Annika, et al. (1993). Stressful life events, social support, and mortality in men born in 1933. *British Medical Journal.*

Rosenthal, Robert, & Jacobson, L. (1968). *Pygmalion in the classroom.* New York: Holt, Rinehart and Winston.

Rothwell, J. Dan. (1982). *Telling it like it isn't: Language misuse and malpractice/what we can do about it.* Englewood Cliffs, NJ: Prentice-Hall.

Ruben, Brent D. (1985). Human communication and cross-cultural effectiveness. In Larry A. Samovar & Richard E. Porter (Eds.), *Intercultural Communication: A Reader* (4th ed, pp. 338–346). Belmont, CA: Wadsworth.

Ruben, Brent D. (1988). *Communication and human behavior* (2nd ed.). New York: Macmillan.

Rubenstein, Carin (1993, June 10). Fighting sexual harassment in schools. *The New York Times,* p. C8.

Rubin, Rebecca. (1982). Assessing speaking and listening competence at the college level: The communication competency assessment instrument. *Communication Education 31,* 19–32.

Rubin, Rebecca, & McHugh, Michael. (1987). Development of parasocial interaction relationships. *Journal of Broadcasting and Electronic Media 31,* 279–292.

Rubin, Zick. (1973). *Liking and loving: An invitation to social psychology.* New York: Holt, Rinehart and Winston.

Rubin, Zick, & McNeil, Elton B. (1985). *Psychology: Being Human* (4th ed.). New York: Harper & Row.

Ruggiero, Vincent Ryan. (1987). *Vital speeches of the day 53.*

Ruggiero, Vincent Ryan. (1990). *The art of thinking: A guide to critical and creative thought* (3rd ed.). New York: Harper-Collins.

Rundquist, Suellen. (1992). Indirectness: A gender study of Fluting Grice's Maxims. *Journal of Pragmatics 18,* 431–449.

Sapadin, Linda A. (1988). Friendship and gender: Perspectives of professional men and women. *Journal of Social and Personal Relationships 5,* 387–403.

Schafer, R. B., & Keith, P. M. (1980). Equity and depression among married couples. *Social Psychology Quarterly 43,* 430–435.

Scherer, K. R. (1986). Vocal affect expression. *Psychological Bulletin 99,* 143–165.

Schoenberger, Nancy E., Kirsch, Irving, Gearan, Paul, Montgomery, Guy, et al. (1997). Hypnotic enhancement of a cognitive behavioral treatment for public speaking anxiety. *Behavior Therapy 28,* 127–140.

Schwartz, Marilyn, and the Task Force on Bias-Free Language of the Association of American University Presses. (1995). *Guidelines for bias-free writing.* Bloomington: Indiana University Press.

Seidman, I. E. (1991). *Interviewing as qualitative resarch: A guide for researchers in education and the social sciences.* New York: Teachers College, Columbia University.

Shannon, Jacqueline. (1987). Don't smile when you say that. *Executive Female 10,* 33, 43.

Shapiro, Debra, & Bies, Robert J. (1994). Threats, bluffs, and disclaimers in negotiations. *Organizational Behavior and Human Decision Processes 60,* 14–35.

Sharkey, William F., & Stafford, Laura. (1990). Turn-taking resources employed by congenitally blind conversers. *Communication Studies 41,* 161–182.

Shaw, Marvin. (1981). *Group dynamics: The psychology of small group behaviors* (3rd ed.). New York: McGraw-Hill.

Siegert, John R., & Stamp, Glen H. (1994). "Our First Big Fight" as a milestone in the development of close relationships. *Communication Monographs 61,* 345–360.

Simpson, Jeffry A. (1987). The dissolution of romantic relationships: Factors involved in relationship stability and emotional distress. *Journal of Personality and Social Psychology 53,* 683–692.

Sincoff, Michael Z., & Goyer, Robert S. (1984). *Interviewing.* New York: Macmillan.

Skopec, Eric William. (1986). *Situational interviewing.* Prospect Heights, IL: Waveland Press.

Sommer, Robert. (1969). *Personal space: The behavioral basis of design.* Englewood Cliffs, NJ: Prentice-Hall Spectrum.

Spitzberg, Brian H. (1991). Intercultural communication competence. In Larry A. Samovar & Richard E. Porter (Eds.), *Intercultural Communication: A Reader* (pp. 353–365). Belmont, CA: Wadsworth.

Spitzberg, Brian H., & Cupach, William R. (1984). *Interpersonal communication competence.* Beverly Hills, CA: Sage.

Spitzberg, Brian H., & Cupach, William R. (1989). *Handbook of interpersonal competence research.* New York: Springer-Verlag.

Spitzberg, Brian H., & Hecht, Michael L. (1984). A component model of relational competence. *Human Communication Research 10,* 575–599.

Sprecher, Susan. (1987). The effects of self-disclosure given and received on affection for an intimate partner and stability of the relationship. *Journal of Social and Personal Relationships 4,* 115–127.

Sprecher, Susan, & Metts, Sandra. (1989). Development of the "romantic beliefs scale" and examination of the effects of gender and gender-role orientation. *Journal of Social and Personal Relationships 6,* 387–411.

Starkey, Judith A. (1996). *Multicultural communication strategies.* Chicago, IL: JAMS Publishing.

Stecker, Ivo (1993). Cultural variations in the concept of "Face." *Multilingua 12,* 119–141.

Steil, Lyman K., Barker, Larry L., & Watson, Kittie W. (1983). *Effective listening: Key to your success.* Reading, MA: Addison-Wesley.

Steiner, Claude. (1981). *The other side of power.* New York: Grove.

Steiner, Claude E., & Perry, Paul. (1997). *Achieving emotional literacy.* New York: Avon.

Stephan, W. G., & Stephan, C. W. (1985). Intergroup anxiety. *Journal of Social Issues 41,* 157–176.

Stephan, W. G., & Stephan, C. W. (1996). *Intergroup relations.* Dubuque, IA: Brown & Benchmark.

Sternberg, Robert J. (1987). Questions and answers about the nature and teaching of thinking skills. In Joan Boykoff Baron & Robert J. Sternberg (Eds.), *Teaching thinking skills:*

Theory and practice (pp. 251–259). New York: W. H. Freeman.

Stewart, Charles J., & Cash, William B., Jr. (1988). *Interviewing: Principles and practices* (4th ed.). Dubuque, IA: Wm. C. Brown.

Stewart, Sandra. (1996). Stop searching and start finding. *The Net 2,* 34–40.

Styles, R. P. (1985). *Vital speeches of the day 51.*

Swann, W. B., Jr. (1987). Identity negotiation: Where two roads meet. *Journal of Personality and Social Psychology 53,* 1038–1051.

Szapocznik, Jose. (1995). Research on disclosure of HIV status: Cultural evolution finds an ally in science. *Health Psychology 14,* 4–5.

Tannen, Deborah. (1990). *You just don't understand: Women and men in conversation.* New York: Morrow.

Tannen, Deborah. (1994a). *Gender and discourse.* New York: Oxford University Press.

Tannen, Deborah. (1994b). *Talking from 9 to 5: How women's and men's conversational styles affect who gets heard, who gets credit, and what gets done at work.* New York: William Morrow.

Taub, Marci. (1997). *Interviews.* New York: Random House.

Tersine, Richard J., & Riggs, Walter E. (1980). The Delphi technique: A long-range planning tool. In Stewart Ferguson & Sherry Devereaux Ferguson (Eds.), *Intercom: Readings in organizational communication* (pp. 366–373). Rochelle Park, NJ: Hayden Book.

Thibaut, J. W., & Kelley, H. H. (1959). *The social psychology of groups.* New York: Wiley.

Thorne, Barrie, Kramarae, Cheris, & Henley, Nancy. (Eds.). (1983). *Language, gender and society.* Rowley, MA: Newbury House Publishers.

Ting-Toomey, Stella. (1985). Toward a theory of conflict and culture. *International and Intercultural Communication Annual 9,* 71–86.

Ting-Toomey, Stella. (1986). Conflict communication styles in black and white subjective cultures. In Yun Kim Young (Ed.), *Interethnic communication: Current research* (pp. 75–88). Thousand Oaks, CA: Sage.

Trager, George L. (1958). Paralanguage: A first approximation. *Studies in Linguistics 13,* 1–12.

Trager, George L. (1961). The typology of paralanguage. *Anthropological Linguistics 3,* 17–21.

Tyler, Patrick E. (1996, July 11). Crime (and punishment) rages anew in China. *The New York Times,* pp. A1, A8.

Valenti, Jack. (1982). *Speaking up with confidence: How to prepare, learn, and deliver effective speeches.* New York: William Morrow.

Veenendall, Thomas L., & Feinstein, Marjorie C. (1996). *Let's talk about relationships: Cases in study* (2nd ed.). Prospect Heights, IL: Waveland Press.

Ventura, Michael. (1998). Taboo: Don't even think about it. *Psychology Today 31,* 32–38, 66, 68.

Verderber, Rudolph. (1997). *The challenge of effective speaking* (10th ed.). Belmont, CA: Wadsworth.

Vernon, JoEtta A., Williams, J. Allen, Phillips, Terri, & Wilson, Janet. (1990). Media stereotyping: A comparison of the way elderly women and men are portrayed on prime-time television. *Journal of Women and Aging 4,* 55–68.

Wallace, Karl. (1955). An ethical basis of communication. *Communication Education 4,* 1–9.

Wardhaugh, Ronald. (1998). *An introduction to sociolinguistics* (3rd ed.). Malden, MA: Blackwell.

Watson, Arden K., & Dodd, Carley H. (1984). Alleviating communication apprehension through rational emotive therapy: A comparative evaluation. *Communication Education 33,* 257–266.

Watzlawick, Paul. (1977). *How real is real? Confusion, disinformation, communication: An anecdotal introduction to communications theory.* New York: Vintage Books.

Watzlawick, Paul. (1978). *The language of change: Elements of therapeutic communication.* New York: Basic Books.

Watzlawick, Paul, Helmick Beavin, Janet, & Jackson, Don D. (1967). *Pragmatics of human communication: A study of interactional patterns, pathologies, and paradoxes.* New York: W. W. Norton.

Weinstein, Eugene A., & Deutschberger, Paul. (1963). Some dimensions of altercasting. *Sociometry 26,* 454–466.

Westwood, R. I, Tang, F. F., & Kirkbride, P. S. (1992). Chinese conflict behavior: Cultural antecedents and behavioral consequences. *Organizational Development Journal 10,* 13–19.

Wetzel, Patricia J. (1988). Are "powerless" communication strategies the Japanese norm? *Language in Society 17,* 555–564.

Weyant, James M. (1996). Application of compliance techniques to direct-mail requests for charitable donations. *Psychology and Marketing 13,* 157–170.

Wheeless, Lawrence R., & Grotz, Janis. (1977). The measurement of trust and Its relationship to self-disclosure. *Human Communication Research 3,* 250–257.

Wiemann, John M. (1977). Explication and test of a model of communicative competence. *Human Communication Research 3,* 195–213.

Wiemann, John M., & Backlund, P. (1980). Current theory and research in communicative competence. *Review of Educational Research 50,* 185–199.

Wilson, A. P., & Bishard, Thomas G. (1994). Here's the dirt on gossip. *American School Board Journal 181,* 27–29.

Wilson, R. A. (1989). Toward understanding E-prime. *Etc.: A Review of General Semantics 46,* 316–319.

Wolfson, Nessa. (1988). The bulge: A theory of speech behaviour and social distance. In J. Fine (Ed.), *Second language discourse: A textbook of current research* (pp. 21–38). Norwood, NJ: Ablex.

Wolpe, Joseph. (1957). *Psychotherapy by reciprocal inhibition.* Stanford, CA: Stanford University Press.

Won-Doornink, Myong Jin. (1991). Self-disclosure and reciprocity in South Korean and U.S. male dyads. In Stella Ting-Toomey & Felipe Korzenny (Eds.), *Cross-cultural interpersonal communication* (pp. 116–131). Newbury Park, CA: Sage.

Won-Doornink, Myong-Jin. (1985). Self-disclosure and reciprocity in conversation: A cross-national study. *Social Psychology Quarterly 48,* 97–107.

Wood, Julia T. (1982). Communication and relational culture: Bases for the study of human relationships. *Communication Quarterly 30,* 75–83.

Wood, Julia T. (1994). *Gendered lives: Communication, gender, and culture.* Belmont, CA: Wadsworth.

Woodward, Gary C., & Denton, Robert E. (1996). *Persuasion and influence in American life* (3rd ed.). Prospect Heights, IL: Waveland Press.

Yun, Hum. (1976). The Korean personality and treatment considerations. *Social Casework 57*, 173–178.

Zima, Joseph P. (1983). *Interviewing: Key to effective management.* Chicago, IL: Science Research Associations, Inc.

Zincoff, M. Z., & Goyer, Robert S. (1984). *Interviewing.* New York: Macmillan.

Zuckerman, M., Klorman, R., Larrance, D. T., & Spiegel, N. H. (1981). Facial, autonomic, and subjective components of emotion: The facial feedback hypothesis versus the externalizer–internalizer distinction. *Journal of Personality and Social Psychology 41*, 929–944.

Zunin, Leonard M., & Zunin, Natalie B. (1972). *Contact: The first four minutes.* Los Angeles, CA: Nash.

Index